Palgrave Studies in Agricultural Economics and Food Policy

Series Editor
Christopher B. Barrett, Cornell University, Ithaca, NY, USA

Agricultural and food policy lies at the heart of many pressing societal issues today and economic analysis occupies a privileged place in contemporary policy debates. The global food price crises of 2008 and 2010 underscored the mounting challenge of meeting rapidly increasing food demand in the face of increasingly scarce land and water resources. The twin scourges of poverty and hunger quickly resurfaced as high-level policy concerns, partly because of food price riots and mounting insurgencies fomented by contestation over rural resources. Meanwhile, agriculture's heavy footprint on natural resources motivates heated environmental debates about climate change, water and land use, biodiversity conservation and chemical pollution. Agricultural technological change, especially associated with the introduction of genetically modified organisms, also introduces unprecedented questions surrounding intellectual property rights and consumer preferences regarding credence (i.e., unobservable by consumers) characteristics. Similar new agricultural commodity consumer behavior issues have emerged around issues such as local foods, organic agriculture and fair trade, even motivating broader social movements. Public health issues related to obesity, food safety, and zoonotic diseases such as avian or swine flu also have roots deep in agricultural and food policy. And agriculture has become inextricably linked to energy policy through biofuels production. Meanwhile, the agricultural and food economy is changing rapidly throughout the world, marked by continued consolidation at both farm production and retail distribution levels, elongating value chains, expanding international trade, and growing reliance on immigrant labor and information and communications technologies. In summary, a vast range of topics of widespread popular and scholarly interest revolve around agricultural and food policy and economics. The extensive list of prospective authors, titles and topics offers a partial, illustrative listing. Thus a series of topical volumes, featuring cutting-edge economic analysis by leading scholars has considerable prospect for both attracting attention and garnering sales. This series will feature leading global experts writing accessible summaries of the best current economics and related research on topics of widespread interest to both scholarly and lay audiences.

Andaleeb Rahman · Prabhu Pingali

The Future of India's Social Safety Nets

Focus, Form, and Scope

palgrave
macmillan

Andaleeb Rahman
Tata Cornell Institute
Cornell University
Ithaca, NY, USA

Prabhu Pingali
Tata-Cornell Institute
Cornell University
Ithaca, NY, USA

ISSN 2662-3889 ISSN 2662-3897 (electronic)
Palgrave Studies in Agricultural Economics and Food Policy
ISBN 978-3-031-50746-5 ISBN 978-3-031-50747-2 (eBook)
https://doi.org/10.1007/978-3-031-50747-2

This Palgrave Macmillan imprint is published by the registered company Springer Nature Switzerland AG
The registered company address is: Gewerbestrasse 11, 6330 Cham, Switzerland

Paper in this product is recyclable.

Series Editor's Foreword

The idea of "inclusive growth" has been widely embraced by policymakers. This concept holds enormous appeal for the simple reason that economic growth that does not raise standards of living for all is both politically divisive and ethically suspect. But how to engineer inclusive growth remains a controversial topic among both scholars and policymakers. The pursuit of inclusive growth poses special challenges for low- and lower-middle-income countries still undergoing structural transformation from predominantly rural, agrarian economies to manufacturing-and-services-based, mainly urban ones. Such nations are building both an adequate tax base and the administrative capacity to implement extensive government-funded safety net programs intended to ensure that all residents can share rising standards of living in a growing economy.

The issue of how to engineer inclusive growth is especially salient in India, the world's most populous country, its largest electoral democracy, and one of the fastest-growing economies in the world, but also home to more poor or undernourished people than any other nation on Earth. India's constitution, supported by subsequent acts of parliament, recognizes individuals' right to food and right to work and attempts to honor those rights through specific safety net programs, the largest in the world. The political economy of enacting and implementing policies and programs is complex and fascinating. Meanwhile, the evidence of impacts remains quite mixed and expert assessments as to how best to modify or reform elements of the nation's social safety net system remain hotly contested.

Making sense of these important issues is difficult. But in the ten chapters that follow, Dr. Andaleeb Rahman and Prof. Prabhu Pingali manage to do so skillfully. They walk the reader through each of India's various social safety net policies. They helpfully synthesize and interpret the substantial prior scholarship on massive programs like India's Public Distribution System for staple foods and its Mahatma Gandhi National Rural Employment Guarantee Scheme. They also explain and assess less well-studied social safety net programs, like the Mid-day Meal Scheme and the Indira Gandhi National Old Age Pension Scheme. Anyone wanting details on specific programs would do well to start with this volume and to trace its meticulously referenced arguments and sources.

The greater value addition of this book, however, comes in its integrative conceptualization of the social safety net system supporting development resilience—what I like to refer to as 'shock-proofing continuous improvement in the human condition'—for all Indians. Andaleeb and Prabhu emphasize why it is essential to focus not only on the currently poor, but also on the prospectively poor, to mitigate the risk of individuals sliding into poverty in the wake of random misfortune, perhaps irreversibly. Taking a life-cycle perspective on how the state can knit together different forms of transfers or support, the authors clearly articulate a vision of an adaptive system in which no one program tries to meet all needs for all peoples at all times, but rather the complex of individual schemes in aggregate does so. This is important not least of which because of the myriad implementation challenges that beset each individual program, especially in low—and lower-middle-income countries experiencing rapid structural transformation.

The authors dedicate considerable thought and space to what they term the 'three I's of policymaking': the *ideas* that motivate citizen welfare, the *institutions* designed to deliver benefits flowing from those ideas, and the political *interests* that shape implementation (which could be a fourth I). They trace the ideas back to the moment of India's independence, citing the words of Jawaharlal Nehru, India's first and longest-serving prime minister. They explain how subsequent scholarship and policy debates have refined the ideas usefully. And they enumerate and assess the supporting institutions and their implementation, as well as the interests that have shaped, and reshaped, the various components of India's social safety net system. It is an absolutely fascinating read.

Andaleeb and Prabhu—along with two co-authors—previously wrote a brilliant and impactful volume for the Palgrave Studies in Agricultural Economics and Food Policy series, *Transforming Food Systems for a Rising India*. I am thrilled that they have now crafted an equally insightful volume on this closely related topic of India's social safety net system. I strongly recommend this outstanding book to all students of India, of social safety net design and practice, and of inclusive growth.

Christopher B. Barrett
Cornell University
Ithaca, NY, USA

Preface

Fragility of human lives and the importance of public action—state and non-state—received global recognition in the wake of the pandemic COVID-19. Social assistance—welfare transfers by governments—emerged as a central policy instrument of reducing the unprecedented economic hardship suffered by the people. While governments in developed countries like the United States sent checks to people to support their incomes, developing countries like India predominantly distributed free food to its people. Neither governments nor its citizens declared this as a generosity measure, rather it was a recognition of any nation's commitment to its citizens. These welfare transfers are not always emergency measures—the requirements surely get heightened during a period of crisis—but a part of the citizen-state social contract. In low-income countries, such contracts are relatively underdeveloped contributing to its underdevelopment.

In this book, we focus on India's social protection architecture, its successes, and failures, and envisage its future given the country's stunted structural transformation and limited administrative capacity. India stands at an interesting point in history. It recently surpassed China to become the most populous nation in the world. Over 1.3 billion people in the country are one of the most diverse populations in the world. The last three decades have brought substantial economic progress and creation of wealth in the country. Indian entrepreneurs and technocrats lead global corporation and are thought leaders in many other disciplines.

Alongside these stellar accomplishments, and a rapidly expanding middle class, India is also home to largest number of poor, undernutrition among children remains persistent, and inequality of opportunity and social exclusion portend significant political challenges. As a result, while India's rising economic influence remains noteworthy, its sustainability has aroused concerns. Inequality in economic opportunities has widened the schism between those who live in cities, possess land, and can afford quality education. This contrasting narrative about India's progress typifies a greater need for the social safety nets to protect the poor and those vulnerable to economic and social shocks to promote broad-based prosperity.

Since 2000s, India has made a commendable progress in expanding social protection programs to its citizens, with a particular focus on vulnerable groups such as women, children, and the elderly. Rights-based parliamentary guarantees for work and food have sustained the social welfare architecture bolstered further by the introduction of subsidized health insurance and direct cash assistance to farmers in later years. By the sheer size of its population, it operates some of the world's largest social safety nets which include direct food transfers, employment generation through public works program, subsidized health insurance, and cash transfers to farmers and the elderly. The semblance of a social minimum—which has emerged late in the history of democratic nation—continues to be a work in progress with challenges associated with political will, implementational capacity, corruption, and limited fiscal space. In this book, we discuss and analyze these and many other issues associated with the emergence of various social protection policies and programs in India in this book. We delve into the historical antecedents of these programs, identify the key issues and challenges faced in implementing these policies and assesses their impact on the lives of beneficiaries. We also highlight the subnational differences in the performance of social welfare programs.

The central focus of this book is on envisaging future social protection as an essential part of the development strategy, a marquee economic support system which spans an individual's lifetime. The life-cycle approach allows us to argue that deprivations begin before a person's birth and manifest themselves in multiple forms in later life. Our conceptualization of a social protection system moves the focus away from isolated welfare schemes toward a system where investments in better public systems are equally important. By public systems, we mean a citizen-oriented developmental state which prioritizes complementary investments in public and merit goods, is high on administrative capacity, and espouses greater public accountability.

Throughout this book, we appeal to an interdisciplinary scholarship where economic development is about enhancing human capabilities and the role of state is paramount in ensuring social justice. Our evaluation of the Indian social welfare programs spans the cutting-edge empirical research evaluating the array of social programs in the country from multiple perspective and over different periods of time. A birds-eye evaluation of the social protection system allows us to avoid the fallacy of seeing woods for the trees. It also allows us to provide a more nuanced perspective on the nature of emerging social protection system amidst India's middling state capacity.

We provide an in-depth evaluation of the various safety nets (say, child nutrition from health insurance) in separate chapters and bring them all together in the concluding one to delineate how the social protection system might look like in the future. This allows us to reach an audience which might have a specific or a general interest in the issue of social protection and development policy.

Through this book, we hope to contribute to the growing body of literature on social protection and development policy in India and beyond. The Indian case is similar to the expansion of social protection in other countries of the Global South, including Brazil, South Africa, and Indonesia. We believe that this book would prove to be an equally valuable resource for policymakers, researchers, practitioners, and students alike sparking an interest in the many intriguing challenges of social policy and its implementations.

No research product is possible without regular feedback. We are extremely grateful to Raghav Puri, Aditya Srinivas (who was involved in the early stages of the book), Chris Barrett, Neeraj Prasad, Digvijay Negi, Anaka Aiyar, Nafis Hasan, S Chandrasekhar, Kidjie Ian Saguin, Sumit Mishra, Deepak Malghan, Mehr Mumtaz, and the research community at the Tata-Cornell Institute (TCI) for many stimulating, critical, insightful, and encouraging conversations during various stages of the writing process. Lastly, this could not have been possible without the TCI support staff, copy editor Patricia Mason, and enormous patience of the editorial staff of Palgrave Macmillan.

Finally, we hope that this book becomes an important capstone study on why (also, how) a social democracy facilitates economic growth and the inherent challenges (economic and political) of building a strong social protection system in a globalizing world. Despite its focus on India, we believe the book's takeaways are applicable to other developing countries where the process of structural transformation—urbanization, services-led economic growth, and informality of labor—is contributing to disparities in income and inequality of opportunity leading to a greater demand for safety nets.

Ithaca, USA

Andaleeb Rahman
Prabhu Pingali

Praise for *The Future of India's Social Safety Nets*

"Social policy received very little attention in India for a long time, despite its prominence in the Constitution. In the last twenty years, there have been significant moves towards a possible social security system. This critical review of recent initiatives is an invaluable springboard for further research and action in this field."

—Jean Drèze, *Ranchi University*

"As technology trends intensify market inequalities, as climate trends exacerbate uncertainties, and as trends in political polarization threaten to undermine social cohesion, there is no question that public safety nets will be a central part of policies to navigate the political economy of the coming decades. But what exactly should these safety nets look like? What design features will enhance their contribution to equality and to efficiency? And what does experience teach us about implementation of safety nets? This excellent volume presents a comprehensive and rigorous assessment of the Indian experience, and in doing so shows the way forward for India and at the same time contributes to the global debate. It will become a standard reference in the literature."

—Ravi Kanbur, *Cornell University*

"From Independence, India has enshrined basic rights including the rights to dignity and freedom from exploitation. The nature and scope of programs to ensure these rights have evolved as the rural economy transformed and as the planned economy liberalized. Rahman and Pingali clearly elucidate the interaction of this economic transformation and the evolution of social welfare policy detailing the importance of historic and regional contexts. Despite gaps in implementation, they present a vision of the potential for social policy to move beyond palliative measures towards a resilient and inclusive social contract."

—Harold Alderman, *International Food Policy Research Institute (IFPRI), Washington D.C.*

"In many ways, India is a global barometer of social protection—a harbinger of developments to come elsewhere in the world. Through thoughtful analysis and novel insights, Andaleeb Rahman and Prabhu Pingali take us on an extraordinary tour of key debates affecting Indian social protection policy, research, and practice. A must read for those that want to understand the past, present, and future of social protection in the country and beyond."

—Ugo Gentilini, *World Bank*

Contents

Abbreviations

AAY	Antyodaya Anna Yojana
ANM	Auxiliary Nurse and Midwife
APC	Agriculture Price Commission
APCAPS	Andhra Pradesh Child and Parents Study
APL	Above Poverty Line
ASHA	Accredited Social Health Activist
ASPIRE	Atlas of Social Protection Indicators of Resilience and Equity
AWC	Anganwadi Center
AWW	Anganwadi Worker
BPL	Below Poverty Line
CAG	Comptroller and Auditor General
CCT	Conditional Cash Transfers
CHC	Community Health Center
CM	Chief Minister
CMCHIS	Chief Minister's Comprehensive Health Insurance Scheme
CMIE	Center for Monitoring of Indian Economy
DAY	Deen Dayal Antyodaya Yojana
DoH	Department of Health
DPEP	District Primary Education Programme
DUET	Decentralized Urban Employment and Training
EAS	Employment Assurance Scheme
EGS	Employment Guarantee Scheme
EWSS	Employment Wage Subsidy Schemes
FC	Finance Commission
FCI	Food Corporation of India
GDP	Gross Domestic Product

GOI	Government of India
GST	Goods and Services Tax
HCI	Human Capital Index
HDI	Human Development Index
HIC	High-income Countries
IAY	Indira Awas Yojana
ICDS	Integrated Child Development Scheme
IGMSY	Indira Gandhi Maternity Support Scheme
IGNDPS	Indira Gandhi National Disability Pension Scheme
IGNOAPS	Indira Gandhi National Old Age Pension Scheme
IGNWPS	Indira Gandhi National Widow Pension Scheme
IHDS	India Human Development Survey
ILO	International Labor Organization
IRDP	Integrated Rural Development Program
IVRS	Interactive Voice-Response Systems
JGSY	Jawahar Gram Samridhi Yojana
JRY	Jawahar Rozgar Yojana
JSY	Janani Suraksha Yojana
LIC	Low-income countries
LMIC	Low—and Medium—Countries
MDG	Millenium Development Goals
MDMS	Mid-day Meal Scheme
MGNREGS	Mahatma Gandhi National Rural Employment Guarantee Scheme
MKSY	Mukhyamantri Khadyann Sahayata Yojana
MMFES	Mufti Muhammad Sayeed Food Entitlement Scheme
MNP	Minimum Needs Program
MoRD	Ministry of Rural Development
MoWCD	Ministry of Women and Child Development
MSP	Minimum Support Price
NAC	National Advisory Council
NCD	Non-Communicable Diseases
NEP	New Education Policy
NFBS	National Family Benefit Scheme
NFHS	National Family Health Survey
NFSA	National Food Security Act
NHM	National Health Mission
NHPS	National Health Promotion Scheme
NHS	National Health Services
NNM	National Nutrition Mission
NP-NSPE	National Programme of Nutritional Support to Primary Education
NREGA	National Rural Employment Guarantee Act

NREP	National Rural Employment Program
NRHM	National Rural Health Mission
NRLM	National rural Livelihood Mission
NRY	Nehru Rozgar Yojana
NSAP	National Social Assistance Programme
NSLP	National School Lunch Program
NSSO	National Sample Survey Organization
NUHM	National Urban Health Mission
NULM	National Urban Livelihood Mission
OFM	One Full Meal
ONORC	One Nation One Ration Card
OOP	Out-of-Pocket
PDS	Public Distribution System
PHC	Public Health Insurance
PLFS	Periodic Labor Force Survey
PM	Prime Minister
PMAY	Prime Minister Awas Yojana
PMIUPEP	Prime Minister's Integrated Urban Poverty Eradication Programme
PMJAY	Pradhan Mantri Jan Arogya Yojana
PM-JDY	Pradhan Mantri Jan Dhan Yojana
PMMVY	Prime Minister's Maternity Assistance Scheme
POSHAN	Prime Minister's Overarching Scheme or Holistic Nourishment
PPP	Public Private Partnership
PROGRESA	Programa de Educacion, Salud y Alimentacion
PUCL	People's Union for Civil Liberties
RLEGP	Rural Livelihood Employment Guarantee Program
RSBY	Rashtriya Swastha Bima Yojana
RTE	Right to Education
SDG	Sustainable Development Goal
SGSY	Swarnajayanti Gram Swarozgar Yojana
SHG	Self-Help Group
SJSRY	Swarna Jayanti Shahari Rozgar Yojana
SNAP	Supplemental Nutritional Assistance Program
THR	Take-Home Ration
TPDS	Targeted Public Distribution System
UBI	Universal Basic Income
UHC	Universal Health Coverage
UIDAI	Unique Identification Authority of India
ULB	Urban Local Body
WIC	Special Supplemental Nutrition Program for Women, Infants, and Children
WPR	Workforce Participation Rate

List of Figures

List of Tables

CHAPTER 1

In the Quest of a Social Democracy

> The future beckons to us. Whither do we go and what shall be our endeavour? To bring freedom and opportunity to the common man, to the peasants and workers of India; to fight and end poverty and ignorance and disease; to build up a prosperous, democratic and progressive nation, and to create social, economic and political institutions which will ensure justice and fullness of life to every man and woman.
>
> —*Tryst With Destiny*, speech delivered by Jawaharlal Nehru to the Constituent Assembly of India in New Delhi on August 15, 1947.

In his historic speech at the dawn of independence from colonial rule India's first Prime Minister, Jawaharlal Nehru emphatically declared that the freedom from colonial rule also provides a collective responsibility toward "the ending of poverty and ignorance and disease and inequality of opportunity." Yet, more than seven decades hence, India's performance on social indicators is sobering. While the country has made considerable progress emerging as one of the global economic giants, yet the behemoth's 'feet of clay' belies its strength.[1] In 2023, India is far wealthier,

[1] Pranab Bardhan famously referred to both India and China as 'awakening giants' with 'feet of clay.' He argued that long-run economic growth in China's could be hindered by its authoritarian political structure, while India's poor democratic governance and political accountability system is a persistent impediment to sustainable and equitable economic growth. See Bardhan (2012).

A. Rahman and P. Pingali, *The Future of India's Social Safety Nets*, Palgrave Studies in Agricultural Economics and Food Policy,
https://doi.org/10.1007/978-3-031-50747-2_1

more entrepreneurial, skilled, educated, urban, and higher life expectancy than in 1947. During the last 75 years, it has seen a substantial decline in poverty, and improvement in the quality of life. The certitude of India's glorious achievements is however weakened by the persistence of human deprivation, most importantly the ignominy of being home to the largest number of poor people and malnourished children in the world.[2] While countries at similar levels of economic development at the end of the colonial era in the postwar era have managed to reduce poverty, with some of them now classified as advanced nations, India continues to languish. Broad-based prosperity seems far in sight.

India of today faces a peculiar development challenge which is a combination of developed and developing country problems. It has a problem of scarcity as well as plenty; greater agricultural productivity amidst growing susceptibility to climate threats; improved medical technologies along with rising costs of treatment; higher educational attainments but low employability; and joblessness amidst rising educational levels and economic growth. Spatially, some parts of the country have begun to reflect developmental challenges of middle-income countries like over-nutrition, non-communicable diseases, while one would find traditional symptoms of deprivation—poverty, undernutrition, ill-health, gender disparities, unemployment, conflicts (along caste and religion), and poor public services—continue to characterize the rest. Overall, while famine-like conditions and mass food insecurity are sporadic (if any), prevalence of high malnutrition, joblessness, income insecurity, gender empowerment, and informality in India continue to dot global headlines. The unrealized human potential of millions of citizens portends democratic disenfranchisement, lack of trust in the government, and the risks of intergenerational poverty which are indicative of subdued future growth potential of the nation.[3]

[2] Dreze and Sen (2013) provide the most definitive account of the 'uncertain glory' which shadows India's remarkable economic progress during the seven decades of democratic rule.

[3] Krishna (2017) explains this paradox as inequality of opportunity, or a 'broken ladder' of social mobility in India. He argues that those who live in remote areas and lack the skills or physical capital required to be a part of the services-driven economic structure—majority of the population—have benefited negligibly from the economic opportunity. The India success story is however mostly about a narrower share of elites with access to quality education, social networks, urban residence, and access to credit, apart from their upper caste privilege.

In India's development process, failures of the state policy to cure poverty—in its various appearances—is conspicuous which goes against the idea of a vibrant social democracy.[4] The process of democratic nation-building requires a strong social contract—political, social, and economic—to the ideals of justice, fairness, and equity to increase trust in the government and build fealty to the nation.[5] The strength of these commitments, the kind of endeavors undertaken, and the institutions primed for attaining these goals determine the nature of long-run economic, social, and human development. While the epigraph of this chapter harps upon the fact that the foundational ethos of the nation-building was based upon this very social pledge of equitable growth, the pathos-filled account of deprivation and suffering of the poor, however, contradicts that such a promise was ever paid obeisance during the seven decades of democratic rule.

Calamitous failure of Indian state to support its poor—from deprivation on multiple counts and enhance their developmental capability—has given rise to a wealth of scholarship discerning this predicament. Proponents of the 'free market' earmark India's state-controlled economic planning as the limiting factor in increasing opportunities for the poor, while those who see a larger role of the government in the economy argue that lack of emphasis on social policy—redistribution, public investments in essential services, and civic empowerment—has restrained India's human potential.[6] Neither of these, however, deny India's significant economic progress as well as the enormous challenge of poverty reduction and sustainable growth. The difference fundamentally lies in the role and design of social policy in facilitating economic development.

[4] Under a social democracy, governments have a right to legal obligation to provide certain social rights such as universal access to essential public services such as education, health care, employee compensation, and other services for the vulnerable sections like children and the elderly. See Bardhan (2011) on the lack of social democratic ideals in Indian policy frameworks. Also refer to Kohli (1987) for the politics of state-led redistribution in the pre-reform era.

[5] See Hickey (2011) for a discussion.

[6] This contrast is best summarized through the perspectives of Dreze and Sen (2013) and Bhagwati and Panagariya (2013).

Scope of This Book

This book focuses on a specific aspect of India's social policy—social welfare programs—which is increasingly at the forefront of public debates, academic theorizing, and even electoral sloganeering.[7] Social welfare programs—which include food assistance, nutritional support to children or pregnant mothers, public works program, social pensions, subsidized health insurance, and cash transfers for various purposes—have emerged as the most important policy instruments to alleviate poverty and risk in the country during the last two decades. This has led to a polarized debate around its need, population coverage, financial feasibility, political undernotes, economic impact, and the ability of the Indian government to deliver welfare to its citizens. Believers in market-based solutions prefer cash and other market-based instruments such as insurance as a more efficient form of welfare transfer, while those wary of the market imperfections rely on commodity-based direct welfare assistance because of India's patriarchal social norms, underfunded public systems, inefficient markets, limited citizen empowerment, and a fledgling infrastructure. As the debate gets more intense and policy relevant, there is a greater need to understand the source of these tensions and learn from economic theory, global experiences, and its own subnational variation in policy design and implementation to think about the issues of poverty, deprivation, and the role of social safety nets. This book provides a framework to understand India's social welfare policies—its historical evolution, impact, current limitations, and ideas for the future.

According to 2022 union budget, India spends around 4% of its GDP on social welfare programs. Public Distribution System (PDS) and Mahatma Gandhi National Rural Employment Guarantee Scheme (MGNREGS) which address food security and rural poverty concerns respectively, are the world's largest welfare programs of their kind. Under PDS, 820 million people benefit from subsidized food every month while MGNREGS provides 100 days of guaranteed work in a calendar year to more than 100 million people in rural India. In addition, India operates several complementary safety net programs such as the Mid-day Meal

[7] Social safety nets are different from social security which is generally understood to be associated with employment status. Social welfare (or assistance) programs, social protection schemes, or safety nets, are used interchangeably to describe many tools of social policy where citizens (mostly poor) are provided direct assistance by the government.

Scheme (MDMS), old age pension scheme, and a public health insurance program, targeted to specific demographic groups to address health, malnutrition, and related vulnerability. Despite these measures, India has nearly a quarter of the world's poor population, highest number of unemployed youths, and the largest number of malnourished children in the world. *Why did it take so long for the Indian social policy to recognize social welfare policies as a key tool for redistribution and inclusive growth? How did welfare policies suddenly storm their way into the center of social policy debate in the 2000s? What has been its impact on the poor? How can a country which guarantees its citizen legal 'rights' to work and food exhibit extreme forms of poverty and deprivation? How can the Indian state improve its effectiveness in delivering welfare to the poor?*

These are questions which require a book length answer to the many challenges of effectively conceptualizing, designing, and implementing a welfare strategy which gets to the bottom of the developmental challenge of a democratic nation which is beginning to modernize yet remains backward on various economic, social, and political indicators. We place this question in a historical context, beginning from period of economic planning in the 1950s and trace its evolution to the current times—a period of 75 years in which India has fundamentally transformed in every regard, social welfare policy included. Across multiple chapters of this book, we deliberate upon the policy design, implementation, and welfare impacts of the array of the welfare programs which have been introduced, rolled back, or re-packaged by the Indian government. We place these policy proclamations as a response to the economic exigencies, demographic changes, and political compulsions of the times.

We argue that India's development trajectory had two epochal events—agricultural productivity enhancing Green Revolution during the 1970s and the economic reforms of the 1991—which influenced the incidence of poverty as well as the design of anti-poverty policy. While Green Revolution initiated the process of rural poverty decline and arrested food security concerns, economic reforms—globalization and reduction in state-control of the economy—animated the rise of India as a global economic power. A substantial structural transformation which India has undergone since then is characterized by high growth rates, declining importance of agriculture in output and employment, urbanization, rising middle class, greater economic opportunities, and changing dietary patterns. The process of structural transformation, however, has failed to 'lift all boats' because economic opportunities arising from agricultural productivity increase as well as services-led growth were differentiated along access to education, credit, capital assets, and social networks. With the skill-based services sector driving this growth process, the larger share of the labor force—larger unskilled or less employable skills—remains in the informal sector, without any employer based social security against loss of employment, illness, or disability. The retrospective analysis of the impact of social welfare programs allows us a more informed engagement with the social policy question going into the future. *How can the current safety net system be transformed in an emerging economy, as diverse as India? What ought to be its developmental goal? Should it cover only the poor and the vulnerable, or everyone? What is the most cost-effective way of achieving these goals? How reliable are technological innovations in plugging the traditional leakages in the welfare delivery systems? How to build resilience for the poorest of the poor?*

These questions also make us review the fundamental premise of social safety nets—its theoretical underpinnings, institutional design, socio-political context of policy implementation, fiscal requirements, and effectiveness for long-term development. We argue that while standalone welfare schemes are important to address various forms of human deprivation, it is imperative to think about social welfare as a 'system' of programs (welfare support) with 'development resilience' as its overarching objective (*scope*).[8] A systems approach to social welfare addresses the multiple dimensions of poverty along the life cycle of individuals which not only provide a safeguard against risks, but also facilitate full realization of human capital through continuum of assured assistance against various plausible shocks thereby arresting any possible decline in human capabilities and build resilience. The welfare system, therefore, ought to address not only current poverty, but also the slide into future poverty with a *focus*

[8] The idea of resilience is central to thinking about systems because it can account for the many complex individual-specific socio-economic and behavioral factors which explain poverty and deprivation (Barrett and Constas 2014) to the meso-level factors such as geography, political institutions, and citizen empowerment (Lade et al. 2017) which together determine the nature of citizen-state contract, essential for sustainable reduction in poverty and economic growth. Graduation programs are a good example of creating such a system where safety nets not only involve the provision of food, but also skills and livelihood training which enhance individual earning capacity (Banerjee et al. 2015, 2021; Banerjee et al. 2022a). However, these interventions are undertaken as part of charitable giving motivated by the concerns of effective altruism concerns, while social welfare programs are a promise of the state toward its citizens which not only takes place at a large scale but has a significant feedback effect on the politics.

on both the poor and the non-poor, however the *forms* of welfare support may differ depending upon the nature of vulnerability. In this book, we argue that if the process of development is not about enhancing human capabilities—instead of just getting individuals over an artificially defined poverty line—safety nets should be envisaged as a tool of enhancing the ability to hold one's own in the wake of unforeseen calamity. Building household resilience, therefore, ought to be the *scope* of social welfare systems.

We do not envisage the welfare system to be composed only of the social welfare programs, but it ought to include robust public systems—higher public investment in health, education, and essential public services—which must work in unison to foster an enabling environment for sustained human progress.[9] While visible public infrastructure (such as roads or markets) along with essential public services (education, health, post offices, etc.) is a key responsibility of the state to reduce physical and financial constraints to economic opportunities, the attainment of these opportunities is realized through the investments in 'invisible' infrastructure—state capacity, citizen, empowerment, and public action—essential to ensure public systems work for the poor.[10] A stronger citizen-state social contract is key to build this system where the state commitment to welfare is clearly laid out along with the pathways to achieve so. Resilient societies are the one where there is a collective commitment and shared responsibility toward uplifting the most downtrodden and marginalized members of the community. Building such social democracy would require strengthening of enabling institutions, overcoming perverse political interests, and resolving multiple clashes of ideas.

To build resilience, social welfare policies need to be more encompassing in their approach given the low initial endowments among the

[9] This system is similar in spirit to the graduation programs, where the poorest are provided consumption support, income assistance, skills and training, and physical capital to allow them to 'graduate' out of poverty on the path to prosperity. While these programs have successfully tested through NGOs conducting randomized control trials (RCTs) on small populations, scaling up such an idea requires monumental government support which is unlikely. Social welfare programs, however, could be thought of a close resemblance to the idea of graduation where multiple developmental deficits of a human being are plugged.

[10] See Page and Pande (2018) for a discussion on the role of 'invisible' infrastructure for poverty reduction. To understand the role of public action for social welfare, see Drèze and Sen (1991) and Sen (1981).

poor and the persistence of low-productivity and informal occupation in the developing countries which is bereft of any employment-based social security. Low capital endowments and the absence of market-based insurance mechanisms and decreasing community-based social insurance, economic risks arising from a loss of a job, crop failure, illness, or disability, are always lurking. Demand from the government for social assistance, therefore, becomes the only alternative for the poor and the vulnerable. In a social democracy, government responds to these requests as an essential part of the citizen-state social contract. We, therefore, argue for a wider population coverage (*focus*) to extend social protection to address the needs of those who got stuck in poverty trap as well as to those who are vulnerable to it. Welfare assistance, therefore, must be designed within the realm of the country's structural transformation and the ensuing nature of poverty and deprivation which characterizes the various sections of the population. There are multiple alternatives of welfare transfers (*form*)—food, cash, nutritional assistance, health insurance, etc.—and we highlight that the decision to pick one over the other ought to be situated to socio-economic and political context. Moreover, while each of the multiple social welfare policies work with a developmental goal (*scope*), a resilient welfare system would be achieved when they are able to collectively able to address various dimensions of deprivation along the human life cycle.

Social Safety Nets as an Enabler of Development Resilience

State intervention in the form of social safety nets is primarily motivated from concerns of redistribution, filling in for missing markets or market failures than inhibits a household's ability to cope with shocks and invest in productive asset accumulation, or reducing household's behavioral constraints.[11] Poor households are vulnerable to frequent crop loss, unemployment, untimely death, or famine which leads to loss of income, livelihood, and property in the short run and impairs their long-term ability to function in full capacity. Such risks are particularly high for those with low endowments of human and physical capital. In the developing

[11] See Hanna and Karlan (2017).

countries where markets (labor, credit, and insurance) are underdeveloped, welfare transfers provide a protective or safety floor against the likelihood of falling into 'poverty trap' through state intervention to fill in for market imperfections.[12]

Social safety nets have emerged as one of the most important policy instruments to alleviate poverty and risk in the last two decades. According to the most recent estimates, around 2.5 billion people globally are covered by safety nets, through which 36% of the very poor have managed to escape from extreme poverty (World Bank 2018). Social protection policies were also utilized globally as perhaps the most potent policy tool to address economic insecurity created by unprecedented exogenous shock of the pandemic, COVID-19.[13]

Historically, the advanced nations of today relied upon a slew of state-sponsored welfare programs during their modernization process since the early twentieth century to support its working population against the newer risks which emerged from the process of industrialization, decline in community-based mutual insurance, greater rural to urban migration, and a more complex economic structure.[14] As developing countries are

[12] The poverty trap framework has been instrumental in unpacking the process of economic development through exposing the many key facets of the functioning of markets, the role of endowments—physical and human capital, nutritional investments, and others—which propagate propel human growth. Based upon a 11-year-long panel data collection, Balboni et al. (2022) find credible empirical support for the poverty trap argument—there is a minimum threshold of asset endowment which is essential for people to come out of the poverty trap on a sustainable basis. For a review of theoretical and empirical literature on poverty trap, refer to Kraay and McKenzie (2014) and Barrett et al. (2019).

[13] See Gentilini (2022) and Gentilini et al. (2022).

[14] Social welfare policies in Europe have been attributed to the structural issues with the labor markets—political economy contestations over the rising commodification of labor capital under capitalism in the wake of industrialization—which led to three models of welfare systems: liberalism, conservatism, and social democracy (Esping-Andersen 1990). The liberal welfare system provides a modest amount of targeted assistance (restrictive *scope* and *focus*). In the conservative model, welfare transfers are provided through the employer and hence social differences are maintained (*focus* on the employed). Social democratic welfare regimes are the one with a strong interventionist state which prioritizes equality as its overarching *scope* with generous benefits and full commitment to livelihood and income protection. While pioneering in the field of social policy, these distinctions have their limits when being applied to other nations, yet it would be not wrong to classify Indian social policy till the rights-based act came into being as conservative in its approach. This is also true of advanced Asian economies of Japan and Korea till democratic reforms of 1993 and 1987 respectively led to new ideas around more expansive social welfare programs (Kwon

undergoing structural transformation, there has been a concerted attempt at creating an expansive social protection architecture. The safety nets *agenda*, promoted by the World Bank and other global agencies in the 1990s, has also accorded prominence to it in the "global fight against poverty."[15] Cash transfers—unconditional and conditional—as pioneered by Brazil, Mexico, China, and South Africa have particularly championed these reforms which have spread to other developing countries like Ethiopia, India, Indonesia, and Bangladesh who have enunciated various other social welfare programs. Yet, in the low-income countries, only 20% of the population is protected through any form of safety net which implies that the redistributive impact has been below its potential, with the poorest of the poor still being left behind.[16] Limited financial resources, inadequate state capacity to implement welfare programs, and weak citizen-state social contract are offered as potential examples for lack of a comprehensive welfare strategy in the poorer countries. Concomitantly, the effectiveness of welfare programs is also influenced by how its need—the nature of poverty and deprivation—is theoretically conceived by the economic planners.

Until very recently, the development thinking—across both academic and practice communities—envisaged safety nets as a policy tool to ensure that standard of living of the poorest person does not fall below a minimum subsistence level.[17] Re-conceptualization of safety nets, however, recognizes it not only as a response to existing poverty but also

1997). Similar is the case in a majority of Latin American countries where economic crises and political actors have refashioned ideas and institutions around social welfare leading to a reduction in poverty and inequality (Barrientos 2009; Levy and Schady 2013). Also see Ravallion (2015), Deaton (2013), and Piketty (2020).

[15] While state-provided social assistance—in limited amount—has always existed in the developing countries, it is characterized by lack of resources, political will, and implementational inconsistencies. Refer to Barrientos (2013) for an in-depth discussion on social assistance in developing countries.

[16] For empirical studies, see Fiszbein et al. (2014), Margitic and Ravallion (2019), and Ravallion (2016).

[17] The principal cause of poverty is attributed to unequal human endowment at birth and the existence of risk and uncertainty in income streams (Banerjee and Duflo 2007; Collins et al. 2009). Livelihood risks, scarcity, and day-to-day struggle for sustenance further lead to suboptimal choices by individuals and households which push them into intergenerational poverty (Ghatak 2015).

as an adaptive strategy to unforeseen adverse economic shocks.[18] The scholarship on poverty and risks has evolved to account for the variation within the poor as well considering the vulnerability of non-poor to falling into poverty, arising out of the multiple kinds of market failures.[19] Households at different levels of human endowments require a different policy response and therefore an equivalent amount of transfer is not likely to have the same benefit to all households. As a result, the state response to poverty requires more progressive transfers which brings the poorest households to a certain 'social minimum' while protecting the non-poor against any possible slide into poverty.[20]

Research has shown that a limited amount of social assistance allows *only* those who are just below the poverty threshold to escape the poverty trap with a negligible effect on those at a very low level of well-being.[21] Therefore, while the poorest households may benefit from more progressive transfers, the vulnerable but non-poor groups can benefit from some form of contingent transfers to sustain themselves above a subsistence consumption level.[22] Keeping everyone outside the poverty trap, above a minimum level of consumption, therefore has a multiplier effect on the economy which increases overall welfare. As a result, anti-poverty policies not only need to address the structural inequalities in financial

[18] Devereux and Sabates-Wheeler (2004) conceptualize safety nets as a policy instrument to 'transform' human lives and stem intergenerational poverty. See Bowen et al. (2020) for the adaptive role of social safety nets.

[19] To understand the vulnerability of non-poor to falling into poverty in the wake of a catastrophic shock like illness or death, see Krishna (2010). Similarly, refer to Barrett et al. (2019) for an account of the multiple poverty traps and market failures.

[20] Economic theory suggests that households are either stuck in poverty because they are born with poor human and physical capital endowments and are therefore employed in low-income activities, or they fall into poverty because of some exogenous shock such as loss of life, livelihood, or erosion of their resource base. To transition out of this situation, they are required to acquire a minimum amount of capital so that their earnings and earning capacity could increase leading to a further expansion in their human capabilities. Overall individual gains also bring about an investment in productive capital, the ability to acquire skills, and a wider set of economic opportunities which pushes overall wages upwards. While social transfers can have a role to pull people out of poverty, but this escape is pre-conditioned upon a certain minimum amount of human and physical capital. See Banerjee et al. (2022b) for an economic formalization of this idea in the context of social protection policies in developing countries.

[21] Refer to Balboni et al. (2022) and Barrett and Carter (2013).

[22] Ikegami et al. (2018) provide a theoretical illustration.

and human capital endowments, but also provide them sufficient support in the wake of economic losses—crop, livelihood, or health. A robust anti-poverty strategy, as a result, need to address both—transitions in and out of poverty—for infusing resilience into the development process. By providing an opportunity to escape poverty, safety nets can help improve the standard of living, arrest the erosion of physical capital, provide human dignity, and reduce interpersonal inequality. However, such a transformational impact requires *timely*, *sustained*, and *formidable* amount of welfare transfer.

Contributions to the Indian Social Policy Debate

Social welfare programs have been one of the most researched aspects of social policy in India lately. The credibility revolution in economics, the mantra of 'evidence-based policy' in development practice, availability of rich household survey data, creative research designs, and gigabytes of public available administrative data on various schemes have made program evaluation a key component of any empirically minded economist's curriculum vitae. India's range of social welfare has provided an abundant field to scholars domestically and abroad to test their theoretical and empirical tools to suggest ways to improve the 'plumbing' of the various social welfare schemes through analyzing their imperfect implementation, welfare impacts and offered novel solutions to improve performance.[23] The wealth of scholarship which has emerged in the last two decades on the impact of social welfare programs however lacks a unifying framework to understand the rising importance of social welfare policies, their impact, and future innovations within the realm of India's economic transformation, social change, and democratic strengthening.

The burgeoning empirical research on India's safety nets reflects is beset with a fundamental challenge. These isolated studies—focusing on the effectiveness of specific welfare schemes, at a certain point in time—focus on a narrow plumbing question without much cognizance to the welfare system architecture. We would show in later parts of the book that

[23] At the prestigious Richard Ely Lecture at the American Economic Association meeting in 2017, Nobel Laureate economist, Esther Duflo famously suggested that the work of an economist is akin to a plumber wherein they bring their technical expertise to fix tap-design in the policy house, identify ruptures in the system, test and suggest solutions, and create an architecture for policy ideas to flow. See Duflo (2017).

the same welfare schemes could have a favorable impact in one region, while not in the other. Several contextual factors could explain this difference, which is not often observable to the researcher or beyond their theoretical paradigms. Program evaluations, despite their crucial importance, could "miss the woods for the trees." Such oversight is particularly common when evaluations of social welfare programs depend upon the quality of program implementation, population coverage, along with the nature of poverty and overall economic structure which are neither time-invariant nor spatially uniform across a country as large as India. This book's contribution therefore lies in extending beyond the limited set of plumbing tools to carry out a comprehensive 'house-inspection' of the emerging social welfare architecture. In doing so, while we deliberate upon the planning and design of the various schemes, we also theorize and envisage how these schemes working together could foster a resilient development process in the future.

To the best of our knowledge, there are only two benchmark study of similar scope.[24] In 2011, World Bank came out with a report which contained a detailed review of all the major social protection programs in India with suggested policy measures. Economist Jean Drèze similarly edited a volume which had a collection of empirical research on various social safety nets in India, from the many volumes of the policy journal, *Economic and Political Weekly*. In the last decade, social welfare policies have undergone a rapid transformation—in terms of their *focus*, *form*, and *scope*—which we update but more importantly this book is not about technocratic solutions to 'fix' the problems but rather it makes us think about the nature of the problem itself, its relevance under the current contextual nuances (economic as well as political) with a vision for the future. While analyzing each of the welfare programs—against the development needs against which they were created (*scope*), the intended beneficiaries of the program (*focus*), and the nature of welfare support (*form*)—our focus is always on the 'big picture' question of long-term improvement in human welfare.

This book is also an important contribution to the study of social development in India. While several other scholars of repute have highlighted the limited success of Indian state in reducing poverty and deprivation, the point of departure for this book lies in the singular focus on

[24] See World Bank (2011) and Drèze (2016).

social welfare programs.[25] We analyze social policy change and its drivers through carefully scrutinizing policy documents since the 1950s, multiple government reports, news pieces, and tomes of scholarly work on India's development trajectory. Big-picture economic thinking, however, cannot disregard politics. The social welfare question, specifically, is a political one both in design as well as implementation. In this book, we delve into great length to argue that future of welfare programs and its reforms lies in political coalition building with citizen at the center. The insights offered here combine a range of scholarship—theoretical and empirical—on poverty, social policy, economic development from a comparative perspective.

In terms of theoretical innovations, this book brings a systems approach to the social welfare debate in India and argues for *development resilience* as the scope of this system. We approach the social welfare question not merely as a tool of improving the many metrics of human deprivation, but as an enabler of human resilience through various *forms* of welfare interventions which address current as well as the future incidence of poverty in its various expressions. We envisage the expansion of social safety nets not only as a policy tool to support the poor, but to build their capability with the ideas of bridging the endowment gaps between the *haves and have-nots*—or *India* versus *Bharat* (India's pre-historical name)—and foster resilience against the fragility of economic lives in the wake of impending economic, social, or environmental change.

[25] While one set of the research is focused on social policies in general, the other focuses on social welfare policies directly. Dreze and Sen (2002, 2013) discuss the causes and consequences of inadequate success on social development indicators and human capabilities in India. Based upon many decades of field work, Krishna (2017) provides a perspective on the limited opportunities for social mobility for the majority of Indians. Kohli (2012) deliberates on the failures of redistributive policy in the country. Gupta (2012) focuses upon the structure of bureaucracy which limits effectiveness of social policies. Mody (2023) sketches out the decadal changes in the politics of poverty between 1947 and 2022. Basu (2017) pens a personal account of his experience as a policymaker when social welfare programs were being reformed. Banerjee et al. (2019) highlight the developmental challenges of the country considering the economic change since 2000s. Drèze (2019) masterfully narrates how social policies have impacted human lives from the eyes of an activist-economist of first grade. Chiriyankandath et al. (2020) describe policy changes between 2004 and 2014 which led to the expansion of social protection in India. Tillin et al. (2015) highlight the political factors which explain the rise of Indian subnational units as the torchbearers of social welfare reforms. Pellissery (2021) argues that the 'social' question in Indian policy has traditionally focused on political empowerment to the marginal group.

In their most recent book, *Good Economics for Hard Times*, Nobel Laureate economists, Abhijit Banerjee and Esther Duflo, remark that the "goal of social policy, in these times of change and anxiety, is to help people absorb the shocks that affect them without allowing those shocks to affect their sense of themselves. Unfortunately, this is not the system we have inherited. Our social protection still has its Victorian overlay, and all too many politicians do not try to hide their contempt for the poor and disadvantaged. Even with a shift in attitude, social protection will require a profound rethinking and an injection of lots of imagination." They further note that, "we clearly don't have all the solutions, and suspect nobody else does either. We have much more to learn. But as long as we understand what the goal is, we can win." This book has a similarly modest aim. We do not claim to have an answer to all the challenges of social safety net in India. Rather, we have provided a framework which allows us to pose relevant questions and generate a debate which is theoretically sound and empirically grounded in India's economic reality. Economist John Maynard Keynes is often attributed (erroneously, it seems) to have remarked that "it is better to be roughly right than precisely wrong."[26] In truly Keynesian spirit (even if it is wrongly attributed to him), our policy prescriptions are based upon the economic structure inherited from past policies and the forces of globalization which are unfolding and would likely shape the future. There are assumptions—some of which may reflect our biases—which may or may not hold the test of time. What is important, however, is to have an informed deliberation around questions which we care about amidst the changing nature of economic risks, vulnerabilities, and the quest for a resilient society.

Roadmap

In the subsequent chapters of the book, we begin focusing on individual programs, deliberate upon their origins, evidence around their effectiveness, and how they could be redesigned in the future.

We begin by describing a general schema for the global expansion of social welfare policies along the path of structural transformation in Chapter 2. Based upon theoretical underpinnings of 'social welfare' and the learning around the implementation of social welfare in India and

[26] https://www.oxfordreference.com/display/10.1093/acref/9780191866692.001.0001/q-oro-ed6-00016758;jsessionid=4571412CE821B186DF3A8386F8E641E5.

abroad, we highlight the rising importance of more demand-side promotive measures (to stop the flow into poverty) of social assistance along with the traditional preventive measures (consumption support to the already poor). We place these arguments in the context of changing economic structure of the developing countries which is characterized by questions around informal employment, gig economy, and the ensuing livelihood risks and vulnerability. In this chapter, we frame poverty as a multidimensional, multi-scalar, and dynamic concept which allows us to approach the issue of social protection as a system, and not only as standalone schemes. The ideas presented here become a source of motivation for the chapters to follow where we focus on the Indian context.

In Chapter 3, we analyze India's reliance on social welfare policies as a response to various developmental deficits from a historical perspective which allows us to review the successes and failures of these schemes in terms of their design, implementation, and welfare impact in the context of India's structural transformation and poverty reduction. We discuss the variety of anti-poverty programs—food transfers, public works, mother and child support, social pensions, and health insurance—as they were progressively introduced over the course of last seven decades. In this chapter, we also highlight the subnational differences in economic and human development outcomes to show that the poorest regions have been lacking in enhancing the effective implementation of welfare programs. Looking into the future, we argue that welfare programs of the future must be attuned to the changing economic and demographic transformation of the economy—as characterized by stagnant farm income, slower pace of urbanization, deindustrialization of the economy, and rising informality of employment—to facilitate a resilient development process.

In the following chapters (Chapters 4–7), we discuss a family of social protection schemes under a common developmental objective (such as income, food security, or nutrition), unpack its theoretical rationale, provide its historical imperative, deliberate upon the implementation design, summarize its impact, discuss policy relevance, and conclude with suggestions for the future. In Chapter 4, we lay out the nature of poverty, livelihood arrangements, economic structure, and ensuing developmental challenges facing the country. Drawing upon the economic policy documents, we specifically discuss how poverty has been synonymous with famines and hunger, in rural India, which gets reflected in the design of social safety nets. As the most important instrument of rural poverty reduction, we discuss the importance of the public works program in contributing to rural prosperity, along with an emphasis on social pensions for the elderly, and newly introduced cash transfers for the farmers. We also highlight that with changes in economic and demographic structure, urban livelihood challenges are now as rampant prominent with rising informality of employment. Lack of employer-based social security and rising threats of climate change have also exacerbated vulnerability for the non-poor. We, therefore, argue for a more dynamic and encompassing social welfare policies in the future which not only need to expand their focus to urban poor but are also geared toward addressing the emerging sources of poverty and vulnerability.

In the following chapter (Chapter 5), we investigate the role of in-kind food transfers through PDS in reducing hunger and improving nutrition. PDS, arguably the most debated of all social welfare schemes in India, has a long history going back to its introduction as a relief measure for urban workers during the Second World War. It continues to be a major source of relief for the poor, with food transfers being a major source of welfare support during the ongoing COVID-19 crisis. Yet, it is beset with numerous challenges, fundamental to which is its reliance upon the state-driven farm procurement of food grains, which has distortionary market effects and compromises food system diversity and ecological sustainability. We deliberate upon these factors, including the political economy of it which abets the procurement–stocking–distribution 'gordian knot' to argue that any replacement of PDS with cash transfers—a key social policy debate—is essentially tied to the reforms in the agricultural sector.

It is widely known that early life nutritional assistance has a transformational effect on human capabilities through improvements in child health outcomes which further increase cognitive skills, work productivity, and halts the intergenerational persistence of poverty. Social welfare policies in India, however, did not pay much attention to these programs till very recently. Currently, nutritional assistance for mother and child under Integrated Child Development Scheme (ICDS) and free school afternoon meal under the Mid-day Meal Scheme (MDMS), along with maternity transfers to encourage institutional delivery are the key programs to address early life undernutrition and child health issues. In Chapter 6, we study the performance of such programs which are ameliorating intergenerational poverty. We argue that despite success in improving child outcomes, these are beset with operational challenges that could make them more potent instruments of addressing child malnutrition.

We highlight these challenges as overworked, demotivated, and underpaid staff at the ICDS centers, poor quality of meals in schools, and narrowly targeted maternal cash transfers for institutional delivery. Put together, these factors highlight the limited state capacity of the public systems which are essentially designed to cater to the poorer sections of the population as the relatively well-off sections of the population have already moved on toward private provisions of school and health, in the expectation of better quality.

While food and nutritional assistance have been the traditional *forms* of social safety nets in India, the *scope* of safety nets in improving health outcomes and supporting households against health shocks has been recognized only lately in the country. In Chapter 7, we discuss the importance of improved health as a fundamental pillar of economic development. Health continues to be an ignored area of social policy despite an agreement on adverse health shocks as a primary reason for slides into poverty, even for the non-poor. India's health care was designed along the lines of the British National Health Services (NHS) where seeking health care would be free for all. Yet, the availability and quality of health care in India has been abysmally poor while has led to a de facto private health care system which is expensive and unaffordable even to non-poor. In the early 2000s, subsidized public health insurance, targeted at the poor, has been introduced as a newer form of safety net. However, health insurance has had moderate success in India due to a poor health infrastructure, both in quality and reach. With the rising burden of no communicable diseases (NCDs) and increasing out-of-pocket patient health costs, health insurance will grow in importance to stem the tide of poverty. An emerging but sparse empirical literature on India suggests its limited effectiveness in Northern India, where other forms of social safety nets have lesser effectiveness, too, further calling into question the regional disparities in governance and state capacity across the country.

Chapter 8 discusses why social welfare schemes in India have been unable to build resilience despite the expansion of social welfare programs. Approaching this question through the lens of policymaking, we argue that the potential welfare impacts of social safety nets have been undermined because of restrictive *ideas* of human welfare and poverty, perverse political *interests*, and discriminatory last-mile *institutions*. The three *I's* of policymaking also allow us to deliberate upon the subnational differences in welfare outcome through laying out the divergent *ideas* which motivate citizen welfare, the *institutions* which were designed to deliver the welfare benefits, and how it shaped political *interests*, in this chapter. The arguments presented here—which suggest a failure of social policy in building an inclusive social welfare system—rely upon a rich vein of scholarship on policy science, institutional economics, and comparative politics.

Given a book with such a broad scope, we cannot shy away from engaging with the most pressing contemporary debates around social safety nets in country. In Chapter 9, we focus on the following central questions which hold the talisman for the future design of Indian social welfare policies: Can food transfers be replaced with cash? Would universalization of welfare programs increase its effectiveness? How can technological innovations overcome implementational hurdles which have traditionally plagued the welfare delivery systems? Is universal basic income (UBI) a feasible alternative to the array of poorly implemented welfare schemes in the country? Does India have the fiscal wherewithal and organization capability to manage and fund an expansive set of social safety nets?

Chapter 10 concludes the discussions in this book with a summary of the various insights generated in each of the chapters and lays out suggestions for the design of social welfare policies in the future. We highlight the need to imagine a social welfare *system* rather than just a mixture of independent schemes to engender a resilient development process.

References

Balboni, C., O. Bandiera, R. Burgess, M. Ghatak, and A. Heil. 2022. "Why Do People Stay Poor?*" *The Quarterly Journal of Economics* 137 (2): 785–844. https://doi.org/10.1093/qje/qjab045.

Banerjee, A., E. Duflo, N. Goldberg, D. Karlan, R. Osei, W. Pariente, J. Shapiro, B. Thuysbaert, and C. Udry. 2015. "A Multifaceted Program Causes Lasting Progress for the Very Poor: Evidence from Six Countries." *Science* 348 (6236): 1260799. https://doi.org/10.1126/science.1260799.

Banerjee, A., E. Duflo, and G. Sharma. 2021. Long-Term Effects of the Targeting the Ultra Poor Program. *American Economic Review: Insights* 3 (4): 471–86. https://doi.org/10.1257/aeri.20200667.

Banerjee, A., G. Gopinath, R. Rajan, and M.S. Sharma. 2019. *What the Economy Needs Now*. New Delhi: Juggernaut.

Banerjee, A., D. Karlan, R. Osei, H. Trachtman, and C. Udry. 2022a. "Unpacking a Multi-Faceted Program to Build Sustainable Income for the

Very Poor." *Journal of Development Economics* 155: 102781. https://doi.org/10.1016/j.jdeveco.2021.102781.

Banerjee, A., R. Hanna, B.A. Olken, and D. Sverdlin-Lisker. 2022b. "Social Protection in the Developing World." *Mimeo.*

Banerjee, A.V., and E. Duflo. 2007. "The Economic Lives of the Poor." Journal of Economic Perspectives 21 (1): 141–67. https://doi.org/10.1257/jep.21.1.141.

Bardhan, P. 2011. "Challenges for a Minimum Social Democracy in India." *Economic and Political Weekly*, 39–43.

Bardhan, P. 2012. "Awakening Giants, Feet of Clay: Assessing the Economic Rise of China and India." In *Awakening Giants, Feet of Clay*. Princeton: Princeton University Press. https://doi.org/10.1515/9781400845002.

Barrett, C.B., and M.R. Carter. 2013. "The Economics of Poverty Traps and Persistent Poverty: Empirical and Policy Implications." *The Journal of Development Studies* 49 (7): 976–90.

Barrett, C.B., M.R. Carter, and J.-P. Chavas, eds. 2019. *The Economics of Poverty Traps*. Chicago: The University of Chicago Press.

Barrett, C.B., and M.A. Constas. 2014. "Toward a Theory of Resilience for International Development Applications." *Proceedings of the National Academy of Sciences* 111 (40): 14625–30. https://doi.org/10.1073/pnas.1320880111.

Barrientos, A. 2009. "Labour Markets and the (Hyphenated) Welfare Regime in Latin America." *Economy and Society* 38 (1): 87–108. https://doi.org/10.1080/03085140802560553.

Barrientos, A. 2013. *Social Assistance in Developing Countries*. Cambridge: Cambridge University Press.

Basu, K. 2017. *An Economist in the Real World: The Art of Policymaking in India* (First MIT Press paperback edition). Cambridge: MIT Press.

Bhagwati, J. and Panagariya, A., 2013. *Why growth matters: How economic growth in India reduced poverty and the lessons for other developing countries*. Hachette UK.

Bowen, T., C. Del Ninno, C. Andrews, S. Coll-Black, K. Johnson, Y. Kawasoe, A. Kryeziu, B. Maher, and A. Williams. 2020. *Adaptive Social Protection: Building Resilience to Shocks*. Washington, DC: World Bank Publications.

Chiriyankandath, J., D. Maoirano, J. Manor, and L. Tillin. 2020. *The Politics of Poverty Reduction in India: The UPA Government, 2004 to 2014*. Hyderabad: Orient BlackSwan.

Collins, D., J. Morduch, S. Rutherford, and O. Ruthven. 2009. *Portfolios of the Poor*. Princeton: Princeton University Press. https://doi.org/10.2307/j.ctt7rzr4.

Deaton, A. 2013. *The Great Escape: Health, Wealth, and the Origins of Inequality*. Princeton: Princeton University Press.

Devereux, S., and Sabates-Wheeler, R. 2004. *Transformative Social Protection*. Brighton: Institute of Development Studies.

Drèze, J., ed. 2016. *Social Policy*. New Delhi: Orient BlackSwan.

Drèze, J. 2019. *Sense and Solidarity: Jholawala Economics for Everyone*. Oxford: Oxford University Press.

Drèze, J., and A. Sen. 1991. "Public Action for Social Security: Foundations and Strategy." In *Social Security in Developing Countries*, 3–40. Oxford: Oxford University Press.

Dreze, J., and A. Sen. 2002. *India: Development and Participation*. Oxford, UK: Oxford University Press.

Dreze, J., and A. Sen. 2013. *An Uncertain Glory: India and Its Contradictions*. Princeton: Princeton Press.

Duflo, E. 2017. "The Economist as Plumber." *American Economic Review* 107 (5): 1–26.

Esping-Andersen, G. 1990. *The Three Worlds of Welfare Capitalism*. Princeton: Princeton University Press.

Fiszbein, A., R. Kanbur, and R. Yemtsov. 2014. "Social Protection and Poverty Reduction: Global Patterns and Some Targets." *World Development* 61: 167–177.

Gentilini, U. 2022. *Cash Transfers in Pandemic Times: Evidence, Practices, and Implications from the Largest Scale Up in History*. Washington, DC: World Bank. https://doi.org/10.1596/37700.

Gentilini, U., M.B.A. Almenfi, T. Iyengar, Y. Okamura, J.A. Downes, P. Dale, M. Weber, D.L. Newhouse, C.P. Rodriguez Alas, and M. Kamran. 2022. *Social Protection and Jobs Responses to COVID-19*. Wessington, DC: World Bank.

Ghatak, M. 2015. "Theories of Poverty Traps and Anti-Poverty Policies." *The World Bank Economic Review* 29 (suppl 1): S77–S105. https://doi.org/10.1093/wber/lhv021.

Gupta, A. 2012. *Red Tape: Bureaucracy, Structural Violence, and Poverty in India*. Durham: Duke University Press.

Hanna, R., and D. Karlan. 2017. "Designing Social Protection Programs: Using Theory and Experimentation to Understand How to Help Combat Poverty." In *Handbook of Economic Field Experiments*, vol. 2, 515–53. Amsterdam: Elsevier.

Hickey, S. 2011. "The Politics of Social Protection: What Do We Get from a 'Social Contract' Approach?" *Canadian Journal of Development Studies/ Revue Canadienne d'études Du Développement* 32 (4): 426–38. https://doi.org/10.1080/02255189.2011.647447.

Ikegami, M., M.R. Carter, C.B. Barrett, and S. Janzen. 2018. "Poverty Traps and the Social Protection Paradox." In *The Economics of Poverty Traps*, 223–56. Chicago: University of Chicago Press.

Kohli, A. 1987. *The State and Poverty in India: The Politics of Reform*. Cambridge: Cambridge University Press.

Kohli, A. 2012. *Poverty Amid Plenty in the New India*. Cambridge: Cambridge University Press.

Kraay, A., and D. McKenzie. 2014. "Do Poverty Traps Exist? Assessing the Evidence." *Journal of Economic Perspectives* 28 (3): 127–48. https://doi.org/10.1257/jep.28.3.127.

Krishna, A. 2010. *One Illness Away: Why People Become Poor and How They Escape Poverty*. New York: Oxford University Press.

Krishna, A. 2017. *The Broken Ladder: The Paradox and Potential of India's One-Billion*. Cambridge: Cambridge University Press.

Kwon, H.-J. 1997. "Beyond European Welfare Regimes: Comparative Perspectives on East Asian Welfare Systems." *Journal of Social Policy* 26 (4): 467–84. https://doi.org/10.1017/S004727949700514X.

Lade, S.J., L.J. Haider, G. Engström, and M. Schlüter. 2017. "Resilience Offers Escape from Trapped Thinking on Poverty Alleviation." *Science Advances* 3 (5): e1603043. https://doi.org/10.1126/sciadv.1603043.

Levy, S., and N. Schady. 2013. "Latin America's Social Policy Challenge: Education, Social Insurance, Redistribution." *Journal of Economic Perspectives* 27 (2): 193–18.

Margitic, J., and M. Ravallion. 2019. "Lifting the Floor? Economic Development, Social Protection and the Developing World's Poorest." *Journal of Development Economics* 139: 97–108.

Mody, A. 2023. *India Is Broken: A People Betrayed, Independence to Today*. Stanford: Stanford University Press.

Page, L., and R. Pande. 2018. "Ending Global Poverty: Why Money Isn't Enough." *Journal of Economic Perspectives* 32 (4): 173–200. https://doi.org/10.1257/jep.32.4.173.

Pellissery, S. 2021. "Social Policy in India: One Hundred Years of the (Stifled) Social Question." In *One Hundred Years of Social Protection*, edited by L. Leisering, 121–56. New York: Springer International Publishing. https://doi.org/10.1007/978-3-030-54959-6_4.

Piketty, T. 2020. *Capital and Ideology*. Cambridge, MA: Harvard University Press. https://doi.org/10.4159/9780674245075.

Ravallion, M. 2015. *The Economics of Poverty: History, Measurement, and Policy*. New York: Oxford University Press.

Ravallion, M. 2016. "Are the World's Poorest Being Left Behind?" *Journal of Economic Growth* 21 (2): 139–164.

Sen, A. 1981. "Public Action and the Quality of Life in Developing Countries." *Oxford Bulletin of Economics and Statistics* 43 (4): 287–319.

Tillin, L., R. Deshpande, and K. Kailash. 2015. *Politics of Welfare: Comparisons Across Indian States*. New Delhi: Oxford University Press.

World Bank. 2011. *Social Protection for a Changing India: Main Report*. Washington, DC: World Bank. https://openknowledge.worldbank.org/handle/10986/2745.

World Bank. 2018. *The State of Social Safety Nets 2018*. Washington, DC: The World Bank. https://doi.org/10.1596/978-1-4648-1254-5.

CHAPTER 2

Development Resilience as the *Scope* of Social Protection

Introduction

According to the latest estimates, every tenth person in the world (689 million people) lives in extremely poverty.[1] These numbers are surging further as we write this book. The novel coronavirus pandemic, COVID-19, has wrecked lives and livelihoods at an unprecedented scale. In just a few months following the economic lockdown in 2020, poverty levels in India returned to 2016 levels, as almost 3% of the labor force lost jobs and many others suffered economic and health setbacks—a new cohort of poor were added while those already poor were threatened by destitution.[2] Many more young children would therefore be born or raised in poverty with diminished human capital, and therefore, poorer future life outcomes. While pandemics are once in a lifetime phenomenon, economic lives of the poor are exposed to multifarious unavoidable risks over the course of their lifetime which diminishes their ability to invest in long-term productive assets, consigns them to *poverty traps*, and thereby

[1] According to the World Bank (2018), extreme poverty is measured as an expenditure of less than $1.90 a day. According to the same measure, global poverty stood at 9.2% in 2017 (Schoch and Lakner 2020).

[2] The figures come from the monthly panel surveys conducted by the Centre for Monitoring of the Indian Economy (CMIE). https://doi.org/10.1596/978-1-4648-1640-6.

A. Rahman and P. Pingali, *The Future of India's Social Safety Nets*,
Palgrave Studies in Agricultural Economics and Food Policy,
https://doi.org/10.1007/978-3-031-50747-2_2

perpetuates intergenerational poverty.[3] While some are able to escape poverty, vulnerability of non-poor to exogenous shocks such as loss of income, livelihoods, or illness ensures there is also a steady inflow of people into poverty. Lives and livelihoods, therefore, are fragile.

In traditional cultures, voluntary charitable assistance to the needy—often motivated through religious, moral, or social injunctions—acted as a form of social insurance against daily risks. Emperors and rulers maintained certain normative commitment to protecting the vulnerable against starvation during times of scarcity and famine.[4] In the modern day of nation-states and democratic forms of governance, providing citizens with social security or social protection is a part of the economic and political commitment—*social contract*—which provides the state the social legitimacy to govern and builds fealty to the nation among citizens.[5] But these commitments by the states are often absent in practice, weak or fractured, and also open to manipulations which leaves the poor behind and economic inequality across the world.

Organized state action to improve human welfare and eradicate poverty was influenced by industrial revolution-led economic transformation, suffering incurred in the World Wars in the early twentieth century, and the political need for solidarity and nation-building exercise.[6] By 1960s, most advanced nations had introduced various social protection programs as a part of their democratic responsibilities. A strong social welfare system financed with progressive taxation and economic efficiency, along with the ideals of equality of opportunity and social justice, led

[3] See Banerjee and Duflo (2007) for a survey.

[4] During the imperial era of Egyptian and Roman civilizations, free distribution of food to the people was particularly common. These measures served to ensure peace, avoid civic unrest, maintain law and order, and ensure suzerainty of the kings and rulers.

[5] Social contract signifies the formal and informal reciprocal rights and obligations of citizens and the nation-state with each other, as commonly understood in the social science literature. The notion of social contract varies by democratic culture, electoral competition, civil society, and nation-state ideals.

[6] Bismarck proclaimed the first social insurance law in Germany in 1880. In a decade's time, Denmark, New Zealand, and Australia introduced old age pension schemes. Subsequently, Britain legislated compensation for unemployed workers, old age pensions, and an insurance program for the sick and disabled in the early 1900s. Across the Atlantic, US President Roosevelt introduced a massive public works program in response to the Great Depression of the 1930s, and consequently, a welfare state came into being in America with the "New Deal" legislation. In the midst of the Second World War, Britain and France announced their own ambitious welfare state plans.

to a resounding success in lowering poverty, inequality, and improved overall human and economic development in the Western nations.[7] East Asian economies ramped up their social protection programs in order to recover from the economic crisis of 1997–1998, even though they were at a more modest level of economic development than the Western nations.[8] Subsequently the idea of social protection spread to the poorer countries of Global South (Brazil, Mexico, India, South Africa, Indonesia, Ethiopia, among others) much like a 'quiet' revolution motivated by foreign aid, rights-based humanitarian concerns, threats of informality of labor, leading to various innovations in social safety net designs brought about by technological advancements and political considerations.[9]

Social protection systems in the developing countries, however, despite the recent expansion continue to be small, weak, and benefit only a few.[10] The developed nations spend a large share of their overall gross domestic product (GDP) on tax-financed social protection policies which includes unemployment benefits, social insurance, and other forms of assistance (Fig. 2.1). Most notably, the Scandinavian countries famously known for the Nordic welfare model—where every citizen is covered under a variety of programs that ensure they do not fall through the cracks and maintain a certain minimum standard of living—stand out. In most developed countries, the social contract is built around a much larger role of the state in ensuring its citizens live their life with dignity and respect. Developing countries, on the other hand, have a weaker social contract where rights and responsibilities to a better life rests more on the individuals than the

[7] The twin pillars of market-based capitalism and democratic socialism, on which the postwar Western economies were built, created a hybrid system—varying by countries—making them far from the ideal welfare states, as many thinkers have conceptualized. Yet, the *welfarist* turn of the advance nations has indeed been exemplary in generating domestic prosperity. See Esping-Andersen (1990, 1999).

[8] The East Asian example highlighted the risks of globalization to domestic poverty and expansion of social protection in response showed that an social inclusion and economic growth together are possible. Interested readers can refer to Kwon (2005) for more detailed description of social protection reforms in East Asian countries.

[9] See Hanlon et al. (2012).

[10] Barrientos (2013) provides a comprehensive review of reforms what challenges with the social assistance policies in developing countries.

state. As a result, they have a relatively underdeveloped social protection system and suffer from much higher rates of poverty and deprivation.[11]

The last few decades, however, have seen a concerted attempt at creating a social protection architecture in the low-income countries (LICs), as the concerns of poverty and redistribution have been at the center of global development.[12] Millennium Development Goals (MDGs) and its successor, Sustainable Development Goals (SDGs) explicitly invoke the need for social protection as a 'global' social contract in order to achieve the poverty reduction commitments (Birdsall 2008). This is in continuation of the safety nets *agenda*, promoted by the World Bank and other global agencies during the late 1990s—in the wake of economic restructuring and globalization in developing countries—in the

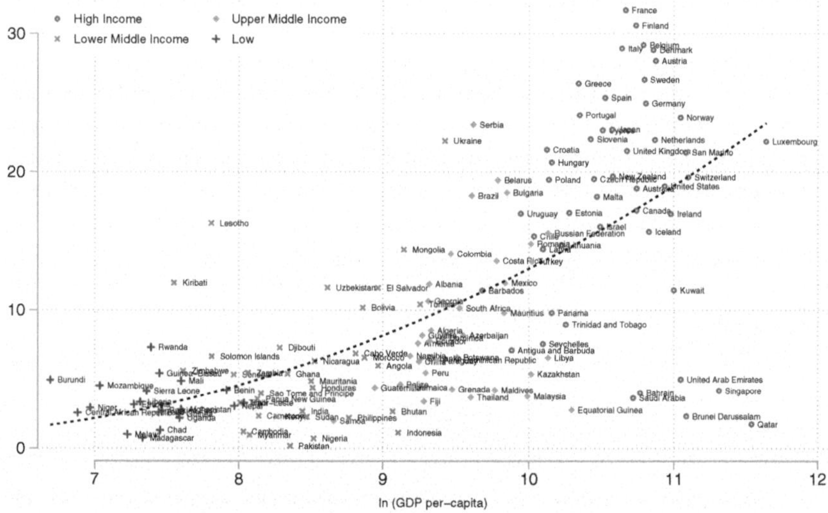

Fig. 2.1 Expenditure on social protection and per capita income (2017) (*Source* International Labour Organization [ILO])

[11] For a more elaborate discussion on the linkages between social protection and social contract, refer to Hickey (2011).

[12] Global development commitments in the form of Millennium Development Goals (MDGs) and its successor, Sustainable Development Goals (SDGs) explicitly invoke social protection as a tool for anti-poverty policy. These commitments are also considered to be a sort of 'global' social contract (Birdsall 2008).

"global fight against poverty." The social risks framework as espoused by the World Bank envisaged safety nets—a combination of programs—as a bulwark against everyday economic risks and catastrophic exogenous shocks which make households vulnerable and potentially descend into poverty.[13] Yet, despite the significant expansion of the social protection programs in the developing countries, it has not enabled the poorest of the poor to break through the poverty trap on a scale, as expected.[14]

This book is an attempt at diagnosing the ineffectiveness of the social safety nets and providing a framework which allows us to envisage social safety nets as a tool for building *resilience*—reducing current poverty along with an enhanced human capability to reduce the likelihood of future poverty. The key contribution of this book is to argue the following: long-term success of social welfare lies in transcending the narrow conceptualization of welfare as 'schemes for a problem' toward a more encompassing social welfare 'systems' which *provides support for all, at all stages of life* in order to allow a life of dignity. Focusing on India, we provide policy perspective on how to operationalize a social welfare system which leaves no one behind and contributes to long-term gains in economic and human development.

Conceptualizing social protection as mere safeguard or a risk-reducing instrument—in the form cash or in-kind transfer, or public employment against an exogenous adverse shock, which could be addressed through smoothening the consumption gap—has been a major undoing of the social safety nets in bringing about transformational impact on poverty.[15]

[13] Safety nets were considered essential to safeguard the poor against the risks of loss to livelihood, displacement, illness, etc. (World Bank 2000). Through a slew of programs, their aim is to "protect a person or household against two adverse outcomes in welfare: chronic incapacity to work and earn (*chronic poverty*) and a decline in this capacity from a marginal situation that provides minimal means for survival with few reserves (*transient poverty*)" (Subbarao et al. 1997, p. 2).

[14] While social transfers have enabled 36% of the very poor to escape extreme poverty, cross-country analysis by Margitic and Ravallion (2019) suggests that the rise in spending on social protection in LICs has lifted the 'subsistence floor' as a whole, the poorest are often left behind in benefiting from the spending. The poorest therefore are 'left behind.'

[15] Safety nets are effectively designed with the aim of stemming the descent of transitory poor into chronic poverty. Such conceptualization ignores those who are chronically poor. Barrett (2005, p. 48), therefore, points out to need for another class of interventions, which he refers to as "cargo nets" to pull the chronic poor out of their condition.

Comprehensive social safety nets not only need to provide social assistance to stem the descent of households into poverty or pull them out of poverty traps, but also need to provide an opportunity to take off on the path to prosperity.[16] We argue that safety net interventions need to move from merely preventive cures to the problems of poverty to building household resilience to have a transformative impact. Anti-poverty transfers should not only target consumption assistance, which removes resource constraints and enhances productive capacity in the short run, but should also promote capital accumulation over the long run.

While the empirical context of this study is rooted to India, we believe the relevance of this book goes beyond the present context. The present chapter sets the tone for this book where we highlight some of the fundamental aspects of social protection policies—its conceptualization and purported impacts—essential for long-term reduction in global poverty. We provide a framework and build a taxonomy of social safety nets to argue that for social protection programs to succeed in reducing poverty and vulnerability, one must expand the *scope* of them beyond the narrow objectives of social safety nets as merely instruments of safeguarding against the risks of poverty. For a transformative welfare impact, social welfare policies need to move the *focus* away from poverty—measured as a money metric—to those identified as poor. Poverty manifests itself multi-dimensionally—deprivation along the dimensions of health, education, and nutrition—and each of them require a different lever of the social welfare apparatus to promote the potential human capability.[17] Similarly, the *form* of social protection needs to adapt to the changing nature of deprivation along the development trajectory of a nation. A more expansive *scope, form, and focus* of an anti-poverty program would enable a more resilient development process and bring about transformational change.

[16] In the parlance of social protection, their role as a "trampoline" was used by World Bank (2000) in the *World Development Report 2000/2001: Attacking Poverty*, while Barrett (2005, p. 48) introduced the term "cargo net" as a means to pull households out of chronic poverty.

[17] For a detailed discussion on poverty, entitlements, and human capability, see Sen (2001).

Enabling Development Resilience

We invoke the concept of ***development resilience*** as an overarching theme or scope of progress through social safety nets. Resilience, as a developmental objective, has been an important part of the global debate around increasing the "the ability of countries, communities, and households to manage change by maintaining or transforming living standards in the face of shocks or stress" (DFID 2011, p. 6).[18] Safety nets, through insuring against such risks—either due to covariate (conflicts or natural disasters) or idiosyncratic shocks (health, etc.)—enhance individual or household resilience. While such risks are disproportionately more acute on the poor, they are equally threatening those around the poverty line, even above it.

For resilient development, welfare policy should not only concern itself with current levels of poverty and deprivation, but also to vulnerability to poverty in the future as well. The strategy for addressing poverty, present and future, should also depend upon where households lie on the scale of deprivation. Those pushed into poverty because of an adverse shock, since they lie closer to the poverty line, can be served through social assistance, which covers their consumption or income decline. For the extreme poor, however, merely the stability of consumption through safety nets may not suffice in pulling them from poverty, and hence, need much stronger support on multiple fronts of development, providing them with suitable opportunities to accumulate more assets so that they make a sustainable transition out of poverty.[19] Both of these sets of households are at risk of being trapped in poverty but require different policy responses—the latter, a more comprehensive one.[20] Although the poorest

[18] In more technical terms, development resilience is conceptualized as promoting the "stochastic dynamics of individual and collective human well-being" (Barrett and Constas 2014, p. 14625).

[19] While highlighting the role of safety nets as an important source of breaking out of the poverty trap, Barrett and Carter (2013) pointed out that social assistance of a limited amount can help escape poverty only for those just below the poverty threshold, with a negligible effect on those at the extreme.

[20] This is based upon the idea of multiple poverty traps introduced by Ikegami et al. (2019). They argued that existence of multiple poverty traps implies that not all households have the same ability to benefit from a transfer of equivalent amount. There are some households that are perpetually poor, while some are vulnerable to poverty but have a slight ability to accumulate assets when they are able to anticipate risks, *ex ante*.

households may benefit from progressive transfers, the vulnerable but non-poor groups might benefit from contingent transfers, so that they remain above the subsistence level through a multiplier effect.[21] The resilience approach requires incorporating the goals of long-term response and transformative development, without which safety nets can only serve a palliative response of support against risks, at best.

The essential idea behind social protection, or safety nets, is that it should cease to exist or at least, over time, a very low proportion of individuals would require the support. It should progressively become an option only for those who are not able to sustain a minimum standard of living through their livelihoods. Such a situation is possible only when there is an improvement in the ability of households to accumulate human and physical assets essential to fully exercise their capabilities. Adapting to risks and the ability to withstand health shocks, or loss of jobs, essentially emanate from a certain different kind of deprivation in skills, education, or nutrition. Lack of education and skills leads to unemployment or under-employment. Similarly, poor nutrition or health undermines cognitive potentials; and certain cultural or exclusionary practices, such as participation of women in the labor force, further hinder economic growth and transformation. Social safety should play a role in promoting resilient development by addressing many such developmental shortfalls—often during the most appropriate life-cycle window, or for a specific subpopulation or geography—to have a ***transformational*** effect (Sabates-Wheeler and Devereux 2007).

To bring about this transformational change, the scope of social welfare policies should be more expansive, which not only ensures the maintenance of a minimum of consumption needs but also addresses structural inequalities, promotes equal opportunities for all, and stems the intergenerational persistence of poverty. A more ambitious social safety architecture with a wider set of objectives—like addressing livelihood insecurity, or nutritional capabilities, or promoting asset accumulation—can engender greater synergies among many of the standalone schemes, thereby increasing overall welfare impact. By combining the various

[21] Ikegami et al. (2019, p. 242) built a dynamic stochastic model of consumption and asset accumulation, relevant to the developing country context and argued for a hybrid social protection system that combines traditional means-tested cash transfers with a "state of the world contingent transfers" (SWCTs) to be made to those who are vulnerable to negative shocks in the future, but non-poor currently.

aspects of social assistance—addressing essential needs; prevention of the fall into poverty; building assets and human capabilities—a resilient development process can be stimulated that leads to greater prosperity and ensures that the poorest are not left behind.[22] The scope of social welfare should enhance human functioning and capabilities. Social safety nets, which engender resilience through an expansion of human functioning and capabilities, fulfill the ideals of social justice that underpin the moral philosophy of social assistance of any form.

Consistency with the Social Justice Paradigm

Welfare, in the form of state support for the poor, destitute, or vulnerable emanates from moral imperatives of social justice, where a society's progress needs to be judged by its ability to improve the well-being of the poorest person (Rawls 1971).[23] The state, as Rawls argued, needs to have "strains of commitment" to a "social minimum" essential for citizens to lead a "decent life, and... more" (Rawls 2001, pp. 129–30). The justice-based concept of a social minimum moves beyond merely a subsistence-level consumption floor of basic needs toward basic rights and the political participation of the poor. Rawls' social minimum seeks to ensure all citizens have equal access to *primary goods*, which include fundamental individual liberty, choice, income, wealth, and a sense of self-respect, so that they are able to participate in economic cooperation on an equal footing. The state, he argued, should engage therefore in some form of redistribution through transfers, so that all citizens have a "social minimum" of primary goods, thereby increasing the well-being of those on the lowest strata of society (Rawls 2001, p. 130). The social minimum in the Rawlsian world is, therefore, developmental and transformative.

Nussbaum and Sen (1993) extended the same idea further, influencing global thinking around basic needs and what constitutes a good quality of life, especially in the developing countries. In his influential essay, *Justice:*

[22] Leaving no one behind is also the theme of SDGs. See UN (2017).

[23] In his classical treatise, *A Theory of Justice*, John Rawls (1971, p. 136) had argued that principles of justice as chosen from behind a "veil of ignorance"—when there is natural awareness of one's own abilities, stature, sex, race, or tastes—ought to affirm a system that seeks to minimize inequality through elevating the position of the poorest person.

Means Versus Freedom, Sen extends the Rawlsian formulations of distribution and puts forth his idea that the equality of primary goods (liberty, choice, economic status, and self-respect, in the Rawlsian world), should be replaced with human capabilities (Sen 1990).[24] The capability-based approach, as it is commonly known, recognizes the undue disadvantages that occur to some through a "natural lottery," as a result of disability, gender, health, etc. The 'capability set' in Sen's framework, "stands for the actual freedom of choice a person has over alternative lives that he or she can lead" (Sen 1990, p. 114). A social minimum, therefore, should be based upon enhancing the actual capabilities that people need to prosper and pursue their own desired outcomes, whatever they may be. It enshrines the citizen with the "entitlements" they have over their human worth and dignity, as instrumental to further pursuits of human flourishing (Nussbaum 2000).

The social justice framework that a society's progress should be judged by is its ability to improve the well-being of the poorest person in the society, most notably reflected in the UN's Sustainable Development Goals (SDGs), which advocate for a development paradigm where "no one is left behind" (UN 2017).[25] Yet, the ideals of state commitment to a social minimum have remained limited to maintaining people above subsistence, especially in LICs. Using social protection to achieve social

[24] Sen (1990, p. 114) is critical of Rawls' selection of primary goods as the set of desirable outcomes 'every rational man is presumed to want.' According to Sen, Rawls is silent on the differential ability of various individuals to utilize these goods as valuable "functionings." What is the benefit of having more primary goods than others, if one requires more effort to attain the same level of functioning due to some impairment or disability?

[25] Even the Preamble of the Swiss Constitution proclaims, "the strength of a people is measured by the well-being of its weakest members" (Switzerland 1999). In the context of India, it is important to add that Gandhi's *talisman*, or his social thoughts, resonated with the welfare of the most destitute. Gandhi is reported to have said:

> Whenever you are in doubt, or when the self becomes too much with you, apply the following test. Recall the face of the poorest and the weakest man [woman] whom you may have seen, and ask yourself, if the step you contemplate is going to be of any use to him [her]. Will he [she] gain anything by it? Will it restore him [her] to a control over his [her] own life and destiny? In other words, will it lead to *Swaraj* [freedom] for the hungry and spiritually starving millions? Then you will find your doubts and your self melt away (Gandhi 2004, p. 1).

justice outcomes still remains a far cry from the norm, though newer forms of social contracts between states and citizens can be seen in many countries, like India with a rights-based approach.[26]

Resilience Through Social Safety Nets: Expanding Upon Focus, Form, and Scope

The principal reason why so many fall outside of the welfare system in developing countries is that the welfare system is designed for a very few, addressing a narrow dimension of poverty and deprivation. Let us explain this further by distinguishing between the various forms of social protection.[27] Unpacking what is meant by *social protection* also allows us to understand how the welfare policies differ across developed and developing countries.

Social protection policies, very broadly, comprise a set of public actions that stem from the government's desire to address social risks, reduce vulnerability, and deprivation. It includes "all public and private initiatives that provide income or consumption transfers to the poor, protect the vulnerable against livelihood risks, and enhance the social status and rights of the marginalised; with the overall objective of reducing the economic and social vulnerability of poor, vulnerable and marginalised groups" (Devereux and Sabates-Wheeler 2004, p. iii). A schematic representation of the various social protection strategies is provided in Fig. 2.2. There are three arms to it—direct social assistance, social insurance, and labor regulations—each of which implies a distinct type of public action. Social assistance involves direct transfers—money or food—to the needy, which includes the elderly, disabled, or unemployed. Similarly, nutritional supplementation or deworming medicines are also a part of direct transfers, which address some manifestations of poverty, such as malnutrition and poor health. Many of the developing countries also use public work programs, as a form of income assistance, to provide gainful livelihoods. Since economic shocks could be consequential to many, and not only for the poor and unemployed, strategies for social protection also include employer-based insurance. Often, the government contributes to

[26] For a comprehensive discussion on rights-based human development in India, refer to Hirsch et al. (2019).

[27] Until now, we have used social protection, safety nets, and social assistance synonymously. We will distinguish between them now.

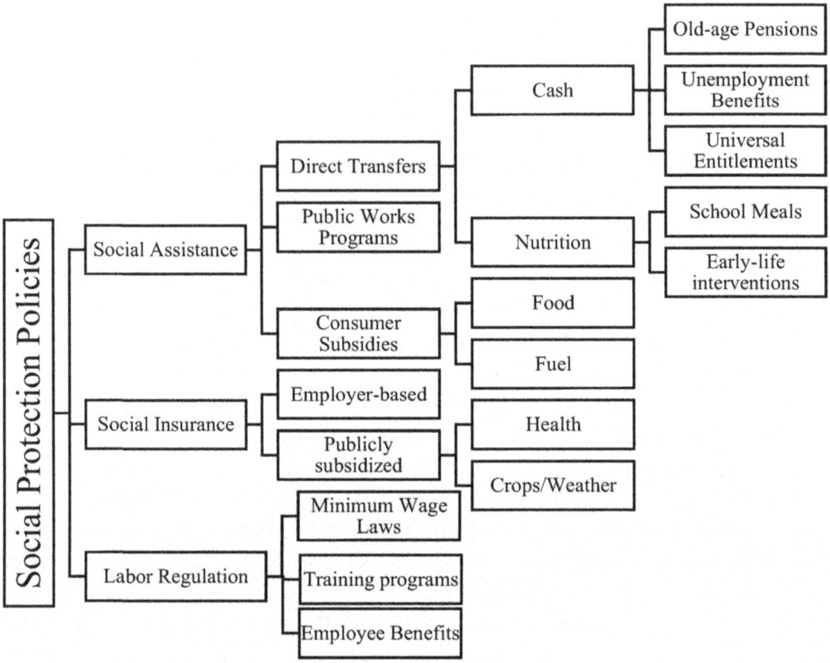

Fig. 2.2 Components of social protection policies (*Source* Authors' depiction)

the insurance premium in poorer countries where formal sector jobs are fewer and insurance markets underdeveloped. Government can also intervene to provide social protection in the form of unemployment insurance, training programs, or other benefits. As part of their social protection strategy, developed countries also developed labor regulation policies.

Social Protection Strategies Across Countries: Coverage and Instruments

The choice of public action rests on the nature of risk, the conception of poverty among policymakers, and the available monetary resources, apart from the political commitment to address these risks. Most of the LICs and low-and-middle-income countries (LMICs), despite having the largest share of poor people in the world, have a narrower set of social welfare schemes which provides protection coverage to only less than 40% of the poor. They have a narrower set of social welfare schemes (Panel A, Fig. 2.3). Developed countries, on the other hand, mostly rely upon social insurance and labor market policies as instruments to protect people against social risks. Among the range of social assistance strategies possible, in-kind transfer of food remains the most prominent choice, followed by unconditional cash transfers and conditional cash transfers (CCTs) (Panel B, Fig. 2.3) among the LICs and LMICs. Lower population coverage has meant that social assistance policies in the developing countries have largely been beneficial only to those closer to the subsistence consumption level, suggesting that the *poorest* have been left behind (Margitic and Ravallion 2019).

At this point, it is important to remind readers of the history of modern welfare states. Expanded social welfare in the developed world came about as a result of the forces of economic transformation. Greater industrialization facilitated rural-to-urban migration, which led to a decline in

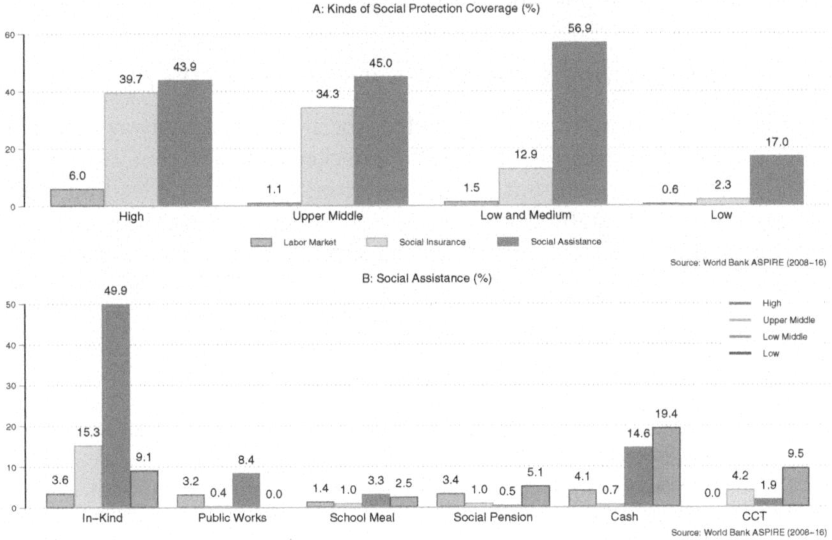

Fig. 2.3 Social protection coverage by income classification (*Source* World Bank ASPIRE [2008–2016]. See https://www.worldbank.org/en/data/datatopics/aspire)

the traditional community-based self-insurance mechanisms. Cities had to cope with rising populations, which led to strains on the urban public infrastructure, such as water, housing, schools, etc.[28] The movement of labor from rural to urban areas created economic insecurity for the wage earners, as the work was casual in nature; employees could be laid off easily in times of lower demand. As the threat of mass unemployment, and therefore, impoverishment became imminent, workers began to unionize. The organized labor movement emerged as a potent industrial and political force, and the advanced nations were forced to consider their demands for social security and redistribution.[29] As the suffering of the poor had an effect on the overall economy, it came to be realized that answers to these problems should be sought in public action.[30] State response varied depending upon the existing economic condition and demographic structure at the turn of the twentieth century. The ability of the state to address the vulnerabilities of the poor was boosted, however, by administrative capacity that had expanded enormously during wartime and was used to bring about social and economic reconstruction with the ideals of a social commitment to the people.

Challenges of Safety Nets in the Developing World

Although some form of state-provided social assistance always existed in developing countries, its history is checkered by lack of resources, political will, and inconsistent implementation; yet, they are leading their own march toward establishing a welfare architecture. Countries in Latin America, Southeast Asia, South Asia, and sub-Saharan Africa have seen an emergence of social protection schemes since the 1990s, which include

[28] Greater population density in the cities also increased the challenges of crime and spread of contagious diseases, which affected the quality of life for the poor as well as the rich. Existing systems of private and community-led social provisions were breaking down as a result of the changing economy and sectoral shifts in output share.

[29] The focus of the welfare system in the Western world in the early twentieth century was, therefore, primarily to address income insecurity as a result of loss of unemployment brought about by sickness, loss of job, or disability. Since the burden fell more on those with larger family sizes or dependents (children and elderly), the vulnerable members were provided extra assistance.

[30] Employers, too, realized the usefulness of social insurance—in promoting the health, welfare, and education of the workers—as advantageous to their firms, as it expanded the human capacities on which they relied upon to innovate and further economic growth.

various forms of cash and in-kind transfers, social insurance, and health care to provide a modicum of security to the vast populations that the countries contain.[31] Welfare policies in the developing countries, like in the postwar advanced societies, have responded to a change in the socio-economic situation, albeit under a different set of circumstances. Instead of industrialization and the rise of labor organizations, social policies of the developing countries have been a response to structural adjustment and the forces of globalization, which have distributional concerns arising from these factors. Economic integration of the developing countries with advanced ones has opened opportunities, while also exposing developing nations to vulnerabilities due to the changes in global markets, with greater risks falling on the less powerful countries and their residents. As a result, globalization has played an important role in increasing the demand for social protection among developing countries (Rodrik 1998). Maturing of the democratic systems in developing countries has further empowered citizens to voice their concerns and exercise their political rights. As a result, in the last decade of the twentieth century, developing countries began to use social protection programs as key components of their social policies with the aim of addressing poverty.[32]

The conceptualization of welfare assistance in the developing countries, however, has been different. Unlike in advanced nations, the demand for social safety nets has come in developing countries when they were largely rural and with underdeveloped industrial structures. With a largely agrarian economy, developing countries have had to focus more on the economic risks that emanate from risks to agriculture and agriculture-based livelihoods. The poor, mainly in rural areas, relying on agriculture-based livelihoods, are prone to risks, such as loss of a crop, unemployment, untimely death, or famine, all of which expose individuals to multiple kinds of economic distress. Further, they are also constrained in their ability to partake in the economic activities, outside of agriculture, which could improve their well-being. They are, therefore, vulnerable to a host of risks—economic, social and natural. The urban populations in

[31] Barrientos and Hulme (2009) considered it as a "quiet revolution" in area of social protection.

[32] Despite its limited coverage, there is no doubt that social safety nets have been instrumental in reducing poverty among developing countries; yet, much needs to be done in terms of having the desired impact on reducing poverty and inequality (Fiszbein et al. 2014).

these countries are prone to the similar nature of risks present in the postwar advanced economies, and more. Much of the manufacturing and service sector jobs are informal in nature, with little or poor legal institutions to support workers in times of job losses. Therefore, even in developing countries, with a larger share of urban population, it has been difficult to create a welfare system similar to the West, because the organizational power of the labor force in these countries is lower (Rudra 2008).[33] Developing countries with abundant low-skilled labor nut divided along multiple axes of identity are less likely to form a potent coalition that could petition the state for welfare concerns. As a result, developing countries have a set of welfare programs—mainly social assistance, as a form of relief against livelihood shocks—which are much more limited compared to the population's needs (Barrientos 2013, p. 8). This is in contrast to the developed world, where noncontributory social assistance is only a 'residual' part of the overall social protection strategy meant for the very few who are not captured through the more advanced forms of social protection—through social insurances or labor regulations in place—largely because of the greater formal sector jobs which means that the social protection or social security is often tied to the employer.

Social safety nets, merely as instruments of emergency relief or risk mitigation, have constrained its transformative potential in developing countries. Fundamental to addressing poverty or vulnerability is first understanding its causes and then employing a range of tools, that is, social protection programs to address it. National policy choices—the amount, intended beneficiaries, and forms of transfer—are not independent of the understanding of poverty, policy ideas, economic states, and political ideals at that point in time. The process of structural transformation and a country's position along the path of economic development therefore has an influence on the nature of social welfare policies required (Ravallion 2015). However, even a pro-poor safety net program could ignore the concerns of citizen right and social equity—in the philosophical moorings of promoting social justice—which are fundamental components of transformative social policy design.

[33] In the European countries, in fact, social welfare payments have increased as a response to globalization.

Expansion in Scope, Focus, and Form

The background presented here helps lay out the essential framing of our framework, according to which social safety nets should be expanded along three fundamental dimensions: *scope*, *form* and *focus* (Fig. 2.4). By *scope*, we mean the developmental objectives of safety net programs; *focus* refers to the beneficiaries; and *form* refers to the instrument or the design of the respective programs. Since social policies have multiple objectives, which evolve over time along a country's development trajectory, safety net policies—in *scope*, *form* and *focus*—should consider welfare objectives beyond addressing economic risks, poverty traps, and asset accumulation that can help to arrest the further slide into poverty. Therefore, social protection policies should offer a *menu* of assistance, which not only ensures that human deprivation and basic needs are taken care of, but also prevents household consumption to fall below a socially accepted minimum in the current time and in the future. The policies should also allow individuals to partake equally in economic opportunities as they arise; and the policies should develop human capabilities that allow for full exercise of "human functioning" to which the social justice paradigm appeals.

Citizens in developing countries do not have the luxury of abundant resources and strong political systems to ensure the social contract is strongly in their favor. Yet, democratic accountability has led to a surge in social protection architecture, even though it remains residual in nature. To design safety nets in the future, one must first recognize that developing countries have human developmental deficits myriad in *scope*, and as a result, the solutions need to be equally varied. A resilient system has to encounter multiple challenges, which include provision of basic needs for some, addressing the risks to lives and livelihoods for many, while also providing an enabling environment through appropriate regulations to create equitable economic opportunities to all, for an overall transformation and gain in human capabilities. Although the developed world may have to worry more about the later stage's challenges, developing countries have to worry about all of them at the same time, while adapting to their own typical economic transformation trajectory.

As noted previously, social assistance in the developing countries in the early stages of development has been mostly of providing for basic provisions—food transfers focused narrowly on a certain population or region. Learning from the growth process along with the democratic

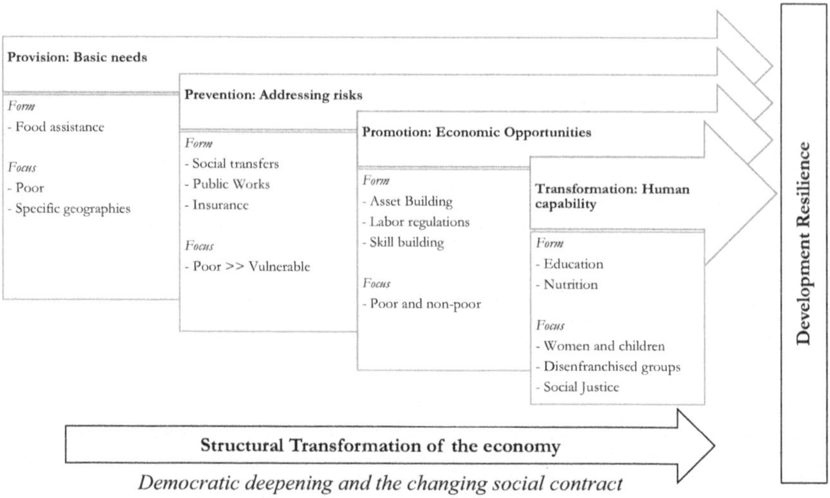

Fig. 2.4 A conceptual framework to explain the role of social protection policies in enhancing development resilience (*Source* Author's construction)

deepening has further led to a demand side, as well as supply side, push for preventive measures, arising out of various individual- and community-level risks. This has led to a greater stress on other forms of transfers, which address the various manifestations of poverty and the likelihood of a poverty trap. As a result, public works, child nutrition, and other forms of social insurance, which prevent people from falling into poverty, have been instituted. Insurance, health, or employment are good examples of the same, as they also prevent people from falling into poverty. Once provisions of basic consumption needs and risk prevention are installed, a large-scale transition out of poverty into prosperity is possible only when social assistance allows for asset accumulation to benefit from opportunities.[34] This implies a further expansion in the *form* of assistance, which

[34] These economic transitions, like the process of economic development, are in no way linear in nature. Economic or political upheavals are part of the development process, and at times, they abet or hinder these transitions, as we argue in the case of India in the following chapter. Similarly, exogenous factors like globalization have further affected domestic ideals of redistribution and welfare policies. In Latin American and East Asian countries, autocratic rule abetted a transition to welfare policies. The simplistic description we represent here delineates how basic needs and state response (the social contract) have

extends the *focus* to the non-poor as well. The transformative aspect of social assistance would be realized when human flourishing, to use Sen's framing, is not inhibited by deficiencies in human capabilities, such as education and nutrition. At the same time, the social welfare system becomes all-encompassing when it is able to address issues pertinent to the disenfranchised and vulnerable groups, so that social justice goals are achieved. These processes and stages overlap, as different sections of the population or geography may be deprived more and on multiple fronts.

We have described earlier how economic progress and progressive political mobilization in the developed world led to a more encompassing *form* of social welfare program in the developed world, where gradually, social assistance of the kind in which transfers were merely to support basic (provisions) needs faded away. Industrialization and formalization of jobs ensured further prosperity, and livelihood risks were largely covered through employers, who also provided health insurance, or else, the government covered it. With lower levels of poverty and higher human development, the state's responsibility largely relied on ensuring people had something to fall back upon when they were transitioning between jobs. A more urbanized economy meant less exposure to adverse, weather-induced, exogenous shocks; and better institutions ensured more egalitarian public systems, with greater equality of opportunity, thereby ensuring a resilient development process. Developing countries, on the other hand, have a large share of the population engaged in agriculture, albeit declining. Nonfarm workers are mostly engaged in informal wage labor, which again implies a form of livelihood risk. Poorly developed health systems further expose these workers to other forms of morbidity-related vulnerability, especially at young ages. Developing countries, along their path of economic development, encounter many of these changes, and social welfare policies need more encompassing *systems* of social protection to promote development resilience.[35]

evolved along with the process of development, globally. See Chapter 8 for a discussion on social policymaking.

[35] Despite a similar objective, the *focus* population of safety nets is markedly different, depending upon a country's development trajectory. This difference emanates from the composition of the labor force and the kind of risks they face. The *scope* of the program relies on that, too. While the *scope* of welfare programs in the developed world spans prevention of extreme hardship, promotion of inclusion, and maintaining social cohesion with the aim of self-sufficiency, developing countries restrict themselves to a rather narrower scope—reducing absolute or extreme poverty.

The adaptation of social welfare strategy will vary depending upon the nature of poverty and its understanding among the policymakers. Largely, the developing world is characterized by a preponderance of safety net schemes that are focused on reduction of absolute or extreme poverty, depending upon the developmental concern of the times. For example, the Programa de Educacion, Salud y Alimentacion (PROGRESA) in Mexico was aimed at reducing intergenerational poverty, while the Mahatma Gandhi National Rural Employment Guarantee Scheme (MGNREGS) in India focused on reducing seasonal unemployment. Since the various schemes aim at different objectives, it is helpful to classify them accordingly. The representation in Table 2.1 is rather simplistic, but still useful to illustrate the point around the specific role each of form of safety net can play in terms of building development resilience. In-kind transfers, the most common form of assistance, are essential to maintaining consumption levels, especially in the context of absent or underdeveloped markets. However, income—targeted or untargeted—goes to smoothening consumption, but also has the ability to promote the accumulation of productive assets. If focused on a particularly vulnerable group—like the disabled, elderly, widows, etc.—who cannot actively participate in the labor market, concerns of equity are addressed, too. For long-term development concerns, the debates around public action and state support have, therefore, led to a wider portfolio, which includes what economists called the "graduation approach" into sustainable livelihoods.[36] Yet, any one program fails to address the risks and vulnerability across the life cycle of an individual—from nutritional deprivation in early life, to livelihood and health risks in later years—and the challenges of inequitable intra-household resource allocation.

[36] Graduation programs are an integrated approach to social protection, livelihood development, and financial services. Here, consumption support is provided to households along with "life skills coaching." Households are further provided with financial assistance to engage in livelihoods using the training they received. The most successful application has been shown in Bangladesh through the help of the nongovernmental organization (NGO), Bangladesh Rural Advancement Committee (now Building Resources Across Communities, BRAC).

Table 2.1 A taxonomy of social safety nets

Transfers	*Form*	*Focus*	*Scope*
In-kind	Food	Poor, Children	Food security Consumption smoothing Nutritional capability
Income	Pensions Unemployment benefits Universal basic income (UBI)	Elderly Disabled	Consumption smoothing Accumulating productive assets
Income + Assets	Public work program Conditional cash transfers (CCTs)	Livelihoods Children	Consumption smoothing Community assets Human capital Local infrastructure
Income + Assets + Training	Graduation programs	Livelihoods Skills	Consumption smoothing Accumulating productive assets Entrepreneurship skills Addressing exclusion and building capabilities

Safety Nets for the Future

Social safety nets in the developing countries have proven to be useful but not effective enough.[37] The poorest of the poor have been left behind, as only a third of the families in the poorest quintile receive any direct social assistance. They are stuck in ***dynamic*** poverty traps, a low-level

[37] Margitic and Ravallion (2019) used household data from multiple countries (developing and developed) and found that spending on social protection has enabled a 7 percentage point reduction in the headcount poverty rate, while the poverty gap index has declined by 5.1 percentage points to 5.8% between 1998 and 2014. Higher social welfare spending has enabled a further rise in the consumption floor of subsistence, which implies that it has benefited the poor. Among the range of social protection programs, contributory pensions have been the most effective, while social assistance has contributed to a mere 2 percentage point decline in the incidence of poverty. Across the developing countries, social protection policies have been most effective where overall welfare spending is higher, but welfare gains have been larger for those closer to the subsistence consumption level than those at the extreme end of the distribution, suggesting that while the poor, on average, have benefited from social assistance, the *poorest* have been left behind.

equilibrium, and are unable to benefit from the current set of social safety nets because of inadequate coverage for the poor (Margitic and Ravallion 2019).[38] This naturally leads to the question: how should we pursue a rethinking of safety nets, relying upon decades of experience in development practice as well theoretical refinement around these issues? This book proposes that the *scope, focus,* and *form* of social safety net strategies should revolve around the issues discussed in the following section.

Newer Form of Risks and Existing Poverty Traps

Economic adversity could arise from a variety of shocks—idiosyncratic or covariate—which could lower individual income or impair earning capacities. Idiosyncratic reasons include loss of employment, damage to the crops and poor harvest, illness, or death in the family, among other individual specific shocks. Covariate shocks, on the other hand, could occur due to natural disasters, famine-like conditions, or closure of an industrial plant, which affect a large set of people. Such abrupt livelihood and income decline or uncertainties lead to economic deprivation, which can force households into transient as well as chronic poverty. A transient decrease in income implies a short-term loss, mostly reflected in consumption expenditure. Chronic poverty, on the other hand, refers to a structural problem where the adverse conditions hinder the ability to work, and hence, further decrease the accumulation of productive capacity. Both of these adverse economic outcomes, at the household or individual levels, affect overall productive capacity of the economy and inhibit optimal use of the economic resources. Overall higher poverty levels could produce further systemic risks to social harmony, engendering a plausible democratic backlash. Most governments, therefore, put into place some form of assistance programs that ensure safety against these risks.[39]

Scholars have also argued that poverty persists not only because of poor lack of employment opportunities, but often the work pays little,

[38] This should be read along with the findings of Ravallion (2016), which suggested that the growth process also largely benefited those who live close to the consumption floor.

[39] The success of European states, in terms of their spectacular human development outcomes and lower inequality, is partly attributed to the active welfare policies of governments in the region.

often below the subsistence needs. Since returns to work depend upon the quality of skills and educational training, largely classified as human capital, the poor lack the opportunity for higher returns, and therefore, they are stuck in a "poverty trap." The rise in anti-poverty policies, such as social safety nets, has been inspired by the idea of eliminating the poverty trap.[40] Poverty traps also emerges from nutritional deprivation, savings constraints, barriers to mobility, or geographical disadvantages. In developing countries, particularly, these risks are more pronounced, as private forms of insurance, such as credit markets are absent. Market failure, therefore, is more commonplace. Not only do markets function poorly, but there are information failures, which imply asymmetric knowledge when carrying out economic transactions (Barr 1992). Although households undertake possible strategies of risk management, it turns out to be rather imperfect in resource-constrained scenarios. Adverse shocks significantly impair the welfare outcomes, thereby eroding the asset base—physical, financial, and human—for future wealth creation (Morduch 1995; Dercon 2002). Initial endowments, therefore, need to be enhanced to break out of this trap and achieve greater potential. The *poverty trap* argument, therefore, suggests that sufficiently large, positive wealth or income shocks could work toward moving individuals or households above the critical threshold of a poverty trap (Carter and Barrett 2006). This intrinsically implies that sustainable poverty reduction strategies require an intervention of some sort, which breaks this limited endowment barrier. These kinds of transfers are sort of "big push" policies that require concerted government interventions, one of which is often the social safety net transfers.[41]

Asset Accumulation and Redistribution

Social protection programs, in general, and noncontributory safety nets, in particular, therefore aim to safeguard vulnerable populations from

[40] Using social protection policies to address shocks and crises has a long history, which dates back to around 300 B.C. In his classical work, *The Science of Material Gain* (*Arthashastra* in Sanskrit), Kautilya advised Indian rulers to provide employment through public works programs to maintain social harmony and economic stability.

[41] We would like to emphasize that we are talking about poverty traps at the individual or household level and not at the country level. On a larger scale, the "big push" refers to foreign aid or loans, which could help LICs cross the threshold.

poverty and address redistributive concerns. Hanna and Karlan (2017) classified the programs into four types, based upon the underlying motivation for intervention: redistributive concerns; filling in for the missing insurance markets; behavioral constraints faced by households inhibiting productive investments; and market failures that erode productive asset accumulation. All of these responses essentially seek to transfer resources to the poor—depending upon the policy objectives—which lowers vulnerability to future poverty and accumulates productive assets. Social protection programs in the developing world have sought to achieve three main objectives. First, the programs aim to ensure a minimum level of consumption for the poor or those vulnerable to falling into poverty. Second, the programs assume that this support—in-kind or cash—would facilitate investments in productive assets—human, physical, and financial—which potentially provides an escape from the likelihood of future poverty. Third, it should improve social standing of the poor—as political actors and citizens—thereby increasing their agency.

Since poverty traps emerge from a loss of income or deprivation in nutritional or physical capital, various forms of safety nets specifically address these deficiencies. Consumer food subsidies are particularly aimed at addressing hunger and food security through maintaining a minimum level of food consumption. Many countries, like India, have large programs that specifically address this issue. Hunger, in many contexts, has shaped the contours of social policy, as a prerequisite to human functioning. Since, hunger itself could manifest in multiple forms, particular policies address hunger and nutritional deprivation among schoolchildren and pregnant and lactating mothers, as the intervention has longer-term benefits. Specifically focusing on vulnerable populations also takes care of inequitable intra-household distribution of resources. Public work programs, in addition to creating public infrastructure, also reduce involuntary unemployment and augment family income. Direct cash to older and vulnerable people is a common form of assistance to control mortality and destitution. One of the primary causes of poverty in developing countries is related to illness of a family member. This becomes a particular challenge if the health shock is particular to an earning member of the household, which not only erodes accumulated assets but also implies less future income through the duration of illness. Subsidized health insurance, therefore, has emerged as a newer form of safety net programs by which government contributes to the insurance premiums.

Many of these schemes involve long and tedious bureaucracy, which often usurps the intended benefits, thereby depriving the beneficiaries. Newer forms of direct transfers, such as cash payments, are therefore being tried, instead of food assistance. Some schemes are now beginning to discuss universalizing a certain minimum income to households, so that they are able to maintain a certain minimum standard of living. Yet, safety net policies seem to be designed to ensure *at least* the poorest are not left behind. The question of development resilience comes only as a desired by-product.

Changing "Future of Work"

As developing countries could see the sectoral share of output and employment moving away from agriculture, there would be a greater share of people employed in wage-based work outside of agriculture—within and outside of the rural areas.[42] Structural transformation of the economy would therefore constantly require the policy paradigm to evolve and rethink ways to address existing as well as newer forms of risks to livelihoods. In the developed world, emergence of welfare systems evolved out of similar concerns with wage insecurities, as a result of technological progress which assisted industrialization, and therefore, promoted rural–urban labor mobility. To imagine safety nets for the future, it is particularly important to understand the changing nature of work in the developing world.

Rapid changes in technological advancements in the twenty-first century have changed the global debates around the "future of work." The nature of work and the worker–employer contract have changed over the years, as economic activities have shifted away from industrial production and manufacturing-based employment, toward more service- and technology-based work, which requires more skill and training. Automation and artificial intelligence (AI) is further transforming how businesses operate, and labor productivity is rewarded, as a result of it. Compared to earlier times, where workers worked for the same organization for all of their careers, they now work at multiple places or do various *gigs*. Currently, around 40% of the people in the European Union are either

[42] At the same time, the demand for food changes along with the economic transformation away from staple grains toward those that are richer in protein and nutrient content, as well as the processed and convenience-based items.

engaged in self-employment or work under a contract which is not full time (EC 2018). In the United States, a person of average working age is likely to hold around 11 jobs in their life course, often holding multiple jobs, at once (BLS 2020). Even in developing countries, where agriculture continues to be the largest employer, changes were felt in the demand for labor. As labor moved out, agricultural productivity would increase, but to maximize poverty reduction, there needed to be gainful complementary employments avenues, especially which improved the cultivation environment, such as irrigation facilities or encouraging mixed cropping (Christiaensen and Martin 2018).

The International Labor Organization (ILO) estimates that around 61% of the employed population globally works in the informal economy, with little or no access to any form of employer-based social protection (ILO 2018).[43] For developing countries, this number is as high as 91%. Although not everyone in the informal economy is poor, most of the people employed as informal workers face a higher risk of poverty because of the uncertainties around coping with shocks. It is in this context that the *World Development Report 2019*, titled *Changing Nature of Work*, calls for "rethinking the social contract" between the state and citizens through the provision of appropriate social safety nets (World Bank 2019, p. viii). The report calls for a "broader and more permanent coverage than most social assistance programs currently provide" (World Bank 2019, p. 109). The rising informality in developing countries should also be understood in terms of the precariousness of the "working poor" (Fields 2012).

Poverty in developing countries, along their structural transformation process, moves from the rural to urban areas, too. Although the traditional, weather-related risks continue to be relevant for the rural cultivators, the lack of jobs and not having sufficient income increasingly become important, as salaries or wages become a major source of household income. The poor, in these contexts, are largely dependent upon their labor to escape poverty, but may still remain in poverty because of lower wages due to surplus labor availability. While economic development brings about improved markets—credit and factor markets—the

[43] The report defines informal sector employment as working in enterprises of being an own account worker, working in family-owned business, or having own business that does not involve any social protection contributions or paid annual and paid sick leave from the employer.

transitions are not smooth, but depend upon the nature of economic restructuring. For many developing countries, opening of markets to global trade did bring about a reduction in poverty, but it also exposed them to the risks of higher inequality. Safety nets, therefore, have an important role to play to improve human development, as the nature of work is changing and households are exposed to a greater variety of risks—even when markets are developed—which inhibit asset accumulation needed to arrest future poverty.

Moving from Schemes to Systems

The success of safety nets to take a transformative role is hindered by a rather myopic view of the developmental policies, where they are seen as singular ways to address the concerns of development at particular points in time; for example, hunger, unemployment, poverty, or malnutrition. The nature of vulnerability itself is dynamic and multi-scalar. When there exist poverty traps and deprivation along multiple dimensions, "small adjustments often fail to move people out of low-level dynamic equilibria unless they happen to be carefully targeted at precisely the context-specific mechanism and threshold that trap people in poverty. Rather, systems must change, major poverty shocks must occur, or both" (Barrett et al. 2016, p. 322).[44] A common characteristic of social safety nets across developing countries is the use of self-standing welfare schemes, aimed at the removal of poverty, hunger, and other forms of human deprivation. These schemes, without being institutionalized, are only an edifice, which is an elementary structure for social policies to work. The other most important aspect of social safety net strategy is to conceptualize and implement it in a context-specific way, in tune with the specific developmental requirements for long-term growth (Gentilini 2009). This would require greater synergy across the social welfare programs for the welfare system to promote economic resilience.

[44] An example of a safety net system can be found in the Graduation programs, being implemented on a pilot basis through NGOs in many developing countries (Barrett et al. 2016, p. 321).

Lessons for India

The framework presented here lays out the fundamental arguments for a robust social protection architecture and provides a valuable lesson for India. India has not been able to reduce poverty—in money-metric and other various dimensions—to the desired low levels, despite economic growth and many social protection programs. Here, we argue that social protection policies have a fundamental role in ensuring a more resilient development process in the country. Subsequent chapters in this book build upon our arguments. First and foremost, we argue for a more nuanced understanding of the nature of deprivations or human development deficits—at present and in the future—and then conceptualize ways through which various social safety net programs can address these deficits. Subsequently, we focus on specific programs aimed at poverty and livelihoods, food and nutrition, and mitigating shocks, with the idea that individuals face different kinds of risk and vulnerability through their life cycle. For an effective social protection strategy, the state must act on all of these risks, and therefore, there have been multiple programs. We focus on each of these programs, study their impacts, highlight how they should have worked more effectively, and consider potential improvements in different chapters. A synthesis of these programs calls for greater synergy between them and a greater readiness among policymakers to innovate upon these to achieve a resilient development process. We call for a social protection system in the future where *no one is left behind*, as we are seeing a changing economic structure. Given that the nature of poverty will be increasingly linked with work and wages, while weather-related shocks will continue to affect farmers, social protection policies need to be more encompassing, transformative, and not just palliative.

References

Banerjee, Abhijit V., and Esther Duflo. 2007. "The Economic Lives of the Poor." *Journal of Economic Perspectives* 21 (1): 141–68.

Barr, Nicholas. 1992. "Economic Theory and the Welfare State: A Survey and Interpretation." *Journal of Economic Literature* 30 (2): 741–803.

Barrett, Christopher B. 2005. "Rural Poverty Dynamics: Development Policy Implications." *Agricultural Economics* 32 (S1): 45–60.

Barrett, Christopher B., and Michael R. Carter. 2013. "The Economics of Poverty Traps and Persistent Poverty: Empirical and Policy Implications." *Journal of Development Studies* 49 (7): 976–90.

Barrett, Christopher B. and Mark A. Constas. 2014. "Toward a Theory of Resilience for International Development Applications." *Proceedings of the National Academy of Sciences* 111 (40): 14625–30.

Barrett, Christopher B., Teevrat Garg, and Linden McBride. 2016. "Well-Being Dynamics and Poverty Traps." *Annual Review of Resource Economics* 8 (1): 303–27.

Barrientos, Armando. 2013. *Social Assistance in Developing Countries*. Cambridge, UK: Cambridge University Press.

Barrientos, Armando, and David Hulme. 2009. "Social Protection for the Poor and Poorest in Developing Countries: Reflections on a Quiet Revolution." *Oxford Development Studies* 37 (4): 439–56.

Birdsall, Nancy. 2008. "The Development Agenda as a Global Social Contract; or, We Are All in This Development Boat Together." Speech to the Dutch Scientific Council, The Hague, December 8, Center for Global Development. Accessed April 25, 2021. https://www.cgdev.org/sites/default/files/Birdsall_Jan_28_Netherlands.pdf.

BLS (Bureau of Labor Statistics). 2020. "Number of Jobs, Labor Market Experience, and Earnings Growth: Results from a National Longitudinal Survey." News Release, August 22, 2019, Bureau of Labor Statistics, US Department of Labor. Reissued October 7, 2020. Accessed April 29, 2021. https://www.bls.gov/news.release/pdf/nlsoy.pdf.

Carter, Michael R., and Christopher B. Barrett. 2006. "The Economics of Poverty Traps and Persistent Poverty: An Asset-Based Approach." *Journal of Development Studies* 42 (2): 178–99.

Christiaensen, Luc, and Will Martin. 2018. "Agriculture, Structural Transformation and Poverty Reduction: Eight New Insights." *World Development* 109: 413–16.

Dercon, S. 2002. "Income Risk, Coping Strategies, and Safety Nets." *World Bank Research Observer* 17 (2): 141–66.

Devereux, Stephen, and Rachel Sabates-Wheeler. 2004. "Transformative Social Protection." IDS Working Paper 232, Institute of Development Studies, Brighton, Sussex, UK. Accessed April 26, 2021. https://www.unicef.org/socialpolicy/files/Transformative_Social_Protection.pdf.

DFID (Department for International Development). 2011. "Defining Disaster Resilience." DFID Approach Paper, DFID, London. Accessed April 25, 2021. https://www.fsnnetwork.org/sites/default/files/dfid_defining_disaster_resilience.pdf.

EC (European Commission). 2018. "Commission Adopts Proposals for a European Labour Authority and for Access to Social Protection." Press release, March 13, Strasbourg. Accessed April 29, 2021. https://ec.europa.eu/commission/presscorner/detail/en/IP_18_1624.

Esping-Andersen, G. 1990. *The Three Worlds of Welfare Capitalism*. Princeton, NJ: Princeton University Press.

Esping-Andersen, G. 1999. *Social Foundations of Postindustrial Economies*. Oxford, UK: Oxford University Press.

Fields, Gary S. 2012. *Working Hard, Working Poor*. Oxford: Oxford University Press.

Fiszbein, Ariel, Ravi Kanbur, and Ruslan Yemtsov. 2014. "Social Protection and Poverty Reduction: Global Patterns and Some Targets." *World Development* 61: 167–77.

Gandhi, Mahatma. 2004. *Learning from Gandhi: Gandhiji's Thoughts on Environment and Development*. New Delhi: Energy and Resources Institute.

Gentilini, Ugo. 2009. "Social Protection in the 'Real World': Issues, Models and Challenges." *Development Policy Review* 27 (2): 147–66.

Hanlon, J., A. Barrientos, and D. Hulme. 2012. *Just Give Money to the Poor: The Development Revolution from the Global South*. Sterling, VA: Kumarian Press.

Hanna, R., and D. Karlan. 2017. "Designing Social Protection Programs." In *Handbook of Economic Field Experiments*, vol. 2, 515–53. Amsterdam: North-Holland.

Hickey, Sam. 2011. "The Politics of Social Protection: What Do We Get from a 'Social Contract' Approach?" *Canadian Journal of Development Studies/Revue Canadienne d'Études du Développement* 32 (4): 426–38.

Hirsch, Moshe, Ashok Kotwal, and Bharat Ramaswami. 2019. *A Human Rights Based Approach to Development in India*. Vancouver: UBC Press.

Ikegami, Munenobu, Michael R. Carter, Christopher B. Barrett, and Sarah Janzen. 2019. "Poverty Traps and the Social Protection Paradox." In *The Economics of Poverty Traps*, edited by Christopher B. Barrett, Michael R. Carter, and Jean-Paul Chavas, 223–56. Chicago: University of Chicago Press.

ILO (International Labour Organization). 2018. *Women and Men in the Informal Economy: A Statistical Picture*, 3rd ed. Geneva: ILO. Accessed April 29, 2021. https://www.ilo.org/wcmsp5/groups/public/---dgreports/---dcomm/documents/publication/wcms_626831.pdf.

Kwon, H. J. 2005. *Transforming the Developmental Welfare State in East Asia*. London: UNRISD/Palgrave.

Margitic, Juan, and Martin Ravallion. 2019. "Lifting the Floor? Economic Development, Social Protection and the Developing World's Poorest." *Journal of Development Economics* 139: 97–108.

Morduch, Jonathan. 1995. "Income Smoothing and Consumption Smoothing." *Journal of Economic Perspectives* 9 (3): 103–14.

Nussbaum, Martha C. 2000. *Women and Human Development*. Cambridge, UK: Cambridge University Press.

Nussbaum, Martha C., and Amartya Sen. 1993. *The Quality of Life*. UNU-WIDER Studies in Development Economics. Oxford: Oxford University Press.

Ravallion, Martin. 2016. "Are the World's Poorest Being Left Behind?" *Journal of Economic Growth* 21 (2): 139–64.

Ravallion, M., 2015. *The economics of poverty: History, measurement, and policy*. Oxford University Press.

Rawls, John. 1971. *A Theory of Justice*. Cambridge, MA: Harvard University Press.

Rawls, John. 2001. *Justice as Fairness: A Restatement*. Cambridge, MA: Harvard University Press.

Rodrik, Dani. 1998. "Has Globalization Gone Too Far?" *Challenge* 41 (2): 81–94.

Rudra, Nita. 2008. *Globalization and the Race to the Bottom in Developing Countries*. Cambridge, UK: Cambridge University Press.

Sabates-Wheeler, Rachel, and Stephen Devereux. 2007. "Social Protection for Transformation." *IDS Bulletin* 38 (3): 23–8.

Schoch, Marta, and Christoph Lakner. 2020. "Global Poverty Reduction Is Slowing, Regional Trends Help Understanding Why." World Bank Data Blog, November 5. Accessed April 24, 2021. https://blogs.worldbank.org/opendata/global-poverty-reduction-slowing-regional-trends-help-understanding-why.

Sen, Amartya. 1990. "Justice: Means Versus Freedoms." *Philosophy & Public Affairs* 19 (2): 111–21.

Sen, Amartya K. 2001. *Development as Freedom*. Oxford: Oxford University Press.

Subbarao, K., Aniruddha Bonnerjee, Jeanine Braithwaite, Soniya Carvalho, Kene Ezemenari, Carol Graham, and Alan Thompson. 1997. "Safety Net Programs and Poverty Reduction: Lessons from Cross-Country Experience." World Bank, Washington, DC. Accessed April 25, 2021. http://documents1.worldbank.org/curated/en/666481468781474860/pdf/multi-page.pdf.

Switzerland. 1999. Switzerland's Constitution of 1999 with Amendments Through 2014. constituteproject.org with content provided by the Swiss Federal Chancellery. Accessed April 26, 2021. https://www.constituteproject.org/constitution/Switzerland_2014.pdf?lang=en.

UN (United Nations). 2017. *Leaving No One Behind: Equality and Non-Discrimination at the Heart of Sustainable Development*. United Nations System Shared Framework for Action. New York: United Nations. Accessed April 26, 2021. https://unsceb.org/sites/default/files/imported_files/CEB%20equality%20framework-A4-web-rev3.pdf.

World Bank. 2000. *World Development Report 2000/2001: Attacking Poverty.* New York: Oxford University Press. Accessed April 25, 2021. https://openknowledge.worldbank.org/handle/10986/11856.

World Bank. 2018. *The State of Social Safety Nets 2018*. Washington, DC: World Bank.

World Bank. 2019. *World Development Report 2019: The Changing Nature of Work*. World Bank, Washington, DC. Accessed April 29, 2021. https://doi.org/10.1596/978-1-4648-1328-3.

CHAPTER 3

India's Economic Development and Social Safety Nets

Introduction

The debate around India's social policies has largely centered around two competing ideological narratives.[1] One side of the debate pushes forward the idea that market reforms and economic growth is the principal antidote to poverty, while the other side rallies about the role of state driven public investments in human development as central to sustaining a virtuous cycle of growth. The former group, therefore, blames historically stunted growth rates on state-sponsored protectionist economic policies in place until the 1980s. They claim that the embrace of market-oriented reforms, beginning 1991, unshackled India's economic development from state control and put it on the path of prosperity. Those on the other side of debate call for greater state intervention to promote human development, highlighting the limited impact of market-driven growth on human development, inequality, social mobility, and undernutrition. Development policy debates in India, including social welfare policies, therefore, are highly polarized, and often the policy instrument depends upon the political ideology of the government in power.

The dissonance between human development and growth is clearly evident when comparing India with other countries (Fig. 3.1). India is

[1] See Drèze and Sen (2013) versus Bhagwati and Panagariya (2013).

A. Rahman and P. Pingali, *The Future of India's Social Safety Nets*, Palgrave Studies in Agricultural Economics and Food Policy, https://doi.org/10.1007/978-3-031-50747-2_3

home to 28% of world's poor population—the second largest number of poor households in the world. On the Human Development Index (HDI), India is ranked 129, much lower than many countries with an equal level of per capita income. On a recent metric for human capital, the Human Capital Index (HCI), the World Bank ranked India 115 among 157 countries, where it scored lower than most of its neighbors in South Asia, including Bangladesh, Sri Lanka, Myanmar, and Nepal.

As Indian economic prospects are glorified for giving competition to China, in terms of growth numbers, its human development indicators, most notably nutrition, resemble that of sub-Saharan Africa. The rapid expansion in primary schooling, leading to universal school enrollment, has not contributed much to child learning outcomes. Surplus food production has ensured that food stocks are plentiful, yet the specter of nutritional security poses a major threat. With the success story for every million capitalists emerging, there must be sordid tales of hundreds of millions of poor living in squalor and somehow trying to eke out a living without access to adequate health care, credit, or basic infrastructure. It is in this context that some of the leading scholars in India refer to as

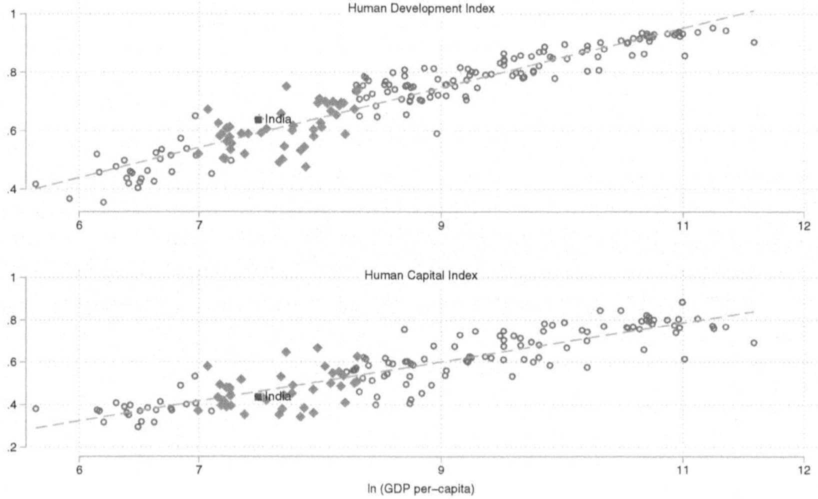

Fig. 3.1 Association between human development and per capita GDP in 2017 (*Source* World Bank WDI | UNDP HDR 2017)

"islands of California within Sub-Saharan Africa," or a hybrid of a rupee–dollar economy.[2] The debate, therefore, on whether India is an *emerging giant* in global economy, or whether its recognition as an economic power, an *uncertain glory*, depends a lot on whether the growth is sustainable and distributed equitably. This is where a robust social protection program can contribute building resilience through ensuring a more equitable redistribution of the fruits of growth.

An array of social welfare programs with varying *form*, *focus*, and *scope* characterizes India's social policy toward addressing some of the fundamental issues of underdevelopment such as poverty, nutrition, or health (see Table 3.1). Through provisions of basic human needs in the *form* of food, cash, employment, or other forms of subsidy, these social welfare programs work with the *scope* of maintaining minimum level of household consumption, preventing hunger, and reducing poverty. Recognizing that poor are most likely to be vulnerable—deficient in terms of food access, nutritional inputs, income, or livelihood opportunities—they remain the primary *focus* or the intended beneficiaries of these programs. These transfers could also promote further acquisition of human and physical capital through guarding against various risks and vulnerabilities across the life cycle which could imbue household resilience and have a transformational impact. A transformational safety net system therefore not only transforms human lives by reducing deprivation and raising human functioning, but also has the potential of engendering a virtuous cycle of economic growth, which is inclusive and leaves no one behind.

Promising as it may sound, the impacts of social safety net programs remain hotly contested, even while its importance in social policy and overall expenditure on social welfare programs has gained eminence in the last two decades. These programs are beset with a host of design and implementation issues which limit their effectiveness in facilitating

[2] Drèze and Sen (2013, xi) invoked India as being akin to "islands of California within sub-Saharan Africa." Anirudh Krishna (2017) considers India to be a hybrid of a rupee–dollar economy, while Arvind Adiga's (2008, 5) protagonist in *The White Tiger* mentions an "India of Light" and an "India of Darkness." On the other hand, the Indian growth story has been hailed through books titles, such as *Propelling India* (Virmani 2006), *India Arriving* (Dossani 2008), *India: Emerging Power* (Cohen 2001), *In Spite of the Gods: The Strange Rise of Modern India* (Luce 2007), *Awakening Giants, Feet of Clay: Assessing the Economic Rise of China and India* (Bardhan 2010). Similarly, Nayyar (2006) contrasts competing images of India's growth process as a 'lumbering elephant' with a 'running tiger.'

Table 3.1 Major social safety net programs in India

	Form	*Focus*	*Scope*	*Implications*
Public Distribution System (PDS)	In-kind	Poor	Consumption smoothing	Preventive
Mahatma Gandhi National Rural Employment Guarantee Scheme (MGNREGS)	Income Public Assets	Rural poor Employment	Consumption smoothing Livelihood vulnerability Women's employment	Provision Prevention Promotion
Integrated Child Development Scheme (ICDS)	In-kind	Early life nutrition (mother and children)	Nutritional deprivation Intergenerational poverty	Provision Prevention Promotion
Mid-day Meal Scheme (MDMS)	In-kind	Early life nutrition (school going children)	Classroom hunger School enrollment Intergenerational poverty	Provision Prevention Promotion
Pensions (elderly/widowed/disabled)	Income	Work-vulnerable	Consumption	Provision
Maternity entitlements (JSY)	Income	Pregnant women	Infant/maternal mortality	Prevention
PM *Jan Ayushman Yojana* (PM-JAY)	Subsidized Health Insurance	Family	Consumption smoothing Risks to poverty	Prevention Promotion
PM–Kisan	Income	Rural poor	Livelihood vulnerability	Prevention

development resilience. Nevertheless, social welfare programs have been a key tool in keeping people away from abject poverty through basic life provisions, despite their limited transformational impact.

In this chapter, we review the changing historical landscape of social welfare policies in India with respect to the country's developmental trajectory. Reflecting upon the evolution of social policy allows us to highlight the importance of designing policies with respect to the economic structure of the country. We highlight the key aspects of India's structural transformation policy which creates the need for more inclusive and expansive social protection 'system' for a resilient development process.

Economic Growth, Poverty, and Developmental Challenges

To understand how economic growth has not led to a commensurate decline in poverty and human development, it is useful to begin with an overview of India's development trajectory.[3] India followed a planning model to economic development wherein the government would come up with its policy priorities for every five years. The 5-year plans, as they were called began in 1951 and followed the ideals of Fabian socialism of the erstwhile Soviet Union type. As a result, the planning process adopted a closed economy model wherein the state-controlled industries were primed as the engines of growth. As part of state policy, important sectors were reserved only for public sector enterprises. The initial impetus was to promote industrial development as an engine of economic growth, despite India being a largely rural country. The focus, however, shifted toward agriculture with the demise of India's first Prime Minister Nehru—who championed the cause of 5-year plans and state-controlled industrialization—in 1964. During this time, famines and hunger were common occurrences and India had to rely on import of food grains from abroad for domestic consumption. During the tenure of Nehru's successor, Lal Bahadur Shastri, however, there was a shift toward the agriculture sector not only as a source of food but also a source of economic development. This shift coincided with agricultural productivity growth because of the Green Revolution, which led to increase in farm income and decline in poverty.[4] But these benefits were regionally concentrated, and as a result the overall income growth continued to grow at a slow rate.[5]

During the first three decade of India's planning process, per capita income in the country remained low but stable with agriculture being the major contributor to overall GDP (Panels A-B, Fig. 3.2). Poverty levels, as measured by consumption expenditure, in India when it was largely rural,

[3] For a recent review of the Indian economy, refer to Basu (2018).

[4] See Datt and Ravallion (1998).

[5] It is also important to highlight that these benefits were regionally concentrated, and therefore overall income growth continued to grow at a slow rate. Per-capita GDP in the country grew at just over 1% per year between 1950 and 1980. Often referred to as the "Hindu rate of growth," this coincided with a massive population increase as mortality rates came down and life expectancy improved.

remained consistently high from the early 1950s until the mid-1970s (Ravallion and Datt 1996). In 1973–74, almost half of the population was classified as poor—in both rural and urban areas (Panel C, Fig. 3.2). Acceleration in the growth process began in the 1980s on the back of rural productivity increase led by technological improvements, irrigation facilities, and expansion in the rural credit infrastructure leading to greater household savings.[6] Greater savings with banks not only meant that they could lend to households but also to corporations, which helped promote greater private investments in manufacturing and machinery, adding to the growth process.

The year 1991 was a watershed moment when India had to open up its borders to international trade which marked an "attitudinal shift" of

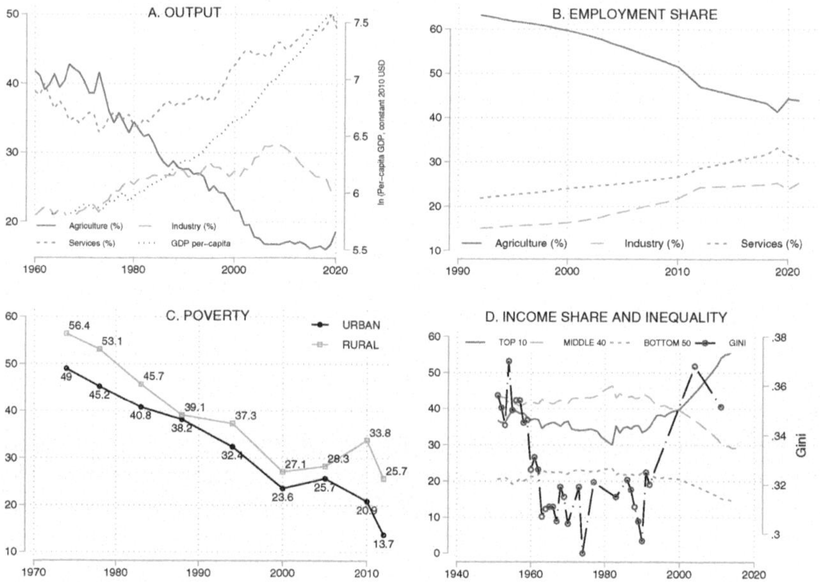

Fig. 3.2 Economic development and poverty in India (*Source* World Development Indicators, World Bank, the World Inequality Database, WID.world, and the United Nations University-World Institute of Development Economics [UNU-WIDER] database)

[6] See Athukorala and Sen (2002), and Burgess and Pande (2005) for more details.

the government away from the stringent regulation of domestic private trade and various to imports (Rodrik and Subramanian 2005).[7] From a closed economy relying on import substitution and state-driven industrialization—which also hindered domestic entrepreneurship, and inhibited competition—often conveyed through the aphorism "license–permit–quota raj"—economic reforms introduced the forces of globalization and international trade competition to the domestic markets. The era of globalization led to a significant increase in economic opportunities, reduced poverty, and brought about an increase in the quality of life. Share of Indian classified as poor declined to 13.7% and 25.7% in urban and rural areas respectively in 2011–12 (Panel C, Fig. 3.2). India's subsequent stable growth has been heralded as a major global success—with the sobriquet, *Shining India*—of engineering growth through an embrace of market-oriented reforms.

The post-reform economic growth has been characterized by a decline in the share of output from agricultural in GDP which has been compensated service sector led growth process in which the industrial sector's share in total output has remained stagnant (Panel A, Fig. 3.2). Yet, despite the decline in the share of sectoral output from agriculture, it continues to employ the greatest number of people in the workforce, while services employ the lowest share of the labor force. For the 18% of the gross domestic product (GDP) that the agriculture sector contributes to, it employs 42% of the labor engaged in any form of productive work (Panel B, Fig. 3.2). This is where India's development trajectory has veered away from the classical theory of structural transformation—while the share of agriculture in the total output has declined with increase in per-capita income during the last seven decades, its share of labor force has not shown a commensurate decrease. As a result, the economy's transition from unskilled agricultural labor to labor-intensive manufacturing sector or skill-intensive service sector employment is considered

[7] There were, however, some very limited, industrial liberalization measures taken up during the 1980s, in addition to the lowering of tax rates and support for imports, which increased private incentives for trade. Official embrace of global markets did not take place until 1991.

'stunted.'[8] It is important to note that while the agricultural productivity-led growth in the pre-reform era not only lowered poverty levels but also reduced inequality by raising the welfare of the poorest of the poor, not only those close to the poverty line (Panel D, Fig. 3.2). However, since the opening of the economy in 1991, the decline in rural poverty has been driven by urban consumption growth, in contrast to the earlier period.[9] As a result, there has been a widening of interpersonal inequality, posing a threat to future growth prospects.[10] Fruits of economic growth in the post-liberalization era have been largely limited to those with access to high quality education, social networks, and sufficient physical capital in the top 10% of the income bracket.[11] Rising inequality remained a feature

[8] During the process of structural transformation, output, and employment shares shift from low to high productivity sectors accompany increase in per-capita income (Johnston 1970; Timmer 1988). In the initial stage, output and labor moves from agriculture to low-skilled manufacturing, and then, to high-skilled manufacturing, and eventually to the services sector in the following phase. In terms of global comparisons, the first stage also coincides with the transition of an economy from the low- to middle-income category, while the second phase occurs in the middle-income stage, providing a further impetus to the growth process (Eichengreen and Gupta 2011). During the initial transition, there is a spur in economic activities, which are informal in nature, but the graduation to the second phase is driven by formal, high-skilled sectors such information technology (IT), banking, and finance. India's development trajectory, however, has defied the canonical models of structural transformation by leapfrogging from an agriculture-driven economy to a service-driven one. Binswanger-Mkhize (2013) famously dubbed India's structural transformation as "stunted."

[9] The contribution of agriculture to poverty reduction has decreased from about 40% before 1991 to less than 10% of the decline in overall poverty since then. The main contributor to the decline in poverty, therefore, has been the tertiary sector, that is, services contributing around 60% while the secondary sector growth, including manufacturing and construction, providing the rest (Datt et al. 2019). This stronger rural–urban inter-sectoral linkage and decline in rural poverty in the recent past has largely emerged from the growth of secondary towns rather than big cities (Gibson et al. 2017). These towns have seen a growth in service sector-based employment but largely of an informal nature.

[10] Some of the quantitative assessment of inequality in post-reform India include Deaton and Dreze (2002), Jayadev et al. (2007), Motiram and Naraparaju (2015), and Subramanian and Jayaraj (2016).

[11] As a departure from the "license-permit-raj" of the socialist per-reform era, Chancel and Piketty (2019) refer to post-reform decades as "billionaire raj" era during which the top 1% of the Indian population have seen the highest increase in income making it one of the most unequal countries in the world. For a careful analysis of widening inequality, through examination of historical national income and consumption surveys, as well as tax data, see Chancel and Piketty (2019).

of both urban and rural sectors. In the urban areas, wages became more unequal with a greater demand for skilled labor as industrial technology improved, and hence, a higher wage premium to the few but skilled workers.[12] Rural inequality, on the other hand, is mainly attributed to differential land endowments, which has increased subsequently with land fragmentation and greater pressure on land.[13]

This inequality is reflected in the division of workers into two broad classes differentiated by the possession of education and skill—a tiny proportion of white-collar formal sector employees while a majority share is either employed as blue-collar unskilled workers or is engaged in farming.[14] Across these two sections of the workforce, there is a stark difference not only in income but also security of livelihoods and access to social security. While the formal sector employees benefit from secured monthly pay checks and other associated health and pension benefits from their employer, rest of the workers are devoid of any employment security, regularized salary structure, or any form of employer-based social protection in times of distress. Even among farmers, around 90% of them are smallholders who try to eke out a living at close to minimum wage.

Put simply, adverse circumstances are likely to be a less consequential for the high-skill formal sector worker and large land holders, while they could be debilitating for the poorer. The significance of this disadvantage is likely to persist in future income and opportunities with grave implications for intergenerational mobility, pathways out of the poverty trap, and for the engendering of development resilience. One must note

[12] See Kijima (2006), Chandrasekhar and Mukhopadhyay (2010), and Vakulabharanam and Motiram (2012).

[13] Naraparaju and Chandrasekhar (2022) and Chakravorty et al. (2019) compute rural inequality through decomposing income sources over time and space in India, while Anand and Thampi (2016) and Bharti (2018) assess the source of wealth inequality.

[14] Krishna (2017) classifies the differential status of workers as those tapped into the *dollar economy* vis-à-vis the *rupee economy*, hearkening to the post-reform era where India's success at a global economy is based upon its comparative advantage in outsourced finance and IT-based services. While the latter group of workers have enjoyed socio-economic mobility, opportunity ladder for the latter group appears broken. Kohli (2012) blames Indian 'poverty amidst plenty' on policy prioritization of economic growth objectives above social ones. As a result, money-metric measures of poverty might show a decline, more durable indicators of progress such as nutrition does not show a commensurate decline (Deaton and Drèze 2009). Even the distribution of poverty suggests a huge share of the non-poor population lies very close to the poverty line implying a high level of vulnerability to poverty (Kotwal et al. 2014).

that the vulnerable groups constitute most of Indian citizens. The role of social protection policies therefore becomes important in ensuring that those who are left behind in the market-based growth process are supported through various forms of interventions, allowing them to overcome their deficiencies through a more equitable, fair, and inclusive growth process.[15]

India's Social Welfare Regime: *Form*, *Focus*, and *Scope*

The importance of social welfare scheme in India has been recognized only in the last two decades. Prior to that, there were very few programs which sought to address the scale of deprivation prevalent in the country. While widespread hunger and anti-poverty policies occupied the political rhetoric, state action was lackadaisical reflecting a "monumental neglect of social inequalities and deprivation in public policy" (Drèze and Sen 2002, p. xv). Whatever little episodes of state action which emanated to address poverty and deprivation arose out of the exigencies of famine-like conditions, rather than a concerted planning around how to overcome large-scale poverty and improve human development outcomes. The narrative around social safety nets is therefore punctuated with numerous historical events which overlapped with the economic and political imperatives of the times (sketched out in Fig. 3.3) thereby determining its *form*, *focus*, and *scope*—the three concepts which we introduced in the previous chapter.

Hunger Mitigation as the Scope of Poverty Reduction

Specter of hunger and famine has traditionally loomed largely over India's social policy which implies that the *focus* and *scope* of social welfare policies have largely been around rural population and food security, respectively. The year 1943, synonymous with the abominable famine in Bengal, was a watershed moment. Bengal famine of 1943 brought to light the

[15] Refer to Chapter 2 for greater details on the importance of social protection for sustainable growth and development resilience.

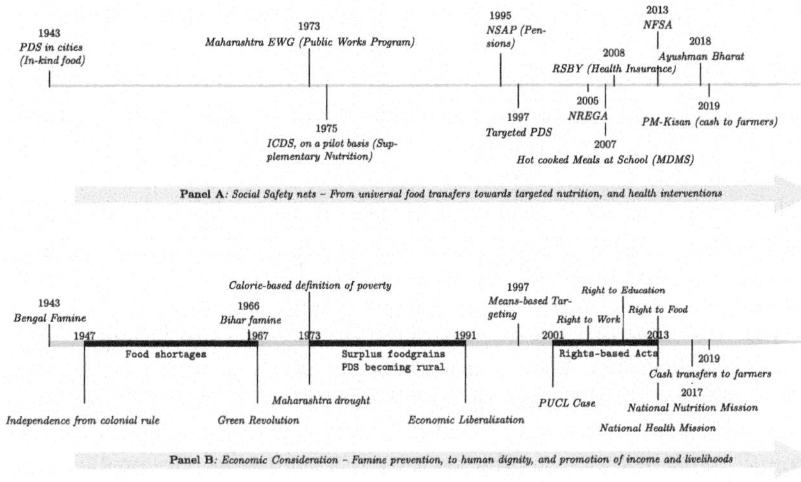

Fig. 3.3 Evolution of India's social safety nets—form, focus, and scope (*Source* Author's representation)

sheer mismanagement of resources during the colonial rule, which led to massive starvation despite sufficient food supplies.[16] The massive humanitarian loss induced by the famine, and particularly, its man-made nature insinuated many of the nationalist leaders no less. Elimination of hunger, therefore, emerged as a national imperative, which continues to be the logic of the food policy to date. Early 1940s also coincided with the introduction of food rations in urban areas for the industrial workers as an emergency response during the Second World War period, which provisioned universal transfer of essential items—food grains, kerosene, and sugar—at subsidized rates. Rations continued to be a part of public policy in India, even after its independence from colonial rule in 1947, under the name of the Public Distribution System (PDS).

Frequent episodes of hunger and famines across the country built up the Malthusian fear and therefore the preoccupation with ensuring people

[16] It is quite remarkable that the memories of the 1943 famine inspired Amartya Sen's inquiries into the nature of poverty and its root cause, which continue to inspire any scholarship in this genre. See Sen (1976) and Drèze and Sen (1989). For a historian's insight into the influence of Bengal famine on India's food and agricultural policies, see Siegel (2018).

had enough to eat. It intensified during the 1960s, when Bihar and Maharashtra—two big states—faced conditions of famine. The drought of 1966–67 was felt, in fact, across the country, and the Malthusian pessimism around hunger was felt widely.[17] In the wake of such misery, Maharashtra, suffering from three consecutive spells of drought from 1970–71 to 1972–73, introduced a public works program, known as Employment Guarantee Scheme (EGS)—an unconditional promise of employment to *anyone* who wished to join the public works program—which acted as an important insurance against famine-induced starvation, mortality, and undernutrition to around 5 million people.[18] One must note that the *scope* of EGS was restricted, however, to providing relief in the wake of droughts. State action through EGS was aimed at reducing rural income loss in the wake of poor rainfalls.

Self-sufficiency in domestic food production with the advent of Green Revolution meant India was able to solve its *food availability* problem and the emphasis moved on to the issue of *food access*.[19] Household access to food however continued to remain an issue because of lower purchasing power for a large share of the population. The policy of 'grow more food' was therefore utilized as a tool to expand the *focus* of PDS from urban to rural areas, leading to massive expansion of the retail outlets (known as fair price shops, FPS) in the hinterland.[20] Food transfers through PDS became the dominant *form* of social protection in the country, with food

[17] A brilliant exposition of the famines during the colonial period and in the early years of independent India is provided in Drèze (1988).

[18] EGS served as an example for the right to work legislation introduced in 2004, and subsequently, named the Mahatma Gandhi National Rural Employment Guarantee Act (MGNREGA). See Khera (2011) for more details.

[19] Food availability, access and affordability are three aspects of food security. With Green Revolution, self-sufficiency in food production brought an end to the frequent droughts and famines like situation. As the food stocks swelled Food Corporation of India (FCI) was established to procure food grains at assured prices, so that surplus production would not push down prices. Price stabilization policies had their roots during the 1960s, when the Agricultural Price Commission (APC) was established in the 1964. In the 1970s, the procurement from farmers went up massively along with food production. Access to food however continued to remain an issue because of lower income among the households. A large section of the population could not benefit from PDS due to corruption and inefficiencies in the system, on which we will elaborate in later chapters.

[20] By the end of 1980s, roughly 75% of the FPS were located in rural areas, and 70% of rice and about 55% of wheat was sold in rural areas (Mooij 1998).

consumption support and hunger removal as the primary policy *scope*.[21] PDS, despite being the only active safety net during that time, was beset with operational problems and political economy challenges which we would discuss later in the book.[22]

The *scope* of anti-poverty policies as food and hunger mitigation policies got further entrenched in the social policy when the official poverty line was anchored in the notion of a 'minimum calorie requirement' essential to maintain a healthy living.[23] Subsequently, to cut down upon the mounting fiscal deficits, the government restricted the *focus* of PDS to the "identified poor." In 1997, means-tested 'pro-poor' targeting was introduced for the first time in the country, classifying households into below poverty line (BPL) and above poverty line (APL). PDS had been beset with problems—inefficiencies in targeting, pilferage, leakages, and rampant corruption—which escalated its operational costs.[24] The Government of India, as it adopted the open market policy in 1991, began to find ways to prune fiscal expenses, and therefore, resorted to targeting benefits toward the poorer regions in 1994, and then, only for the poor in 1997. While this was done mainly for the PDS, as it was the only national-level active social welfare scheme at that time, the APL/BPL distinction continues to be a feature of most other schemes now.

[21] Maharashtra EGS slowly lost its prominence in due time. See Dev (1996).

[22] The procurement-storage-distribution network of food grains however also implied a gradual rise in the political clout of the large farmers cultivating rice and wheat (primarily in the agriculturally rich states of Punjab, Haryana, and parts of Andhra Pradesh and Uttar Pradesh) with a greater influence on food policy encouraging greater procurement at the assured minimum prices fueling government stock of grains. See Chapter 5 for more details.

[23] Dandekar and Rath (1971) came up with the first measurement of a poverty line defined as the percentage of individuals who are not able to afford a "subsistence bundle" of food items, which could provide them with a recommended minimum calorie or energy requirement necessary for survival. Anchored in the calorie norms, the poverty estimates were to be revised and updated with relevant changes in the price levels and food consumption basket. It was only in 2009, that the Tendulkar committee report, for the first time, expanded the scope of the poverty measure by incorporating expenses on health and education.

[24] For details, see Dev (2000), Howes and Jha (1994), and Kotwal and Ramaswami (2014).

Social Pensions to the Vulnerable

Article 41 of the Indian constitution suggests provisions for public assistance to its citizens—within the limits of economic capacity—in case of 'unemployment, old age, sickness and disablement and in other cases of undeserved want' within the limit of its economic capacity and development.' It took more than four decades for the Indian social policy to recognize this with the introduction of National Social Assistance Programme (NSAP) in 1995. It took some more years before NSAP could be scaled up further.

With the *scope* of supporting the vulnerable elderly and disabled population whose income-earning capacities are limited, NSAP *focused* on the elderly, widows, and disabled in the *form* monthly pensions to ensure that they can "live with dignity." NSAP is comprised of the following schemes: Indira Gandhi National Old Age Pension Scheme (IGNOAPS), Indira Gandhi National Widow Pension Scheme (IGNWPS), Indira Gandhi National Disability Pension Scheme (IGNDPS), National Family Benefit Scheme (NFBS), and the Annapurna. Under IGNOAPS, a monthly stipend of Rs. 200 (approximately US$3) is provided to the poor above 60 to 79 years of age and Rs. 500 (~US$5) for those 80 years and older. For widows between 40 and 59 years of age, a monthly pension of Rs. 200 (~US$3) is allotted, provided they belong to households that fall under the BPL category. The same monthly pension is allotted for the poor who have serious or multiple disabilities. For every death of the primary breadwinner falling between 18 and 64 years, the households is entitled to a lump sum of Rs. 10,000 (~US$150) under the NFBS. Under the *Annapurna* scheme, 10 kg of food grains every month are provided free to senior citizens who are although eligible for, remain uncovered under NOAPS. Funded by the central government, implementation of NSAP lies with the states with the latter responsible for identifying beneficiaries and discretion on adding to the benefits levels. Several state governments have therefore expanded upon the *focus* of the scheme by supplementing IGNOAPS with their own budgets.

Rights-Based Social Welfare Legislation

Despite food self-sufficiency and reduction in poverty rates, scarcity and hunger persisted in the 1990s, with little succor to the vulnerable in the form of safety nets. Despite overflowing food stocks, as procurements of rice and wheat from the farmers at assured prices continued, starvation-related deaths were not unheard of.[25] It was a classic case of what Amartya Sen theorized as "entitlement failure"—lack of access to food despite its availability.[26]

A crucial moment in India's social welfare policy came about in early 2001, when severe droughts induced starvation deaths in seven districts of the country. The People's Union for Civil Liberties (PUCL), a human rights organization, following these death reports, took the Government of India to court, and in its writ petition, called out the insensitivity of the government—how can a country with overflowing stocks of food grains not stop starvation-related deaths? The petition made an appeal to the court to allow the grains to be distributed through the various statutory food and nutrition programs, which are present only in policy documents. In the wake of this case (*PUCL v. Union of India and Others, Writ Petition [Civil] 196 of 2001*), famously known as the "right to food case," the Supreme Court of India ordered food to be distributed to every child in the government schools through the Mid-day Meal Scheme (MDMS) and to infants and mothers through the Integrated Child Development Scheme (ICDS). This case, arguably ushered in recent reforms and expansion of India's social welfare programs (Drèze 2017).

The PUCL case was central to the revival of the moribund ICDS and MDMS, primarily targeted at child nutrition. The *focus* on child welfare had germinated earlier in 1974, as part of the National Policy for Children. ICDS was subsequently introduced in 1975, as a pilot program in a few districts by the Ministry of Women and Child Development. The *scope* of ICDS was to reduce the incidence of mortality, morbidity, and malnutrition, through providing health and nutritional requirements to mothers and children under the age of six years. The pilot program, however, was

25 PDS even after becoming a targeted program continued to perform poorly. A government report, highlighted that around 58% of the food grains do not reach the poor because of multiple issues—targeting errors, pilferages, and rampant corruption—which implied that for every rupee government spends, less than a third of it reaches the poor (Planning Commission 2005).

26 An individual's exchange entitlements depend upon a host of factors, which include employment status and wage, the value of non-labor assets, returns on output, the ability to buy resources; and then returns after paying the taxes. In exchange for its labor, the individual would purchase food and invest in productive capital with the rest of the savings, so that its resource base is not eroded in the wake of an exogenous shock. See Sen (1982) for more details.

retracted in 1978, only to be reintroduced later. MDMS, on the other hand, provides free, hot-cooked meals during school hours for children, introduced in some regions as part of the expansion of primary schooling infrastructure under the National Programme of Nutritional Support to Primary Education (NP–NSPE) in 1995 to promote school enrollment and address "classroom hunger." Both MDMS and ICDS got a fresh lease on life after the Supreme Court directed those reserved stocks of food grains should be used to feed poor children, under these programs, in response to the PUCL case. ICDS and MDMS, therefore, not only expanded their geographic *focus*, but also expanded in *scope* to address more than calorie supplementation. MDMS also benefited from greater school enrollment as the Right to Education (RTE), which was passed by the Parliament in 2009, allowed for "free and compulsory" school education for every child between 6 and14 years of age. Recognizing the need to address intergenerational poverty—emanating through undernutrition in early life—the *scope* of social policy expanded from hunger to nutrition, with an added *focus* on mother and children.

Food-focused social welfare programs achieved constitutional legitimacy in 2013, when "right to food" was legislated in the Parliament as the National Food Security Act (NFSA). Under the NGSA, government ought to "provide for food and nutritional security in human life cycle approach, by ensuring access to adequate quantity of quality food at affordable prices to people to live a life with dignity and for matters connected therewith or incidental thereto" (Government of India 2013, p. 1). NFSA, therefore became an umbrella legislation, subsuming various aspects of food and nutritional schemes, with a "life-cycle approach." Under the NFSA, 50 and 75% of the urban and rural poor, respectively, were considered as "priority" households, thereby expanding the narrow *focus* from only on the poor. It is important to mention that the explicit *focus* on the life-cycle approach, rather than the erstwhile food provisions, expanded the *scope* of public policy to nutritional requirements specific to age—from pregnant woman to the elderly and destitute. The life-cycle approach, ingrained in the NFSA, incorporated specific roles for women, such as ration cards in their names; additional take-home rations for pregnant women; nutritional, health and education support to adolescent girls; and separate provisions for elderly, disabled, and single women.[27]

Income Support Through Public Works Program

The right to food legislation followed the "right to work" legislation, which was enshrined in the Constitution under the name of National Rural Employment Guarantee Act (NREGA) in 2005. NREGA, later rechristened as the Mahatma Gandhi National Rural Employment Guarantee Act (MGNREGA), drew its inspiration from the Maharashtra EGS. The primary *scope* of MGNREGS is to provide income support to rural workers, with the added advantage of using the labor to generate and improve rural infrastructure. Under the program, any individual above the age of 18 years could enroll and seek a job card with the local government, guaranteeing 100 days of wage payment in a year, regardless of whether the work is available or not.[28] MGNREGA has a special provision for women, who are underrepresented in employment and are often paid lower wages for equivalent work. Under the MGNREGA, wages are equal for men and women. There is a special provision for childcare facilities at the place of work, so that women can participate in greater numbers. Public assets, as created through the MGNREGA, further add to the rural economic development. Social safety nets in the *form* of MGNREGA, therefore, not only aim to expand the *focus* of livelihood opportunities to everyone in rural areas, but also tries to facilitate greater participation of women in the labor force, creating rural infrastructure (wells, watershed, roads, etc.) that are part of the major *scope* for increasing development resilience in the country.

[27] Under NFSA, "The eldest woman who is not less than eighteen years of age, in every eligible household, shall be head of the household for the purpose of issue of ration cards" (Government of India 2013 (13[1])).

[28] Since independence, a number of rural development programs were implemented in India with the aim of increasing productivity, better infrastructure, and livelihood opportunities. Yet, most of them failed to have the desired impact, as they were beset with administrative issues of design, implementation, and resources. We will get into these attempts and failures at length, later in this book in Chapter 4.

From Symptoms of Poverty to Its Causes: Recognizing Health Shocks

In 2008, the Government of India launched a new welfare scheme, *Rashtriya Swasthya Bima Yojana* (RSBY), under which all the BPL households would be covered with a health insurance of Rs. 5 lakhs (~7000 USD), with the government paying the significant share of the insurance premium. In 2018, RSBY was subsumed under the larger scope of the *Ayushman Bharat* (Healthy India), as the National Health Protection Scheme (NHPS) aimed to cover almost half of the population, expanding upon the *focus*, which was restricted to the BPL households under the RSBY. Expansion of the *scope* of safety nets to health has been a gradual progress beginning with the National Rural Health Mission (NRHM) in 2005. In 2013, the National Urban Health Mission (NUHM) was launched as a part of the overarching National Health Mission (NHM), which also incorporated the NRHM within it. NHM aims to expand the supply of public health infrastructure, especially in remote rural areas. It also included *Janani Suraksha Yojana* (JSY), a safe motherhood intervention, to encourage institutional child delivery, with the *scope* of reducing maternal and neonatal mortality. JSY involves cash payments and delivery and post-delivery care for the mother and her newborn child.

Publicly subsidized health insurance as a novel *form* of social welfare program in the country has been especially welcome as health shocks are globally considered to be a major cause of slide into poverty.[29] The emerging *focus* on 'causes' of poverty, rather than its symptoms expands the *scope* of social policy toward improved health marks a welcome departure from traditional in-kind welfare payments *focused* on the rural poor. Publicly subsidized health insurance is included in the demand-side aspect of social protection rather than the supply-driven public health infrastructure. This *form* of social protection allows vulnerable people to an option to seek health care in private hospitals if they like.

Development resilience requires a broader range of social programs. The expansion of *focus* from poverty, hunger, and nutrition toward health as a "social minimum," therefore, is a much a desired one. One notes that restricting subsidized health insurance to only the poor is likely to ensure errors of exclusion and limit its effectiveness, but at least it breaks away from policy stasis, which considers poverty to be synonymous with living in rural areas and driven by bad weather. As India is urbanizing, with

[29] See Krishna (2011).

greater reliance on wage-based employment, the likelihood of poverty would increasingly be based upon adverse health shocks and the ability to counter it, even within well-nourished and non-poor households.

Toying with the Idea of Cash Transfers

Introduced in one of the economic surveys in recent years, cash transfers in the *form* of a "basic income" are now being considered as an idea that is worth debating in order to reframe the social protection architecture.[30] Cash transfers seem to improve economic efficiency, not only by avoiding intermediaries, which often siphon off the resources, but also providing people with the choice of items they would like to consume. Providing the deserving beneficiaries with cash transfers, however, requires a robust delivery system architecture, which involves identification of beneficiaries, tracking them over time, fixing an inflation-indexed amount, and ensuring beneficiaries receive timely payments. The Government of India seeks to leverage its financial inclusion project under the *Jan Dhan Yojana*, enrollment for the unique biometric identity card called *Aadhaar*, and near universal penetration of (M)obile technology, often referred to as the "JAM" trinity to roll out payments.

While it has not yet been fully implemented, the idea is to use the JAM infrastructure to create a database of beneficiaries and provide them with benefits without risk of the recipients being cheated, as was often the case with earlier social welfare programs. Very recently, given the poor agricultural remunerations, the Government introduced the scheme, *Pradhan Mantri Kisan Samman Nidhi* (PM–Kisan), in 2018, through which each farmer is expected to receive up to Rs. 6,000 (~US$84) as yearly income support. PM–Kisan, along with pensions and maternity benefits, have been some of the newer *forms* of welfare programs, the *scope* of which moves away from merely food provisions to a more dignified living through improved nutritional intake, and health and educational outcomes.

[30] Economic surveys are annual summaries of the current economic status and the government's thinking around those issues, released each year by the government in the Parliament, along with the annual budget. The idea of cash transfers primarily originated as an alternative to expensive PDS.

Emerging Social Contract: Provisions to Entitlements

Modern nation-states have used welfare systems to promote democratic citizenship—the fundamental principles on which nationhood itself is sustained. A strong citizen-state *social contract* increases the accountability of the state toward its citizens instills in them the idea of 'citizenship rights' and equality thereby promoting social integration, solidarity, and a sense of dignity.[31] The performance of Indian state in this regard though sketchy, exhibits substantial progress. Instead of developing a "social minimum" for all its citizens, social welfare policy frameworks limited themselves to ad hoc 'schemes' and 'programs' with a *scope* of addressing the symptoms of poverty rather than addressing the underlying structural issues. With poorly designed and implemented welfare policies around basic provisions—consumption smoothing through food and income transfer—instead of broad-based redistributive policies to address the structural inequalities in initial endowments, transformation was beyond the *scope* of social policy. This trend is however changing with a greater policy recognition to the cause of social welfare.

Civil society push for social welfare reforms legitimize them through rights-based constitutional legislation in 2000s and helped move the needle in developing a new social contract which led to an expansion of its safety net programs in all three aspects—*form, focus,* and *scope.*[32] Yet, while this expansion of social safety nets provides the basic scaffoldings for a 'welfare system,' concerted action is required to build a system of entitlement protection as well as promotion which can be leveraged not

[31] Theories of social contract owe its origins to political philosophers who dwelled upon the political authority and obligations that rulers have to their citizens with further extension toward upholding citizenship rights in democratic systems. For a perspective on how the need for social protection or welfare emerges from the social contract theory, see (Hickey 2011). The Indian social contract has been characterized as an "interventionist" model of welfare that mainly was aimed at food provisions, quite in contrast to the Western notion of welfare, which is more "developmentalist" in character (Jayal 1994). Despite the expansion of social welfare schemes, it is still considered to be residual in nature because of low levels of social expenditure and a mixed review of its impact on social welfare outcomes (Barrientos 2013; Kühner and Nakray 2017).

[32] The defining force in creating a social safety net architecture in India was the National Advisory Council (NAC) that was pushed forward by the "rights-based agenda," which social activists had been advocating for some time. Rights to education, work, and food were subsequently passed between 2003 and 2013. Also, this was partly made possible by the improved fiscal capacity of the government, as a result of economic growth in the last decade or so.

only to provide relief to the poor but also to propel them toward greater opportunities through broad-based public action— involving both state and citizens—to build resilience and facilitate transformation.[33]

Subnational Economic Development and Welfare Regimes

Before we move on to discuss the sources of deprivation, risks, and vulnerability which necessitate social welfare programs in India, it is important to highlight that the national narrative presented above needs a subnational twist. India comprises of 30 states—many of them being the size of nation-states—each of which have had a very different trajectory of economic growth, social development, and the nature of social contract. While India's structural transformation has been atypical, another unique feature of its development trajectory has been divergence in the subnational growth patterns.[34] In terms of social welfare policies, the importance of state governments as implementing agencies has led to radical innovations, suggesting greater importance of subnational governments in being the torchbearer of reforms in the social welfare system.[35]

In terms of structural transformation, while Punjab, Haryana, and parts of Andhra Pradesh benefited from a spurt in agricultural productivity due to the Green Revolution, Gujarat and Maharashtra took the manufacturing route to transform their economy. Other states, such as Karnataka and Tamil Nadu made use of a combination of manufacturing and skill-based services, while Kerala's growth model owes largely to its higher human development and remittances from abroad.[36] Social welfare policy

[33] See Drèze and Sen (1991) for a discussion on entitlement protection, entitlement promotion, and social security.

[34] Refer to Pingali et al. (2019) for an in-depth classification of subnational growth trajectories.

[35] The rise of multi-party coalition politics at the union level provided greater political importance to subnational regional parties which were able to utilize this as an opportunity to improve better delivery mechanisms and expand on the programs creating new subnational regimes. Improved performance of social welfare programs created greater electoral credibility of the subnational governments (Tillin 2022). Subnational differences in social welfare schemes remains a recurring theme in the book. For a discussion on the socio-political origins of different commitment to welfare, see Deshpande et al. (2017) and Tillin et al. (2015).

[36] See Sinha (2005).

at the subnational level followed a different logic. More committed to a social democracy, and redistribution, and political unity through by linguistic subnational identity, South Indian states invested more in public service delivery leading to better human development outcomes.[37]As a result of these socio-economic changes, poverty levels, human development outcomes, and the degree of urbanization vary widely across these states, and therefore, their developmental challenges are unique.

Among the major states of India, higher per capita GDP is associated with a lower share of agriculture in total output (Panel A and B, Fig. 3.4). Among the more advanced states, traditionally *agriculture-driven* states like Punjab, Haryana, and Andhra Pradesh continue to have a relatively greater share of agricultural output. Other richer states like Gujarat, Himachal Pradesh, and Maharashtra, however, have a greater share of industrial output. In comparison, the more urbanized states—Tamil Nadu, Karnataka, or Kerala—have an economy dominated by services.

The structural transformation process is more stunted in some of the poorer and populous states like Bihar and Uttar Pradesh. A closer look at the workforce participation rates (WPR) suggests in that poorer states despite a low share of agriculture in total output, employ a disproportionately greater share of labor in the sector. In fact, agriculture remains the most important employer of workers with little variation across the two richest and the poorest states in the country (Panel C, Fig. 3.4). However, there is a substantial variation in the labor force participation in manufacturing—the poorest states progressively perform the worst. Among poorer states, a large share of the workers, despite living in rural areas, are employed in the wholesale and retail trade, which is largely informal in nature. This suggests that poorer states, with greater pressure on land, are participating in the rural nonfarm informal employment for livelihood. Manufacturing sector has traditionally been the source of large-scale employment of unskilled workers while services not only require more skilled and trained workforce, it employs lesser share of the population. The lack of manufacturing sector as a source of employment

[37] Indian states were organized along the lines of linguistic identity. A strong subnational identity and a long history of community action through political mobilization among the lower castes created a more egalitarian social contract in South India with better public services, redistribution, which led to empowerment of the poor (Dreze and Sen 2002; Kalaiyarasan and Vijayabaskar 2021; Lee 2019; Singh 2015).

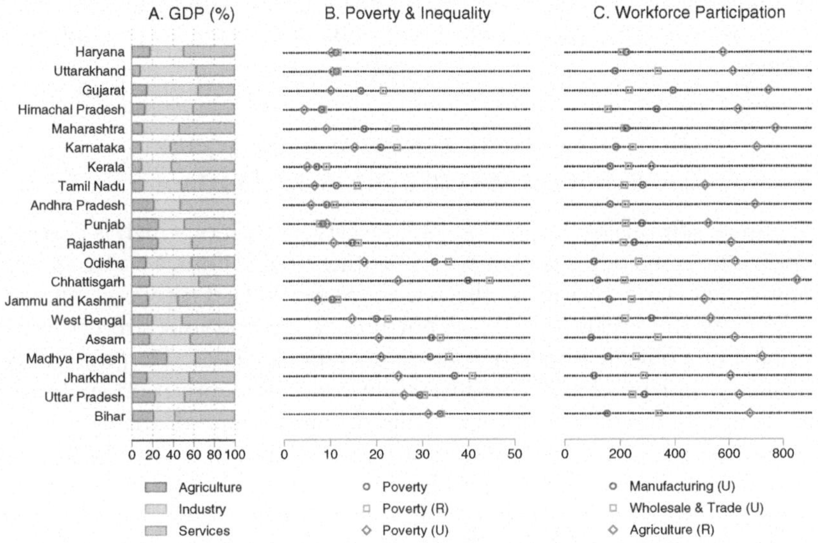

Fig. 3.4 State-level output shares, workforce participation, poverty, and inequality ranked by per capita output (*Source* Output data from the Economic and Political Weekly Research Foundation [EPWRF] for 2017–18. Other figures based upon the National Sample Survey Office [NSSO] 2011–12)

in the poorer states has led to the movement of unskilled labor toward poor quality, service-based employment, which portends a combination of agricultural and nonagricultural livelihood-based risks that now exist in rural areas.

The variegated nature of structural transformation and performance of social welfare programs reflects the differential risks and vulnerability of households across the country. For example, social risks in relatively richer and more urbanized states might emerge from loss of employment, informality of livelihood, health shocks, while in relatively rural states, earning loss is additionally accounted by weather shocks, lack of markets, or access to public services. The scope of social welfare policies in both these contexts is to protect as well as to promote their entitlements with varying importance. More advanced regions may require stronger promotional measures such as growth-oriented strategies which build greater skills and human capital, while the poorer regions require greater state support in protecting their fragile livelihoods in addition to promotional strategies.

Building Resilience as the *Scope* of Social Safety Nets in India

Living in conditions of destitution and poverty—much of which is beyond an individual's agency—is akin to an "entitlement failure," and requires strong public action to assist the needy (Sen 1982). Protecting human entitlements and creating equal opportunities for everyone are not only a moral but political imperative in democratic societies. Despite plenty of schemes and programs to address poverty and deprivation in India, concerted public action is lacking. While diagnosing and describing many of these failures in the earlier section of this chapter, we would like to highlight some key economic considerations which are essential to address in imagining social safety nets of the future. These concerns primarily arise from the precarity generated by the stunted structural transformation of the Indian economy and the fixation with money-metric poverty measures as the scope of social policy.

Moving Beyond the Preoccupation with Poverty Line

Let's first discuss the challenges fraught with poverty reduction as the singular scope of social policy. Resilience is the ability to withstand adverse shocks and maintain a reasonable standard of living. For human development, such resilience stems from human and physical capital endowments. For social safety net architecture to have a transformational impact on human development, the policy scope must move beyond its preoccupation with poverty.

The money-metric poverty line is a concept fraught with theoretical and operational challenges. It creates an artificial boundary between the poor and the non-poor, while ignoring how economic lives among both these groups are so variegated, and vulnerability is differentiated based upon geography, social group, occupation, and physical, human, and social capital. Social welfare programs that are targeted toward the poor—means-tested benefits—often run the risk of lower support among the non-beneficiaries, thereby lowering their effectiveness. At the same time, the amount of transfers has not been able to fundamentally change the relative ownership bundles—physical and human capital—for the poor. At best, they provide temporary relief, which may help the recipients cope with shocks to some extent but does not increase their resilience. At a time when most Indian households continue to be asset poor with a widening of the gap between the haves and have-nots in terms of most productive assets, such as land and income, it is important to *focus* beyond poverty to have a bigger developmental *scope*.

Poverty metrics, income or calorie-based, conceal wide fluctuations in household economic circumstances, often within a given year. In the rural areas, income fluctuations arise from the quality of harvest, although it could be due to loss of jobs in the urban areas. Monthly consumption expenditure estimates, as used to measure poverty in India, could vary if made right after the harvest or later. Given the uncertainties of income, by season in developing countries, an accurate understanding of poverty requires a more nuanced understanding of the everyday lives of the poor.[38] As India is moving toward a more market-based economy, the ability to purchase a preferred consumption basket, including food and other assets, depends upon the returns from livelihood—returns to cultivation for farmers and wages for the labor.

Income, asset, or expenditure-based poverty estimates shy away from some of the most important factors which influence the current living conditions, such as concerns about security of livelihood, access to common property resources, and essential public infrastructure, including drinking water, health, and education. Many of these non-income factors create conditions of chronic poverty and poverty traps through food insecurity, malnutrition, mortality, and reduction in overall productivity. Food insecurity may lead to malnutrition, which causes reduced physical capacity and stunting, inhibits learning, and may have long-term nutritional, health, and productivity-related effects for present and future generations. An important finding in studies on poverty in India is that most poor households continue to be poor over time, suggesting they

[38] Inadequate returns to cultivation to farmers, lower real wages for workers in agriculture or industry, and unremunerative self-employment lead to income poverty (Kathuria and Raj S.N. 2016). Even in rural India, low wages—wage-based livelihood is the most important income source in rural areas—are the major reason for higher poverty, having increased with a decline in agricultural output share and low-productivity services sector. See Banerjee and Duflo (2007) for a thicker description of the 'economic lives of the poor.'

experience chronic conditions of poverty trap.[39] Those suffering from chronic poverty are not necessarily poor in terms of consumption expenditure, as it is often measured, but due to very low levels of initial endowments of physical and human capital, like land, assets, education, health, and employment, which affect their risk-bearing capacities and their abilities to invest in acquiring employable skills to enhance labor productivity.

Social Safety Nets to Address Multiple Dimensions of Poverty

Comparing India with other countries on various development indicators presents a dismal picture (Fig. 3.5). India's performance on some of the most important indicators of long-term development outcomes fare the worst. If children are the future of a nation, India is not only home to largest share of undernourished children in the world, but it also holds the ignominious record of having the highest prevalence of anemia among pregnant women across the globe.

Although these are symptoms of poverty to a large degree, without direct support in early childhood, these developmental deficits will not be reduced merely by growth. Distributional consequences of growth have not been very progressive, as inequality has risen since the 1990s. Poor childhood nutrition further brings down human capital attainments. Despite a near universal, free primary education, learning outcomes of children have not improved considerably, and there is a massive dropout rate in their transition to secondary schools. With poor human capital attainment, gainful and secure livelihood opportunities are likely to be sparse in a service sector-driven economy, with return to education strongly tied to skills. As a result, a very small proportion of Indians are able to afford any annual savings. With land and livelihood, both unequally distributed, a very large section of the people are exposed to various kinds of shocks including adverse weather conditions for farm-based workers, unemployment for wage-based ones and health shocks in general. India has one of the highest rates of slide into poverty on account of the high out-of-pocket (OOP) health expenditures. This is where safety net programs—imagined not as a collection of schemes but as a portfolio of initiatives creating a system of protection and promotion through

[39] Refer to Kapur Mehta and Shah (2003) for greater details.

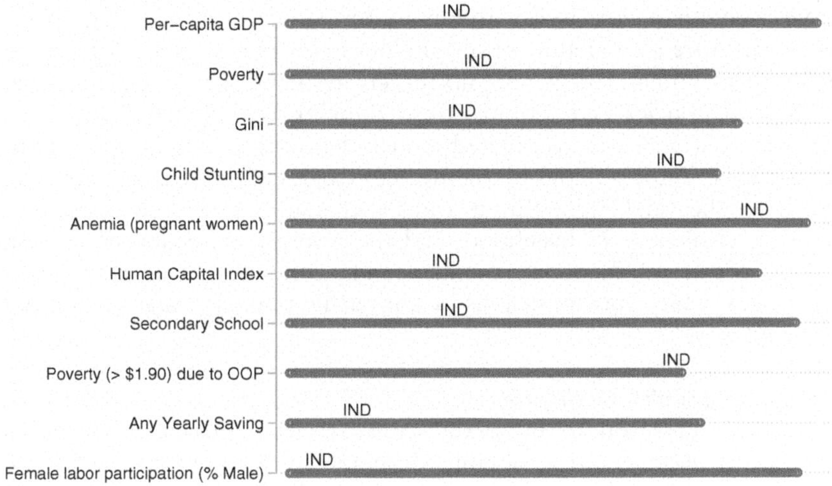

Fig. 3.5 India's global rankings on development indicators: The numbers of countries depend upon the data availability for the year 2017 (*Source* World Development Indicators, World Bank)

the life cycle—can foster a resilient development process that is not only broad-based but is also inclusive and potentially transformative.

Protecting Entitlements in a Deindustrializing Economy

A defining feature of Indian economy which creates various risks and vulnerabilities is its stunted structural transformation. The current state of Indian economy has been characterized by "premature deindustrialization [and] precocious servicification" wherein the comparative advantage of abundant supply of unskilled labor has been lost (Lamba and Subramanian 2020).[40] An aspirational India which is urbanizing (albeit, at a

[40] This is also an important point of departure between India's experience with that of China's, which through its exports of labor-intensive manufacturing products, lifted a large share of its population out of poverty. The same, however, was not true for India, as it relied mainly upon the export of skill-intensive products such as IT, which employs only 1% of the total labor force (Bardhan 2010). Even the associated subsectors, including finance, IT-enabled services, and telecommunications, comprise a small share of the total output in the service sector.

slower pace than expected) with limited formal sector jobs, unremunerative agriculture (dominantly of smallholder type), persistent human capital deficiencies, and archaic gender norms, creates newer challenges for social protection policies and requires fresh thinking on how to break from the past policies which considered human deprivation merely as failure of food access. Vulnerabilities of the future, in a globalized market, portends greater upheaval. Highlighting India's changing economic structure, poverty, challenges of livelihood, and the divergent subnational growth pattern is particularly useful to understanding the current developmental challenges, which further help us in approaching policy designs in a more nuanced way.

Premature Deindustrialization

Premature transition to high-skill service sector employment leads to regional divergence in economic development, as not all states are endowed with a similar nature of economic opportunities, especially in the formal sector, whether in industry or the service sector. Lack of skill-intensive growth implies that labor productivity would continue to be high in the capital-scarce states. In the poorer states of India, where poverty is largely concentrated, the manufacturing sector, especially the formal one, fares worse. At the individual level, a clear labor market segmentation differentiated by education and skill levels would perpetuate inequality, dividing workers by placing them in so-called white-collar and blue-collar jobs, with stark differences not only in income but also in security of livelihoods and access to social security. The differential wages and labor productivities between the high-skill and low-skill workers have been issues of active debate in India, especially after the period of market liberalization, in which some of the workforce (very few) tapped into the *dollar economy* vis-à-vis the low-skill workers (a huge share), who are still stuck in the *rupee economy* (Krishna 2017). As a result, redistribution not only of current income, but also of future income and opportunities, remains the most essential of developmental challenges, with grave implications for intergenerational mobility, pathways out of the poverty trap, and for the engendering of development resilience.

Urban Informality

Economic transformation is synonymous with urbanization. Welfare of the rural-to-urban migrant is facilitated by the quality of urban employment. As a result of the premature deindustrialization in India, much of the labor movement has been absorbed in informal, low-skill service sector jobs. According to an estimate by the International Labor Organization (ILO), informal workers constitute 93% of the labor force in India. This amounts to 82% of the total nonagricultural labor force in the country. Informal labor is also typically low in education attainment, with little specialization and skills.

The informal nature of wage-based employment renders a large share of the labor force outside the purview of any form of employer-based safety nets. According to the Periodic Labor Force Survey (PLFS) conducted by the Government of India in 2017–18, 71.1% of the people working as wage or salaried employees in the nonagricultural sector had no written job contracts, 54.2% were ineligible for any paid leave, and 49.6% did not have access to any social security benefits. If one adds these numbers to the self-employed workers—another large share of workers in the urban space—most of the workers have little protection against livelihood risks.

As urban employment is largely in the form of self-employment, small industrial firms, or the service sector, collective action through organized labor fronts has been increasingly difficult. Informal workers are not officially recognized by their employers in the same way as those formally on their payrolls. Being outside the purview of legal regulation, and not supported in anyway during labor retrenchment or illness, laborers face a perpetual exposure to job loss and frequent periods of unemployment, which makes them vulnerable to long-term unemployment and poverty. Many of those working in the informal labor force are migrants—*footloose labor*, moving from one urban center to the another, originally belonging to villages, but in search of work elsewhere (Breman 1996). Not only do they lack the social network they left behind in their villages, but they are more liable to be cheated through denial or underpayment of wages in the labor market, as a study of casual "*day labor*" markets on the outskirts of Mumbai shows (Naraparaju 2016). As contract enforcements in the informal labor market are difficult and employer-based social protection programs on the wane, the workers have turned to the state for social protection in the wake of economic losses (Agarwala 2013). With a reduction in the power of urban informal workers as employees, instead of demanding traditional work benefits from employers, these workers demand, on the basis of their "citizenship," welfare from the state. Yet, most of the welfare programs have been *focused* on the rural poor, and urban poor often suffer from dispossession, pauperism, and vagrancy (Breman 2016, 2019). The desperate scenes of migrant laborers walking to their homes, after the economy-wide lockdown in the wake of COVID-19 induced social distancing, was a painful reminder of the precariousness of the urban labor market situation.

Stagnant Farm Income

While the urban poor, largely a part of informal sector, suffer from precarious livelihoods, farmers in the hinterland are currently struggling with lower returns to cultivation. A major challenge for the Indian economy in the recent past has been the lack of commensurate increase in farm income. In 2016, Prime Minister Narendra Modi, in his Independence Day speech, proclaimed the government's ambition of doubling farm income by 2022. This declaration came in the wake of stagnant farm income in the preceding decade. However, as this book goes to press, we have not seen much progress on that front, except for the announcement of cash transfers to farmers in the form of PM-Kisan. Yet, the transfer of money, while a commitment to farmers' concerns, fails to address the issue of farm productivity, an issue which requires curative reforms rather than palliative care.

Stagnant farm incomes—around 1% since 2011–12—have been a grave policy concern, as a large share of the rural population (61% of the total population) relies on it, directly or indirectly (Chand et al. 2015). The National Sample Survey suggests that during a decade (2003–13), the income of agricultural households grew by a mere 34% in real terms (Chandrasekhar and Mehrotra 2016). Much of this increase, however low, came from other sectors, such as livestock and other nonfarm enterprises, rather than from cultivation. The increase in income was differentiated by the size of landholdings, with the smallholders faring worst. Are there ways to think of how safety nets could be leveraged to promote rural incomes? Income through guaranteed employment, through the Mahatma Gandhi National Rural Employment Guarantee Act (MGNREGA), has been one such program to reduce rural poverty, but it does little to increase farm income, which is related to productivity increase and better market access. From the perspective of this book, it is therefore useful to assess what is the role of existing safety nets in propelling farm income and addressing rural poverty in the future.

Rural Nonfarm Employment

Along with the urban labor, rural agricultural labor has a peculiar problem. Increasingly, as farm sizes have become smaller, and the rural economy grows in the shadow of urban growth, the nonfarm sector has become a necessary part of the Indian rural economy by absorbing surplus labor from agriculture. Between 1983 and 2004, rural nonfarm output grew at faster pace (7.1%), compared to overall agricultural output growth (2.6%), creating more remunerative livelihoods (Himanshu et al. 2011). A large share of the farming households (88%) engage in a portfolio of other activities, such as livestock or wage/salaried employment to diversify their earnings stream (Chandrasekhar and Mehrotra 2016). In fact, the growth of rural nonfarm employment has been instrumental, therefore, in reducing poverty, promoting social mobility, and increasing food security in the Indian villages (Himanshu et al. 2013; Rahman and Mishra 2020). Not only has nonfarm employment been pro-poor in India, but it has also provided an effective insurance against the uncertainty of farm-based income (Lanjouw and Murgai 2009).

The diversification is especially important from the perspective of smallholders, as the rising population burden on land has led to a reduction in average land size in rural India. Between 1970–71 and 2015–16, total operational holdings almost doubled from 71.01 million to 146 million, but the average farm size halved from 2.28 ha to 1.08 ha. This has led to an increase in the share of small landholders who currently cultivate 47.3% of the operational agricultural land and possess 86.21% of the total landholdings. Without diversification into nonfarm activities, one-fourth of smallholders are likely to fall, therefore, below the official poverty line (Chand et al. 2011). Yet, despite this diversification, as greater numbers of people own smaller parcels of land—their principal physical asset—the risk to agricultural income, the most stable type of income in rural areas, has increased. Any incidence of bad harvest, job loss, or any form of health shock is likely to put these farmers at risk of falling below the poverty line. The subsistence earning, which nonfarm employment has managed to provide, has only ensured sustenance with very little asset accumulation to develop resilience against shocks.

Scope of This Book: Leveraging Social Safety Nets to Promote Development Resilience

Given India's current economic structure and the persistent human development deficit, this book tries to imagine a social safety net architecture that promotes development resilience. This chapter marks out the basic contours of India's economic development trajectory and the emergence of a social welfare architecture in the country—as relief-induced state intervention to citizens' rights along its path of economic development, and democratic deepening—against the persistent human developmental challenges. From the vantage point of many years of learning from various social welfare programs, within and outside of the country, we provide a theoretically and empirically grounded analysis of how India's social welfare programs need to be reoriented to achieve development resilience in the future.

We argue that while the safety net policies in maintaining a "social minimum" of human needs has expanded in *scope* from basic food provisions to nutrition, income, and health, the performance of social safety nets has left much to be desired in terms of have a transformational effect. Although safety nets have provided relief to the poor, they have not promoted development resilience such that the poor are able to overcome their low initial resource endowments and the non-poor are able to sustain themselves continuously at higher levels of development. Studying the social safety nets in India, in terms of their *focus, scope*, and *form*, we provide a comprehensive review of the set of programs that provide the basic social protection scaffolding and speculate upon future policy directions. Safety nets in the future, in our framework, should be aligned with the changing forms of risk and vulnerability along the path of structural transformation.

Policy debates around the nature of assistance (in-kind food or an equivalent amount of cash), nutritional assistance in utero and in early childhood, free school meals, public works employment, and health insurance have evolved according to the policy imperatives of the time, political initiatives, and the technological infrastructure of public service delivery. We argue that the expansion in *scope* of safety nets continues to lack synergies across developmental objectives, and various social safety nets work in isolation, therefore, remaining limited in overall impact. The design of these programs, in terms of their *focus* and *form*, is further afflicted because it was designed for an agrarian population when poverty was considered a rural issue. Economic growth and structural transformation have not only brought about prosperity but also created newer forms of economic risks and social vulnerability, especially when the fruits of growth have been unequally distributed—across regions and people. Economic redistribution through social safety nets, therefore, remains key to a more resilient and sustainable development path. As a result, we study social welfare policies, looking forward to an India of the future, which would be more urbanized, service sector-driven, and with greater reliance on nonfarm employment, even in rural areas. In such a setting, socio-economic risks would therefore emanate from the loss of livelihood and income-earning capacities arising out of exogenous health and weather shocks.

References

Adiga, A., 2008. *The white tiger: A novel.* Simon and Schuster.

Agarwala, Rina. 2013. *Informal Labor, Formal Politics, and Dignified Discontent in India.* Cambridge: Cambridge University Press.

Anand, Ishan, and Anjana Thampi. 2016. "Recent Trends in Wealth Inequality in India." *Economic and Political Weekly* 51 (50): 59–67.

Athukorala, Prema-Chandra, and Kunal Sen. 2002. *Saving, Investment and Growth in India.* New Delhi: Oxford University Press.

Banerjee, A.V. and Duflo, E., 2007. The economic lives of the poor. *Journal of economic perspectives*, 21(1), pp.141-167.

Bardhan, Pranab. 2010. *Awakening Giants, Feet of Clay: Assessing the Economic Rise of China and India.* Princeton: Princeton University Press.

Barrientos, Armando. 2013. *Social Assistance in Developing Countries.* Cambridge: Cambridge University Press.

Basu, Kaushik. 2018. "A Short History of India's Economy." WIDER Working Paper 2018/124.

Bhagwati, J. and Panagariya, A., 2013. *Why growth matters: How economic growth in India reduced poverty and the lessons for other developing countries.* Hachette UK.

Bharti, Nitin Kumar. 2018. "Wealth Inequality, Class and Caste in India, 1961–2012." WID. World Working Paper 14.

Binswanger-Mkhize, Hans P. 2013. "The Stunted Structural Transformation of the Indian Economy." *Economic and Political Weekly* 48 (26–27): 5–13.

Breman, Jan. 1996. *Footloose Labour*. Cambridge: Cambridge University Press.

Breman, Jan. 2016. *On Pauperism in Present and Past.* New Delhi: Oxford University Press.

Breman, Jan. 2019. *Capitalism, Inequality and Labour in India*. New Delhi: Cambridge University Press.

Burgess, Robin, and Rohini Pande. 2005. "Do Rural Banks Matter? Evidence from the Indian Social Banking Experiment." *American Economic Review* 95 (3):780–95. https://doi.org/10.1257/0002828054201242.

Chakravorty, Sanjoy, S. Chandrasekhar, and Karthikeya Naraparaju. 2019. "Land Distribution, Income Generation and Inequality in India's Agricultural Sector." *Review of Income and Wealth* 65 (S1). https://doi.org/10.1111/roiw.12434.

Chancel, Lucas, and Thomas Piketty. 2019. "Indian Income Inequality, 1922–2015: From British Raj to Billionaire Raj?" *Review of Income and Wealth* 65 (S1). https://doi.org/10.1111/roiw.12439.

Chand, Ramesh, Lakshmi Prasanna, and Aruna Singh. 2011. "Farm Size and Productivity: Understanding the Strengths of Smallholders and Improving Their Livelihoods." *Economic & Political Weekly* 46 (26/27): 5–11.

Chand, Ramesh, Raka Saxena, and Simmi Rana. 2015. "Estimates and Analysis of Farm Income in India, 1983–84 to 2011–12." *Economic & Political Weekly* 50 (22): 139–45.

Chandrasekhar, S., and Nirupam Mehrotra. 2016. "Doubling Farmers' Incomes by 2022." *Economic & Political Weekly* 51 (18): 10–13.

Chandrasekhar, S., and Abhiroop Mukhopadhyay. 2010. "Poverty and Well-Being in Indian Cities During the Reforms Era." *Poverty & Public Policy* 2 (2): 189–209.

Dandekar, Vishnu Mahadeo, and Nilakantha Rath. 1971. "Poverty in India-I: Dimensions and Trends." *Economic and Political Weekly*, 25–48.

Datt, Gaurav, and Martin Ravallion. 1998. "Farm Productivity and Rural Poverty in India." *Journal of Development Studies* 34 (4): 62–85. https://doi.org/10.1080/00220389808422529.

Datt, Gaurav, Martin Ravallion, and Rinku Murgai. 2019. "Poverty and Growth in India over Six Decades." *American Journal of Agricultural Economics*. https://doi.org/10.1093/ajae/aaz043.

Deaton, Angus, and Jean Dreze. 2002. "Poverty and Inequality in India: A Re-examination." *Economic and Political Weekly* 37 (36d): 3729–48.

Deaton, Angus, and Jean Drèze. 2009. "Food and Nutrition in India: Facts and Interpretations." *Economic and Political Weekly* 47 (7): 42–65. https://doi.org/10.2307/40278509.

Deshpande, Rajeshwari, K. K. Kailash, and Louise Tillin. 2017. "States as Laboratories: The Politics of Social Welfare Policies in India." *India Review* 16 (1): 85–105. https://doi.org/10.1080/14736489.2017.1279928.

Dev, S. Mahendra. 1996. "Food Security: PDS vs EGS: A Tale of Two States." *Economic and Political Weekly* 31 (27): 1752–64.

Dev, S. Mahendra. 2000. "Agricultural Development and PDS: Lack of Major Initiatives." *Economic and Political Weekly* 35 (13): 1046–49.

Drèze, Jean. 1988. "Famine Prevention in India." In *Political Economy of Hunger Vol. 2*, edited by A. K. Sen and J. Drèze, 13–122. Oxford: Oxford University Press.

Drèze, Jean. 2017. *Sense and Solidarity: Jholawala Economics for Everyone*. Oxford, UK: Oxford University Press.

Drèze, Jean, and Amartya Sen. 1989. *Hunger and Public Action*. New York: Oxford University Press.

Drèze, Jean, and Amartya Sen. 1991. "Public Action for Social Security: Foundations and Strategy." In *Social Security in Developing Countries*, 3–40. Oxford: Oxford University Press.

Drèze, Jean, and Amartya Sen. 2002. *India: Development and Participation*. Oxford, UK: Oxford University Press.

Drèze, J. and Sen, A., 2013. *An uncertain glory: India and its contradictions*. Princeton University Press.

Eichengreen, Barry, and Poonam Gupta. 2011. "The Service Sector as India's Road to Economic Growth." NBER Working Paper No. 16757.

Gibson, J., Datt, G., Murgai, R. and Ravallion, M., 2017. For India's rural poor, growing towns matter more than growing cities. *World Development*, 98, pp.413-429.

Government of India. 2013. The National Food Security Act. *The Gazette of India*. New Delhi: Ministry of Law and Justice.

Hickey, Sam. 2011. "The Politics of Social Protection: What Do We Get from a 'Social Contract' Approach?" *Canadian Journal of Development Studies/ Revue Canadienne d'études Du Développement* 32 (4): 426–38. https://doi.org/10.1080/02255189.2011.647447.

Himanshu, Peter Lanjouw, Abhiroop Mukhopadhyay, and Rinku Murgai. 2011. "Non-Farm Diversification and Rural Poverty Decline: A Perspective from Indian Sample Survey and Village Study Data," 1–49. ASIA Research Centre Working Paper 44.

Himanshu, Peter Lanjouw, Rinku Murgai, and Nicholas Stern. 2013. "Nonfarm Diversification, Poverty, Economic Mobility, and Income Inequality: A Case Study in Village India." *Agricultural Economics* 44 (4–5): 461–73. https://doi.org/10.1111/agec.12029.

Howes, Stephen, and Shikha Jha. 1994. "Public Distribution of Food in India: A Comment." *Food Policy* 19 (1): 65–68. https://doi.org/10.1016/0306-9192(94)90009-4.

Jayadev, Arjun, Sripad Motiram, and Vamsi Vakulabharanam. 2007. "Patterns of Wealth Disparities in India During the Liberalisation Era." *Economic and Political Weekly* 42 (38): 3853–63.

Jayal, Niraja Gopal. 1994. "The Gentle Leviathan: Welfare and the Indian State." *Social Scientist* 22 (9/12): 18. https://doi.org/10.2307/3517911.

Johnston, Bruce F. 1970. "Agriculture and Structural Transformation in Developing Countries: A Survey of Research." *Journal of Economic Literature* 8 (2): 369–404.

Kalaiyarasan, A., and M. Vijayabaskar. 2021. *The Dravidian Model: Interpreting the Political Economy of Tamil Nadu*. Cambridge: Cambridge University Press.

Kathuria, V. and Raj SN, R., 2016. Do informal sector wages explain rural poverty? Evidence from India. *Journal of Poverty*, 20(1), pp.73-101

Khera, Reetika, ed. 2011. *The Battle for Employment Guarantee*. Oxford and New York: Oxford University Press.

Kijima, Yoko. 2006. "Why Did Wage Inequality Increase? Evidence from Urban India 1983–99." *Journal of Development Economics* 81 (1): 97–117. https://doi.org/10.1016/j.jdeveco.2005.04.008.

Kohli, Atul. 2012. *Poverty Amid Plenty in the New India*. Cambridge: Cambridge University Press.

Kotwal, Ashok, and Bharat Ramaswami. 2014. "Delivering Food Subsidy: The State and the Market." In *The Oxford Handbook of Food, Politics, and Society* (September), 301–301. Oxford and New York: Oxford University Press.

Kotwal, Ashok, Bharat Ramaswami, and Wilima Wadhwa. 2014. "Economic Liberalization and Indian Economic Growth : What's the Evidence ?" *Journal of Economic Literature* 49 (4): 1152–99.

Krishna, Anirudh. 2011. *One Illness Away: Why People Become Poor and How They Escape Poverty*. Oxford: Oxford University Press.

Krishna, Anirudh. 2017. *The Broken Ladder*. Cambridge: Cambridge University Press.

Kühner, Stefan, and Keerty Nakray. 2017. "India's Emerging Social Policy Paradigm: Productive, Protective or What?" *Journal of Asian Public Policy* 10 (1): 40–56. https://doi.org/10.1080/17516234.2016.1258521.

Lamba, Rohit, and Arvind Subramanian. 2020. "Dynamism with Incommensurate Development: The Distinctive Indian Model." *Journal of Economic Perspectives* 34 (1): 3–30.

Lanjouw, Peter, and Rinku Murgai. 2009. "Poverty Decline, Agricultural Wages, and Nonfarm Employment in Rural India: 1983–2004." *Agricultural Economics* 40 (2): 243–63. https://doi.org/10.1111/j.1574-0862.2009.00373.x.

Lee, Alexander. 2019. *Development in Multiple Dimensions: Social Power and Regional Policy in India*. Ann Arbor: University of Michigan Press.

Mehta, A.K. and Shah, A., 2003. Chronic poverty in India: Incidence, causes and policies. *World Development*, 31(3), pp.491-511.

Mooij, Jos. 1998. "Food Policy and Politics: The Political Economy of the Public Distribution System in India." *Journal of Peasant Studies* 25 (June 2015): 77–101. https://doi.org/10.1080/03066159808438667.

Motiram, Sripad, and Karthikeya Naraparaju. 2015. "Growth and Deprivation in India: What Does Recent Evidence Suggest on 'Inclusiveness'?" *Oxford Development Studies* 43 (2): 145–64. https://doi.org/10.1080/13600818.2014.988693.

Naraparaju, Karthikeya. 2016. "Impediments to Contract Enforcement in Day Labour Markets: A Perspective from India." *Journal of Institutional Economics* 12 (3): 651–76. https://doi.org/10.1017/S1744137415000442.

Naraparaju, Karthikeya, and S. Chandrasekhar. 2022. "Poverty Reduction in Rural India During 2004–2005 to 2011–2012: Role of Growth, Redistribution, and Population-Shifts." *Review of Income and Wealth* 68 (S2): 295–316. doi: https://doi.org/10.1111/roiw.12557.

Nayyar, D., 2006. Economic growth in independent India: Lumbering elephant or running tiger?. *Economic and Political Weekly*, pp.1451-1458.

Pingali, Prabhu, Anaka Aiyar, Mathew Abraham, and Andaleeb Rahman. 2019. *Transforming Food Systems for a Rising India.* Cham: Springer International.

Planning Commission. 2005. *Performance Evaluation of Targeted Public Distribution System (TPDS).* New Delhi: Government of India.

Rahman, Andaleeb, and Sumit Mishra. 2020. "Does Non-Farm Income Affect Food Security? Evidence from India." *The Journal of Development Studies* 56 (6): 1190–1209. https://doi.org/10.1080/00220388.2019.1640871.

Ravallion, Martin, and Gaurav Datt. 1996. "India's Checkered History in Fight Against Poverty: Are There Lessons for the Future?" *Economic and Political Weekly* 31 (35/37): 2479–85.

Rodrik, Dani, and Arvind Subramanian. 2005. "From 'Hindu Growth' to Productivity Surge: The Mystery of the Indian Growth Transition." *IMF Staff Papers* 52 (2): 193–228. https://doi.org/10.2307/30035894.

Sen, Amartya. 1976. "Famines as Failures of Exchange Entitlements." *Economic and Political Weekly* 11 (31/33): 1273–80.

Sen, Amartya. 1982. *Poverty and Famines: An Essay on Entitlement and Deprivation.* Oxford: Oxford University Press.

Siegel, Benjamin Robert. 2018. *Hungry Nation: Food, Famine, and the Making of Modern India.* Cambridge: Cambridge University Press.

Singh, Prerna. 2015. *How Solidarity Works for Welfare.* Cambridge: Cambridge University Press.

Sinha, Aseema. 2005. *The Regional Roots of Developmental Politics in India: A Divided Leviathan.* Bloomington: Indiana University Press.

Subramanian, S., and D. Jayaraj. 2016. "The Quintile Income Statistic, Money-Metric Poverty, and Disequalising Growth in India: 1983 to 2011–12." *Economic and Political Weekly* 51 (5): 73–79.

Tillin, Louise. 2022. "Does India Have Subnational Welfare Regimes? The Role of State Governments in Shaping Social Policy." *Territory, Politics, Governance* 10 (1):86–102. https://doi.org/10.1080/21622671.2021.1928541.

Tillin, Louise, Rajeshwari Deshpande, and K. K. Kailash. 2015. *Politics of Welfare: Comparisons Across Indian States*. New Delhi: Oxford University Press.

Timmer, C. Peter. 1988. "The Agricultural Transformation." *Handbook of Development Economics* 1: 275–331.

Vakulabharanam, Vamsi, and Sripad Motiram. 2012. "Understanding Poverty and Inequality in Urban India since Reforms: Bringing Quantitative and Qualitative Approaches Together." *Economic and Political Weekly* 47 (47/48): 44–52.

CHAPTER 4

Anti-Poverty Transfers: Policy Successions with Little Success

Introduction

Individuals are poor because they were born into poor households, or because they are pushed into poverty in the wake of adverse economic shocks. Asset-poor households in low-resource settings are particularly vulnerable to poverty traps and require sustained efforts—state support, entrepreneurial zeal—to be able to improve their well-being. Development resilience implies enhancing the ability of poor to accumulate assets, withstand negative shocks, and increase their adaptation options to sustain a reasonable standard of living and emerge from the poverty trap (see Barrett and Constas 2014). In a resilient system, non-poor households are either able to resist the ill-fare caused by negative stressors or bounce back to the same level of welfare in quick time. Loss of livelihood is considered the most common form of shock that exposes a household's economic vulnerability. While farmers face unanticipated risks of poor harvest, or loss of crops, a wage-based worker is vulnerable to the risk of potential job loss. Agricultural risks and the risk of unemployment are commonplace and contribute to current as well as future vulnerabilities. Persistently high poverty, in the long run, slows down the economic growth process. Anti-poverty policies, therefore, not only have a moral imperative but are a necessary device for sustaining economic progress and building development resilience. The policy instrument for anti-poverty transfers, however, is variegated across contexts. Advanced nations, with a smaller share of

A. Rahman and P. Pingali, *The Future of India's Social Safety Nets*, Palgrave Studies in Agricultural Economics and Food Policy,
https://doi.org/10.1007/978-3-031-50747-2_4

farmers, design their social protection policies for the wage-based workers in the form of labor social insurance or labor regulation policies. Developing countries, on the other hand, face a greater risk that emanates from having a large share of rural population who are prone to climate-related risks and greater amount of informality among urban livelihoods.

For poorer households, either because of a transitory income loss or poor resource endowment to begin with, a resilience development process would call for appropriate support to reduce the number of poor—to lift people out of poverty—and subsequently, to reduce the likelihood of future poverty. Unemployment and livelihood vulnerability is the most immediate determinant of current as well as future poverty. As a result, developing countries like India focus on direct social assistance, such as direct food assistance, public employment programs, social pensions, and cash transfers.[1]

India has experimented with implementing some of the world's largest rural anti-poverty programs, including rural public works, public infrastructure investments, rural livelihoods, and social pensions, which have been at the center of global debate on social protection and have had varying degrees of success and failure. In this chapter, we review the stated *scope, focus, and form* of these policies and deliberate upon how anti-poverty social safety nets in the future might look in the wake of India's stunted structural transformation, evident by its stagnant farm income, rising nonfarm employment, urbanization without industrialization, and informality of livelihoods.[2]

Poverty Reduction Strategy in India's Planning Process

The pursuit of economic growth through industrial development—with the assumption that the fruits of growth would "trickle down" to the poor—without a deliberate redistributive policy has proved a bane for India's structural transformation. The state-led push toward industrialization did not create large-scale employment and led to a neglect of

[1] Social protection policies in relatively affluent countries, in contrast, take the form of social insurance or labor regulation policies because of greater formal sector labor forces. See Chapter 2 for more details.

[2] In Chapter 3, we have provided a detailed discussion of India's economic development trajectory and the resulting need for robust social safety net.

other sectors—agriculture, primary education, and public health infrastructure—in the early years of economic planning which hindered broad-based economic development and the creation of a skilled and productive labor force. Although the agricultural sector did benefit subsequently from the technological advancements brought about by Green Revolution, these benefits were restricted to relatively well-endowed regions (in terms of irrigation potential) and landed groups which widened regional and interpersonal inequalities.[3]

Indirect Attacks on Poverty Reduction

Given the history of famines during the colonial era, the post-independence planning process continued to view poverty as synonymous with hunger in rural India. As a result, state policy pursued the path of "grow more food" to reduce hunger.[4] While food security—sufficient food availability at the national level—was attained through Green Revolution, issues of hunger and food access for the poor, continued to remain a major concern.[5] Rural poor neither possess economically viable amounts of land to cultivate, nor do they have employable skills to leave agriculture or agriculture-based employment. Yet, there was no direct action on poverty, except for some small-scale and ad hoc interventions, until the 6th Five-Year Plan (1980–85).

Admitting to the "failures of the past three decades of planning," the 6th Five-Year Plan document, for the first time, discussed the ideals of a *social minimum*: a minimum needs program (MNP) to support consumption and provide social services to enhance overall quality of life and eradicate poverty) (Government of India 1981). It highlighted the immediate need to assist the poor with "an appropriate package of skill development, technologies, services and productive asset transfer programme and wage employment." A menu of *rural development programs* and

[3] See Pingali et al. (2019) for a discussion on the state-level differences in agriculture-led structural transformation in India.

[4] The Bengal drought in 1943 and the ones across other states in 1966 and 1969 meant hunger always remained in the public consciousness (Siegel 2018). The Indian Famine Codes, written in 1880s under colonial rule, continued to guide famine prevention policies in independent India until 1970s. See Chapter 5 for a detailed discussion of these policies.

[5] Food distribution through the Public Distribution System (PDS) became the most important means of poverty reduction. See Chapter 5.

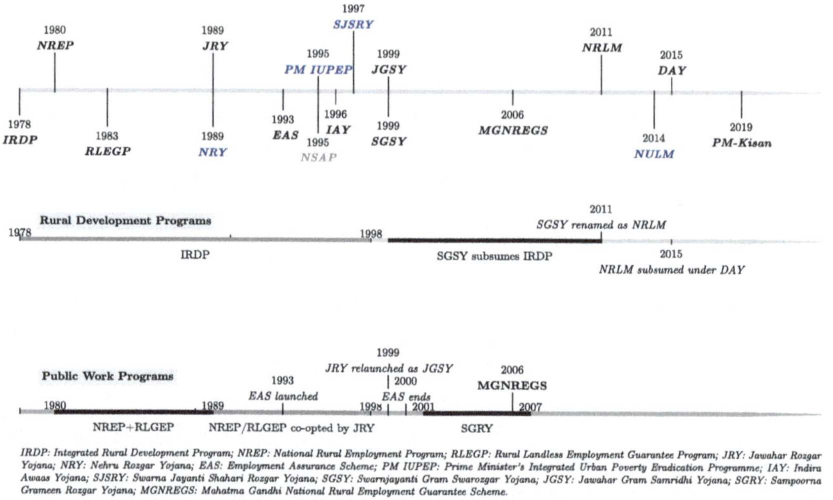

Fig. 4.1 Anti-poverty programs over time, with a focus on rural development and public work schemes (*Source* Author's conceptualization)

employment-generating public works program—the two-pronged strategy for reducing rural poverty—were introduced as the means of redistribution, increasing agricultural productivity, and support for the poor. These programs were not a huge success, and therefore, were constantly rebranded and reintroduced (see Fig. 4.1).[6]

Rural Development and Agricultural Productivity

Inadequate rural infrastructure and markets were identified as key causes of rural poverty. With the *scope* of reducing long-term poverty, the Integrated Rural Development Programme (IRDP), composed of a matrix of subprograms, was introduced by the central government in 1978, expanding to cover the entire nation in 1980.[7] The *scope* of rural poverty

[6] For an appraisal of the anti-poverty policies in the economic planning document, see Bandyopadhyay (1988). Similarly, refer to Gaiha (2000) for a detailed analysis on why anti-poverty programs fail to reach the poor in India.

[7] Components of IRDP included the *Training of Rural Youth for Self-Employment* (TRYSEM), the *Development of Women and Children in Rural Areas* (DWCRA), the

reduction principally relied upon increasing agricultural productivity through providing the rural poor with income-generating assets—agricultural inputs, subsidies, and credit. IRDP, however, did not succeed. The targeted *focus* on poor, as measured by the income levels, not only led to errors of inclusion but also failed to ignore the distinctions between chronic and transient poverty. By prioritizing subsidized credit as the *form* of transfer, instead of a broad-based array of productive assets, its *scope* of increasing agricultural productivity was further undermined.[8] The top-down design of the program further led to pervasive corruption in providing benefits to the last-mile beneficiaries.[9] The 7th Five-Year Plan admitted to the flaw in the design of IRDP and stressed for the need for shifting resources toward self-targeted rural employment programs instead, which would provide wage income while creating durable rural infrastructure at the same time (Government of India 1985).[10]

Public Works Programs

The *focus* on programs that increase agricultural productivity may not serve the needs of the chronically poor and landless. The employment-generating public works programs, the National Rural Employment Programme (NREP) and the Rural Labour Employment Guarantee Programme (RLEGP), were therefore envisaged as supplemental *forms* of social assistance.[11] Without much impact, both NREP and RLGEP

Supply of Improved Toolkits to Rural Artisans (SITRA), and *Ganga Kalyan Yojana* (GKY), in addition to other rural development programs.

[8] Refer to Dreze (1990) and Rath (1985) for a description of IRDP, its limited scope, and its inability to bring about large-scale poverty reduction.

[9] One must note, however, that in relatively prosperous parts of the country, such as Andhra Pradesh and Tamil Nadu with more empowered citizens, IRDP did have some positive impact. See Subbarao (1985).

[10] The 7th Five-Year Plan pointed to the following flaws. First, the identified beneficiaries were extremely poor, unable to make economic use of the provided credit and public infrastructure. Second, their disempowerment was further exacerbated by corruption, where only a small portion of the benefits were received.

[11] RLGEP was introduced in 1983, with the same characteristics as NREP, but it catered to only landless households. Its aim was the provision of at least 100 days of assured employment to at least one member of every landless laborer household.

were merged into *Jawahar Rozgar Yojana* (JRY, or the Jawahar Employment Scheme) in 1989.[12] Subsequently, the Employment Assurance Scheme (EAS) was launched in selected poorer regions in 1993, with a national expansion in 1997, with a primary objective of providing "gainful employment in manual work during lean agricultural seasons to all able-bodied adults in rural areas who are in need of work, but cannot find it" and a secondary objective of creating "economic infrastructure and community assets for sustained employment and development." In 1999, JRY was restructured as *Jawahar Gram Samridhi Yojana* (JGSY, or the Jawahar Village Advancement Scheme), which changed its primary *scope* from employment generation to creation of rural public infrastructure—construction and maintenance of public infrastructure, such as irrigation projects, road construction, flood protection, drainage works, ecological conservation, and drinking water supply schemes, etc. Given the similarities in *focus, scope*, and *form*, EAS and JGSY were combined into *Sampoorna Grameen Rozgar Yojana* (SGRY, or the Universal Rural Employment Programme) in 2001, with a twofold *scope*: rural public infrastructure creation and generation of wage-based employment.[13] The importance of a public works program in social welfare policies, however, gradually declined until the National Rural Employment Guarantee Act (NREGA) was passed in 2005.[14]

[12] It is interesting to note that NREP, when introduced, co-opted the Food for Work Programme (FWP), which was introduced by the government in 1977–78. Both RLGEP and JRY included *Indira Awaas Yojana* (Indira Housing Scheme or IAY), a grant-in-aid credit and subsidy scheme that became an independent program in 1996 to assist the rural poor and the most marginalized caste groups in either constructing houses or converting semi-permanent structures into a permanent ones. It was restructured as *Pradhan Mantri Awaas Yojana* (Prime Minister Housing Scheme, or PMAY) in 2015, expanding its *scope* to housing for the urban poor as well.

[13] The fundamental difference between JRY and EAS was that the former required top-down allocations while the latter was envisaged as a demand-driven scheme. Gradually, the primary scope of JRY became rural infrastructure creation, while EAS accorded primacy to wage-based employment generation.

[14] It is important to note here that the first direct attack on poverty—in the wake of frequent droughts with loss of livelihood—was conceptualized in the *form* of the Employment Guarantee Scheme (EGS), in the state of Maharashtra in 1972. EGS, with the slogan of "*Magel tyala kam*" (whoever desires work will get it), guaranteed employment to all adults above the age of 18 years to do unskilled manual work at a predefined minimum wage rate. To finance EGS, the Maharashtra government levied a special tax on all urban and salaried person in the state. The *scope* of the program was twofold: support household consumption during the lean season (short run) and leverage the rural public assets

From Agricultural Productivity Enhancement to Self-Employment

IRDP was restructured in 1999, and was subsequently reintroduced as *Swarnajayanti Gram Swarozgar Yojana* (SGSY, or Golden Jubilee Rural Self-Employment Programme). SGSY departed significantly from its predecessor in terms of program *scope*. Instead of providing credit and subsidies to improve agricultural productivity, SGSY aimed to promote self-employment among the rural poor by organizing them into self-help groups (SHGs) and providing them with the required infrastructural and technical support, such as technology, credit, and marketing infrastructure to facilitate the establishment of microenterprises.[15] SGSY, unfortunately, suffered from the same faulty design as the IRDP. Neither the *form* of assistance—credit, subsidies, and skills—suffices in ensuring income-generating activity for the poor, nor does the *focus* on poor ensure better targeting of the beneficiaries. Only 22% of the 25 million households, which organized themselves into SHGs by 2010, succeeded in accessing bank credit. Further, by restricting the *scope* of the program to a single livelihood activity, it failed to adequately meet the multifarious livelihood requirements of the poor. The subsidy without sufficient mobilization and collectivization of the SHGs led to high attrition among its members. The only laudable aspect of SGSY was recognition of women as "economic beings" in economic policy, through mandating 40% of the employment should be for women. SGSY was later renamed the National Rural Livelihood Mission (NRLM) or *Aajeevika* in 2011, to be later merged into

generated through the program for strengthening rural infrastructure, and hence, overall rural development (in the long run). In 1977, the Food for Work Programme (FWP) was added to EGS, so that food was provided in addition to wages to the workers. FWP was subsequently renamed as NREP in 1980. Maharashtra EGS slowly lost popularity after an increase in wage rates to twice the earlier amount. It led to rationing of jobs to fewer people, and slowly, the program lost its significance. FWP was initiated again in 2001, to be merged with the Mahatma Gandhi National Rural Employment Guarantee Scheme (MGNREGS) in 2006.

[15] The objectives of allied schemes in the IRDP, such as TRYSEM (Training of Rural Youth for Self-Employment), DWCRA (Development of Women and Children in Rural Areas), SITRA (Supply of Improved Toolkits to Rural Artisans), GKY (Ganga Kalyan Yojana), and MWS (Million Wells Schemes) reached the forefront. The focus on local bodies and SHGs, at the same time, coincided with administrative reforms in India's decentralized governance system (73rd and 74th amendments to the Constitution), which empowered local bodies (rural and urban) to work as "institutions of self-government."

the *Deen Dayal Antyodaya Yojana* (DAY), which also included urban livelihood issues within its fold in 2015.

Unlike SGSY, which relied upon allocation of resources from central government, NRLM adopted a demand-driven strategy, in which state governments had greater autonomy in implementing the program.[16] Central allocation would depend upon approval of annual action plans to be submitted by the state governments. Most importantly, the identification of the poor in the NRLM, instead of through a state-identified poverty classification (BPL), would be done through a participatory identification of the poor. NRLM was motivated by a "livelihoods approach" to reducing rural poverty and sought to "increase household income through sustainable livelihood enhancements and improved access to financial services," with a specific focus on women-led SHGs.[17] Under NRLM, the poor can assert their developmental needs, access entitlements, or seek assistance for self-employment and job skills, instead of seeking state-provided, unconditional social safety net benefits to bail them out of poverty.

Urban Poverty as a Residual of Rural Poverty

Poverty was considered a rural phenomenon in social policy until the 7th Five-Year Plan (1985–90), with the assumption that urban poverty is a spillover of rural poverty. Given that a large share of the Indian population was classified as rural, anti-poverty policies were exclusively focused on risks related to agriculture and landlessness, as discussed in the earlier section. Gradual deregulation of economic activity from state control in the 1980s encouraged private enterprise, and gradually, greater urbanization and rural–urban labor mobility alerted policymakers to the concerns of migrants, to the proliferation of slums, and the rise of low-wage, unskilled work in urban areas, leading to a growing share of informality dominating urban employment patterns.

Continuing the trend of promoting self-employment, as in rural areas, *Nehru Rozgar Yojana* (NRY, or the Nehru Employment Scheme)—the urban version of JRY—was launched in 1989, with the *scope* of

[16] For more details, see Deshpande (2022).

[17] In a short span, NRLM has been successful in improving livelihoods, by getting more women into the labor market and ensuring higher savings for the rural households, but it has had limited or no effect on income and assets (Pandey et al. 2019).

providing self-employment avenues to the poor unemployed and underemployed individuals through required training and subsidized credit assistance to set up small businesses. For the Class II cities (with a population of 50,000–100,000), the Prime Minister's Integrated Urban Poverty Eradication Programme (PMIUPEP) was introduced in 1995, with similar aims. Yet, these programs failed for similar reasons: lack of clear targeting rules, lack of integration of urban poverty reduction plans with other development plans, and the inadequate involvement of community-based organizations to coordinate demand and monitor these schemes. NRY and PMIUPEP were phased out during the 9th Five-Year Plan, and a new program, *Swarna Jayanti Shahari Rozgar Yojana* (SJSRY), was introduced in 1997. Similar in spirit to its predecessor, sought to promote self-employment as well as wage employment. Under the program, across all urban local bodies (with populations less than 500,000), wage-based employment to the identified poor was to be provided, for the creation of socially and economically useful public assets. The 10th Five-Year Plan, however, noted that SJSRY has been unsuccessful and recommended inclusion of contributory benefits such as insurance against the death of the primary breadwinner, or against sickness or disability, and old age benefits with matching contributions from the government. The 11th Five-Year Plan further called out the ineffectiveness of SJSRY, suggesting a restructuring of the program. In 2013, the scheme was renamed the National Urban Livelihood Mission (NULM, then DAY–NULM in 2014), with a similar *scope* of reducing "poverty and vulnerability of the urban poor households by enabling them to access gainful self-employment and skilled wage employment opportunities, resulting in an appreciable improvement in their livelihood on a sustainable basis, through building grassroots level institutions of the poor."

Despite the rising share of urban population, social safety nets for the urban poor have largely been ignored. Anti-poverty policies aimed at the urban poor have been designed around creating gainful livelihood opportunities through facilitating access to market for credit, providing skills, and market-based employment to those identified as poor. These programs, however, have done little to alter the initially skewed human or physical endowments among the population. Global evidence on using self-employment generation activities to reduce poverty has also highlighted their limited abilities to bring about transformational change, as they are beset with implementation problems—most importantly, in identifying the poor. Urban Local Bodies (ULBs)—central to identifying beneficiaries, liaising with the banks, and assisting beneficiaries in the selection of projects, allotment of sites, and other related matters—are hardly autonomous and empowered to be effective. Although the 74th Amendment of the Parliament in 1992 provides ULBs with functional, financial, and administrative autonomy to be self-governing institutions, they are still struggling to be fully decentralized and autonomous.[18]

MGNREGS: Rural Employment Program Back in Vogue

The Mahatma Gandhi National Rural Employment Guarantee Scheme (MGNREGS) has arguably been the most impactful anti-poverty program in India. Unlike earlier other programs, which promised employment but did not provide an entitlement to work, NREGA enshrines "right to work" as a constitutional guarantee to every citizen in rural areas. It is the largest public works program in the world—600 million rural residents are eligible to receive its benefits, and 0.5% of India's GDP goes to its funding. Under MGNREGS, anybody in rural India who is willing to work at a pre-announced minimum wage rate will receive work from the government for at least 100 days. The guaranteed employment under the MGNREGS, therefore, has reduced economic insecurity, which no earlier program provided. Contrary to other programs, its effectiveness relies largely on the "self-selection" aspect of it, which ensures that the program's benefits are not captured by the privileged elites, as has happened in earlier programs. MGNREGS also addresses another major developmental challenge in the country: very low participation of women in the labor force. It encourages the participation of women by providing work and childcare facilities (within 5 km of a participant's village), with wages in parity with men. It, thus, provides higher wage bargaining power to the workers, especially women. MGNREGS, therefore, provides the safety of a next-best livelihood opportunity being available around one's village, without incurring any search costs. Self-selection into the program often happens in the wake of a job loss, crop failure, or death of livestock, even for those households that would otherwise have sufficient assets. Given the nature of work—unskilled labor which requires no training—MGNREGS also reduces inequality, as only the poorest

[18] For the challenges facing ULBs, refer to Sharma (2020).

enroll into the program. Since the public works, for which the labor is employed, are used to create community public infrastructure, the program also contributes to improvements in agricultural productivity, which along with greater income among the wage workers, contributes to overall economic growth.

The idea of MGNREGS was initially viewed with a great degree of skepticism. It was criticized as populist "make-work" or "dig-and-fill-hole" wasteful expenditures, with little potential for asset creation.[19] Such assertions implied that the program's primary objective is employment generation and asset creation was just a residual gain. While some of this criticism was based upon earlier employment creation schemes that had failed to work, there was also concern about India's inadequate state capacity to implement such a program efficiently. It was believed that a rules-based social welfare program, which is open to political and bureaucratic manipulation and local corruption, could not last long in India. The success of MGNREGS, however—with around 600 million people eligible to work under it—belied many of these speculations, despite the limited administrative capacity of the Indian state, especially at the local level. The criticisms around MGNREGS not creating sufficient public infrastructure was also misplaced, as around 36 million assets had been created under the scheme by 2019.[20] Although we would not assert that MGNREGS is the best answer to India's poverty problem, surely the program is among the most important components of social protection in India and has helped in engendering development resilience in rural India.

It is important to look at the ways by which MGNREGS has affected rural poverty and economic development.[21] Overall, MGNREGS led to an increase in the aggregate economic output by 1–2% per capita (Cook and Shah 2020), including several intermediate contributing welfare gains, such higher market wages (Imbert and Papp 2015), economic security against rainfall shock (Berg et al. 2018; Zimmermann 2020),

[19] For a detailed description of the struggles of the program, see Khera (2011).

[20] See https://rural.nic.in/press-release/assets-created-under-mgnrega. Accessed on January 15, 2022.

[21] The developmental impact of MGNREGS has amassed a very rich array of empirical work—arguably, the most among any public works program. The sequential rollout of the program in three phases made the program amenable to measurement of precise causal effects. For details, see Sukhtankar (2017).

agricultural intensification (Deininger et al. 2016; Gehrke 2019; Bhargava 2021), greater female labor force participation (Azam 2012), and reduction in seasonal migration (Imbert and Papp 2020).[22] In addition to economic contributions, NREGA has been instrumental in ecological restoration. By employing labor to work on restoring soil fertility and groundwater conservation, conditions have improved for millions of Indian farmers whose livelihoods are affected by declining soil fertility and destruction of watersheds (Esteves et al. 2013; Ranaware et al. 2015). What is most impressive is the incredible diversity of rural public works that have *transformative* implications for rural development, as they enhance rural income, improve productivity, build ecological resilience, and assist in disaster-related management (Narayanan 2016). The rural infrastructure created has helped the small and marginal farmers, especially, who are the most vulnerable to economic shocks.[23] To summarize, MGNREGS allowed the complementarity of public and private investment needed to bring about a transformative development.

Why did MGNREGS succeed? A variety of reasons, which are also important for designing social safety nets in the future, must be highlighted. The universally applicable program had people self-selecting into it, which allowed the most vulnerable to *demand* work, avoiding the challenges of a targeted program (Liu et al. 2020). Through decentralization of work decisions—the nature and choice of work along with site selection as discussed in open assemblies (*gram sabhas*) and approved by village councils (*gram panchayat*)—MGNREGS engendered participatory decision-making and strengthened local democracy and public consciousness of their rights (Shah 2007).[24] Mandated social audits of the program further increased transparency and accountability in delivery

[22] The second order household-level benefits of MGNREGS include higher consumption, nutrient intake, and assets (Bose 2017; Deininger and Liu 2019); and higher investment in children's education (Afridi et al. 2016; Li and Sekhri 2020). It also led to reduction in violence and insurgency in parts of the country (Dasgupta et al. 2017; Khanna and Zimmermann 2017; Fetzer 2020).

[23] See Ranaware et al. (2015).

[24] *Gram panchayats* are a collection of villages, which have elected local village councils that deliberate on local issues at public forums, known as *gram sabhas* (village assemblies). These local institutions form the most important component of decentralized democracy in India (Sanyal and Rao 2018).

systems.[25] Transfer of wages to beneficiaries in their bank accounts or post office accounts reduced the incentive of local officials to cheat.[26] With the use of biometrics smartcards to authenticate payments, leakages, corruption, and delayed payments to the beneficiaries have subsequently been reduced, leading to a greater overall impact of MGNREGS (Muralidharan et al. 2016).

Direct Income Support to Farmers

While MGNREGS provides an employment avenue for farmers during lean seasons, farming itself has been unremunerative in India for a large share of small and marginal farmers. A major debate in the Indian policy has, therefore, been how to increase farm income. The most recent statistics from the government, *Situation Assessment of Agricultural Households and Land and Holdings of Households in Rural India 2018–19*, suggests that income from cultivation has declined for farmers from 48 to 38% between 2012–13 and 2018–19. With a decline in the share of income from cultivation for the farm households and lack of formal employment outside of the farm sector, rural livelihoods remain vulnerable. One must note that while rural poverty reduction was brought about by productivity growth during the 1970s and 1980s, urban demand has contributed to poverty reduction since the 1990s (Gibson et al. 2017; Datt et al. 2020). However, there are limits, especially when the urban economy has not been able to absorb the surplus agricultural labor and increase agricultural productivity.

Given the stagnancy in farm income, the Government of India, in 2019, announced an annual direct cash transfer of Rs. 6,000 (US$84)—under the name of *Pradhan Mantri Kisan Samman Nidhi* (PM–Kisan) scheme—as minimum income support to all small and marginal landholder farmer families who collectively own cultivable land of up to 2 hectares.[27] The introduction of PM–Kisan came on the back of Prime

[25] For a discussion on the role of social audits in MGNREGS, see Aiyar and Samji (2009) and Vij (2011).

[26] See Banerjee et al. (2020).

[27] There are certain exemptions to it. Refer to the website, www.pmkisan.nic.in, for more details.

Minister Modi's proclamation of doubling farmer's income by 2022.[28] The idea of direct income transfer followed a similar announcement by the Government of Telangana under the name of *Rythu Bandhu* in 2018. The government of Andhra Pradesh, later in 2019, supplemented the transfer with Rs. 9000 (US$125) more, as part of their scheme named *Annadatha Sukhibhava*. Income support to farmers, instead of addressing productivity issues and seasonal risks, has its precedence in the waiving of farm loans periodically by successive governments. Since only institutional credit could be waived, and most smallholders rely upon informal lending sources, loan waivers did not benefit the poorest households. And there has been substantial unrest among the small farmers, who also comprise the largest share of voters. The restricted *focus* only on farmers is especially problematic when a large share of the rural population is engaged in nonfarm labor employment. It is also not clear what the *scope* is of such transfers. If it is an income support, without adequate incentive to increase agricultural productivity, there is certain to be demand for incremental increases in such transfers in the future.

Social Pensions

Social transfers, such as pensions for the elderly and vulnerable with limited ability to engage in gainful employment, not only provide human dignity, but also build household resilience through smoothing consumption in the short term and arresting the intergenerational persistence of poverty. This most vulnerable section of the population traditionally relies upon family and community support for their sustenance. While those with accumulated savings and strong support networks can rely upon this support in times of distress, the miseries of the vulnerable persons in poorer household's only increases. Indian social welfare policies until 1995—when the National Social Assistance Program (NSAP) for the elderly, sick, widowed, and disabled was introduced—did not *focus* on assisting the elderly, sick, widowed, and disabled. NSAP has five components: Indira Gandhi National Old Age Pension Scheme (IGNOAPS);

[28] Initial survey-based findings on the impact of PM–Kisan suggest a positive effect on productive investments. Based upon a telephone survey of 1,789 households in North India, Varshney et al. (2021) find that every additional INR 1000 (US$12) of transfers led to a 6.8% increase in the likelihood of greater investment in agricultural inputs, like seeds, fertilizer, and pesticides.

Indira Gandhi National Widow Pension Scheme (IGNWPS); Indira Gandhi National Disability Pension Scheme (IGNDPS), National Family Benefit Scheme (NFBS), and *Annapurna*. These schemes cover both rural and urban households. IGNOAPS is a noncontributory transfer under which the elderly (60–79 years), possessing a BPL card, are eligible to receive a monthly pension of INR 200 (US$3). For those above the age of 80, the pension is higher at INR 500 (US$7.5). Widows (40–79 years old) are entitled to INR 300 (US$4) a month under IGNWPS, while IGNDPS benefits are fixed at INR 200 (US$3) a month. Various state governments supplement these pensions and relax the eligibility rules. As a result, IGNOAPS beneficiaries may receive anywhere between INR 200 to INR 2,500 per month, depending on state. NFBS is a one-time, lump-sum transfer of INR 20,000 (approximately US$300) to a bereaved family, upon the death of the primary breadwinner. Under the *Annapurna* scheme, instead of cash, a monthly quota of 10 kg of food grains is provided instead to the elderly who are not covered under IGNOAPS.

Social pensions are among the few schemes that are highly efficient with low targeting errors, corruption, or leakages, even in areas of poor governance (Dutta et al. 2010; Gupta 2013; Chopra and Pudussery 2014). Although NSAP suffered from underutilization during its early years, there has been steady improvement with time. Around 30 million people benefited from these schemes with an overall outlay of INR 92,000 million (US$1,250 million) in 2019–20. Yet, there are limitations to social pensions building resilience. In terms of their *focus*, using BPL cards as the identification criteria to ration the eligible households has led to a persistence of errors, much to the detriment of the poorest (Asri 2019). Also, monthly pensions are sufficiently low to cover only basic needs of individuals, without allowing them to access quality health care. State governments, however, have taken a lead in expanding IGNOAPS, beyond the BPL households and with additions to the monthly pension amount, and expanding coverage beyond the BPL households. Yet, targeting errors remain high (Bhattacharya et al. 2015).

The impact of social pensions on reducing poverty, as well as redistributive aspect and overall resilience, is immense. These transfers are an important resource for the household to fall back upon during times of calamity for intergenerational transfers in resource-constrained societies with multigenerational co-residence as a social norm.[29] IGNOAPS, despite being a small benefit, has been an important source of poverty reduction, improving health care access and intergenerational transfer for the benefiting households (Kaushal 2014; Unnikrishnan and Imai 2020; Unnikrishnan 2022).

Absence of an Integrated Anti-Poverty Strategy

India's action on poverty and redistribution can be classified as a classic case of "policy successions" in which schemes and programs, without the desired impact, have been repeatedly repackaged and reintroduced.[30] Often designed in the wake of a calamity and reoriented with political regime change and ideological orientation, these schemes not only have suffered from a poor understanding of the causes of poverty and vulnerability—structural and transient—but also from meager state capacity for effective implementation.[31] While poor implementation is a function of lower administrative capacity and corruption, faulty conceptualization of the schemes has resulted from incoherent policy design and only lip service paid to redistributive social welfare, with limited *focus, form,* and *scope* (Table 4.1).[32]

By focusing solely on the poor (without the means to identify them) and providing market-based subsidies or supply-driven employment avenues (either through rural development or public works program), Indian social policy incurred some of the most vexing problems from which redistributive policies in developing countries suffer. First, in the absence of information about a household's socio-economic situation, the identification of poor is most likely to be erroneous. Second, there

[29] Case and Deaton (1998) provided theoretical arguments and an illustration from South Africa. Also, see Duflo (2003) for intergenerational benefits.

[30] The term policy succession is used in public policy literature to represent replacement of a previous policy or scheme with a new one with the same *scope* (Hogwood and Peters 1982). The newer policies are continuation of the policy ideas from the preceding programs.

[31] See Table 1 in Bahal (2020) for the timing and outlay on various rural welfare programs in India since 1980.

[32] Of course, some states have been the exceptions, and we highlight that fact later in the book.

Table 4.1 Anti-poverty programs: Focus, form, and scope

	Focus	*Form*	*Scope*
IRDP	Poor	Credit-cum-subsidy	Rural infrastructure Agricultural productivity
NREP/RLGEP/SGRY	Poor	Public works	Consumption support Rural infrastructure
SGSY/DAY	Poor Women	SHG membership Credit-cum-subsidy Skill and training	Self-employment Market participation
MGNREGS	Universal Women	Public works	Income support Rural infrastructure
Social pensions	Elderly Widowed Disabled	Cash	Income support
PM–Kisan	Small farmers	Cash	Income support

is a great amount of variation in the degree of deprivation and human needs within the poor. The ideas that fruits of growth would "trickle down" or that market-based subsidies through IRDP or self-employment programs could lead to a reduction in poverty not only belied India's acute poverty status but further exacerbated the socio-economic disparity among people. Also, the success of these schemes has relied upon a strong political commitment and state capacity to effectively deliver benefits. Poorly developed local institutions—rife with corruption and elite capture—have acted only as an impediment.

Recognizing these concerns, there have been clarion calls for introducing cash transfers as a substitute in multiple schemes and programs to overcome the pervasive "culture of immunity in public administration and weakened local government" (Subramanian et al. 2008, pp. 86).[33] Over the last seven decades, as India's economic and governance system has improved, cash transfers—through social pensions and farm support programs like PM–Kisan—are gaining in importance. We would like to highlight here again that the *focus* and *forms* of anti-poverty transfers in India have been intrinsically linked to the economic structure and political ideology of the times. Rural development and wage-based employment (*scope*) were the developmental concerns of a primarily agrarian economy

[33] Such sweeping redirection of social policy, however, is not entirely radical and has existed since 1938. See Srinivasan (2016).

during India's initial planning years. The *focus* of these programs was largely to help the poor. Current challenges of India are, however, different, and therefore, the social policies need to be tailored accordingly.

Anti-Poverty Policy in the Future

Building anti-poverty policies for the future must be attuned with India's changing demographic and economic structure. There are some keys facts to be considered. While agriculture contributes to a little less than a fifth of overall GDP, it employs more than 50% of the labor force. Eighty-nine percent of farmers are smallholders, with a significant share of income from occupations beyond cultivation, and with no substantial increase in income for more than a decade.[34] Also, smallholders are working on declining sizes of their farms. The average landholding size in rural Indian has declined from 2.28 hectares in 1970–71, to 1.55 hectares in 1990–91, and in 2015–16, it stands at 1.08 hectares per landholding (Panel A, Fig. 4.2). Furthermore, while the anti-poverty policies continue to be *focused* on rural areas, India is also urbanizing. Settlement patterns from the last five decades exhibit a secular decline in the share of rural areas, and in smaller hamlets, in particular (Panel B, Fig. 4.2). While India's urbanization has been slower than anticipated based upon the urban-rural classifications defined by the census, urbanization of built structure and related livelihood opportunities are fairly apparent.

The proliferation of smaller towns has been an important source of rural poverty reduction, by providing markets and employment opportunities for the villagers, but urbanization patterns have been exclusionary generally, creating classes of small formal and larger informal sector workers with inequitable access to quality housing and public services for the urban poor. The informality aspect of India's employment structure is fairly concerning, as a large share of the nonagricultural workforce is casual in nature (Panel C, Fig. 4.2). Even among the wage earners or salaried workers, 67.3% had no written job contract, and 54.2% do not have access to any form of employment-based social security.[35] Self-employed persons comprise the largest share of the workforce (dominated

[34] Eighty-eight percent of the farming households are also engaged in some of form of employment outside of agriculture (Chandrasekhar and Mehrotra 2016).

[35] Based on the Periodic Labor Force Survey (PLFS) 2019–20. See https://pib.gov.in/PressReleaseIframePage.aspx?PRID=1738163. Accessed on June 27, 2022.

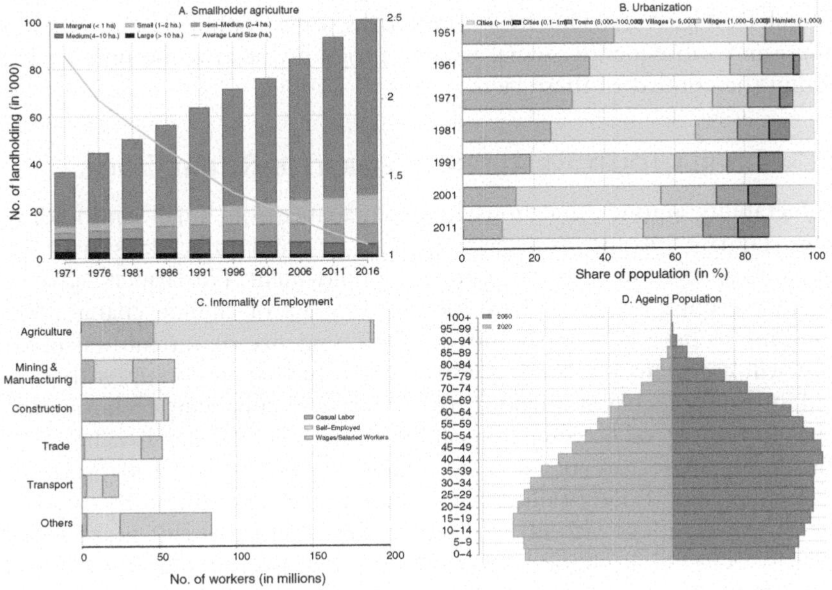

Fig. 4.2 Economic structure and newer forms of vulnerabilities

by the agricultural workforce); they are outside the formal sector and thus, do not have access to social security.[36]

Many of the farmers, who want to move away from agriculture, find themselves in the informal sector without the required skills to get formal sector jobs, which further limit sustainable income opportunities. As a result, around 100 million people in India migrate internally from one place to another for work, but on a short term or seasonal basis, with only a low rate of permanent migration, which further inhibits a faster pace of structural transformation. Lastly, India's demographic composition (population age pyramid), with increasing life expectancy and declining fertility rates, is expected to bulge toward a greater share of elderly population (60 years and above) by 2050, reversing the current youth dividend

[36] Self-employed implies "own account workers (who run small enterprises alone or with help from family members but without hiring workers); unpaid family helpers; and employers (who hire workers for their enterprise)."

(Panel D, Fig. 4.2). Thus, economic risks, catastrophic shocks, poverty traps, and subsequently, social welfare programs need to be understood within the context of these facts.

Livelihood Resilience for the Rural Poor

Vulnerability among rural households emanates from small landholding size, stagnant income from farming, lack of employable skills, and the precariousness of wage-based, informal employment. For farmers, adverse weather events, heightened by looming threats of climate change, will continue to pose risks in the future. Declining size of agricultural holdings will constrain the household resources further in coping with risks and in being capable of introducing productivity-enhancing technologies. The movement of farming households toward nonfarmer livelihoods—the dominant feature of rural household income—is no less prone to economic risks. Poorly skilled rural labor is ever susceptible to employment and wage loss with no recourse to formal employment-based social security. Overall livelihood vulnerability—not only farming risks—will affect the demand for social welfare policies in the future, as the share of rural population continues to be sizable, especially as a political force.

Notwithstanding the importance of traditional social safety nets—rural development and wage employment programs—development resilience can be achieved only through sustainable farm and nonfarm livelihood opportunities to further facilitate an enhancement of the physical and human asset base of rural households. It must be recognized that the *scope* of household anti-poverty transfers in the *form* of wages or cash assistance is to address the immediate needs of the vulnerable households. Households trapped in chronic poverty need the economic floor of sustenance, as provided by existing anti-poverty programs, like MGNREGS or cash transfers. The *transformative* effect of anti-poverty policies should rely on how the gamut of social safety net programs works in unison—some *prevent* immediate poverty, while others *protect* against the future likelihood of poverty—which will lead to *transformation* through quality education, market infrastructure, and employment avenues. For those vulnerable to livelihood loss, cash transfers through PM–Kisan or wage-based employment through MGNREGS will continue to be important *forms* of social policy to address immediate rural vulnerabilities.

Strengthening MGNREGS in Poorer States

Looking ahead, MGNREGS should continue to play a key role in sustaining the income of the vulnerable households, sustaining the rural economy, if there is surplus labor in the rural economy. Furthermore, income earned through MGNREGS is likely to boost the rural economy, especially for private sector development, by raising demand for consumption or production inputs. By bringing more women into the local workforce, MGNREGS can also reduce the stigma around female labor force participation in rural India. MGNREGS has substantial *scope* to contribute to the future through arresting the emerging challenge of environmental degradation, poor quality of rural infrastructure, and the strengthening of participatory grassroots democracy—all very important components of developing resilience. In the future, even when higher prosperity may reduce demand for the MGNREGS, the *scope* of quality rural infrastructure creation, especially for climate-proofing against climate change effects, need to be recognized as a significant role. It could help increase agricultural productivity and stem environmental degradation.

A key challenge for MGNREGS is the improvement of its performance in the poorer states of the country, such as Bihar, Uttar Pradesh, and Jharkhand.[37] The failure of MGNREGS in poorer states brings to fore an important factor to the success of social protection programs in India—politics. The implementation of a demand-driven, decentralized social safety net like MGNREGS relies essentially upon engendering empowerment—political, civic, and eventually, economic—and an improvement in administrative accountability. The poor beneficiaries in economically backward regions are often denied their entitlements because of a lack of information on the program, reduced citizen bargaining power, and pervasive rent-seeking among the local bureaucracy perpetuates corruption and underdevelopment.[38] To harness the transformative potential of

[37] Interested readers can refer to Dutta et al. (2014) for a discussion on the failures of MGNREGA in poorer states.

[38] At a macro level, historical inequality in landownership and resultant concentration of political power creates an unfavorable political economy for MGNREGA's effectiveness across districts (Misra 2019). The micro-politics of MGNREGA emerges from its implementation reliance upon on the relative ability of citizens to interact with elected representatives and bureaucrats, which creates opportunities for rent-seeking and

MGNREGS, the demand as well as sufficient supply for work need to be freed of the impediments of local politics.

Cash Transfers Through PM–Kisan

The idea behind cash transfers through PM–Kisan, with a *scope* of increasing rural income, is to provide liquidity in the hands of poor smallholder farmers. The extra income can provide for seasonal consumption needs and increase demand for the local economy, but its transformative potential can only be realized when the farmers are able to invest in productivity-enhancing technologies. Although such transfers are important, one must note that the *scope* of such programs is to address the temporary loss of income, while stagnant farm income is a longstanding issue and not the structural cause of rural poverty. Farmers are poor or at risk of poverty owing to their low-resource endowments. A landless rural labor force is poor because of insufficient economic opportunities and human capital endowments. A sufficient number of PM–Kisan transfers do open avenues for productivity-enhancing investments—in and out of agriculture. To have a transformative effect, rural anti-poverty transfers cannot avoid addressing the structural issues that hold back economic potential for farmers. Such transfers must be combined with rural livelihood missions (DAY–NRLM) to impart employable skills to the workers, especially women, to increase the quality of the labor force and its gender composition.

Urbanization of Poverty and Livelihood Risks

As India is urbanizing, the vulnerability of urban livelihoods is increasingly coming to the fore. A large part of the urban labor force engages in casual work, with unwritten job contracts, and therefore, no job security or employer-based social protection. As a result, the urban household consumption is found to be at a higher risk to idiosyncratic negative shock, relative to a rural household (Gupta and Kishore 2021). With

clientelism (Marcesse 2018). Differential "agency" of the citizens and the nature of state responsiveness also contribute to the uneven performance of MGNREGA at the subnational level (Fischer and Ali 2019).

the rise of a platform economy and "gig" work (firms such as Uber, Ola, Zomato, Swiggy, Flipkart, Urban Clap, and Dunzo being household names in Indian cities), employer–employee relationships are increasingly becoming unconventional, and workers are more vulnerable to transitory income losses. The plight of workers, including many migrants, in the wake of COVID-19-induced economic lockdowns and resultant loss of jobs, has been an unfortunate testimony to the economic fragility of urban livelihoods. Concerns have risen about the "urbanization of poverty," a situation in which the overall headcount ratio of poverty declines both in rural and urban areas, but the total number of poor in urban areas increase.[39]

Vulnerability of urban livelihoods is a by-product of the "stunted" structural transformation of the economy, wherein economic activity and urbanization are spatially concentrated, and service sector employment creates a gulf between a tiny proportion of high-skilled jobs with social security and a huge proportion of informal employment. Demographically, India's urbanization, which theoretically creates more formal employment, is characterized by *in-situ* growth—natural population growth and reclassification of rural areas as urban, rather than the movement of labor from villages to towns and cities.[40] This *subaltern urbanization*—the morphing of larger villages into urban areas—without relying on agglomeration economies or "anchor industries" runs the risk of further reproducing the informality of the rural employment structure.[41] Social welfare policies must expand the *focus* toward the urban poor and their sources of vulnerability, which emerge from the "informalization" of employment.

Labor informality in India is not only a characteristic of informal business enterprises but also of formal sector firms, which are increasingly hiring workers on a temporary or informal basis to reduce costs (Srivastava 2012; Abraham 2019; Bertrand et al. 2021). Lack of social

[39] See Ravallion (2002) and Ravallion et al. (2007) for detailed discussions.

[40] Thirty percent of India's urban population increase between 2001 and 2011 has come about through reclassification of villages as new "census towns," while migration accounts for around 22 percent of the urban population increase. The rest is natural urban population increase. See Roy and Pradhan (2018).

[41] Employment in large villages, likely to be reclassified as urban, consists of construction, manufacturing and trade, and services, mostly of casual wage and self-employment types (Chatterjee et al. 2015).

support for such workers exposes them to the risk of falling into poverty in the aftermath of health shocks or loss of jobs, despite being classified as non-poor. What makes the issue of vulnerability of the urban labor force more acute is that many of these workers live in poor quality dwelling and squatter settlements, rendering them more vulnerable to a host of ailments, which leads to health-related expenditures. In this context, expanding the *focus* of social safety nets toward the working poor becomes even more important.[42] It is important to note here that the public health insurance scheme was first launched to address the vagaries of employment and health for informal labor and was later scaled up to the larger population.[43]

The policy document of the urban livelihood mission does recognize the multiple dimensions of urban poverty emanating primarily from three forms of vulnerability: residential (poor access to land, shelter, and basic services), social (deprivations graded along the axes of gender, age, caste, and religion; inadequate social protection; and lack of political voice), and occupational (precarious livelihoods, informal employment with lack of job security, and poor working conditions). It further states that while residential vulnerability could be addressed through low-cost housing programs like the *Pradhan Mantri Awas Yojana (PMAY)*, occupational and social vulnerability can only be addressed through sufficient earning opportunities with access to credit and through promotion of skill development and self-employment, which are precisely where the DAY–NULM focuses. The impact of DAY–NULM, however, on urban poverty has not been noteworthy, despite its potential.

There is also a need to strengthen protection for workers in the organized sector. Social Security Code Bill 2020 is an attempt to provide workers in the unorganized sector, including platform or the gig economy, with social insurance (life and disability), health and maternity benefits, saving funds, and opportunities for upgrading skills. The bill, however, lacks a clear framework, outline, and legal mandates to ensure a "social minimum" for unprotected workers. These benefits also need

[42] Refer to Fields (2012) for a comprehensive discussion on the working poor, with a particular reference to India.

[43] See more details in Chapter 7.

to be expanded for all workers, including self-employed own-account workers who fall outside of social security in the informal sector.[44]

Urban Employment Program

Since access to formal sector employment remains limited, the idea of job guarantee programs in urban areas, like MGNREGS, is being debated. Although this idea may not be entirely unprecedented, or even the most ideal solution, the debate around urban livelihood support is timely and critical. In the run up to the 2020 presidential election in the United States, Democrats, like Bernie Sanders and Alexandria Ocasio-Cortez, broached the idea of having employment guarantee programs. UK Prime Minister Gordon Brown had also debated the feasibility of such programs. In other European countries, Employment Wage Subsidy Schemes (EWSS) have been a common policy instrument that provides subsidy vouchers to approved private enterprises to hire workers who register for public employment programs. Similar urban employment program could therefore be introduced as an extension of the "right-to-work" entitlement for urban poor in India.

A recent symposium called for *Decentralized Urban Employment and Training* (DUET) as a wage subsidy in the wake of a high rate of unemployment rates in the country. Jean Drèze, one of the architects of the MGNREGS proposed it as a job stamps program, run by and for urban women at approved public institutions—schools, colleges, government departments, health centers, municipalities, neighborhood associations, urban local bodies, etc.—where the government would cover the wage bill based upon the statutory minimum wage (Drèze 2020, 2021). In the short run, this proposal would enable risk mitigation and an increasing female labor force participation; the long-term effects could be harnessed by using the same labor to strengthen urban local bodies and build capacities through imparting on-the-job training and providing apprenticeships, which would allow the beneficiaries to graduate into formal sector jobs or entrepreneurship ventures with necessary skills.[45] Certainly, there will be multiple issues to resolve, such as deciding upon the work

[44] Mehrotra (2020) provided a detailed discussion on the current draft of the social security bill and its limitations. Bordoloi et al. (2020) highlight the weak legislative and enforcement aspects of the bill.

[45] See Basole (2019) for a detailed discussion.

and matching the labor with employers, within malfunctioning and less participatory urban local bodies, among others, which could prove to be an administrative nightmare to implement. The gravity of urban labor market precariousness, however, demands such a scheme, at least a pilot trial of it.[46] Urban employment guarantee schemes introduced in 2020 to fight the COVID-19-induced employment losses by the governments of Odisha, Himachal Pradesh, and Jharkhand, and the urban guarantee program in the state of Kerala existing since 2010, may provide useful insights over time (Pallath 2021).

Migrants and Access to Welfare Programs

Around 100 million people in India migrate internally from one place to another for work. At the same time, another 80–140 million workers move on a short-term or seasonal basis to work away from their homes every year. A large part of work-related migration is from rural to urban areas on account of differential wages, which attract labor to cities and towns. However, what often gets unacknowledged in this process of transformation is that migration is often a result of desperate economic situations, unemployment, indebtedness, or persecution of the marginalized.

The stunted structural transformation of the country has reproduced rural vulnerability in urban settings, albeit with different drivers. Low-income migrants in India are often relegated to the boundaries of city precincts where they are deprived of access to basic public amenities and opportunities. Living in poor quality housing conditions exposes them to various natural hazards and threats of dislocation. Flash floods and cyclones in the coastal cities of Mumbai or Chennai have exposed these vulnerabilities. While workers migrate for better economic opportunities, mobility also means reduced access to social safety nets, which are tied to their place of permanent residence. In fact, the association of social safety nets to their place of residence has been found to be a major hindrance to interstate migration in the country. Urbanization has been, therefore, also considered as "exclusionary" in the Indian cities.

[46] One must also caution, however, against considering DUET a silver bullet to the urban unemployment problem. A wage subsidy and training program in Argentina has found little effect on employment and no effect on income (Galasso et al. 2004). India's own experience with MGNREGA has not met with success in some of the poorer states.

If one follows the trajectory of migrants, underdeveloped states like Odisha, Bihar, Uttar Pradesh, and West Bengal are the source of migration to more developed states like Maharashtra, Gujarat, Delhi, and the southern states. Migrants, mostly short-term, in their places of work are deprived of their villages' informal social insurance. Working in informal employment adds to the vulnerability of job losses and health care costs, despite earning a higher income than their rural counterparts. It was only the wake of the mass movement of labor into the hinterlands that brought the vulnerability of migrants into the national consciousness. Access to food subsidies through PDS has, therefore, been untied from the state of residence, and there has been some action on creating a database of workers—migrants and non-migrants—in an unorganized sector to provide them with welfare measures. Although such initiatives are laudable, unless there is concerted social welfare policy support for those in vulnerable livelihoods, a mere registry of workers would be futile.

Social Pensions for the Aging of India

India is getting older at a faster pace than it is getting richer (Jain and Goli 2021). According to UN projections, 20% of India's population will be 60 years or above by 2050, with a large share of them being female and rural residents. Increased life expectancy and lowering fertility rates imply that growth of the elderly in the population is destined to reverse the current "youth dividend" in the coming few decades. An aging society, especially a relatively poorer one, brings a newer set of vulnerabilities. Research has shown that poverty is higher among the elderly once they are no longer capable of earning for themselves.[47] The provision of a life of dignity, care, and access to affordable health services for the older population, when they have little or no earnings of their own, ought to be an active *scope* of social welfare policy in the future.

The common practice of cohabitation with the elderly parents or in-laws, in an aging country, implies a further budget squeeze, with greater pressure on family members to spend and save for their elders, within already resource-constrained households. The rising burden of noncommunicable diseases and higher costs of medical care puts a higher burden on intra-household allocation of resources. A stronger focus on old age

[47] For a review of old age poverty in developing countries, see Barrientos et a. (2003).

social pensions, therefore, is only expected to increase, as the elderly not only have high out-of-pocket health expenditures—a large share of them would have been either farmers, unemployed (mostly women), or employed in informal work during their working lives—with scarce savings and a meager provision of social security in later years.[48]

Social pensions for the elderly are common in the developed world with high life expectancies, and therefore, greater shares of older populations. Developed nations have had sufficient time to craft social security policies and welfare institutions to address the old age vulnerability problem. A smoother process of structural transformation—as a large share of the population had access to social protection, financial institutions, and therefore, savings for later years—abetted such change.

India has a daunting challenge, as the country has aged relatively faster than a commensurate gain in economic strength. NSAP has been encouraging initiatives in this regard, but still falls short of the challenge. The Task Force on Restructuring NSAP in 2013, therefore, proposed multiple recommendations to the scheme, which includes a significant expansion in coverage (*focus*) and the stipulated pension amount. India has much to learn from countries like South Africa, Brazil, or China, which have successfully implemented generous social pension programs that have helped stem the skewed income distribution.[49] China's New Rural Pension Scheme (NRPS), larger than MGNREGS in terms of coverage and financial outlay, has a near universal coverage of pensions that has not only enabled addition to household income but also lowered manually intensive, farm-related work for the elderly, and improved their food security, contributing to better health and lower mortality rates (Huang and Zhang 2021). Expenditures on noncontributory pension programs in Brazil and South Africa are around 1% of overall GDP of each of the two

[48] The parts of the organized sector employment (public or private) are eligible for benefits under various acts, including the Employees' Provident Fund Act 1952, Family Pension Scheme 1971, Payment of Gratuity Act 1972, Deposit-linked Insurance Scheme 1976, Group Insurance and General Provident Fund Scheme 1982, and finally, the National Pension Scheme (NPS) that was introduced in 2004.

[49] Brazil, a country with similar economic conditions to India, introduced a nationwide pension scheme much earlier, in 1967, with the Rural Workers' Assistance Fund (RWAF), at a time when urban workers already had access to pension schemes. Similarly, while South Africa has a longer history of social pensions for the elderly, restricted mainly to the white population in the beginning, means-tested, old age pension is now ubiquitous, efficient, and generous (pegged at twice the median income of an African household).

countries, similar to what the Indian government spends on PDS. The old age and disability pension program in India is much smaller.[50] There is a need to make noncontributory pensions more expansive—universally applicable with a commitment to index the pension to inflation, and an overhaul of the multiple set of independent schemes, such as by placement under the NSAP umbrella for greater effectiveness.

Conclusion

This chapter argues that social welfare programs in the future need to anticipate and adapt to changing economic situations. Path-dependent anti-poverty policies over many decades of the planning process have had modest success, mainly, because of a poor understanding of poverty. Social welfare policies have largely tried to remedy the symptoms of poverty, while not paying sufficient attention to the structural facet of poverty—underlying unequal resource endowment and the risks associated with it. The poor are deprived because of multiple hindrances to accumulation of productive capital, and therefore, no single anti-poverty social welfare program can be considered a silver bullet. Social welfare policies of the future need to initially take stock of the nature of socio-economic vulnerability and its long-term implications to determine its *form*, *focus*, and *scope*.

India's stunted or atypical transformation suggests that although vulnerabilities associated with a rural economy will persist, changes in the economic and demographic structure call for a concerted action on the increasing risks to urban livelihoods, to financial protection to the aging population, and to the challenges of managing an informal workforce. This broad categorization of the economy has many layers; most important is the large subnational variation in the nature of transformation and its associated risks. The *form* of anti-poverty transfers in the future, therefore, must adhere to a design that is context-specific. Subnational

[50] Recently introduced contributory old age pension schemes—*PM Mazdoor Samman Nidhi* and *Atal Pension Yojana*—targeted at those outside of formal employment are exemplars of modest success of voluntary social insurance in developing countries (Mehrotra 2022). Contributory pension programs targeted at the poorer section of the population in India have the problem of reaching a population sector that is characterized by a smaller reach with poor awareness among potential beneficiaries and lower financial allocation from the government, thus rendering them to obscurity as part of the social safety nets (Rajasekhar et al. 2017).

developmental needs and priorities should be an important component of the design. A restricted *focus* on means-tested poor as the beneficiaries of many of the schemes is prone to targeting errors and escalates fiscal costs. Research as well as variation in the success of social safety nets in the country have clearly shown that more widely targeted or universal programs are more effective. Future policy, therefore, must not err on the side of narrow targeting of benefits. Lastly, the *scope* of anti-poverty policies must address vulnerabilities along multiple dimensions and not just income. Expanding the focus to non-income well-being indicators will push the collective goal further toward a transformative and resilient development process.

References

Abraham, Rosa. 2019. "Informal Employment and the Structure of Wages in India: A Review of Trends." *Review of Income and Wealth* 65 (S1): S102–S122. https://doi.org/10.1111/roiw.12435.

Afridi, Farzana, Abhiroop Mukhopadhyay, and Soham Sahoo. 2016. "Female Labor Force Participation and Child Education in India: Evidence from the National Rural Employment Guarantee Scheme." *IZA Journal of Labor & Development* 5, Article 7. https://doi.org/10.1186/s40175-016-0053-y.

Aiyar, Yamini, and Salimah Samji. 2009. "Transparency and Accountability in NREGA: A Case Study of Andhra Pradesh." AI Working Paper No. 1, February, Accountability Initiative, Centre for Policy Research, New Delhi.

Asri, Viola. 2019. "Targeting of Social Transfers: Are India's Poor Older People Left Behind?" *World Development* 115: 46–63. https://doi.org/10.1016/j.worlddev.2018.11.001.

Azam, Mehtabul. 2012. "The Impact of Indian Job Guarantee Scheme on Labor Market Outcomes: Evidence from a Natural Experiment." IZA Discussion Paper No. 6548, Institute for the Study of Labor (IZA), Bonn.

Bahal, Girish. 2020. "Estimating the Impact of Welfare Programs on Agricultural Output: Evidence from India." *American Journal of Agricultural Economics* 102 (3): 982–998. https://doi.org/10.1093/ajae/aaz030.

Bandyopadhyay, Debabrata. 1988. "Direct Intervention Programmes for Poverty Alleviation: An Appraisal." *Economic and Political Weekly* 23 (26): A77–81, A83–88.

Banerjee, Abhijit, Esther Duflo, Clément. Imbert, Santhosh Mathew, and Rohini Pande. 2020. "E-Governance, Accountability, and Leakage in Public Programs: Experimental Evidence from a Financial Management Reform in India." *American Economic Journal: Applied Economics* 12 (4): 39–72. https://doi.org/10.1257/app.20180302.

Barrett, Christopher B., and Mark A. Constas. 2014. "Toward a Theory of Resilience for International Development Applications." *Proceedings of the National Academy of Sciences* 111 (40): 14625–14630. https://doi.org/10.1073/pnas.1320880111.

Barrientos, Armando, Mark Gorman, and Amanda Heslop. 2003. "Old Age Poverty in Developing Countries: Contributions and Dependence in Later Life." *World Development* 31 (3): 555–570. https://doi.org/10.1016/S0305-750X(02)00211-5.

Basole, Amit. 2019. *State of Working India 2019*. Bengaluru: Centre for Sustainable Employment, Azim Premji University.

Berg, Erlend, Sambit Bhattacharyya, D. Rajasekhar, and R. Manjula. 2018. "Can Public Works Increase Equilibrium Wages? Evidence from India's National Rural Employment Guarantee." *World Development* 103: 239–54. https://doi.org/10.1016/j.worlddev.2017.10.027.

Bertrand, Marianne, Chang-Tai Hsieh, and Nick Tsivanidis. 2021. "Contract Labor and Firm Growth in India." NBER Working Paper 29151, National Bureau of Economic Research, Cambridge, MA.

Bhargava, Anil Kumar. 2021. "Do Labor Market Interventions Incentivize Technology Adoption? Impacts of the World's Largest Rural Poverty Program." *Economic Development and Cultural Change*. https://doi.org/10.1086/714269.

Bhattacharya, S., M. M. Jos, S. K. Mehta, and R. Murgai. 2015. "From Policy to Practice: How Should Social Pensions Be Scaled Up?" *Economic and Political Weekly*, 60–67.

Bordoloi, Mridusmita, Mohammad Hamza Farooqui, and Sharad Pandey. 2020. "Social Security for Informal Workers in India." Research Brief, November, Centre for Policy Research, Accountability Initiative. https://accountabilityindia.in/wp-content/uploads/2021/01/Brief_SocialSecurity_InformalWorkers_8Jan2021.pdf.

Bose, Nayana. 2017. "Raising Consumption through India's National Rural Employment Guarantee Scheme." *World Development* 96: 245–263. https://doi.org/10.1016/j.worlddev.2017.03.010.

Case, Anne, and Angus Deaton. 1998. "Large Cash Transfers to the Elderly in South Africa." *The Economic Journal* 108 (450): 1330–1361. https://doi.org/10.1111/1468-0297.00345.

Chandrasekhar, S., and Nirupam Mehrotra. 2016. "Doubling Farmers' Incomes by 2022: What Would It Take?" *Economic & Political Weekly* 51 (18): 10–13.

Chatterjee, Urmila, Rinku Murgai, and Martin Rama. 2015. "Employment Outcomes Along the Rural-Urban Gradation." *Economic and Political Weekly* 50 (26/27): 5–10.

Chopra, Saloni, and Jessica Pudussery. 2014. "Social Security Pensions in India: An Assessment." *Economic and Political Weekly* 49 (19): 68–74.

Cook, C. Justin, and Manisha Shah. 2020. "Aggregate Effects from Public Works: Evidence from India." NBER Working Paper 27395, National Bureau of Economic Research, Cambridge, MA.

Dasgupta, Aditya, Kishore Gawande, and Devesh Kapur. 2017. "(When) Do Antipoverty Programs Reduce Violence? India's Rural Employment Guarantee and Maoist Conflict." *International Organization* 71 (3): 605–632. https://doi.org/10.1017/S0020818317000236.

Datt, Gaurav, Martin Ravallion, and Rinku Murgai. 2020. "Poverty and Growth in India over Six Decades." *American Journal of Agricultural Economics* 102 (1): 4–27. https://doi.org/10.1093/ajae/aaz043.

Deininger, Klaus, and Yanyan Liu. 2019. "Heterogeneous Welfare Impacts of National Rural Employment Guarantee Scheme: Evidence from Andhra Pradesh, India." *World Development* 117: 98–111. https://doi.org/10.1016/j.worlddev.2018.12.014.

Deininger, Klaus, Hari Nagarajan, Sudhir Singh, and Hari Krishnan Nagarajan. 2016. "Short-term Effects of India's Employment Guarantee Program on Labor Markets and Agricultural Productivity." Policy Research Working Paper No. 7665, World Bank, Washington, DC.

Deshpande, Ashwini. 2022. *Rural Livelihoods Programs in India: Lessons from the Past as a Guide to the Future.* https://thedocs.worldbank.org/en/doc/62141abf1152d94953e76c11345c869f-0310022021/related/SARL-India-Final-Report-Final-May22.pdf.

Dreze, Jean. 1990. "Poverty in India and the IRDP Delusion." *Economic and Political Weekly* 25 (39): A95–A104.

Drèze, Jean. 2020. "DUET: A Proposal for an Urban Work Programme." *Ideas For India*. Poverty & Equality, September 9. https://www.ideasforindia.in/topics/poverty-inequality/duet-a-proposal-for-an-urban-work-programme.html.

Drèze, Jean. 2021. "DUET Re-Examined." *Ideas For India*, Poverty & Equality, March 9. https://www.ideasforindia.in/topics/poverty-inequality/duet-re-examined.html.

Duflo, Esther. 2003. "Grandmothers and Granddaughters: Old-Age Pensions and Intrahousehold Allocation in South Africa." *World Bank Economic Review* 17 (1): 1–25. https://doi.org/10.1093/wber/lhg013.

Dutta, Puja, Stephen Howes, and Rinku Murgai. 2010. *Small but Effective: India's Targeted Unconditional Cash Transfers. 2010–18.* Canberra: Australian National University, Australia South Asia Research Centre.

Dutta, Puja, Rinku Murgai, Martin Ravallion, and Dominique van de Walle. 2014. *Right to Work?: Assessing India's Employment Guarantee Scheme in Bihar*. Washington, DC: World Bank.

Esteves, Tashina, K. V. Rao, Bhaskar Sinha, S. S. Roy, Bhaskar Rao, Shashidharkumar Jha, Ajay Bhan Singh, Patil Vishal, Sharma Nitasha, Shashanka Rao, Murthy I. K., Rajeev Sharma, Ilona Porsche, Basu K., and N. H. Ravindranath. 2013. "Agricultural and Livelihood Vulnerability Reduction through the MGNREGA." *Economic and Political Weekly* 48 (52): 94–103. http://www.jstor.org/stable/24477901.

Fetzer, Thiemo. 2020. "Can Workfare Programs Moderate Conflict? Evidence from India." *Journal of the European Economic Association* 18 (6): 3337–3375. https://doi.org/10.1093/jeea/jvz062.

Fields, Gary S. 2012. *Working Hard, Working Poor: A Global Journey*. Oxford: Oxford University Press.

Fischer, Harry W., and Syed Shoaib Ali. 2019. "Reshaping the Public Domain: Decentralization, the Mahatma Gandhi National Rural Employment Guarantee Act (MGNREGA), and Trajectories of Local Democracy in Rural India." *World Development* 120: 147–158. https://doi.org/10.1016/j.worlddev.2018.09.013.

Gaiha, Raghav. 2000. "Do Anti-Poverty Programmes Reach the Rural Poor in India?" *Oxford Development Studies* 28 (1): 71–95. https://doi.org/10.1080/713688307.

Galasso, Emanuela, Martin Ravallion, and Agustin Salvia. 2004. "Assisting the Transition from Workfare to Work: A Randomized Experiment." *ILR Review* 58 (1): 128–142. https://doi.org/10.2307/4126640.

Gehrke, Esther. 2019. "An Employment Guarantee as Risk Insurance? Assessing the Effects of the NREGS on Agricultural Production Decisions." *World Bank Economic Review* 33 (2): 413–435. https://doi.org/10.1093/wber/lhw067.

Gibson, John, Gaurav Datt, Rinku Murgai, and Martin Ravallion. 2017. "For India's Rural Poor, Growing Towns Matter More than Growing Cities." *World Development* 98: 413–429. https://doi.org/10.1016/j.worlddev.2017.05.014.

Government of India. 1981. "6th Five Year Plan." Planning Commission, Yojana Bhavan, New Delhi. https://niti.gov.in/planningcommission.gov.in/docs/plans/planrel/fiveyr/welcome.html.

Government of India. 1985. "7th Five Year Plan." https://niti.gov.in/planningcommission.gov.in/docs/plans/planrel/fiveyr/welcome.html.

Gupta, Aashish. 2013. "Old-Age Pension Scheme in Jharkhand and Chhattisgarh." *Economic and Political Weekly* 48 (34): 54–59.

Gupta, Manavi, and Avinash Kishore. 2021. "Unemployment and Household Spending in Rural and Urban India: Evidence from Panel Data." *Journal of Development Studies*. https://doi.org/10.1080/00220388.2021.1983171.

Hogwood, Brian W., and B. Guy Peters. 1982. "The Dynamics of Policy Change: Policy Succession." *Policy Sciences* 14 (3): 225–245.

Huang, Wei, and Chuanchuan Zhang. 2021. "The Power of Social Pensions: Evidence from China's New Rural Pension Scheme." *American Economic Journal: Applied Economics* 13 (2): 179–205. https://doi.org/10.1257/app.20170789.

Imbert, Clément., and John Papp. 2015. "Labor Market Effects of Social Programs: Evidence from India's Employment Guarantee." *American Economic Journal: Applied Economics* 7 (2): 233–263. https://doi.org/10.1257/app.20130401.

Imbert, Clément., and John Papp. 2020. "Short-Term Migration, Rural Public Works, and Urban Labor Markets: Evidence from India." *Journal of the European Economic Association* 18 (2): 927–963. https://doi.org/10.1093/jeea/jvz009.

Jain, Neha, and Srinivas Goli. 2021. "Demographic Change and Economic Growth in India." (September 2, 2021). Available at SSRN: https://ssrn.com/abstract=3916157 or https://doi.org/10.2139/ssrn.3916157.

Kaushal, Neeraj. 2014. "How Public Pension Affects Elderly Labor Supply and Well-being: Evidence from India." *World Development* 56 (C): 214–25. https://doi.org/10.1016/j.worlddev.2013.10.029.

Khanna, Gaurav, and Laura Zimmermann. 2017. "Guns and Butter? Fighting Violence with the Promise of Development." *Journal of Development Economics* 124: 120–141. https://doi.org/10.1016/j.jdeveco.2016.09.006.

Khera, Reetika, ed. 2011. *The Battle for Employment Guarantee*, 1st ed. New Delhi: Oxford University Press.

Li, Tianshu, and Sheetal Sekhri. 2020. "The Spillovers of Employment Guarantee Programs on Child Labor and Education." *World Bank Economic Review* 34 (1): 164–178. https://doi.org/10.1093/wber/lhy027.

Liu, Yanyan, Christopher B. Barrett, Nancy H. Chau, Upasak Das, Klaus Deininger, Sara Gustafson, Sudha Narayanan, Megan Sheahan, and Vidhya Soundararajan. 2020. Targeting and the Impacts of India's MGNREGS. *IFPRI Project Note, March, International Food Policy Research Institute, Washington, DC.* https://doi.org/10.2499/p15738coll2.133768.

Marcesse, Thibaud. 2018. "Public Policy Reform and Informal Institutions: The Political Articulation of the Demand for Work in Rural India." *World Development* 103: 284–296. https://doi.org/10.1016/j.worlddev.2017.10.024.

Mehrotra, Santosh. 2022. "Can India Universalize Social Insurance Before Its Demographic Dividend Ends? The Principles and Architecture for Universalizing Social Security by 2030." Bath Papers in International Development and Wellbeing, no. 67. Centre for Development Studies, University of Bath, UK.

Misra, Karthik. 2019. "Does Historical Land Inequality Attenuate the Positive Impact of India's Employment Guarantee Program?" *World Development* 124: 104662.

Muralidharan, Karthik, Paul Niehaus, and Sandip Sukhtankar. 2016. "Building State Capacity: Evidence from Biometric Smartcards in India." *American Economic Review* 106 (10): 2895–2929. https://doi.org/10.1257/aer.20141346.

Narayanan, Sudha. 2016. "MNREGA and Its Assets." *Ideas For India*, Poverty & Inequality. http://www.ideasforindia.in/topics/poverty-inequality/mnrega-and-its-assets.html.

Pallath, Shreehari. 2021. "How Urban Employment Schemes Can Offer Social Security to the Poor and Empower Women." Scroll.in, August 18. https://scroll.in/article/1003041/how-urban-employment-schemes-can-offer-social-security-to-the-poor-and-empower-women.

Pandey, Vivek, Abhishek Gupta, and Shivani Gupta. 2019. "Labor and Welfare Impacts of a Large-Scale Livelihoods Program: Quasi-Experimental Evidence from India." Policy Research Working Paper 8883, World Bank, Washington, DC.

Pingali, Prabhu, Anaka Aiyar, Mathew Abraham, and Andaleeb Rahman. 2019. *Transforming Food Systems for a Rising India*. Cham: Springer International Publishing.

Rajasekhar, D., Santosh Kesavan, and R. Manjula. 2017. "Are Our Contributory Pension Schemes Failing the Poor." *Economic & Political Weekly* 52 (27): 77–85.

Ranaware, Krushna, Upasak Das, Ashwini Kulkarni, and Sudha Narayanan. 2015. "MGNREGA Works and Their Impacts: A Study of Maharashtra." *Economic and Political Weekly* 50 (13): 53–61.

Rath, Nilakantha. 1985. "Garibi Hatao': Can IRDP Do It?" *Economic and Political Weekly* 20 (6): 238–246.

Ravallion, Martin. 2002. "On the Urbanization of Poverty." *Journal of Development Economics* 68 (2): 435–442. https://doi.org/10.1016/S0304-3878(02)00021-4.

Ravallion, Martin, Shaohua Chen, and Prem Sangraula. 2007. "New Evidence on the Urbanization of Global Poverty." *Population and Development Review* 33 (4): 667–701. https://doi.org/10.1111/j.1728-4457.2007.00193.x.

Roy, Shamindra, and Kanhu Pradhan. 2018. "Predicting the Future of Census Towns." *Economic and Political Weekly* 53 (49): 70–79.

Sanyal, Paromita, and Vijayendra Rao. 2018. *Oral Democracy: Deliberation in Indian Village Assemblies*. Cambridge, UK: Cambridge University Press.

Shah, Mihir. 2007. "Employment Guarantee, Civil Society and Indian Democracy." *Economic and Political Weekly* 42 (45/46): 43–51.

Sharma, Purva. 2020. "Opportunities and Struggles of Decentralized Governance Reform for Urban Municipalities in India." *World Development Perspectives* 17: 100174. https://doi.org/10.1016/j.wdp.2020.100174.

Siegel, Benjamin Robert. 2018. *Hungry Nation: Food, Famine, and the Making of Modern India*. Cambridge, UK: Cambridge University Press.

Srinivasan, T. N. 2016. "Minimum Standard of Living for All Indians." *Ideas for India*. Poverty & Inequality, September 30. https://www.ideasforindia.in/topics/poverty-inequality/minimum-standard-of-living-for-all-indians.html.

Srivastava, Ravi. 2012. "Changing Employment Conditions of the Indian Workforce and Implications for Decent Work." *Global Labour Journal* 3 (1). https://doi.org/10.15173/glj.v3i1.1113.

Subbarao, K. 1985. "Regional Variations in Impact of Anti-Poverty Programmes: A Review of Evidence." *Economic and Political Weekly* 20 (43): 1829–1834.

Subramanian, Arvind, Devesh Kapur, and Partha Mukhopadhyay. 2008. "The Case for Direct Cash Transfers to the Poor." *Economic and Political Weekly* 43 (15): 37–41, 43.

Sukhtankar, Sandip. 2017. "India's National Rural Employment Guarantee Scheme: What Do We Really Know about the World's Largest Workfare Program?" *India Policy Forum* 13 (1): 231–285.

Unnikrishnan, V., 2022. "The Welfare Effects of Social Assistance Programs for Women in India." *The Journal of Development Studies*: 1–20.

Unnikrishnan, Vidhya, and Katsushi S. Imai. 2020. "Does the Old-Age Pension Scheme Improve Household Welfare? Evidence from India." *World Development* 134: 105017. https://doi.org/10.1016/j.worlddev.2020.105017.

Varshney, Deepak, Anjani Kumar, Ashok K. Mishra, Shahidur Rashid, and Pramod K. Joshi. 2021. "COVID-19, Government Transfer Payments, and Investment Decisions in Farming Business: Evidence from Northern India." *Applied Economic Perspectives and Policy* 43 (1): 248–269. https://doi.org/10.1002/aepp.13144.

Vij, Nidhi. 2011. "Collaborative Governance: Analysing Social Audits in MGNREGA in India." *IDS Bulletin* 42 (6): 28–34. https://doi.org/10.1111/j.1759-5436.2011.00269.x.

Zimmermann, Laura. 2020. "Why Guarantee Employment? Evidence from a Large Indian Public-Works Program." GLO Discussion Paper 504, Global Labor Organization (GLO), Essen.

CHAPTER 5

Food Policy: A Case of Punctuated Equilibrium

Introduction

Food transfers through the Public Distribution System (PDS) are the oldest, and arguably, the most debated of all social welfare schemes in India. Accounting for around 1% of GDP and 60% of social welfare spending, PDS benefits around 800 million people, but the value chain of its operation—procurement, storage, and distribution of food grains—has traditionally been rife with leakages, corruption, and inefficiencies. While these inefficiencies have been reduced in recent years, an active debate has also emerged around replacing food grains with an equivalent amount of cash. Giving the poor cash instead of food grains would not only make the system more efficient by saving the rising cost of its value chain, but also provide people with an option of purchasing more nutritious food of their choice. Such postulations, however, lead naturally to questions. From the welfare perspective, would it not undermine food security if the transferred money was wasted on nonessential items? From an administrative point of view, does India have the organization wherewithal—from identification of beneficiaries to efficient delivery mechanisms—to move toward a cash-based program? Finally, there is a political economy question: how can cash transfers be introduced when distribution of grains is inextricably linked to the state-led procurement of food from the farmers?

While these questions on the reform of the PDS have been fodder for debate among academics and policymakers, the steady improvement

A. Rahman and P. Pingali, *The Future of India's Social Safety Nets*, Palgrave Studies in Agricultural Economics and Food Policy,
https://doi.org/10.1007/978-3-031-50747-2_5

in the PDS—even in the states with a poor welfare policy governance record—has led to its greater relevance for the poor. For instance, the extra provision of free food grains through the PDS during the COVID-19 pandemic has provided a much needed relief to the already suffering.[1] So, why is there a need to change the form of an already functioning social assistance program that apparently delivers?

Indeed, the PDS has been a lifeline for the poor, as it addresses the most basic need of food and ensures a "social minimum" for a dignified life, in the short run. The long-term question, however, for a resilient development process is: will the PDS promote a healthy diet and nutritional security in the future by providing calorie-rich food grains? As the country is going through its nutrition transition—decreasing household expenditure on staple cereals—with greater incidence of obesity-related non-communicable diseases (NCDs), along with high micronutrient deficiencies, would the PDS be the right policy instrument to address the nutritional challenge? Would continuing with the staple food grains—rice and wheat—as the subsidized food commodities through the PDS not harm long-term agricultural diversification and bear environmental costs? These are some of the questions we grapple with in this chapter as we deliberate upon the future of the PDS—in *focus, form, and scope*—to facilitate a resilient development process.

Social Welfare Through the PDS

Food assistance has been a feature of state support to the poor and needy since time immemorial.[2] Currently, more than 90 billion USD is spent annually on food-based safety nets—comprising a core component of global social protection schemes—benefiting around 1.5 billion

[1] As part of the COVID-19 relief, the Government of India (GoI) offered additional 5 kg of wheat or rice free of cost for three months through the PDS, over and above their monthly entitlement of subsidized food grains, under the aegis of *Pradhan Mantri Garib Kalyan Anna Yojana* (PMGKAY). Some states made the PDS free, even for the non-poor. See Roy et al. (2020) for details.

[2] Distribution of food in Egyptian and Roman courts during times of famine is famously cited as one of the earliest records of food assistance programs.

people.[3] PDS has been a lifeline for the poor in India. Despite its historically changing *focus*—in terms of geographical coverage and targeted population—PDS is one of the most powerful component of the social protection and food security in the country. According to India's National Food Security Act (NFSA), 921 million (67% of the population) should be covered under the PDS. Since the poor spend almost half of their expenditures on food, subsidized food grains, through the PDS, provide a substantial consumption support, which could be allocated to other food and nonfood expenditures for improved welfare. Critics of the PDS argue that households could benefit more from moving to cash transfers while reducing the inefficiencies of the system.[4] Yet, we have seen an expansion of the PDS across the country with better performance and reduced corruption.[5]

To unravel this conundrum, one must understand the interlocked incentives—which tie consumer subsidy through PDS with the agricultural policies of assured prices—which underlie the PDS value chain. Food grains for the PDS are distributed to the consumers at subsidized prices by first procuring them from farmers at assured prices. Farmers (most importantly, in Punjab and Haryana, and now in Madhya Pradesh for wheat) contribute to a central pool of food grain stock that is distributed through the PDS at ration shops across the country. Any move toward cash transfers, in lieu of food grains from the PDS, would imply either that the government stops procuring grains from farmers at the minimum support price (MSP), or stores the grains and sells them to private players domestically or on the international market. The interlocked producer–consumer incentive, therefore, restricts much of the innovation needed

[3] In fact, about 44% of individuals benefiting from any form of social safety nets are reported to receive in-kind food (World Bank 2015). Food transfers are the predominant form of social assistance, particularly in low- and middle-income countries (LMICs), covering about 20% of the population. Prominent among them, in addition to the PDS, are *Raskin* in Indonesia (62 million people), Supplemental Nutritional Assistance Program (SNAP) in the United States (46 million people), and Ration Card and *Baladi Bread* programs in Egypt (150 million people). For more details, see Alderman et al. (2018).

[4] See Gulati and Saini (2015), Kapur et al. (2008), Kotwal et al. (2011), and Svedberg (2012) for arguments in favor of cash transfers. Narayanan (2011) presents a cautionary note against imagining cash as the 'silver bullet' because cash transfers are not devoid of the same vexing challenges of providing food transfers such as identifying beneficiaries, and likelihood of local corruption.

[5] See Drèze and Khera (2015) and Rahman (2014).

for a move from the PDS to cash transfers.[6] The continuation and expansion of the PDS, in its current form, has, however, served the interests of the political class, who have used this as an opportunity to demonstrate their commitment to social welfare policies. It is important, therefore, to understand the rationale for the continued relevance of the PDS in India. We consider its origins and how it evolved—in *scope, focus, and form*—as we imagine its future and how it can promote development resilience.

Changing Scope, Focus, and Form

While remaining an important tool of addressing poverty, the *scope* and *focus* of the PDS has evolved considerably since its inception—from wartime relief focused on urban populations to consumption support for maintaining food security—with varying degrees of effectiveness. For the PDS to be a tool for facilitating a resilient development process, however, we need to move its scope beyond food to nutritional security, through improving the PDS delivery system, stemming the negative externalities it creates, and gradually, moving toward a cash-based system. Although the argument for cash is theoretically sound, India's economic realities, current infrastructural deficits, and most importantly, the realpolitik of food policy all act as unyielding constraints. To understand these barriers, we must understand first the evolution of the PDS and economic policy scenario around it.[7]

The PDS has gone through multiple stages of changes in its targeted population (*focus*) and policy objective (*scope*) (Table 5.1). When it was introduced in the 1940s, it was mainly used as a tool to ensure there was sufficient food supplies for workers in the major industrial cities, limited largely to Bombay, Calcutta, and Cochin. Gradually, by the end of 1943, it was expanded to other urban centers with more than 100,000 inhabitants, and by 1946, 771 cities were covered under the PDS in an attempt to safeguard consumers against higher and volatile prices in the wake of recurrent famines and exigencies of the Second World War. The scope

[6] For a detailed discussion on what inhibits innovations in food policy at large, refer to Pingali et al. (2017).

[7] The history and evolution of the PDS has been studied extensively. For instance, see Banerjee et al. (2014), Bhatia (1970), Chopra (1988), Frödin (2010), Landy (2009) and Venugopal (1992).

Table 5.1 Historical evolution of food assistance through PDS

Stages	*Focus*	*Scope*
Inception (1940–1960)	Urban	Safeguarding urban consumers from high food prices
Consolidation (1960–1990)	Urban to rural	Price stability and farm income support
Reformation (1990–2005)	Pro-poor targeted (TPDS)	Rural poverty and food security
Expansion and NFSA (2005–2020)	"Priority" but not all households	Household poverty and food security

of the PDS operations was to maintain low food prices for the urban workers.

Rationing and Price Control in Industrial Towns

Until the late 1960s, India suffered from frequent famines in various parts of the country, highlighting the fact that food insecurity occurred largely because of lack of food availability as well as access.[8] The colonial era policies, therefore, continued with the aim of ensuring price stability, even when the demand for food exceeded the domestic supplies, and India relied upon substantial imports of food grains from abroad to supply its people through the PDS. Since India's economic planning priorities relied upon domestic industry-led growth, the focus of the PDS on the urban working class served the industrial owners and the urban-based, politically important middle class well, as it could enable some degree of social equilibrium in industrial and urban areas (Mooij 1998). It was feared that rise in the prices of food (which comprised more than 70% of monthly food expenditures at that time) would further erode the purchasing power of the workers. As a result, urban centers had a universal entitlement to rationed amounts of food. And more urbanized states,

[8] One must note that India faced the most ravaging of famines in 1943—the Bengal famine—which brought to light the willful negligence of the colonial rule in ensuring food access. The famine has had a major bearing on independent India's food policy, in which starvation, inadequate access to food, and poverty have been recurrent themes. The importance of state intervention in this sphere has been highlighted most comprehensively in Sen (1982) and Dreze and Sen (1990).

like Maharashtra, Tamil Nadu, and West Bengal, with the metropolitan cities of Bombay, Madras, and Calcutta, received larger shares of the PDS allocations (Suryanarayana 1995).

Emergence of the Interlocked Production–Consumption Incentive

Consolidation of the PDS, as it expanded through the rural hinterland—where most Indians resided and poverty was more acute—came about because of breakthrough gains in agricultural productivity, resulting from the Green Revolution (GR). The GR solved the issue of food availability, as India became self-sufficient in staple food production. Food production—mainly, rice and wheat—was incentivized not only through better varieties of seeds, fertilizers, and irrigation infrastructure, but also through active involvement of the government in assuring farmers that excess supplies would not lead to a glut and lowering of market prices. The government set up two key public institutions: the Food Corporation of India (FCI) and the Agriculture Price Commission (APC) to manage the food supply chain. The APC would set up a MSP, at which the government promised to buy all the farmers' produce if the farmers wished to sell to the government. The FCI was entrusted with the task of procurement, storage, transportation, distribution, and sale of the food grains. As a result, the FCI became a nationwide supply chain, which connected food surplus and food deficit areas in the country. For instance, rice from surplus states like Punjab or Haryana would be shipped as far as Tamil Nadu and Kerala, through the FCI. The food availability issue was resolved through the territorial integration of the country via the food management system.[9] But, as PDS consolidated its expansion across the nation, its *scope* increasingly got intertwined with the policy of price support to farmers.

The expansion of PDS also coincided with changing economic policy in the country which put a greater emphasis on agricultural development.[10] India's rural elites, bolstered by economic gains from the GR, began to exert their political clout in influencing food policy. Mooij, a

[9] See Frödin (2010) and Landy (2009).

[10] The second Prime Minister of India, Lal Bahadur Shastri focused more on farmers than his predecessor Jawaharlal Nehru, who imagined industrialization as the measure of economic progress. Nehru died in 1964. Shastri's tenure was also a short-lived one, as he passed away under unceremonious circumstances in 1966, but he was instrumental in

scholar of social policy and economic change in India, highlighted this shifting policy and the political scenario through the changing composition of elected representatives in the Parliament. She notes, '... the ratio of representation of agricultural to business and industrial interests was 2:1 in favour of the agriculturalists in the first Lok Sabha in 1951, it increased steadily to 3:1 in the second (1957), 4:1 in 1976 as the Green Revolution was gaining momentum, 5:1 in 1971, and 9:1 in 1977' (Mooij 1998).[11] The agricultural lobby, especially the large farmers of Punjab and Haryana, firmly consolidated their political influence during this period and played a key role in advocating for higher MSPs (Varshney 1993). The emergence of producer-friendly policies undermined the representation of consumer's interests (Parikh et al. 1988). While the higher prices benefited the large farmers, consumers (often also small farmers) suffered from higher prices, even during times of surplus food, as artificially high MSPs kept the open market prices above the market-clearing ones in the absence of procurement (Chetty and Srinivasan 1990; Dantwala 1967; Hayami et al. 1982).[12] As a result of this system, massive stocks of food grains have been procured and stored in the FCI warehouses, despite the expansion in the PDS (Fig. 5.1).

Inefficiencies and the Call for Reforms

Gradually, the inefficiencies in the system became evident leading to calls for reforms. The 9th Five-Year Plan (1997–2002) noted that the PDS

changing the course of food policies in India. Varshney (1998) provided the most comprehensive discussion on the rural–urban political competition in India since independence, until the economic liberalization of 1991.

[11] The planning document for 1985–1990 clearly states the role of the PDS: "... as a permanent feature of the strategy to control prices, reduce fluctuations and achieve an equitable distribution of essential goods" (GoI 1985–1990, Sec. 20.2). Further, it called for "...increasing the number of fair price shops in the hitherto under-served and unserved areas and on organising mobile shops in far-flung regions. The main thrust of expansion is in the rural areas with special attention to remote and inaccessible areas, so that the public distribution system becomes supplementary to the poverty alleviation programme" (GoI 1985–1990, Sec. 20.4).

[12] High consumer subsidy has become a detriment to farmer interests in the long run with poor investments in private market infrastructure and trade restrictions for agricultural products, domestically and internationally (Gulati et al. 2020).

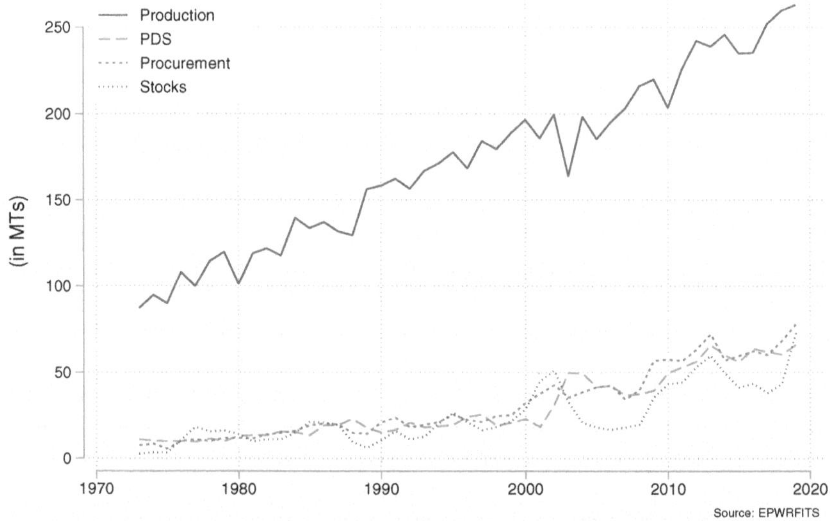

Fig. 5.1 Historical trends in the production, procurement, distribution, and government stocks of food grains (rice and wheat) (*Source* EPWRFITS)

"...has failed to translate the macro level self-sufficiency in food production achieved by the country into household level food security for the poor" (GoI 1997–2002, Sec. 2.3.1). The planning document further states that, "... [with] the mounting food subsidy in recent years, coupled with the fact that the PDS did not reach the poor, a view has emerged that the universal coverage of the PDS is neither sustainable nor desirable" (GoI 1997–2002, Sec. 2.3.2). These proclamations were based on two aspects. First, it was noted that despite the presence of the program, the poorest regions of the country, such as Orissa, Bihar, Madhya Pradesh, and Uttar Pradesh, had very low PDS offtakes from the ration shops. Second, the government took the view that universal access to the PDS (to the poor as well as the non-poor households) implied a lower per capita entitlement to each household and higher amount of procurement from the farmers.

Calls for PDS reform followed the macroeconomic restructuring of 1991, which fundamentally called for a reduction in subsidies and state control over economic activities in the country. With reference to the

PDS, it called for a narrower *focus*—on those households that were identified as poor.[13] As a result, in 1997, the system came to be labeled as the Targeted Public Distribution System (TPDS), dividing households based upon their economic status: Below Poverty Line (BPL) and Above Poverty Line (APL) for access to the PDS.[14] In 2002, another ration card classification was introduced for the poorest of the poor among the BPL households, who were also disadvantaged in other ways, such as widows and the disabled, under the scheme *Antyodaya Anna Yojana (AAY)*.

The 'targeting' aspect of PDS, however, ushered in the fundamental challenge of identifying the 'deserving' beneficiaries of the scheme. Identifying the poor, especially on a real-time basis, with limited information on household incomes and assets, was destined to be an administrative nightmare. Complications further arose from regional variation in poverty levels as PDS delivery is the responsibility of state governments but the share of the poor is determined by the central government. The central government had to decide upon the resources to share with the state governments based upon poverty estimates from the National Sample Survey Office (NSSO) and the corresponding population from the Census, while the state governments distributed APL/BPL cards based upon their proxy means-tested poverty criteria, leading to serious errors of exclusion and inclusion.[15] An evaluation of the TPDS, in 2005, noted that around 58% of the food grains meant for poor do not reach them. Errors of targeting, inefficient operation, and corruption in the implementation of the TPDS lead to only 27% of the budgeted consumer expenditure reaching the poor.[16] As a result, the government contemplated food coupons as an alternative *form* of the PDS in the Ninth

[13] One must note that targeting in the PDS was initially introduced in 1992. The "revamped PDS" or RPDS focused on regional targeting through provision of more generous benefits to backward (drought prone or desert areas), tribal, and remote regions while gradually withdrawing benefits from relatively developed regions.

[14] Some states, like Tamil Nadu or Himachal Pradesh, continued with a universal PDS, paying the surplus amount out of their own budgets. Some amount of ration to APL households was continued for a time, for a gradual phase-out, but the APL households paid a higher price. Subsequently, the APL quota became a conduit of leakages and corruption in the system, as Khera (2011) argues.

[15] For targeting errors in the BPL surveys, refer to Khera (2008) and Hirway (2003).

[16] See Planning Commission (2005).

Five-Year Plan (1997–2002) concluded that replacing the PDS might not be acceptable, despite the systemic inefficiencies in the current system.[17]

Economic planners recognized that the PDS relies upon the system of MSP and procurement operations which are a part of the current agricultural price policy. Replacing the PDS with a new system of food coupons is therefore fraught with administrative problems such as secured printing of coupons, corruption in distribution, periodic indexation of the coupons, etc. It was also feared food coupons, like cash, could be misused, and the greater purchasing power could further increase demand for food grains, thereby bidding their prices upward, with adverse consequences for the poor. Concerns around the inefficiencies of the PDS, and food stamps as a solution, were echoed again in the Tenth Five-Year Plan (2002–2007) along with the possibility of introducing smart cards (in the form of a food credit/debit card) but both these options were ruled out subsequently.

The Tenth Five-Year Plan however brought about newer ideas. For the first time, it was recognized that in addition to hunger (the incidence of which is on the decline), the *scope* of PDS could also be expanded to addressing micronutrient deficiencies (referred to as, hidden hunger) by including subsidized coarse grains, pulses, and iodized or double fortified salt to the program. On the procurement side, the Plan highlighted the need to re-examine the MSP scheme, which leads to the interlocked procurement–storage–distribution system, saying it "has served its purpose."[18] To supply non-cereals through PDS, the Plan suggested price incentives for pulses and oil seeds. The subsequent Economic Plan (2007–2012) highlighted the limited *focus* of the PDS as restrictive in attaining wider welfare gains. It stated that, "food-insecure households may be much higher than the official poverty ratios," and therefore,

[17] Food coupons of an equivalent amount meant that households could purchase cereals or other food items from the local market. Food stamps, in the United States, are the primary form of food assistance to the needy.

[18] MSP operations traditionally have been successful only in a few food grains surplus states which supply to PDS. But the erstwhile 'food deficit states' have gradually started generating food. Since every region has the right to benefit from the MSP policy, the Plan suggested decentralized system of procurement and distribution of food grains because it would be unfair to restrict the benefits only to the major producing states, like Punjab and Haryana. Under the decentralized procurement scheme, introduced in 1997–1998, the state governments undertake direct procurement of paddy and wheat on behalf of the FCI. The agencies of the state governments procure, store, and distribute food grains for the TPDS within the states. The deficit is to be supplemented by the FCI.

using the 1993–1994 data projected to the population in 2000 to determine food allocations may be misleading (GoI 2007–2012, §4.136, 136). Further, it highlighted the differential ways in which state governments identify the poor, which further makes the central allocation ineffective.[19] Highlighting the inefficiencies in the TPDS, it noted that, stemming this leaky system would require "political commitment and participation of the people in the [PDS] delivery process," along with an "effective use of IT including introduction of a unique ID-based smart card system" (GoI 2007–2012, §4.1.43, 137). The plan document further stressed the issue of nutrition security as a *scope* of the PDS.[20]

While the *focus* and *scope* of PDS were being deliberated upon, studies evaluating the effectiveness of PDS as a tool of hunger and poverty reduction during this period highlighted its gross failures. Because of rampant corruption in the system, a sizable portion of the food did not reach the intended beneficiaries. Even for those households which could access PDS, the transferred amount was too low to have a meaningful impact on consumption or nutrition of the targeted.[21] The most pressing challenges were threefold. First, identification of the poor (*focus*) through proxy means tests in the absence of fine-grained data on individuals, their residence and socio-economic status in a vast country as India is a monumental exercise fraught with its own challenges of targeting errors. Second, the value chain of PDS, right from procurement to distribution has been rife with corruption. Grains being swindled off from the warehouses is a common occurrence, and so is the sale of subsidized grains by FPS dealers in the open market, or the presence of 'ghost' beneficiaries on the ration card. Third, the identified beneficiaries were often not provided the benefits, provided less than their entitlement, or grains of

[19] For instance, 87% of the rural households in Andhra Pradesh have a BPL ration card, according to the NSSO 2011–2012, although poverty rates are considerably lower.

[20] Similar in spirit to the erstwhile plan, the Eleventh Five-Year Plan stated "If nutrition security is one of the considerations of TPDS, the government may explore the possibility of including more commodities under TPDS. For example, cereals such as jowar, bajra, and also pulses could be introduced in TPDS because of nutritional considerations" (GoI 2007–2012, §4.1.44, 137).

[21] See Planning Commission (2005), Kochar (2005), Tarozzi (2005), and Kaushal and Muchomba (2015). Kochar (2005) found a modest improvement in calorie intake as a result of the move toward targeted PDS but the elasticity of calorie intake with the food subsidy value to be as low as 0.07. Similarly, Tarozzi (2005) found negligible effects of the lower price of PDS in Andhra Pradesh on the incidence of child nutrition.

very poor quality owing to corruption, lack of local power dynamics and poor accountability mechanisms.

New-Style PDS

The late 2000s saw the debate around the PDS intensifying, yet the performance of PDS continued to improve, albeit with a high degree of geographical variation. Drèze and Sen (2018) referred to it as the "new style" PDS which included a wider participation in the PDS and a reduction in corruption. Across the country, there was a massive increase in the share of households which benefited from the PDS. With greater coverage of the population and lowered prices of subsidized grains, the share of households reporting consumption from foods provided through the PDS increased from a modest 24% in 2004–2005 to 44.5% in 2011–2012 (Panel A, Fig. 5.2). It also led to a reduction in as leakages—the loss of grains in the value chain from procurement to actual sale at the fair price shop (FPS)—by a significant amount (Panel B, Fig. 5.2). Greater consumption of food grains led to an increase in the corresponding, implicit food transfers to intended beneficiaries by almost three times in real terms—from INR 31 in 2004–2005 to INR 85 in 2011–2012 (Rahman 2014).[22] The income effect of increased food transfers to poor households not only reduced the poverty-gap index of rural poverty by 18–22% (Drèze and Khera 2013), but also led to substantial improvements in nutrition and diversification of the food basket of poor households (Kaul 2013; Kishore and Chakrabarti 2015; Krishnamurthy et al. 2017; Rahman 2016). This improvement at an all-India level came about largely because of the improvements in the PDS across North and East Indian states, since the South Indian states have performed better on PDS traditionally.

Credit for this reform goes largely to the state governments that pushed the reforms with a renewed political commitment and to the central government for their subsequent plans that gave encouragement to carrying forward these initiatives with greater vigor.[23] As a first step,

[22] Implicit monetary value of the food transfers are computed as the amount saved by the households had they purchased the subsidized amount from the open market at prevailing prices.

[23] Other initiatives like door-step delivery and text messages to beneficiaries when the ration arrives at the FPS has improved access and generated demand for the PDS.

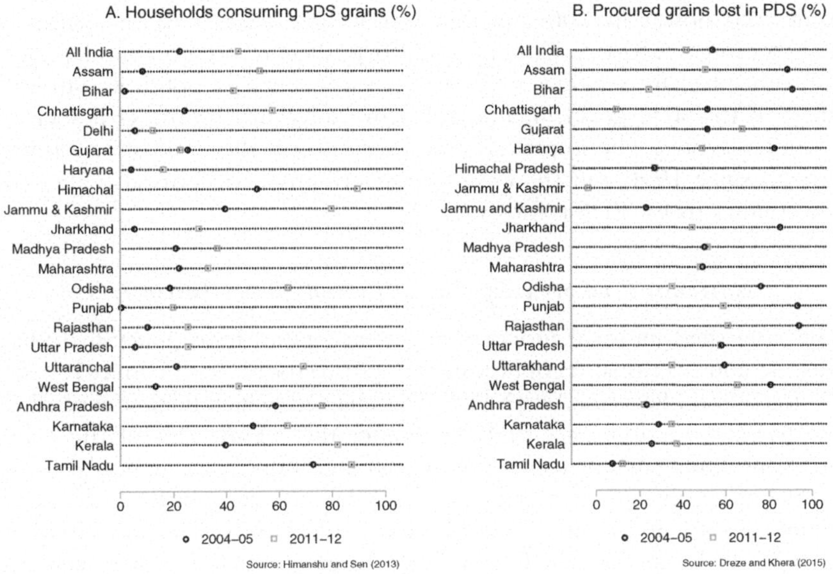

Fig. 5.2 Improvements in the PDS: greater participation and reduced leakages

many state governments, which had targeted programs, reevaluated their BPL lists and expanded the coverage of PDS to larger sets of beneficiaries. Second, greater incentives were provided to consumers as well as FPS owners. Lowering of the price at the PDS shops incentivized the beneficiaries to access the PDS, while higher commission to the PDS shop owners lowered their incentives of cheating and corruption.[24] Third, an updated database of the beneficiaries, FPS owners, and an improved monitoring system enabled by IT-based systems (end-to-end computerization) has further brought down inefficiencies.[25] This period also saw a change in the government, with the Congress government, which

[24] The government of Chhattisgarh, in fact, shifted the management of the PDS from private dealers to self-help groups, cooperatives, or other community-based organization (Puri 2012).

[25] For a detailed coverage of the various changes, refer to Khera (2011), Himanshu and Sen (2013), and Rahman (2014).

came into power in 2004, pushing its welfare agenda to the front.[26] The National Advisory Council (NAC) pushed reforms in food policy and other welfare schemes while there was a renewed political commitment of the state governments and active advocacy by the civil society advocacy group. The improved fiscal position on the back of economic growth since 1990 and the ensuing redistributive concerns also abetted the conditions for PDS reforms.

National Food Security Act, 2013 and Newer Initiatives

The watershed moment in expanding the scope of food policy in India, was the constitutional recognition to "right to food" Act.[27] In 2013, the National Food Security Act (NFSA) was enacted, which further expanded the *focus, form,* and *scope* of PDS. Under the NFSA, 75% of the rural population and 50% of urban population are "priority households" with a total monthly ration entitlement of 5 kg of rice, wheat, and coarse grains at INR 3, 2, and 1 per kilogram, respectively. The introduction of the NFSA was identified as an opportunity to include coarse cereals, pulses, and other edibles in the PDS, but the decision was left to the state governments, as food demand patterns vary regionally. NFSA also major landmark in making women as the head of household, under whose name the ration card would be issued, allowing for greater agency in intra-household decision-making.[28]

Early experiences from the NFSA suggest that the PDS coverage in most states increased, with considerable improvements in previously lagging states of Bihar, Madhya Pradesh, Odisha, West Bengal, and many of India's poorer states (Drèze et al. 2019; Drèze and Khera 2017; Puri

[26] For a discussion on the changing policy social welfare policy landscape, refer to Chapter 3.

[27] In Chapter 3, we discuss how the writ petition by People's Union for Civil Liberties (PUCL), in response to the starvation deaths in the state of Rajasthan in 2001, forced the central government to release excessive food grain stocks to the PDS. The litigation, which was intended initially as a relief measure in response to starvation deaths, paved the way for several food security reforms in the country.

[28] Section 13 of the NFSA mandates the 'oldest woman of a family, who is not less than 18-year old' as the head of a household on whose name PDS supplies would be issued.

2017).[29] The income effect from large increases in the generosity of PDS transfers after the NFSA substantially improved nutrition and dietary diversity of beneficiary households (Shrinivas et al. 2018).

The expansion of PDS necessitated better organizational capacity of the system which benefited from the greater use of information technology (IT) and digitalization in service delivery. It led to greater efforts at database creation for the 'priority' households, some states issued smart cards, along with the investments in digitizing every transaction to avoid the last-mile delivery challenges which have traditionally affected the performance of PDS, With 'right to food' being an Act of parliament, it also became a political imperative—at local and national scale—to ensure PDS reaches its rightful beneficiaries.

Beneficiary Database and Electronic Records of Transactions

As part of the initiative to streamline the operations of the PDS, there has been an "end-to-end computerization" of the system.[30] Detailed records of all transactions, purchases at the FPSs through electronic point of sale (e-PoS) devices, and GPS-enabled movement and storage of grains in the supply chain have made the system more efficient, reducing the leakages and corruption in the system. A digitized database of all ration card-holding families has further helped to discard "ghost cards" and improve last-mile delivery to the beneficiaries. By making the database publicly available—for beneficiaries to verify the status of their monthly entitlements—with grievance redressal systems (online and toll-free helpline numbers), the government has expressed its commitment to improve the performance of PDS.[31]

[29] For a summary of state-level reforms in PDS before and after NFSA, refer to Puri (2022a, b).

[30] By March 2021, more than 92% of the FPSs have ePoS devices and facility for biometric identification, according to the government. See the Ministry of Consumer Affairs press release, "Department of Food & Public Distribution implemented a scheme on End-to-end Computerization of TPDS Operations in 31 States/UTs": https://www.pib.gov.in/PressReleasePage.aspx?PRID=1703481. Accessed on January 13, 2022.

[31] A shift toward more technology-based transfers through end-to-end computerization of the PDS operations to save costs was discussed in the Twelfth Five-Year Plan (2012–2017) which further envisaged using the *Aadhaar*-based authentication platform for PDS delivery, giving the beneficiaries the choice of commodities or the ration shop purchases.

Aadhaar-Based Biometric Authentication

Although the beneficiary database and computerization of the PDS supply chain have been unanimously welcomed, the most polarizing innovation has been the use of *Aadhaar*-based biometric authentication (pejoratively referred to as ABBA, meaning father, by its critics) for PDS transactions. Launched in 2010, *Aadhaar* is a 12-digit unique identification (UID) number—stored in a central database—assigned to every Indian resident. While it is similar to the Social Security Number (SSN) issued in the United States, the uniqueness of *Aadhaar* lies in the added information on biometric markers (fingerprints and iris patterns) stored with the UID in addition to other socio-economic and demographic information. By connecting PDS with the *Aadhaar* allows for 'automated' recognition of the beneficiary and her entitlements. The system also updates each time the beneficiary buys from the FPS which provides a check on the prevailing corrupt practices.

It is this uniqueness of biometrics-based authentication that has been considered as dangerous to individual privacy, as well as a source of exclusion.[32] *Aadhaar* assignment, which began as a voluntary exercise, has become a *sine qua-non* to access state welfare programs, including the PDS. To be eligible for the PDS, beneficiaries are first required to link their *Aadhaar* number with the PDS database, which the FPS dealer uses along with the fingerprints to authenticate every transaction. According to the government, it helps them deliver food to the authenticated beneficiaries, cutting down on last-mile corruption, and therefore, keeping the system fiscally efficient. Every purchase through the PDS, therefore, requires the presence of a functioning ePOS, high-speed Internet, and the correct recognition of fingerprints. Field-based reports have documented how these technologies are very "fragile" yet in helping the most marginalized, who live in remote areas with poor Internet connections and the elderly and manual wage workers, biometrics often do not clearly register. Such seemingly minor technological "glitches" have robbed the poor of significant state support, with critics dubbing ABBA as a tool of exclusion or "pain without gain," as it has been unable to reduce the malpractices of the FPS dealers in undercutting the stipulated rationed

Many of the state governments began the digitization process much before the NFSA 2013 came into being, as discussed in the earlier section.

[32] See Khera (2019) for a discussion.

quantity (Drèze et al. 2017).[33] In fact, poor beneficiaries, unable to link their card to *Aadhaar*, lost out on their precious entitlements (Muralidharan et al. 2020). The criticism, however, is not against the ePOS but about allowing for offline authentication and the hassle of matching fingerprints for every transaction. Such last-mile innovations, however, in no way enhance the operational credibility of the system where the PDS is mired in local corruption.[34]

Several states have experimented therefore with smart cards as an alternative.[35] Smart cards, with a PDS-like ration card number, not only do away with the unreliable "register" system of the old, but also enable more authentic bookkeeping. Smartcards do not require the use of matching biometrics-based authentication or internet connectivity requirement, thereby avoiding the ABBA-enabled exclusion of deserving beneficiaries.[36] Yet, technology has been less than inclusive. Consider, for example, the decision of the Andhra Pradesh government to make the PDS benefits portable across any FPS in the state. Among those who benefited from the portability option, the poor and socially disadvantaged had a significantly lower share mostly because the lower-caste households were disallowed to access shops in neighborhoods inhabited by the upper castes (Allu et al. 2022).

These findings are similar to the global evidence around the pitfalls of digital IDs as they are 'subject to failure to deliver on high expectation' (World Bank 2016, p. 196). For digital IDs such as *Aadhaar* to succeed as a tool for welfare recipients, supportive legal framework, adequate financial and human resource, committed leadership, and high trust between citizen and state is required. India fares poorly on most of these preconditions for success and therefore a unique ID could at best

[33] Even the most ardent proponents of ABBA for social welfare delivery, argue for additional offline authentication in the local POS machine as the biometrics authentication often fails. See Muralidharan et al. (2022).

[34] A good example of a reform of the PDS not reducing local corruption is the unsuccessful move of the PDS in Bihar from in-kind to cash vouchers. See, for example, Choithani and Pritchard (2015).

[35] See Allu et al. (2019).

[36] A simple swipe of the smart card would allow the FPS dealer to verify the buyer's identity and PDS entitlements. The transaction would be recorded in the system for future reference, reducing the incentive to report false purchases.

be one component of the social policy and not the be-it-all source of beneficiary identification.[37]

One Nation One Ration Card

A major development in the PDS has been the introduction of the One Nation, One Ration Card (ONORC) which makes the PDS benefits portable outside of the state. Unlike earlier times, when every beneficiary was tied to an FPS within the state of residence, beneficiaries can now receive their PDS entitlement in any part of the country which makes it particularly useful for the migrant population. The operationalization of ONORC is based upon linking all ration cards with *Aadhaar*-based biometric authentication and electronic point of sale (e-PoS) devices at the FPSs. The ONORC is now enabled across the country, covering nearly 690 million beneficiaries (86% of the NFSA beneficiaries) in the country, according to the latest economic survey.[38] It has been lauded most recently as a major provision of relief via state support to migrant workers, who suffered disproportionate losses during the COVID-19 pandemic.

PDS, the Story Thus Far

The 70-year-old story of the PDS in India can be characterized as a classic case of *punctuated equilibrium*.[39] While the *scope* and *focus* of PDS has evolved in response to economic and political ideals of the times, yet, this evolution has been spurred by crisis, rather than by an organic advancement of policy ideals toward addressing the incremental challenges of human development and welfare. Although the PDS came about as a war relief program, unprecedented agricultural productivity gains led to

[37] For a cross-country review of biometrics and perils of development policy, refer to Gelb and Clark (2013).

[38] See the *Economic Survey 2020–21*, Vol. 2, Agriculture and Food Management, Ch. 7: https://www.indiabudget.gov.in/economicsurvey/doc/vol2chapter/echap07_vol2.pdf. Accessed on February 28, 2022.

[39] The theory of "punctuated equilibrium" characterizes policy decisions as both stable and incremental—long periods of inertia, punctuated by dramatic bursts of change (Jensen 2009). Since policies are embedded in a politician's reelection motivation, a significant or radical policy change, therefore, happens when there is an active constituency for this change. Otherwise, there are long and dormant periods of inattention to the issue.

its consolidation. The economic reforms of 1991 led to a narrowing of its focus, but civil society activism steered toward restricting the PDS with the NFSA. The emerging subnational political landscape further provided for the use of the PDS as an opportunity to seek electoral gains, leading to its further expansion and improvement. In a nutshell, the recent reforms, which have improved household welfare at least in the short run, can be attributed to the rights-based social policy agenda, politically motivated initiatives by state governments, and improvements in technology. PDS reforms, however, are still stuck in the older paradigm of food assistance, because of the political economy of farm support and struggles with identifying the poor for targeting, which hinder an innovation in the *form* of transfer.

Interlocked Incentive Structure and Negative Externalities

The major impediment to reforming PDS is the interlocked incentives to the farmers to grow rice and wheat. PDS reforms—movement to cash or food vouchers—are impossible without bringing about carefully crafted agricultural policy reforms and appropriate safeguards for households against the risk of higher food prices. Currently, the production incentives that the system provides to the rice–wheat-producing regions, through increased MSPs, lead to negative externalities, such as inhibiting agricultural diversification and more intensive use of natural resources, eventually harming progress on nutrition and environmental sustainability.[40] Persistence in incentivizing only staple crops may distort optimal crop allocations and crowd out production of other nutrient-rich crops, such as course cereals and pulses, undermining nutritional security for the future.[41] Intensive cultivation of rice and wheat has led to further ecological degradation, such as ground water depletion.[42] An additional

[40] Pingali (2012) and Davis et al. (2019) deliberate upon the challenges of the post-Green Revolution cereal-based food systems in India. For a discussion on India's agricultural markets, price variations, and the implications of procurement, refer to Chatterjee and Kapur (2016).

[41] Refer to the discussion in Pingali et al. (2017).

[42] The water footprint estimates from different studies are as high as 3,150 l/kg for rice cultivation in India (Balasubramanian et al. 2017). Chatterjee et al. (2022) illustrate how the expansion of wheat procurement in Madhya Pradesh led to the lowering of the water table in the state.

negative externality of rice cultivation in Punjab and Haryana, which has received greater attention in recent times, is the massive burning of crop residue after harvest that contributes as much as half of the particulate pollution in some cities in India during harvest seasons.[43] Such atmospheric pollution has been found to have detrimental effects on health and mortality.[44] Yet, the conversations around the need to rethink MSPs for rice and wheat to eventually reform the *form* of the PDS remain on the sidelines.[45]

It would be reasonable to say that simply eliminating MSPs could be disastrous—economically as well as politically—in the absence of appropriate marketing infrastructure and regulation of agricultural trade. Expenditures on staple food grains still continue to be more than half of the household budgets for the poor, and an abrupt rise in prices could undermine their food security and resilience. Similarly, a large share of farmers, even smallholders, sell at their crops at MSPs or rely on the floor prices set through its operations to sustain their livelihoods (Gupta et al. 2021). The rise of Madhya Pradesh and other states, in using decentralized procurement to expand procurement operations has further complicated the enactment of any reforms which could break the interlocked incentives. In fact, greater public procurement is increasingly being used by state governments to assert themselves in national food policy.[46]

[43] See Cusworth et al. (2018) and Venkataraman et al. (2006) for more discussion. Depletion of ground water has been particularly aggravated during the mid-1990s with the introduction of a new short-duration rice variety that allowed farmers to complete two crop cycles in one season (April–October), which delayed the planting season of rice to May. In response resort to burning the crop residue. Crop residue burning after rice harvest has been increasing at an alarming rate, with significant effects on air pollution, and consequently, on health and mortality.

[44] For instance, Pullabhotla (2019) estimated the infant mortality costs of pollution from crop residue burning in India to be nearly 94,000 additional infant deaths per year attributable to an ambient air pollution risk of a 10 unit increase in PM10. In other words, an increase of five upwind fires each year increases the infant mortality rate by 10%.

[45] In the agricultural reforms that were introduced recently, there was not much conversations around the need to rethink MSPs for rice and wheat (Narayan 2020).

[46] Krishnamurthy (2012) refers to it as a "radical new centrality" in India's regional politics.

Subnational Politics

Food policy reforms, largely, have been a central part of the emerging social policy narrative at the subnational level, which does not preclude the PDS. It has been widely recognized that much of the action concerning the PDS has been championed by the forces of subnational politics. Since the 1990s, India's federal polity changed from two central parties to a proliferation of regional parties and a coalition government at the center. Improved welfare benefits through the PDS were particularly useful for the state Chief Ministers (CMs) in their electoral pitches. For example, the states of Odisha and Chhattisgarh, with high levels of poverty and poor governance, became the torchbearers of PDS reforms.[47] These initiatives inspired other poorer states, such as Jharkhand, Bihar, and Uttar Pradesh to push for PDS reforms. Similarly, along with the governments of Madhya Pradesh and Chhattisgarh, states like Bihar and Uttar Pradesh are also pushing for state-driven procurement of food grains to feed the PDS supply chain. State governments, therefore, have been referred to as "laboratories" of social welfare policy reforms, with welfare entitlements as powerful political strategies to mobilize votes (Deshpande et al. 2017).[48]

It is interesting to note that the politics of the "new style PDS" is similar to the North Indian states, which have traditionally performed worst on social welfare, following the leads of their Southern counterparts. Chief Ministers in the other states have taken a leaf out of the book of South Indian politics. It is quite well documented how the southern states of India used the PDS and other social welfare measures for electoral politics, regime legitimacy, and individual popularity. In 1960s, C. N. Annadurai, the founder and leader of the political party Dravida Munnetra Kazhagam (DMK) in Tamil Nadu had swept the elections with

[47] Raman Singh, then CM of Chhattisgarh often came to be referred by the sobriquet of "chawal baba" ("rice daddy") and won three consecutive electoral terms. The parent state of Madhya Pradesh began pushing for greater production and procurement of wheat for PDS, providing its CM with many consecutive electoral victories.

[48] However, state governments vary in their distinct policy preferences, levels of clientelism, and political incentives, which has led to the PDS reforms (Tillin 2021). Even in 2011–2012, states were in very different stages of PDS reforms. Uttar Pradesh, Bihar, and Jharkhand, for example, were still not able to compete with Odisha and Chhattisgarh—states with similar track records of underdevelopment and poor state capacity (Rahman et al. 2018).

his slogan "three measures of rice for Re 1."[49] Similarly, in Karnataka, CM Ram Krishna Hegde's government expanded the PDS in rural areas with higher entitlement through the Green Card Scheme in 1985. N. T. Rama Rao from the Telugu Desam Party (TDP) famously announced the 'two-rupees per kilo rice scheme' through the PDS, after winning the elections in 1983. He sought to use the scheme—as CMs of Odisha and Chhattisgarh have done in recent times—to create an image of a benefactor for the Telugu people (residents of Andhra Pradesh), with colorful pamphlets showing his photo and the nickname of Anna-Varam (meaning "big brother's gift").[50]

Even before the NFSA was enacted, the Chhattisgarh government had announced its own state-level NFSA-like scheme in 2007, labeled as *Mukhyamantri Khadyann Sahayata Yojana* (MKSY, or the CM's food relief scheme), which expanded PDS coverage to almost a universal one. Many of the other CMs have similarly tried to appropriate the expansion of the PDS and the NFSA as a strength of their own pro-poor commitment. The CMs in Uttar Pradesh and Telangana distributed the new ration cards with their own pictures on them. K. Chandrasekhar Rao, the CM of Telangana, defended this action, saying that the state government is offering an extra subsidy of INR 1 per kg of rice. The Karnataka government introduced *Anna Bhagya Yojana* in 2013—rice through the PDS at a symbolic price of INR 1/kg—as the first executive decision of the Siddaramaiah government after his election victory. Madhya Pradesh's Shivraj Singh Chouhan introduced the *Mukhyamantri Annapurna Scheme* offering rice through the PDS at INR 1/kg. Both the states sold rice at lower than the NFSA-stipulated Rs. 3 per kg. Some CMs expanded the PDS-eligible population. Mamata Banerjee, CM of West Bengal, announced that the state would include an additional 17 million people, which were above the 67% "priority households." After being elected as CM of Jammu and Kashmir, Mehbooba Mufti announced the Mufti Muhammad Sayeed Food Entitlement Scheme (MMSFES), named after her father, providing a greater allocation and expanded coverage than NFSA.

[49] One measure is considered equivalent to 4.5 kg, which implies 13.5 kg for INR 1. NFSA prices are reasonably less than that in real terms, which speaks of the generosity of the benefits, scaled up to the national level.

[50] See Olsen (1989) for a discussion.

With the weakening of party cadre structure and mass political organizations, the CMs have increasingly asserted their charisma as being "development oriented" for electoral gains (Manor 2016). The electoral appeal of low inflation and subsidized staple foods seem to have worked. Why would political leaders care about changing the *form* of food assistance? Cash or vouchers do not carry the same visual appeal of personal offerings from the charismatic benefactor. Therefore, any nuanced discussion around PDS reforms cannot ignore the political economy challenges of MSP and assured procurement.

Reframing the Reformed Public Distribution System

The PDS has significantly improved, albeit gradually, in most states to become a form of social protection against food price inflation, for stabilizing consumption, and for increasing dietary diversity—at least in rural India, over the last two decades. These improvements have principally come about for two reasons: greater political commitment to welfare and improvements in the last-mile delivery systems such as better targeting and technology-based monitoring of the value chain to lower corruption. These improvements, perhaps, have not yet led to big bang reform, that is, to dismantle the PDS system in favor of food coupons or cash transfers, much to the dismay of the system's critics. The economic rationale for dismantling the current system is one of efficiency, while the reason for its persistence is path-dependent politics and imperfect institutions—political institutions and markets—which sustains this punctuated equilibrium. We argue that the way out of the policy stasis is to reframe the PDS debate and ask the following question: how can we leverage the PDS infrastructure to improve nutrition?

Nutrition as the Scope of PDS

It is important to put nutrition at the center of this debate for multiple reasons. First, nutrition is, first, about the quality and quantity of food. The current form of the PDS provides a minimum level of calorie sufficiency, but essential micronutrients (leading to hidden hunger) are insufficient through staple foods. Can we address these nutritional needs through the PDS? Second, India is undergoing a nutrition transition in which the triple burden of malnutrition—undernutrition concurrent with over-nutrition (obesity) and micronutrient deficiency—is the major challenge. There is declining trend in calorie consumption with sedentary lifestyles and better hygiene. Improvements in sanitation practices and less manually intensive occupations in the future will lower calorie requirements further and potentially increase obesity and non-communicable diseases (NCDs). We should ask, therefore, what should be the role of the PDS in the future? Third, structural transformation will mean greater urbanization, with a higher rate of migration and more nonagricultural employment. Automation of jobs implies a greater gulf between the skilled and unskilled workforce. Greater inequality could be fueled by rising informality in employment, without employer-based social protection, leading to greater demand for state support. High population density will put stress on urban water and sanitation infrastructure, leading to fears of disease epidemic. Any form of consumption support without being nutrition-sensitive would make households more vulnerable to shocks—of health and livelihood—impeding the process of development resilience. While the NFSA, as enshrined in the Constitution provides citizens their "right to food," one should begin thinking instead of the "right to adequate nutrition."

Need for a Gradual, and Not Hasty Move to Cash Transfers

The case in favor of cash is straightforward.[51] It saves administrative costs while providing households with the ability to purchase what they would like. Arguments against cash transfers stem from multiple reasons.[52] First, the value of the cash transfer could be eroded by inflation, and the promise of indexing the cash transfer by inflation may not be deemed credible by people. Lack of appropriate revisions in the old age or disability pensions with inflation are a case in point. Sometimes, local price increase could lower the value of a transfer, as prices vary across the rural–urban areas or even across states is substantial.[53] Second, Indian

[51] See Kapur et al. (2008), Kotwal et al. (2011), and Svedberg (2012).

[52] Refer to the discussion in Drèze (2019) and Khera (2014).

[53] PDS beneficiaries might prefer food transfers as an insurance against price risk, against only an implicit income transfer (Gadenne et al. 2021). As a result, in-kind transfers are more beneficial than cash, especially for the poorer households in ensuring a minimum amount of calories. The risk of fluctuating market prices has been cited as a

families are highly patriarchal and intra-household allocation of food is inequitable. The powerful members of the family could use the money on non-food items, often spending on nefarious activities, undermining household welfare. Third, the financial payment infrastructure has to step up to reach every beneficiary.[54] Many of these reasons contribute to the low popularity currently of cash among the masses.

One must understand that the question of "cash versus food" is highly embedded in the economic and political context.[55] With greater economic development, better market infrastructure, and nutritional awareness, cash transfers could become more prudent and also politically popular.[56] A hasty transition to cash from the current system exposes many of the poor to the vagaries of the market, undermine their food and nutritional security, and inhibit resilience to shocks. Experimental evidence also supports the argument that remote and underdeveloped regions exhibit an increase in price of food when cash, instead of food, is provided to the households. In the Indian context, hunger and starvation continue to be a major concern in the remote parts of the country, and the PDS provides a formidable safety net. Although in urban centers, cash transfers could be easier, a hasty shift might adversely affect the poorer regions.[57] A *cash versus the PDS* experiment in Delhi found cash to be useful in improving diet intake (Gangopadhyay et al. 2015). On the contrary, a similar state-sponsored experiment in the poorer state of Jharkhand led to loss of benefits because of the fragile infrastructural and institutional system around *Aadhaar*-based identification and delivery

reason for preferring food instead of cash by poorer households (Khera 2014). Even in other contexts, like Ethiopia, where cash transfers are common, food insecure households express their preference for some kind of in-kind transfers in lieu of cash (Hirvonen and Hoddinott 2021).

[54] While it is envisaged that under *Prime Minister Jan Dhan Yojana* (PMJDY), Somanchi (2020) and Pande et al. (2020) looked at the proliferation of PMJDY among the poor for COVID-19 relief and found the financial coverage of the poor inadequate.

[55] For a detailed discussion, refer to Currie and Gahvari (2008) and Gentilini (2016).

[56] Even the staunchest supporter of the PDS, Jean Drèze recognized the merit of cash transfers, but possibly at some point in the future when the "banking system has a wider reach and the food security problem has been resolved" (Drèze 2011), but a hasty transition to cash when there is serious shortage of banking infrastructure, and a glut of food grains in the FCI warehouses could be premature.

[57] Under NFSA, Direct Benefit of Transfer (or DBT), in lieu of food, has already begun in the more urban Chandigarh, Puducherry, and Dadra and Nagar Haveli.

(Barnwal and Pandey 2019). Therefore, the transition to cash could be most successful when there is already an effective system of social protection in place, such that cash transfers are another option in the "menu" of social protection devices that are complementary to the supply-side food or nutritional assistance (Narayanan 2011). Cash, indeed, is a better alternative once the appropriate financial infrastructure for a smooth transition is available, and the social policy architecture becomes more beneficiary-centric, rather than that of administrative ease.[58] Continuing with the PDS with a better monitoring system—as it is happening currently—would eventually pave the way for an architecture useful to transfer cash. Until then, the clamor for immediate change could be premature and possibly ignorant of India's socio-political context.[59]

In the next few years, the PDS can continue in its current *form* with an expanded *focus* on addressing not merely the basic consumption support and calorie supplementation, but also hidden hunger and improved nutrition. Expansion of the nutritional *scope* of the PDS should include non-cereals, such as pulses and coarse cereals, in the PDS.[60] While some states have begun to include other nutritious food items such as oilseeds and pulses as part of the NFSA, progressively, one can move to a greater quantity of these non-cereals. Remaining with the current PDS and the provision of a diversified basket would imply not only continuing with the procurement–storage–distribution system that inhibits agricultural diversification, but also the need for a procurement infrastructure for non-cereals. Creating a procurement structure for coarse cereals has its own challenges.[61] While one can only speculate on when it would

[58] Various forms of unconditional cash transfers are already in place through scholarships to students, old age/widow/disability pensions, along with cash transfers conditional on institutional delivery.

[59] Based on the experience of 10 low- and middle-income countries, along with the United States, Bhattacharya et al. (2017) argued that choice of the form of transfer—food or cash—in India depends upon four factors—financial access and literacy, people's perception of cash versus food, integration and competitiveness of food markets, and political economy factors. Currently, numerous hurdles need to be surmounted to be able to get to the ease of cash transfers being implementable.

[60] Around 2007–2008, some states added small quantities (1–3 kg/household/month) of pulses at subsidized prices through the PDS. Following the NFSA, Odisha and Karnataka have provided coarse cereals at INR 1/kg, while Rajasthan and Tamil Nadu have provided edible oil at subsidized rates through the PDS.

[61] With the assumption that coarse grains are not only more nutritionally sensitive food systems but are also climate-resistant which could contribute to healthy and sustainable

be politically feasible and economically sound, there is no doubt that the MSP has to be eventually dismantled to achieve agricultural diversification and ecological sustainability. It, however, needs to be supplemented with adequate income support to the farmers. Expansion of *PM-Kisan*—cash transfers to small farmers—could be an option. Price support could be gradually replaced with income support. Further, development of rural markets and emerging demand for diversified foods could allow production diversification in the regions where large-scale procurement takes place.

Global experience suggests that some of the largest food assistance programs, such as *Raskin, Baladi Bread, or Samrudhi*, too, have evolved gradually rather than through radical reforms.[62] None of these transition experiences were however smooth because of the fundamental challenges of design of an efficient delivery system for cash—identifying beneficiaries (*focus*) and the appropriate mode of payment (*form*)—in determining what is acceptable politically. In India, replacing the current PDS with cash or vouchers would imply the dismantling of the producer subsidy or compensating the producers accordingly. While we were writing this book, the farmer lobbies—mainly from Punjab and Haryana, from where the government largely procures food grains—led a massive protest against the agricultural marketing reforms which could have a bearing on the procurement system. The government eventually backed out which implies that current mode of procurement, stocking, and distribution of food grains would continue. It is evident that policy change in a democratic country often suffers from being slow and incremental. Reforming the PDS would fundamentally entail a monumental political risk. While one can say little about which regime and when such risk could be taken, or who would have the courage to take it, reframing nutritional security as the *scope* of the PDS could possibly be the game-changer in bridging the gap between ideologies and political ideals to bring about desired change.

food systems, many of the Indian states introduce them (in smaller quantities) in the PDS basket (Rampal et al. 2021). Karnataka, for example, introduced the whole grain, ragi, in the PDS after the NFSA, but it had to be discontinued because of supply-side constraints. While it eventually became available again at the FPS, some households wanted to stick with the starchy rice, while others exhibited specific regional preferences for millet (Raju et al. 2018).

[62] For a comprehensive review, refer to Alderman et al. (2018).

References

Alderman, Harold, Ugo Gentilini, and Ruslan Yemtsov. 2018. *The 1.5 Billion People Question: Food, Vouchers, or Cash Transfers?* Washington, DC: World Bank.

Allu, Rakesh, Sarang Deo, and Sripad Devalkar. 2019. "Alternatives to Aadhaar-Based Biometrics in the Public Distribution System." *Economic & Political Weekly* 54 (12): 30–37.

Allu, Rakesh, Maya Ganesh, Sarang Deo, and Sripad Devalkar. 2022. "Portability in the Public Distribution System." *Economic & Political Weekly* 57 (2): 50–57.

Balasubramanian, Rudrasamy, Venkatachalam Saravanakumar, and Kovilpillai Boomiraj. 2017. "Ecological Footprints of and Climate Change Impact on Rice Production in India." In *The Future Rice Strategy for India*. London: Elsevier.

Banerjee, O., T. Darbas, P. R. Brown, and C. H. Roth. 2014. "Historical Divergence in Public Management of Foodgrain Systems in India and Bangladesh: Opportunities to Enhance Food Security." *Global Food Security* 3 (3–4): 159. https://doi.org/10.1016/j.gfs.2014.06.002.

Barnwal, Barun Kumar, and Mrityunjay Pandey. 2019. "Troubles with Cash Food Subsidy a Case Study of Jharkhand Villages." *Economic and Political Weekly* 54 (43): unpaginated.

Bhatia, B. M. 1970. *India's Food Problem and Policy Since Independence*. Bombay: Somaiya Publications

Bhattacharya, S., Falcao, V.L. and Puri, R., 2017. The public distribution system in India. in Alderman, H., Gentilini, U., Yemtsov, R. (Eds.), *The 1.5 Billion People Question*: Food, Vouchers, or Cash Transfers? The World Bank: Washington D.C.

Chatterjee, Shoumitro, and Devesh Kapur. 2016. "Understanding Price Variation in Agricultural Commodities in India: MSP, Government Procurement, and Agriculture Markets India Policy Forum." *India Policy Forum* 3: 12–13.

Chatterjee, S., Lamba, R. and Zaveri, E., 2022. The role of farm subsidies in changing India's water footprint.

Chetty, V. K., and P. V. Srinivasan. 1990. "Welfare Effects of Selected Food-Grain Policies in India." *Agricultural Economics* 4 (2): 179–92. https://doi.org/10.1016/0169-5150(90)90031-U.

Choithani, Chetan, and Bill Pritchard. 2015. "Assessing Bihar's Coupon-Based PDS: Importance of Local Context." *Economic and Political Weekly* 50 (3): 61–68.

Chopra, R. N. 1988. *Food Policy in India. A Survey*. New Delhi: Intellectual Publishing House.

Currie, Janet, and Firouz Gahvari. 2008. "Transfers in Cash and In-Kind: Theory Meets the Data." *Journal of Economic Literature* 46 (2): 333–83. https://doi.org/10.1257/jel.46.2.333.

Cusworth, Daniel H., Loretta J. Mickley, Melissa P. Sulprizio, Tianjia Liu, Miriam E. Marlier, Ruth S. Defries, Sarath K. Guttikunda, and Pawan Gupta. 2018. "Quantifying the Influence of Agricultural Fires in Northwest India on Urban Air Pollution in Delhi, India." *Environmental Research Letters* 13 (4). https://doi.org/10.1088/1748-9326/aab303.

Dantwala, M. L. 1967. "Incentives and Disincentives in Indian Agriculture." *Indian Journal of Agricultural Economics* 22 (2): 1.

Davis, Kyle Frankel, Ashwini Chhatre, Narasimha D. Rao, Deepti Singh, Suparna Ghosh-Jerath, Anvi Mridul, Miguel Poblete-Cazenave, Nabin Pradhan, and Ruth DeFries. 2019. "Assessing the Sustainability of Post-Green Revolution Cereals in India." *Proceedings of the National Academy of Sciences of the United States of America* 116 (50): 25034–41. https://doi.org/10.1073/pnas.1910935116.

Deshpande, Rajeshwari, K. K. Kailash, and Louise Tillin. 2017. "States as Laboratories: The Politics of Social Welfare Policies in India." *India Review* 16 (1): 85–105. https://doi.org/10.1080/14736489.2017.1279928.

Drèze, Jean. 2011. "The Cash Mantra." *Indian Express*, May 11.

Drèze, Jean. 2019. *Sense and Solidarity: Jholawala Economics for Everyone*. Oxford: Oxford University Press.

Drèze, Jean, and Reetika Khera. 2013. "Rural Poverty and the Public Distribution System." *Economic and Political Weekly* 48 (45–46): 55–60.

Drèze, Jean, and Reetika Khera. 2015. "Understanding Leakages in the Public Distribution System." *Economic and Political Weekly* 50 (7): 39–42.

Drèze, Jean, and Reetika Khera. 2017. "Recent Social Security Initiatives in India." *World Development* 98: 555–72. https://doi.org/10.1016/j.worlddev.2017.05.035.

Dreze, Jean, and Amartya Sen. 1990. *Hunger and Public Action*. Oxford: Clarendon Press.

Drèze, Jean, and Amartya Sen. 2018. *An Uncertain Glory*. Princeton: Princeton University Press.

Drèze, Jean, Nazar Khalid, Reetika Khera, and Anmol Somanchi. 2017. "Aadhaar and Food Security in Jharkhand: Pain Without Gain?" *Economic and Political Weekly* 52 (50): 50–60.

Drèze, Jean, Prankur Gupta, Reetika Khera, and Isabel Pimenta. 2019. "Casting the Net: India's PDS After the Food Security Act." *Economic & Political Weekly* LIV (6): 36–47.

Frödin, Olle. 2010. *Feeding India. The Spatial Parameters of Food Policy*. Vol. 22. New Delhi: Manohar Publishers.

Gadenne, Lucie, Samuel Norris, Monica Singhal, and Sandip Sukhtankar. 2021. *In-Kind Transfers as Insurance*. Vol. 28507. Cambridge, MA: National Bureau of Economic Research. https://doi.org/10.3386/w28507.

Gangopadhyay, Shubhashis, Robert Lensink, and Bhupesh Yadav. 2015. "Cash or In-Kind Transfers? Evidence from a Randomised Controlled Trial in Delhi, India." *Journal of Development Studies* 51 (6): 660–73. https://doi.org/10.1080/00220388.2014.997219.

Gelb, Alan, and Julia Clark. 2013. "Identification for Development: The Biometrics Revolution." *SSRN Electronic Journal*. https://doi.org/10.2139/ssrn.2226594.

Gentilini, Ugo. 2016. "Revisiting the 'Cash Versus Food' Debate: New Evidence for an Old Puzzle?" *World Bank Research Observer* 31 (1): 135–67. https://doi.org/10.1093/wbro/lkv012.

Gulati, Ashok, and Shweta Saini. 2015. "Leakages from Public Distribution System (PDS) and the Way Forward." Working Paper.

Gulati, Ashok, Devesh Kapur, and Marshall M. Bouton. 2020. "Reforming Indian Agriculture." *Economic and Political Weekly* 55 (11): 35–42.

Gupta, Prankur, Reetika Khera, and Sudha Narayanan. 2021. "Minimum Support Prices in India: Distilling the Facts." *SSRN Electronic Journal*. https://doi.org/10.2139/ssrn.3791859.

Hayami, Yujiro, Keijiro Otsuka, and K. Subbarao. 1982. "Efficiency and Equity in the Producer Levy of India." *American Journal of Agricultural Economics* 64 (4): 655–63. https://doi.org/10.2307/1240574.

Himanshu, Abhijit Sen, and A. Sen. 2013. "In-Kind Food Transfers-I." *Economic & Political Weekly* 48 (45–46): 45–55.

Hirvonen, Kalle, and John Hoddinott. 2021. "Beneficiary Views on Cash and In-Kind Payments: Evidence from Ethiopia's Productive Safety Net Programme." *The World Bank Economic Review* 35 (2): 398–413. https://doi.org/10.1093/wber/lhaa002.

Hirway, Indira. 2003. "Identification of BPL Households for Poverty Alleviation Programmes." *Economic and Political Weekly* 38 (45): 4803–8.

Jensen, C. 2009. Policy punctuations in mature welfare states. *Journal of Public Policy* 29 (3): 287–303.

Kapur, Devesh, Partha Mukhopadhyay, and Arvind Subramanian. 2008. "The Case for Direct Cash Transfers to the Poor." *Economic and Political Weekly* 43 (15): 37–43.

Kaul, Tara. 2013. "Household Responses to Food Subsidies: Evidence from India." *Economic Development and Cultural Change* 67: 95–129.

Kaushal, Neeraj, and Felix M. Muchomba. 2015. "How Consumer Price Subsidies Affect Nutrition." *World Development* 74: 25–42. https://doi.org/10.1016/j.worlddev.2015.04.006.

Khera, Reetika. 2008. "Access to the Targeted Public Distribution System: A Case Study in Rajasthan." *Economic and Political Weekly* 43 (44): 51–56.

Khera, Reetika. 2011. "Revival of the Public Distribution System: Evidence and Explanations." *Economic & Political Weekly* 46 (44): 36–50.

Khera, Reetika. 2014. "Cash vs. In-Kind Transfers: Indian Data Meets Theory." *Food Policy* 46: 116–28. https://doi.org/10.1016/j.foodpol.2014.03.009.

Khera, Reetika. 2019. *Dissent on Aadhaar: Big Data Meets Big Brother*. Hyderabad: Orient BlackSwan.

Kishore, Avinash, and Suman Chakrabarti. 2015. "Is More Inclusive More Effective? The 'New Style' Public Distribution System in India." *Food Policy* 55: 117–30. https://doi.org/10.1016/j.foodpol.2015.06.006.

Kochar, Anjini. 2005. "Can Targeted Food Programs Improve Nutrition? An Empirical Analysis of India's Public Distribution System." *Economic Development and Cultural Change* 54 (1): 203–35. https://doi.org/10.1086/431260.

Kotwal, Ashok, Milind Murugkar, and Bharat Ramaswami. 2011. "PDS Forever?" *Economic and Political Weekly* 46 (21): 72–76.

Krishnamurthy, Mekhala. 2012. "States of Wheat: The Changing Dynamics of Public Procurement in Madhya Pradesh." *Economic and Political Weekly* 47 (52): 72–83.

Krishnamurthy, Prasad, Vikram Pathania, and Sharad Tandon. 2017. "Food Price Subsidies and Nutrition: Evidence from State Reforms to India's Public Distribution System." *Economic Development and Cultural Change* 66 (1): 55–90. https://doi.org/10.1086/694033.

Landy, Frédéric. 2009. *Feeding India: The Spatial Parameters of Food Grain Policy by Frédéric Landy*. New Delhi: Manohar Publishers & Distributors.

Manor, J. 2016. India's states: The struggle to govern. *Studies in Indian Politics* 4 (1): 8–21.

Mooij, Jos. 1998. "Food Policy and Politics: The Political Economy of the Public Distribution System in India." *Journal of Peasant Studies* 25 (2): 77–101. https://doi.org/10.1080/03066159808438667.

Muralidharan, Karthik, Paul Niehaus, and Sandip Sukhtankar. 2020. *Identity Verification Standards in Welfare Programs: Experimental Evidence from India*. Cambridge, MA: National Bureau of Economic Research. https://doi.org/10.3386/w26744.

Muralidharan, Karthik, Paul Niehaus, and Sandip Sukhtankar. 2022. "Integrating Biometric Authentication in India's Welfare Programs: Lessons from a Decade of Reforms." In *India Policy Forum 2021*, 139–66. New Delhi: National Council of Applied Economic Research.

Narayan, Sudha. 2020. "The Three Farm Bills. Is This the Market Reform Indian Agriculture Needs?" *The India Forum*, October.

Narayanan, Sudha. 2011. "A Case for Refraining the Cash Transfer Debate in India." *Economic and Political Weekly* 46 (21): 41–48.

Olsen, Wendy K. 1989. "Eat Now Pay Later: Impact of Rice Subsidy Scheme." *Economic & Political Weekly* 24 (28): 1597–1611.

Pande, R., S. Schaner, C. T. Moore, and E. Stacy. 2020. "COVID-19 Relief: Assessing the Reach of PMJDY Cash Transfers in India."

Parikh, Ashok, Alain De Janvry, and K. Subbarao. 1988. "Agricultural Price Policy and Income Distribution in India." *The Economic Journal* 98 (389): 208. https://doi.org/10.2307/2233533.

Pingali, Prabhu L. 2012. "Green Revolution: Impacts, Limits, and the Path Ahead." *Proceedings of the National Academy of Sciences of the United States of America* 109 (31): 12302–8. https://doi.org/10.1073/pnas.0912953109.

Pingali, Prabhu, Bhaskar Mittra, and Andaleeb Rahman. 2017. "The Bumpy Road from Food to Nutrition Security—Slow Evolution of India's Food Policy." *Global Food Security* 15: 77–84. https://doi.org/10.1016/j.gfs.2017.05.002.

Planning Commission. 2005. *Performance Evaluation of Targeted Public Distribution System (TPDS).* New Delhi: Government of India.

Pullabhotla, Hemant K. 2019. "Air Pollution and Infant Mortality: Evidence from Agricultural Fires in India." Working Paper 1049.

Puri, Raghav. 2012. "Reforming the Public Distribution System: Lessons from Chhattisgarh." *Economic and Political Weekly* 47 (5): 21–23.

Puri, Raghav. 2017. "India's National Food Security Act (NFSA): Early Experiences." *LANSA Working Paper Series* 2017 (14): 1–33.

Puri, Raghav. 2022a. India's National Food Security Act (NFSA): Early Experiences. 2022. in Ruchita Beri, Anjoo Sharan Upadhyaya, and Åshild Kolås (Eds.) *Food Governance in India*: Rights, Security and Challenges in the Global Sphere. Routledge.

Puri, Raghav. 2022b. Improving In-Kind Food-Based Safety Nets: The Case of India's Public Distribution System, in Ugo Gentilini (Eds.) Social Protection, *Food Security and Nutrition: An Update of Concepts, Evidence and Select Practices in South Asia and Beyond*. Washington DC: World Bank.

Raju S., Rampal, P., Bhavani, R.V. and Rajshekar, S.C. 2018 'Introduction of millets in PDS lessons from Karnataka', *Review of Agrarian Studies*, vol. 8, no. 2, pp120–136.

Rahman, Andaleeb. 2014. "Revival of Rural Public Distribution System Expansion and Outreach." *Economic and Political Weekly* 46 (20): 62–68.

Rahman, Andaleeb. 2016. "Universal Food Security Program and Nutritional Intake: Evidence from the Hunger Prone KBK Districts in Odisha." *Food Policy* 63 (June): 73–86. https://doi.org/10.1016/j.foodpol.2016.07.003.

Rahman, Andaleeb, Prabhu Pingali, and Bhaskar Mittra. 2018. "Food Security and Nutrition in Rural India: Understanding State Level Heterogeneity." *World Food Policy* 4 (2). https://doi.org/10.18278/wfp.4.2.7.

Rampal, P., Pradhan, A., Panda, A.K., Raju, S. and Bhavani, R.V., 2021. Millets in farming systems in support of nutrition and social safety net programmes. *Orphan Crops for Sustainable Food and Nutrition Security: Promoting Neglected and Underutilized Species*, pp.319-326.

Roy, Devesh, Ruchira Boss, and Mamata Pradhan. 2020. *How India's Food-Based Safety Net Is Responding to the COVID-19 Lockdown*. Washington, DC: International Food Policy Research Institute. https://doi.org/10.2499/p15738coll2.133762_24.

Sen, Amartya. 1982. *Poverty and Famines: An Essay on Entitlement and Deprivation*. New Delhi: Oxford University Press.

Shrinivas, Aditya, Kathy Baylis, Ben Crost, and Prabhu Pingali. 2018. "Do Staple Food Subsidies Improve Nutrition?"

Somanchi, Anmol. 2020. "Covid-19 Relief: Are Women Jan Dhan Accounts the Right Choice for Cash Transfers?" Ideas for India.

Suryanarayana, M. H. 1995. "PDS: Beyond Implicit Subsidy and Urban Bias—The Indian Experience." *Food Policy* 20 (4): 259–78. https://doi.org/10.1016/0306-9192(95)00025-9.

Svedberg, Peter. 2012. "Reforming or Replacing the Public Distribution System with Cash Transfers?" *Economic and Political Weekly* 47 (7): 53–62.

Tarozzi, Alessandro. 2005. "The Indian Public Distribution System as Provider of Food Security: Evidence from Child Nutrition in Andhra Pradesh." *European Economic Review* 49 (5): 1305–30. https://doi.org/10.1016/j.euroecorev.2003.08.015.

Tillin, Louise. 2021. "Does India Have Subnational Welfare Regimes? The Role of State Governments in Shaping Social Policy." *Territory, Politics, Governance*: 1–17. https://doi.org/10.1080/21622671.2021.1928541.

Varshney, Ashutosh. 1993. "Self-Limited Empowerment: Democracy, Economic Development and Rural India." *The Journal of Development Studies* 29 (4): 177–215. https://doi.org/10.1080/00220389308422299.

Varshney, Ashutosh. 1998. *Democracy, Development, and the Countryside: Urban-Rural Struggles in India*. Cambridge: Cambridge University Press

Venkataraman, Chandra, Gazala Habib, Deep Kadamba, M. Shrivastava, Jean Francois Leon, B. Crouzille, Olivier Boucher, and D. G. Streets. 2006. "Emissions from Open Biomass Burning in India: Integrating the Inventory Approach with High-Resolution Moderate Resolution Imaging Spectroradiometer (MODIS) Active-Fire and Land Cover Data." *Global Biogeochemical Cycles* 20 (2): 1–12. https://doi.org/10.1029/2005GB002547.

Venugopal, K. R. 1992. *Deliverance from Hunger: The Public Distribution System in India*. New Delhi: Sage.

World Bank. 2015. *The State of Social Safety Nets 2015*. Washington, DC: World Bank.

World Bank. 2016. *World Development Report 2016: Digital Dividends*. Washington, DC: World Bank

CHAPTER 6

Early Life Interventions for Intergenerational Prosperity

Introduction

A resounding testimony to India's modest achievements on human development is the poor state of child nutrition in the country. India is home to the largest number of malnourished children in the world. Economic growth and poverty reduction haven't led to commensurate improvements in child health outcomes. Almost one-third of children under the age of 5 years are stunted (less than required height-for-age) and underweight (weight-for-age), while one in fifth is wasted (weight-for-height) (See Fig. 6.1). More than half of the pregnant women, at the same time, are anemic—with low levels of iron supplement intake—which makes them likely to give birth to the children at non-institutional health centers, exacerbating mortality risks—to the child as well as the mother—and further nutritional deprivations.

If development resilience is defined as an enhancement in "…the capacity over time of a person, household or other aggregate unit to avoid poverty in the face of various stressors and in the wake of myriad shocks" (Barrett and Constas 2014, p. 14,626), undernourishment among children becomes a source of economic fragility.[1] Undernourished children are less likely to suffer from adverse functional consequences which

[1] In this book, we have framed the *scope* of safety nets as an enabler of development resilience. See Chapter 2.

A. Rahman and P. Pingali, *The Future of India's Social Safety Nets*,
Palgrave Studies in Agricultural Economics and Food Policy,
https://doi.org/10.1007/978-3-031-50747-2_6

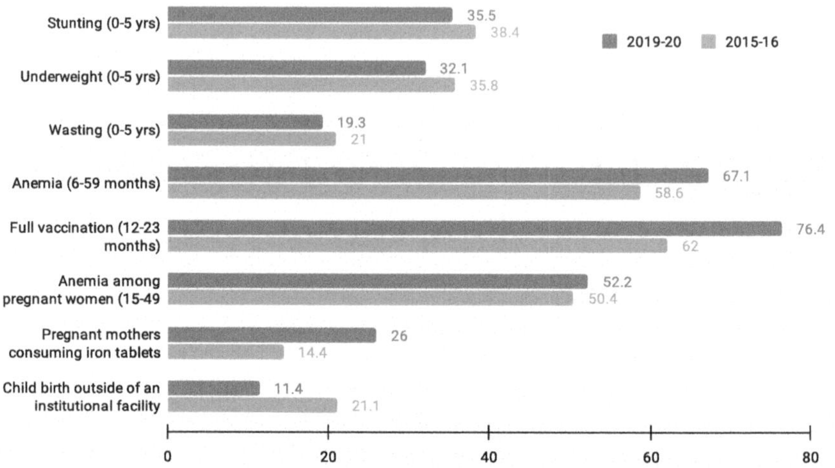

Fig. 6.1 State of maternal and child malnutrition in India (in %) (*Source* National Family Health Survey [2019–2020, 2015–2016])

limit their cognitive potential and impair human capital accumulation depriving them of the potential economic opportunities which they would have otherwise commanded—had it not been for their undernourished status—leading to intergenerational poverty.[2] Since the seeds of future individual economic achievements and interpersonal disparities germinate early in life, appropriate interventions correcting this imbalance in the formative years of children is essential to build resilience.[3] These interventions are often along the maternal–child biological pathway—in the form of nutritional supplements to the pregnant mother, encouragement for safe institutional child birth delivery, vaccinations to mother and children,

[2] See Alderman et al. (2006), Behrman (1993), Hoddinott et al. (2008), Maluccio et al. (2009), and the references cited therein.

[3] In his classical introductory textbook of economics, *Principle of Economics*, Alfred Marshall labeled child poverty as an "evil [that] is cumulative," because the more undernourished children are, "the less they earn when they grow up, and the less will be their power of providing adequately for the material wants of their children; and so on to following generations" (Marshall 1980). For a review on the economic effects of early childhood influences on adult life outcomes, see Currie and Almond (2011).

and nutritional supplementation to the infant—along with the provision of free school meals to the young children.[4]

To address the inequalities which develop early in life—and are likely to persist across generations—the Indian government, like many other developed and developing nations, has a range of social welfare programs with a *focus* on maternal and child health. These interventions take the *form* of targeted nutritional assistance to pregnant and lactating women and infant children, cash transfers as maternity benefits to mothers, free and compulsory primary schools, free meals to schoolchildren in public schools, and cash payment to mothers for institutional childbirth. The *scope* of these independent schemes is not only to improve child and maternal nutrition but also to stem higher levels of child and maternal mortality. Yet, despite the active presence of these programs, poor nutritional outcomes continue to be a blot on India's progress on human development.

In this chapter, we will discuss the relevance of social safety nets along the maternal–child biological pathway and early childhood for long-term gains for India. We begin with a global review of evidence on early life intervention hypothesis, followed up by a discussion of India's strategy of reducing early life nutrition—its *form*, *focus*, and *scope*—and its impact. We conclude the chapter with some suggestions on how to improve the current programs to build development resilience through improving mother and child nutritional outcomes.

Early Life Risks and Adverse Intergenerational Outcomes

Early life economic disadvantage leads to deprivation on two of the most fundamental human capital inputs to long-term developmental outcomes—nutrition and education. Children growing up in poverty

[4] Among the developed countries, Scandinavian nations provide a comprehensive set of early life health programs—which include prenatal, maternity, and well-infant care—to all families. In the USA, Supplemental Nutrition Program for Women, Infants, and Children (WIC) is provided to pregnant mothers and children and free school meals through the National School Lunch Program (NSLP). Early life assistance programs have been instrumental in reducing infant mortality in the short term with significant long-run benefits which include greater adult mortality, lower morbidity, and improved education, and labor market outcomes (Aizer et al. 2022; Wüst 2022). In the developing world, preschool nutrition component of Mexico's *Progresa/Oportunidades* and Brazil's *Bolsa Familia* are prominent examples of early life interventions.

are less likely to attend school and, therefore, to be cognitively disadvantaged, which further lowers labor productivity and dampens earning capacity as an adult.[5] Undernourished children are therefore likely to be poorer adults, who in turn, would give birth to poorer children. Child undernutrition and poverty therefore perpetuate a vicious cycle of intergenerational poverty created and sustained through the poor's inability to invest in their children's nutrition and education during early and later stages in life.

There is a unanimous agreement in the scientific community on the importance of investing during a "critical window" in early child life—in utero and beyond—for long-term development.[6] This line of argument draws upon the influential *fetal origins* hypothesis, which posits that long-term health outcomes of an individual depend upon a critical period in fetal life and early childhood (Barker 1990).[7] *Lancet,* a premier scientific journal in the field of epidemiology and medicine subsequently published a special series on early childhood development in 2007, 2011, and 2017.[8] One of the studies finds that 39 percent of children under the age of 5 in low-income and middle-income countries (LMICs) are at the risk of remaining below their developmental potential, which implies, on average, a deficit of 19.8 percent of annual income in adulthood (Grantham-McGregor et al. 2007). Newer estimates pitch the numbers at an even higher level—43 percent (250 million children) of children under the age of 5 in LMICs are the risk of not being able to "develop the intellectual skills, creativity, and wellbeing required to become healthy and productive adults" (Black et al. 2017). Recent research has further expanded the idea of the "critical window" of early life to include middle

[5] See Almond et al. (2018) and Case et al. (2002).

[6] Refer to Prentice et al. (2013) for more details.

[7] In an exhaustive summary of the empirical work that investigates this hypothesis (Currie and Almond 2011) showed that events in children's lives before their fifth years *do* have an enormous impact on their economic outcomes well into adulthood and beyond.

[8] The 2017 series, *Advancing Early Childhood Development*, notes that the "The science of early childhood development and its underlying neurobiology are increasingly invoked in the global discourse on education, health, social and child protection, and human capital formation" (Shonkoff et al. 2017, p. 14). The series provided in-depth reviews of existing evidence around early childhood development and health and well-being later in life, in the context of developing countries (Grantham-McGregor et al. 2007; Lake and Chan 2015).

childhood and adolescence, too, when physical growth consolidates itself, and cognitive and intellectual development stabilize (Bundy et al. 2018).

However, scholars studying the fetal origins hypothesis or the science of early childhood development strongly believe that the early life disadvantages can be remedied through appropriate investments "across health, nutrition, education, child protection, and social protection sectors that should be accessible to all families and young children…[through appropriate interventions] particularly in the first 1000 days of a child's life" (Machel 2017).[9] Most countries, including India, therefore, have a range of early childhood intervention programs that work to break the intergenerational cycle of deprivation and promote more inclusive economic growth and development. Examples of such intervention include free and compulsory primary schooling, prenatal and antenatal care, provision of free meals in schools, and tying together of many other public benefits, conditional on such programs ensuring that nutritional and educational needs of children are met.

A simplistic representation of the early life risks and a potential amelioration through appropriate interventions during the critical window are presented in Fig. 6.2. Early life deprivation begins from a mother's womb. In most developing countries, children born into poor households suffer from poor access to quality nutrition and health care for the mother. Essential routine visits to the doctor during and after pregnancy is not a common practice. In many cases such as in India, the quality of public health care is absent, poor, or unaffordable that mothers give birth to children outside of institutional facilities at home which increases the risks of maternal and child mortality. Lack of immunization facilities and access to nutrition further undermine the growth potential of a child. Further into adolescence, lack of access to quality schooling is commonplace which hinders cognitive development and labor market outcomes. This intergenerational transmission of poverty could, however, be stymied through strong public action early in the life cycle through improved neonatal and antenatal care along with better educational facilities for children. Such a reversal of fortune for those deprived early in life—with a *focus* on women and children—has the transformative potential for human development.

[9] The first 1000 days are counted as the child's life from conception until the age of 2 years.

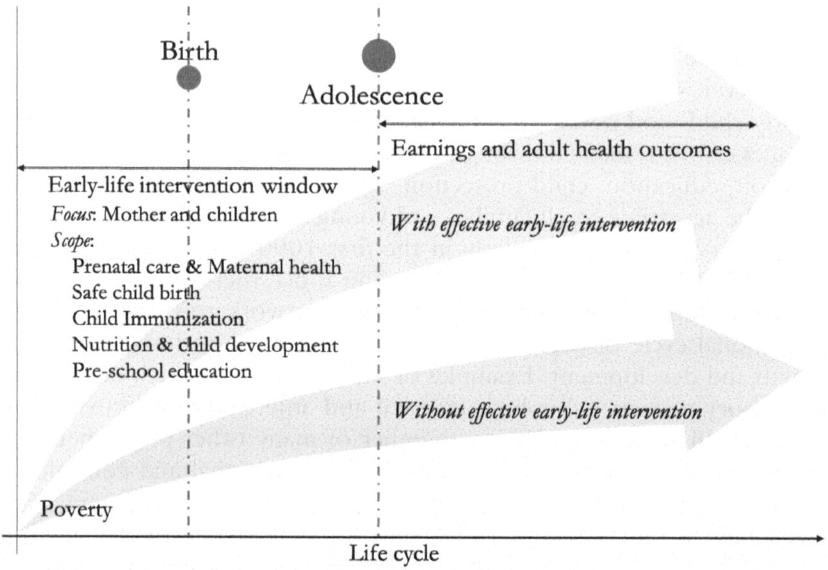

Fig. 6.2 Early life intervention and its long-term effects

The Role of Women as Primary Caregivers and Empowered Economic Agents

Women play an important role in the maternal–child biological pathway to improve nutritional outcomes. This pathway essentially relies upon the physical and economic status of women. If human capital investments determine long-term human achievements, then women as primary caregivers for children are most influential in shaping their health, cognitive ability, and future life outcomes. It is widely known that poorer economic conditions of women lead to worse child health in utero and at birth, thereby contributing to intergenerational poverty (Aizer and Currie 2014).[10] Similar, nutritional status of mothers is key for infant child health. Women who are underweight before pregnancy and do

[10] To quote Alfred Marshall, "*The most valuable of all capital is that invested in human beings; and of that capital the most precious part is the result of the care and influence of the mother*" (Marshall 1980). As a result, conditional transfers are mainly targeted toward women, because they are more likely to use the resources on children with respect to food, education, or health. Studies have shown that this targeting has not only led to

not gain sufficient weight during pregnancy are likely to give birth to children who are less likely to survive infanthood, and if they do, the children are prone to undernourishment later, which further comprises their cognition and economic productivity in adulthood (Coffey 2015). This situation becomes particularly ominous in countries like India, where 'son preference' continues to be rife despite increase in education and overall growth.[11] Gender-based discrimination is therefore a societal norm leading to inequitable intra-household allocation of resources including those as basic as food, lowered agency, and overall disempowerment for women. This is particularly common for the young and newly married women who fall at the bottom of household hierarchies, are expected to acquiesce to the household cultural norms of doing most of the daily chores, keeping quiet, and eating little.[12]

Apart from their caregiving role, greater economic opportunity for women in the ability to command employment, assets, and social status is also an essential part of the intergenerational development process (Duflo 2012; Mammen and Paxson 2000). Research suggests that, even in developed countries, women are more likely to live in poverty than men (Casper et al. 1994). Children born to poorer women are likely to suffer from the adverse consequences of poverty in terms of acquiring the requisite human capital to succeed in life. Further, improving the educational status of the women, which affects decision-making in health care, family planning, and spousal communication, adds to their own health outcomes, thus contributing to the initial health stock, and thus

better child outcomes, but also improved bargaining power among women and reduced domestic violence (Bardasi and Garcia 2014).

[11] Preference for a boy child is common in patriarchal societies. While countries like South Korea—with similar preference for sons few decades ago—have undergone a reform, India continues to lag with 'missing women' from all aspects of daily life (Sen 1992, 2003). Preference for son has led to considerable disempowerment for the girl child in terms of poor girl child health (Pande 2003), nutrition (Behrman 1988; Jayachandran and Kuziemko 2011), higher fertility (Drèze and Murthi 2001), adverse sex ratios (Jha et al. 2006), poor educational outcomes (Azam and Kingdon 2013), persistence of dowry system (Bhalotra et al. 2020), and overall intra-household inequality (Rosenzweig and Schultz 1982).

[12] To understand the role of family structure on female autonomy, see Debnath (2015).

improving the future health outcomes of their children, too (Chen and Li 2009; Heckert et al. 2019).[13]

Global Evidence on Effective Interventions Targeting Women and Children

Recognizing the importance of women and children in the development process, economically advanced nations introduced cash transfer programs targeted at widows with young children in the early twentieth century. This was backed by constitutional legislation that assured minimum years of schooling, and restricted child labor and unsafe working environments for children. In the United States, Mothers' Pension was expanded across the country in the form of welfare transfers as cash payments to poorer widows and single mothers with dependent children.[14] Currently, the Supplemental Nutrition Assistance Program (SNAP), Special Supplemental Nutrition Program for Women, Infants, and Children (WIC), and the National School Lunch Program (NSLP) form the three pillars of food and nutrition-related schemes in the United States (Currie 2003). The scope of WIC is limited to the early life nutritional challenges with a focus on pregnant, postpartum, or lactating women, along with infants and children less than five years of age. Through WIC, the policy tries to address specific nutritional goals, and therefore, hot cooked, vitamin-rich meals are provided for immediate consumption along with nutrition education and access to basic health services.[15] Under NSLP, on the other

[13] Similarly, the provision of a public works program, as discussed in an earlier chapter, is another example where betterment of women's agency through social and economic empowerment could add to the initial health endowment, with its positive intergenerational effect throughout the life of their children, well into adulthood.

[14] Long-term evaluation by Aizer et al. (2016) found that children, whose mothers benefited from the pensions program, attained better schooling outcomes, lived longer, and earned a higher wage in the labor market.

[15] WIC, in principle, is similar in spirit to the Integrated Child Development Scheme (ICDS) in India, albeit with a slightly different design. WIC is a federally run program and has a cap on the amount of money allocated to it. Many deserving women and children, despite suffering from "nutritional risk," could be deprived of the benefits when the allocated money runs out. ICDS, on the contrary, is a universal scheme in which any child or women can have access to it.

hand, meals are provided to students at the school, similar to India's Midday Meal Scheme (MDMS), with the scope of providing minimum daily requirements of key nutrients, focusing on only those classified as poor.[16]

These safety net programs were instrumental in ameliorating the "early origin" disadvantages in the United States. In his seminal work on human capital formation, Heckman notes that early life interventions are a 'rare public policy initiative' which 'promotes fairness and social justice and at the same time promotes productivity in the economy and in society at large' by investing in the human capital development potential of disadvantaged children. In his assessment, "early interventions targeted toward disadvantaged children have much higher returns than later interventions such as reduced pupil-teacher ratios, public job training, convict rehabilitation programs, tuition subsidies, or expenditures on police" (Heckman 2006, p. 1902). Evaluating the effect of Food Stamps program in the United States, Hoynes et al. (2016) find that in utero exposure to nutrition from mothers with who participated in the Food Stamps program, and hence, acquired access to food, had a significant long-term effect into adulthood for the offspring, with improved health outcomes, such as with decreased incidence of NCDs. Mothers, exposed to this program, exhibited an increase in economic self-reliance through greater educational outcomes and earning capacity. Similarly, children with access to the food stamps benefited from long-term improvements on an expansive set of development outcomes, such as increase in human capital, self-sufficiency, neighborhood quality, longevity, and reduced likelihood of incarceration (Bailey et al. 2020). Among the range of social welfare policies in the United States, those targeted at low-income children's health and education have historically proven to have useful return (Aizer et al. 2022; Hendren and Sprung-Keyser 2020). Social expenditures on such policies, therefore, pay themselves off in the long run through additional taxes collected from the beneficiaries later in their lives, as more productive adults, which also led to reduced transfers for the next generation.

Developing countries have gradually learned from this experience, as they have taken on the challenge of reducing child malnutrition in the last two decades. Prominent among them are Bangladesh, Ethiopia, and countries from Latin America like Brazil, which successfully adopted a

[16] Recently, NSLP also recognized the reduction in the incidence of overweight as a program goal.

combination of targeted nutrition-specific and nutrition-sensitive interventions that addressed the issue of malnutrition as well as its causes (Webb et al. 2018). Brazil and Mexico experienced a decline in child stunting through their flagship *Bolsa Familia* and *Opportunidas/Progresa* programs, in addition to a decline in poverty and income stability generally (Falcão et al. 2022; Farfán et al. 2022). The suite of welfare measures designed around the conditional cash transfers (conditional on school enrollment and visits to public health centers) also engendered greater gender equity through female education and lower fertility levels. Ethiopia, albeit still with a high level of undernourishment among its population, considered nutrition to be a multisector challenge and employed numerous ministries, along with improved sanitation infrastructure (Berhane et al. 2017). Bangladesh has a been a torch bearer in reducing child malnutrition—57 percent in 1997 to around 36 percent in 2014—despite low levels of income. The decrease was brought about not only by an increase in rural income, but also through community nutrition-sensitive interventions, with a concerted focus on the poor, including education of young girls, greater gaps between births, smaller family size, and an overall improved access to health care infrastructure (Headey et al. 2015).

India's Performance on Early Life Intervention

Persistence of child undernutrition in India emanates from multiple social, behavioral, and infrastructural factors.[17]

State action on eradicate undernutrition however has traditionally suffered from the limited *scope* of India's social safety nets in controlling hunger through the Public Distribution System (PDS) or protecting livelihoods through the public works program. For quite a long time in independent India's history, nutrition (child's or mother's) was not particularly an area of importance. The *scope* of safety nets remained limited to addressing some of the manifestations of poverty without regard to its

[17] Lack of a direct correspondence between income and child undernutrition gathers a lot of attention (Deaton and Drèze 2009; Ramalingaswami et al. 1997). Less nutritive diets (Maitra et al. 2013), poor sanitation practices, and prevalence of open defecation (Spears 2013, 2020), son preference leading to intra-household resource inequality (Jayachandran and Pande 2017), and short birth spacing (Dhingra and Pingali 2021) have been proposed as some of the reasons behind lower height of Indian children.

long-term implications. Hence, any explicit focus on women and children was largely missing. It was only in 2013, with the National Food Security Act (NFSA) passed in the parliament, that the life-cycle approach to food and nutritional well-being gained more prominence.

By recognizing that overall food and nutrition security must begin earlier, the NFSA provides constitutional guarantees to women to complete schooling and to be empowered enough to participate in household decision-making, leading to smaller, healthier, and well-nourished families. Such a conceptualization makes investment in women transformative, as an educated and healthy woman not only raises well-nourished children but is also better equipped to pursue business or employment opportunities that contribute to overall well-being. While the effective implementation of NFSA is still ongoing, it is useful to visit the many milestones, successes, and failures along the road to the historic NFSA legislation as we aim to think about its future. We will be focusing on the four central schemes (Table 6.1) while also discussing some of the state-level initiatives.

Table 6.1 India's safety net programs that focus on early life interventions

Schemes	*Focus*	*Scope*	*Form*
Integrated Child Development Scheme (ICDS)	<6-year-old children Pregnant/lactating mothers	Nutritional supplements Immunization Primary health check-up Non-formal education	Take-home food at the Anganwadi (ACW)
Mid-day Meal Scheme (MDMS)	6–14-year-old students in public schools	Reduction in "classroom hunger"	Free primary school Free hot cooked meal
Pradhan Mantri Matru Vandana Yojana (PMMVY)	Pregnant women	Maternity benefits Immunization	Conditional cash transfer
Janani Suraksha Yojana (JSY)	Pregnant women	Institutional child birth (reduced mother and child mortality)	Cash transfers

Integrated Child Development Scheme

The earliest initiative that focused on women and child development was the Integrated Child Development Scheme (ICDS), which aimed at ensuring child survival. It was introduced in 1975, at a time during when child mortality in India was at an unacceptably high level. One must keep in mind that it was only by the 1970s, that India was close to achieving self-sufficiency in food production and combatting hunger (as conceptualized in overall availability of food) was beginning to be less of a policy concern. Yet, policies largely focused on food, and so did ICDS. At the time of its introduction, ICDS had the following stated objectives:

- Improve the nutritional and health status of children in the age-group 0–6 years
- Lay the foundation for proper psychological, physical, and social development of children
- Reduce the incidence of mortality, morbidity, malnutrition, and school drop out
- Achieve effective coordination of policy and implementation among the various departments to promote child development
- Enhance the capability of the mother to look after the normal health and nutritional needs of the child through proper nutrition and health education

To achieve these objectives, ICDS offered a package with six kinds of services, which included supplementary nutritional assistance, preschool non-formal education, nutrition and health-related education, immunizations at centers, routine health check-ups, and hospital referral services. These services were to be provided through designated village focal points known as *Anganwadi* centers (AWCs).[18] Local women (educated up to 8th or 10th grade) would be selected to be the principal functionaries, in charge of the service provisioning, and were called Anganwadi Workers (AWWs).[19]

ICDS is now the world's largest mother-and-child welfare program in the world under which supplementary nutrition (once daily for 25 days

[18] A village *Anganwadi* implies a courtyard of the village.

[19] In areas that were difficult to reach or more backward, the educational requirements for an *Anganwadi* worker could be relaxed.

each month) is provided to every eligible person. By September 2016, its outreach had expanded to 101.06 million children and mothers. Under the scheme, children under the age of 3 and their mothers are provided with take-home rations (THR), and home-cooked food is provided to children between the age of 3 and 6 years at the designated AWCs. Food rations are mandated to provide 500 kilocalories (kcal) of energy and 12–15 g of protein to each child per day and 600 kcal of energy and 18–20 g of protein per day to pregnant or lactating mothers.[20] In addition to the supplementary nutrition, AWCs, under the ICDS, also provide immunization, health check-ups, and referral services with the aim of reducing short-term morbidity. AWCs, therefore, have become the node where preschool children, pregnant women, and lactating mothers come to receive health, nutrition, and education services.[21] AWCs, along with the Accredited Social Health Activist (ASHA), who is part of the local health infrastructure, are responsible for the services.

In the initial years, ICDS suffered from severe underperformance. A review of ICDS, as part of the appraisal of the 11th Five-Year Plan (2007–2012), highlighted its low impact on reducing child malnutrition. It was criticized for the poor infrastructure at the AWCs, overworked but unskilled staff, inadequate nutritional supplies, poor targeting of beneficiaries, misappropriation of funds, and abysmal monitoring systems in place. In order to address many of these concerns, the government increased its allocation and put better systems in place during the 12th Five-Year Plan, with the aim of "strengthening and restructuring" the ICDS (Government of India 2010, 13[1]). It brought institutional and management reforms, which in combination with judicial activism in the country, led to substantial improvement in the performance of ICDS (Balarajan and Reich 2016). There was a massive turn around in its performance, because of these changes, which were also abetted by the "right to food" campaigns. Between 2005–2006 and 2015–2016 (the two rounds of the National Family Health Surveys [NFHSs]), the share of people benefiting from the supplementary food assistance from ICDS increased from a mere 9.6 percent to 37.9 percent. Similarly, the usage

[20] Severely malnourished children are provided extra take-home rations (800 kcal and 20–25 g of protein content).

[21] In 1975, ICDS was introduced in 33 blocks, which covered 4891 Anganwadi centers. Each administrative block loosely consisted of 100 rural villages with a total population of approximately 100,000 people.

of child-specific services, such as immunization and growth monitoring, increased from 10.4 percent to 24.2 percent. These benefits accrued to the marginalized social groups, yet their outreach to the poorest of the poor lags behind yet. Similarly, there has been a substantial variation in the coverage of ICDS across states, with the poorer states who need early life assistance the most, lagging behind.

However, ICDS has improved overall in its performance, leading to substantial short-term and long-term developmental gains to welfare outcomes, such as improved nutrition, educational attainments, and cognitive ability. Using the 2005–2006 NFHS data, (Kandpal 2011) found that the presence of an ICDS center in a village improved the height-for-age z-score for children by 5 percent (4 and 6 per cent for boys and girls, respectively).[22] Similarly, (Jain 2015) found that girls (0–2 years) who received food from the ICDS grew up to be 1.2 cm taller and 0.48 standard deviation less likely to be stunted (higher height-for-age), compared to those who did not have access to ICDS (Dhamija and Sen 2020) extended the analysis further using the second round of the India Human Development Survey (IHDS), to find that the positive effects of ICDS on nutrition persists into later ages. For example, the Andhra Pradesh Child and Parents Study (APCAPS) conducted in one of the districts found that children exposed to ICDS in early life, when observed in their teenage (13–18 years) were likely to be 1.4 cm taller and of better cardiovascular health (Kinra et al. 2011; Kulkarni et al. 2014; Nandi et al. 2015).

While these studies might look at the short-term *prevention* or *promotional* aspects of the ICDS, others have looked at its *transformational* aspects, which are greater educational outcomes or cognitive abilities for children who benefited from ICDS. When adults within the ages of 20–25 years are observed, those born in villages that had ICDS were 9 and 11 percent more likely to complete secondary and graduate-level education, respectively (Nandi et al. 2018). The combination of services at the ICDS centers—food supplementation, immunizations, and health interventions—also leads to an improvement in the cognitive abilities of children benefiting from these services (Vikram and Chindarkar 2020). The beneficiary children were more likely to be employed or enrolled

[22] A previous evaluation of ICDS by (Lokshin et al. 2005) found no significant impact on children's nutrition. Positive effects of the ICDS, therefore, are a result of the improvements in its functioning, of late.

in higher education, suggesting long-term benefits (Nandi et al. 2018). A more detailed, subsequent study reiterated the educational benefits of ICDS—for men 15–54 years and women 15–49 years, exposure to a ICDS center during the first three years of their lives led to an increase 0.1–0.3 grades of schooling (Nandi et al. 2019). The early life benefit accrued more to women of comparable ages. ICDS not only improved the cognitive abilities of children, with improvements in reading and math scores, but also improved health and employment outcomes as adults, including higher wages (Ravindran 2018). ICDS has also led to positive spillovers in the family. Older siblings (6–14 year olds) of children, who benefited from ICDS, are more likely to enroll and complete primary schooling, especially their sisters (Jain 2018).[23] The educational benefits of ICDS are particularly important, not only for the individual's long-term welfare but also for India's human capital, in general. School drop-out rates, though on the increase, especially among women, remain a particularly important challenge. The draft National Educational Policy (NEP), therefore, recognizes the critical role of early childhood care and education.

Yet, despite its success, ICDS only addresses one of the contributors to malnutrition. ICDS focuses on the narrow *critical window* from pregnancy until the age of 6 years. While potential gains to child nutrition are most fecund during this period, malnourishment results from a number of other factors, such as poor diets in terms of calories and micronutrient content, water and sanitation facilities, or poor status of mother's health emanating from poverty and other associated factors. Most importantly, ICDS does not address the mortality risks that emanate from low levels of institutional birth delivery in the country.[24]

Encouraging Institutional Childbirth and Improving Maternal Health

Higher rates of pregnancy-related complications and maternal mortality are a common occurrence in developing countries, including India.

[23] However, some concerns around the positive net effects of ICDS have been the negative spillovers on siblings, as parents reallocated their investments away from other siblings (Ravindran 2018).

[24] Birth deliveries at home through poorly trained midwives have traditionally led to higher maternal and child mortality.

Recognizing this issue, a safe motherhood intervention scheme was introduced by the government called *Janani Suraksha Yojana* (JSY) with the *scope* of incentivizing access to institutional care during childbirth for the poor.[25] Since non-institutional childbirth is more common among the poor, JSY provides cash transfers to mothers in lieu of institutional delivery and post-delivery care. The impact of JSY has been encouraging. The incidence of institutional delivery in rural India has trebled from an abysmally low 18 percent of childbirths in 2005–2006 to 52 percent in 2015–2016. Evaluation of JSY found a significant impact on institutional delivery and antenatal care for both the newborn and the mother (Lim et al. 2010; Powell-Jackson et al. 2015). It has also led to a reduction in perinatal and neonatal deaths—progress on two of the most critical health indicators.

Another important aspect of India's maternal health status is the high rate of anemia among women. Because of high levels of poverty, many women continue to work late into their pregnancies or are unable to procure sufficient nutritious food, which affects not only their health but that of their unborn child. In cognizance of the in utero nutritional risks, the Government of India introduced a maternity benefits program, *Indira Gandhi Matritva Sahyog Yojana* (Indira Gandhi Maternity Support Scheme, IGMSY) in 2011 which was later renamed as *Pradhan Mantri Matru Vandana Yojana* (Prime Minister's Maternity Assistance Scheme, PMMVY) in 2017. PMMVY now is a part of the National Food Security Act, 2013 as part of its life-cycle focus. Under the PMMVY, a cash transfer of Rs. 6000 (USD 80) is provided (in three installments) to the mother, conditional on the registration of birth, antenatal check-up, and the appropriate vaccination of the child. Together with this central scheme, some of the states introduced their own maternity benefit programs, like *Mamata* in Odisha and *Kasturba Yojana* in Gujarat. Tamil Nadu, however, has had its own *Muthulakshmi Maternity Benefit Scheme* since 1987. Short-term evaluation of the nationwide

[25] JSY forms one of the initiatives under the National Rural Health Mission (NRHM), which was introduced in 2005. NRHM was aimed at integrating and improving the poor and fragmented health infrastructure in the most backward regions of the country. Under NRHM, many reforms were introduced with the aim of establishing an integrated but decentralized health delivery system. The idea was to create inter-sectoral convergence at all administrative and departmental levels to ensure a simultaneous attack on the main determinants of poor health outcomes in India—water, sanitation, education, nutrition, and social and gender parity.

expansion of PMMVY suggests modest effect. While it has led to greater access to the health system, immunization rates (especially among girls)—which was the *scope* of the scheme—did not have much effect on the long-term health outcomes of children, such as underweight, stunting, or anemia (von Haaren and Klonner 2021). The state-level schemes have higher payments and have been more effective in delivering benefits.

POSHAN Abhiyan or the National Nutrition Mission

Continuing its *focus* on mother-and-child nutrition, and the importance of early life intervention, the government launched the National Nutrition Mission (NNM) as the apex body in 2018, with the aim to "monitor, supervise, fix targets and guide the nutrition-related interventions across the Ministries," with the aim of reducing stunting, undernutrition, anemia, and underweight incidence at the annual rates of 2, 2, 3, and 2 percent, respectively. NNM was introduced with the idea of creating a synergy between the suite of schemes that sought to improve the nutritional status of children and pregnant and lactating women. It was realized that the schemes lack synergy with one another, despite having a common goal. NNM would, therefore, become an umbrella mission that worked toward such a convergence. The mission proposal aimed at several targets, including mapping these schemes, creating synergies across them, and using better means of monitoring the workers as well as the beneficiary performance of regular health measurements at the AWCs. It seeks to improve greater accountability of the AWCs and AWWs through regular social audits, setting up regular community meetings (*Jan Andolan*) and Nutrition Resource Centers, while also incentivizing the subnational governments to effectively work toward meeting the nutrition targets. The Nutrition Mission was later rechristened as the Prime Minister's Overarching Scheme or Holistic Nourishment (POSHAN).

Free School Meals Through the Midday Meal Scheme

Although early life interventions like ICDS and JSY *focus* on the critical window from pregnancy until the age of 6 years, school feeding programs have been employed to address nutritional needs of children in school. Once a child is beyond infancy, safety nets focused upon enabling human capital accumulation through incentivizing school enrollment and ensuring that pupils receive quality education can have long-term economic gains. With due recognition of the role of education, the Government of India launched the District Primary Education Programme (DPEP) in 1993–1994, which expanded public primary schools across the country. Later in 2001, primary education was declared "free and compulsory" to all children between the ages of 6 and 14. Immediately following the DPEP, the government launched the school meals program, the Mid-day Meal Scheme (MDMS), in a bid to encourage greater enrollment in primary schools.[26] MDMS is the largest school feeding program in the world for primary and upper primary schoolchildren and has led to substantial reduction in "classroom hunger." Currently, MDMS provides meals that contain 300 cal and 8–12 g of protein daily to all children who attend primary schools. However, it took a while for the MDMS to bring kids to school, which it eventually did leading to almost 100 percent primary school enrollment in India.[27] The program struggled with hot-cooked meals and could only obtain "cooked meals," and "dry ration" for distribution in the schools. Owing to pressures from the judicial system and civil society organizations, hot-cooked meals became mandatory, which brought in many students to attend classes.

There has been a substantial improvement in school enrollment with the institution of the MDMS. Even before school meals were made mandatory by the SC, they were shown to be particularly effective, especially for making education accessible to girls (Drèze and Khera 2009; Drèze and Kingdon 2001).

MDMS has led to a substantial increase in the nutrient intake of schoolgoing children, in terms of calories as well as dietary iron content,

[26] The name of MDMS has been changed to PM-POSHAN (*Pradhan Mantri Poshan Shakti Nirman*) Scheme, in the beginning of September 2021. We, however, continue to use the term MDMS for the school meals program to prevent confusion for the readers who have been more familiar with the earlier nomenclature.

[27] The *focus* on children and their ability to continue in school has been an important policy objective. Similarly, it is important to understand how the policymakers thought about it. One of the primary reasons why children drop out of school is the inability of parents to pay for the fees during times of adverse income shocks; another is when children work instead of attending school if the household needs more working hands. The Supreme Court (SC) of India, therefore, passed an order in 2004, directing all public schools in drought-affected areas to serve midday meals, even when schools are closed during regular vacations.

and the nutritional gains outweigh the costs of cooked meals (Afridi 2010). One might ask if the school lunches provided could be just substitutes for a similar meal at home, leading to little or no nutritional gains. However, Afridi (2010) found the opposite to be true. MDMS supplements the home-cooked meal at home, as the quantity of school meal is too small from the perspective of a household resource allocation.[28] MDMS has been particularly successful among poor households, prone to exogenous livelihood shocks. By acting as a transfer—of money through free schooling and nutrition through meals—MDMS has been able to arrest the nutritional poverty trap for farming households in times of drought. Child poverty is often due to adverse household shocks, which lead to lower resources affecting the schooling and nutrition of children. MDMS has acted as an important safety net for children's nutrition, especially in times of adverse weather shocks. Observing the same cohort of children at multiple points in time, (Singh et al. 2014) found that in drought, in which there is an expected height and weight loss of 0.77 and 0.44 standard deviations from average, MDMS could entirely correct for the losses. The gains from MDMS are not restricted to compensating for the likelihood of stunting or underweight among children when the household is affected by livelihood risks; the program also facilitates growth in heights and catch-up and remediation of nutritional deprivations, previously considered impossible at the first 2–3 years of age.

Once children can attend school and access nutrition there, intergenerational persistence of poverty could be further alleviated through improvements in cognitive ability of children. Long-term evaluation of the MDMS provides credible evidence for its continuation. Using the multi-year Annual Status of Education Report (ASER) data set on child learning outcomes, (Chakraborty and Jayaraman 2019) found that MDMS increases test scores by 18 and 9 percent, respectively, pertaining to reading and math ability for those exposed to 5 years of MDMS, compared to those with a single year of exposure.[29] The intergenerational *transformational* gains from MDMS have been realized through

[28] Afridi (2010) argued that the calorie content of the meal from the program was too small from the perspective of the average family's needs, with almost seven members (including four adults), to lead to resource redistribution within households.

[29] Based upon a field experiment, Afridi et al. (2019) arrive at the same finding. Children who benefited from the MDMS performed better on cognition tests by 13–16 percent, compared to those who did not.

greater nutritional support to girls who benefited from school meals. The exposure of schoolgirls to MDMS led to a reduction in malnutrition among their children, as it increased the girls' ability to learn, control their fertility decisions, and utilize the institutional health system when they reached maturity (Chakrabarti et al. 2021b). Nutritional supplementation through MDMS, therefore, remains a very useful source of long-term gains, but probably not sufficient for all children, especially those at the economic margins.

The Way Forward

Well-nourished and healthy mother and children are the key to development resilience as pathways to progress need to be unlocked early in life. India has a long way to go, both in improving the status of women in the society—which contributes to a large share of the developmental challenge—and reducing undernutrition among young children. Having said that, one must highlight the greater focus on these issues in recent years. Nutrition has emerged as a major policy *scope* which has led to an expansion of the various social safety nets *focused* on maternal and child health. The congratulatory aspect of these schemes—ICDS, MDMS, and JSY—is that they have the desired impacts when they are functioning well. An improvement in their performance, especially in recent years, has been instrumental in preventing and promoting human development outcomes in the short run. There is also evidence for their transformational roles in the long run. However, for a truly transformational impact, which ensures that the development process is resilient, these schemes need to function better through enhancement in the quality of their services and by building greater state capacity and generating a renewed political commitment to deliver and sustain these services *across* the country. Each of these schemes, given their individual *scope*, *focus*, and *form*, face a distinct challenge.

Integrated Child Development Scheme

The effectiveness of ICDS is hindered by poor institutional capacity of the government to provide the basic services and monitor child growth. Certain improvements in the functioning of ICDS could greatly reduce India's malnutrition problem. To begin with, *Anganwadis* need an infrastructural upgrade and expanded coverage. AWCs, the first centers of care and learning for children, are often not child-friendly. They function out of buildings with poorly built infrastructure—dilapidated, cramped, and rented buildings—with poor health and hygiene provisions. Out of almost 14,00,000 AWCs in the country, 3,62,940 do not have a toilet and 1,59,568 do not have drinking water facilities. The Union Budget of 2021 has recognized this deficit with an extra allocation for infrastructure upgrade, as part of the *Saksham Anganwadi* initiative. In terms of coverage, there is a still a long way to go. Only 53.6 percent of eligible children (0–6 years) and 54.7 of pregnant mothers availed benefits from the program.

A critical aspect of ICDS, especially in terms of its *scope*, is the nutritive value of food provided. Infants and young children need not only sufficient amounts of safe food but also high-quality nutrition, which ICDS, by focusing largely on the calorie content of the food, does not provide sufficiently yet. While ICDS is no longer just a calorie-assistance program, as envisaged in initial years, it still does not adequately address the most vexing issues of nutrition—the need for greater consumption of protein and micronutrients among children and mothers. Eggs, which could be a vital source of protein and almost all essential nutrients for children, are often missing from ICDS for political reasons in many states. Notions of ritual purity, which lead to the anti-egg sentiments, limit the possibilities ICDS has to offer in reducing undernutrition in the country.[30] It has also been observed that the take-home-ration (THR) component of ICDS leads to sharing of the food intended for lactating mothers.[31] As a result, many states are now trying to incorporate a One Full Meal (OFM) program as part of the ICDS (see, for example, Kachwaha et al. [2021]). OFM is akin to a midday meal for women. These meals comprise of proteins and micronutrients in the form of milk and green leafy vegetables, which are relatively expensive if purchased from the market.[32] Similar

[30] Only 9 states provide eggs as part of the ICDS. For details, see "In maps: India's vulnerable children are paying the price of upper-caste prejudice with their bodies": https://scroll.in/article/983137/indias-most-vulnerable-children-are-paying-the-price-of-upper-caste-prejudice-with-their-bodies. Accessed on July 7, 2022.

[31] Andhra Pradesh, Telangana, and Karnataka were the earliest states to incorporate spot feeding, or wet meals, as part of ICDS for mothers.

[32] There have also been debates around replacing the take home ration component of ICDS with cash transfers as it provides greater choice. For a detailed discussion, refer to Narayanan and Saha (2020) and Nair et al. (2021).

innovative initiatives that aim to address the various kinds of nutritional gaps in early life are key to the success of ICDS. Fortification of food with micronutrients is one such scheme, given the high incidence of micronutrient deficiencies in the population. While the government has issued advisories to the states to mandate the use of fortified wheat flour and edible oils in ICDS and MDMS, the adoption rates have been low.

Finally, the quality of services at ICDS depend significantly on the performance and motivation of the last-mile providers, that is, the AWWs. AWWs often complain of being overworked and underpaid. Duties and accountability of AWWs have increased substantially with the policy emphasis directed toward ICDS, as it has acquired multiple objectives, which go beyond its original conception as a source of take-home rations or daycare for children. AWWs are now expected to encourage vaccination among mothers and children and prepare meals for the children, in addition to administrative tasks and often home visits.[33] Greater duties, though, have not come with higher salaries. AWWs and their helpers (AWHs) are considered honorary workers with a monthly ***honorarium*** of Rs. 4500 and 2250 per month, respectively.[34] For AWWs, it amounts to US$2 per day for a full-time job, which is less than the minimum wage rate and with low levels of social security. Since work at an *Anganwadi* is considered as honorary service (for about 4 h per day), the legal wage rule does not apply. AWWs have regularly staged protests and organized strikes demanding higher wages, without much policy change.[35] While many state governments have provided greater monetary incentives to the AWWs, it is still too low to ensure they provide their services with full enthusiasm and efficiency.[36]

The neglect of the frontline workers addressing India's nutrition challenge poses a serious challenge in not only sustaining ICDS but also in

[33] Time use surveys of AWWs suggest that a significant portion of their time is spent on administrative duties, which undermines care for the children (Jain et al. 2020).

[34] There is an added component of performance-linked incentive under the *POSHAN Abhiyaan*. For details, refer to the 2019 government notification: https://pib.gov.in/PressReleasePage.aspx?PRID=1602394. Accessed January 26, 2022.

[35] See Krishnaprasad and Peer (2019).

[36] For instance, Karnataka has increased wages, but the AWWs are still unhappy on account of being overburdened with work and often receiving delayed payments. For a detailed field report, see: https://thewire.in/health/icds-anganwadi-workers-helpers-midday-meals-minimum-wage-protest.

undermining development resilience. Research has shown that financial incentives, such as fixed bonuses and performance pay, to the AWWs and adding more AWWs have long-term benefits for child outcomes.[37] AWWs are often demotivated as their aspirations of being teachers do not align with the beneficiary expectations, who want them to provide immunizations and food, rather than function as nutrition workers.[38] Delayed wage payments, lack of clarity in hiring, and corruption by their supervisors affect their job satisfaction (John et al. 2020). The other organizational challenge is to professionally train the AWWs with sufficient knowledge around health and nutrition for them to be the agents of transformation who could then bring about behavioral change in the community around maternal and childcare.

Given that ICDS involves continuous monitoring of children, it can only be assessed through regular check-ups on child growth (as measured through anthropometric indicators) and mother's health and immunization records. Recordkeeping and data management on a real-time basis form a key component of the success of ICDS. State capacity to maintain these records currently is low, with poor quality of data on children, mothers, and AWWs. Better recordkeeping would facilitate more robust empirical evaluation of the program, which requires fairly detailed longitudinal data on the households, particularly, for women and children, who received these benefits and their well-being—income, health, and nutrition. Such recordkeeping implies further time spent on it by AWWs, at the cost of time spent on caregiving and preschool education. Augmenting the state capacity at these local nutritional centers, through healthy and nutritive food, better infrastructure, better paid staff, and accountability, is therefore key to fulfilling the mission of ICDS.

Midday Meal Scheme

MDMS is doing reasonably well in terms of its reach. It is now a regular feature of all government schools in the county, spread throughout the country, with near-universal primary school enrollment—the *scope* of the

[37] See Ganimian et al. (2021) and Singh and Masters (2017) for a positive effect of AWW performance—as reflected in improved child nutrition—through experimental studies with added capacity and performance pay incentives, respectively.

[38] A smaller percentage of pregnant and lactating women seek health check-ups or health and nutrition education from the AWWs than receive supplementary food.

program. It has built in *prevention* and *promotional* aspects by encouraging children to attend school, addressing the issue of classroom hunger, and providing supplementary calories to poor children, so that they are not deprived of essential human capital inputs. Its *transformative* impact lies in engendering a virtuous cycle of improved health condition, higher labor productivity, and thereby, income gains, thereby building development resilience. Prioritizing not only education and nutrition, but also health through important messaging, could be key for MDMS in the future.

The provision of safe and nutritive meals is the first step in that direction. The most common complaint is often captured in newspaper headlines about reports of illnesses and even deaths due to contaminated food. Lack of basic cooking infrastructure at the schools, such as cooking sheds, refrigeration, drinking water, and essential hygiene practices make poor children vulnerable to stomach-related diseases and food poisoning. What also characterizes MDMS are the monotonous meals provided. Greater community participation that monitors the quality of schooling infrastructure and the nature of food provided should be encouraged, as it leads to a great accountability among the school administrators and teachers.[39] Further, sensitizing children early in life to eat healthily is key to future prosperity. School Nutrition (kitchen) gardens through MDMS, giving children a first-hand experience with nature, along with an awareness of potential micronutrient deficiencies, has been a step in the right direction. Even if at a fledgling stage, such innovations serve as the right example in setting the agenda or the scope of MDMS to evolving nutritional needs and challenges of overweight children. Another important innovation has been to provide iron and folic acid (IFA) supplementation through MDMS, but with little success.[40] Fortification of food through MDMS is another consideration, given that micronutrient deficiency seems to be a major component of the triple-burden of malnutrition in the country. Experimental case studies, such as the one from Bihar, has shown that introduction of doubly fortified salt as part of the midday meal

[39] Global evidence around increasing educational outcomes suggest the importance of community participation in improving school performance and teacher accountability (Glewwe and Muralidharan 2016).

[40] (Berry et al. 2020) found no effect on the hemoglobin levels in children who experienced breaks in supplementation, either due to inconsistent distribution of IFA tablets or the constraints of a school calendar, which limits its long-term impact.

preparation has led to a significant reduction in iron deficiency among children, along with higher test scores (Krämer et al. 2020).

Finally, MDMS can truly be used to bring about a *transformational* change when the required nutritional gains and learning outcomes are sufficiently high (Alderman and Bundy 2012). While the nutritional and health gains are connected through food, educational gains also rely on complementary essential schooling inputs like high-quality teachers and educational infrastructure. As more and more children, even among poorer but aspirational households, are now switching toward private schools, the policy must also start thinking about providing nutrition for schoolchildren who opt out of public schooling.

Janani Suraksha Yojana and Pradhan Mantri Matru Vandana Yojana

The *scope* of JSY is to encourage institutional childbirth. Empirical studies have highlighted its success as having been largely driven by greater usage of the primary health centers or community health centers. Since there is a great amount of subnational variation in health services, the impact of JSY on health outcomes has been concentrated in regions with better institutional capacity and implementation of the program (Carvalho and Rokicki 2019). JSY, in fact, performs worst in regions where mortality rates are the highest (Das et al. 2011).[41] In those regions, the program suffers from tardy and uneven implementation of the program, owing to corruption, inadequate quality, and substantial out-of-pocket expenditure on institutional delivery, which limits its success. The success of maternal cash entitlement depends upon the quality of maternity services and the referral system, which are of poor quality in the public sector. Emergency obstetric care in the public facilities, especially in the poorer region of the country has been the worst. As a result, the success in reducing maternal mortality has been four times faster in richer regions, compared to the poorest regions (Randive et al. 2014).[42]

[41] For instance, the infant mortality rate (IMR) in Kerala is similar to that of Mexico; in Madhya Pradesh, it is closer to that of Ethiopia.

[42] Through JSY, while financial incentives for institutional delivery have encouraged safer childbirth and reduced mortality rates, it might have unintended health effects with an increase in fertility, which could potentially undermine the objectives of the program.

PMMVY has had little success in improving health-seeking behavior by women, principally because of low administrative capacity and reluctance of local bureaucrats in improving service delivery (von Haaren and Klonner 2021; Puri 2021).[43] In addition to improving the delivery system, it has been restrictive in scope, with the maternity benefits applying *only* for the first living child and discriminating against those with more than one child. The cumbersome application process, which requires a long list of documents to be submitted, often hinders timely payments (Drèze et al. 2021). Maternity benefits, to be successful, in their objective need to expand their *focus* to all women, that is, universalization of the program—and for every child. Given that the amount is not much to the well-off, they are expected to opt out of the detailed paperwork needed to avail themselves of the benefits.

Synergy Across Departments and Schemes

Addressing the issue of mother-and-child nutrition needs a continuum of action along the life cycle. Different schemes, therefore, need to function in synergy, complementing each other, and filling in for various deprivations. The holistic program of *Poshan Abhiyan,* under the National Nutrition Mission was launched with the idea of creating a synergy between different schemes and departments toward a common goal of better nutrition. It aimed at a multi-ministerial convergence in order to monitor, supervise, set nutritional goals as targets, and implement related interventions. The idea of convergence, however, has been slow to percolate right to the local level where schemes are often implemented. Local officials and departments, in a decentralized system, have been struggling with their respective roles, adversely affecting the implementation. For example, action on early life nutrition principally relies upon the *Anganwadi* workers, their helpers, and the local public health delivery systems, which include the ASHAs (Accredited Social Health Activists) and Auxiliary Nurse Midwives (ANMs), as the principal drivers of better health information and service delivery. The success of maternal and child nutrition programs in states like Karnataka or Odisha are illustrative of how

[43] In Odisha, where the coverage of a similar scheme is much better—with greater awareness levels, beneficiary application rates, and received benefits—it has increased access to health care, health outcomes, and food security (Chakrabarti et al. 2021a; Raghunathan et al. 2017).

convergence across government departments and ministries—Women and Child Development (MoWCD), Health (DoH), Rural Development and Panchayati Raj (MoRD), and Food (MoF)—have been instrumental in ensuring supplies and services.[44] There is a lot to learn in other states as well when it comes to bridging the gap between interdepartmental synergies in action and effective local delivery.[45]

Finally, one must highlight the role of a robust healthcare system, from local public health centers to super-specialized hospitals, for all of these schemes to bring about a transformational change to human development. Globally, improvements in maternal and child health have come about from improvements in the health coverage structured around an array of schemes that constitute the health system (Bishai et al. 2016). For India, therefore, to surmount the challenge of intergenerational poverty in general and nutritional outcomes in particular—to facilitate a resilient development process—a robust health system is necessary in the first place.

References

Afridi, Farzana. 2010. "Child Welfare Programs and Child Nutrition: Evidence from a Mandated School Meal Program in India." *Journal of Development Economics* 92 (2): 152–65. https://doi.org/10.1016/j.jdeveco.2009.02.002.

Afridi, Farzana, Bidisha Barooah, and Rohini Somanathan. 2019. *Hunger and Performance in the Classroom*. 12627.

Aizer, A., and J. Currie. 2014. "The Intergenerational Transmission of Inequality: Maternal Disadvantage and Health at Birth." *Science* 344 (6186): 856–61. https://doi.org/10.1126/science.1251872.

Aizer, Anna, Shari Eli, Joseph Ferrie, and Adriana Lleras-Muney. 2016. "The Long-Run Impact of Cash Transfers to Poor Families." *American Economic Review* 106 (4): 935–71. https://doi.org/10.1257/aer.20140529.

[44] Practitioners, like Uma Mahadevan, report from their experiences on how effectiveness of these programs depend upon how the DoH responds to the demands of MoWCD for micronutrient supplements at the AWCs, in the case of OFM. See "Community Action, with a Focus on Women's Well-Being, Can Fight Malnutrition": https://indianexpress.com/article/opinion/columns/equal-wages-women-men-mgnrega-gender-equality-malnutrition-7132922/ Accessed on June 26, 2022.

[45] An internal review of the Poshan Abhiyan by the government accepts this underperformance and mentions that there are very few examples of effective and efficient convergence, in practice. For more details, see: http://www.niti.gov.in/sites/default/files/2020-10/AbhiyaanMonitoringReport.pdf.

Aizer, Anna, Hilary Hoynes, and Adriana Lleras-Muney. 2022. "Children and the US Social Safety Net: Balancing Disincentives for Adults and Benefits for Children." *Journal of Economic Perspectives* 36 (2): 149–74. https://doi.org/10.1257/jep.36.2.149.

Alderman, H., and D. Bundy. 2012. "School Feeding Programs and Development: Are We Framing the Question Correctly?" *The World Bank Research Observer* 27 (2): 204–21. https://doi.org/10.1093/wbro/lkr005.

Alderman, Harold, John Hoddinott, and Bill Kinsey. 2006. "Long Term Consequences of Early Childhood Malnutrition." *Oxford Economic Papers* 58 (3): 450–74.

Almond, Douglas, Janet Currie, and Valentina Duque. 2018. "Childhood Circumstances and Adult Outcomes: Act II." *Journal of Economic Literature* 56 (4): 1360–446. https://doi.org/10.1257/jel.20171164.

Azam, Mehtabul, and Geeta Gandhi Kingdon. 2013. "Are Girls the Fairer Sex in India? Revisiting Intra-Household Allocation of Education Expenditure." *World Development* 42: 143–64.

Bailey, M. J., H. W. Hoynes, M. Rossin-Slater, and R. Walker. 2020. *Is the Social Safety Net a Long-Term Investment? Large-Scale Evidence from the Food Stamps Program*. 26942.

Balarajan, Yarlini, and Michael R. Reich. 2016. "Political Economy of Child Nutrition Policy: A Qualitative Study of India's Integrated Child Development Services (ICDS) Scheme." *Food Policy* 62 (October 1975): 88–98. https://doi.org/10.1016/j.foodpol.2016.05.001.

Bardasi, Elena, and Gisela Garcia. 2014. *Social Safety Nets and Gender : Learning from Impact Evaluations and World Bank Projects*. Washington, DC: World Bank.

Barker, D. J. 1990. "The Fetal and Infant Origins of Adult Disease." *BMJ* 301 (6761): 1111. https://doi.org/10.1136/bmj.301.6761.1111.

Barrett, Christopher B., and Mark A. Constas. 2014. "Toward a Theory of Resilience for International Development Applications." *Proceedings of the National Academy of Sciences* 111 (40): 14625–30. https://doi.org/10.1073/pnas.1320880111.

Behrman, Jere R. 1988. "Intrahousehold Allocation of Nutrients in Rural India: Are Boys Favored? Do Parents Exhibit Inequality Aversion?" *Oxford Economic Papers* 40 (1): 32–54.

Behrman, Jere R. 1993. "The Economic Rationale for Investing in Nutrition in Developing Countries." *World Development* 21 (11): 1749–71. https://doi.org/10.1016/0305-750X(93)90081-J.

Berhane, Guush, John F. Hoddinott, and Neha Kumar. 2017. *The Impact of Ethiopia's Productive Safety Net Programme on the Nutritional Status of Children: 2008–2012*, vol. 1604. Intl Food Policy Res Inst.

Berry, James, Saurabh Mehta, Priya Mukherjee, Hannah Ruebeck, and Gauri Kartini Shastry. 2020. "Implementation and Effects of India's National

School-Based Iron Supplementation Program." *Journal of Development Economics* 144: 102428. https://doi.org/10.1016/j.jdeveco.2019.102428

Bhalotra, Sonia, Abhishek Chakravarty, and Selim Gulesci. 2020. "The Price of Gold: Dowry and Death in India." *Journal of Development Economics* 143: 102413. https://doi.org/10.1016/j.jdeveco.2019.102413.

Bishai, David M., Robert Cohen, Y. Natalia Alfonso, Taghreed Adam, Shyama Kuruvilla, and Julian Schweitzer. 2016. "Factors Contributing to Maternal and Child Mortality Reductions in 146 Low- and Middle-Income Countries between 1990 and 2010" edited by N. Speybroeck. *PLOS ONE* 11 (1): e0144908. https://doi.org/10.1371/journal.pone.0144908.

Black, Maureen M., Susan P. Walker, Lia C. H. Fernald, Christopher T. Andersen, Ann M. DiGirolamo, Chunling Lu, Dana C. McCoy, Günther Fink, Yusra R. Shawar, Jeremy Shiffman, Amanda E. Devercelli, Quentin T. Wodon, Emily Vargas-Barón, and Sally Grantham-McGregor. 2017. "Early Childhood Development Coming of Age: Science through the Life Course." *The Lancet* 389 (10064): 77–90. https://doi.org/10.1016/S0140-6736(16)31389-7

Bundy, Donald A. P., Nilanthi de Silva, Susan Horton, George C. Patton, Linda Schultz, Dean T. Jamison, Amina Abubakara, Amrita Ahuja, Harold Alderman, Nicolas Allen, Laura Appleby, Elisabetta Aurino, Peter Azzopardi, Sarah Baird, Louise Banham, Jere Behrman, Habib Benzian, Sonia Bhalotra, Zulfiqar Bhutta, Maureen Black, Paul Bloem, Chris Bonell, Mark Bradley, Sally Brinkman, Simon Brooker, Carmen Burbano, Nicolas Burnett, Tania Cernuschi, Sian Clarke, Carolyn Coffey, Peter Colenso, Kevin Croke, Amy Daniels, Elia De la Cruz, Damien de Walque, Anil Deolaikar, Lesley Drake, Lia Fernald, Meena Fernandes, Deepika Fernando, Günther Fink, Rae Galloway, Aulo Gelli, Andreas Georgiadis, Caroline Gitonga, Boitshepo Giyosa, Paul Glewwe, Joseph Gona Nzovu, Amber Gove, Natasha Graham, Brian Greenwood, Elena Grigorenko, Cai Heath, Joan Hamory Hicks, Melissa Hidrobo, Kenneth Hill, Tara Hill, T. Deirdre Hollingsworth, Elissa Kennedy, Imran Khan, Josephine Kiamba, Jane Kim, Michael Kremer, D. Scott LaMontagne, Zohra Lassi, Ramanan Laxminarayan, Jacqueline Mahon, Lu Mai, Sebastián Martínez, Sergio Meresman, Katherine A. Merseth, Edward Miguel, Arlene Mitchell, Sophie Mitra, Anoosh Moin, Ali Mokdad, Daniel Mont, Arindam Nandi, Joaniter Nankabirwa, Daniel Plaut, Elina Pradhan, Rachel Pullan, Nicola Reavley, Joan Santelli, Bachir Sarr, and Susan M. Sawyer. 2018. "Investment in Child and Adolescent Health and Development: Key Messages from Disease Control Priorities, 3rd Edition." *The Lancet* 391 (10121): 687–99. https://doi.org/10.1016/S0140-6736(17)32417-0

Carvalho, Natalie, and Slawa Rokicki. 2019. "The Impact of India's Janani Suraksha Yojana Conditional Cash Transfer Programme: A Replication Study." *The Journal of Development Studies* 55 (5): 989–1006. https://doi.org/10.1080/00220388.2018.1506578.

Case, Anne, Darren Lubotsky, and Christina Paxson. 2002. "Economic Status and Health in Childhood: The Origins of the Gradient." *American Economic Review* 92 (5): 1308–34. https://doi.org/10.1257/000282802762024520.

Casper, Lynne M., Sara S. McLanahan, and Irwin Garfinkel. 1994. "The Gender-Poverty Gap: What We Can Learn from Other Countries." *American Sociological Review* 59 (4): 594. https://doi.org/10.2307/2095933.

Chakrabarti, Suman, Anwesha Pan, and Parvati Singh. 2021a. "Maternal and Child Health Benefits of the Mamata Conditional Cash Transfer Program in Odisha, India." *The Journal of Nutrition*. https://doi.org/10.1093/jn/nxab129.

Chakrabarti, Suman, Samuel P. Scott, Harold Alderman, Purnima Menon, and Daniel O. Gilligan. 2021b. "Intergenerational Nutrition Benefits of India's National School Feeding Program." *Nature Communications* 12 (1): 4248. https://doi.org/10.1038/s41467-021-24433-w.

Chakraborty, Tanika, and Rajshri Jayaraman. 2019. "School Feeding and Learning Achievement: Evidence from India's Midday Meal Program." *Journal of Development Economics* 139: 249–65. https://doi.org/10.1016/j.jdeveco.2018.10.011.

Chen, Yuyu, and Hongbin Li. 2009. "Mother's Education and Child Health: Is There a Nurturing Effect?" *Journal of Health Economics* 28 (2): 413–26. https://doi.org/10.1016/j.jhealeco.2008.10.005.

Coffey, Diane. 2015. "Prepregnancy Body Mass and Weight Gain during Pregnancy in India and Sub-Saharan Africa." *Proceedings of the National Academy of Sciences* 112 (11): 3302–7. https://doi.org/10.1073/pnas.1416964112.

Currie, Janet. 2003. "U.S. Food and Nutrition Programs." In *Means-Tested Transfer Programs in the United States*, edited by R. A. Moffitt. Chicago: Chicago Press.

Currie, Janet, and Douglas Almond. 2011. "Human Capital Development before Age Five." In *Handbook of Labor Economics*, vol. 4b, 1315–1486. Amsterdam: Elsevier.

Das, Abhijit, Deepa Rao, and Amy Hagopian. 2011. "India's Janani Suraksha Yojana: Further Review Needed." *The Lancet* 377 (9762): 295–96. https://doi.org/10.1016/S0140-6736(11)60085-8.

Deaton, Angus, and Jean Drèze. 2009. "Food and Nutrition in India: Facts and Interpretations." *Economic and Political Weekly* 47 (7): 42–65. https://doi.org/10.2307/40278509.

Debnath, Sisir. 2015. "The Impact of Household Structure on Female Autonomy in Developing Countries." *The Journal of Development Studies* 51 (5): 485–502. https://doi.org/10.1080/00220388.2014.983909.

Dhamija, Gaurav, and Gitanjali Sen. 2020. "Lasting Impact of Early Life Interventions: Evidence from India's Integrated Child Development Services." *The Journal of Development Studies* 1–33. https://doi.org/10.1080/00220388.2020.1762861

Dhingra, Sunaina, and Prabhu L. Pingali. 2021. "Effects of Short Birth Spacing on Birth-Order Differences in Child Stunting: Evidence from India." *Proceedings of the National Academy of Sciences* 118 (8): e2017834118. https://doi.org/10.1073/pnas.2017834118

Drèze, J. P., and R. Khera. 2009. "Mid-Day Meals in Primary Schools." In *Elementary Education in India: Issues and Challenges*. New Delhi: Uppal.

Drèze, Jean, Reetika Khera, and Anmol Somanchi. 2021. "Maternity Entitlements in India: Women's Rights Derailed."

Drèze, Jean, and Geeta Gandhi Kingdon. 2001. "School Participation in Rural India." *Review of Development Economics* 5 (1): 1–24. https://doi.org/10.1111/1467-9361.00103

Drèze, Jean, and Mamta Murthi. 2001. "Fertility, Education, and Development: Evidence from India." *Population and Development Review* 27 (1): 33–63. https://doi.org/10.1111/j.1728-4457.2001.00033.x.

Duflo, Esther. 2012. "Women Empowerment and Economic Development." *Journal of Economic Literature* 50 (4): 1051–79. https://doi.org/10.1257/jel.50.4.1051.

Falcão, Ila Rocha, Rita de Cássia Ribeiro-Silva, Flávia Jôse Oliveira Alves, Naiá Ortelan, Natanael J. Silva, Rosemeire L. Fiaccone, Marcia Furquim de Almeida, Júlia M. Pescarini, Cinthia Soares Lisboa, Elzo Pereira Pinto Júnior, Enny S. Paixao, Andrea J. F. Ferreira, Camila Silveira Silva Teixeira, Aline dos Santos Rocha, Srinivasa Vittal Katikireddi, M. Sanni Ali, Ruth Dundas, Alastair Leyland, Laura C. Rodrigues, Maria Yury Ichihara, and Mauricio L. Barreto. 2022. "Evaluating the Effect of Bolsa Familia, Brazil's Conditional Cash Transfer Programme, on Maternal and Child Health: A Study Protocol." *PLOS ONE* 17 (5): e0268500. https://doi.org/10.1371/journal.pone.0268500

Farfán, Gabriela, María Eugenia Genoni, Luis Rubalcava, Graciela Teruel, and Duncan Thomas. 2022. "Scaling Up Oportunidades and Its Impact on Child Nutrition."

Ganimian, Alejandro, Karthik Muralidharan, and Christopher Walters. 2021. *Augmenting State Capacity for Child Development: Experimental Evidence from India*. Cambridge, MA: National Bureau of Economic Research. https://doi.org/10.3386/w28780.

Glewwe, P., and K. Muralidharan. 2016. "Improving Education Outcomes in Developing Countries," 653–743.

Grantham-McGregor, Sally, Yin Bun Cheung, Santiago Cueto, Paul Glewwe, Linda Richter, and Barbara Strupp. 2007. "Developmental Potential in the First 5 Years for Children in Developing Countries." *The Lancet* 369 (9555): 60–70. https://doi.org/10.1016/S0140-6736(07)60032-4.

von Haaren, Paula, and Stefan Klonner. 2021. "Lessons Learned? Intended and Unintended Effects of India's Second-Generation Maternal Cash Transfer Scheme." *Health Economics* 30 (10): 2468–86.

Headey, Derek, John Hoddinott, Disha Ali, Roman Tesfaye, and Mekdim Dereje. 2015. "The Other Asian Enigma: Explaining the Rapid Reduction of Undernutrition in Bangladesh." *World Development* 66: 749–61.

Heckert, Jessica, Deanna K. Olney, and Marie T. Ruel. 2019. "Is Women's Empowerment a Pathway to Improving Child Nutrition Outcomes in a Nutrition-Sensitive Agriculture Program?: Evidence from a Randomized Controlled Trial in Burkina Faso." *Social Science & Medicine* 233: 93–102. https://doi.org/10.1016/j.socscimed.2019.05.016.

Heckman, James J. 2006. "Skill Formation and the Economics of Investing in Disadvantaged Children." *Science* 312 (5782): 1900–2. https://doi.org/10.1126/science.1128898.

Hendren, Nathaniel, and Ben Sprung-Keyser. 2020. "A Unified Welfare Analysis of Government Policies." *The Quarterly Journal of Economics* 135 (3): 1209–1318. https://doi.org/10.1093/qje/qjaa006.

Hoddinott, John, John A. Maluccio, Jere R. Behrman, Rafael Flores, and Reynaldo Martorell. 2008. "Effect of a Nutrition Intervention during Early Childhood on Economic Productivity in Guatemalan Adults." *The Lancet* 371 (9610): 411–16.

Hoynes, Hilary, Diane Whitmore Schanzenbach, and Douglas Almond. 2016. "Long-Run Impacts of Childhood Access to the Safety Net." *American Economic Review* 106 (4): 903–34. https://doi.org/10.1257/aer.20130375.

Jain, Anoop, Dilys M. Walker, Rasmi Avula, Nadia Diamond-Smith, Lakshmi Gopalakrishnan, Purnima Menon, Sneha Nimmagadda, Sumeet R. Patil, and Lia C. H. Fernald. 2020. "Anganwadi Worker Time Use in Madhya Pradesh, India: A Cross-Sectional Study." *BMC Health Services Research* 20 (1): 1130.https://doi.org/10.1186/s12913-020-05857-4

Jain, Monica. 2015. "India's Struggle Against Malnutrition—Is the ICDS Program the Answer?" *World Development* 67: 72–89. https://doi.org/10.1016/j.worlddev.2014.10.006.

Jain, Monica. 2018. "A Vaccination for Education: Early Childhood Development Programme and the Education of Older Girls in Rural India." *The Journal of Development Studies* 54 (1): 153–73. https://doi.org/10.1080/00220388.2017.1288218.

Jayachandran, Seema, and Ilyana Kuziemko. 2011. "Why Do Mothers Breastfeed Girls Less than Boys? Evidence and Implications for Child Health in India." *The Quarterly Journal of Economics* 126 (3): 1485–538.

Jayachandran, Seema, and Rohini Pande. 2017. "Why Are Indian Children So Short? The Role of Birth Order and Son Preference." *American Economic Review* 107 (9): 2600–29. https://doi.org/10.1257/aer.20151282.

Jha, Prabhat, Rajesh Kumar, Priya Vasa, Neeraj Dhingra, Deva Thiruchelvam, and Rahim Moineddin. 2006. "Low Male-to-Female Sex Ratio of Children

Born in India: National Survey of 1·1 Million Households." *The Lancet* 367 (9506): 211–18. https://doi.org/10.1016/S0140-6736(06)67930-0.

John, Aparna, Nicholas Nisbett, Inka Barnett, Rasmi Avula, and Purnima Menon. 2020. "Factors Influencing the Performance of Community Health Workers: A Qualitative Study of Anganwadi Workers from Bihar, India" edited by A. (Neeloy) Alam. *PLOS ONE* 15(11): e0242460. https://doi.org/10.1371/journal.pone.0242460.

Kachwaha, Shivani, Rasmi Avula, Purnima Menon, Vani Sethi, William Joe, and Avula Laxmaiah. 2021. *Improving Maternal Nutrition in India through Integrated Hot-Cooked Meal Programs: A Review of Implementation Evidence.* New Delhi: International Food Policy Research Institute.

Kandpal, Eeshani. 2011. "Beyond Average Treatment Effects: Distribution of Child Nutrition Outcomes and Program Placement in India's ICDS." *World Development* 39 (8): 1410–21. https://doi.org/10.1016/j.worlddev.2010.12.013.

Kinra, Sanjay, KV Rameshwar Sarma, Michelle Hards, George Davey Smith, and Yoav Ben-Shlomo. 2011. "Is Relative Leg Length a Biomarker of Childhood Nutrition? Long-Term Follow-up of the Hyderabad Nutrition Trial." *International Journal of Epidemiology* 40 (4): 1022–29. https://doi.org/10.1093/ije/dyr074

Krämer, Marion, Santosh Kumar, and Sebastian Vollmer. 2020. "Improving Child Health and Cognition: Evidence from a School-Based Nutrition Intervention in India." *The Review of Economics and Statistics* 1–51. https://doi.org/10.1162/rest_a_00950

Krishnaprasad, Suchita, and Karan Peer. 2019. "An Ongoing Battle for Rights: The Case of Anganwadi Workers with Special Reference to Maharashtra." In *Globalization, Labour Market Institutions, Processes and Policies in India: Essays in Honour of Lalit K. Deshpande*, edited by K. R. Shyam Sundar, 341–67. Singapore: Springer.

Kulkarni, B., H. Kuper, K. V. Radhakrishna, A. P. Hills, N. M. Byrne, A. Taylor, R. Sullivan, L. Bowen, J. C. Wells, Y. Ben-Shlomo, G. Davey Smith, S. Ebrahim, and S. Kinra. 2014. "The Association of Early Life Supplemental Nutrition With Lean Body Mass and Grip Strength in Adulthood: Evidence From APCAPS." *American Journal of Epidemiology* 179 (6): 700–9. https://doi.org/10.1093/aje/kwt332.

Lake, Anthony, and Margaret Chan. 2015. "Putting Science into Practice for Early Child Development." *The Lancet* 385 (9980): 1816–17. https://doi.org/10.1016/S0140-6736(14)61680-9.

Lim, Stephen S., Lalit Dandona, Joseph A. Hoisington, Spencer L. James, Margaret C. Hogan, and Emmanuela Gakidou. 2010. "India's Janani Suraksha Yojana, a Conditional Cash Transfer Programme to Increase Births in

Health Facilities: An Impact Evaluation." *The Lancet* 375 (9730): 2009–23. https://doi.org/10.1016/S0140-6736(10)60744-1.

Lokshin, M., M. Das Gupta, M. Gragnolati, and O. Ivaschenko. 2005. "Improving Child Nutrition? The Integrated Child Development Services in India." *Development and Change* 36 (4): 613–40. https://doi.org/10.1111/j.0012-155X.2005.00427.x.

Machel, Graça. 2017. "Good Early Development—The Right of Every Child." *The Lancet* 389 (10064): 13–14. https://doi.org/10.1016/S0140-6736(16)31700-7.

Maitra, Pushkar, Anu Rammohan, Ranjan Ray, and Marie-Claire Robitaille. 2013. "Food Consumption Patterns and Malnourished Indian Children: Is There a Link?" *Food Policy* 38: 70–81. https://doi.org/10.1016/j.foodpol.2012.10.004.

Maluccio, John A., John Hoddinott, Jere R. Behrman, Reynaldo Martorell, Agnes R. Quisumbing, and Aryeh D. Stein. 2009. "The Impact of Improving Nutrition during Early Childhood on Education among Guatemalan Adults." *The Economic Journal* 119 (537): 734–63.

Mammen, Kristin, and Christina Paxson. 2000. "Women's Work and Economic Development." *Journal of Economic Perspectives* 14 (4): 141–64. https://doi.org/10.1257/jep.14.4.141.

Marshall, Alfred. 1980. *Principles of Economics [1930]*. London: Macmillan.

Nair, Divya, Aditi Gupta, Will Thompson, Signe Stroming, Rohan Raj, Kuldeep Shukla, and Debendra Nag. 2021. *Improving Implementation of the Take Home Ration Programme Under ICDS: Findings from Rajasthan and Jharkhand. Project Report*. New Delhi: IDinsight.

Nandi, Arindam, Ashvin Ashok, Sanjay Kinra, Jere R. Behrman, and Ramanan Laxminarayan. 2015. "Early Childhood Nutrition Is Positively Associated with Adolescent Educational Outcomes: Evidence from the Andhra Pradesh Child and Parents Study (APCAPS)." *The Journal of Nutrition* 146 (4): 806–13. https://doi.org/10.3945/jn.115.223198.

Nandi, Arindam, Jere R. Behrman, Sanjay Kinra, and Ramanan Laxminarayan. 2018. "Early-Life Nutrition Is Associated Positively with Schooling and Labor Market Outcomes and Negatively with Marriage Rates at Age 20–25 Years: Evidence from the Andhra Pradesh Children and Parents Study (APCAPS) in India." *The Journal of Nutrition* 148 (1): 140–46. https://doi.org/10.1093/jn/nxx012.

Nandi, Arindam, Jere R. Behrman, and Ramanan Laxminarayan. 2019. "The Impact of a National Early Childhood Development Program on Future Schooling Attainment: Evidence from ICDS in India." *Economic Development and Cultural Change* 703078. https://doi.org/10.1086/703078

Narayanan, Sudha, and Shree Saha. 2020. *Take Home Rations (THR) and Cash Transfers for Maternal and Child Nutrition: A Synthesis of Evidence in India.* 2020–039.

Pande, Rohini P. 2003. "Selective Gender Differences in Childhood Nutrition and Immunization in Rural India: The Role of Siblings." *Demography* 40 (3): 395–418. https://doi.org/10.1353/dem.2003.0029

Powell-Jackson, Timothy, Sumit Mazumdar, and Anne Mills. 2015. "Financial Incentives in Health: New Evidence from India's Janani Suraksha Yojana." *Journal of Health Economics* 43: 154–69. https://doi.org/10.1016/j.jhealeco.2015.07.001.

Prentice, A.M., Ward, K.A., Goldberg, G.R., Jarjou, L.M., Moore, S.E., Fulford, A.J. and Prentice, A. 2013. "Critical windows for nutritional interventions against stunting." *The American of Clinical Nutrition* 97 (5): 911–918.

Puri, Raghav. 2021. "Can Conditional Cash Transfers Improve Maternal and Child Health? Evidence from India's Maternity Benefit Program."

Raghunathan, Kalyani, Suman Chakrabarti, Rasmi Avula, and Sunny S. Kim. 2017. "Can Conditional Cash Transfers Improve the Uptake of Nutrition Interventions and Household Food Security? Evidence from Odisha's Mamata Scheme" edited by S. Horton. *PLOS ONE* 12 (12): e0188952. https://doi.org/10.1371/journal.pone.0188952.

Randive, Bharat, Miguel San Sebastian, Ayesha De Costa, and Lars Lindholm. 2014. "Inequalities in Institutional Delivery Uptake and Maternal Mortality Reduction in the Context of Cash Incentive Program, Janani Suraksha Yojana: Results from Nine States in India." *Social Science & Medicine* 123: 1–6. https://doi.org/10.1016/j.socscimed.2014.10.042.

Ravindran, Saravana. 2018. *Parental Investments and Early Childhood Development: Short and Long Run Evidence from India.*

Rosenzweig, Mark R., and T. Paul Schultz. 1982. "Market Opportunities, Genetic Endowments, and Intrafamily Resource Distribution: Child Survival in Rural India." *The American Economic Review* 72 (4): 803–15.

Sen, Amartya. 1992. "Missing Women." *BMJ: British Medical Journal* 304 (6827): 587.

Sen, Amartya. 2003. "Missing Women—Revisited." *BMJ* 327 (7427): 1297–98.

Shonkoff, J.P., Radner, J.M. and Foote, N. 2017. "Expanding the evidence base to drive more productive early childhood investment." *The Lancet* 389 (10064): 14–16.

Singh, Abhijeet, Albert Park, and Stefan Dercon. 2014. "School Meals as a Safety Net: An Evaluation of the Midday Meal Scheme in India." *Economic Development and Cultural Change* 62 (2): 275–306. https://doi.org/10.1086/674097.

Singh, Prakarsh, and William A. Masters. 2017. "Impact of Caregiver Incentives on Child Health: Evidence from an Experiment with Anganwadi Workers in

India." *Journal of Health Economics* 55: 219–31. https://doi.org/10.1016/j.jhealeco.2017.07.005.

Spears, Dean. 2013. *How Much International Variation in Child Height Can Sanitation Explain?* The World Bank.

Spears, Dean. 2020. "Exposure to Open Defecation Can Account for the Indian Enigma of Child Height." *Journal of Development Economics* 146: 102277. https://doi.org/10.1016/j.jdeveco.2018.08.003.

Ramalingaswami, V., U. Jonsson, and J. Rohde. 1997. "Malnutrition: A South Asian Enigma." In *Malnutrition in South Asia: A Regional Profile*. https://www.popline.org/node/274083.

Vikram, Kriti, and Namrata Chindarkar. 2020. "Bridging the Gaps in Cognitive Achievement in India: The Crucial Role of the Integrated Child Development Services in Early Childhood." *World Development* 127: 104697. https://doi.org/10.1016/j.worlddev.2019.104697.

Webb, Patrick, Gunhild Anker Stordalen, Sudhvir Singh, Ramani Wijesinha-Bettoni, Prakash Shetty, and Anna Lartey. 2018. "Hunger and Malnutrition in the 21st Century." *BMJ* k2238. https://doi.org/10.1136/bmj.k2238.

Wüst, Miriam. 2022. "Universal Early-Life Health Policies in the Nordic Countries." *Journal of Economic Perspectives* 36 (2): 175–98. https://doi.org/10.1257/jep.36.2.175.

CHAPTER 7

Public Health Insurance: Reducing Poverty or Access to Equitable Health Care?

Introduction

While traditional forms of social safety nets work with the *scope* of assisting people in getting out of poverty, a certain set of people are still falling into poverty. Health shocks or medical expenditures—ubiquitous with improvement in life expectancy and rise in the incidence of noncommunicable diseases (NCDs)—are the predominant causes of descents into poverty. Health shocks are different from other economic shocks. Not only is ill health likely to befall upon the poor, but the idiosyncratic nature of the shocks also triggers multiple coping strategies, which in the absence of affordable health care infrastructure relegates even the non-poor into poverty. Once poor, the climb out of poverty becomes difficult because the health shocks not only cause an expenditure loss in the short run, but may also amount to loss of household assets, employability, and therefore, the ability to accumulate productive assets in the future. Most vulnerable households are, therefore "one illness away" from falling into poverty.[1]

[1] Krishna (2010) provided a seminal account of the drivers and consequences of health-induced descent into poverty. To understand the effects of illness on household consumption, income, and wages, please refer to Kochar (1995), Gertler and Gruber (2002), and Wagstaff (2007). Further, Wagstaff and Lindelow (2014) described how the adaptability to or the impacts of a health shock are distributed along initial endowments of wealth and income.

A. Rahman and P. Pingali, *The Future of India's Social Safety Nets*, Palgrave Studies in Agricultural Economics and Food Policy, https://doi.org/10.1007/978-3-031-50747-2_7

A North Indian farmer, Heera Gujar narrated his account of his descent into poverty, in Anirudh Krishna's (2010) seminal book, *One Illness Away: Why People Become Poor and How They Escape Poverty.*

> The bad days began when my father fell ill about 18 years ago. They say he was stricken by TB [tuberculosis]. We took him several times to the district hospital, about 35 kilometers away. Each time we spent a considerable amount of money. We must have spent close to 25,000 rupees on his treatment, but to no avail. When my father died, we performed the customary death feast, spending another 10,000 rupees. We sold our cattle, and we also had to take out some loans.
>
> We worked harder in order to repay these debts. Then, about 10 years ago, my wife fell seriously ill, and she has still not recovered. We borrowed more money to pay for her medical treatments. More than 20,000 rupees were spent for this purpose. It became hard to keep up with our debts. Somehow, we could make do for another two or three years. Then, the rains failed for three years in a row, and that was the end of the road for us. We sold our land.
>
> Now, my sons and I work as casual labor, earning whatever we can from one day to the next. On some days, we find work. On other days, there is nothing.

Heera Gujar's misfortunes are not isolated occurrences. About a fifth of the Indian population face health shocks that could potentially be impoverishing, with 4% of them (55 million people) becoming poor because of catastrophic expenditures associated with the health shocks.[2] A resilient development process calls for not only pulling people out of poverty but instituting effective safeguards or insurance against potential descent into poverty. Residents of developed countries benefit from well-developed financial markets, and health insurance with a monthly premium is an important part of employment benefits. For the poor and those living in less developed financial markets, health insurance premiums are the last form of investment for which households' budget. Even when they do, precautionary savings could reduce investments in capital accumulation, inhibiting development resilience. As a result, designing subsidized

[2] See Selvaraj et al. (2018).

health care programs is becoming a priority of social policy in low- and middle-income countries (LMICs).[3]

Economic benefits and the social value of health insurance are, therefore, vast. Household welfare responds to economic fluctuations. Poor people, devoid of secure paychecks, face instability based on the low level of income they earn. The insurance against such risks is provided through community, family, or the state. The poor also live in impoverished communities and families. They live in places where either credit markets are absent, or they are not considered "safe" borrowers by the lending institutions. In the wake of an adverse shock, the economic conditions of the poor are worsened, so that they can resort neither to their family nor to financial institutions, thereby inhibiting their ability to accumulate assets and lift themselves out of poverty. As the earlier example of Heera Gujar reflects, even the assets of the non-poor get eroded, leading to poverty if the exogenous shock is large enough. Health shocks, being large enough, are therefore the leading cause of descent into poverty or being stuck in poverty traps. Health insurance, by covering for unanticipated expenditures, provides a "safety net" against a potential decline in income and earning capacity. Such social insurance, provided to those in the formal economy through employer or self-contributory investments, is absent for the poor and vulnerable. Publicly subsidized health insurance, therefore, has emerged globally as a key strategy against catastrophic health expenditure.

In the Indian social policy dialogue, the importance of publicly provided health insurance has risen considerably, which reflects a shift in the *scope* of social welfare programs from addressing symptoms of poverty toward focus on its immediate causes. Such a change has been correlated with the higher burden of diseases, rise in private health care services that are expensive, and a greater share of informal workers with

[3] Examples include *Regimen Subsidiado* (SR) in Columbia (introduced in 1993), *Seguro Popular de Salud* in Mexico (introduced in 2005), National Health Insurance Scheme (NHIS) in Ghana (2004), Community Based Health Insurance in Rwanda (*Mutuelle*, 1999), *Seguro Facultativo de Salud* in Nicaragua (introduced in 2007), and *Jaminan Kesehatan Nasional* (JKN) in Indonesia (2014), among others. A systematic review of the impact of these insurance programs is provided in Acharya et al. (2013) and Erlangga et al. (2019).

no recourse to employment-based social security.[4] The idea of unorganized labor without any form of social assistance, in the wake of a health shock, inspired the Indian Prime Minister Manmohan Singh to launch a national health insurance scheme, *Rashtriya Swasthya Bima Yojana* (National Health Insurance Scheme, RSBY), focused on the poor in 2008. In his 2005 speech, marking the Golden Jubilee of the All-India Institute of Medical Sciences (AIIMS), he is reported to have said, "We recognise health as an inalienable human right that every individual can justly claim. So long as wide health inequalities exist in our country and access to essential health care is not universally assured, we would fall short in both economic planning and in our moral obligation to all citizens."[5] The emphasis on universal assurance of health care, being a "moral obligation" of the state toward citizens, echoed other changes in the social policy—right to work and food, for instance, around the same time. RSBY, therefore, marked a major paradigm shift in social protection policy in the country: from *social assistance* to *social insurance*.

RSBY subsequently was rechristened as *Pradhan Mantri Jan Arogya Yojana* (Prime Minister's Healthy Living Scheme, PM-JAY) in 2018, as a more expansive, publicly funded health insurance program with the *scope* of providing secondary and tertiary care hospitalization health care coverage up to Rs. 5 lakhs (~US$6,500) per household annually to over 107.4 million poor and vulnerable families, which would benefit the bottom 40% of the Indian population (500 million people). At the time

[4] Existing models of financial protection against health shocks included the Employees' State Insurance Scheme (ESIS) and the Central Government Health Scheme (CGHS), but the focus of these schemes was blue-collar employees, working in registered firms, and government employees, respectively. Under ESIS, blue-collar workers (subject to a monthly income ceiling) who are employed in the private sector can seek free treatment in empaneled hospitals. The contributions to ESIS are made by the employer, and some nominal premium by the employee. The benefits cover the employee's entire family. CGHS is a network of health care facilities, which provide insurance against health-related expenses, only for the central government. Similarly, public sector employees in railways, defense services, and others have special provisions of financial protection against health shocks through their own dispensaries/hospitals, often within the residential premises/township allocated for them, or receive reimbursements of claims through their employers. Together, these employees comprise a very small section of the working population, exposing a large share of the individuals to health-related risks. For details, refer to Ellis et al. (2000).

[5] Speech by Prime Minister Manmohan Singh at AIIMS, October 2005.

of this announcement, 80% of the population did not have health insurance. In terms of the sheer number of targeted beneficiaries, PM-JAY is the world's largest public health insurance scheme. PM-JAY forms a key component of the larger *Ayushman Bharat*, or the National Health Protection Scheme (NHPS)—an expansion in the primary health care centers to provide maternal and child health services, cure NCDs, and distribute free essential drugs and diagnostic services—with the aim of achieving Universal Health Coverage (UHC).

Although the expansion in demand-driven health insurance schemes is laudable, challenges to the promise of UHC abound. Health care systems are broken. Less than two years after PM-JAY was rolled out, as COVID-19 wreaked havoc in the country, the fragility of health care system in the country was laid bare.[6] Those who could afford the costs struggled to find testing centers, doctors, hospital beds, emergency medicines, and oxygen; the poor were left to their own devices. The pandemic aside, the surging NCD epidemic—cardiovascular disease, high blood pressure, various kinds of cancer, chronic respiratory diseases, diabetes, and mental health, mostly driven by lack of attention to preventive care—has escalated medical costs and impoverishment.[7] The largest share of expenditures for NCD treatment is on medicine and diagnostic tests, which are not covered under any form of public health insurance program.[8]

In such a context, where health infrastructure is brittle and public health insurance still in its infancy, how much can a public health insurance like PM-JAY act as a source of *resilience*: to stem the flow of households into poverty, allowing them to bounce back, and to increase future well-being? Although the short-run answer to this question depends on how well the government is able to iron out the logistics of implementation and program delivery of the massive program, its long-term assessment would be based on whether PM-JAY can effectively create an equitable health system for the poor and improve overall health.

[6] It has been estimated that around 3.1–3.4 million people died in India because of COVID-19 between June 1, 2020, and July 1, 2021 (Jha et al. 2022).

[7] Predominantly three kinds of NCDs—cardiovascular diseases, respiratory diseases, and diabetes—are a cause of premature mortality for around 4 million Indians annually (Arokiasamy 2018).

[8] Medicines comprise about 40% of the treatment, followed by expenditures on diagnostic tests (15%) and transportation costs (Behera and Pradhan 2021).

Privatized Health Expenditure, Despite Public Health Infrastructure

Around 55 million Indians (4% of households) are pushed into poverty every year because of high out-of-pocket (OOP) expenditures on health.[9] For those who are already poor, health shocks become a source of further destitution.[10] These figures are astonishingly high for a country that boasts of one of the largest networks of a publicly run free health care system.[11] The devil, as the saying goes, lies in the detail. Despite the expansive public health infrastructure, a greater share of Indian households relies on private providers for treatment, which are often expensive. The most recent estimates by the National Sample Survey Organization (NSSO) suggest that 55% of Indians received treatment in private hospitals in 2017–2018. Treatment in private facilities costs six times more than in public ones. Households—poor and non-poor, without financial protection through health insurance against such expenses—are at risk for catastrophic expenses.

Low Public Investment in Health

Health is among the primary responsibilities of government.[12] However, there are different models of health care systems across the world. For example, the United Kingdom provides free health care through the government-run National Health Service (NHS), while in Canada, health care is provided by private sector, but the government finances health insurance premiums for all. France, Italy, Norway, and Sweden have similar models to the United Kingdom, in which private health insurance to cover additional expenses is optional. In some other European countries, like Switzerland and the Netherlands, health insurance is provided

[9] See Selvaraj et al. (2018).

[10] Refer to van Doorslaer et al. (2006) for multi-country findings on how health care payments increase the poverty gap ratio.

[11] While treatments in government hospitals are free, patients do have out-of-pocket expenditures on user fees, medicines, diagnostic tests, and other supplies.

[12] During the First World Health Assembly, in 1948, which met to adopt a constitution for the World Health Organization (WHO), it stressed the role of the state in health care provisions and mentioned, "Governments have a responsibility for the health of their people which can be fulfilled only by the provision of adequate health and social measures."

exclusively by private providers, but the insurance premiums are subsidized by the government. State-financed *Medicaid* for the poor, *Medicare* for elderly provide, along with employer-provided or personal health insurance is used to pay for health care (privately provided) in the United States. Overall, richer countries spend a substantially higher amount of their GDP on health and attain better health outcomes. Residents in low-income countries, with lower public spending on health, suffer from the risks of catastrophic and impoverishing health expenditures.[13] As a result, there is a negative association between total health expenditures and impoverishment because of health shocks (Wagstaff et al. 2018a, b).

India's public expenditures on health remain abysmally low—around 1% of GDP—despite a significant rise in overall income in the country over the last two decades. These figures pale in comparison with other LMICs, which spend almost twice the share (Panel A, Fig. 7.1). As a result of the low public investment on health, OOP expenditure on health is high. Even among countries with similar levels of economic development, India's OOP remains at a much higher level, at around 60% of the total health expenditure (Panel B, Fig. 7.1). For instance, Ghana and Nicaragua, with well-developed public health insurance, incur substantially lower OOP expenditures.

Inefficient Supply-Driven Public Health Care Infrastructure

The Indian health system is a hybrid of public and private services, with the former responsible for affordable health care for the poor.[14] The public health care system follows a three-tiered structure. Free public health centers (PHCs) and their subsidiaries are the primary source of care, with community health centers (CHCs) at the sub-district level providing the second layer of health care services. Hospitals and medical colleges provide the tertiary form of care at the district level. At the time of its design—under the leadership of Sir J. W. Bhore, who headed the first Health Survey and Development Committee set up by the British Government in 1943—India's public health infrastructure was envisaged

[13] While there is variation in its definition, WHO classifies health expenditure as catastrophic when it equals or exceeds 40% of a household's capacity to pay, that is, the surplus income or expenditure available after meeting the basic needs.

[14] For a typology of public–private service-dominated health care systems in low-income countries, refer to Mackintosh et al. (2016).

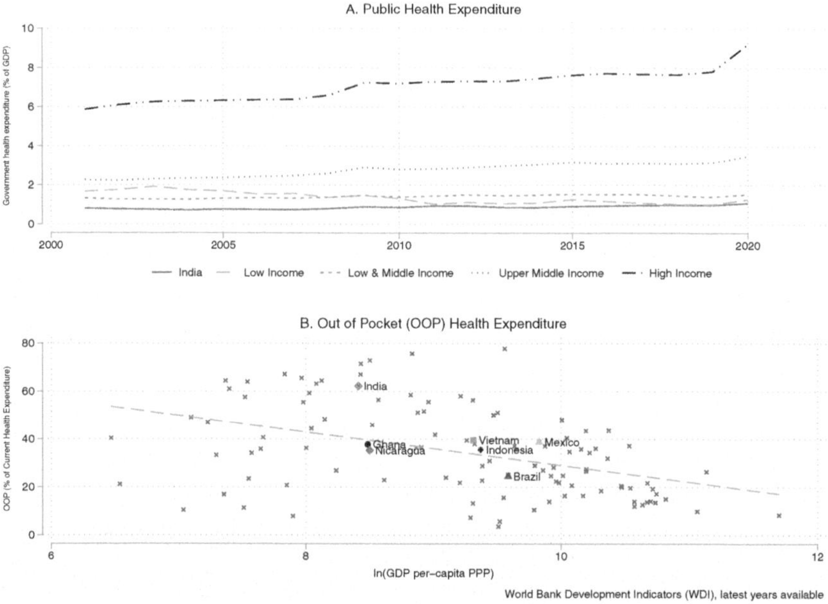

Fig. 7.1 Patterns of health expenditure—public and OOP—across countries (*Source* World Bank Indicators [WDI]. https://data.worldbank.org/indicator)

along similar lines as the United Kingdom's National Health Service. As of March 31, 2020, it consists of 810 district hospitals, 1,193 subdivisional hospitals, 5,649 CHCs, 30,813 PHCs, and 157,921 subcenters spread across the health care; however, it has failed to deliver effectively on the promise of affordability, equity, and quality (Balarajan et al. 2011). Health care is a classic case of "government failure" in most parts of the country, marred by high rates of absenteeism, lack of professionalism, and poor quality of services, which not only exacerbate the cost of health care but also reduce satisfaction with public services in general (Hammer et al. 2007). This has led to the gradual expansion of private health care providers—heterogeneous in quality and qualification—which are generally more competent and responsive to patient needs (Das and Hammer 2005; Das et al. 2016). Poorer regions of the country fare worse in both the quantity and quality of public health care, leading to higher cost of care and potentially greater health-induced impoverishment (Das et al. 2020).

The early emphasis on publicly owned health care infrastructure was motivated by the idea of curing the most important health issue of that time—child and maternal mortality. As the nature of the disease burden has moved toward NCDs from infectious ones, the public health care system's response has been slow, except for highly specialized health facilities. However, there is a continued effort to expand the public health system in the form of the National Health Mission (NHM), which aims to achieve "universal access to equitable, affordable and quality health care services that are accountable and responsive to people's needs."[15] NHM has specifically focused on reproductive, maternal, neonatal, child, and adolescent health (RMNCH+A), along with the spread of communicable and noncommunicable diseases. Among its stated goals, NHM seeks to "reduce household out-of-pocket expenditure on total health care expenditure." The idea behind NHM is to improve the existing health system—improved physical infrastructure, greater availability, professional upgrading of human resources, greater supply of doctors, better management of the system, encouragement of community participation, and use of information technology for tracking care performance. It further created a new cadre of community health care workers in rural areas—Accredited Social Health Workers (ASHAs)—female residents who are paid an honorarium and some task-based incentives to raise community awareness about health and its social determinants and facilitate access to health services—as the interface between the community and the public health system.[16] The National Health Policy 2017 further highlighted the role of government in "shaping health systems in all its dimensions—investments in health, organization of health care services, prevention of diseases and promotion of good health through cross sectoral actions, access to technologies, developing human resources, encouraging medical

[15] NHM subsumed the National Rural Health Mission (NRHM, launched in 2005) and the National Urban Health Mission (NUHM, launched in 2013). https://nhm.gov.in.

[16] According to the National Health Mission (NHM) guidelines, any "woman resident of the village—married/widow/divorced, and preferably in the age group of 25 to 45 years... with formal education up to eighth class" is eligible to work as an ASHA worker. Together, with the mandated auxiliary nurse midwifes (ANMs) at the subcenter of each PHC, and the Anganwadi Workers (AWWs) at ICDS centers, ASHA workers provide the first point of contact for the community to avail itself of health services. Since most of such services are focused on mother and child nutrition, women are responsible for these jobs.

pluralism, building knowledge base, developing better financial protection strategies, strengthening regulation and health assurance" (GoI 2017, p. 1). Corruption in NHM is, however, rife and its focus primarily on maternal and child health services does not yet provide the necessary financial protection against much of the OOP health care expenses.[17]

OOP Health Expenditure and Its Financing

Poor quality of public health infrastructure and high costs of health care in private facilities escalate health-related OOP expenditure, in the absence of adequate financial protection such as insurance against health shocks. Before PM-JAY was launched, only 14.1 and 19.1% of the rural and urban populations, respectively, reported having any form of health expenditure coverage (Panel A, Fig. 7.2). Insurance coverage is particularly low for the poor; individuals in the bottom expenditure quintiles had lower coverage. Health insurance in the rural areas is largely dominated by RSBY and other state-level initiatives.[18] This is true in urban areas that are dominated by informal employment as well. Only 1% of the rural population and 6% of the urban population reported having an employment-based insurance to cover health-related expenses (Panel B, Fig. 7.2). Poor financial protection against health shocks leads to significant OOP expenditure because around 60% of treatment takes place in the private sector. For those seeking health care in the public system, expenses of medicines comprise the largest share of expenditures (Panel C, Fig. 7.2). Further additional expenses add to OOP in private health facilities, which are financed largely through savings or borrowings that can often be catastrophic to the poor (Panel D, Fig. 7.2).

Lack of financial protection against health shocks is detrimental for household welfare in the anticipation (*ex ante*) as well in the coping strategy adopted (*ex post*). Devoid of access to quality health care infrastructure and missing markets for health insurance, households tend to "save for the rainy day" against the expectations of future illness or related health shocks. These precautionary savings—among low resource-endowed households—affect both their short- and long-term investment choices, with negative consequences for investments in productive

[17] See Shukla (2012) for a discussion of corruption in the NRHM.

[18] We will discuss the state-level health insurance programs later in this chapter.

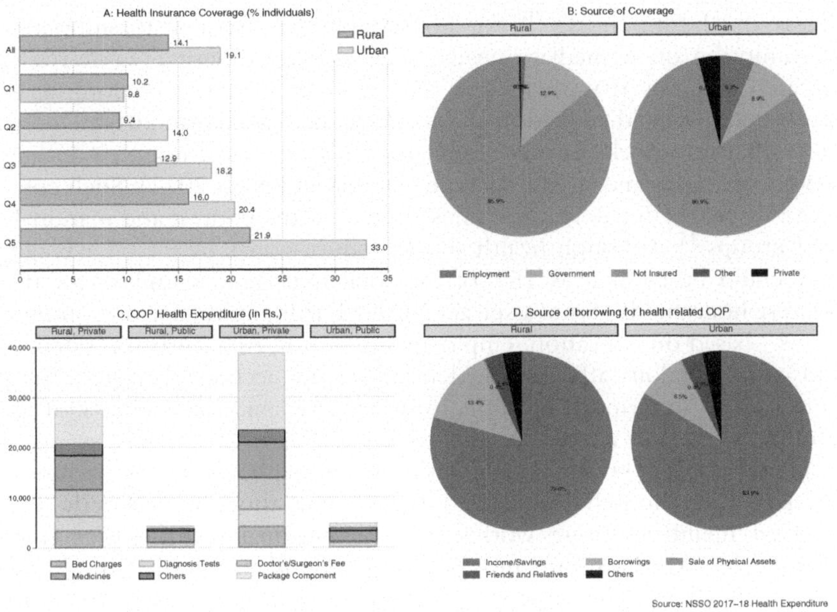

Fig. 7.2 Health insurance, OOP expenditure, and its financing (*Source* NSSO 2017–2018 Health Expenditure)

assets—and except for health shocks—perpetuating the cycle of ill health and poverty (Kochar 2004). *Ex post*, lack of social insurance against income shocks leads to large welfare losses to households near the subsistence standard of living, through risky economic decisions such as taking children out of school or reduced spending on long-term investments (Chetty and Looney 2006).[19]

Research has shown that a large share of Indian households, similar to other LMICs—with meager savings and access to financial resources—is unable to smoothen their consumption over time and often resort to coping mechanisms that further perpetuate poverty when faced with

[19] Findings from a wide range of contexts suggest a positive spillover effect of health insurance on improvements in labor and educational outcomes. See Chen and Jin (2012), Alcaraz et al. (2017), Wherry et al. (2018), Del Valle (2021), and Khiem and Kuo (2021), among others.

illness and health shocks.[20] For households that are able to smoothen consumption on immediate needs, such as food, housing, or festivals, research suggests that there is a reduction in spending on long-term investments in child education and food security (Mohanan 2013; Dureja 2021). Health shocks further reduce monthly earnings through a decline in wage earnings and overall income (Dureja and Negi 2022). Such costs prove disproportionately more catastrophic for the poorest and marginalized groups.[21] Although health shocks reduce wages by 5% on average, they could be as high as 15% of the total household spending for the poorest households (Srinivas et al. 2021). Furthermore, socio-economic status—based on education, employment, wealth, rural/urban residence, and caste/religious affiliations—determines the accrued damage arising out of OOP, in terms of both the losses incurred and the coping strategy adopted (Sangar et al. 2019).

Disadvantaged groups—rural residents with poorer access to health infrastructure, households headed by women, those with elderly and disabled members, those working in the informal sector, lower caste groups, and Muslims—are most likely to be affected by health shocks (Dhanaraj 2016). The same set of households are more likely to resort to risky coping strategies, such as sale of assets or borrowing credit, which further lowers their ability to prosper and undermines household resilience. Insurance can improve resilience by providing financial incentives to the most vulnerable and addressing persistent disparities by offering greater access to health care and ensuring more equitable intra-household distribution of resources. For example, Aiyar and Sunder (2022) found that RSBY contributed to long-term health gains through a decline (around 5%) in the child mortality rate, with greater benefits to the poorest households, resulting in more favorable outcomes for female children and children born later in families, who are reported to receive lesser expenditure on health care.[22] These effects were largely mediated by greater access to maternal health services.

[20] For a review on burden of health-related OOP and its source of financing in LMICs, refer to Alam and Mahal (2014).

[21] See Wagstaff and Lindelow (2014) for a detailed discussion.

[22] Conti and Ginja (2020) also found a convergence in infant mortality rates across poor and rich municipalities in Mexico since the introduction of *Seguro Popular* (SP).

The Emergence of Demand-Driven Health Insurance

To provide insurance against health-induced OOP expenditures and their potentially catastrophic impact, the first nationwide, publicly subsidized health insurance program, RSBY, was developed in 2008. RSBY was introduced as a part of the "welfare agenda" of the Congress Party-led government, which also introduced other rights-based legislations—food and work—that form the two important pillars of existing social welfare architecture in the country. Recognizing the limitations of the public health care infrastructure in reducing OOP health expenditure and health insurance for the poor, RSBY was introduced with the *scope* of providing financial protection against the expensive access to expensive quality medical care (Virk and Atun 2015).[23] The insurance route (*form*)—instead of strengthening the demand-oriented public health systems, like the British NHS, which were already in place—was chosen because of the inherent inefficiencies and poor accountability in existing health systems. It was argued that the demand-side insurance model would entail patients seeking health care providers of their choice while the government worked with professional insurance agencies to monitor each transaction and to reimburse them accordingly. Such a program would also foster greater demand for better quality health care providers and create competition in the health care industry for overall welfare. In its initial conceptualization, the *focus* of RSBY was on poor, unorganized, informal workers who lacked employer-based social security, but the program was targeted specifically at those identified as poor, that is, in possession of a BPL (below poverty line) ration card.[24]

There were two key features of RSBY that were unprecedented among other any other social welfare programs in the country. First, it was designed as a public–private partnership (PPP) exercise, wherein the

[23] We must mention to our readers that one of the first provisions for financial protection against health shocks in the country was introduced in 1997 under the aegis of *Rashtriya Arogya Nidhi* (RAN), which aimed to provide one-time monetary assistance to poor patients suffering from cancer or rare and life-threatening diseases for treatment in government hospitals. While the scheme continues to be in existence, it is hardly utilized. Only 591 patients benefited from it in 2017–2018 (https://pib.gov.in/Pressreleaseshare.aspx?PRID=1524808).

[24] The Ministry of Labor and Employment, rather than the Ministry of Health, as a result, was entrusted with the task of creating the RSBY architecture.

government funded the scheme, but private insurance companies were the implementing agencies. It was believed that the private insurance firms, by virtue of being more experienced than the government in the insurance sector, would bring efficiency to the scheme. Encouraging the enrollment of beneficiaries would increase profits and pool risks to bring down operational costs. In building the entire infrastructure, the reliance upon information and communications technology to vet every transaction through the RSBY smart card, which allowed for portability, was the second key feature of the scheme.

The nature of health care expenses covered under the scheme was limited only to hospitalization expenses—up to 30,000 INR (US$400) annually—with the expectation that outpatient care costs a negligible amount in state-run PHCs.[25] Eligible households (BPL cardholders) could obtain biometrics-based "smart" RSBY cards upon registration for the scheme. There was no copayment component to the scheme, and it relied upon patients presenting the smart card to access in-hospital care. Each transaction would reduce the eligible amount on the card, based on the government's fee for the treatment, until the ceiling was reached. The insurance facilities were provided by private companies, the selection of which was based upon competitive bidding in each district. The insurance companies created a list of empaneled inpatient care facilities—public and private—and reimbursed them for the care provided to the RSBY-cardholding beneficiaries. The insurance claims were paid by the government to the companies. States selected into the implementation of the scheme. Central government contributed to 75% of the premium, while the state governments financed the rest.[26] RSBY reached more than 130 million people within five years of its launch and paved the way for similar health insurance programs in many states.

Initiatives by State Governments

We have highlighted the role of subnational governments in being the driving forces for innovation in social welfare programs and the

[25] The number of family members eligible for benefits was restricted to 5 persons, including the head, spouse, and a maximum of three dependents, and the expenses covered around 700 surgical or medical procedures.

[26] See La Forgia and Nagpal (2012) for a comprehensive review of RSBY, along with other schemes introduced by the state governments.

national health insurance program.[27] RSBY, similarly, had precedent in the *Yeshasvini* (2003) and *Rajiv Aarogyasiri* (2007), two innovative health insurance programs in Karnataka and Andhra Pradesh, respectively. Under the *Aarogyasri* scheme, the state government set up a trust headed by the Chief Minister who, in consultation with insurance and medical professionals, devised the insurance scheme with an insurance premium of Rs. 250 (~US$3) and maximum coverage of health expenses of Rs. 1.5 lakh (US$2,000) per family for inpatient care for a fixed set of treatments. There was a buffer provision of an additional sum of Rs. 50,000 (US$600) if costs exceeded the original allocation. The scheme covered around 85% of the population. *Yeshasvini*, on the other hand, was introduced as community insurance with a *focus* on cooperative rural farmers and informal sector workers. It was a voluntary, not-for-profit, cashless health insurance scheme, with the scope of financial protection against "highly" catastrophic and less discretionary inpatient surgical procedures, with a low level of personal contribution. It provided an annual coverage of Rs. 2 lakh (~US$280) per family.[28] Subsequently, the scheme was merged with the *Arogya Karnataka* scheme, renamed later as *Ayushman Bharat-Arogya Karnataka* (AB-ArK) in 2018, with the health department at its helm.

The success of *Aarogyasiri*, *Yeshasvini*, and RSBY—and the political appeal of these schemes—spurred other states to announce their own independent health insurance schemes. In 2009, Tamil Nadu launched *Kalaignar* Insurance Scheme (renamed in 2012 as Chief Minister's Comprehensive Health Insurance Scheme, or CMCHIS) to provide financial protection against "serious and life-threatening ailments" to the poorest and unorganized sector workers. Yet, by targeting the scheme to

[27] While this is a recurring theme in the book, we would come back to this issue in the following chapters again.

[28] In the community-based insurance, the Department for Co-operation was entrusted with the task of mobilizing members and overseeing the implementation of the program. Cooperative societies organized farmers and other rural workers in rural areas work at the intermediary level to explain the principles of health insurance to the community, mobilize, and implement the program at the grassroots level. Care was sought from designated health care providers, which could be either from the private sector, charitable, or government-run hospitals. Governance of *Yeshasvini* was provided by an independent trust supported by a third-party administrator (TPA), which provided logistical support to insurance companies, such as issuance of ID cards to beneficiaries, processing of claims, and payment delivery.

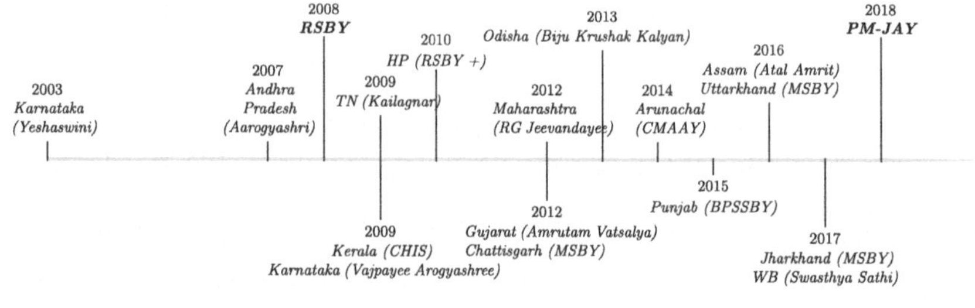

Fig. 7.3 Timeline of introduction of various national and subnational health insurance schemes (*Source* Authors, based upon government sources)

families below an annual income of Rs. 72,000 (~US$1,000), *Kalaignar* included the poorest as well as the lower middle-class families. The insurance covered inpatient medical expenses up to a maximum of Rs. 100,000 (~US$1,250) per family over the four-year insurance period. The competition among state governments to introduce health insurance led to a series of state-sponsored programs, which led to added coverage of treatment, amount, and beneficiaries to the RSBY (Fig. 7.3). In 2018, RSBY was subsumed under PM-JAY, which provided more comprehensive care with a higher insurance coverage for the bottom 40% of the population. Many of the state government schemes subsequently have been rechristened but add to the benefits provided by PM-JAY from their own finances.

The Impact of Health Insurance on Building Resilience

Have these health insurance programs achieved their goals in providing financial protection to the poor? This question has led to a rich body of literature that has evaluated the impact of RSBY and state government schemes. A comprehensive review of such studies, in terms of the impact of health insurance on utilization of health care, willingness-to-pay, and financial risk protection, found that, although the scheme increased utilization of health care services by beneficiaries, the evidence on financial protection—that is, the reduction in OOP—is inconclusive (Sriram and Khan 2020; Reshmi et al. 2021).[29] In fact, there are concerns about the insurance schemes increasing OOP and nonmedical expenditures, arising out of greater health care utilization. The health insurance creates conditions of both adverse selection (greater usage of insurance by those who are ill) and moral hazard (greater usage of insurance by the ill increases insurance premium). While greater access to the medical system is welfare enhancing, lack of reduction in health care costs could either mean warranted expenditures on the required treatment that could have potentially gone undiagnosed (improving health), or an exorbitant increase in the price of health services (undermining the effectiveness of health insurance).[30]

One must note, however, that any generalized argument around the effects of insurance could be misleading when the enrollment in the scheme, its implementation, and the health care provision infrastructure varies widely across regions and over time.[31] The challenges of program evaluation using observational design, unlike transaction-level data, conflate many of the findings.[32]

Yet, there are some generalizable facts important to understanding the potential effects of health insurance in India. First, increasing enrollment in the program remains a major bottleneck to its success, even after a decade of RSBY.[33] States with particularly poor performance on

[29] Refer to Karan et al. (2017) and Azam (2018) and the references cited therein for a comprehensive survey of quantitative evaluation of the RSBY.

[30] See Sengupta and Rooj (2019) for the moral hazard and adverse selection debates.

[31] Bauhoff and Sudharsanan (2021) provided a useful framework, a "insurance cascade" to sequentially study the impact of health insurance through incremental and subsequent steps toward financial protection—enrollment of beneficiaries, awareness of benefits, choice of empaneled hospital, and utilization of the entitled services. It provides a systematic way to think about why and how health insurances might or might not work for the poor.

[32] There are challenges of statistical inference in using observational data to study health insurance programs (Nandi et al. 2015). To understand the challenges of evaluation in the Indian context, refer to Vellakkal and Ebrahim (2013).

[33] Health insurance is an "experience good." Lack of familiarity with the concept of insurance, or any previous experiences (good or bad) with health or any other kinds of insurance product, affects the enrollment in and usage of the product (Banerjee et al. 2014). Difficulties in enrollment in public health insurance have been found to be a common challenge in low- and middle-income countries which have similar programs (Acharya et al. 2013). For more details, see Das and Leino (2011) and Banerjee et al. (2021).

governance, and also have the poorest share of the population and inferior health infrastructure, fare the worst in terms of enrollment (Nandi et al. 2013). There is also a low level of awareness among people of the scheme and its benefits, and often, the commercial insurance agencies resist creating awareness (Hooda 2015). Second, given the program's *focus* on the poor, there is a high degree of targeting errors. The deserving beneficiaries are often left behind while the undeserving gain access (Fan et al. 2012).[34] Therefore, the poorest have been unable to benefit from the health insurance programs, as intended, which implies that despite the insurance, health inequalities persist (Selvaraj et al. 2021).[35] Third, one of the main challenges to financial protection against rising OOP is the high cost of outpatient care and medicines, which are not covered under the insurance. Expenditures on medicine comprise a substantial share (72%) of the total OOP payments and hence, do not adequately protect the poor against impoverishment (Shahrawat and Rao 2012). Fourth, with the growing strength of private insurance companies and private health care systems, overtreatment or unnecessary health expenses potentially inflate the costs of health care, much to the detriment of the poor. There have been many reports of denial of care for the empaneled households because of delayed reimbursement from the government (Rajasekhar et al. 2011; Ghosh 2014). Often the health care providers charge for services not covered by the insurance or participants are forced to buy expensive drugs and diagnostic tests (Devadasan et al. 2013). Together, these concerns suggest that subsidized health insurance programs have provided a "partial" financial protection for the poor, at best.

Financial protection—through health insurance—can facilitate greater access to health care and more equitable distribution of resources within the household. For example, RSBY has contributed to a decline (around 5%) in the infant mortality rate among children. Greater benefits have accrued to female children and children born later in families, who are

[34] The issue of identifying the poor and misclassification involving the BPL cards—necessary to obtaining RSBY cards in most contexts—have been subjects of major debate in India. See Hirway (2003) and Niehaus et al. (2013).

[35] It might be useful to consider the example of *Yeshaswini* in Karnataka, which increased health care use among insured households, and yet, there was a greater preference for private facilities. While the insurance program reduced the need to borrow money or sell assets for treatment, the relatively better off households benefited more, as they were not only more aware but also better equipped to handle the other costs associated with hospitalization (Aggarwal 2010).

reported to receive lesser expenditures on health care. These effects are mediated through greater access to maternal health services.

Facilitating Resilience: Equitable Health Care and Improved Health Outcomes

Catastrophic income loss due to illness is becoming increasingly important, as India is undergoing an epidemiological transition, with the burden of disease shifting from infectious diseases to NCDs, even among the poor. Public health infrastructure, which was traditionally designed to address the spread of communicable diseases, is particularly constrained in providing quality care to everyone. Private providers remain the dominant providers of health care services, making health care expensive. As a result, the Indian health care system has been criticized for being inefficient as well as inequitable. Public hospitals provide a low quality of treatment while subsidized health insurance fails to provide adequate financial protection against OOP health expenditure. The emerging question, therefore, is how can subsidized health insurance programs like PM-JAY facilitate equitable access to health care?

We would like to argue that the *raison d'etre* for a robust health care system is to improve health at the lowest possible cost to patients, and therefore, the *scope* of health insurance policies should be earmarked as UHC and for improvement in health outcomes.[36] Financial protection for the poor should be an intermediate goal. Health insurance, as a *form* of safety net, therefore, is only a key "intermediate" step in accessing health care.[37] Otherwise, insurance subsidy *focused* on the poor would remain as just another tool of an anti-poverty policy, which could fall short of the transformational aims of building resilience. With the *scope* of affordable and equitable access to quality health care, health insurance

[36] Unlike fire or accident insurance, where insurance is purchased to cover for financial damages and not the incidence of an accident or fire hazard, the *scope* of health insurance ought to include improvement in health outcomes, too, apart from providing financial protection.

[37] Subsidized public health insurance is not necessarily a silver bullet to achieving UHC, but together with other social safety net schemes, it remains a vital "cog in the wheel" in protecting households against everyday risks. Studies show no discernible difference in health outcomes among OECD countries, regardless of the health care model used—an insurance based one with private providers or a tax-financed public health care system (Wagstaff 2009; Radojicic et al. 2020).

programs would not only allow households to cope with shocks but also continue investing in productive investments (improved health and its impact on productivity and income), which is key to building resilience.[38] In order to get there, numerous hurdles need to be surmounted, which are discussed below.

Increasing Enrollment

First and foremost, there is an urgent need to increase enrollment rates in the health insurance programs, which currently stand at very low levels. Lower enrollments in health insurance are caused by lack of literacy and awareness among the beneficiaries, or low rates of scheme utilization in their networks.[39] India's poor only recently received universal bank accounts, and their financial literacy remains very limited. Information campaigns by the government through widespread use of education and communication (IEC) methods, which include information pamphlets, health camps, etc., should be undertaken on a large scale to increase awareness about the health insurance scheme, its benefits, and clarify eligibility criteria in a simple manner. Such campaigns have proven successful in some states, such as Karnataka, in increasing the uptake and utilization.[40] Insurance agencies often subcontract such campaigns to third-party agencies, which have little incentive or ability to increase awareness. Awareness drives need to be accompanied by enrollment drives, helplines, and grievance redressal systems. In the villages, awareness meetings are particularly helpful, as they are well attended and the spread of word in the social network could have a cascading effect in awareness, as well as utilization.[41] The need for awareness is particularly high in regions where the utilization of the scheme is low and social networks are denser.

[38] We have already discussed how health status and poverty have a feedback loop. The poor have limited access to quality health care. Worsened health conditions lower productivity. Reduced labor productivity perpetuates poverty. Improved financial protection against large medical expenses protects income and assets, enabling households to invest in more productive activities, leading to improved well-being.

[39] Refer to Fadlallah et al. (2018) and Platteau and Ontiveros (2013) for more details.

[40] See Puri and Sun (2021) and Das and Leino (2011).

[41] Debnath and Jain (2020) showed how social networks are important to access health insurance in India.

Expanding Health Care Coverage Beyond Hospitalization

Narrow focus on secondary and tertiary care hospitalization has been a major criticism of India's public health insurance model. Traditionally, India's public health has concerned itself with the aims of eradicating infectious diseases, immunization, and encouraging family planning, with curative care responsibility remaining with the patients. The importance of financial protection against health shocks is expected to rise as the nature of the disease burden changes.[42] Countries, along their path of economic and demographic transformation, also go through an epidemiological transition, in which NCDs emerge as more important health hazards than the infectious, maternal, neonatal, and nutritional diseases, which are traditionally the causes of high mortality rates in early stages of economic development. While maternal and child mortality has declined substantially in India, NCDs now amount for 55% of the disease burden (Dandona et al. 2017). NCDs include cardiovascular diseases, high blood pressure, diabetes, neurological disorders, cancers, musculoskeletal disorders, and chronic kidney disease, which have substantially higher costs of inpatient and outpatient medical care. PM-JAY and most other state-level health insurance programs do not cover the NCDs.

Medicines and diagnostic tests comprise about 80–85% of the outpatient treatment costs.[43] Providing financial protection against preventive outpatient expenditures on doctor fees, diagnostic tests, and medication has long-term effects on reducing costly curative inpatient expenditures later. Encouraging the use of preventive health care facilities would not only improve community health through regular check-ups but also reduce the financial burden for the government in the long run through a reduced need for subsidized catastrophic health expenditure. To directly address the cost of medicines, initiatives like *Jan Aushadhi* (translates as "drug store for the people"), which subsidized generic drugs, have not been noteworthy but limited in reducing OOP health expenditure.[44]

[42] NCDs typically comprise half of the average households' OOP spending on health care in India (Engelgau et al. 2012). Treatment for NCDs such as cancer is highly associated with the risk of indebtedness (Joe 2015).

[43] These numbers are based upon Statement 3.31 of the NSSO 75th round Social Expenditure Survey.

[44] Launched in 2008, under the scheme, *Jan Aushadhi*, a network of dedicated outlets is supposed to provide generic medicines at affordable prices. On an average, these medicines are 50–90% cheaper than branded products. By August 2021, 8,012 such

Designated stores under the scheme are mostly located in more urbanized and developed districts which means a larger share of the population does not have access to them. There are also concerns about quality. Lack of regulatory oversight on substandard and spurious drugs, along with doctors' preferences for branded medicines, reduces the popularity of the generic drugs among patients.[45]

Social health insurance for curative care, with the rising cost of preventive medicines, is therefore only likely to delay the burden of disease and the incurrence of OOP health expenditure, with little impact on either financial protection against health shocks or improving long-term health outcomes.

Expanding Coverage: Move Toward Universality

Subsidized health insurance for the poor such as PM-JAY leaves a substantial proportion of the middle-income population (around 400 million individuals) without financial protection against illness, exposing them to the risk of potentially catastrophic descents into poverty. The "missing middle," which comprises about 30% of the population, overlaps substantially with the section of population—the self-employed, farmers, and workers in the formal and informal sector that lack employer-based social security—which RSBY for which initially intended to provide coverage. A recent report of India's planning body has suggested that PM-JAY should be extended to include the middle-income population, because the catastrophic effect of OOP health expenditure is not limited to the poor but impacts all segments of the population (Sarwal and Kumar 2021).[46] The policy paper recommends a newer insurance product in the medium term—once PM-JAY is functioning and people are familiar

outlets were available throughout the country. For more details, visit. http://janaushadhi.gov.in/pmjy.aspx.

[45] See Singh et al. (2020) and Thawani et al. (2017) for more details.

[46] Working group members for the report were affiliated with private insurance agencies, and the report did not acknowledge any contributions from civil society, social policy experts, or health/development practitioners. Here, we offer the famous quote by Adam Smith without comment: "*The proposal of any new law or regulation which comes from [businessmen], ought always to be listened to with great precaution, and ought never to be adopted till after having been long and carefully examined, not only with the most scrupulous, but with the most suspicious attention. It comes from an order of men whose interest is never exactly the same with that of the public, who have generally an interest to deceive and even*

with how health insurance works—the product could be considered as PM-JAY+ with voluntary insurance premiums.[47] The aim is to provide low-cost health insurance coverage to 80% of the population with free and subsidized premiums.

Although the government has yet to announce any concrete plans around the proposed scheme, it is expected that providing a larger share of the population with health insurance coverage would pool risks and bring insurance premiums down. The challenge for such a program, however, is in *identifying* the "missing middle." It is relatively easier to identify the poor, based on the possession of a BPL or RSBY card, as forms of proof of poverty. The absence of information about who occupies the middle-income distribution of the population, thus, could create an administrative nightmare. The absence of civil registry data, weak administrative capacity, and the requirement to pay partial insurance premiums pose challenges to increasing enrollment and the continuation of beneficiaries in the program.Experimental evidence from India highlights these concerns in identifying the non-poor for public health insurance.[48]

Despite the challenges, the idea of expanding insurance coverage is important, as errors of targeting often exclude the deserving. Including a

to oppress the public, and who accordingly have, upon many occasions, both deceived and oppressed it" (Smith 1776, pt. xi, 10).

[47] A similar program exists in Indonesia, *JKN Mandiri*—although legally mandatory with financial penalties for missing monthly payments—with a *focus* on non-poor, informal worker households (around 30% of the population), who must contribute insurance premiums out of their own pockets to seek health care—primary, secondary, and tertiary—at any private or public facilities. There is no restriction on the kind of treatment, except for cosmetic, infertility, or other lifestyle procedures.

[48] In a randomized control trial (RCT) conducted to understand the uptake of health insurance among non-poor in India, Malani et al. (2021) found that full subsidy for health insurance premiums led to a considerably greater enrollment (78.7%) than partial subsidy coverage (59.9%). Challenges in expanding health insurance coverage to informal workers with partial subsidies have been seen in many other Asian countries, like Indonesia, Vietnam, and the Philippines (Bredenkamp et al. 2015). In the case of Indonesia—a context very similar to India's with a network of PHCs as the first source of contact for patients and a mix of private and public health care providers for more complicated health needs—lack of civil registry and poor capacity of the health infrastructure has made the expansion of health insurance to non-poor informal workers particularly challenging (Banerjee et al. 2021). For informal workers, financial hardship makes regular monthly payments difficult (Dartanto et al. 2020). See Mboi (2015) for details on the Indonesian health care system and the implementation of its health insurance program, *JKN*.

wider set of beneficiaries would further increase utilization, as awareness gaps would be plugged. Instead of charging premiums for the non-poor as PM-JAY+ envisages, it may be more prudent to learn from the initiatives of various state governments that already have programs providing greater coverage for health insurance—in terms of population as well as health care costs—than PM-JAY. For example, anyone with an annual income below Rs. 72,000 (~US$1,000) in Tamil Nadu, which is much higher than the median income, is eligible for the insurance scheme. In Odisha and Haryana, all residents are entitled to public health insurance, while Andhra Pradesh, Karnataka, and Chhattisgarh also cover significant shares of non-poor families. Instead of a PM-JAY+, a more reasonable policy would be an expanded PM-JAY to cover all sections of the population, which would reduce targeting costs and improve access. Once the Indian population is more "experienced" with the insurance product, the non-poor may be charged a small amount. Universal enrollment would also create a larger pool of the insured population—many of which healthier—which could be eventually bring down the insurance premium for the government. A continued incremental effort toward expanding beneficiary coverage is therefore essential to achieving the goals of UHC.[49]

Investment in Public Health Care Infrastructure

How useful is access to health insurance without adequate quality health services? Very little. Overall, the capacity of health systems—both private and public—is poor, even by developing country standards. Health care infrastructure (per 1,000 people)—hospital beds, physicians, and primary care staff—in India needs substantial improvement (Fig. 7.4). The poor numbers also mask a huge gulf between the qualities of care across regions and the rural-urban divide. For example, it is widely known that public health infrastructure is significantly better in Tamil Nadu and Kerala when compared to poorer states like Bihar, Odisha, UP, or Jharkhand. Within states, secondary and tertiary care health care facilities are largely located in urban areas which increases the cost (transportation and accommodation) of care. Demand-drive health-focused social insurance

[49] The incremental approach to universal health care, despite the many limitations of state capacity, health infrastructure, and political inertia, has been championed by Thailand and is considered to be a model for many LMICs. See Tangcharoensathien et al. (2019).

to be successful therefore needs to be matched with the corresponding supply-side availability of quality health infrastructure (doctors, hospitals, pharmacies, equipment, medicines, etc.). Lower-level service providers at the public health infrastructure are overworked, and underpaid, while doctors are often absent and put in less effort in treatment.

The National Health Policy, 2017, proposed to increase public health expenditure to 2.5% of the GDP by 2025. Under the *Ayushman Bharat* scheme, there are further plans to increase primary public health infrastructure through the creation of 150,000 Health and Wellness Centers—which includes upgrading existing PHCs and subcenters—along with the use of PM-JAY to cover secondary and tertiary care. Greater spending, however, may not be done so equitably. Increasing the quality of health

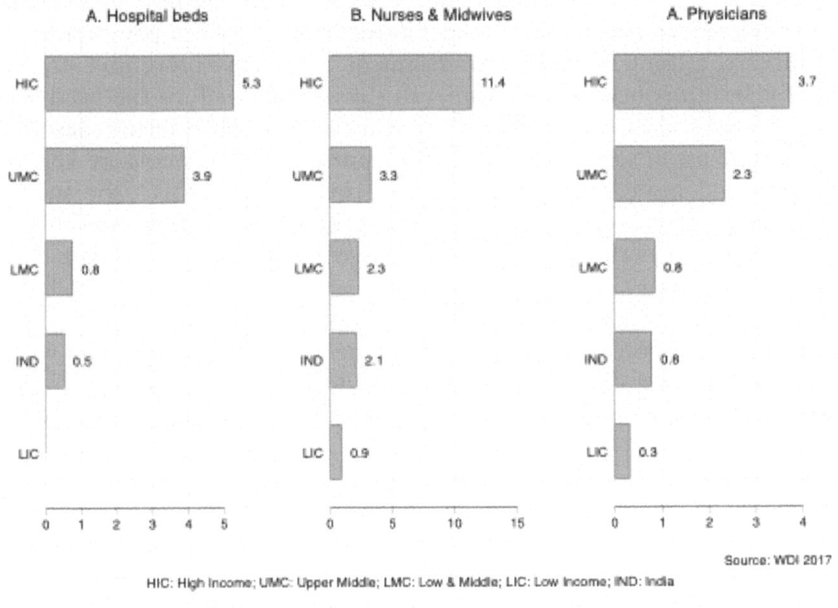

Fig. 7.4 Number of health care facilities per 1,000 people in India compared with countries in other income classes (*Source* World Development Indicators 2017. https://openknowledge.worldbank.org/handle/10986/26447)

services and motivation for health care providers currently stands as the most important supply-side hindrance to increasing access to health.[50]

Although investment in public health infrastructure without improving quality is certainly a futile effort, one cannot *throw the baby with the bath-water*, as the proverb goes.[51] The fragmented public health system needs a new lease on life. PHCs, along with ASHAs, provide the first point of contact for patients with health care workers and have been instrumental in eradicating smallpox, polio, improving maternal health, and currently, in fighting against the COVID-19 outbreak by providing door-to-door information campaigns and vaccinations. As part of the *Ayushman Bharat* program, improved management of PHCs, better training of staff, and coordination with secondary care should be promoted to provide equitable access to quality preventive care, especially in underserved regions. It is well established that the poor, often residing in regions with underdeveloped public health infrastructure, tend to pay more for health care, causing further impoverishment.[52] Effective preventive strategies for health concerns, therefore, can substantially reduce the need for complicated and expensive curative care at the specialized tertiary level.

Investments in secondary and tertiary public health systems are key to spurring and motivating private health providers. In LMIC, the structure and performance of the public sector health institutions are linked to public sector performance.[53] A healthy competition between the two sectors is necessary, as the private health care providers tend to collude and set higher prices or encourage unnecessary hospitalization expenditures. In the absence of an alternative option—a public health system with free quality health care—health shocks could have an increasingly catastrophic impact, even for common illnesses.[54] Maintaining high quality

[50] See Mohanan et al. (2016).

[51] Based upon qualitative interviews with various stakeholders in the design of RSBY, Virk and Atun (2015) highlighted that the choice of an insurance model for financial protection against illness was largely motivated by the fact that there was a feeling in the government that public health infrastructure leaves a "lot to be desired."

[52] See Dash and Mohanty (2019).

[53] See Morgan et al. (2016) for a discussion.

[54] Patient claims of a health insurance scheme for women, VimoSEWA, show that the insured are more likely to be hospitalized, even for common illnesses, such as fever, diarrhea, or malaria, which generally do not warrant inpatient treatment (Desai 2009; Sinha et al. 2014). Even without insurance, private health care providers are found to

secondary and tertiary public health infrastructure has further long-term benefits. For instance, the presence of a strong public health system in Tamil Nadu has allowed the state to keep the health care costs to the patient, as well as for the exchequer, low. The strong and competitive public health system in Tamil Nadu has contributed to the lower prices charged in private hospitals, and better quality has led to a large share of the insurance-backed treatment being made available at public hospitals. To achieve UHC, the role of public health care infrastructure, therefore, is paramount, despite the increasingly important role of private health care providers in the health insurance program.

Improved Regulatory Oversight over Perverse Private Incentives

The behavior of private health care providers depends upon the institutional environment in which they operate (Bennett et al. 1994). While India's public health care has been faulted for its inefficiency, profit-driven private health care systems have also been criticized for their exploitative practices. Patients are not only charged higher fees but referred for irrelevant and excessive diagnostic tests and for inpatient care beyond need. Corruption in the health sector is a fairly well recognized "dirty open secret" and the "opportunity to engage in corrupt practices by dint of being in a position of power in a system with inadequate oversight; financial, peer, or personal pressures felt by officials; and a culture that rationalises and accepts corruption" is a typical feature of the Indian medical fraternity (Jain et al. 2014).[55] Often, private hospitals provide time-specific "financial targets" to doctors, which they achieve through prescribing expensive—but unnecessary and even harmful—tests and surgical treatments, increasing the health-seeking costs for patients.[56] While private hospitals provide better quality, and therefore, attract patients with public insurance cover, they tend to charge governments and patients more, by manipulating claims and charging for free services.[57] Qualitative studies also suggest that patients often do not

overprescribe drugs, even if the quality of care they provide is of higher quality (Bhatia and Cleland 2004).

[55] For a review of corruption in the Indian health care sector, refer to Vian (2007).

[56] See Kay (2015).

[57] Analyzing more than 1.5 million insurance claims and follow-up, large-scale patient surveys, Jain (2021) showed that private hospitals in less competitive markets use "balance

understand the various costs and coverage of services they are entitled to, and as a result, often end up spending a significant amount on OOP expenses (Ahlin et al. 2016; Nandi and Schneider 2020a, b; Ecks 2021). Conspicuous by its absence, in the contract design between the government and the insurance agencies, monitoring strategy and mechanisms do not find mention with discussion around the role of incentives for the various stakeholders for effective implementation of the program and the quality of care.[58] There is little recourse for patients if they are denied the benefits based on empaneled (rostered) care. As a result, contractual breaches are commonplace. Often, beneficiaries are not provided information about treatment packages, location of hospitals, transportation cost coverage, or food during hospitalization. Such malpractices not only lead to high OOP but also have negative consequences for equity and access, two important parameters of UHC.

Given the poor state of India's current health system, the idea, while laudable, of health insurance anointing the private sector to deliver essential services such as health care as a PPP model is fraught with challenges: there is limited institutional oversight, regulatory frameworks, monitoring, and optimal price-setting. Malpractices in the Indian health care sector are rampant because of a weak regulatory climate, with poor quality standards and no institutional mechanisms to address grievances against ethical violations. This weakness leads to a low level of trust in in the health care sector—both public and private—that could further lower health-seeking behavior until absolutely necessary, leading to poor overall health. As a result, a study summoned by India's planning body suggested that to ensure health insurance models achieve the objectives of equity, there is a need for a "robust regulatory system for quality and price control, supported by periodic technical and social audits" to discourage private health care from becoming unaffordable (Reddy et al. 2011). Addressing these regulatory issues first requires upgraded data and monitoring systems that can provide real-time records of each transaction undertaken—diagnosis, treatment, price, provider, length of stay in the hospital, patient history, etc.—sharable across the service providers and which can then be used to dynamically update the cost of treatment

billing" to compensate for low reimbursement rates by the government through increasing the amount of patient claims without increasing quality.

58 See Khetrapal et al. (2019) and Sheikh et al. (2015) for in-depth case studies around failures of regulatory mechanisms from different contexts in India.

and quality of care (Morton et al. 2016).[59] Such a database would also allow regulators to monitor, authenticate, and arbitrate patients' claims or when the government finds reimbursement claims suspicious. It would also facilitate quality ratings of service providers and create a national benchmark, which potentially allows for pricing treatments differentially according to the service provided.[60] This might foster more competition among the providers, bidding down the price of health care coverage.

In the absence of appropriate data systems and regulatory mechanisms, there is little monitoring of the value chain beginning from patient benefits received, claims made by providers to the government, and the subsequent payment made to the insurance firms, which makes the system vulnerable to malpractice. In response to such malpractices by the insurance agencies, many of the state governments, which are entrusted with the task of implementation using funds allocated by the central government, are increasingly switching to a trust-based model or a mixture of trust-based and private insurance agency models.[61] Insurance companies hesitate to share patient claims, which puts the legitimacy of the treatment under scrutiny. Although the short-term issue of trust may be fixed in a PPP model, it also creates doubt about the long-term sustainability of trust-based or mixed models, as the government appointed trusts are inexperienced insurers. There is an urgent need to rethink the delivery mode of an insurance-based health system in India which generates synergies between both public and private health care infrastructure and strengthen the quality of fragmented health care delivery systems.[62]

[59] *Ayushman Bharat Digital Health Mission* is a step in this direction for monitoring that needs to be strengthened.

[60] Unlike PM-JAY and many other states that have flat rates, the price of treatment at the empaneled hospitals in Tamil Nadu are based upon the quality ranking of the hospitals. The government hospitals are at the top of rankings, which further allows the government to gain economically from delivering better quality treatment. See Choudhury et al. (2019).

[61] For instance, *Arogyasri*, which began with a PPP model with an insurance company in 2007, switched to a trust-based model after a few years. Similarly, Karnataka and Andhra Pradesh moved to a trust-based system.

[62] For interested readers, we would like them to refer a set of readings essential to gaining an understanding of the challenges of the Indian health system, a mixture of private and public health providers. See Berman (1998), Mahal (2002), GoI (2011), Reddy et al. (2011), Das and Hammer (2012).

Recognizing the "Right to Health"

Finally, while public health insurance programs, such as RSBY and PM-JAY, have been key *incremental* steps toward the *scope* of providing financial protection and access to UHC in India, continuity of these initiatives and their long-term success must rely upon recognizing "right to health" as an inalienable part of the citizen-state social contract. While financial protection needs have motivated the need for health insurance, the success of the programs will rely on thinking them as basic citizenship "rights," essential for human flourishing. It would be useful to look at the reforms in other emerging economies, such as Brazil, Thailand, Indonesia, Turkey, or South Africa, at how public health insurance schemes incorporate health care as a "right." Such an approach would enable addressing the equity aspects of health care through creating institutional arrangements that advance the *scope* of health insurance as equitable access to health care and improved health outcomes, rather than as solely financial protection per se.

Experience from other social safety nets—the Public Distribution System (PDS) and the Mahatma Gandhi National Rural Employment Guarantee Scheme (MGNREGS)—has suggested that their recent successes have relied significantly on the recognition of the rights to food and to work. Health, being an inalienable right of citizens, was recognized at the time when RSBY was introduced, but there has been little movement on this issue since then.[63] Recognizing health as a fundamental right would provide the necessary boost to the fragmented service-delivery model of Indian public health systems. It would also establish a clear set of legal obligations of government to its citizens, which would not only put

[63] India's Prime Minister, Manmohan Singh, an economist by training and the driving force behind RSBY, reportedly said that investments in health, despite being the harbinger of economic progress, cannot be motivated purely by economic considerations alone, but must recognize health as an "inalienable human right that every individual citizen can justly claim" (from a speech by Prime Minister Manmohan Singh at AIIMS, October 2005). The *High Level Expert Group Report on Universal Health Coverage for India* also argued that "..it is imperative to consider the right to health as the key underlying theme" to achieve UHC (GoI 2011, p. 44). The World Health Organization's Constitution (1946) too envisages "...the highest attainable standard of health is one of the fundamental rights of every human being without distinction of race, religion, political belief, economic or social condition" (WHO [1946] 2020, p. 1). Guided by the aim of UHC and building upon the Bhore Committee Report of 1943, a *Lancet* Citizens' Commission has been appointed to examine the barriers and opportunities in creating a resilient health system. See Patel et al. (2021, 2022).

health on the political agenda but also empower citizens in demanding their right to improved quality of health care. Greater involvement of citizens would increase accountability of service providers, public or private, and pave the way for regulatory reforms that could provide patients with greater influence and trust in the health system.

Summing Up

There is no one definitive and correct path toward reducing poverty or improving health. Multiple arms of social policy are needed to cope against economic shocks. Subsidized public health insurance is one only such tool, which is increasingly becoming an important lever of anti-poverty policies in developing countries, as the costs of health care—partly driven by rising NCDs—have increased along with the inability of public health infrastructure to provide quality care to a rising share of the population. India's public health insurance is still in its infancy, with a shockingly low share of expenditure on health, limited insurance coverage (in terms of people covered and types of health expenditures), poor quality of health infrastructure, lack of financial literacy, and poor regulatory institutions to check perverse incentives for the private health providers. As a result, although health insurance has increased health access, it has not yet been able to deliver either on reducing out-of-pocket health expenditures or on improving health outcomes that increase household resilience. Long-term, broad-based gains from the health insurance program can only be realized once there is a credible political commitment to universal health care, which, in turn, can only begin by recognizing the "right to health" as a fundamental right of the citizens.

References

Acharya, A., S. Vellakkal, F. Taylor, E. Masset, A. Satija, M. Burke, and S. Ebrahim. 2013. "The Impact of Health Insurance Schemes for the Informal Sector in Low- and Middle-Income Countries: A Systematic Review." *The World Bank Research Observer* 28 (2): 236–66. https://doi.org/10.1093/wbro/lks009.

Aggarwal, Aradhna. 2010. "Impact Evaluation of India's 'Yeshasvini' Community-Based Health Insurance Programme." *Health Economics* 19 (S1): 5–35.

Ahlin, Tanja, Mark Nichter, and Gopukrishnan Pillai. 2016. "Health Insurance in India: What Do We Know and Why Is Ethnographic Research Needed." *Anthropology & Medicine* 23 (1): 102–24. https://doi.org/10.1080/13648470.2015.1135787.

Aiyar, Anaka, and Naveen Sunder. 2022. "Health Insurance and Infant Mortality: Evidence from India." In *9th Annual Conference of the American Society of Health Economists*.

Alam, Khurshid, and Ajay Mahal. 2014. "Economic Impacts of Health Shocks on Households in Low and Middle Income Countries: A Review of the Literature." *Globalization and Health* 10 (1): 21. https://doi.org/10.1186/1744-8603-10-21.

Alcaraz, Carlo, Daniel Chiquiar, María José Orraca, and Alejandrina Salcedo. 2017. "The Effect of Publicly Provided Health Insurance on Education Outcomes in Mexico." *The World Bank Economic Review* 30 (Supplement_1): S145–56.

Arokiasamy, Perianayagam. 2018. "India's Escalating Burden of Non-Communicable Diseases." *The Lancet Global Health* 6 (12): e1262–63. https://doi.org/10.1016/S2214-109X(18)30448-0.

Azam, Mehtabul. 2018. "Does Social Health Insurance Reduce Financial Burden? Panel Data Evidence from India." *World Development* 102: 1–17. https://doi.org/10.1016/j.worlddev.2017.09.007.

Balarajan, Yarlini, Selvaraj Selvaraj, and S. V. Subramanian. 2011. "Health Care and Equity in India." *The Lancet* 377 (9764): 505–15.

Banerjee, Abhijit, Esther Duflo, and Richard Hornbeck. 2014. "Bundling Health Insurance and Microfinance in India: There Cannot be Adverse Selection If There Is No Demand." *American Economic Review* 104 (5): 291–97. https://doi.org/10.1257/aer.104.5.291.

Banerjee, Abhijit, Amy Finkelstein, Rema Hanna, Benjamin A. Olken, Arianna Ornaghi, and Sudarno Sumarto. 2021. "The Challenges of Universal Health Insurance in Developing Countries: Experimental Evidence from Indonesia's National Health Insurance." *American Economic Review* 111 (9): 3035–63. https://doi.org/10.1257/aer.20200523.

Bauhoff, Sebastian, and Nikkil Sudharsanan. 2021. "Evaluating Health Insurance Programmes." *Economic and Political Weekly* 56 (23): 7–8.

Behera, Sasmita, and Jalandhar Pradhan. 2021. "Uneven Economic Burden of Non-Communicable Diseases Among Indian Households: A Comparative Analysis." *PLoS One* 16 (12): e0260628. https://doi.org/10.1371/journal.pone.0260628.

Bennett, Sara, George Dakpallah, Paul Garner, Lucy Gilson, Sanguan Nittayaramphong, Beatriz Zurita, and Anthony Zwi. 1994. "Carrot and Stick: State Mechanisms to Influence Private Provider Behaviour." *Health Policy and Planning* 9 (1): 1–13. https://doi.org/10.1093/heapol/9.1.1.

Berman, Peter A. 1998. "Rethinking Health Care Systems: Private Health Care Provision in India." *World Development* 26 (8): 1463–79. https://doi.org/10.1016/S0305-750X(98)00059-X.

Bhatia, Jagdish, and John Cleland. 2004. "Health Care of Female Outpatients in South-Central India: Comparing Public and Private Sector Provision." *Health Policy and Planning* 19 (6): 402–9.

Bredenkamp, Caryn, Timothy Evans, Leizel Lagrada, John Langenbrunner, Stefan Nachuk, and Toomas Palu. 2015. "Emerging Challenges in Implementing Universal Health Coverage in Asia." *Social Science & Medicine* 145: 243–48. https://doi.org/10.1016/j.socscimed.2015.07.025.

Chen, Yuyu, and Ginger Zhe Jin. 2012. "Does Health Insurance Coverage Lead to Better Health and Educational Outcomes? Evidence from Rural China." *Journal of Health Economics* 31 (1): 1–14.

Chetty, Raj, and Adam Looney. 2006. "Consumption Smoothing and the Welfare Consequences of Social Insurance in Developing Economies." *Journal of Public Economics* 90 (12): 2351–56. https://doi.org/10.1016/j.jpubeco.2006.07.002.

Choudhury, Mita, Shruti Tripathi, and Jay Dev Dubey. 2019. *Experiences with Government Sponsored Health Insurance Schemes in Indian States: A Fiscal Perspective*. New Delhi: National Institute of Public Finance and Policy.

Conti, Gabriella, and Rita Ginja. 2020. "Who Benefits From Free Health Insurance: Evidence from Mexico." *Journal of Human Resources* 58 (1): 1117-9157R2. doi: https://doi.org/10.3368/jhr.58.3.1117-9157R2.

Dandona, Lalit, G. Rakhi Dandona, D. K. Anil Kumar, Vinod K. Shukla, Kalpana Balakrishnan Paul, Dorairaj Prabhakaran, Nikhil Tandon, Sundeep Salvi, A. P. Dash, A. Nandakumar, Vikram Patel, Sanjay K. Agarwal, Prakash C. Gupta, R. S. Dhaliwal, Prashant Mathur, Avula Laxmaiah, Preet K. Dhillon, Subhojit Dey, Manu R. Mathur, Ashkan Afshin, Christina Fitzmaurice, Emmanuela Gakidou, Peter Gething, Simon I. Hay, Nicholas J. Kassebaum, Hmwe Kyu, Stephen S. Lim, Mohsen Naghavi, Gregory A. Roth, Jeffrey D. Stanaway, Harvey Whiteford, Vineet K. Chadha, Sunil D. Khaparde, Raghuram Rao, Kirankumar Rade, Puneet Dewan, Melissa Furtado, Eliza Dutta, Chris M. Varghese, P. Ravi Mehrotra, Tanvir Kaur Jambulingam, Meenakshi Sharma, Shalini Singh, Rashmi Arora, Reeta Rasaily, Ranjit M. Anjana, Viswanathan Mohan, Anurag Agrawal, Arvind Chopra, Ashish J. Mathew, Deeksha Bhardwaj, Pallavi Muraleedharan, Parul Mutreja, Kelly Bienhoff, Scott Glenn, Rizwan S. Abdulkader, Ashutosh N. Aggarwal, Rakesh Aggarwal, Sandra Albert, Atul Ambekar, Monika Arora, Damodar Bachani, Ashish Bavdekar, Gufran Beig, Anil Bhansali, Anurag Bhargava, Eesh Bhatia, Bilali Camara, D. J. Christopher, Siddharth K. Das, Paresh V. Dave, Sagnik Dey, Aloke G. Ghoshal, N. Gopalakrishnan, Randeep Guleria, Rajeev Gupta, Subodh S. Gupta, Tarun Gupta, M. D. Gupte, G. Gururaj, Sivadasanpillai

Harikrishnan, Veena Iyer, Sudhir K. Jain, Panniyamamkal Jeemon, Vasna Joshua, Rajni Kant, Anita Kar, Amal C. Kataki, Kiran Katoch, Tripti Khanna, Ajay Khera, Sanjay Kinra, Parvaiz A. Koul, Anand Krishnan, Avdhesh Kumar, Raman K. Kumar, Rashmi Kumar, Anura Kurpad, Laishram Ladusingh, Rakesh Lodha, P. A. Mahesh, Rajesh Malhotra, Matthews Mathai, Dileep Mavalankar, Murali Mohan BV, Satinath Mukhopadhyay, Manoj Murhekar, G. V. S. Murthy, Sanjeev Nair, Sreenivas A. Nair, Lipika Nanda, Romi S. Nongmaithem, Anu M. Oommen, Jeyaraj D. Pandian, Sapan Pandya, Sreejith Parameswaran, Sanghamitra Pati, Kameshwar Prasad, Narayan Prasad, Manorama Purwar, Asma Rahim, Sreebhushan Raju, Siddarth Ramji, Thara Rangaswamy, Goura K. Rath, Ambuj Roy, Yogesh Sabde, K. S. Sachdeva, Harsiddha Sadhu, Rajesh Sagar, Mari J. Sankar, Rajendra Sharma, Anita Shet, Shreya Shirude, Rajan Shukla, Sharvari R. Shukla, Gagandeep Singh, Narinder P. Singh, Virendra Singh, Anju Sinha, Dhirendra N. Sinha, R. K. Srivastava, A. Srividya, Vanita Suri, Rajaraman Swaminathan, P. N. Sylaja, Babasaheb Tandale, J. S. Thakur, Kavumpurathu R. Thankappan, Nihal Thomas, Srikanth Tripathy, Mathew Varghese, Santosh Varughese, S. Venkatesh, K. Venugopal, Lakshmi Vijayakumar, Denis Xavier, Chittaranjan S. Yajnik, Geevar Zachariah, Sanjay Zodpey, J. V. R. Prasada Rao, Theo Vos, K. Srinath Reddy, Christopher J. L. Murray, and Soumya Swaminathan. 2017. "Nations Within a Nation: Variations in Epidemiological Transition Across the States of India, 1990–2016 in the Global Burden of Disease Study." *The Lancet* 390 (10111): 2437–60. https://doi.org/10.1016/S0140-6736(17)32804-0.

Dartanto, Teguh, Alin Halimatussadiah, Jahen Fachrul Rezki, Renny Nurhasana, Chairina Hanum Siregar, Hamdan Bintara, Wahyu Pramono Usman, Nia Kurnia Sholihah, Edith Zheng Wen Yuan, and Rooswanti Soeharno. 2020. "Why Do Informal Sector Workers Not Pay the Premium Regularly? Evidence from the National Health Insurance System in Indonesia." *Applied Health Economics and Health Policy* 18 (1): 81–96. https://doi.org/10.1007/s40258-019-00518-y.

Das, Jishnu, Benjamin Daniels, Monisha Ashok, Eun-Young Shim, and Karthik Muralidharan. 2020. "Two Indias: The Structure of Primary Health Care Markets in Rural Indian Villages with Implications for Policy." *Social Science & Medicine* 112799. https://doi.org/10.1016/j.socscimed.2020.112799.

Das, Jishnu, and Jeffrey Hammer. 2005. "Which Doctor? Combining Vignettes and Item Response to Measure Clinical Competence." *Journal of Development Economics* 78 (2): 348–83. https://doi.org/10.1016/j.jdeveco.2004.11.004.

Das, Jishnu, and Jeffrey Hammer. 2012. *Health and Health Care Policy in India: The Case for Quality of Care*. Oxford: Oxford University Press.

Das, Jishnu, Alaka Holla, Aakash Mohpal, and Karthik Muralidharan. 2016. "Quality and Accountability in Health Care Delivery: Audit-Study Evidence from Primary Care in India." *American Economic Review* 106 (12): 3765–799. https://doi.org/10.1257/aer.20151138.

Das, Jishnu, and Jessica Leino. 2011. "Evaluating the RSBY: Lessons from an Experimental Information Campaign." *Economic and Political Weekly* 46 (32): 85–93.

Dash, Anjali, and Sanjay K. Mohanty. 2019. "Do Poor People in the Poorer States Pay More for Healthcare in India?" *BMC Public Health* 19 (1): 1020. https://doi.org/10.1186/s12889-019-7342-8.

Debnath, Sisir, and Tarun Jain. 2020. "Social Connections and Tertiary Healthcare Utilization." *Health Economics* 29 (4): 464–74. https://doi.org/10.1002/hec.3996.

Del Valle, Alejandro. 2021. "The Effects of Public Health Insurance in Labor Markets with Informal Jobs: Evidence from Mexico." *Journal of Health Economics* 77: 102454.

Desai, Sapna. 2009. "Keeping the 'Health' in Health Insurance." *Economic and Political Weekly* 44 (38): 18–21.

Devadasan, Narayanan, Tanya Seshadri, Mayur Trivedi, and Bart Criel. 2013. "Promoting Universal Financial Protection: Evidence from the Rashtriya Swasthya Bima Yojana (RSBY) in Gujarat, India." *Health Research Policy and Systems* 11 (1): 29. https://doi.org/10.1186/1478-4505-11-29.

Dhanaraj, Sowmya. 2016. "Economic Vulnerability to Health Shocks and Coping Strategies: Evidence from Andhra Pradesh, India." *Health Policy and Planning* 31 (6): 749–58. https://doi.org/10.1093/heapol/czv127.

Dureja, Abhishek. 2021. "Smoothing Consumption in Times of Sickness: Households Recourse Mechanisms." 2021 Annual Meeting, August 1–3, Austin, TX: Agricultural and Applied Economics Association.

Dureja, Abhishek, and Digvijay S. Negi. 2022. "Coping with the Consequences of Short-term Illness Shocks: The Role of Intra-household Labor Substitution." *Health Economics*. https://doi.org/10.1002/hec.4514.

Ecks, Stefan. 2021. "'Demand Side' Health Insurance in India: The Price of Obfuscation." *Medical Anthropology* 40 (5): 404–16. https://doi.org/10.1080/01459740.2021.1929208.

Ellis, Randall P., Moneer Alam, and Indrani Gupta. 2000. "Health Insurance in India: Prognosis and Prospectus." *Economic and Political Weekly*, 207–17.

Engelgau, Michael M., Anup Karan, and Ajay Mahal. 2012. "The Economic Impact of Non-Communicable Diseases on Households in India." *Globalization and Health* 8 (1): 9. https://doi.org/10.1186/1744-8603-8-9.

Erlangga, Darius, Marc Suhrcke, Shehzad Ali, and Karen Bloor. 2019. "The Impact of Public Health Insurance on Health Care Utilisation, Financial Protection and Health Status in Low- and Middle-Income Countries: A Systematic Review." *PLoS One* 14 (8): e0219731. https://doi.org/10.1371/journal.pone.0219731.

Fadlallah, Racha, Fadi El-Jardali, Nour Hemadi, Rami Z. Morsi, Clara Abou Abou. Samra, Ali Ahmad, Khurram Arif, Lama Hishi, Gladys Honein-AbouHaidar, and Elie A. Akl. 2018. "Barriers and Facilitators to Implementation, Uptake and Sustainability of Community-Based Health Insurance Schemes in Low- and Middle-Income Countries: A Systematic Review." *International Journal for Equity in Health* 17 (1): 13. https://doi.org/10.1186/s12939-018-0721-4.

Fan, Victoria Y., Anup Karan, and Ajay Mahal. 2012. "State Health Insurance and Out-of-Pocket Health Expenditures in Andhra Pradesh, India." *International Journal of Health Care Finance and Economics* 12 (3): 189–215. https://doi.org/10.1007/s10754-012-9110-5.

Gertler, Paul, and Jonathan Gruber. 2002. "Insuring Consumption Against Illness." *American Economic Review* 92 (1): 51–70. https://doi.org/10.1257/000282802760015603.

Ghosh, Soumitra. 2014. "Publicly-Financed Health Insurance for the Poor: Understanding RSBY in Maharashtra." *Economic and Political Weekly* 49 (43/44): 93–99.

GoI. 2011. *High Level Expert Group Report on Universal Health Coverage for India.* New Delhi: Planning Commission.

GoI. 2017. *National Health Policy 2017.* New Delhi: MoHFW.

Hammer, Jeffrey, Yamini Aiyar, and Salimah Samji. 2007. "Understanding Government Failure in Public Health Services." *Economic and Political Weekly* 42 (40): 4049–57.

Hirway, Indira. 2003. "Identification of BPL Households for Poverty Alleviation Programmes." *Economic and Political Weekly* 38 (45): 4803–8.

Hooda, Shailender. 2015. "Health Insurance, Health Access and Financial Risk Protection." *Economic and Political Weekly* 50 (50): 63–72.

Jain, Radhika. 2021. "Private Hospital Behavior Under Government Insurance: Evidence from Reimbursement Changes in India." https://scholar.harvard.edu/rjain/research.

Jain, A., S. Nundy, and K. Abbasi. 2014. "Corruption: Medicine's Dirty Open Secret." *BMJ* 348 (jun25 9): g4184. doi: https://doi.org/10.1136/bmj.g4184.

Jha, Prabhat, Yashwant Deshmukh, Chinmay Tumbe, Wilson Suraweera, Aditi Bhowmick, Sankalp Sharma, Paul Novosad, Sze Hang Fu, Leslie Newcombe, Hellen Gelband, and Patrick Brown. 2022. "COVID Mortality in India: National Survey Data and Health Facility Deaths." *Science.* https://doi.org/10.1126/science.abm5154.

Joe, W. 2015. "Distressed Financing of Household Out-of-Pocket Health Care Payments in India: Incidence and Correlates." *Health Policy and Planning* 30 (6): 728–41. https://doi.org/10.1093/heapol/czu050.

Karan, Anup, Winnie Yip, and Ajay Mahal. 2017. "Extending Health Insurance to the Poor in India: An Impact Evaluation of Rashtriya Swasthya Bima Yojana on out of Pocket Spending for Healthcare." *Social Science & Medicine* 181: 83–92. https://doi.org/10.1016/j.socscimed.2017.03.053.

Kay, Meera. 2015. "The Unethical Revenue Targets That India's Corporate Hospitals Set Their Doctors." *BMJ*. https://doi.org/10.1136/bmj.h4312.

Khetrapal, Sonalini, Arnab Acharya, and Anne Mills. 2019. "Assessment of the Public-Private-Partnerships Model of a National Health Insurance Scheme in India." *Social Science & Medicine* 243: 112634. https://doi.org/10.1016/j.socscimed.2019.112634.

Khiem, Phuong Huu, and Yu-Chen Kuo. 2021. "Health Insurance Reform Impact on Children's Educational Attainment: Evidence from Vietnam." *Review of Economics of the Household* 20 (1): 1255–85.

Kochar, Anjini. 1995. "Explaining Household Vulnerability to Idiosyncratic Income Shocks." *The American Economic Review* 85 (2): 159–64.

Kochar, Anjini. 2004. "Ill-Health, Savings and Portfolio Choices in Developing Economies." *Journal of Development Economics* 73 (1): 257–85. https://doi.org/10.1016/j.jdeveco.2003.02.001.

Krishna, Anirudh. 2010. *One Illness Away: Why People Become Poor and How They Escape Poverty*. Oxford: Oxford University Press.

La Forgia, Gerard, and Somil Nagpal. 2012. *Government-Sponsored Health Insurance in India: Are You Covered?* Washington, DC: The World Bank.

Mackintosh, Maureen, Amos Channon, Anup Karan, Sakthivel Selvaraj, Eleonora Cavagnero, and Hongwen Zhao. 2016. "What Is the Private Sector? Understanding Private Provision in the Health Systems of Low-Income and Middle-Income Countries." *The Lancet* 388 (10044): 596–605. https://doi.org/10.1016/S0140-6736(16)00342-1.

Mahal, Ajay. 2002. "Assessing Private Health Insurance in India: Potential Impacts and Regulatory Issues." *Economic and Political Weekly* 37 (6): 559–71.

Malani, Anup, Phoebe Holtzman, Kosuke Imai, Cynthia Kinnan, Morgen Miller, Shailender Swaminathan, Alessandra Voena, Bartosz Woda, and Gabriella Conti. 2021. *Effect of Health Insurance in India: A Randomized Controlled Trial*. w29576. Cambridge, MA: National Bureau of Economic Research. doi: https://doi.org/10.3386/w29576.

Mboi, Nafsiah. 2015. "Indonesia: On the Way to Universal Health Care." *Health Systems & Reform* 1 (2): 91–7. https://doi.org/10.1080/23288604.2015.1020642.

Mohanan, Manoj. 2013. "Causal Effects of Health Shocks on Consumption and Debt: Quasi-Experimental Evidence from Bus Accident Injuries." *Review of Economics and Statistics* 95 (2): 673–81. https://doi.org/10.1162/REST_a_00262.

Mohanan, Manoj, Katherine Hay, and Nachiket Mor. 2016. "Quality of Health Care in India: Challenges, Priorities, and the Road Ahead." *Health Affairs* 35 (10): 1753–58. https://doi.org/10.1377/hlthaff.2016.0676.

Morgan, Rosemary, Tim Ensor, and Hugh Waters. 2016. "Performance of Private Sector Health Care: Implications for Universal Health Coverage." *The Lancet* 388 (10044): 606–12. https://doi.org/10.1016/S0140-6736(16)00343-3.

Morton, Matthew, Somil Nagpal, Rajeev Sadanandan, and Sebastian Bauhoff. 2016. "India's Largest Hospital Insurance Program Faces Challenges in Using Claims Data to Measure Quality." *Health Affairs* 35 (10): 1792–99. https://doi.org/10.1377/hlthaff.2016.0588.

Nandi, Arindam, Ashvin Ashok, and Ramanan Laxminarayan. 2013. "The Socioeconomic and Institutional Determinants of Participation in India's Health Insurance Scheme for the Poor." *PLoS One* 8 (6): e66296. https://doi.org/10.1371/journal.pone.0066296.

Nandi, Arindam, E. Phoebe Holtzman, Anup Malani, and Ramanan Laxminarayan. 2015. "The Need for Better Evidence to Evaluate the Health & Economic Benefits of India's Rashtriya Swasthya Bima Yojana." *The Indian Journal of Medical Research* 142 (4): 383.

Nandi, Sulakshana, and Helen Schneider. 2020a. "Using an Equity-Based Framework for Evaluating Publicly Funded Health Insurance Programmes as an Instrument of UHC in Chhattisgarh State, India." *Health Research Policy and Systems* 18 (1): 50. https://doi.org/10.1186/s12961-020-00555-3.

Nandi, Sulakshana, and Helen Schneider. 2020b. "When State-Funded Health Insurance Schemes Fail to Provide Financial Protection: An in-Depth Exploration of the Experiences of Patients from Urban Slums of Chhattisgarh, India." *Global Public Health* 15 (2): 220–35.

Niehaus, Paul, Antonia Atanassova, Marianne Bertrand, and Sendhil Mullainathan. 2013. "Targeting with Agents." *American Economic Journal: Economic Policy* 5 (1): 206–38. https://doi.org/10.1257/pol.5.1.206.

Patel, Vikram, Shubhangi Bhadada, Kiran Mazumdar-Shaw, Arnab Mukherji, Tarun Khanna, and Gagandeep Kang. 2022. "A Historic Opportunity for Universal Health Coverage in India." *The Lancet* 400 (10351): 475–77. https://doi.org/10.1016/S0140-6736(22)01395-2.

Patel, Vikram, Kiran Mazumdar-Shaw, Gagandeep Kang, Pamela Das, and Tarun Khanna. 2021. "Reimagining India's Health System: A Lancet Citizens' Commission." *The Lancet* 397 (10283): 1427–30. https://doi.org/10.1016/S0140-6736(20)32174-7.

Platteau, Jean Philippe, and Darwin Ugarte Ontiveros. 2013. *Understanding and Information Failures: Lessons from a Health Microinsurance Program in India*, 39. Belgium: University of Namur.

Puri, Raghav, and Changqing Sun. 2021. "Increasing Utilization of Public Health Insurance Programs: Evidence from an Experiment in India." *World Development* 139: 105321.

Radojicic, Milan, Veljko Jeremic, and Gordana Savic. 2020. "Going Beyond Health Efficiency: What Really Matters?" *The International Journal of Health Planning and Management* 35 (1): 318–38. https://doi.org/10.1002/hpm.2914.

Rajasekhar, D., Erlend Berg, Maitreesh Ghatak, R. Manjula, and Sanchari Roy. 2011. "Implementing Health Insurance: The Rollout of Rashtriya Swasthya Bima Yojana in Karnataka." *Economic and Political Weekly* 46 (20): 56–63.

Reddy, Srinath, Sakthivel Selvaraj, Krishna Rao, Maulik Chokshi, Preeti Kumar, Vandana Arora, Sachin Bhokare, and Isheeta Ganguly. 2011. *A Critical Assessment of the Existing Health Insurance Models in India*. New Delhi: Public Health Foundation of India.

Reshmi, Bhageerathy, Bhaskaran Unnikrishnan, Eti Rajwar, Shradha S. Parsekar, Ratheebhai Vijayamma, and Bhumika Tumkur Venkatesh. 2021. "Impact of Public-Funded Health Insurances in India on Health Care Utilisation and Financial Risk Protection: A Systematic Review." *British Medical Journal Open* 11 (12): e050077. https://doi.org/10.1136/bmjopen-2021-050077.

Sangar, Shivendra, Varun Dutt, and Ramna Thakur. 2019. "Distress Financing of Out-of-Pocket Health Expenditure in India." *Review of Development Economics* 23 (1): 314–30. https://doi.org/10.1111/rode.12540.

Sarwal, Rakesh, and Anurag Kumar. 2021. "Health Insurance for India's Missing Middle." *Open Science Framework*. https://doi.org/10.31219/osf.io/s2x8r.

Selvaraj, Sakthivel, Habib Hasan Farooqui, and Anup Karan. 2018. "Quantifying the Financial Burden of Households' Out-of-Pocket Payments on Medicines in India: A Repeated Cross-Sectional Analysis of National Sample Survey Data, 1994–2014." *British Medical Journal Open* 8 (5): e018020. https://doi.org/10.1136/bmjopen-2017-018020.

Selvaraj, Sakthivel, Anup K. Karan, Wenhui Mao, Habib Hasan, Ipchita Bharali, Preeti Kumar, Osondu Ogbuoji, and Chetana Chaudhuri. 2021. "Did the Poor Gain from India's Health Policy Interventions? Evidence from Benefit-Incidence Analysis, 2004–2018." *International Journal for Equity in Health* 20 (1): 159. https://doi.org/10.1186/s12939-021-01489-0.

Sengupta, Reshmi, and Debasis Rooj. 2019. "The Effect of Health Insurance on Hospitalization: Identification of Adverse Selection, Moral Hazard and the Vulnerable Population in the Indian Healthcare Market." *World Development* 122: 110–29. https://doi.org/10.1016/j.worlddev.2019.05.012.

Shahrawat, R., and K. D. Rao. 2012. "Insured Yet Vulnerable: Out-of-Pocket Payments and India's Poor." *Health Policy and Planning* 27 (3): 213–21. https://doi.org/10.1093/heapol/czr029.

Sheikh, Kabir, Prasanna S. Saligram, and Krishna Hort. 2015. "What Explains Regulatory Failure? Analysing the Architecture of Health Care Regulation in Two Indian States." *Health Policy and Planning* 30 (1): 39–55. https://doi.org/10.1093/heapol/czt095.

Shukla, Shubhlakshmi. 2012. "India Probes Corruption in Flagship Health Programme." *The Lancet* 379 (9817): 698. https://doi.org/10.1016/S0140-6736(12)60293-1.

Singh, Prachi, Shamika Ravi, and David Dam. 2020. "Medicines in India: Accessibility, Affordability and Quality." Brookings India. Research Paper No. 032020-01.

Sinha, Tara, Sapna Desai, and Ajay Mahal. 2014. "Hospitalized for Fever? Understanding Hospitalization for Common Illnesses Among Insured Women in a Low-Income Setting." *Health Policy and Planning* 29 (4): 475–82.

Smith, Adam. 1776. *The Wealth of Nations: An Inquiry into the Nature and Causes of the Wealth of Nations*. Petersfield: Harriman House Limited.

Srinivas, Aditya, Suhani Jalota, Aprajit Mahajan, and Grant Miller. 2021. "Illness and Wage Loss: Longitudinal Evidence from India (and Implications for the Universal Health Coverage Agenda)." MedRxiv.

Sriram, Shyamkumar, and M. Mahmud Khan. 2020. "Effect of Health Insurance Program for the Poor on Out-of-Pocket Inpatient Care Cost in India: Evidence from a Nationally Representative Cross-Sectional Survey." *BMC Health Services Research* 20 (1): 839. https://doi.org/10.1186/s12913-020-05692-7.

Tangcharoensathien, Viroj, Walaiporn Patcharanarumol, Anond Kulthanmanusorn, Nithiwat Saengruang, and Hathairat Kosiyaporn. 2019. "The Political Economy of UHC Reform in Thailand: Lessons for Low- and Middle-Income Countries." *Health Systems & Reform* 5 (3): 195–208. https://doi.org/10.1080/23288604.2019.1630595.

Thawani, Vijay, Abin Mani, and Neeraj Upmanyu. 2017. "Why the Jan Aushadhi Scheme Has Lost Its Steam in India?" *Journal of Pharmacology & Pharmacotherapeutics* 8 (3): 134.

van Doorslaer, Eddy, Owen O'Donnell, Ravi P. Rannan-Eliya, Aparnaa Somanathan, Shiva Raj Adhikari, Charu C. Garg, Deni Harbianto, Alejandro N. Herrin, Mohammed Nazmul Huq, Shamsia Ibragimova, Anup Karan, Chiu Wan Ng, Badri Raj Pande, Rachel Racelis, Sihai Tao, Keith Tin, Kanjana Tisayaticom, Laksono Trisnantoro, Chitpranee Vasavid, and Yuxin Zhao. 2006. "Effect of Payments for Health Care on Poverty Estimates in 11 Countries in Asia: An Analysis of Household Survey Data." *The Lancet* 368 (9544): 1357–64. https://doi.org/10.1016/S0140-6736(06)69560-3.

Vellakkal, Sukumar, and Shah Ebrahim. 2013. "Publicly-Financed Health Insurance Schemes: Concerns About Impact Assessment." *Economic and Political Weekly* 48 (1): 24–27.

Vian, T. 2007. "Review of Corruption in the Health Sector: Theory, Methods and Interventions." *Health Policy and Planning* 23 (2): 83–94. https://doi.org/10.1093/heapol/czm048.

Virk, A. K., and R. Atun. 2015. "Towards Universal Health Coverage in India: A Historical Examination of the Genesis of Rashtriya Swasthya Bima Yojana—The Health Insurance Scheme for Low-Income Groups." *Public Health* 129 (6): 810–17. https://doi.org/10.1016/j.puhe.2015.02.002.

Wagstaff, Adam. 2007. "The Economic Consequences of Health Shocks: Evidence from Vietnam." *Journal of Health Economics* 26 (1): 82–100. https://doi.org/10.1016/j.jhealeco.2006.07.001.

Wagstaff, Adam. 2009. *Social Health Insurance vs. Tax-Financed Health Systems—Evidence from the OECD.* Washington, DC: The World Bank.

Wagstaff, Adam, Gabriela Flores, Justine Hsu, Marc-François Smitz, Kateryna Chepynoga, Leander R. Buisman, Kim van Wilgenburg, and Patrick Eozenou. 2018a. "Progress on Catastrophic Health Spending in 133 Countries: A Retrospective Observational Study." *The Lancet Global Health* 6 (2): e169–79. https://doi.org/10.1016/S2214-109X(17)30429-1.

Wagstaff, Adam, Gabriela Flores, Marc-François Smitz, Justine Hsu, Kateryna Chepynoga, and Patrick Eozenou. 2018b. "Progress on Impoverishing Health Spending in 122 Countries: A Retrospective Observational Study." *The Lancet Global Health* 6 (2): e180–92. https://doi.org/10.1016/S2214-109X(17)30486-2.

Wagstaff, Adam, and Magnus Lindelow. 2014. "Are Health Shocks Different? Evidence from a Multishock Survey in Laos." *Health Economics* 23 (6): 706–18. https://doi.org/10.1002/hec.2944.

Wherry, Laura R., Sarah Miller, Robert Kaestner, and Bruce D. Meyer. 2018. "Childhood Medicaid Coverage and Later-Life Health Care Utilization." *Review of Economics and Statistics* 100 (2): 287–302.

WHO (World Health Organization). [1946] 2020. "Constitution." In *Basic Documents*, 49th ed., 1–19. WHO, Geneva. https://apps.who.int/gb/bd/pdf_files/BD_49th-en.pdf#page=1.

CHAPTER 8

Incommensurate Welfare Gains: The Role of Ideas, Institutions, and Interests

Introduction

Despite the array of social safety nets—each addressing a particular feature of human deprivation—why do India's poor and those close to poverty continue to be vulnerable to economic uncertainty with long-lasting adverse consequences? There are two ways to answer this. First, social welfare programs are often inefficient in reaching their citizens of *focus* (targeted beneficiaries), which could emerge from flaws in design (*form*), corruption, or ineffective implementation. Second, the social welfare programs may not alone be sufficient to create development resilience (*scope*) and require other enablers to work in unison. In this chapter, we would focus on the first explanation, which has often been attributed to the poor performance of social welfare programs in the country.

Let us consider some facts. Forty percent of grains earmarked for the poor through PDS fails to reach its beneficiaries.[1] There remains a substantial unmet demand for work at MGNREGS in many of the poorest regions. It is often reported that wage payments at the MGNREGS

[1] These are the latest figures, but unfortunately more than a decade old based upon the computations by Dreze and Khera (2015) using the National Sample Survey Organization (NSSO), 2011–2012. While we strongly believe that the leakages have come down since then, but there is no data to back this claim.

A. Rahman and P. Pingali, *The Future of India's Social Safety Nets*, Palgrave Studies in Agricultural Economics and Food Policy, https://doi.org/10.1007/978-3-031-50747-2_8

sites is either delayed or paid a lower amount than stipulated.[2] The quality of school meals under MDMS remains nutritionally poor and hygiene quality remain a lingering concern. ICDS centers are known to be understaffed, and *Anganwadi* workers grossly underpaid, overworked, and demotivated to adequately fulfill their ever-increasing responsibilities as caregivers, teachers, and health workers, all at the same time.[3] A larger share of the poor is still unaware of the benefits of the health insurance program, and incapable to figure out the rigmarole of what coverage it provides, the associated costs of care, and the risk of being overcharged for seeking healthcare.[4] Maternity benefits, despite using computerized payment methods frequently get transferred to wrong bank accounts.[5] Most importantly, the inability to prove their poverty status arising from complex paperwork debars the poor from availing any benefits meant for them.[6] These are not field anecdotes or isolated journalistic accounts but generalizable findings across multiple academic research papers and reports which highlight the fledgling but poorly developed India's social safety nets architecture. Yes, there are exceptions—some states do a better job and protecting the poor—yet for most of the poor, the transformational impact of the social welfare schemes remains illusory.

This chapter focuses on these bottlenecks—design faults and implementational hurdles—which limit the effectiveness of social welfare programs and thereby development resilience. Our proposed answers are

[2] A note prepared by the Peoples' Action for Employment Guarantee estimates that 15.5 million workers did not get work under MGNREGS despite asking for it in 2020. Majority of this unmet demand for work was concentrated in the poorer states: Uttar Pradesh (27%), Madhya Pradesh (22%) and Bihar (20%). See https://www.im4change.org/upload/files/PAEG%20press%20conference_10%20September%202020.pdf. Accessed November 20, 2022. Also refer to Narayanan et al. (2020) for a discussion. Analyzing over 9 million wage payments under MGNREGS in 2016–2017, Narayanan et al. (2019) show that only 21% of the payments were made within the stipulated duration of 15 days from work.

[3] https://gcnf.org/wp-content/uploads/2021/05/State-Survey-of-School-Meal-Programs-in-India-Report-with-Annexes.pdf Time-use survey of Anganwadi workers suggests that a substantial amount of their time is spent on administrative tasks which compromises upon their time on providing direct care, while they are unpaid at the same time (Jain et al. 2020; Razavi and Staab 2010).

[4] See Parisi et al. (2022).

[5] https://www.thehindu.com/news/national/one-in-three-payments-for-maternity-benefit-scheme-credited-to-wrong-account/article30891111.ece. Accessed October 1, 2022.

[6] See Gupta (2012).

grounded in a careful analysis of policy *ideas*—conceptualization of the nature of citizen-state social contract on the subsistence floor—and the institutional structure—responsible for designing and implementing the programs—which undergirds the success of any social welfare system.[7]

Ideas, Institutions, and Interests

The challenge of public policy is to come up with an *idea* on how to utilize key welfare *institutions*—markets, state, and society—to support citizen welfare.[8] In the context of low- and medium-income countries, markets are underdeveloped, and societies provide mutual social insurance to its members. State, therefore, takes a 'developmental' role where its primary responsibility is not only to protect property rights, and maintain law and order, but also 'to be a guide, coordinator, stimulator, and a catalytic agent for economic activities' ... [because, for]...various historical and structural reasons, the development process [in such contexts] has been atrophied and the path forward is darkened by all kinds of missing information and incomplete markets' (Bardhan 2016, pp. 864). Implicit in this arrangement, are the *ideas* around rights and obligations—explicit or implicit—of the state toward its citizens, referred to as the citizen-state *social contract*.[9]

[7] Mehta and Walton (2014) provide a rich description of the politics of development and change in India using the concepts of ideas, institutions, and interests. Varshney (1989), in his seminal work, also appeals to the importance of these concepts for understanding Indian agricultural policymaking process and the rural-urban divide. Similarly, Mukherji (2014) uses changes in ideas, institutions, and interests to explain India's embrace of globalization policies and institutional change toward market-based model of development in the 1990s. Recently, Baloch (2021) has engaged with the role of ideas—of nationhood, and socio-economic deprivation—on democratic practice and corruption in contemporary India.

[8] In their recent book (Acemoglu and Robinson 2020) demonstrate how a strong state and society—creating a 'corridor' of competition and collaboration where potentially despotic action is checked by the society, while state's commitment toward basic societal needs tempers social upheavals—is essential for human flourishing.

[9] The analytical lens of social contract allows one to study the development process of a nation through the changing nature of state-society relationship over time. The strength of social contract is increasingly gaining attention as an important explanation of the persistence of underdevelopment—with deep-rooted inequalities, poor quality of public services, lack of or weak institutions, and resistance to reforms—across the developing world (Cloutier et al. 2021). See Hickey (2011) and Hickey and King (2016) for the role of social contracts in the politics of social protection.

There is wide variation in the nature and strength of social contract as high inequality, weak civil society, and entrenched elite *interests* perpetuate non-democratic institutions and therefore weaken the bargaining power of citizens with the state.[10] A citizen-oriented *social contract*, on the other hand, promotes equal opportunity, economic empowerment, and social cohesion, with a greater role of social protection against economic insecurity. Ideas around the nature of social contract and redistributive welfare policy are, however, imbedded in the contextual political, and socio-cultural norms or economic needs thereby determining the nature of welfare mix while the effective implementation necessitates appropriate governance arrangements which includes allocation of funds, assignment of responsibilities, enactment of regulations, and local bureaucratic appointments to deliver the welfare services. Long-term success of such a design hinge on the cohesiveness of ideas around redistribution, political commitment to those ideals, and a capable state to efficiently implement welfare programs. This is only possible through a perfect trifecta of *ideas*, *interests*, and *institutions* aligned to enact, deliver, and innovate on the social welfare policies for human resilience which is a central challenge for the developing countries with poor institutions, vested political interests, and often ill-conceived ideas around welfare.

Borrowing from the textbook models of policymaking, we present a framework in Fig. 8.1 to describe the intricate linkages across *ideas*, *institutions*, and *interests* which determine the *focus*, *form*, and *scope* of social welfare policies and its reform over time.[11] We argue that while the ideational process is a culmination of the collaboration between macro-level ideas and institutions, and the influential interest groups they foment, implementation of welfare schemes depends upon the program design and local institutions—state capacity, bureaucratic effectiveness, and the nature of social contract.[12]

[10] Weak social contracts in countries with imperfect markets and poor state capacity create mutually reinforcing conditions of high inequality in income and opportunity, disempowered citizens, and lower demands for redistribution. See Bénabou (2000) for a theoretical exposition.

[11] See Gough (2008) for more details.

[12] Ideas around universal values—equality, solidarity, social justice, or security—have been the hallmark of welfare policy in the welfare states in advanced nations. To understand the role of ideational process and its connectedness with political institutions and policy legacies, refer to Béland (2005). Also see Leisering (2021) for an ideational approach to social protection policies in Brazil, India, China, and South Africa, four

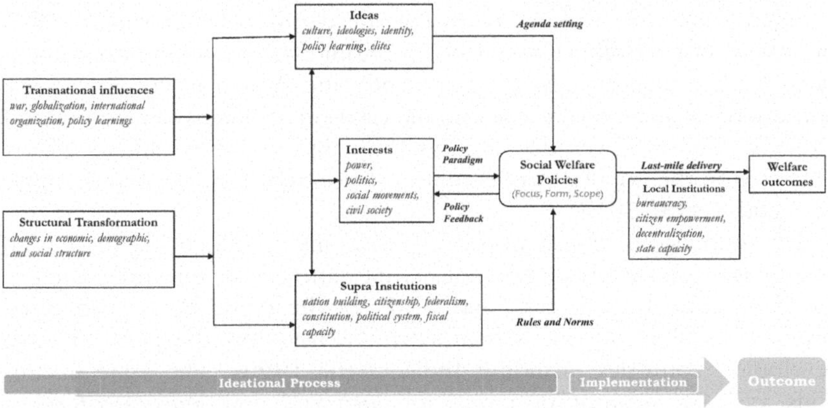

Fig. 8.1 The role of ideas, interests, and institutions in social welfare policy design (Adapted from Gough [2008])

Ideas Set Forth the Welfare Agenda

Ideas, simply put, represent the historically formed cognitive beliefs, perceptions, and the intrinsic values held by the policy actors which allow them to frame their understanding of the social problem, and offer suggestions, thereby initiating an 'agenda setting' process (Kingdon and Stano 1984). Policy ideas—the preferred ideological narrative of the policy actors within the nature of citizen-state social contract—are formed with respect to the national economic transformation (declining importance of agriculture, industrialization, urbanization, changing demographic share of the population, etc.) which create newer forms of vulnerability, along with transnational influences such as global consensus on certain development goals, international aid, or transferable policy learnings on best practices in program delivery.

Despite distinct models of welfare policies in the advanced nations, they have all been associated with the structural issues with the labor markets and economic change in the wake of industrialization (Esping-Andersen 1990). East Asian economies of Japan and Korea too developed *ideas* around a more expansive social welfare programs in response to

of the major countries in Global South which have embarked on expanding social safety nets since the 1990s.

changing economic realities following the democratic reforms of 1993 and 1987, respectively (Kwon 1997). Among the developing economics, social welfare programs in a majority of Latin American countries were introduced as a result of the economic crises in 1990s which led political actors to develop newer ideas around reductions in poverty and inequality which led to the popularity of conditional cash transfers (Barrientos 2009; Levy and Schady 2013).

The influence of transnational organizations in influencing the design of domestic policies is conspicuous. International organizations such as the International Monetary Fund (IMF) or the World Bank propagated targeted social protection schemes with a *focus* on the poor in most developing countries including India in the 1990s. The same institutions are now promoting a case for *universal* and *guaranteed* social protection highlighting the *rights-based* ideas of social security of every citizen (World Bank 2019). This shift in policy ideals reflect the changing global paradigm in favor of human rights and dignity of citizens as a basis of social protection against the earlier views around fiscal profligacy. Similarly, international donor organizations have also influenced the expansion of social welfare programs while in some cases countries there is a diffusion of social policy ideas across nations (Graham 2002; Weyland 2005).[13]

The perceptions of current development challenges (or the *scope* of the social problem), identification of the deserving beneficiaries (*focus*), and the nature of prescribed solutions (*form*) to it—cash benefits, food transfers, old age pensions, social health insurance—therefore reflect the underlying *ideas* of the policymaker around the nature of welfare mix to be designed in a particular economic and political context.

[13] Ethiopia's Productive Safety Net Program (PSNP) in mid-2000s is an example of the former, while expansion of welfare programs in Korea and Taiwan represents the latter case. Sustainable Development Goals (SDGs) 1.3 and 3.8 further mandate country-specific minimum level of social protection floor and universal health coverage respectively which affects domestic social welfare policies. In the wake of COVID-19, UN General Assembly at the 47th Human Rights Council Meeting decided upon a global fund for social protection to allow low-income countries to guarantee a minimum standard of living through social assistance programs.

Institutions: Conduit of Welfare

Scholarship on the role of institutions for long-run economic development and growth is vast.[14] *Institutions* referred as to the set of 'rules and norms'—formal (property rights, legal codes, democratic constitution, bureaucracy, etc.) and informal (social sanctions, customs and traditions, and corruption among others)—shape and govern political and economic exchange in a society. Some institutions ease the challenges of coordination, while others could be disruptive to fair exchange.[15] Policy actors prescribe their policy *ideas* with regard to their understanding of the presence of institutions and their effectiveness.

During the ideational process, *supra-institutions*—legislative frameworks, political system, and financial strength as—determine the framing of policy paradigms. These *supra-institutions*, backed by legal frameworks, are influenced by a multitude of *ideas*—constitutional democracy, electoral systems, federalism, bureaucratic structure, citizen rights, etc.—which are aligned with the nation-state's cultural norms, religious practices, or social structure.[16] *Local institutions*, on the other hand, mediate the delivery of welfare policies. Formal state machinery—bureaucrats, elected representatives, non-governmental service providers, etc.—and its interaction with the informal social norms and practices governs the

[14] See North (1990), Greif (2006), Glaeser et al. (2004), Rodrik et al. (2004) and Acemoglu and Robinson (2008) among others. For the role of institutions in charting welfare policymaking, refer to Béland (2007) and Blyth (2002).

[15] For example, property rights, efficient contract enforcement, or credit institutions promote exchange, bureaucratic corruption or institutional hierarchy is an impediment to fair returns to this exchange. The latter inhibits both the efficiency and equity in an economic system. In order to understand which institutions may matter and which may not, see Bardhan (2005).

[16] The institution of race and persistent racial prejudice is referred to as an important impediment to progressive social welfare policies in the United States compared to countries at a similar level of economic development in the Europe. Racial minorities in the USA are highly overrepresented among those eligible for welfare benefits. Political rhetoric positions the colored minorities, mainly the Black population, as lazy recipients of welfare suppresses redistribution (Alesina et al. 2001). Within the USA, welfare expansion was resisted for a long time. Agricultural interests of the Southern region discouraged civil rights movement because it was likely to hinder the availability of cheap labor. This resistance lasted until agricultural technologies such as mechanization in the late 1950s and early 1960s reduced the demand for labor (Alston and Ferrie 1999). Similarly, old age pensions in South Africa were meant only for the white citizens until the apartheid era came to an end.

everyday nature of exchange between citizens determine the success of local institutions. But local traditions, rituals, and entrenched hierarchies often inhibit fair terms of exchange within societies and resist formation of voluntary associations which lowers the quality of citizen-state engagements. It could also abet bureaucratic corruption, identity-based discrimination, and poor grievance system which implies that welfare recipients are often deprived of their entitlements.[17] The unevenness in the performance of local *institutions,* therefore, has been attributed to the divergence local state capacity for improved well-being (Bardhan 2016).

Perverse Interests Undermine the Welfare Agenda

Policies create politics through a feedback process. The emerging politics could potentially shape policy outcomes depending upon whether it benefits the masses or the elite *interest* groups (Campbell 2012).[18] Where institutions are poorly developed and state accountability is low, *institutions* are prone to being manipulated for political *interests* thereby reducing the policy process—from ideation to delivery—an inherently political exercise. Supra-level institutions create strategic opportunities for the political actors to further their *interests,* be it maximizing electoral gains, claim rule legitimacy, or social mobilization. As a result, there is often resistance to a necessary change among the elites, causing stasis in the ideational process much to the detriment of long-term development.

[17] In most developing countries, corruption or discrimination is rampant and such an intrinsic part of social life that lack of bureaucratic accountability and bribery is considered a 'norm' (Basu 2011, 2018). These norms are legitimized or rather enforced through lack of political voice of the disadvantaged. In the case of local public services, social networks among the elites (Cruz et al. 2020) and culture of coercion might impinge upon public action (Rao and Walton 2004). Local collective action, however, which overcomes the distinctions between people, and creates solidarity groups can overcome some of these challenges (Ostrom 1990). Improvements in the local governance in India has been cited as one of the reasons for improved public services, however, its unevenness is explained by the supra state, i.e. the subnational ideas of democratic empowerment (Rao and Sanyal 2019).

[18] Political interests affect the design of economic policies (Persson and Tabellini 2002). For example, agricultural price support policies across the globe have created newer political interests and community mobilization around sustaining such policies as it provides disproportionately high benefits to certain groups of the society at the expense of others and larger developmental goals. Refer to Pierson (1993, 1996) for a comprehensive discussion on the politics of welfare.

The institution of federalism adds another layer to the politics of welfare policies with its own distinct subnational policy ideas, institutional norms, and political interests.[19]

Local *interests* are often served through clientelistic practices, elite capture, and street-level bureaucratic inefficiencies may undermine the success of well laid out policy design of formal supra-institutions through discrimination, rent seeking, and corruption in service delivery. To avoid the last-mile delivery concerns—rampant in the developing countries—the citizen-state social contract, as designed at the supra level, needs to be supplemented with sufficient motivation, incentive, and accountability of local state institutions.[20] Developing local state capacity through democratic institutions such as decentralization of governance which empower citizens and increase accountability are therefore essential to improve delivery. Empowered citizens imply greater voice to the citizens in building a more compact social contract further influencing ideas around the *focus*, *form*, and *scope* of social welfare policies.

Ideas, Institutions, and Interests Co-evolve

Policymaking process is not static, yet it is a slow or gradual process constantly evolving in response to changing economic, political, and institutional considerations.[21] Ideas, too, instead of being dogmatic ideological stances, are shaped by (and also shape) the institutions and

[19] The nature of federal system its interaction with central and local institutions are instrumental in influencing social policies. Pierson (1995) provide its theoretical underpinnings with a comparative study of social policies in United States and Canada.

[20] See Drèze and Sen (1991) for a discussion on failure of public service delivery in India.

[21] The status-quo in policy stance emerges despite its inefficiency emerges from the political uncertainty about the consequences of reform. Ex-ante, who stands to gain or lose from the change is not determined. Gradualism, through partial reforms, which slowly ease out these political constraints are therefore more politically sustainable than a 'big bang' policy change. See Rodrik (1996) for more discussion on the challenges of policy reform.

interests within the emerging policy paradigms over time.[22] Some perpetuate vested interests thereby inhibiting change, while others force their way into civic consciousness.[23] For example, the emergence of universal concepts (such as human rights, malnutrition, or social inclusion) or specific group-based upliftment ideals (elderly, or marginalized ethnicities) have created broad-based moral consciousness around the need for a 'social minimum.' Accepting these goals as 'socially desirable' creates a political consensus around the need for appropriate institutions, the design of which—in the *form* of delivery or the beneficiary *focus*—might still differ across *ideas* held by the policy actors. The disagreement may be mediated by the respective *interests* of the policy actors in establishing the *policy paradigms* at a specific point in time. While short-term vested *interests* might hinder change, *ideas* can potentially act as catalyst for long-term change, especially when the policy actor stands to gain from it in the future.[24]

[22] For instance, the dominant ideas around social welfare policies during the early twentieth century was economic recovery from the Great Depression and recovery from the World Wars. In the 1970s and 1980s however, the political efforts to dismantle those benefits were motivated by the ideas that white working-class citizens are paying for the benefits received by the predominantly black welfare recipients. Focusing on the low-income countries, Lavers and Hickey (2016) argue that the ideas around social protection need to be studied within the broader real of domestic and transnational political economy changes as democratic deepening and globalization have contributed significantly to expansion of welfare programs in the Global South.

[23] Lavers and Hickey (2016) argue that a social protection in developing countries has primarily become a political tool to maintain stability and legitimacy of political rule rather than as a lever of advancing development. Success or failure of social protection in developing countries therefore must be understood as a corollary of vested interests of the policy actors. Studying the introduction of social welfare programs in sub-Saharan Africa, Lavers and Hickey (2021) highlight the role of transnational influences such as global policy coalitions in the introduction and adoption of social protection *ideas*, while political *interests* arising from the presence of democratic *institutions* such as competitive elections further entrench or institutionalize the social transfers programs. They argue that in countries where electoral competition is low, elite's perception of vulnerability and impending distributional crisis which could pose a potential threat to the 'legitimacy of rule' aids expansion of social welfare programs.

[24] Rodrik (2014) argues that the political economy models often overemphasize vested political interests as a cause of underdevelopment leading to pessimistic interpretation of reforms. According to him, *ideas* act a catalyst for policy and institutional change as interests are also nothing but pre-conceived ideas of future benefits. Institutional transformations such as prohibition of slavery, universal suffrage, or democratic institutions are after all ideas of equality and hope for a better world. Using a political economy model

Long-Term Success of Social Welfare Programs

Long-term success of social welfare strategies requires the emergence of a compact *social contract* with clearly articulated *ideas* around the role of state and its commitment to social welfare, along with the institutional apparatus to identify and deliver welfare to the intended beneficiaries. Such a social contract requires broad-based political support and democratic consensus across policy actors and citizens on what ought to be the socially desired 'basic minimum.' These deliberations are however an ongoing process—which includes the challenges of developmental priority, institution building, political bargaining, and fiscal considerations—amid which the *form*, *focus*, and *scope* of social welfare programs are determined.

While the short-term success of social welfare programs is often measured through a combination of many attributes—namely, appropriateness, adequacy, equity, cost-effectiveness, incentive compatibility, sustainability, and dynamism—long-term benefits include not only a reduction in poverty and extent of deprivation but also a reduction in the future likelihood of falling into poverty, along with empowering citizens, thereby building development resilience.[25] There is no golden rule, however, for what is the most appropriate *form* or an adequate amount of social transfers. It depends upon the developmental challenge at hand—extent and nature of deprivation—and the government's ideas (or solutions) around what should be the minimum subsistence floor for its citizens (*scope*), who are the people in need (*focus*) and how to best help achieve that (*form*). When the policy actors do not have a perfect understanding of the 'developmental problem' or the financial and institutional wherewithal to address it—which is most often the case in developing countries—policy *ideas* are often a kind of experiments—suited to the interests of the policy actors, even when informed by theory—with uncertain outcomes. The proposed ideas around welfare therefore emerge and

of ideas and policy change, Mukand and Rodrik (2018) reckon that "in the very short run, it is all about interests. In the long run, it is all ideas."

[25] See Grosh et al. (2008) for the desirable attributes of a successful social welfare program.

evolve within a particular form of economic, social, and political setting where good *ideas* often clash with perverse *interests*.[26]

Diagnosing Incommensurate Welfare Outcomes

The framework presented in Fig. 8.1 is useful to understand the disconnect between social safety net policies, their implementation, and the actual welfare outcomes in India. We use it to make two points. First, we argue, as we have done throughout the book, that social welfare programs in the country have a short-term focus, and myopic approach toward sustainable development. A weak *social contract* has only provided band-aid solutions to poverty reduction with little recognition to long-term strategy toward human capability and resilience building. Second, the fledgling social welfare architecture is further handicapped by poor institutional arrangements—weak state capacity—to deliver the welfare benefits. Unless the local institutions—social and political—are empowered sufficiently, elite ideas driven ideational process might not be able to achieve broad-based success—in implementation, as well as impact.

Fledgling, Yet Feeble 'Social Contract'

India's centralized economic planning, in the early years of its planning period, prioritized economic growth over redistribution with the *idea* that fruits of economic growth would trickle down to the poor.[27] The

[26] Institutions influence, and are influenced, by such contestations for welfare delivery. Mukand and Rodrik (2005) argue that while economic *ideas* are transferable, they are not institution-free. Institutions, germane to the success of welfare programs, are however distinct across contexts. Economic concepts of incentives, competition, budget constraints, fiscal sustainability, and property rights which are central to the reform process do not map directly into institutional solutions. As a result, reforms successful in one context may be a poor policy option in others. They provide examples of two-track reform which may have worked well in China but not in Soviet Union. Similarly, import substitution may lead to competitive industrial structure in Brazil, but not in Argentina. Understanding the success of social welfare policies—in terms of *focus*, *form*, and *scope*—therefore requires a rigorous engagement with the nature of ideas and institutions which allowed the introduction and functioning of particular social welfare programs along with the political interests it generates.

[27] Economic planning in the early years had committed itself to the *ideals* of 'socialist' path of economic development—state driven industrialization—where agriculture was meant to be a source of inputs for manufacturing sector. The socialist approach, however,

responsibility of social welfare was assigned to the subnational governments which did not express much interest in distributional objectives.[28] The 5th five-year economic plan (1974–1979), for the first time, brought about the idea of a 'Common Minimum Needs Program.'[29] Subsequently, newer anti-poverty schemes were introduced, yet expenditure on social safety nets received only a 'residual' budgetary allocation.[30]

Inadequate attention to social welfare policies could be explained by an "absence of a real commitment among state elites, poor quality peripheral bureaucracy, but most of all, powerful vested interests" (Kohli 2012). Social institutions marked by multiple axes of identity-based divisions—subnational, religious, linguistic, caste, and class—provided sufficient distraction for the new democratic nation to generate a strong *social contract*. Elite interests—of farmers and businessmen—dominated policy ideas, and the citizen voices were suppressed by the social divisions within these groups. It was therefore in the interest of policy actors to harbor upon group identities and the form of politics it created to undermine citizen mobilization for ensuring a social minimum. The 'social question,'

remained limited to matters of economy as institutional agrarian reforms—such as redistribution of land, devolving power to local bodies, or establishment of cooperatives—was resisted by local landed political elites. See Varshney (1998) and Mehta and Walton (2014) for a detailed discussion on the political ideas, and competing interests on issues related to the development process and subnational responsibilities in India's planning process.

[28] Subnational politics was dominated by elite *interests*—landed farmers—who resisted land reforms thereby leaving the largest share of the people shorn of basic physical assets essential to break out of the poverty trap. The farmer elites, in subsequent years, got further emboldened with gains from the 'grow more food' agricultural policies to fight famines. The idea of poverty reduction was synonymous with starvation, and famines in those years, and the government therefore emphasized agriculture. See Chapters 2–5 for more details.

[29] It is important to note that Indian Constitution aims to achieve economic democracy along with political democracy. The ideals of economic welfare are enshrined in its Directive Principles of State Policy (Article 38) but are not legally binding. Article 38 of the Indian Constitution states, "i) The State shall strive to promote the welfare of the people by securing and protecting as effectively as it may a social order in which justice, social, economic and political, shall inform all the institutions of the national life. ii) The State shall, in particular, strive to minimise the inequalities in income, and endeavour to eliminate inequalities in status, facilities and opportunities, not only amongst individuals but also amongst groups of people residing in different areas or engaged in different vocations."

[30] See Guhan (1995) for a discussion.

however, was addressed through identity-based political representation rather than citizenship 'rights.'[31]

The ideas of redistribution under the slogans of '*gharibi hatao*' (eradicate poverty) emerged in the 1970s only when the Congress party—which held unopposed political power till then—began to face political pressures with a rising influence of identity-based political parties—language, region, and caste—at the subnational level. It led to a slew of anti-poverty policies—institutional support through expansion of agricultural credit and irrigation services—with the scope of addressing rural poverty, but the performance of these programs was unsatisfactory in reducing mass poverty.[32] It benefited primarily the *interests* of the landed agricultural class leaving the structure of poverty intact with families, religious, and caste affiliations continuing to be the source of social insurance during times of need.

The next two decades, 1980s and 1990s, brought about an 'attitudinal shift' in the government, away from state-led economic planning to greater reliance on private trade and global markets for economic growth (Rodrik and Subramanian 2004).[33] Policies which hindered private entrepreneurship—an array of license requirements, land and labor regulations, and other controls—were replaced with a greater 'pro-business' shift in the planning process. The *idea* of development through redistribution, as espoused during the 1970s, was quickly relegated to the backburner with priority being accorded to the "growth first" strategy (Kohli 2007). The strategy of economic liberalization put India on a path of unprecedented growth and structural transformation of the

[31] India's constitution outlawed caste-based untouchability—a defining feature of the caste system—and provided for affirmative action policies in politics, education, and employment to the most marginalized of the groups, scheduled castes (*Dalits*) and scheduled tribes (*Adivasis*) subsequently. See Pellissery (2021) for a discussion on the stifled 'social question' in India.

[32] See Chapter 4 for a more detailed discussion.

[33] Economic planning in the early years had committed itself to the *ideals* of 'socialist' path of economic development—state driven industrialization—where agriculture was meant to be a source of inputs for manufacturing sector. The socialist approach, however, remained limited to matters of economy as institutional agrarian reforms—such as redistribution of land, devolving power to local bodies, or establishment of cooperatives—was resisted by local landed political elites. Varshney (1998) comprehensively portrays the clash of ideals and interests in the early years of Indian policymaking.

economy, yet achievements on human development outcomes continue to be lacking.[34]

While economic deregulation did increase economic growth rates and led to a reduction in consumption-based poverty, it didn't 'trickle down' to generate broad-based prosperity and therefore widened interpersonal and spatial inequality.[35] Commensurate improvements in human development outcomes such as undernutrition, health, or learning outcomes among children remain lacking. The growth process also did little to hasten the pernicious role of 'sticky' social institutions and cultural norms—unequal intra-household bargaining power, poor sanitation and hygiene practices, and low female labor force participation—while improvements in the quality of public infrastructure, which are essential for a broad-based reduction in poverty remained slow. These outcomes, however, should not be surprising if one believes that the attitudinal shift toward economic deregulation "was shaped largely by the economic problems of the government rather than by the economic priorities of the people or by long-term development objectives" (Nayyar 2017, p. 47).

The emergence of rights-based social protection demands in the 2000s proved to be a watershed moment which changed the policy *ideas* around redistribution. These *ideas* emerged from redistributive concerns arising out of a globalizing economy, urbanization, informalization of labor, and democratic strengthening. Government planning document also echoed its vision for 'inclusive growth' which "yields broad-based benefits and

[34] What distinguishes India from these other countries which went through structural transformation in the postwar era is the lack of long-term ideas around social policy. The structural transformation process in the East Asian countries was driven by a rising share of both manufacturing and the service sector in the total output and investment in social welfare as part of their structural transformation. Service-sector growth of the Indian economy created a dual labor market—earning epithets like India of light and darkness, the dollar-rupee economy or islands of California with sub-Saharan Africa—where high-skilled and educated urban work force enjoyed the fruits of employment provided social security while the rest of labor force was devoid of any support in times of adversity. As a result, only less than 10% of India's workforce has the provision of employment based social security currently. See more details in Chapters 3 and 4.

[35] Any serious student of poverty debate would highlight the limitations of money-metric measure of consumption-based poverty lines. Kotwal et al. (2014) therefore contend that if one considers poverty at twice the government identified poverty line, poverty levels in India remain unchanged between 1983 and 2004 at a staggering 80% of people falling under poverty. Refer to Chapters 3 and 4 for a comprehensive discussion.

ensures equality of opportunity for all" (Government of India 2006, p. 2). Social welfare programs were now backed by the constitutional 'rights' created *institutional* guarantees to welfare transfers. Newer social welfare schemes were introduced while the poorly performing ones got a new lease of life, even in regions traditionally known for poor governance and corruption in public service delivery.[36] Civil society groups, the prime architects of this change, hailed it is a great triumph for the democratic process. Legitimacy to the concerns of poor and their political empowerment provided a proof that the "demands of the underprivileged majority can prevail over privileged interests" (Drèze 2010).

Economic growth in the subsequent years had allowed substantial financial resources to be spent on welfare, and greater political competition (especially at a subnational level) contributed to a more progressive social welfare policy. The *ideas* around *scope*, *focus*, and *form* of the social welfare programs however continue to be subservient to the perverse political *interests* and underdeveloped *institutions*. For example, despite its widely established nutritional benefits, political leadership in most states are hesitant to add eggs to the school meals or early life nutritional interventions, fearing its punitive electoral outcomes. The introduction of eggs is likely to offend the vegetarian lobby, leading to a clash of *interests* much to the detriment of improved development outcomes. While employment and food are considered citizen entitlements backed by constitutional legislations, right to affordable healthcare has not gathered the same support. Similarly, big farmer's political *interests* inhibit innovations in farm income support programs and agricultural diversification, while public health insurance policies are often held ransom by the profit-driven *interests* of private healthcare providers.

At the implementation level, however, ideas matter less, but locally relevant social institutions, and state bureaucracy, become important. The efficacy of welfare systems depends upon the administrative structure responsible for delivery of benefits. Once the *form, focus*, and *scope* of policies are decided, fiscal allocations are made by the federal or subnational government which is funneled to villages and municipalities. Local bureaucrats and politicians work jointly to identify and distribute these benefits to deserving citizens. District and sub-district bureaucrats act as

[36] For a systematic review of the policymaking process, key actors which influenced it and their interests behind the introduction and reforms of anti-poverty programs between 2004 and 2014, refer to Chiriyankandath et al. (2019).

the state representatives while elected politicians are the people's representatives in ensuring the deserving citizens get their welfare entitlement. An efficient, motivated, and adequately incentivized bureaucracy at the local level along with political empowerment of the citizens, therefore, is required for an egalitarian distribution of benefits to the citizens. While local state capacity and state institutions are becoming more participatory leading to greater benefits to the citizens, they continue to be underdeveloped, leading to an inefficient social welfare delivery system.

Underdeveloped Local Institutions

Persistent inefficiencies of the local *institutions* lead to an uneven translation of welfare *ideas* into human welfare, which has been the bane of Indian social policy, with the ignominy of being described as a *flailing state*—"a nation-state in which the head, the elite institutions at the national (and in some states) level remain sound and functional but this head is no longer reliably connected via nerves and sinews to its own limbs" (Pritchett 2009). Poor attendance of public health and teaching staff at workplace, frequent closure of shops which provide food to the poor and often malpractices by the shop owners, poor hygiene of school meals, lower increase educational learning, and lack of motivation among the lower level of public service providers reflect this problem.

Rent seeking behavior among local politician and bureaucrats is a typical characteristic of *institutional* failures of the state which lowers citizen's trust in the public delivery system thereby acting as a deterrent to reforms such as better payment to the lower level staff and investment in local state capacity (The World Bank 2016). Local governance institutions (arms and limbs of the state) have not developed commensurately in India.[37] Trying to unpack the success as well the failures of the Indian state, Kapur (2020) notes that the Indian state succeeds mostly in episodic delivery of services or mission-mode projects such as holding free and fair elections, emergency relief, providing digital identity,

[37] Indian public administration has 5 tiers—nation, subnational states, districts, subdistricts, and village/municipality. It has been argued that the subnational elites hoarded power and did not allow the third tier of local government—such as the village councils (*panchayats*) and the municipal corporations—to develop. See Evans and Heller (2019) for a comparative review of state directed development process across countries in Asia and India's unique challenge.

building toilets, public schools, road infrastructure but when it comes to the everyday service delivery such as continued provision of social welfare programs, teacher, or health staff attendance, it lets its citizens down. The failure, he argues, emanates from the lack of local state capacity to deliver services, the nation's struggles associated with a democratic transition amid widespread poverty and weak fiscal capacity, and the poor bargaining power of citizens through pervasive divisions along the lines of hierarchy and status in the society—religion, caste, class, and patriarchy—which promotes rent seeking and patronage, thereby debilitating local accountability.[38] While incentives such performance pay bonuses to local state actors have been put forwarded as solutions to ensure better accountability, and the use of technology to monitor performance, but it somehow hasn't been able to change the culture of frontline bureaucracy.

Below, we discuss key features of the local state institutions, essential to understand the inefficiencies inherent in the last-mile delivery of the social welfare programs.

Local State Capacity and Implementation Deficits

Last-mile service delivery concerns—be it public goods or social safety net programs—have long been recognized as a 'binding constraint' to development.[39] Information asymmetry between the local state and higher authorities further creates avenues for rent seeking behavior by the local bureaucrats and politicians creating a 'leaky' public system which increases fiscal costs of the programs and reduces public support for welfare, in the long run.[40] Leakages in the PDS, lower take up of the health insurance, poor implementation of MGNREGS, overworked health and *Anganwadi* workers, and modestly funded primary health centers are some of the

[38] The term 'state capacity' signifies the ability of the government to reach its citizens, hear their grievances, enumerate them, collect taxes, create physical infrastructure, ensure law and order, and provide basic citizenship rights.

[39] Providing welfare services to the poor, in the remotest part of the world, has been identified as a major challenge to development policy. See World Bank (2003).

[40] For the effect of corruption on social spending and redistribution policy of the state, see Olken (2006).

most glaring examples state failure. Overcoming this constraint requires an active local state, and its enhanced capacity to deliver.[41]

Local state capacity, however, is one of the most tenuous aspects of governance as it most intimately connected to the variegated local institutions—archaic norms and beliefs, coercive power structure, conflicts, etc.—which largely emanates from information asymmetry on the part of the state around everyday lives of its citizens and how they negotiate with the local bureaucracy. Local state institutions—bureaucracy and political leadership—are often seen as insensitive to public concern and inefficient in their daily operations with complete disregard to formal and fair procedures.[42] Popular mass-media such as TV and movies have popularized this vision of frontline bureaucracy in India where citizen's engagements with the local state are rarely rules-based, time consuming, and beset

[41] For the role of state capacity in economic development, refer to Acemoglu, García-Jimeno, and Robinson (2015) and Besley and Persson (2009).

[42] Max Weber, the founder of the study of administration, defined bureaucracy as an 'organizational structure that is characterized by many rules, standardized processes, procedures and requirements, number of desks, the meticulous division of labor and responsibility, clear hierarchies and professional, almost impersonal interactions between employees' (Weber 2009). Indian bureaucracy is far from the Weberian one because the various agencies responsible for program delivery and the local power structures influencing fairness in the system. Enrollment in social welfare programs entail a prolonged and complicated application process. Often the information around eligibility is unclear, and there are transaction costs to enroll in the program, which encourages rampant corruption and rent seeking. For example. getting local politicians and bureaucrats to vet and approve application form and several supporting documents—an identity proof, proof of address and marital status (for maternity transfers), bank account information, etc.—itself to begin enrollment in welfare programs is a cumbersome process which acts as a greater discouragement to enroll among those with lower levels of literacy (often women). In an experimental study of widow pensions, Gupta (2017) shows that lower take-up of the program among many women can attributed to bureaucratic frictions which hinders successful enrollment.

with discrimination.[43] Critics of the state intervention use these experiences to argue that the Indian state is bloated and inefficient. The reality, though, is mixed. There is plenty of evidence to show that local bureaucrats are often corrupt, inefficient, and apathetic to citizen concerns, but it is also important to note that performance is marred by lack of sufficient resources (human and financial) at their disposal to serve 1.3 billion residents of the nation.

Lower-level bureaucracy in India is considerably smaller compared to other countries. The share of local government employees in United States and China are five times to that of India, and the Indian state spends only 3% of its total expenditure on local government, while United States and China spend 27 and 51% of their total expenditure respectively (Kapur 2020). At the same time, despite a proliferation of administrative units and the rising managerial responsibilities of implementation and monitoring of various welfare schemes and infrastructural projects has not met with a commensurate increase in hiring posing a particularly acute challenge for the effectiveness of local state institutions and welfare delivery (Somanathan and Natarajan 2022). At the upper administrative echelons of the local state, district and sub-district level bureaucrats have increasingly become overburdened. A time-use survey of local officials in the country by Dasgupta and Kapur (2020) suggests that this 'bureaucrat overload' affects program implementation as well as the politician's incentive to intervene. Resource constrained officials implement programs poorly because of the time constraints, and poor implementation further discourages devolution of funds to that administrative unit from higher political authorities, thereby significantly reducing state capacity and possibly welfare benefits to the deserving.

[43] Before the advent of cable television, comedian Jaspal Bhatti's show on national television, *Ultra Pulta* was principally centered around the theme of daily corruption. Almost a decade later, each episode of actor Pankaj Kapoor's show, *Office Office*, portrayed the mundane struggles of a common man muddling his way through wily local officials trying to get basic services like driving license, passport, or death certificate made. *Bhrashtachaar* (corruption), or *sifarish* (leaning on a powerful person to get something done) are common phrases used to represent local state in Northern India. These issues are as salient in accessing social welfare programs, beginning from proving eligibility status, getting the required identity documents approved, maintaining the documentation, and availing the benefits. See Gupta (2012) and Corbridge et al. (2005) for an inquiry into citizen-state interaction and corruption in rural India.

Technological innovations such as IT-enabled payment services, smart-cards, and unique identification number in the form of *Aadhaar* have surely reduced the reliance of welfare beneficiaries on local state, thereby contributing to building state capacity.[44] Yet, lower staffing remains a lingering concern for improving long-term development outcomes. For example, while augmenting staff strength at the early childhood welfare scheme, ICDS, in a large-scale experiment by Ganimian, Muralidharan, and Walters (2021) shows a significant effect on improving learning and nutritional outcomes for children—representing two potentially large transformative impact of—ICDS workers continue to be poorly paid and overworked leading to low levels of motivation.[45]

Expansion of state capacity, however, is more than hiring more people or creating a disciplined bureaucracy. Local state actors in India are notoriously known for extracting private benefits from the public resources they are responsible for. To stop such practices, greater state capacity also includes improvements in the prevalent 'culture' of bureaucratic practices which includes "the incentives, beliefs and expectations, or norms, shared among state personnel about how others are behaving" (Khemani 2019). Such practices are intrinsically connected to the nature of politics—both at local and federal level.

Elite Capture and Clientelism

Low state capacity and the ensuing implementational deficits in the delivery of social welfare are part of the larger malaise with the local institutions in India which is subservient to elite interests which work through personalistic ties. The entrenched structure of power in the local institutions is sustained through the information asymmetry inherent in the last-mile delivery systems and clientelistic local politics leads to 'fragmented and unequal' social welfare program implementation (Keefer and Khemani 2003).[46] Clientelistic practices—preferential treatment based

[44] See Muralidharan et al. (2016) for the benefits of smartcard based payment in MGNREGS.

[45] For more details, see Chapter 6.

[46] Surmounting elite capture at the local level is difficult of the information possessed by the last-mile actors who are responsible to identifying the poor and delivering benefits. Higher level actors, therefore, are bound to work within a limited information setting. For an anthropological account of the Indian state—from higher level bureaucrats to

upon caste, religion, and party affiliations—allow for politically targeted spending and strategic transfers.[47] Local elites—bureaucrats and elected representatives—possess discretionary power through the arbitrariness in beneficiary identification and the discretionary allocation of benefits, which perpetuates a culture of rent seeking and corruption.

Targeting errors—of inclusion and exclusion—are often a function of who the elites consider poor, and the process involves corruption and favoritism. A survey by Niehaus et al. (2013) found that welfare beneficiaries—as identified by the possession of a below poverty line (BPL) card—are often misclassified. They find that 70% of the ineligible households possessed BPL cards while 13% of the eligible households did not get one. Around 75% of the households reported paying a price above the statutory fee for the BPL card. Such forms of corruption emanate not only from the logistical challenges of identification, but also discriminatory partisan networks.[48] In schemes where participation is not targeted, local corruption and elite capture is of a different kind. The demand for work in the universal public works program, MGNREGS is mediated through local politicians who aggregate citizen demand and work with the state officials to get the program going. It is often reported that increase in MGNREGS wages are not passed on to the workers by the officials (Niehaus and Sukhtankar 2013b) and overreporting of number of days worked and underpayment of wages is a norm (Niehaus and

local ones—in implementation of MGNREGS in Andhra Pradesh, refer to Veeraraghavan (2021).

[47] Caste preferences are pervasive when it comes to the delivery of public goods in India and its persistent across the administrative system despite political empowerment of the lower castes. Studying more than 100,00 local representatives in the state of Bihar, Sharan and Kumar (2021) finds that political representatives in the lower administrative geography are discriminated against from higher caste political officials in the higher geography. Further, using data from all villages in India, Bharathi et al. (2018) show that villages with a larger share of lower caste people have lower incidence of state-provided public goods, which is largely explained by discrimination from top-down in the administration. See Bardhan and Mookherjee (2000) for a theoretical debate on elite capture and rural governance in India.

[48] Using a nationally representative survey, Panda (2015) shows that local political connections influence the possession of below poverty line (BPL) card which essential to access most pro-poor targeted programs. Similarly, Asri (2019) finds that large share of the poor who do not have the right political connections are not able to get a BPL card, and hence are deprived of their old age pension. The deprived ones are also disproportionately poorer.

Sukhtankar 2013a).[49] Similarly, there is substantial evidence which shows that identity-based networks facilitate access to subsidized food through PDS or nutritional assistance through ICDS.[50] Social welfare programs, therefore, often fail to reach the most marginalized and deserving.

Decentralization and Public Action

The pernicious effects of elite capture, and bureaucratic harassment, could potentially be overcome by empowerment of citizens and greater public action, through participatory governance which leads to a more deliberative citizen-state engagement. Administrative decentralization, therefore, emerged as an important instrument to improve state capacity for the implementation of social welfare programs. Decentralization which entails a formal devolution of power to local actors has two key components: civic participation and political accountability. Under a decentralized regime, citizens elect their local leaders and partake in local governance through highlighting the relevant developmental issues. Elected local politicians are further held accountable through the electoral processes. India's 73rd and 74th Constitutional Amendment Acts, 1992 provided legal status to the panchayati raj institutions (PRIs) and urban local bodies

[49] Using sub-district level flow of MGNREGS funds into the state of Rajasthan, Gupta and Mukhopadhyay (2016) show that the Congress party, which brought in the right-to-work legislation allocated greater amount of funds were to regions where it had a lower seat share, despite the fact that MGNREGS is a demand-based and not supply-side scheme. Similarly, in a survey from West Bengal, Das (2015) finds that workers who support the local ruling political party, are not only more likely to participate in MGNREGS, but also report greater number of days of work and earnings from participation in the program. Survey evidence from Andhra Pradesh strengthens this argument by showing that politically active households benefited more from MGNREGS, and the program was used by the incumbent party to expand its base to attract newer voters (Chau et al. 2021). However, improved accountability measures and transparency mechanisms through social audits have worked to reduce partisan behavior in the state of Andhra Pradesh. See Maiorano et al. (2018) and Sheahan et al. (2018), for example.

[50] Using a survey data from Uttar Pradesh villages, Nagavarapu and Sekhri (2016) show that the marginalized caste groups are more likely to buy grains when the PDS shop owner belongs to their own caste. In Bihar, another state with high rates of poverty and poor implementation of social welfare programs, the distribution of food coupons was done along the lines of partisan affiliations, depriving many of the poor of their entitlements, while allowing the undeserving non-poor to benefit from the program (Choithani and Pritchard 2015). For caste-based discrimination in access to ICDS, refer to Mamgain and Dilip Diwakar (2012) and Thorat and Sadana (2009).

(ULBs) in rural and urban areas respectively, for greater administrative decentralization and community involvement in planning and implementing various developmental schemes. Gram Panchayats, meaning village councils, acts as a cabinet council from a collection of villages which engages with the local population through commonly held gram *sabhas* (village council meetings).[51]

The success of MGNREGS partly lies in its decentralized implementation. Being a demand driven social protection program, panchayats are responsible for drawing up plans to determine labor allocation and selection of development projects to employ workers under MGNREGS which allows for greater accountability toward the program beneficiaries. Similarly, decentralization of ICDS has improved community participation in the program, therefore its effectiveness in some of the poorest regions in the country.[52] Yet, in a country with high levels of inequality, and unequal status across groups, reduction in information asymmetry through participatory local governance does not necessarily guarantee greater accountability and citizen empowerment.[53]

Local elites, despite greater public accountability, continue to hold political power, through their stranglehold over the moral economy of reciprocal exchanges within a rural society. The poor cannot bypass the local elites in claiming the state benefits.[54] Moreover, they continue to

[51] Every gram panchayat serves office for a term of five years and elections are conducted after every term. There is a provision of affirmative action with one-third of the seats, on a rotational basis, reserved for women, and another stipulated share of the historically marginalized groups—scheduled castes (SCs) and scheduled tribes (STs). For more details, refer to Nagarajan et al. (2014).

[52] The devolution of powers to Panchayati Raj in Chhattisgarh has fostered a participatory service delivery system across a range of programs where citizens engage in participatory governance (Chanchani 2022). Similar findings hold true for the state of Odisha. See https://globalnutritionreport.org/resources/case-studies-and-briefings/decentralising-accountability-nutrition-odisha/. Accessed October 18, 2022.

[53] For a discussion on the limited potential of decentralization in contexts with low state capacity and elite capture, see Bardhan (2002).

[54] Moral economy refers to the ideas of economic justice and the mutual obligations in a particular social arrangements (Scott 1977). In rural India, public action to access welfare benefits is determined by the interactions with local state—of oneself and the community—and prevailing social and spatial determinants of the flow of information and ideas (Kruks-Wisner 2018). Krishna (2002) has famously highlighted the importance of 'active' social capital—differentially distributed across citizens—in accessing public services in rural India.

rely on traditional elites for other non-state services such as wage-based employment. As a result, the culture of subordination of the historical disadvantaged communities remains persistent thereby limiting the political freedom and voice which social welfare programs through decentralized system aim to relax.[55] Similarly, while periodic local elections may allow the democratic freedom to dislodge inefficient performers, administrative decentralization may also allow politicians to pursue patronage-based politics in a bid to enhance their political support base.[56] The benefits of decentralization, therefore, can only be realized when the entrenched power structures are weakened sufficiently for the disenfranchised section of the population to become an active participant in the local democratic process.[57] Until then, participatory governance, by itself, is less likely to have a transformative role in providing social welfare support to the most deserving in an efficient manner.

Varying Social Welfare Ideals at the Subnational Level

While a fledgling social contract, low state capacity, and weak local institutions undermine the effectiveness of social welfare programs at the national level, there are noticeable subnational exceptions. Some of the Indian state governments have exhibited greater commitment to social welfare *ideas* than others. They have relied upon a building a political coalition which has worked toward pushing citizen *interests* over private ones and reducing some of the last-mile implementational challenges through empowering local participatory *institutions*. As a result, they have

[55] See Marcesse (2018), Akerkar et al. (2016) and Pellissery (2008) for qualitative accounts of the micro-politics of social welfare program implementation in Uttar Pradesh, West Bengal and Maharashtra, respectively.

[56] Local elections and political representatives, in that case, become a source of principal agent for the central leaders to gather information on their potential voters which allows them to focus on groups and design patronage strategies. Refer to Bohlken (2016) for a detailed argument.

[57] Village public meetings in South Indian villages are an example where the village council deliberates upon the budgetary allocations and beneficiary selection for anti-poverty programs. See Rao and Sanyal (2010, 2019).

been recently referred to as 'laboratories' of social welfare policy formulation in the country.[58] But not all states have been equally enthusiastic in pushing social welfare agenda, as *ideas*, *interests*, and *institutions* around social welfare vary significantly at the subnational level.

India's parliamentary democracy has a federal character. It is imagined as a cooperative federalism under which the legislative domains of the central and central governments are clearly defined. While the central government has the power to legislate and enact new welfare programs, federal governments have the responsibility of implementing them. Federal system of parliamentary democracy is therefore an important *institution* of welfare delivery, where subnational governments, in addition to implementation of welfare programs, can also enact their own programs provided it falls under their purview of state or concurrent list such as agriculture, education, or health among others.[59] They can also add newer programs, innovate upon the *form* of welfare delivery, or increase its *focus* through an expanded set of beneficiaries, out of their own resources. Given the importance of subnational governments in program delivery and design, one observes remarkable variation in the delivery and effectiveness of social welfare programs across Indian states.

To highlight the variations in social welfare program implementation across Indian states, we present some of the social welfare programs performance indicators in Table 8.1. The South Indian states—with a higher per capita income and better human development indicators—clearly perform better. Among other regions, hilly states of Himachal Pradesh and Uttarakhand, along with the poorer states of Chhattisgarh and Odisha which have a tribal huge population are standout better performers.

South India's Historical Exceptionalism

It is quite well-known that the South Indian states historically prioritized citizen welfare. They not only invested more in social welfare programs, but also ensured that the benefits extend to the most marginalized and maintained an efficient bureaucracy to keep last-mile implementational

[58] We have highlighted these innovations across multiple welfare programs in earlier chapter. Also see Deshpande et al. (2017) for political dimension of this change.

[59] Refer to Tillin (2019, 2021) for a detailed discussion on Indian federalism and the national and subnation division of legislative powers.

Table 8.1 State-wise performance on social welfare programs

	MGNREGS[a]		*ICDS implementation (% of child beneficiaries)*[b]		
	Person employed (%) *(1)*	*Person-day employment* *(2)*	*Nutrition* *(3)*	*Immunization* *(4)*	*Preschool* *(5)*
North					
Jammu & Kashmir	38.9	49.5	48.4	26	41.7
Himachal Pradesh	29.0	48.4	70.7	30.2	39.3
Uttarakhand	34.0	40.9	67	52.5	35.5
Punjab	31.4	31.2	48	37.5	35.5
Haryana	20.0	35.4	63.2	53.7	43.4
Rajasthan	32.5	59.0	50.4	49.4	37.7
Uttar Pradesh	24.4	46.0	61.8	57.9	46.3
East					
Assam	29.2	32.3	65.3	34.9	53.9
Bihar	14.7	42.0	41.3	45.3	39.3
Jharkhand	19.4	46.4	59.5	54.9	44
West Bengal	27.0	49.9	77.3	44.2	70.7
Odisha	20.9	47.9	86.5	75.8	74
West & Central					
Gujarat	14.4	43.2	65.7	59.6	57.7
Maharashtra	12.2	41.0	53.5	43.3	48.9
Chhattisgarh	47.0	55.7	78.1	67.3	64.6
Madhya Pradesh	32.1	53.3	75.9	68.5	63.4
South					
Andhra Pradesh	35.4	49.6	75.6	64.6	61.9
Tamil Nadu	50.4	44.0	73.7	61.4	58.8
Telangana	33.6	43.2	69	59	53.2
Karnataka	26.7	50.0	77.3	71.7	69
Kerala	28.8	55.7	52.7	24	31.9

(continued)

Table 8.1 (continued)

	Eggs in MDMS (weekly)[c]	*PDS coverage greater than NFSA*[d]	*Health insurance coverage (%)*[e]	*Old age pension*[f]	
				Coverage (%)	*Additional pension (in Rs.)*
	(6)	*(7)*	*(8)*	*(9)*	*(10)*
North					
Jammu & Kashmir	0	Yes	14	35.2	200
Himachal Pradesh	0	Yes	39	28	1000
Uttarakhand	1	Yes	63	30.2	600
Punjab	0	No	25	54.8	250
Haryana	0	No	26	60.1	1200
Rajasthan	0	No	88	68.9	300
Uttar Pradesh	0	No	16	15.2	100
East					
Assam	0	No	67	29.2	200
Bihar	1	No	17	46.1	400
Jharkhand	2	No	50	34.9	800
West Bengal	1	Yes	34		200
Odisha	2	Yes	48	42.1	100
West & Central					
Gujarat	0	No	44	11.5	200
Maharashtra	0	Yes	22	4.3	400
Chhattisgarh	0	Yes	71	32.3	100
Madhya Pradesh	0	No	38	43.7	75
South					
Andhra Pradesh	5	Yes	80	34.2	800
Tamil Nadu	5	Yes	67	13	800
Telangana	3	Yes	69	24.8	1000

(continued)

Table 8.1 (continued)

	Eggs in MDMS (weekly)[c]	*PDS coverage greater than NFSA*[d]	*Health insurance coverage (%)*[e]	*Old age pension*[f]	
				Coverage (%)	*Additional pension (in Rs.)*
	(6)	*(7)*	*(8)*	*(9)*	*(10)*
Karnataka	0	Yes	32	48.2	300
Kerala	1	Yes	58	34.7	250

Notes

[a]Columns 1–2 depicts the performance of MGNREGS in providing employment. Column 1 presents share of those employment provided under MGNREGS as a fraction of the number of individuals registered, while column 2 is the computed person days of work per registered household. *Source* MGNREGS website, 2019–2020

[b]The ICDS figures (columns 3–5) come from the 2019–2020 round of National Family Health Survey (NFHS). The figures represent the percentage of children under age 6 years who received services from the ***Anganwadi center*** (AWC) in the last 12 months preceding of the survey. For access to preschool under AWC, the sample is restricted to children between 36 and 71 months. Nutritional assistance includes both cooked and take-home ration (THR)

[c]Information on the Number of eggs provided every week in the school meals (column 6) is based upon the performa filled by each state before the annual Programme Approval Board (PAB) Meetings, as available on the MDMS website. The numbers are for the year 2019–2020, and may have changed as this book goes to press

[d]Based upon the poverty figures, the National Food Security Act (NFSA), 2013 allocated a desired population coverage for each state to be covered under the Public Distribution System (PDS). State governments have, however, expanded upon those coverage ratios. *Source* Khera and Somanchi (2020)

[e]Health insurance coverage implies the percentage of households with at least one usual member covered by any health insurance or financing scheme. This could include private health insurance too, but that number is generally very small. It is also important to note that, while the survey was being conducted the expansion of public health insurance program under PM-JAY had not taken place. *Source* NFHS 2019–2020

[f]Columns 9–10 report the coverage of Indira Gandhi National Old Age Pension Scheme (IGNOAPS) for the eligible population (identified as BPL and greater than 60 years of age). Information on column 9 comes from a nationally representative survey, Longitudinal Aging Study in India (LASI) conducted in 2017–2018. Numbers in column 10 represent the additional monthly pension paid by the state governments for those between 60 and 79 years. There is an additional amount for the ones older than that. Source for this data is a parliamentary reply to an unstarred question on 29th November 2019, as provided on government open data website (data.gov.in). These numbers could have changed as this book goes to press

challenges to a minimum. Tamil Nadu and Kerala are the most prominent examples of it, where progressive social policies extended beyond welfare programs to investments in public welfare services such as education, health, and infrastructure, despite having a comparable level of poverty than the rest of India (Dreze and Sen 2002, 2013).[60] Social welfare reforms in other South Indian states of Andhra Pradesh and Karnataka followed the same lead. Progressive social policy in South Indian states have put them on a higher trajectory of economic and human development. Several reasons have been attributed to their exceptionalism, most important being a history of social movements and a united linguistic identity which allowed them to overcome deep-rooted societal divisions, reduce elite capture, and create more egalitarian local institutions, fostering greater public action.[61]

Welfare-oriented *social contract* in Kerala goes back to the pre-independence period when the princely states of Travancore and Cochin made a strong commitment to reduce identity-based distinctions and empowered communities through public investments in literacy and public services. State politics in the post-independence era, continued the same trend, organizing around class-based movements, instead of identity, leading to greater social capital, which has contributed to Kerala's empowered citizenry to demand greater welfare benefits.[62] In Tamil Nadu, on the other hand, mass-led non-Brahmin movement—protesting elite caste's political capture—reduced traditional elite influence and championed the cause of social justice thereby facilitating greater political demand and supply of broad-based public services and social welfare for the citizens. The state championed public school meals and early life nutritional interventions much before they became national level welfare schemes.[63] The southern states had also initiated participatory governance through decentralization of program governance much earlier than

[60] The success of South Indian states in ensuring growth with redistribution has been referred to as a 'Dravidian ideology' where welfare ideas are motivated to benefit the poor as part of the larger pursuits of social justice and reform (Kalaiyarasan and Vijayabaskar 2021; Narayan 2018).

[61] A strong subnational identity allowed some states to accommodate identity-based divisions, creating a syncretic culture and stronger political mobilization for citizen welfare. See Singh (2106) for a detailed exposition.

[62] For a greater deliberation on Kerala's exceptionalism in democratic empowerment, refer to Heller (1996, 2000).

[63] The idea of school meals in India was first introduced by Tamil Nadu Chief Minister, K. Kamaraj in 1956. Under the program, food prepared in central kitchens was delivered on bicycles to various public schools. In 1982, the program was scaled up in the state by M G Ramachandran (popularly known as *MGR*). Similarly, Tamil Nadu Integrated Nutrition Program (TINP) proved to be an important source of learning for the ICDS. See Chapter 5 for more details on how state leaders championed the cause of food

some of the other states. The subnational social welfare *ideas* percolated down to create egalitarian local *institutions* through an efficient bureaucracy. At the same time, citizen empowerment through social justice movements created a stronger sense of collective action which reduced elite *interests* and ensured leaders remain accountable to their promise, thereby contributing to improved welfare delivery systems. What also worked in making the social welfare more effective in these states is that instead of a narrow *focus* on a specific section of the population, most of the schemes are universal in nature, and often free.

Historical trends are persistent. Southern states, despite a significant reduction in poverty, lay a greater emphasis on the ideals of social welfare. It is essential to their politics. Andhra Pradesh, another South Indian state, has been one of the best performers in implementing MGNREGS, and its success comes from a strong political commitment from the state government. The state was also one of the first one in pioneering social audits of the program by the local citizens and bringing in electronic payments. Social audits have now been further extended to other welfare programs.[64] Similarly, direct cash transfers to farmers were first introduced by the newly formed state of Telangana (carved out of Andhra Pradesh), which was subsequently launched as a national level scheme, PM-Kisan.

Emerging Political Populism in North India?

The nature of politics in South India has been key to its successful social welfare policies. A broader political coalition which supported the *ideas* of citizen welfare and created efficient *institutions* in pursuing poverty alleviation policies, as imagined in the South, were lacking in other states. Kohli (2012), observes that the "southern states as a whole share some of these political traits of India's "social democratic" states—a broad power base and competent bureaucracies—but not others—well organized ruling parties and an activist citizenry—creating within them some

assistance programs in South India in the 1980s, and more recently in some of the North Indian states.

[64] Andhra Pradesh also brought in an innovation where MGNREGS work was to be decided by contracted agents, instead of the local village council. These agents had a set target to provide a minimum level of work every year or else they would be laid off (Maiorano 2014).

capacity for poverty alleviation. Hindi- heartland states pretty well lack most of these traits, creating a political landscape in which repeated redistributive failures have by now become a norm." Yet, despite the general pessimism associated with poor social development in North Indian states, incremental positive changes are now visible (Vivek 2015).

Himachal Pradesh and Uttarakhand along with the poorer states of Chhattisgarh and Odisha are at the forefront of this positive change. Himachal Pradesh, like Kerala, has taken a more expansive and deliberative model of social development in the post-independence period, where bureaucratic disciple is strictly adhered to, and collective action (especially around forest and water management) inspires greater public action holding local politicians accountable.[65] The state had undertaken a massive universal education drive in the 1970s and ranks high on most human development indicator currently. Uttarakhand, carved out of Uttar Pradesh in 1999, is another hilly state in the Himalayas, which has taken a similar model as Himachal Pradesh.

The turnaround in the performance of social welfare programs in the relatively poorer states of Chhattisgarh and Odisha is however the most striking.[66] Even before the National Food Security Act, 2013 was implemented in the Indian parliament, Chhattisgarh had enacted its own Food Security Act following up on a massive reform of PDS in the preceding decade. Today, it has the most well-functioning, near-universal PDS which was unimaginable two decades ago. In Odisha, where starvation deaths used to be a common occurrence in the 1990s, improved performance of food and early-child nutrition initiatives, has made it a 'success story' of social welfare program implementation and impact, despite lower state capacity.[67]

A convincing explanation of why some states have seen such a turnaround while others continue to flounder could possibly be a book (or a series of them) in itself. A myriad set of *ideas*, *interests*, and *institutions* have forged the subnational *social contracts*, and the process is

[65] See Mangla (2015) and Saberwal and Chhatre (2006).

[66] Reforms initiated by Chhattisgarh are explained by Puri (2012), while Gillespie et al. (2013) and Gillespie and van den Bold (2017) describe Odisha's success story.

[67] A comparion of Jharkhand and Chhattisgarh—two newly formed mineral-rich states, with a predominant tribal population—suggests that even at low levels of state capacity, performance of social welfare programs could be improved provided there is sufficient political commitment (Chhotray et al. 2020).

still a work in progress. Among the many possible explanations, what stands out is the role of politics and commitment of state leaders.[68] Noted economist and one of the most influential chroniclers of social welfare reforms in India, Jean Drèze, reckons that social welfare—*ideas* of welfare and its effective implementation—is a political problem. Referring to the improvement of PDS in Chhattisgarh, he says[69]:

> Ultimately, however, it is political will that seems to matter most. Somehow, the PDS became a political priority in Chhattisgarh and a decision was made to turn it around, instead of siding with the corrupt dealers who were milking the system. When political bosses firmly direct the bureaucracy to fix a dysfunctional system, things begin to change.
>
> The fact that government functionaries were under enormous pressure to make the PDS work was evident in Lakhanpur. For instance, monitoring grain movements had become one of the top priorities of the patwaris (landrecord officers) and tehsildars (revenue officers). The tehsildar mentioned that the PDS was the first agenda item whenever meetings were held at the district level. The political pressure was also manifest in their willingness to stand up to vested interests, e.g. by arresting corrupt middlemen and sending them to jail if need be.
>
> It would be naïve to think that the revival of the PDS in Chhattisgarh reflects the kindheartedness of the state government, especially in the light of its contempt for people's rights in other contexts. It was a political calculation, nothing more.

Historically, the pursuits of social welfare were a political plank in Southern India, while the North Indian politicians appealed to the narrow politics of identity—mostly caste and religion—appeals to sustain their politics.[70] Since the 1990s, social welfare policies have become a part of

[68] For a comparative study of state-level politics in shaping social policies in recent times, see Tillin et al. (2015). Chiriyankandath et al. (2019) also describe the unearths the constellation of interests that shaped their legislation, and the key roles played by central, state and local governments, senior politicians, bureaucrats, civil activists, courts and the private sector in influencing their agenda. Focusing on political dynamics and the crucial issue of implementation, the authors address how concerns such as coalitions of interest, resource availability, and local and state administrative capacity shaped what was thought possible at the implementation stage.

[69] Drèze (2019, pp. 186–187).

[70] Deshpande et al. (2017) attribute the importance of subnational welfare politics to three factors—political legacy of welfare, broad-based social coalitions which cuts across

political calculations in North India as well as the role of regional parties in central politics has risen.[71] Multi-party fragmentation at the center necessitated a new form of electoral engineering which allowed the subnational governments to design and implement their own distinctive welfare policy agendas (Tillin 2022). Greater influence of subnational politics on the national politics has allowed the state *political bosses*, the chief ministers, to be more assertive in exercising their discretionary powers, and stake claims for the success of welfare programs, thereby increasing their popularity to seek 'regime legitimacy' (Manor 2015, 2016).[72]

The institution of federalism has therefore been key in shaping the ideas of welfare at the subnational level. State governments have not only been actively participating as key actors in the policy design process, but also influencing each other through learning from one another's experience. In that regard, North still has a lot to learn from the South. There are two major aspects to it—sustained commitment to the ideals of social justice, and faster economic growth. It is important to note that the success of Southern states in social policy implementation came from a *longue durée* policy commitment to redistributive ideas which empowered citizens to demand their citizen entitlements and hold state actors accountable for service delivery. These services went beyond social protection programs to public investments in education, health, and other infrastructure, which created a citizen-oriented *social contract*.[73]

social identity and class, the political competition arising out of it, and the extent of political leaders' commitment to welfare delivery.

[71] With the decline of Congress party in the 1990s, regional parties became increasingly important in central politics, which provided state governments to have a greater maneuvering power in the policy space (Kennedy et al. 2013; Manor 2015). Some of these regional parties were emerged from a 'politics of dignity' representing the *interests* of socio-economically marginalized caste groups, and thereby demanding affirmative actions policies and targeted redistribution (Chhibber and Nooruddin 2004; Thachil and Teitelbaum 2015). Aneja and Ritadhi (2022) show that this mobilization of lower caste groups led to an improvement in the performance of food transfer program, PDS.

[72] Chief ministers of state governments, recognizing their ability to claim electoral credit in the eyes of voters, committed themselves to welfare policies, even when the programs were designed and financed by the central governments (Tillin and Pereira 2017). Some of them also introduced their own programs or added to the list of eligible beneficiaries.

[73] When social welfare policies become an instrument of political strategy through the provision of targeted benefits in exchange for political support, there is a risk of underinvestment in public services which are likely to benefit in long-term development outcomes such as the quality of schools, health infrastructure, water, etc. at the expense of

The ability of the state to supply welfare support, on the other hand, emerged from their fiscal ability to generate sustained economic growth. A large share of the North Indian states lack on both these fronts. The politics around social welfare in the North Indian states has emerged as another strategy of political populism, or 'political calculations,' as Jean Drèze remarks in the above quotation, to ensure electoral success as the redistributive *ideas* lack a commitment to social justice and citizen empowerment. This is also reflected in the continued lack of enthusiasm in improving the quality of public services. Similarly, stagnant economic growth in most of the states implies a diminished agency to allocate more funds to welfare programs to improve implementational capacity.

Threats to Subnational Welfare Regimes

Federal relationship is determined by partisan dynamics and the nature of political leadership at the central level, given they control the resources.[74] Subnational welfare regimes thrived in India because they got greater resources from the center, and the state leadership had autonomy to improve implementation. As the power of one central political party declined since the beginning of the 1990s, and consequently, the influence of country's Prime Minister (PM) watered down, subnational leaders began to assert their autonomy. The election of 2014 and the massive victory of BJP in the central elections with PM Modi at its helm, however, marked a break with the central party and PM again becoming important.[75]

Concentration of power at the center has created a tussle between the center and state governments to appropriate the credits of social welfare programs. Many of the programs now have a prefix PM (for "Prime Minister") attached to the programs to signify political leader's benevolence. Centralized transfer of welfare benefits—bypassing the subnational government, leveraging upon the technology to make direct

temporary relief which social welfare programs provide (Khemani 2015). Southern states of India, however, defied this argument with an expansion of social welfare programs along with greater public investments in education, health, and infrastructure.

[74] See Aiyar and Kapur (2019).

[75] CMs, however, when unaligned with the ruling party, have continued to express their autonomy over social welfare schemes, which have again influenced central policies. Income transfers to farmers, PM-Kisan, being one of the examples.

transfers—has further encroached upon the state government's constitutional responsibility and fiscal space causing rift between the central and state governments (Aiyar 2019).[76] Since 2014, a series of flagship schemes have been further launched by the central government, which provides private transfers (such as housing, toilets, cooking gas, and cash) in addition to the social welfare programs to "redefine and to repurpose the welfare state from a right-based and universalistic logic to a logic of rationing and targeting welfare to those who "deserve" it" (Heller 2021, p. 117). The new semantics of pro-poor politics, arising out of electoral necessities, tries to shift social protection paradigm in the country from state support as a citizenship right to personalized gestures of generosity, rather than social upliftment and justice. Such personal politics which centralizes political power in one strong national level leader has the risk of undermining public action through democratic accountability, deliberative local institutions, and citizen participation, essential to sustain a social democracy (Sircar 2020). It also skirts the issue of transforming the state bureaucracy and local institutions, which are still central in identifying the poor, delivering the benefits, and ensuring political accountability (Aiyar and Walton 2015).

Conclusion

Development resilience requires adequate protection against anticipated and unanticipated risks, while developing human capabilities to adapt to such risks over time. Indian state has taken great strides in providing this through an expansion of the coverage of social welfare programs through enacting rights-based legislations, introducing newer social safety net programs, and improving welfare delivery systems, but there is still a long road toward "having found its feet as far as social security programs are concerned" (Drèze and Khera 2017). Such anxieties largely emerge from the politicized nature of the *ideational* process of social welfare programs determined by perverse *interests*. Redistributive ideas motivated by short-term electoral concerns in countries with underdeveloped *institutions* often makes the social welfare program a handmaiden of political *interests* with detrimental implications for a transformational impact on

[76] Recent research suggests that voters are more likely to attribute the receipt of social welfare to the central government despite state governments overseeing welfare program delivery (Deshpande et al. 2019).

poverty and increasing development resilience. The success of some of the state governments in creating a stronger *social contract* regarding welfare however provides some respite to these apprehensions which now seems to be under threat with the rise of new forms of welfarism which does not pay attention to encouraging collective mobilization, civic action, and effective state institutions.

References

Acemoglu, Daron, and James Robinson. 2008. *The Role of Institutions in Growth and Development*. Vol. 10. Washington, DC: World Bank.

Acemoglu, Daron, and James A. Robinson. 2020. *The Narrow Corridor: States, Societies, and the Fate of Liberty*. New York: Penguin.

Acemoglu, Daron, Camilo García-Jimeno, and James A. Robinson. 2015. "State Capacity and Economic Development: A Network Approach." *American Economic Review* 105 (8): 2364–2409.

Aiyar, Yamini. 2019. "Modi Consolidates Power: Leveraging Welfare Politics." *Journal of Democracy* 30 (4): 78–88. https://doi.org/10.1353/jod.2019.0070.

Aiyar, Yamini, and Avani Kapur. 2019. "The Centralization *vs* Decentralization Tug of War and the Emerging Narrative of Fiscal Federalism for Social Policy in India." *Regional & Federal Studies* 29 (2): 187–217. https://doi.org/10.1080/13597566.2018.1511978.

Aiyar, Yamini, and Michael Walton. 2015. "Rights, Accountability and Citizenship: India's Emerging Welfare State." In *Governance in Developing Asia*, 260–95. Cheltenham, UK and Northampton, MA: Edward Elgar Publishing.

Akerkar, Supriya, P. C. Joshi, and Maureen Fordham. 2016. "Cultures of Entitlement and Social Protection: Evidence from Flood Prone Bahraich, Uttar Pradesh, India." *World Development* 86: 46–58. https://doi.org/10.1016/j.worlddev.2016.06.004.

Alesina, Alberto, Edward Glaeser, and Bruce Sacerdote. 2001. "Why Doesn't the United States Have a European-Style Welfare State?" *Brookings Papers on Economic Activity.*

Alston, Lee J., and Joseph P. Ferrie. 1999. *Southern Paternalism and the American Welfare State: Economics, Politics, and Institutions in the South, 1865–1965*. 1st ed. Cambridge and New York: Cambridge University Press.

Aneja, Abhay, and S. K. Ritadhi. 2022. "Can Political Parties Improve Minority Wellbeing? Evidence from India's 'Silent Revolution.'" *Journal of Development Economics* 158: 102931. https://doi.org/10.1016/j.jdeveco.2022.102931.

Asri, Viola. 2019. "Targeting of Social Transfers: Are India's Poor Older People Left behind?" *World Development* 115: 46–63. https://doi.org/10.1016/j.worlddev.2018.11.001.

Baloch, Bilal A. 2021. *When Ideas Matter: Democracy and Corruption in India*. Vol. 16. Cambridge: Cambridge University Press.

Bardhan, Pranab. 2002. "Decentralization of Governance and Development." *Journal of Economic Perspectives* 16 (4): 185–205.

Bardhan, Pranab. 2005. "Institutions Matter, But Which Ones?" *Economics of Transition* 13 (3): 499–532.

Bardhan, Pranab. 2016. "State and Development: The Need for a Reappraisal of the Current Literature." *Journal of Economic Literature* 54 (3): 862–92. https://doi.org/10.1257/jel.20151239.

Bardhan, Pranab K., and Dilip Mookherjee. 2000. "Capture and Governance at Local and National Levels." *American Economic Review* 90 (2): 135–39. https://doi.org/10.1257/aer.90.2.135.

Barrientos, Armando. 2009. "Labour Markets and the (Hyphenated) Welfare Regime in Latin America." *Economy and Society* 38 (1): 87–108. https://doi.org/10.1080/03085140802560553.

Basu, Kaushik. 2011. "Why, for a Class of Bribes, the Act of Giving a Bribe Should Be Treated as Legal."

Basu, Kaushik. 2018. "The Republic of Beliefs." In *The Republic of Beliefs*. Princeton: Princeton University Press.

Béland, Daniel. 2005. "Ideas and Social Policy: An Institutionalist Perspective." *Social Policy & Administration* 39 (1): 1–18.

Béland, Daniel. 2007. "Ideas and Institutional Change in Social Security: Conversion, Layering, and Policy Drift." *Social Science Quarterly* 88 (1): 20–38.

Bénabou, Roland. 2000. "Unequal Societies: Income Distribution and the Social Contract." *American Economic Review* 90 (1): 96–129. https://doi.org/10.1257/aer.90.1.96.

Besley, Timothy, and Torsten Persson. 2009. "The Origins of State Capacity: Property Rights, Taxation, and Politics." *American Economic Review* 99 (4): 1218–44.

Bharathi, Naveen, Deepak Malghan, Sumit Mishra, and Andaleeb Rahman. 2018. "Spatial Segregation, Multi-Scale Diversity, and Public Goods." Charles H. Dyson School of Applied Economics and Management at Cornell University Working Paper Series AEM-WP2018(7).

Blyth, Mark. 2002. *Great Transformations: Economic Ideas and Institutional Change in the Twentieth Century*. Cambridge: Cambridge University Press.

Bohlken, Anjali Thomas. 2016. *Democratization from Above: The Logic of Local Democracy in the Developing World*. Cambridge: Cambridge University Press.

Campbell, Andrea Louise. 2012. "Policy Makes Mass Politics." *Annual Review of Political Science* 15 (1): 333–51. https://doi.org/10.1146/annurev-polisci-012610-135202.

Chanchani, Devanshi. 2022. "Two Cheers for Decentralisation: Unpacking Mechanisms, Politics and Accountability in the ICDS, Central India." *The European Journal of Development Research*. https://doi.org/10.1057/s41287-022-00545-x.

Chau, Nancy H., Yanyan Liu, and Vidhya Soundararajan. 2021. "Political Activism as a Determinant of Strategic Transfers: Evidence from an Indian Public Works Program." *European Economic Review* 132: 103631. https://doi.org/10.1016/j.euroecorev.2020.103631.

Chhibber, Pradeep, and Irfan Nooruddin. 2004. "Do Party Systems Count?: The Number of Parties and Government Performance in the Indian States." *Comparative Political Studies* 37 (2): 152–87. https://doi.org/10.1177/0010414003260981.

Chhotray, Vasudha, Anindita Adhikari, and Vidushi Bahuguna. 2020. "The Political Prioritization of Welfare in India: Comparing the Public Distribution System in Chhattisgarh and Jharkhand." *World Development* 128: 104853. https://doi.org/10.1016/j.worlddev.2019.104853.

Chiriyankandath, James, Diego Maoirano, James Manor, and Louise Tillin. 2019. "The Politics of Poverty Reduction in India: The UPA Government, 2004 to 2014."

Choithani, Chetan, and B. Pritchard. 2015. "Importance of Local Context: Assessing Bihar's Coupon-Based PDS." *Economic & Political Weekly* 50 (3).

Cloutier, Mathieu, Bernard Harborne, Deborah Isser, Indhira Santos, and Michael Watts. 2021. "Social Contracts for Development."

Corbridge, Stuart, Glyn Williams, Manoj Srivastava, and René Véron. 2005. *Seeing the State: Governance and Governmentality in India*. Vol. 10. Cambridge: Cambridge University Press.

Cruz, Cesi, Julien Labonne, and Pablo Querubín. 2020. "Social Network Structures and the Politics of Public Goods Provision: Evidence from the Philippines." *American Political Science Review* 114 (2): 486–501. https://doi.org/10.1017/S0003055419000789.

Das, Upasak. 2015. "Does Political Activism and Affiliation Affect Allocation of Benefits in the Rural Employment Guarantee Program: Evidence from West Bengal, India." *World Development* 67: 202–17. https://doi.org/10.1016/j.worlddev.2014.10.009.

Dasgupta, Aditya, and Devesh Kapur. 2020. "The Political Economy of Bureaucratic Overload: Evidence from Rural Development Officials in India." *American Political Science Review* 114 (4): 1316–34. https://doi.org/10.1017/S0003055420000477.

Deshpande, Rajeshwari, K. K. Kailash, and Louise Tillin. 2017. "States as Laboratories: The Politics of Social Welfare Policies in India." *India Review* 16 (1): 85–105.

Deshpande, Rajeshwari, Louise Tillin, and K. K. Kailash. 2019. "The BJP's Welfare Schemes: Did They Make a Difference in the 2019 Elections?" *Studies in Indian Politics* 7 (2): 219–33.

Drèze, Jean. 2010. "Democracy and the Right to Work: India's Employment Guarantee Act." In *Oxford Companion to Politics in India*, edited by N. Jayal and P. B. Mehta. New Delhi: Oxford University Press.

Drèze, Jean. 2019. *Sense and Solidarity: Jholawala Economics for Everyone*. Oxford, UK: Oxford University Press.

Dreze, Jean, and Reetika Khera. 2015. "Understanding Leakages in the Public Distribution System." *Economic and Political Weekly* 50 (7): 39–42. https://doi.org/10.1177/014473940002000203.

Drèze, Jean, and Reetika Khera. 2017. "Recent Social Security Initiatives in India." *World Development* 98: 555–72. https://doi.org/10.1016/j.worlddev.2017.05.035.

Drèze, Jean, and Amartya Sen. 1991. "Strategies of Entitlement Protection." In *Hunger and Public Action*. Oxford: Oxford University Press.

Dreze, Jean, and Amartya Sen. 2002. *India: Development and Participation*. Oxford, UK: Oxford University Press.

Dreze, Jean, and Amartya Sen. 2013. *An Uncertain Glory: India and Its Contradictions*. Princeton: Princeton Press.

Esping-Andersen, Gosta. 1990. *The Three Worlds of Welfare Capitalism*. Princeton: Princeton University Press.

Evans, Peter, and Patrick Heller. 2019. "The State and Development." In *Asian Transformations*, 109–35. Oxford, UK: Oxford University Press.

Ganimian, Alejandro J., Karthik Muralidharan, and Christopher R. Walters. 2021. "Augmenting State Capacity for Child Development: Experimental Evidence from India."

Gillespie, Stuart, and Mara van den Bold. 2017. "Stories of Change in Nutrition: An Overview." *Global Food Security* 13: 1–11. https://doi.org/10.1016/j.gfs.2017.02.004.

Gillespie, Stuart, Lawrence Haddad, Venkatesh Mannar, Purnima Menon, and Nicholas Nisbett. 2013. "The Politics of Reducing Malnutrition: Building Commitment and Accelerating Progress." *The Lancet* 382 (9891): 552–69. https://doi.org/10.1016/S0140-6736(13)60842-9.

Glaeser, Edward L., Rafael La Porta, Florencio Lopez-de-Silanes, and Andrei Shleifer. 2004. "Do Institutions Cause Growth?" *Journal of Economic Growth* 9 (3): 271–303.

Gough, Ian. 2008. "European Welfare States: Explanations and Lessons for Developing Countries." *Inclusive States: Social Policy and Structural Inequalities*, 39–72.

Government of India. 2006. *11th Five Year Plan (2007–2012)*. New Delhi: Planning Commission.

Graham, Carol. 2002. *Public Attitudes Matter: A Conceptual Frame for Accounting for Political Economy in Safety Nets and Social Assistance Policies*, 0233. Washington, DC: World Bank.

Greif, Avner. 2006. *Institutions and the Path to the Modern Economy: Lessons from Medieval Trade*. Cambridge: Cambridge University Press.

Grosh, Margaret E., Carlo Del Ninno, Emil Tesliuc, and Azedine Ouerghi. 2008. *For Protection and Promotion: The Design and Implementation of Effective Safety Nets*. Washington, DC: World Bank.

Guhan, S. 1995. "Social Expenditures in the Union Budget: 1991–96." *Economic and Political Weekly* 30 (18/19): 1095–1101.

Gupta, Akhil. 2012. *Red Tape: Bureaucracy, Structural Violence, and Poverty in India*. Durham and London: Duke University Press.

Gupta, Bhanu, and Abhiroop Mukhopadhyay. 2016. "Local Funds and Political Competition: Evidence from the National Rural Employment Guarantee Scheme in India." *European Journal of Political Economy* 41: 14–30. https://doi.org/10.1016/j.ejpoleco.2015.10.009.

Gupta, Sarika. 2017. "Perils of the Paperwork: The Impact of Information and Application Assistance on Welfare Program Take-up in India." Unpublished Report, Harvard University, Boston, MA.

Heller, Patrick. 1996. "Social Capital as a Product of Class Mobilization and State Intervention: Industrial Workers in Kerala, India." *World Development* 24 (6): 1055–71. https://doi.org/10.1016/0305-750X(96)00015-0.

Heller, Patrick. 2000. "Degrees of Democracy: Some Comparative Lessons from India." *World Politics* 52 (4): 484–519.

Heller, Patrick. 2021. "The Social Roots of the Authoritarian Turn in India." In *Routledge Handbook of Autocratization in South Asia*, 115–26. New York: Routledge.

Hickey, Sam. 2011. "The Politics of Social Protection: What Do We Get from a 'Social Contract' Approach?" *Canadian Journal of Development Studies/ Revue Canadienne d'études Du Développement* 32 (4): 426–38. https://doi.org/10.1080/02255189.2011.647447.

Hickey, Sam, and Sophie King. 2016. "Understanding Social Accountability: Politics, Power and Building New Social Contracts." *The Journal of Development Studies* 52 (8): 1225–40. https://doi.org/10.1080/00220388.2015.1134778.

Jain, Anoop, Dilys M. Walker, Rasmi Avula, Nadia Diamond-Smith, Lakshmi Gopalakrishnan, Purnima Menon, Sneha Nimmagadda, Sumeet R. Patil, and

Lia C. H. Fernald. 2020. "Anganwadi Worker Time Use in Madhya Pradesh, India: A Cross-Sectional Study." *BMC Health Services Research* 20 (1): 1130. https://doi.org/10.1186/s12913-020-05857-4.

Kalaiyarasan, A., and M. Vijayabaskar. 2021. *The Dravidian Model: Interpreting the Political Economy of Tamil Nadu*. Cambridge: Cambridge University Press.

Kapur, Devesh. 2020. "Why Does the Indian State Both Fail and Succeed?" *Journal of Economic Perspectives* 34 (1): 31–54. https://doi.org/10.1257/jep.34.1.31.

Keefer, Philip, and Stuti Khemani. 2003. "Democracy, Public Expenditures, and the Poor."

Kennedy, Loraine, Kim Robin, Diego Zamuner, Loraine Kennedy, Kim Robin, and Diego Zamuner. 2013. "Comparing State-Level Policy Responses to Economic Reforms in India."

Khemani, Stuti. 2015. "Buying Votes versus Supplying Public Services: Political Incentives to under-Invest in pro-Poor Policies." *Journal of Development Economics* 117: 84–93. https://doi.org/10.1016/j.jdeveco.2015.07.002.

Khemani, Stuti. 2019. "What Is State Capacity?" World Bank Policy Research Working Paper (8734).

Khera, Reetika, and Anmol Somanchi. 2020. "A Review of the Coverage of PDS." Retrieved October 19, 2022. https://www.ideasforindia.in/topics/poverty-inequality/a-review-of-the-coverage-of-pds.html.

Kingdon, John W., and Eric Stano. 1984. *Agendas, Alternatives, and Public Policies*. Vol. 45. Boston, MA: Little, Brown.

Kohli, Atul. 2007. "State, Business, and Economic Growth in India." *Studies in Comparative International Development* 42 (1–2): 87–114. https://doi.org/10.1007/s12116-007-9001-9.

Kohli, Atul. 2012. "State and Redistributive Development in India." In *Growth, inequality and social development in India*, 194–226. Hampshire: Springer.

Kotwal, Ashok, Bharat Ramaswami, and Wilima Wadhwa. 2014. "Economic Liberalization and Indian Economic Growth: What's the Evidence ?" 49 (4): 1152–99.

Krishna, Anirudh. 2002. *Active Social Capital: Tracing the Roots of Development and Democracy*. New York: Columbia University Press.

Kruks-Wisner, Gabrielle. 2018. "The Pursuit of Social Welfare: Citizen Claim-Making in Rural India." *World Politics* 70 (1): 122–63. https://doi.org/10.1017/S0043887117000193.

Kwon, Huck-Ju. 1997. "Beyond European Welfare Regimes: Comparative Perspectives on East Asian Welfare Systems." *Journal of Social Policy* 26 (4): 467–84. https://doi.org/10.1017/S004727949700514X.

Lavers, Tom, and Sam Hickey. 2016. "Conceptualising the Politics of Social Protection Expansion in Low Income Countries: The Intersection of Transnational Ideas and Domestic Politics: Conceptualising the Politics of Social

Protection." *International Journal of Social Welfare* 25 (4): 388–98. https://doi.org/10.1111/ijsw.12210.

Lavers, Tom, and Sam Hickey. 2021. "Alternative Routes to the Institutionalisation of Social Transfers in Sub-Saharan Africa: Political Survival Strategies and Transnational Policy Coalitions." *World Development* 146: 105549. https://doi.org/10.1016/j.worlddev.2021.105549.

Leisering, Lutz, ed. 2021. *One Hundred Years of Social Protection: The Changing Social Question in Brazil, India, China, and South Africa*. Cham: Springer International Publishing.

Levy, Santiago, and Norbert Schady. 2013. "Latin America's Social Policy Challenge: Education, Social Insurance, Redistribution." *Journal of Economic Perspectives* 27 (2): 193–218.

Maiorano, Diego. 2014. "The Politics of the Mahatma Gandhi National Rural Employment Guarantee Act in Andhra Pradesh." *World Development* 58: 95–105. https://doi.org/10.1016/j.worlddev.2014.01.006.

Maiorano, Diego, Upasak Das, and Silvia Masiero. 2018. "Decentralisation, Clientelism and Social Protection Programmes: A Study of India's MGNREGA." *Oxford Development Studies* 46 (4): 536–49. https://doi.org/10.1080/13600818.2018.1467391.

Mamgain, Rajendra P., and G. Dilip Diwakar. 2012. "Elimination of Identity-Based Discrimination in Food and Nutrition Programmes in India." *IDS Bulletin* 43: 25–31. https://doi.org/10.1111/j.1759-5436.2012.00343.x.

Mangla, Akshay. 2015. "Bureaucratic Norms and State Capacity in India: Implementing Primary Education in the Himalayan Region." *Asian Survey* 55 (5): 882–908.

Manor, James. 2015. "Key Issues in the Study of State Politics in India." In *Politics in South Asia: Culture, Rationality and Conceptual Flow*, edited by S. O. Wolf, J. Schöttli, D. Frommherz, K. Fürstenberg, M. Gallenkamp, L. König, and M. Pauli, 73–86. Cham: Springer International Publishing.

Manor, James. 2016. "India's States: The Struggle to Govern." *Studies in Indian Politics* 4 (1): 8–21. https://doi.org/10.1177/2321023016634909.

Marcesse, Thibaud. 2018. "Public Policy Reform and Informal Institutions: The Political Articulation of the Demand for Work in Rural India." *World Development* 103: 284–96. https://doi.org/10.1016/j.worlddev.2017.10.024.

Mehta, Pratap Bhanu, and Michael Walton. 2014. "Ideas, Interests and the Politics of Development Change in India: Capitalism, Inclusion and the State."

Mukand, Sharun, and Dani Rodrik. 2018. "The Political Economy of Ideas: On Ideas versus Interests in Policymaking." National Bureau of Economic Research.

Mukand, Sharun W., and Dani Rodrik. 2005. "In Search of the Holy Grail: Policy Convergence, Experimentation, and Economic Performance." *American Economic Review* 95 (1): 374–83.

Mukherji, Rahul. 2014. *Globalization and Deregulation: Ideas, Interests, and Institutional Change in India.* New Delhi: Oxford University Press.

Muralidharan, Karthik, Paul Niehaus, and Sandip Sukhtankar. 2016. "Building State Capacity: Evidence from Biometric Smartcards in India." *American Economic Review* 106 (10): 2895–2929. https://doi.org/10.1257/aer.20141346.

Nagarajan, Hari K., Hans P. Binswanger-Mkhize, and S. S. Meenakshisundaram. 2014. *Decentralization and Empowerment for Rural Development*. New Delhi: Cambridge University Press.

Nagavarapu, Sriniketh, and Sheetal Sekhri. 2016. "Informal Monitoring and Enforcement Mechanisms in Public Service Delivery: Evidence from the Public Distribution System in India." *Journal of Development Economics* 121: 63–78. https://doi.org/10.1016/j.jdeveco.2016.01.006.

Narayan, S. 2018. *The Dravidian Years: Politics and Welfare in Tamil Nadu.* New Delhi: Oxford University Press.

Narayanan, Rajendran, Sakina Dhorajiwala, and Rajesh Golani. 2019. "Analysis of Payment Delays and Delay Compensation in MGNREGA: Findings Across Ten States for Financial Year 2016–2017." *The Indian Journal of Labour Economics* 62 (1): 113–33. https://doi.org/10.1007/s41027-019-00164-x.

Narayanan, Sudha, Christian Oldiges, and Shree Saha. 2020. "Does Workfare Work? MNREGA during Covid-19." Ideas for India. Retrieved November 27, 2022. (ttp://www.ideasforindia.in/topics/poverty-inequality/does-workfare-work-mnrega-during-covid-19.html.

Nayyar, Deepak. 2017. "Economic Liberalisation in India" (2): 8.

Niehaus, Paul, Antonia Atanassova, Marianne Bertrand, and Sendhil Mullainathan. 2013. "Targeting with Agents." *American Economic Journal: Economic Policy* 5 (1): 206–38.

Niehaus, Paul, and Sandip Sukhtankar. 2013a. "Corruption Dynamics: The Golden Goose Effect." *American Economic Journal: Economic Policy* 5 (4): 230–69. https://doi.org/10.1257/pol.5.4.230.

Niehaus, Paul, and Sandip Sukhtankar. 2013b. "The Marginal Rate of Corruption in Public Programs: Evidence from India." *Journal of Public Economics* 104: 52–64. https://doi.org/10.1016/j.jpubeco.2013.05.001.

North, Douglass C. 1990. *Institutions, Institutional Change and Economic Performance*. Cambridge: Cambridge University Press.

Olken, Benjamin A. 2006. "Corruption and the Costs of Redistribution: Micro Evidence from Indonesia." *Journal of Public Economics* 90 (4): 853–70. https://doi.org/10.1016/j.jpubeco.2005.05.004.

Ostrom, Elinor. 1990. *Governing the Commons: The Evolution of Institutions for Collective Action*. Cambridge: Cambridge University Press.

Panda, Sitakanta. 2015. "Political Connections and Elite Capture in a Poverty Alleviation Programme in India." *The Journal of Development Studies* 51 (1): 50–65. https://doi.org/10.1080/00220388.2014.947281.

Parisi, D., S. Srivastava, D. Parmar, C. Strupat, S. Brenner, C. Walsh, R. Neogi, S. Basu, S. Ziegler, N. Jain, and Allegri M. De. 2022. "Awareness of India's National Health Insurance Scheme (PM-JAY): A Cross-Sectional Study across Six States." *Health Policy and Planning* Czac106. https://doi.org/10.1093/heapol/czac106.

Pellissery, Sony. 2008. "Micro-Politics of Social Protection: Examining the Effectiveness of 'Employment Rights' for the Informal Sector in Rural Maharashtra." *Contemporary South Asia* 16 (2): 197–215. https://doi.org/10.1080/09584930701733530.

Pellissery, Sony. 2021. "Social Policy in India: One Hundred Years of the (Stifled) Social Question." In *One Hundred Years of Social Protection*, *Global Dynamics of Social Policy*, edited by L. Leisering, 121–56. Cham: Springer International Publishing.

Persson, Torsten, and Guido Tabellini. 2002. *Political Economics: Explaining Economic Policy*. Cambridge, MA: MIT Press.

Pierson, Paul. 1993. "When Effect Becomes Cause: Policy Feedback and Political Change." *World Politics* 45 (4): 595–628. https://doi.org/10.2307/2950710.

Pierson, Paul. 1995. "Fragmented Welfare States: Federal Institutions and the Development of Social Policy." *Governance* 8 (4): 449–78. https://doi.org/10.1111/j.1468-0491.1995.tb00223.x.

Pierson, Paul. 1996. "The New Politics of the Welfare State." *World Politics* 48 (2): 143–79. https://doi.org/10.1353/wp.1996.0004.

Pritchett, Lant. 2009. "Is India a Flailing State?: Detours on the Four Lane Highway to Modernization." HKS Faculty Research Working Paper Series.

Puri, Raghav. 2012. "Reforming the Public Distribution System: Lessons from Chhattisgarh." *Economic and Political Weekly*, 21–23.

Rao, Vijayendra, and Paromita Sanyal. 2010. "Dignity through Discourse: Poverty and the Culture of Deliberation in Indian Village Democracies." *The ANNALS of the American Academy of Political and Social Science* 629 (1): 146–72. https://doi.org/10.1177/0002716209357402.

Rao, Vijayendra, and Paromita Sanyal. 2019. *Oral Democracy: Deliberation in Indian Village Assemblies*. Cambridge: Cambridge University Press.

Rao, Vijayendra, and Michael Walton. 2004. *Culture and Public Action*. Washington, DC: World Bank.

Razavi, Shahra, and Silke Staab. 2010. "Underpaid and Overworked: A Cross-National Perspective on Care Workers." *International Labour Review* 149 (4): 407–22. https://doi.org/10.1111/j.1564-913X.2010.00095.x.

Rodrik, Dani. 1996. "Understanding Economic Policy Reform." *Journal of Economic Literature* 34 (1): 9–41.

Rodrik, Dani. 2014. "When Ideas Trump Interests: Preferences, Worldviews, and Policy Innovations." *The Journal of Economic Perspectives* 28 (1): 189–208.

Rodrik, Dani, and Arvind Subramanian. 2004. "From 'Hindu Growth' to Productivity Surge: The Mystery of the Indian Growth Transition."

Rodrik, Dani, Arvind Subramanian, and Francesco Trebbi. 2004. "Institutions Rule: The Primacy of Institutions over Geography and Integration in Economic Development." *Journal of Economic Growth* 9 (2): 131–65.

Saberwal, V., and A. Chhatre. 2006. *Democratizing Nature: Politics, Conservation, and Development in India*. New Delhi: Oxford University Press.

Scott, James C. 1977. "The Moral Economy of the Peasant." In *The Moral Economy of the Peasant*. New Haven, CN: Yale University Press.

Sharan, M. R., and Chinmaya Kumar. 2021. "Something to Complain About: How Minority Representatives Overcome Ethnic Differences."

Sheahan, Megan, Yanyan Liu, Christopher B. Barrett, and Sudha Narayanan. 2018. "Preferential Resource Spending under an Employment Guarantee: The Political Economy of MGNREGS in Andhra Pradesh." *The World Bank Economic Review* 32 (3): 551–69. https://doi.org/10.1093/wber/lhw044.

Singh, Prerna. 2106. *How Solidarity Works for Welfare: Subnationalism and Social Development in India*. New York: Cambridge University Press.

Sircar, Neelanjan. 2020. "The Politics of Vishwas: Political Mobilization in the 2019 National Election." *Contemporary South Asia* 28 (2): 178–94. https://doi.org/10.1080/09584935.2020.1765988.

Somanathan, TV, and Gulzar Natarajan. 2022. *State Capability in India*. Oxford: Oxford University Press.

Thachil, Tariq, and Emmanuel Teitelbaum. 2015. "Ethnic Parties and Public Spending: New Theory and Evidence from the Indian States." *Comparative Political Studies* 48 (11): 1389–1420.

The World Bank. 2016. *Making Politics Work for Development: Harnessing Transparency and Citizen Engagement*. Washington, DC: World Bank.

Thorat, Sukhadeo, and Nidhi Sadana. 2009. "Discrimination and Children's Nutritional Status in India." *IDS Bulletin* 40 (4): 25–29. https://doi.org/10.1111/j.1759-5436.2009.00055.x.

Tillin, Louise. 2019. *Indian Federalism*. Oxford: Oxford University Press.

Tillin, Louise. 2021. "Building a National Economy: Origins of Centralized Federalism in India." *Publius: The Journal of Federalism* 51 (2): 161–85. https://doi.org/10.1093/publius/pjaa039.

Tillin, Louise. 2022. "Does India Have Subnational Welfare Regimes? The Role of State Governments in Shaping Social Policy." *Territory, Politics, Governance* 10 (1): 86–102. https://doi.org/10.1080/21622671.2021.1928541.

Tillin, Louise, Rajeshwari Deshpande, and K. K. Kailash. 2015. *Politics of Welfare: Comparisons across Indian States*. New Delhi: Oxford University Press.

Tillin, Louise, and Anthony W. Pereira. 2017. "Federalism, Multi-Level Elections and Social Policy in Brazil and India." *Commonwealth & Comparative Politics* 55 (3): 328–52. https://doi.org/10.1080/14662043.2017.1327928.

Varshney, Ashutosh. 1989. "Ideas, Interest and Institutions in Policy Change: Transformation of India's Agricultural Strategy in the Mid-1960s." *Policy Sciences* 22 (3/4): 289–323.

Varshney, Ashutosh. 1998. *Democracy, Development, and the Countryside: Urban-Rural Struggles in India*. Cambridge: Cambridge University Press.

Veeraraghavan, Rajesh. 2021. *Patching Development: Information Politics and Social Change in India*. New York: Oxford University Press.

Vivek, S. 2015. *Delivering Public Services Effectively: Tamil Nadu and Beyond*. New Delhi: Oxford University Press.

Weber, Max. 2009. *The Theory of Social and Economic Organization*. New York: Simon and Schuster.

Weyland, Kurt. 2005. "Theories of Policy Diffusion Lessons from Latin American Pension Reform." *World Politics* 57 (2): 262–95. https://doi.org/10.1353/wp.2005.0019.

World Bank. 2003. *World Development Report 2004: Making Services Work for Poor People*. Washington, DC: World Bank.

World Bank. 2019. *World Development Report 2019: The Changing Nature of Work*. Washington, DC: World Bank.

CHAPTER 9

Welfare Reforms and the Leviathan State

Introduction

As social safety nets programs are increasingly recognized for their usefulness in poverty reduction and building resilience in the Indian policy debate, an intensely contested and polarized debate has emerged on how to design and implement the programs more effectively. This debate touches upon the fundamental aspects of the social welfare programs—what is an effective way to reach the vulnerable population (*focus*)? what is the most cost-efficient and welfare enhancing *form* of welfare transfers? Do the transfers improve long-term welfare of the households (*scope*)? These questions have emerged as central to social policy as the economic, demographic, political, and technological change has brought about progress, but also generated newer sources of vulnerability.

In the chapter, we would focus on 4 key questions. First, do cash transfers provide a better alternative to the lengthy value chain of welfare transfer infrastructure beset with implementational deficits? There are auxiliary parts to this question. Shall cash replace food transfers through PDS only, or other welfare programs as well? Should it be narrowly targeted or take the form of a universal income transfer (UBI)? Second, given the implementational deficits in reaching the most deserving, can technology help overcome the governance of social welfare programs? Is payment through a biometrics-based digital identification the panacea to reducing last-mile corruption? Third, given India still being a developing

A. Rahman and P. Pingali, *The Future of India's Social Safety Nets*,
Palgrave Studies in Agricultural Economics and Food Policy,
https://doi.org/10.1007/978-3-031-50747-2_9

country with limited financial resources, does it have to wherewithal to have an expansive social welfare system? Fourth, two decades of expansion of social welfare have now created economic and political disquiets around welfare payments considered as 'freebies.' What does it imply for the future of social welfare programs?

Cash Transfer: Changing the *Form* of Welfare Transfers

Given the inefficient design of welfare delivery system which is beset with administrative inefficiencies, leakages, and promotes corruption and rent seeking, cash transfers have been introduced as a more efficient alternative *form* of welfare delivery. Theoretically, the case for cash is an economically sound one. A lump-sum amount of cash can have multiple benefits. First, it would expand the set of choices beneficiaries have in terms of household resource allocation and does away with the element of paternalism imbedded in the current form of welfare delivery. Cash eases immediate financial constraints and is likely to reduce borrowing from exploitative informal credit markets. Second, replacing in-kind transfers would also imply getting rid of the institutional system of welfare delivery which has not only been a source of corruption hurting beneficiaries but also an impingement to government's fiscal health. Third, in the case of India, a cash transfer is also likely to alleviate the interpersonal and regional inequity in the distribution of subsidies. Currently, food or fertilizer subsidies provide disproportionally high benefits to the economically prosperous rice growing regions of the country as compared to the poorer states.

One of the earliest proposal for cash transfers was made by Subramanian et al. (2008) marking 'a radical shift in the structure and mechanism of spending on poverty reduction programmes.' Their back-of-the-envelope calculation of a potential monthly transfer—computed by dividing the total budgetary expenditure on 30 centrally sponsored major social welfare programs by the number of poor in the country—suggested substantial fiscal savings over what is currently spent on anti-poverty programs. They particularly argue for replacing food transfers, fertilizer subsidy, housing subsidy, and the self-employment assistance program with monthly monetary handouts. Distributing cash, however, would create newer infrastructural requirements. The authors suggested that a unique biometrics-linked identification cards be provided to every citizen in the country, and the poor among then should be identified through the local participatory institution (*panchayati raj institutions*, PRIs) as traditionally done in the country, with frequent revisions to the list. The stipulated cash transfers should finally be provided into the account of a female member of the household.

This much avowed 'revolutionary' idea, however, skirts around some of the structural issues with the existing welfare delivery architecture. Cash transfers with a *focus* on the poor imply reliance on the same set of identification tools which are fraught with targeting errors. It is also unknown how cash transfers would reduce the power of local elites—principal contributor to the implementational deficit—in rural areas are less likely to disappear through participatory governance. Lastly, the required technological infrastructure—identity cards, internet, bank accounts, and financial literacy—is still lacking in most parts of the country, especially those where social welfare programs are of most importance. To sum up, any *form* of welfare delivery must face the grim realities of the Indian state, which is characterized by underdevelopment, low state capacity, bureaucratic apathy, and elite capture.[1]

Implementational challenges aside, the role of cash transfers in bringing about a transformational impact on poverty and make households resilient—assuming it to be the *scope* of cash transfers—requires rigorous empirical scrutiny as the nature of poverty and its determinants are likely to vary across context. There is a growing body of empirical work which supports the argument that 'small, recurrent, and reliable' cash transfers to the poor households improves multiple aspects of their well-being, such as consumption, savings, child nutrition, and mental health among others while lowering the incidence of teen pregnancies, child marriages, and intimate partner violence.[2] Cash transfers prove particularly useful during times of natural calamity and exogenous negative shocks such as COVID-19 in increasing the adaptive capacities of the poor in the short-term.[3] Their medium to long-term impact in increasing

[1] For an in-depth discussion, see this chapter.

[2] See Bastagli et al. (2019) and McGuire et al. (2022) for a survey and meta-analysis on the impact of cash transfers.

[3] As a response to COVID-19, the Indian government introduced cash transfers in addition to expansion of food transfers through PDS under the scheme, *Pradhan Mantri Garib Kalyan Yojana* (PMGKY) (Bhattacharya and Sinha Roy 2021). Refer to Gentilini (2022) for an extensive global review of the cash-based response to the pandemic, COVID-19.

human or physical capital accumulation, however, remains less convincing because sustainable transition out of poverty depend upon the amount of transfer, along with the nature and extent of poverty, and household's initial asset endowment, access to markets, financial infrastructure, and property rights (Balboni et al. 2022; Blattman et al. 2020; Haushofer and Shapiro 2016). As a result, while cash transfers potentially increase short-term welfare of the poor, the transferred income is mostly spent on immediate items of consumption such as rent, food, or energy and therefore the positive gains are not likely to persist even for more than six months (Altındağ and O'Connell 2023). For the poorest of the poor, also referred to as ultra-poor, long-term reduction in poverty, therefore, requires a range of social assistance—consumption support, asset transfer, entrepreneurship training program, etc.—along with cash transfer for a sustainable reduction in poverty (Banerjee et al. 2015, 2022, 2021). Cash transfers, therefore, can't be conceived as the only *form* of social assistance when the *scope* of social policy is to reduce long-term poverty and make households resilient. Surely, it could be one among other forms of welfare support.

The Old Debate: Cash or Food?

Old age pensions, maternity benefits, and farm income support, apart from other subsidies to the poor such as scholarships, cooking gas, are some of the existing cash-based social welfare transfers in India. However, the area where cash transfers have been proffered as the most compelling alternative is the replacement of food with cash. This debate has generated steam as food assistance through PDS has expanded to an unprecedented scale in the recent times.[4]

The theoretical case for cash is a sound one because food transfers amount to a deadweight loss. Staple grains-based food assistance programs entail huge operational costs on the supply side—state-led procurement, storage, and distribution of food grains—and on the demand side, they reduce consumer's food choice. Consumers could

[4] For an overview of the theoretical literature on cash versus food, refer to Alderman et al. (2017), Currie and Gahvari (2008) and Gentilini (2016). Between Kotwal et al. (2011), Kotwal and Ramaswami (2014), Ramaswami and Murugkar (2015), Svedberg (2012), Sinha (2015), Jhabvala and Standing (2010), Standing (2014), Khera (2014) and Narayanan (2011, 2015), readers can get a sense of this debate in the Indian context.

have spent the money on more nutritious food items or incurred essential non-food expenditure. While there is no disagreement on the fiscal argument, the welfare effects on household from cash in lieu of food has been the source of debate. Critics of the cash argument cite market failures (absence of food markets and the fear of inflation), lower state capacity and credibility (government's ability to deliver regular cash payments on time), and behavioral attributes of the beneficiaries (fear of wasteful expenditure, and differential ownership of cash and food in the household) as reasons to continue with the current *form* of food-based assistance. How much of these reservations stand to empirical scrutiny?

Global Experiences with Cash Transfer

Cash transfers increase household welfare in regions where markets are present and average income levels reasonably higher. Comparing cash and in-kind transfers across different regions of Mexico, Cunha, De Giorgi, and Jayachandran (2019) find that in remote areas, in-kind food transfers lead to a reduction in food prices, while cash transfers have the opposite effect. Food transfers, therefore, have greater overall benefit to the consumers than cash transfers of an equivalent amount in the absence of well-functioning markets.[5] Experimental studies from Ecuador, Niger, Congo, and Mexico further reveal that the cash versus food debate also needs to account for the income levels of the context in which the question is asked because household in poorer regions might prefer food even if it is of poor quality, while above a certain income threshold, they may prefer quality over quantity, which thereby affects the estimated welfare impact.[6] As a result, in-kind food assistance is preferable in poorer and inaccessible geographies.

Besides supply and income considerations, poor consumers may value food over cash for various reasons such as gradual erosion of purchasing power because of food price volatility and inflation, inherent transaction costs associated with going to a financial institution to access cash, or confidence in the government institutions. A survey which solicited about this option, an overwhelming majority of the beneficiaries of

[5] In Philippines, Filmer et al. (2021) show that cash transfers can generate negative local spillovers such as higher prices of perishable food products which can potentially undermines the stated welfare objectives of the program.

[6] See Cunha (2014), Hoddinott et al. (2018), Schwab (2020) and Aker (2017).

Ethiopia's Productive Safety Net Program (PSNP) expressed a preference for food transfers, despite cash being the dominant form of payment in the program (Hirvonen and Hoddinott 2021). While households with better access to food markets and financial services preferred cash, the majority responded to in-kind transfers as their preferred *form* of welfare payment. The preference for cash also depends upon the citizen's perception of past government performance and their trust in its ability for redistribution. In a survey in Tanzania, two-thirds of voters expressed approval for spending gas revenues on government services than cash transfers, arguing that "social services encourage a collective voice that helps increase accountability, while cash transfers would focus people on private interests and leave room for corruption" (Sandefur et al. 2015).

Prospects of Cash Transfers in India's Complex Socio-Political Landscape

Cash transfers in lieu of food (mostly calorie-rich, rice and wheat) would surely expand the choice set of the poor Indian consumers to buy more nutritious items, yet a pilot study conducted in Bihar, Muralidharan et al. (2011) finds that respondents do express concerns about moving to a cash-based system. They expressed inflation, delayed or incomplete payments, and the risk of cash being spent on non-food items as reasons for preference of PDS over cash. Further, they elicited a higher amount than the value of PDS subsidy, on an average, as their willingness to pay to move to cash in lieu of food. It can also be argued that disappointments with other cash-based transfers acts such as pensions, and wage payments in the public works programs also influences their stated preference for in-kind transfers (Khera 2014).

Cash in lieu of food might allow Indian poor to buy other food items, but to exercise such an option there needs to be sufficient supply of such food items in the private market at affordable prices. Given the inadequate value chain development of nutritious food products in the country, particularly in rural areas, moving to cash might deprive the poor of food security, the *scope* for which the PDS was designed.[7] The transactions cost

[7] Based upon a sample of around 250 local markets in India, Gupta et al. (2021) highlight the role of markets in making nutritious food affordable to rural households. In some regions, markets are lacking the infrastructure to make nutritious animal-based food items such as milk available throughout the year.

of accessing cash might be more than getting food at the closest PDS shop. Further, food price volatility is a common feature in the country and beneficiaries might worry about the erosion of purchasing power of the cash transfer.[8]

Critics of in-kind transfers argue that there is paternalistic note to continuing with the current system—a belief that poor can't make wise economic decisions on their own. Poor beneficiaries might not spend cash on wasteful expenditure and on temptation' goods such as alcohol or tobacco.[9] Yet, one must also account for India's social context where adverse intra-household bargaining power, and self-control influence the beneficiary preference for food in place of an equivalent amount of cash (Khera 2014; Pradhan et al. 2015). Poor consumers might have a preference for food because it allows them to have a constant supply of food throughout the month, while cash might be spent on one-time bulk purchase of other items.[10] This does not imply that the poor can't make correct economic decisions for themselves, or act impulsively, rather it is a symptom of scarcity itself, which lowers their cognitive bandwidth required to strategize and plan an investment.[11]

Perhaps, a bigger obstacle to the cash versus food debate in India emerges from the unequal agency of women within a household. In an Indian household, women traditionally have a greater say in the control of the kitchen, while men control financial transactions. The move from food to cash could entail an adverse effect on the bargaining power of women who is in charge of the household food security. An incentivized experimental survey from low-income neighborhoods in Nashik, Maharashtra

[8] There is credible empirical evidence that in-kind transfer through PDS buffers households against price shocks. See Gadenne et al. (2021) and Negi (2022).

[9] See Evans and Popova (2017) for a review of existing studies across many countries which debunks the idea that cash transfers are spent on wasteful expenses. The only evidence on this from India comes from a randomized control trial among urban poor in New Delhi where cash transfers were found to be superior to food with no increase in the consumption of temptation goods (Gangopadhyay et al. 2015). The study's generalizability to the rural context where poverty is higher and households are more reliant on PDS for household food security, is however unknown.

[10] Hirvonen and Hoddinott (2021) also find lack of self-control when it comes to spending cash as a reason for beneficiaries preferring in-kind transfer over cash transfer.

[11] There is a rich body of research which discusses the psychological costs of poverty. Lack of resources reduce the cognitive ability of the poor to undertake long-term decision making. See Mani et al. (2013), Mullainathan and Shafir (2013) and Shah et al. (2012).

reveals this behavioral preference (Abbink et al. 2022). Respondents in the survey, mostly women in male-headed households, were asked to choose between varying amounts of cash and the fixed quantity of rice they get from the PDS. Most of them chose a much higher value of cash over the value of the food subsidy that they were receiving, suggesting their preference for in-kind food transfer.

Citizens may also resist cash transfers if they have a lower trust in the government to provide regular payments without administrative hassle. Further, if the promised amount is not revised regularly to account for inflation, it may lead to a loss of welfare to the poor. Old age pension amounts haven't been revised in the last three decades since their inceptions and have been left to the states to revise it upward. The states which have increased the amount are also the one with lower levels of poverty. For cash to be an alternative, the government must provide a credible policy signal. In a survey of 3800 respondents in Bihar, one of the poorest regions in India, 87% preferred investment in public health infrastructure over cash (Khemani et al. 2019). The former was overwhelmingly preferred among the poor and less educated. Insufficient infrastructure and quality of public services lower the trust in government to provide regular payments of cash. Beneficiaries of the conditional cash transfers (replacing bicycle provision for school going children) expressed a clear preference for in-kind payment as the disbursement of money too inordinate time, and often the amount was insufficient to purchase a bicycle (Ghatak et al. 2016). Similarly, the confidence in local institutions to provide the food entitlements may be higher than an electronic money transfer through an impersonal technology and limited financial infrastructure. Currently, around 500,000 PDS shops in the country provide food rations—one shop in 75% of the villages—while banks and post offices which would be required to provide cash payments are present in only 8 and 25% of villages which (Narayan 2015). A pilot study in some of the most urbanized regions of the country shows that 20% of the beneficiaries did not receive the money, while for some who lived farther from the markets and ATM machines were unavailable in the neighborhood, transaction costs—of time and money—were substantially higher than the benefits (Muralidharan et al. 2017). Movement from food to cash transfers therefore creates a huge expectation from the financial system to deliver welfare.

As a result, the debate has now veered toward providing citizens the option of choosing cash or food.[12] The proposed choice-based model relies upon digitization of the PDS value chain, ubiquity of e-POS devices for every transaction, and portability of benefits across different shops where beneficiaries can ask for food or cash whenever they would like. We would discuss later in this chapter, how individual details, along with their bank account information, are now linked to their unique digital identity which allows cash to be transferred into the beneficiary's account, preferably a female member on whose names food ration cards are issued.[13] The option of cash would also incentivize the PDS shop owners to provide better services and reduce diversion of their stock to the open market. This seems a reasonable mid-way solution but would still require addressal of some of the structural issues associated around implementational deficits, credibility of the government to deliver regular payments, intra-household distribution of resources, and the over-reliance on the fragile technology to provide welfare payments to the poor. Food versus cash debate in India, therefore, must be situated in the complex economic, social, and political reality of the nation.

Lastly, the choice of cash versus kind is also a political one. Replacing food with cash implies an end to massive procurement system which was set up five decades ago to increase food security to the consumers and incentivize farmers to produce more through minimum support prices (MSP). Replacement of PDS with cash would require an overhaul not only of the food subsidy to the consumers but also newer ways of social support to the farmers, and agricultural market structure to reduce price volatility and build buffer stocks for emergency. Agriculture market reforms which were initiated in 2020 received a massive backlash from the farmers, and the government had to ultimately roll them back.[14] While a cash transfers through a new social protection scheme, PM-KISAN, has

[12] Refer to Muralidharan et al. (2018) for greater details. Government of Andhra Pradesh is trying such a pilot where beneficiaries would be offered a choice between cash and food. See https://www.hindustantimes.com/india-news/andhra-govt-to-introduce-cash-transfer-scheme-as-alternate-to-pds-rice-supply-101650570168484.html. Accessed on November 2, 2022.

[13] The idea of unique digital identity and financial inclusion was initially designed to enable cash transfers instead of food. Instead, the same technology now has become a source of addressing leakages from the PDS, contributing to the credibility of in-kind transfers. See Masiero (2015a) for more details.

[14] For more details on the proposed agricultural market reforms, see Narayanan (2021).

been launched, the amount is meager especially in the context of stagnant farm income in the country. Moreover, the *scope* of PM-Kisan is to support small farmers (*focus*), while the *scope* of PDS is to remove hunger and food insecurity among the poor. Cash versus food debate, therefore, pits one policy objective against the other and creates a trade-off between the welfare of some citizens at the expense of others. The 'radical shift' toward cash, therefore, requires a fundamental rethinking not only around the *form* of welfare transfers, but also the *scope* and *focus* of state-led welfare programs, in general.

Targeted or Universal Benefits?

Indian social policy has constantly wrestled with the question of whether welfare schemes should *focus* only on poor or span the entire population. Targeted schemes *focus* on the needs of the poor and the vulnerable, allowing for a more concerted attention to the cause of poverty, while using the limited fiscal resources efficiently. The efficiency objective, however, runs into a trade-off with the economic, moral, and political costs of targeting.[15] Targeting errors are inevitable in developing countries where income—to determine poverty status—is not directly observed. Any eligibility criteria are bound to leave out some of the deserving citizens (exclusion errors) and include the non-deserving (inclusion errors). The magnitude of these errors is determined by the choice of targeting criteria, the quality of information on citizen's income and assets, and the extent of last-mile corruption. The acceptability of

[15] Targeting could be of various forms: proxy-means based, community-based, self-reported, or geographic. A means test criteria is the ideal way to target in which a person is considered eligible for the program if their income falls below a certain threshold. In the absence of information on income, a proxy means test (PMT) is used to predict income based upon the observable information (proxy for income) on household wealth, asset, or education. The eligibility threshold is based upon this computed proxy of income. Community-based targeting relies upon the local communities to generate the information on poorer members of the community. Self-targeting means that the individuals apply for a program and the government verifies their credibility based upon the already calculated PMT score. This method reduces the likelihood of targeting errors as non-poor might not apply, while the poor are allowed another chance to make themselves identifiable to the government. Some regions could be poorer than others, and this distinction makes a case for geographic targeting. On the various methods of targeting and an overview of arguments in favor and against targeting, see Besley and Kanbur (1991) and Coady et al. (2004).

these errors, however, depends upon the nature of politics and citizen empowerment. We have discussed earlier in the book that countries with a more progressive social policies prioritize 'universalism' considering it as a part of the social contract where welfare entitlements are the rights of a citizen, while countries with a targeted system devise eligibility rules to determine the 'deserving' population. Most of the developing countries including India mostly employ targeted welfare programs when fiscal resources are limited.[16]

While the benefits and pitfalls of welfare targeting are an old debate, it has gained greater significance in the Indian policy debates along with the greater calls for cash transfers replacing food-based social assistance. The choice of targeting is an ideological choice. Given the importance of early life disadvantages for human capital and intergenerational poverty, social welfare programs with a *focus* on children—nutritional assistance, and school meals—have universal eligibility, while public works program *focus* on the rural labor. Food transfers, public health insurance, and old age pensions, on the other hand, are meant for those identified as poor. Poor and non-poor in India are identified through the above poverty line (APL) and below poverty line (BPL) cards which were introduced when PDS make a targeted program in 1997. With the National Food Security Act (NFSA) in 2013, the PDS coverage has been expanded with households being classified as 'priority' and 'non-priority' households. Other schemes like PM-JAY for health insurance have also expanded the targeted beneficiaries from those identified as BPL households. Beneficiary targeting, however, remains an administrative hassle, a source of exclusion, and contributor to burgeoning fiscal costs in the absence of limited information on household's socio-economic situation. For these very reasons, it has been singled out as one of the primary reasons for a shift away from in-kind benefits to a progressively universal cash transfer.[17]

Amartya Sen had famously said, "benefits meant exclusively for the poor often end up being poor benefits" (Sen 1992). There are several reasons why progressive universalism works better in the Indian case. Over the last two decades, the expansion of beneficiary coverage (*focus*)—as

[16] Grosh et al. (2022) provide an update on the policy dilemmas associated with targeted social welfare programs in the developing countries.

[17] See Kotwal et al. (2011) and Subramanian et al. (2008).

local government have revised targeting criterions—has led to improvements in the performance of social welfare programs.[18] First, finer targeting reduces political support for the programs. Greater share of beneficiaries allows for lesser opposition from any particular interest group and enhances political support behind the program.[19] This not only leads to greater enrollment but also facilitates stronger citizen participation thereby reducing last-mile implementational challenges. Second, targeting is efficient when institutions are transparent and targeting rules are non-discretionary, otherwise it creates an opportune environment for rent seeking and corruption. With limited information on the poverty status of citizens, the poor and non-poor classification is often found to be discretionary despite a list of exclusionary criterions. Targeting errors—both inclusion and exclusion—are often a function of who the local elites consider poor, and the process is replete with corruption and favoritism.[20] With progressive universalization of benefits, these errors have however reduced. Third, targeting precision has been enhanced through several attempts at a systematic database of all citizens of the country. Initiatives like Socio-economic and Caste Census (SECC) 2011, a door-to-door enumeration of citizens and an array of social and economic indicators pertaining to their households conducted by the Ministry of Rural Development, Government of India, allowed for the creation of a large

[18] State government led improvement in PDS performance is one of the prime examples of it, which has led Dreze and Sen (2013) to refer to it as the 'new style' PDS. For example, food assistance through PDS is a universal entitlement in Himachal Pradesh and Tamil Nadu, while Chhattisgarh has 'near universal' eligibility. Similarly, through their own public health insurance and old age pension programs, many of the states have expressed a commitment toward universality of welfare benefits. For a greater discussion on state-led social welfare program innovations, refer to this chapter.

[19] Indian states with a greater coverage of PDS beneficiaries have traditionally performed better (Khera 2011). Progressive universalization of the same program since 2000s has significantly improved the program objectives of food security and diet diversity (Kishore and Chakrabarti 2015; Krishnamurthy et al. 2017; Rahman 2016). With the NFSA expansion of eligibility criteria, there has been incremental improvement (Drèze et al. 2019). See Gelbach and Pritchett (2002) and (Sen 1992) for a theoretical debate on the political economy of targeting.

[20] Numerous studies have highlighted how welfare beneficiaries across the APL and BPL distinctions have proven to be erroneous. See Drèze and Khera (2010), Hirway (2003) and Niehaus et al. (2013) for empirical studies.

database—with its own imperfections—which became the basis of expansion of PDS and other welfare programs.[21] A live roster of citizens is now maintained under digital identity initiative, *Aadhaar*, about which would discuss in the following section, has further enabled in creating a database of potential beneficiaries.[22]

We would like to argue that when the majority of workforce is outside the employer-based social security system, covering a larger set of beneficiaries under social assistance program is key for resilience building—to address current poverty as well as poverty in the future. Throughout this book, we have highlighted that there are poor and there are those who are at the risk of falling into poverty. Building resilience requires social support for the symptoms as well as cause of poverty.[23] Moreover, the poor themselves are variegated—with some closer to the poverty line while others stuck in a state of poverty trap—and household-based poverty line is possibly not the best indicator for the range of vulnerability over a life course for an individual. A progressively universal social welfare, therefore, avoids such errors of exclusion, even when there are errors of inclusion.[24] This trade-off is inherent when targeting is a part of the policy design. Indian social welfare policies have tried to reduce it through progressively expanding the set of beneficiaries as part of the emerging social contract.

Is Universal Basic Income (UBI) the Solution?

There is a strong call for universalization of social safety nets globally with idea of Universal Basic Income (UBI) gaining political traction. Envisaged as an unconditional cash transfer to *every* citizen of a nation, financed

[21] For challenges with SECC, see Saxena (2015).

[22] These initiatives spurred other states like Rajasthan, Haryana, and Madhya Pradesh to create their own citizen registry systems to enroll and verify the 'deserving' beneficiaries. See Mukherjee (2021).

[23] Krishna (2007) provides a comprehensive argument for targeting the causes of poverty over symptoms of poverty.

[24] One must note that errors of exclusion continue to be serious. For example, in the publicly subsidized health insurance program, PM-JAY, which aim to *focus* on the bottom 40% of the population has a greater coverage of those in the top half of the population, contrary to the program objectives (Sheena and Smith 2022). The findings are similar even for other state-level health insurance programs, though some of them may have a more expansive coverage.

through progressive taxation, it would allow for a substantial income redistribution and surmounts the inefficiencies associated with in-kind subsidies and a narrow focus on the identifying 'deserving' citizens.[25] Justifications for UBI are derived from normative concerns of helping the poor as well as the implementational inefficiencies inherent in the current design of the social welfare programs. There is a lot to like about the idea of unconditional assured income to every citizen in a poor country. Universal Basic Income (UBI) is an elegant way to protect risks to livelihoods and ensure a life of dignity. For those, who prefer not to work (or engage in paid work) and those on the search for work, the nominal amount of UBI transfer would allow to sustain a life at least at a 'social minimum.' In a world where every citizen has an address, a bank account, and the agency to use the money at their discretion, benevolent governments can transfer a stipulated amount of UBI to the registered bank account of every resident of a country, like a monthly paycheck.

Economic Survey of India 2016–17, under the leadership of economist Arvind Subramanian, an early proponent of cash-based welfare system, introduced the possibility of a UBI to replace existing welfare schemes (Government of India 2017). The report made a conceptual and philosophical case for UBI as a 'radical new vision' which "puts money into people's hands" and provides the "shortest path to eliminating poverty." It argued that UBI—in lieu of other forms of transfers—would offer a solution to many of the inefficiencies associated with identifying and providing beneficiaries of the welfare payment. It obviates the need of intermediaries—local state institutions such as bureaucrats and politicians—in helping the poor. The semantics used in the survey appealed to the rights-based aspect universal entitlements to cash-based welfare. It said, "every person should have a right to a basic income to cover their needs, just by virtue of being citizens" and further claimed that UBI could become the *form* of welfare transfer which can address some of the fundaments concerns of human development—social justice, individual agency, poverty, and unemployment—in the most efficient manner. UBI, can therefore, replace all existing subsidies provided by the government.

[25] It is quite remarkable that UBI has garnered support from various political quarters—conservatives, libertarians, and progressives alike—which helps build a broad-based coalition across actors from politics, business, and activists. Yet, a clear idea around how to implement it and what its effects might entail remains elusive. See Hanna and Olken (2018) and Banerjee et al. (2019) for a discussion.

The proposal, however, stopped short of the strict universality and instead termed it as a quasi-UBI covering 75% of the population. Based upon the official poverty numbers, an annual UBI of INR 7620 per person (around 100 USD) for the year 2016–17 was computed which was assessed at around 4.9% of the GDP. These numbers subsequently ignited a debate around the feasibility of UBI, the optimal transfer amount, fiscal costs of the transfer, and the required infrastructure to make these transfer work.[26]

In the parlance of this book's framework, the *scope* of UBI is to reduce poverty through a guaranteed welfare transfers in the *form* of cash payments to those in the bottom 75% of the population (*focus*). It would be difficult to imagine cash transfers or UBI to be the single *form* of social safety net which could address vulnerabilities which emanate across the life cycle of a human being. Not all social welfare schemes can be substituted with a cash transfer, especially the early life interventions. The provision of school meals, or nutritional support to pregnant and lactating mothers, along with a menu of care provisions for preschool children is designed because of the missing market for early life care and stoking behavioral nudges which are key to long-term development of child health. It is for this reason, even the developed countries—where it is easier to implement UBI—continue to have an active welfare provision without any discussion on moving to cash transfers. PDS or MGNREGS are the only major scheme which could be a like-to-like replacement for UBI. Other major social safety net programs like maternity benefits, old age pensions, and cash transfers to farmers (with a focus on distinct population groups) are already being provided in the form of cash. Earlier in this chapter, we have discussed the challenges of replacing PDS with cash transfers. Under MGNREGS, beneficiaries are paid wages in their bank account for their labor employed on public works program. If MGNREGS wage payments are provided as monthly cash transfers, rural infrastructure creation as the secondary *scope* of the program—providing income security being the primary one—would be compromised. One must note that the success story of MGNREGS has been its contribution to rural economy on multiple fronts—fallback employment option during times of economic distress, infrastructure creation, improving wages and bargaining power of labor, and facilitating labor force participation of

[26] Interested readers can refer to Gentilini et al. (2020), Khosla (2018) and Mehrotra, Rajagopalan, and Kumar (2020) for discussion on UBI in India. Also see Davala et al. (2015) for pilot studies on cash transfer in the Indian context.

women, among others, thereby facilitating rural resilience.[27] Can UBI be the *tour de force* it is envisaged addressing the multidimension developmental deficits many of these social welfare schemes—as intended in their *scope* and their inadvertent impacts—currently address?

One can only speculate upon the short- and long-term welfare impact of UBI on poverty and equity before it gets implemented. The challenges of implementation, however, are clear. First and foremost, introducing UBI would first requires an institutionalized system of cash transfers which a dynamic database of citizens, which is connected their bank accounts where money would instantaneously get transferred every month. Such an infrastructure, however, has begun to emerge with digital identity and cash transfers to farmers in existence, however, it is fragile with a risk of excluding the poorest and most marginalized, the primary *focus* of welfare programs. Secondly, while cash is the *form* of transfer under UBI, there needs to be consensus on the optimal amount of transfer, whom to target (*focus*), how frequently would the amount be adjusted to the inflation rate, and how does it account for regional variation in prices. While it is inconceivable that UBI could substitute for mother and child nutrition programs, school meals, or health insurance programs, there needs to be a greater deliberation of the schemes it replaces and equity-efficiency trade-offs therein. Lastly, but most importantly, the move toward UBI must also articulate its developmental *scope*. Each of the existing welfare programs have a stated 'welfare objective'—eradication of hunger, poverty, food insecurity, or nutritional advancement, reducing gender inequality etc.—each of which contribute to development resilience in distinct own way. Combining them into a cash-based welfare transfer in the form UBI might increase the short-term income, but whether this income gain translates into a sustainable increase in the standard of living would also depend upon investments in essential public infrastructure, financial market, and public services along with changing social norms around intra-household bargaining power. If spending on UBI crowds out public investments, welfare gains may be limited or non-existent. Folding all (even a few) welfare programs into a UBI would therefore require a new articulation of the *scope* of this transfer.[28]

[27] Refer to Chapter 4 for a detailed review of this issue.

[28] Bardhan (2022) proposes UBI as a guardrail against the pervasive economic insecurity. A small amount of guaranteed income acting as a protection against loss of job,

To summarize, it is early to think of UBI as a replacement for the existing set of social welfare programs, or even a few of them. We make this claim primarily for two reasons. First, the cost of UBI at a minimum level of income support is prohibitively high (around 4% of the country's GDP) when it can't substitute for the other welfare schemes. Increasing public expenditure on health probably should be higher on the policy agenda. Second, a hasty move to UBI might be bad economics as well bad politics given the economic and socio-political ramifications of each of the schemes.[29] Yet, we believe that including UBI to the conversation in social policy design is indeed important. The larger social welfare policy debate, however, should first organize itself around a more fundamental question: "what kind of society people want (and will vote for) as about how to get there" (Banerjee et al. 2019). UBI may or may not be the only or another complementary *form* of welfare measure to the existing ones to get there, but it is more important for the policymakers to decide what ought to be the destination, i.e. the *scope* of their social welfare policy agenda—to reduce visible feature of poverty, to stem the inflow of people into deprivation, or both—and create a *social contract* around achieving them.

illness, crop failures, disability, etc., would also help build a more robust labor market and reduce inequality in the long run. He considers such a transfer as a citizen right.

[29] Even the proponents of efficiency gains from cash transfers concur with it. A more feasible solution would be to use UBI as one of the many forms of social welfare policy strategy policy alongside other conditional welfare programs. Cash transfers to farmers in the form of PM-Kisan is already a step in that direction, along with the existing old age pension schemes. One must note that economic theory suggests that a lump-sum amount of cash might provide some relief to the poor, but it may not be a long-term solution to poverty, especially when the welfare pursuit is of social justice (Ghatak and Maniquet 2019). In this light, an Inclusive Growth Dividend (IGD)—where 1% of per capita income of the country is distributed to all citizens of the country—has been proposed which does not preclude other *forms* of welfare transfers (Ghatak and Muralidharan 2020). While the suggested amount may not be sufficiently high enough to ensure a 'social minimum' to maintain a life of dignity, but it could surely be a step toward a 'practical and symbolic commitment to universally shared prosperity' which could eventually take the form of UBI (avoiding the targeted approach as proposed currently).

Leveraging Technology to build Local State Capacity

The role of technology in identifying poor and the vulnerable, disciplining the local state actors to reduce leakages and rent seeking activities, and thereby contributing to state capacity is a key social policy debate in India. This debate is relevant not only to fix the 'leaky pipes' of current welfare delivery system but also to create an enabling plumbing infrastructure for a gradual transition to market-based *forms* of welfare transfers. There are two kinds of technological innovations introduced to stem leakages in the current welfare delivery system. The first one focuses on transparency and accountability in the entire value chain of welfare transaction. Introduction of GPS tracking in the vehicles transporting food to the PDS shops, e-POS based PDS purchase, text-messages to inform beneficiaries about the delivery of grains at PDS shops, geo-tagging of MGNREGS work, smartcards for portability of services, digital registry of all healthcare providers for beneficiaries of the public health insurance program, MIS system at the ICDS centers, call centers and helplines, public data dashboards where beneficiaries can verify the receipt of benefits, are some of the examples of using digital infrastructure to improve welfare delivery.

The second, perhaps a more significant one, is the provision of a digital identity to every citizen of the country. *Aadhaar*, as the 12-digit unique identity card (UID) is called, assigns a biometric authenticated identity number to every citizen of the country, and connects it to a host of demographic and socio-economic data pertaining to the individual.[30] The unique ID, Aadhaar (A) along with a government financial inclusion program, *Jan Dhan Yojana* (J), which provides every person has a bank account, and the spread of mobile (M) phone to the remotest parts of the country, comprises of the pillars of "JAM trinity" is hailed

[30] Digital identity, globally, is being conceptualized as a platform for building public infrastructure for better governance and service delivery. Porting it seamlessly with other authentication platforms, payment systems, digital signatures, data sharing, KYC systems, consent management, and sectoral delivery platforms, it is expected to create a government stack ecosystem for the future. The World Bank, for example, has a dedicated program which focuses on identity-for-development (ID4D) which is currently supporting many countries through committed financing and technical inputs to implement digital ID and civil registration ecosystems for inclusive development.

by the government as a 'game changer' in the delivery of welfare.[31] It is envisaged as a solution to all last-mile implementation problems through eliminating 'intermediaries and leakages' and reaching 'only those who actually need them' without much influence of the local bureaucracy and political elites.[32]

Challenges with JAM

The JAM digital governance infrastructure is geared to deliver subsidies—cooking gas, old age pensions, farmer income transfer, wages in the public works programs, maternity benefits among others—through a cash-based direct benefit transfer (DBT), which is planned to be extended further to replace food, kerosene, and agricultural subsidies.[33] According to government figures, the new DBT-based governance infrastructure has allowed it to save around 2.8 billion USD by November 2021.[34] The technology-based welfare transfer infrastructure has earned great plaudits from International Monetary Fund (IMF) and the World Bank as a "logistical marvel" in solving problems of poverty.[35] Parameswaran Iyer, the CEO of NItI Aayog—Indian government's planning body—subsequently proclaimed that JAM-based DBT initiative is only "expected to expand further in size and structure as it continues to be the major tool

[31] To reduce the pressure on banking infrastructure and reach the remotest population, the government introduced many business correspondents, known as *Bank Mitra*. These retail agents are appointed by banks who provide various banking services in inaccessible regions where a bank branch/ATM is not present.

[32] Speech by India's Finance Minister, Arun Jaitley, at the 2016 K.R. Narayanan Annual Orations at the Australian National University. This speech is one of the sections in a selection of lectures compiled in Jha (2021).

[33] As of October 2022, 318 government schemes have been using the JAM infrastructure for DBT. https://dbtbharat.gov.in/scheme/scheme-list.

[34] https://dbtbharat.gov.in/estimatedgain. Accessed on December 10, 2022.

[35] The President of the World Bank Group further hailed the initiative urging other nations to learn from India's targeted cash transfer program which are successfully replacing the range of in-kind subsidies. See https://www.livemint.com/news/india/lot-to-learn-from-india-says-imf-on-govt-scheme-11665628152606.html. Accessed on December 10, 2022.

of the government for a more nuanced and targeted intervention towards improving the ease of living."[36]

While it is yet unclear whether *Aadhaar* is a voluntary exercise or constitutionally mandated, JAM-based infrastructure has become a *sine qua-non* to access any form of state-provided subsidies, benefits, and other services.[37] The government's standpoint is the following—JAM allows it to authenticate the beneficiary and reduce 'fake' or 'ghost' registries and reduce the dependency of beneficiaries on corrupt local institutions, both of which ensure significant financial savings to the exchequer. Digitization of transactions on a real-time basis also enables a simpler and faster flow of information and funds which increases efficient monitoring and effective governance of the programs. DBT to their bank accounts, instead of cash or wages in hand, further increase financial inclusion of the poor and encourages the culture of savings in bank accounts.

As of November 2022, more than 1.30 billion live *Aadhaar* numbers covering around 94% of the Indian population.[38] There are 1.2 billion mobile phone subscribers, around 0.5 billion new bank accounts have been opened under the *Jan Dhan Yojana*, and between 0.6–0.8 million banking correspondents are now placed to deliver branchless banking services within 5 km of every village in the country. These infrastructural preconditions are necessary to usher in an era of DBT as the *form* of welfare payment, yet the initiative's potential success continues to be contingent upon the existing institutional challenges which plague the present system. Deficient rural infrastructure, inflexible public systems, and discriminatory social institutions, while creating newer challenges

[36] https://indianexpress.com/article/opinion/columns/how-direct-benefit-transfer-scheme-has-transformed-social-welfare-in-india-8217140/. Accessed on December 10, 2022.

[37] Initially, India's Supreme Court (SC) ruled against mandating against *Aadhaar* as necessary for welfare benefits. However, in March 2016, India's Parliament, passed the *Aadhaar* Bill which permits the government to link the delivery of social welfare schemes to *Aadhaar*. While the Act allows for alternate means to verify the beneficiary's identity for the welfare payment if the person does not yet have an assigned *Aadhaar* ID, the most recently released circular mentions that UID enrollment now stands at almost 99%, and hence Aadhaar ID is a necessity to avail government benefits. See Hindustan Times, August 11, 2022. https://www.livemint.com/news/india/aadhaar-number-mandatory-to-receive-govt-benefits-subsides-check-details-here-11660666638016.html. Accessed December 1, 2022.

[38] https://uidai.gov.in/images/StateWiseAge_AadhaarSat_Rep_30112022_Projected-2022-Final.pdf. Accessed on December 10, 2022.

inherent in an opaque system of electronic transfers and the ensuing citizen-state negotiations.[39] Critics highlight that the promise of digital transfers in bypassing local state intermediaries has failed in both regards—it has neither ensured a more equitable *form* of transfer through becoming potential source of exclusion of the marginalized, nor it has increased efficiency in fiscal resource use (Khera 2017, 2019b).[40]

PM-Kisan is one of the earliest attempts at unconditional cash transfers through DBT. Field-based reports and analyses of government statistics suggest that there are serious concerns around successful seeding of *Aadhaar* with bank accounts, back-end system integration, connectivity failures, and inappropriate grievance redressal system. Despite the use of *Aadhaar*, DBT under PM-Kisan for many people were falsely credited into the bank accounts of ineligible people.[41] Gupta and Hussain (2022) analyzing the record of around 40,000 farmers in the East Godavari district of Andhra Pradesh who are enrolled under the PM-KISAN scheme and did not receive their entitlement. They find that almost 50% of these failures were on account of back-end failures of *Aadhaar* integration into the payment system and duplication of the *Aadhaar* ID. In about 5% of the cases, banks could not validate the account number seeded into the system. A study based in two villages in Telangana which—based upon comparing land records and the number of beneficiaries—estimates these errors to be of the magnitude of 16–20% as land records often do not match beneficiary list prepared by the government (Thomas et al. 2020). At the same time, tenant farmers, who do

[39] See Carswell and De Neve (2022) for an anthropological enquiry into citizen-state negotiations created by smartcards, and biometrics driven welfare transfers in the state of Tamil Nadu, one of the best performer on welfare governance.

[40] The delivery of LPG subsidies through the DBT route under the initiative, ***PAHAL***—launched in June 2013 in 291 districts, which required the consumer to mandatorily link their bank account to receive the subsidy as DBT linked to their *Aadhaar* number—***was*** proclaimed by the government as a flagship success in reducing 'ghost' beneficiaries and black market trading of LPG cylinders leading to substantial fiscal savings (Barnwal 2016; Mittal et al. 2017). The implementation of DBT was, however, also excluded genuine beneficiaries which led to an exaggerated claim on its fiscal benefits (Lahoti 2016).

[41] It is estimated that around an amount of 1.1 billion USD was fraudulently credited to ineligible farmers in the state of Tamil Nadu because of targeting errors as conspired by a syndicate of private contractors and government bureaucrats. See https://www.thehindu.com/news/national/tamil-nadu/pm-kisan-scheme-scam/article56832427.ece. Accessed December 2022.

not own land, and owners of land under litigation lose out on the cash benefits (Masiero and Buddha 2021).[42]

The story is similar for other schemes too. A government report notes that 33% of *Aadhaar* based payments (around 7 million payments) under the Pradhan Mantri Matri Vandana Yojana (PMMVY) got transferred to a different bank account, according to government's own report (NItI Aayog 2020). Kishore et al. (2022), assessing the DBT-based transfer of agricultural subsidies to the farmers report significant lags in payment. Delayed, rejected, diverted, or blocked payments are some of the recurrent issues associated with Aadhaar line MGNREGS payment (Khera and Somanchi 2020b). Corruption in the food transfers through PDS, too, continues to persist as beneficiaries often do not get their full entitlements, biometric authentications often fail, and successful disbursement is recorded despite non-delivery (Hundal et al. 2020). The failures of Aadhaar may not come as a surprise to the ardent students of the Indian state, and the leviathan which it is.[43]

The key marker of success of these technologies—build state capacity and deliver welfare in a more effective manner—is whether they can prioritize citizen's empowerment in a socio-political system where the citizen-state relationship is characterized by asymmetric power. Any technology, after all, is only a tool to serve the interests to which they are designed. In a democratic system, citizens are supposed to be at the center of such design, but often stated citizen interests are undermined by the existing inefficiencies in the public systems. While *Aadhaar* may allow the government to 'see better'—borrowing the phrase from Scott's, Seeing Like a State (1998)—citizen's welfare lies in being 'served better.' From the perspective of citizen empowerment and building resilience into the system, the promise of *Aadhaar* has fallen short of its promise. It also flares up serious concerns from the way the government is forcing it upon the citizens. Making *Aadhaar* compulsory for social welfare

[42] High levels of targeting errors are possibly a lower bound on the overall targeting errors in the country where land records are not yet updated. Before the launch of the program, Telangana government had already undertaken a drive to update and digitize land records—which many states haven't initiated or completed successfully—and issued digital land title to its owners.

[43] See Jayal (1994) and Sinha (2005) for the use of the term 'leviathan' while describing the Indian state.

programs like school meals for children under MDMS or early life nutritional supplements at the ICDS is hardly conceivable as sound economic reasoning.

The purported idea of using *Aadhaar* to weed out 'ghost' beneficiaries might have some arguments for food rations, cash transfers, or public work programs, but its mandatory use for nutritional support to children defies logic. Newly proposed linkage of the Aadhaar database with electoral roles poses further threat to the democratic process as the ensuing *India Stack*—as it is sometimes referred to—allows the information on more than a billion voters to the government as well as other agencies. The ubiquitous reliance of *Aadhaar* in social welfare policy, therefore, faces some serious challenges which we discuss below.

Limited ability to deal with corrupt practices: *Aadhaar* has been proposed as an answer to corruption and frauds in welfare delivery with a limited understanding of what causes are these last-mile malpractices. Local corruption occurs through misclassification of beneficiaries, duplicitous claim on someone else's identity who may be dead or non-existent, or deceitful quantity supplied. Fraudulent quantity claims could either be a complete denial to provide beneficiaries their entitlement, reduce their quantity entitlement, or ask for bribes for the transfers.[44] Inconvenience to welfare beneficiaries also emerge in the case of delayed or irregular payments from the government. Among these many forms of corruption, *Aadhaar* is only useful to address cases of identity fraud through controlling for duplication, at best (Bhatia and Bhabha 2017; Khera 2017).[45]

[44] A field-based report prepared by researchers from Dvara Research, Gram Vaani, Tika Vaani and University of Montreal, (2021) on last-mile implementational challenges in social welfare delivery highlights the prevalence of discretionary denial and quantity fraud by fair price shop officers in PDS. The researchers note that beneficiaries are often "denied their ration or sent away empty-handed or with less ration than the entitled quota, with no clear or documented reasons for the shortfall."

[45] We have discussed in the earlier section on targeting that much of the challenge with social welfare programs arise from misclassification of poor and non-poor, which *Aadhaar* cannot solve. An example from Krishna district in Andhra Pradesh, might be instructive here in understanding the limitations of the JAM technology. In Krishna district, local administration decided to go for complete digitization of all welfare transactions with the *Aadhaar*. While this led to an improvement in service delivery, the first order problem of 'selecting' the beneficiaries—with differing eligibility for various programs—remained unresolved (Aadil et al. 2019). Further, mandatory biometric authentication often failed for the poor elderly as their fingerprints were the hardest to match, depriving them of

Infrastructural Constraints: JAM-based online authentication often fails because of a mismatch in biometric, internet communication failures, server overload, or other technological glitches thereby increasing the transaction costs of obtaining welfare entitlements for the poor. The success of this technology requires regular and high-speed internet connectivity, super-efficient severs, and easier access to banking facilities, which continues to remain underdeveloped, despite an improvement over the years, especially in the remote areas of the country. Digital financial payment systems are not devoid of inconsistencies with a high frequency of delayed, rejected, diverted, or blocked payments in the bank accounts.[46] These infrastructural anomalies hurt the poorest most. Results from the field surveys as well as randomized control trials suggest that despite the presence of these technologies, local corruption remains pervasive, and beneficiaries often lose their precious entitlements. Even the most zealous supporters of JAM-based welfare delivery recognize the limits of fragile rural infrastructure and suggest a more careful scrutiny of its benefits (Muralidharan et al. 2022).

Lack of Legal Protection to Citizen Data: Data privacy, commercial misuse of the data, and risk of state surveillance create some of the ethical issues with the use of *Aadhaar*. Currently, there are no laws which

the pension benefits. In some of the better governed states like Kerala and Karnataka, despite digitization of records, and various e-governance initiatives, issues around population coverage and mistargeting continue to be a policy challenge (Masiero 2015a; Masiero and Prakash 2015).

[46] Narayanan et al. (2021) describe the challenges of *Aadhaar* based payments under MGNREGS through highlighting the challenges with electronic payments its limited role in creating a more transparent system. The job card holder first submits a demand application with the local MGNREGS office where her card details along with the *Aadhaar* number is updated in the system. Upon completion of the work, a fund transfer order (FTO) is generated in her name at the block (sub-district) office which is then sent electronically to the central government in Delhi under the electronic Public Fund Management System (ePFMS). The Ministry of Rural Development (MoRD), which oversees MGNREGS, initiates the payment order to the state government which pushes out an electronic notification to the National Payments Corporation of India (NPCI) which is the nodal agency for payment settlement for welfare transfers. As part of the Aadhaar Payment Bridge System (APBS), NPCI locates the bank to which beneficiary's *Aadhaar* is most recently linked. Once the identity is verified, wages are transferred to this account. Even a single break in this chain of identification-mapping can lead to delayed, rejected, diverted, or blocked payments. Similar payment-related issues persist in social security pensions, maternity benefits, and cash transfers to farmers under PM-Kisan. Khera (2019a) highlights the labyrinth one must traverse to access *Aadhaar*-authenticated PDS.

protect the privacy of the sensitive personal data which not only include biometrics but many other private information about citizens such as their bank accounts, addresses, mobile numbers, tax details, and ration cards which poses hazard to individual right to privacy.[47] The proposed Data Protection Bill in the country has undergone many botched attempts with its most recent draft, Digital Personal Data Protection Bill 2022, being the fourth attempt at it since the Supreme Court of India questioned the government on the privacy safeguards with respect to the *Aadhaar* data. The current draft too has been questioned by digital media researchers in its commitment to protect the 'right to privacy'—recognized as a fundamental right by the Supreme Court—of citizen. While a commitment to citizen privacy was included in the preamble of earlier drafts, it is conspicuous by its absence in the current one. The 2022 draft gives a *carte blanche* to the government agencies to share personal details of Indian citizens with other data fiduciaries—private or public; domestic, or international—at the behest of "sovereignty and integrity of India, security of the state, friendly relations with foreign states, maintenance of public order or preventing incitement to any cognizable offence relating to any of these." Advocacy groups such as the Internet Freedom Foundation have raised concerns that not only can this allow unfettered access of personal to private agencies but could also be a tool of mass surveillance.[48]

Government Audit of the Aadhaar-based transfers: The first independent performance audit of the Aadhaar system by the Comptroller and Auditor General (CAG) of India carried out between 2015 and 2019 points to some of the most glaring inconsistencies in the system (Government of India 2021). It notes that Aadhaar numbers in the database

[47] In 2017, telecom company Airtel allegedly opened bank accounts for its mobile subscribers without their consent. Airtel had utilized its eKYC (electronic 'know-your-customer') license which allows private entities (like a bank or a telecom company) to verify the personal details of an *Aadhaar* ID holder. While UIDAI quickly realized it and imposed a fine on the company and made amendments to the eKYC process, Airtel had already succeeded in routing payments away from original bank accounts to Airtel Payment Bank, belonging to 0.31 million beneficiaries' of the LPG subsidy without their consent. To understand the importance of developing a data protection legal framework in India, refer to (Prasad M and Menon C 2020).

[48] https://www.washingtonpost.com/business/indias-data-protection-bill-has-A-privacy-problem/2022/11/22/972e6a90-6ac2-11ed-8619-0b92f0565592_story.html. Accessed on December 10, 2022.

were often incomplete with biometrics not matched with the address and demographic information of the resident. The report further questions the claims of uniqueness of the UID. Technically, no individual can obtain two Aadhaar IDs, or a person's biometrics cannot be assigned someone else's UID, but as of November 2019, around 0.5 million cases of duplications were found. Despite many subsequent corrections in the system, challenges of faulty identification remain replete. To correct for some of these discrepancies, the Unique Identification Authority of India (UIDAI)—agency responsible for collecting and storing the *Aadhaar* data—places undue responsibility on the citizens themselves, which also comes at a monetary payment. The CAG report states that during 2018–19, more than 73% biometric updates were voluntary undertaken by residents for data entry faults and they had to pay charges to correct their entries. Huge volume of voluntary (around 30 million) indicate poor quality of initial data. CAG further admonishes UIDAI for not having a data archiving policy, a management 'best practice,' especially while storing private information. Building the UID database relies hugely on private contractors which poses an added risk to privacy as many of these third-party agents do not have the same safety safeguards as required. In fact, the data sharing ecosystem of UIDAI with other financial institutions, telecommunication companies, and other agencies to authenticate private services is a breach of privacy compliance and contradicts regulations of the Aadhaar Act itself.[49]

Global evidence around digital IDs suggests that they could be 'subject to failure to deliver on high expectation' (World Bank 2016, 196). For digital IDs such as *Aadhaar* to succeed as a tool for welfare recipients, supportive legal framework, adequate financial and human resource, committed leadership, and high trust between citizen and state is required. India fares poorly on most of these preconditions for success and therefore a unique ID could at best be one component of the social

[49] While the Supreme Court of India, on many instances, has maintained the use of biometric authentication through Aadhaar is meant only for welfare schemes, but many in practice, *Aadhaar* has already became a de facto citizen ID in the country despite the Supreme Court's directives. According to the State of Aadhaar Report, 2019, more than half of those who used *Aadhaar* to open a bank account or get a new SIM card, reported that they were asked for their *Aadhaar* ID while availing non-government services such as hotel reservation, school admissions, etc., which violates the 'voluntary' aspect of UID (Totapally et al. 2019).

policy and not the be-it-all source of beneficiary identification.[50] If social welfare programs, on an average, are already improving in implementation, single-minded focus on JAM-based welfare delivery might amount to "pain without gain" (Drèze et al. 2017). Several states including Kerala, Chhattisgarh, Jharkhand, and Odisha have already suspended Aadhaar-based transfers while others like Madhya Pradesh and Haryana are attempting alternative forms of beneficiary identification methods.[51]

To sum up, it is imperative that one must be aware of what biometric technology can potentially accomplish and the preconditions required for its success. First, JAM-based welfare transfers are effective in reducing only specific kinds of corruption, but not all. Second, in the absence of appropriate data protection laws, such a data architecture is a potential threat to privacy and civil liberty. Lastly and most importantly, the enthusiasm associated with sophisticated technology must reconcile with the sobering reality of the functioning of the Indian state and its public systems, which to put it mildly, are not 'citizen friendly.'[52] The reliance on digital identity, therefore, must be studied in this light with adequate weightage to its benefits and pitfalls.

Technological Efficiency Sans Bureaucratic Incentives

Technology can be used to enhance transparency through digitization of welfare records, public data dashboards, and greater dissemination of on-the ground implementation to the welfare beneficiaries. Digital technology, in the Indian case, has significantly reduced the information gap—which contributes to clientelism, last-mile corruption, and overall program inefficiency—between the higher level authorities who design programs and the lower level implementing institutions. For instance, the MGNREGS website provides a list all the works undertaken, and payment delivered on a real-time basis. Similarly, most state governments now have a list of the PDS ration cards available on the internet with all requisite details which does improve transparency and lowers corruption. One can also check for the status on delivery of pensions and other schemes. The

[50] For a cross-country review of biometrics and perils of development policy, refer to Gelb and Clark (2013).

[51] Refer to Allu et al. (2019) for subnational experiences with other alternatives.

[52] Refer to Chapter 8 for a discussion on the implementational failures of the Indian state when it comes to social welfare programs.

government has also initiated e-governance reforms to ensure information on fund flow within the government departments—from central government to the local institutions—on a real-time basis to increase efficient fund transfers.[53]

Such information disclosure been key source of increased beneficiary welfare—as a facilitator of greater transparency and accountability in the welfare delivery systems—by making information easily available to everyone. It helps political leaders electorally because the beneficiaries are now more 'legible' to them to stake claim for improvements in welfare delivery.[54] There are also added incentive for the upper-level politicians to monitor local party workers and bureaucrats for improved welfare delivery, at a reduced cost, with information on welfare benefits available on a real-time.[55] The state and national leadership have, therefore, been upfront in staking claim for the improvement of welfare programs as a part of their redistributive strategy in their electoral bids.

The use of digital technologies for improved governance and local state capacity, however, has its limits. While the use of technology can certainly improve citizen-state interactions through efficiency enhancing information systems which enables greater compliance to formal rules by the bureaucrats, it does little to reform existing bureaucratic structures—archaic administrative systems, demotivated service providers, and stymied local accountability—which are the typical feature of the *flailing* Indian state and its limited state capacity (Pritchett 2009). Numerous studies show that technological innovations have been undermined by the low levels of motivation and commitment to the public service. Oft-cited examples include staff monitoring technologies and a management 'best practice' in public health service and schools, respectively which failed to have their desired effect.

[53] In the case of MGNREGS, flow of funds from the center to the local offices has been a painfully slow and inefficient process—leading to unspent money and challenges of audit—which encourages financial misappropriation and discouraged performance of the programs. See Banerjee et al. (2020)

[54] In his seminal work, James Scott argues that gathering local information and organizing them into an actionable format renders citizens "legible" to the state officials. See Scott (1998) for more details.

[55] See Wilkinson (2021) for an overall review of political effects of technological innovations for the delivery of social welfare programs in India.

An experimental study under which attendance and effort of nurses in public health facilities was monitored through a time/date-stamping machines, along with a threat of fine imposition in the case of delinquency, failed to have any effect in the long-run, despite its short-term promise (Banerjee et al. 2008). The public health staff utilized the provision of "exempt days" as allowed by the hospital administration to reduce their work hours and effort, while still complying with the official monitoring rules. Subsequently, under the National Rural Health Mission (NRHM), the state of Karnataka, introduced biometrics-based attendance for the health workers—with a threat of pay cut for lower attendance—at public health centers (PHCs) to measure whether it improved staff attendance. An evaluation of this intervention by Dhaliwal and Hanna (2017) shows that while the attendance monitoring technology improved staff attendance, however, it only worked for nurses and pharmacists but not for the doctors. Doctors had access to better outside employment options which nullified the threat of penalty. Similarly, an educational intervention designed to improve management quality in public schools leading to higher learning outcomes among children got reduced to an "exercise in administrative compliance" (Muralidharan and Singh 2020). The schools diligently carried out every mandated administrative task considering the documentation of school improvement plan as the ultimate end goal. The government considered the timely submission of paperwork as a success and scaled-up the program to over half a million schools. Any increase in student learning outcomes, however, was not found. The incentive structure for the local bureaucrats—officials and teachers, here—was designed toward completion of procedures around meeting administrative targets, with little concern toward the *scope* of the intervention—greater learning ability of children.

The success of technology-enabled monitoring system in fixing the 'leaky pipes' of the social welfare delivery architecture, therefore, require necessary complementary inputs—political will, citizen empowerment, flexibility in the public systems, and robust infrastructure. While creation of infrastructure is relatively easier in the short-term, political will, state-citizen interaction norms, and public system reforms require greater commitment to social democracy.

Complementary Inputs: Political Commitment and Citizen Empowerment

Top-down digital technologies like JAM can only reduce, but not solve local corruption or exploitative practices entirely. Technological systems can also exclude the poor and undermine their potential as a 'social good' unless they prioritize democratic empowerment of citizens over their use as an policy instrument of reducing fiscal cost of transfers.[56] Contrasting experience of two states—Jharkhand and Andhra Pradesh—provide a testimony to the mediating role played by political will and priorities in leveraging technology to build state capacity (Muralidharan et al. 2022). JAM succeeded in achieving the twin goals of improving beneficiary welfare as well as economic efficiency in improving MGNREGS payment in Andhra Pradesh because the state government has a strong emphasis on beneficiary experience. Active safeguards were put in place to protect citizen entitlements through timely payments. In Jharkhand, on the other hand, government prioritized fiscal savings as the stated scope of JAM-based food transfers without the short-term concerns of the beneficiary welfare. Some of the beneficiaries were excluded from the benefits, many had to make multiple trips to the PDS shops, and sometimes they got less than their entitlements as the newer system had many technical glitches. Eventually the program was discontinued by the Jharkhand government. Similarly, a new electronic payment system introduced in the state of Bihar to manage the flow of funds from the higher level of government to the implementing agencies in the case of MGNREGS led to a reduction in leakages but also generated greater lags in the payment schedule which worked against worker's interest (Banerjee et al. 2020; Drèze 2020). Hasty implementation of a potentially useful technology and lack of political support behind it can therefore prove to be its undoing.

The use of digital technologies in the last-mile implementation can be leveraged to empower citizens and increase greater accountability among the service providers. A persistent challenge of welfare delivery

[56] Technological systems work within a wider socio-political system and are therefore subservient to powerful interests. Refer to Seth (2022) for a framework to understand the use of technology in reducing the unequal power relationships and promoting more egalitarian citizen-state interaction, with a particular focus on welfare programs in India.

is the lopsided structure of power—bureaucracy's sway over the beneficiaries' welfare claims—which undermines public action. For example, the local officials often engage in quantity fraud through not providing full entitlements to the citizens or they may request a bribe for the service. Greater local accountability among service providers could be encouraged through publicly disseminating statistics on welfare benefits could be another which also allows fostering of local democratic accountability.[57] Proliferation of mobile phones and its use to call and verify beneficiary claims reduces the monitoring costs of the government and have been recommended as a scalable and cost-effective tool to incentivize the local bureaucracy to improve welfare programs.[58]

Welfare Expansion: Good Economics, But Contentious Politics

The expansion of social welfare programs has increased the quality of life of the poor, and made them resilient to multiple, but it has also increased political disquiets around its *form*, *focus*, and *scope*. Political debates have

[57] Das et al. (2021), in an experimental study, show that providing personalized communications and community canvassing—disseminating publicly available information on the provisions of MGNREGS, workers listed, beneficiary wages, and date of receipt—increases the take-up of work and reduces payment delays through increased accountability of local implementing institutions. An experimental study in Indonesia also shows that once the beneficiary lists and their entitlements were made public (through loudspeaker announcements and listing on the wall in the village), it created greater private information to seek welfare benefits and reduced the incentive of the local elite to discriminate against a person or a group (Banerjee et al. 2018).

[58] Numerous experimental studies suggest the use of mobile phones to improve program monitoring. Dodge et al. (2018) found that access to an internet- and mobile-based management and monitoring platform among local bureaucrats led to 29% reduction in wage payment delays under MGNREGS. In the state of Telangana, phone-based monitoring of *Rythu Bandhu*, a cash transfer to farmers in the state, showed a 7.8% reduction in leakages once the sub-district officials were told that beneficiaries would be randomly called via phone to verify claims of cash transfers (Muralidharan et al. 2021). Similarly, Bihar government introduced the Interactive Voice Response Systems (IVRS)— a fully-automated platform under which one teacher in every school would be called daily—to monitor the performance of school meals program which could be cross-verified with a lower frequency evaluation of the same program by designated officials. It helped to weed out 'ghost' students while increasing the overall performance of the program in terms of take-up, sufficiency, and quality of the meals (Sekhri et al. 2022). Elsewhere, Aker and Ksoll (2019) find significant benefits of phone-based monitoring intervention in the case of an adult education program in Niger.

emerged around whether welfare transfers are unproductive handouts or 'freebies' in return for political gains, at the cost of taxpayer's money. At the same time, national as well as subnational governments are competing to stake claims for newer *forms* of programs with a more encompassing *scope*, greater coverage (*focus*), and better delivery of welfare programs. This has led to a tension in the asymmetrical federal structure of the Indian constitution where the central government holds greater financial power, and subnational governments often exceed their fiscal resources in making welfare promise to their voters.

Welfare Transfers or 'Freebies'?

Targeted welfare transfers have been a common source of scorn by the well-off section of the society as populist bargains—referring to them as doles, handouts, or freebies—which makes the poor lazy, spawn corruption, and hollow out fiscal resources.[59] As the *form*, *focus*, and *scope* of social welfare programs have increased in India, concerns have been raised about a rising culture of *freebies*. In 2022, India's Prime Minister (PM) referred it to as *revdi culture*—equating it to the frivolous distribution of sweets—as an attempt to "buy the people by distributing freebies to them" analogous to a form of "bribery" which according to him bodes of a "dangerous" political development.[60] Government institutions have also called for the rationalization of these subsidies.

The apex monetary institution of the country, Reserve Bank of India (RBI), in a June 2022, raised an alarm about rising fiscal debt in some of the states because of the increase in expenditure on direct welfare transfers (Reserve Bank of India 2022). Supreme Court of the country, which had earlier championed the expansion of social welfare reforms in early 2000s, also chimed in suggesting an independent panel of experts be appointed to evaluate the rising expenditure on various kinds of subsidies

[59] The most famous example of it being the stereotypical image of a 'welfare queen' who has relied upon public assistance for many years. US President Ronald Reagan used this caricature to demonize welfare beneficiaries as lazy and undeserving recipient of the state largesse. Someone living on the backs of taxpayer's contribution has historically served as a potent political message to the masses. http://www.slate.com/articles/news_and_politics/history/2013/12/linda_taylor_welfare_queen_ronald_reagan_made_her_a_notorious_american_villain.html. Accessed on January 29, Accessed on January 25, 2022.

[60] https://www.bbc.com/news/world-asia-india-62722592. Accessed on November 29, 2022.

being provided. The Chief Justice expressed the court's concern that the "state largesse dressed as freebies should not bleed the national economy dry."

The RBI report refers to freebies as a "public welfare measure that is provided free of charge" but distinguishes welfare transfers from the provision of free access to services like electricity, water, and public transportation, and waiver of long-standing dues such as pending utility bills and farm loans which are potentially affect credit markets, distort incentives for private investment, and reduced incentives to work." By this definition, meals at school, free or subsidized housing, gas cylinders or credit for education, toilets, free bus passes to women, or cycles to school going girls can also be classified as freebies. Surely, these are not. Rather, they are 'merit goods' with long-run benefits to the larger economy. The *scope* of many such welfare transfers is to improve developmental possibilities for those who can't afford basic essential needs for a dignified living which could take the *form* of publicly provided private goods at a subsidized or no cost. Without school meals, children would suffer from loss of learning. Bicycles would allow girl child to attend school and free commute for women facilitates greater employment among women. Subsidized toilets and housing allow for a dignified living and saves them from various hazards. Similarly, gas cylinders reduce the dependence on cook stove which increase respiratory infections. Free or subsidized access to many private goods, therefore, has multiple positive externalities through increasing the productive ability of its citizens and these transfers ought not to be dubbed as handouts or freebies as the benefits of 'merit goods' exceed their costs to the exchequer in the long run.

Welfare transfers are public investments in human capabilities with positive externalities for growth. Not only were public works program and food transfers instrumental in helping millions escape the wrath of livelihood and income loss during the pandemic, COVID-19, these welfare payments act a source of support for millions of others in the wake of everyday vulnerabilities of a poor household. We have discussed the importance of these welfare programs in building household resilience in the earlier chapters of this book.[61] Demeaning the political commitment of government toward the poor by calling them as freebies is grossly

[61] It must also be noted that government incurs significant financial loss through granting tax holidays, corporate subsidies, stimulus packages, credit write-offs—to encourage productive investments and job creation—which are akin to freebies to the

misplaced for the dignity of the poor as well as building the productive capacity of a nation beset with a high level of multidimensional poverty and deprivation.

Subnational Politics of Welfare Delivery and 'New Welfarism'

The freebies versus welfare debate carries significance beyond its economic rationale. The rising importance of social welfare schemes on the policy agenda has made it a hot-button political issue. In earlier sections of this book, we have highlighted the role played by subnational governments in the early 2000s in moving social welfare policy to the forefront of the social policy debates which thrived under by the welfarist leanings of the central government during this period (2004–14)—Congress government under the leadership of then PM, Manmohan Singh—further enabled an expansion of the centrally sponsored welfare programs. The subsequent PM Narendra Modi, who was in the opposition during this period, however, was a passionate critic of welfare programs. In a famous speech in the parliament, he had once called out MGNREGS as a useless dole to people and sneered at the construction work undertaken under the program as 'living monuments' of the current government's failures.[62] However, once he got power, PM Modi also could not to stymie MGNREGS. On the contrary, there has been increase its budget allocation since and the scheme is now referred to as 'national pride' in improving livelihood opportunities for the poor.[63] Politics, therefore, is key to the continuation of social welfare programs, but the very nature of welfare politics keeps on evolving. One could argue that there is a reasonable amount of continuity in welfare policy with the expansion of various programs and their recognition as anti-poverty instruments. However, the new government also brought about some fundamental changes in the *focus* and *form* of social safety nets along with a greater use of technology to monitor welfare delivery, which together is reshaping the politics around the social welfare policies.

corporates. After all, the welfare effects of these tax exemptions are little known. Welfare impacts of social safety nets—despite their limitations—are however clearly established.

[62] https://scroll.in/article/710095/Modi-says-MNREGA-will-continue-as-A-living-monument-to-Congress-failure. Accessed on December 20, 2022.

[63] https://indianexpress.com/article/explained/why-the-bjp-embraced-mgnrega-the-living-monument-of-the-upas-failures/. Accessed on December 20, 2022.

Using the catch phrase of *sabka saath, sabka vikas* (social solidarity, and collective development), PM Modi embodied a new *idea* of inclusive development which expanded the current *forms* of welfare transfers to subsidized provision of private goods like bank accounts, water, toilets, and cooking gas, along with cash transfer to farmers (PM-Kisan) and expansion of health insurance for the poor. The developmental *scope* of these newer programs was several—improving financial inclusion, better sanitation practices, reducing indoor pollution, insurance against risks, etc.—with clear long-term positive externalities. What was surprising to political analysts, however, is to find the pro-business political party which harped upon creating "minimum government, maximum governance" turning toward a new form of *welfarism* (Jaffrelot 2022). The other major push of the Modi government has been on digitization and extreme reliance on technology (despite their imperfections and challenges) to deliver welfare benefits. Despite the teething challenges of digital infrastructure, technology has brought about a degree of fairness and reduced the stranglehold of political clientelism through eliminating an array of middlemen in the welfare delivery system (Wilkinson 2021). This has allowed the central government to speak to its clients, the beneficiaries, and stake claim for more programmatic service delivery than in the past.

The 'new welfarism'—visible *forms* of direct transfers aided by technology—has surely increased the short-term needs of the poor but most importantly it has proven to be of considerable electoral gains to the central government as a *quid pro quo* bargain (Aiyar 2019).[64] Improvements in the welfare programs which began at the subnational level—owing to greater political competition at the state level—and gradually became an issue of national level social policy is increasingly being used by the central government to gain political legitimacy.[65] Voters in the age of new welfarism increasingly attribute the receipt of social

[64] Using the 2019 post-election survey data, Deshpande et al. (2019) show that voters attributed the receipt of welfare benefits as an important factor in voting for the incumbent government.

[65] Greater political competition, especially at the subnational level, has contributed to the salience of welfare transfers for electoral outcome (Gupta et al. 2022). The subnational political leaders, Chief Ministers (CMs), in many states expressed their commitment to improvement in welfare delivery and carried out multiple reforms which increased the performance of these programs, reduced deprivations, and provided the CMs greater political credibility. However, the central government gradually took much of the credit for these. Using the 2019 post-election survey data, Deshpande et al. (2019) show that

welfare to the central government despite state governments being in charge of welfare program delivery. Using the CSDS *Lokniti* post-election survey for the years 2014 and 2019—when central elections were held—Wilkinson (2021) shows that while the share of welfare beneficiaries haven't changed significantly between 2014–2019, the share of beneficiaries which credit the central government for MGNREGS and PDS has almost doubled (Table 9.1). State governments which are primarily responsible for implementing the program have lost out on the credit they deserve thereby reducing their incentive for better governance. Direct transfers of welfare programs have allowed the central government to bypassing the multiple stakeholders involved in welfare delivery and therefore claim credit for better service delivery. Aggressive political messaging on similar lines through PM's photographs and a renaming of welfare programs with "*Pradhan Mantri*" (Prime Minister) suffixed on helped increase PM's 'connection' with the poor beneficiaries, a unique form of welfare populism.

This new welfarism raises two important concerns from the perspective of long-term development. Centralized transfer of welfare benefits—bypassing the subnational government, leveraging upon the technology to make direct transfers—encroaches upon the state government's constitutional responsibility and fiscal space causing rift in the federal system of

Table 9.1 Greater credit to central government for welfare schemes

	MGNREGS		*PMAY*		*PDS*
	2014	*2019*	*2014*	*2019*	*2019*
Individuals reporting welfare benefits (%)	19.7	20.8	14.9	20.7	43.6
Beneficiary attributing welfare receipt to:					
Central Government	26.9	50.2	22.4	51.1	27.7
State Government	42	31.5	50.2	32.2	57.2
Both		0.7	–	1	1.2
Local politicians	16.1	6.2	14.7	5.9	4.7
Local bureaucrats	4.9	2.8	3.9	2.2	2.4
Others/NA	2	8.5	8.8	7.5	6.8

Source Wilkinson (2021)

voters attributed the receipt of welfare benefits as an important factor in voting for the incumbent central government.

governance (Aiyar 2019). Fiscal centralization has already begun to be a bone of contention between the central and state governments as latter complain getting lesser share of the tax revenues for the welfare schemes. Traditionally, the fiscal devolution—transfer of tax revenues to the subnational government—was decided based upon a formula arrived at through consultations between the Planning Commission and Finance Commission. Since 2015 these transfers have become ad hoc, based entirely on political exigencies as Planning Commission has been scrapped and its replacement, NItI Aayog, does not have the same mandate (Rao 2022). The terms of reference as devised under the 15th Finance Commission in 2018 have further accorded greater power to the center worsening the fiscal health of the subnational governments (Aiyar and Tillin 2020). With Goods and Services Taxes (GST)—a multi-stage indirect tax—replacing many of the other local levies and taxes in 2017, the ability of state governments to raise revenues has already declined. This impinges not only the ability of subnational government to innovate on social welfare programs but also their ability to undertake public investments in services like health and education.[66]

How to allocate resources and prioritize public spending between social services—infrastructure and welfare programs—is the other key policy issue for the future. It has been argued that public provision of private services over social safety nets and investment in 'hard' infrastructure—social services such as basic health, primary education—and productive safety nets might undermine long-term human development benefits such as health and nutritional gains (Abhishek et al. 2020; Anand and Subramaniam 2021). It is ultimately a matter of political priority as long-term gains from public investments are unquestionable and widely known. However, there is no conflict between investments on welfare as well as infrastructure are both are two important levers of a developmental state. What is required is a political commitment to both these efforts but unfortunately in a democratic society, there are more tangible electoral gains of private transfers—often necessary—than public investments on essential services.

[66] The challenges of COVID-19 response—primarily healthcare, which is the responsibility of state governments under Indian federal system—laid bare the limited financial resources possessed by the subnational governments.

Expanding Social Welfare System with Limited Fiscal Resources

Redistributive powers of the state are fundamentally tied to its ability to tax its citizens.[67] Along the process of economic development, governments increase their taxation capacity, broaden the tax base, and improve their tax/GDP ratio which allows them to develop the required state capacity to fulfill their productive and redistributive resposibilities. One of the fundamental reasons for the economic progress of Western countries lies in the role fiscal policy played in generating funds for building infrastructure, investments in essential public services, and a strong social welfare system. In the aftermath of the World War, the Western nations increasingly utilized a progressive fiscal policy using greater tax revenue mobilization to support those who cannot provide for themselves—through investments in education, childcare, health, and retirement benefits—taking on the responsibility of a 'social state'—(Saez 2021).[68]

Western Europe (Germany, France, UK, and Sweden) which is considered as the pioneer of the social state is the best example of efficiently utilizing fiscal resources for public welfare and investments in building human capabilities of its citizens. Piketty (2020) provides an overview of the rise of European social state from 1870s and its effect on higher levels of current human development outcomes. In the early twentieth century, only 2% of the national income was spent on public services while 8% was spent on maintaining law and order. As of 2020, while defense related expenses remain the same, expenditure on public services

[67] In countries where fewer citizens pay taxes, civic culture is underdeveloped which constrains the collective ability to demand public services, hold the government responsible for its deficits, and punish corrupt practices (Besley 2020; Persson and Rothstein 2015). Also see Brautigam et al. (2008) and Besley and Persson (2013) for a discussion on the role of taxation for state building.

[68] In Chapter 2 of this book, we highlighted how the idea of state led redistribution originated early in the advanced nations followed by the East Asian countries as their economies began to grow. As a result, the economically advanced nations spend a greater share of their GDP on social welfare policies. In response to rising inequality in these countries, they have further increased the outlay on social welfare in recent years. In the last few decades, as inequality in the richer nations has increased driven largely by the top 1% of the population, their governments have also garnered greater taxation resources to provide transfers to those in the middle and bottom of the income distribution. A more judicious fiscal policy, therefore, is key to fund a social welfare system and there is a lesson for India here.

and social welfare programs comprises of 37% of the total income (Panel A, Fig. 9.1). Greater public investments were principally brought about by rise in income and its fiscal mobilization through progressive taxation. The same is true of other advanced nations which are part of the OECD which spend around 20% of their GDP on social welfare programs currently, comprising of old age care (7–8% the GDP) followed by health (6%), and family and incapacity-related benefit (2% each).[69]

Nations which can generate greater fiscal capacity, as reflected in their higher tax-GDP ratio, are able to utilize the same for greater investment in social assistance programs. There is a clear positive association between the two using the World Bank ASPIRE database for the most recent years for which the data is available (Panel A, Fig. 9.1). India lies somewhere in the middle with low tax-GDP ratio as well as expenditure of social protection programs.[70] India's inability to generate and allocate commensurate fiscal resources for redistribution and facilitate greater economic opportunity—despite rapid economic growth in the last few decades—has been highlighted as one of its major failings of social policy which has exacerbated inequality and limited its potential for broad-based prosperity (Chancel et al. 2022). An equitable tax-funded welfare architecture in the developing countries like India, therefore, necessitates a broader tax base and fiscal modernization for efficient tax collection. In this section, we would assess the expenditure patterns of the current array of welfare schemes in the country and the discuss ways to raise higher tax revenues to finance them.

Current Expenditure on Social Welfare Programs

India's budget documents unfortunately do not provide a very clear picture of amount allocated under different schemes. At the same time, many state governments have multiple welfare programs of their own or add to the central allocation on specific schemes from their own resources.

[69] Incapacity-related spending refers to compensation by the state on account of sickness, disability, and occupational injury.

[70] It is important to note that the definition of social assistance and the time period for which data is reported is restrictive despite its usefulness. The India figures in the ASPIRE database is based upon expenditure incurred between 2010–16. As we would show in the following section, India's social welfare expenditure on its flagship programs has increased in recent times and is significantly higher than 1.5% of GDP as reported in ASPIRE database.

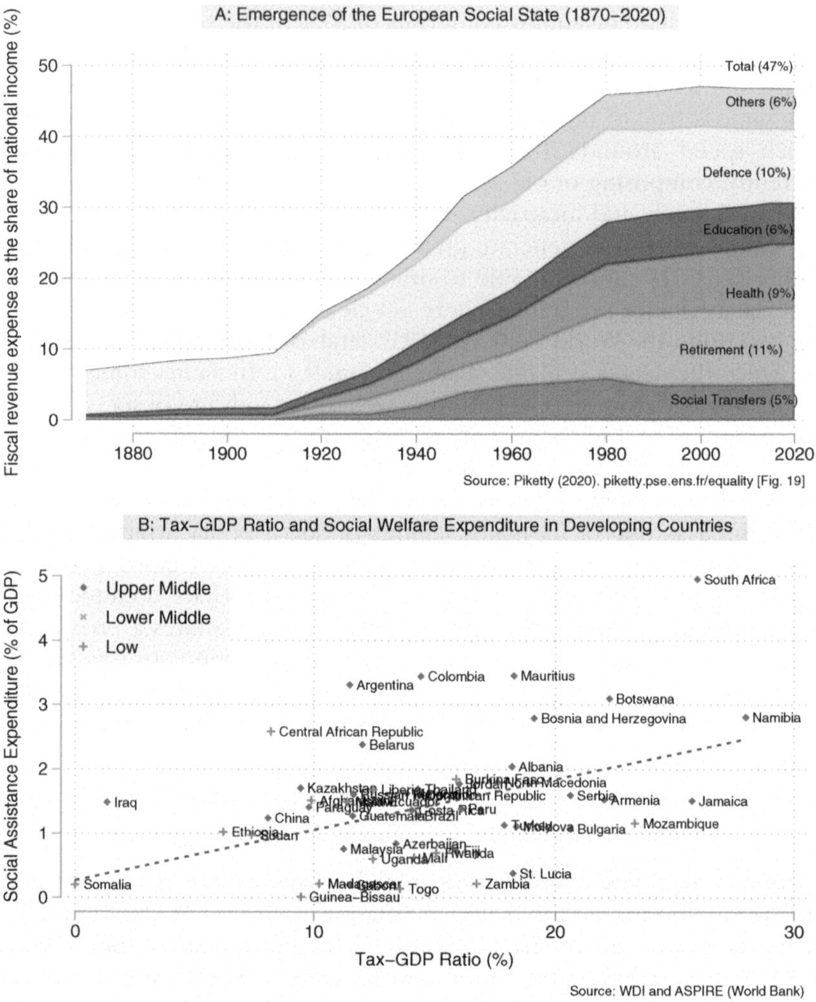

Fig. 9.1 The role of fiscal policy for social welfare program expansion

Getting a sense of the consolidated amount of money spent on various social welfare programs is therefore prone to errors of assumption. Yet, the numbers reported in the central budget of India which includes a combined expenditure (of state and center) on the Centrally Sponsored Schemes (CSS) provides us with useful benchmark estimates. The set of schemes under CSS are predominantly funded by the national government and subnational governments spend a small share out of their own resources. CSS are further classified as core schemes, core of the core schemes, and major central schemes. Not of all the schemes included in the list, however, can be classified as social protection schemes because some of them are solely focused on identity-based marginalized groups, and infrastructure related programs. We would restrict ourselves to the range of major social welfare programs—which span the life cycle of an individual—around which the book has been focused.

Overall expenditure on CSS comprises around 10% of India's GDP, while the major social welfare schemes constitute a little less than half of it, around 5% (Table 9.2). Food assistance under PDS and public work program MGNREGS are the major source of this expenditure (around 3%). Both schemes, as we have discussed in the earlier chapters of the book, have been the mainstay against the daily risks of consumption and livelihood food insecurity. As part of the COVID-19 relief measures, they were the most reliable form of welfare support. Cash transfers to farmers (PM-Kisan) and subsidized housing scheme (PMAY) are the other major social welfare expenditure which are provided in the *form* of cash transfers.

Despite an increase in the outlay on social welfare programs, poverty and vulnerability in India continues to be high. If India aspires to be in the league of more advanced nations, not only its spending on social welfare requires greater effort—in terms of its *form*, *focus*, and *scope*—but also needs to be combined with a rise in public investment in the field of health and education (Fig. 9.2). Lack of public investment in health is a particular concern because beneficiaries of the public system of care largely belong to the poorer sections of the poor. Even by markers of the other lower-middle-income countries, India's performance fares worst.[71] While subsidized public health insurance programs are a newer component of

[71] See more details in Chapter 7.

Table 9.2 Expenditure on major social welfare programs (in Rs. crores)

	2021–22		*GDP (%)*
	INR (crores)	*USD (million)*	
Food Subsidy for Public Distribution System (PDS)	286,219	34,518.0114	2.29
Mahatma Gandhi National Rural Employment Guarantee Program (MGNREGS)	98,000	11,818.8	0.79
Mid-day Meal Scheme (MDMS)	10,234	1234.2204	0.08
Integrated Child Development Scheme (ICDS)	20,000	2412	0.16
Pradhan Mantri Awas Yojna (PMAY)	47,390	5715.234	0.38
Pradhan Mantri Kisan Samman Nidhi (PM-Kisan)	67,500	8140.5	0.54
National Social Assistance Program (NSAP)	8730	1052.838	0.07
Pardhan Mantri Swasthya Suraksha Yojana (subsumes RSBY)	14,900	1796.94	0.12
National Health Mission	34,947	4214.6082	0.28
National Livelihood Mission—*Ajeevika*	12,505	1508.103	0.10
Total	**600,425**	72,411.255	**4.81**

Source India Budget (2022)

the social protection strategy, spending on it forms a tiny proportion of the budget share (See Table 9.2).

Raising Tax Revenues

A common lament among Indian policymakers is the lack of sufficient fiscal ability to expand social welfare programs and increase public investments on health and education. We would discuss here several ways to increase tax revenues for better redistribution which include higher income tax revenues by expanding the tax base, increasing the tax

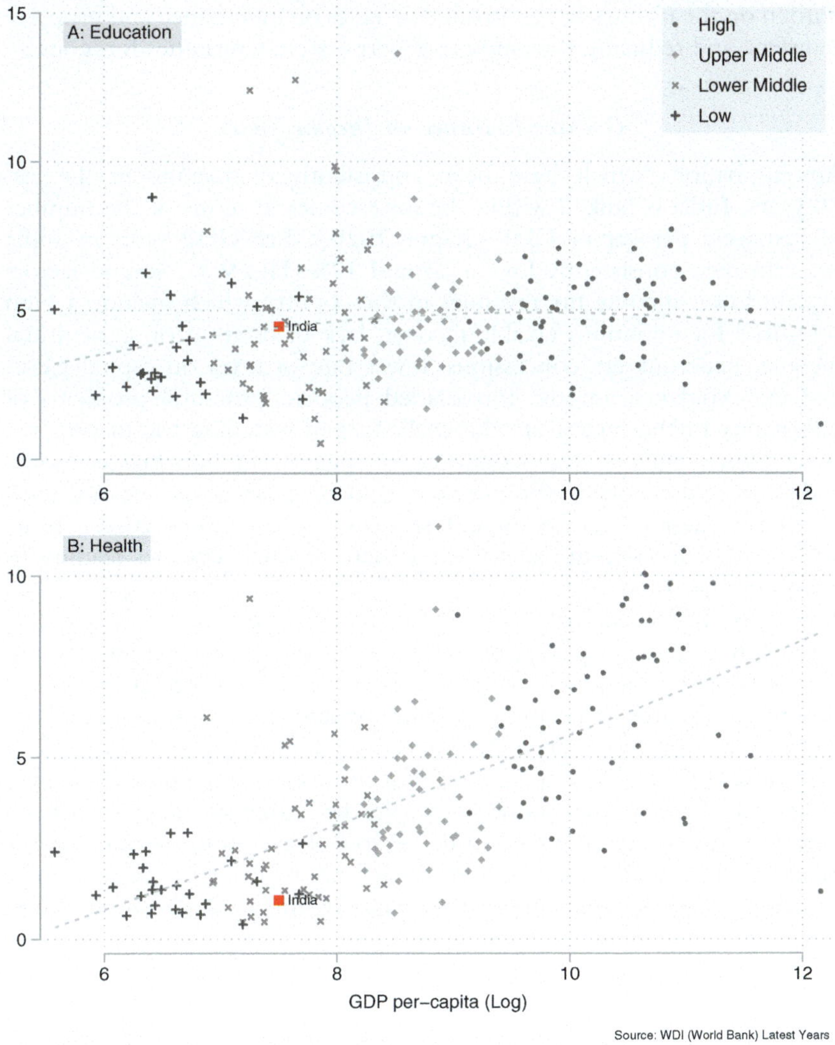

Fig. 9.2 Public expenditure on education and health (% of GDP)

burden on the ultra-rich, re-introducing taxes on inheritance and property transfers, and reducing the amount of corporate tax revenues foregone.[72]

Greater Reliance on Income Taxes

Among nations which have been consistently democratic in the last 50 years, India is ranked within the lowest ones in terms of the number of taxpayers per capita GDP (Kapur 2020). Tax/GDP ratio in India has remained consistently low at around 12% (Fig. 9.3). Several factors explain lower income tax revenues in the country which include a high threshold for minimum taxable income, lack of taxation on agricultural income, generous tax concessions, lower rate of taxes on capital gains, and tax avoidance among non-salaried people. Structural problems of informality further aggravate the challenges of widening the income tax base. Nearly 90% of the workforce is engaged in informal economy and is therefore outside the purview of income taxes. As a result, indirect taxes (mainly on goods and services)—where every citizen bears an equal burden—comprise a greater share of total revenues leading to distributional concerns.

It must be noted that a low tax-GDP ratio does not only a reflect smaller number of taxpayers or low tax rates but is also symptomatic of a poor effort by the government to collect taxes.[73] Inefficient tax collection methods, archaic taxation structure, widespread corruption, and tax concessions to private corporates collectively reduce the ability to collect more taxes in India. When it comes to income taxes, the limited coverage of the tax base in the country—despite its progressiveness—has been attributed to the constant upward revision of exemption levels and tax brackets which makes income taxes apply only to a tiny minority of individuals—2% of the total population contributing to 2–3% of the GDP

[72] Bardhan (2022) also argues that up to 10% of GDP could be mobilized through effective tax policies and rationalization of subsidies given to corporate and relatively well-off section of the population.

[73] Tax-GDP ratio and the source of taxes—direct or indirect and their sub-classifications—depend upon a range of factors which include a nation's economic structural transformation pathway, its political development—the nature of institutions, administrative transparency, sense of national identity—and the socio-cultural norms around compliance to rules and corruption (Besley and Persson 2014).

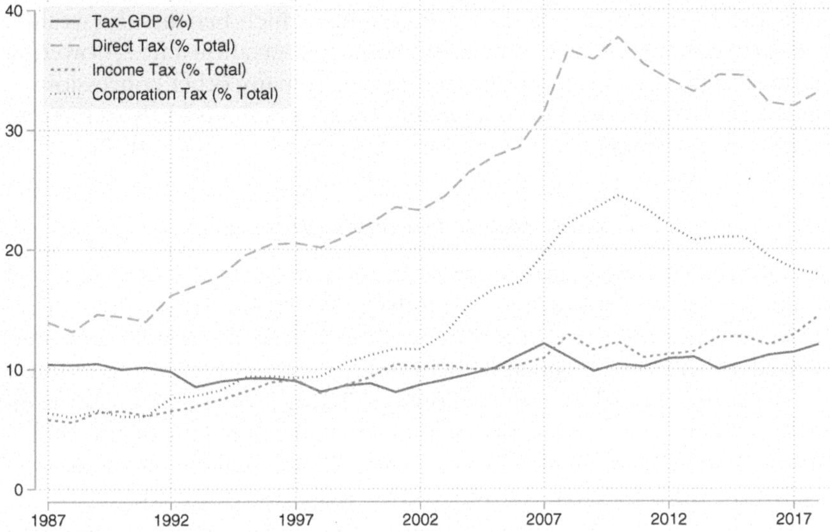

Fig. 9.3 Source of tax revenues in India

(Piketty and Qian 2009).[74] With greater informalization of the labor market and farm income outside the purview of income tax, overall tax base for income tax has continues to remain low. Upward revision of the minimum income bracket for taxation in a highly unequal economy has further limited the potential for greater revenue mobilization. Using Indian data on income taxes between 2011 and 18, Datt et al. (2022) show that that despite a progressive tax structure, it does not lend itself well to greater redistribution because of the lower amount of revenues generated. According to their analysis, greater tax-financed redistribution could be achieved by lowering the income threshold for higher marginal taxes. Another regressive aspect of the India's tax structure is the negligible taxation of income earned from long-term capital gains

[74] Piketty and Qian (2009) attribute the improvement in the tax-GDP ratio in China to a 'combination of fast income growth and under-indexed tax schedule.' As a result, income tax coverage in the country increased from less than 0.1% of the population in 1986 to about 20% in 2008. On the other hand, India which had a similar share of income tax paying population in 1986, could only increase its share to around 2–3% by 2008. Therefore, while income taxes in China are paid by the masses, only a minority of elites pay taxes in India.

on financial investment and dividend earnings which benefits the wealthy disproportionately. Restructuring the country's taxation rates—lowering the threshold for tax exemptions, and reducing many other concessions—in line with that followed in other emerging economies is likely to increase revenue from income taxes by at least 50% (Joumard et al. 2017).

Taxing High Net-Worth Individuals

There has been a significant increase in the concentration of wealth and capital among few individuals in India. The World Inequality Report 2022 computes the share of private wealth (sum of all financial and non-financial assets, net of debts, held by the private sector) in the country as a share of national income at 560% in 2020, a marked increase from 290% in 1980. The report further notes that the top 10% of the Indian citizens hold 57% of the total wealth and 64% of total pre-tax income.[75] Just before the pandemic, Hurun Global Rich List 2021 added 55 new Indian billionaires in the year 2020. It is quite embarrassing to note that a country of 221 billionaires, also has the ignominy of being home to the highest number of poor and malnourished children. The sobriquet of 'billionaire raj' is only befitting not only do these individuals possess much of the nation's wealth but pay far less in taxes.

While India has a progressive tax rate structure in addition to taxes on capital gains, gifts, and a surcharge on income tax on the ultra-rich, but there are sufficient loopholes and lax implementation which allows them to get away. At the same time, the effective tax rate is not progressive with respect to wealth. The ultra-rich Indians on the Forbes List pay less than 0.2% of their wealth—a much smaller tax burden than the liability falling on individuals at median wealth levels—because they misreport income

[75] According to a report by the investment consultancy, Marcellus, 20 most profitable firms in India comprise of the 70% of the total profit, up from a mere 13% three decades ago. Rising concentration of wealth in India is also reflected in the high wealth-income ratio which has returned to its historic peak—from the colonial period—since the 1980s (Kumar 2019). Even among the rich, the ultra-rich have had a phenomenal growth in wealth. Kumar and Anand (2022) estimate that while the richest 1% of Indians have a lower share of total income compared to other countries, but when it comes to the share of income held by those in the top 0.001% of wealth distribution—measured from the list prepared by Forbes Magazine's and the Hurun Global Rich—India comes a close second to Russia. Also see https://marcellus.in/blogs/behold-the-leviathan-the-remaking-of-indian-capitalism#. Accessed on December 15, 2022.

to the government (Singh 2022). The wealthiest citizens of the nation transfer only a miniscule share of their capitals returns to their personal accounts which lowers their tax accountability in the books. Unless the tax system considers total income earned and not just the reported income by the person filing taxes, the affluent groups have no incentive to report their actual income.

Rising wealth of the ultra-rich or the high net-worth individuals (HNI)—even in developing countries—calls for a reconsideration of wealth and inheritance tax.[76] Currently, there are no taxes on bequeathed assets in the country. Inherited property is also not considered for capital gains tax because it is only a transfer of ownership. In 1986, India discontinued inheritance tax citing little revenue from this source as wealthy individuals would often pool their assets into family trusts which fell outside the purview of inheritance tax. This argument, however, is a misplaced because family trusts typically comprise of bank accounts and equity shares with unrealized capital gains. A study based upon the revenues from 'estate tax'—taxes on large bequests—in place between 1953 and 1986 suggests a significant 'wealth leveling' during the period (Kumar 2020), and the findings concur with that of Banerjee and Piketty (2005) who study income inequality in India during this period.

Lack of an inheritance tax—a progressive levy on wealth in one generation—in an economy with increasing concentration of wealth implies an intergenerational curse of higher concentration of wealth, inequality of opportunity, and its associated social consequences such as conflict. We have discussed the role of building state capacity for implementing social welfare programs in many parts of the book. Low tax revenues in India also suffers from the inability of the state to identify and tax the rich in an efficient manner. Infact, inheritance or wealth taxes were removed primarily on the logic that the administrative costs associated with collecting tax revenue outweigh the collected revenue. However, now with *Aadhaar*-linked digitization of tax records, administrative costs are much lower to collect these taxes. Digitization of land records further

[76] Like income taxes, richer countries earn a greater share of income from wealth tax. In rich nations, wealth taxes comprise of 2–3% of national income. The share comes down to 1% in middle-income countries and 0.5% in low-income and emerging countries. See Chancel et al. (2022) for more details.

allows to assess the true value of real estate and property sales which are commonly known to be ludicrously low compared to an estates' market value of the same.

Reducing Corporate Freebies and Non-Merit Subsidies

The government of India provides numerous exemptions, concessions, and deductions in tax payments every year. The idea behind these exceptions is to provide greater incentives for private investments in hitherto underdeveloped sectors and is a common policy followed by governments across the globe. Companies investing areas like scientific research, infrastructure and employment creation, software technology parks, special economic zones (SEZs), the power sector, industries established in backward regions are therefore provided tax breaks or favorable rates. However, these concessions provide an opportunity for massive tax evasion and avoidance in the absence of any metric to assess if indeed private incentives influence investment objectives of the beneficiary firms (Rao 2016). Till 2014–15, the revenue foregone used to hover around 4–6% of the GDP. A change in accounting methodology in 2015–16 subdivided these incentives into conditional and unconditional categories and only the former was considered as foregone revenue. As a result, the tax revenue forgone came down to around 1–2% while the rest.[77] Mundle and Sahu (2020) estimate that around 3% of GDP—more than total public investment in health and education combined—can certainly be mobilized through removing these blanket waivers.

It must also be noted that the foregone tax revenue neither includes dividends earned by individuals from Indian companies and the exemptions provided for long-term capital gains which could be additional sources of fiscal mobilization for more socially responsible investments including social welfare programs. Reducing non-merit subsidies—expenditure on state-provided services other than pure public services and social welfare expenditure—is the other method to create more fiscal space for social expenditure. Currently, the non-merit subsidies, which largely go to better off sections of the population stand at 5.7% of GDP, a reduction of which would further enhance the fiscal space for redistribution (Mundle and Sikdar 2020).

[77] See Khera and Somanchi (2020a) for more details.

Conclusion

A good economic policy advice must be motivated by a sound theoretical framework around understanding of market failures (Townsend 2011), it ought to be grounded in the specific institutional context (Rodrik 2007), and supported by rigorous empirical evidence of its efficacy (Banerjee and Duflo 2011). The best possible advice also needs to be politically feasible, which often it is not, and therefore one must account for the political consequence of policies (Acemoglu and Robinson 2013). Our diagnosis of the current conundrum of India's social welfare policies is mindful of these challenges and therefore for each of the solutions we offer, we also add a cautionary note on the politics it creates.

On the question of cash versus in-kind transfers, we would like to argue that in a world where markets are well developed, social institutions are unhindered by paternalism, patronage and corruption, citizen trust their government, and public systems efficient, cash certainly leads to better welfare outcomes. As India has time to get to such a level of socio-economic development, it is better to wait and consolidate the current programs while testing out the feasibility of cash transfers in particular contexts where greater progress has been made. Metropolitan cities and urban areas progressively are a good place to experiment with cash (through giving beneficiaries an option of cash versus food)—without replacing the current system—on a pilot basis and update policies accordingly. Yet, it is important to note that cash versus food is not a debate independent of government's food procurement policy. If government continues to procure food on a large scale—which has increased in the last decade—food would continue to be the main *form* of transfer. Solution to the procurement issue is first a political one followed by the behavioral aspects of beneficiary preference for cash or food. In a patriarchal society, intra-household inequality—where women have less control over cash—paternalistic arguments of irresponsible use of cash prevail over the idea that poor be left to their own devices in choosing how to spend cash.

The choice between targeted and universal welfare benefits has amassed a wealth of empirical and theoretical literature. The answer is trivial. If it is possible to identify beneficiaries, targeting is a superior alternative. In the Indian context, targeting is arguably the most important source of corruption and inefficiencies in the welfare delivery system. Evidence suggests that states which have followed the policy of progressive universalism have improved performance. It would be natural therefore to err on the side of caution and argue for more universal programs. Progressive universalism is also desirable in the context of India's stunted structural transformation and heightened informality of labor force where even the non-poor are highly prone to falling into poverty given loss of livelihood, an illness, or any other misfortune. In the absence of employer-based protection to almost 90% of the citizens, it is the moral responsibility of the state to provide a support against any potential slide into poverty. Development resilience, which we argue in this book to be the *scope* of social welfare programs, particularly calls for effective safeguards against such risks.

Indian policymakers are fascinated by digital technologies as the be-it-all solution to all problems of corruption, clientelism, and associated last-mile implementational deficits. We have argued that the technology enthusiasts must understand the complexities of the Indian public systems as they envisage the role of digital technologies in developing state capacity for welfare delivery. Technology surely has a role, but it cannot be the ultimate solution when underdevelopment, citizen disempowerment, lower public action, insufficient political will, and bureaucratic indifference to the cause of welfare are the endemic problems which limit the effectiveness of public systems responsible for welfare delivery. The JAM infrastructure, which has been introduced as a tool to surmount these organizational issues, however, continues to be fragile, open to manipulations, and often exclusionary, which has been brought to light by field-based reporters, and most recently by the government audit report. Moreover, in the absence of adequate data protection laws, the fragile JAM infrastructure could encourage financial frauds while posing a threat to privacy and civil liberty. One can only hope that with time, the teething issue with the technology gets resolved over time to realize its purported welfare gains.

The debate around UBI is in infancy even in the most developed countries with abundant fiscal resources, a high level of literacy, financial development, efficient public services, empowerment of women, and most importantly a political system in which citizens demand welfare entitlements as their legitimate dividend from the country's growth process. The idea of UBI treats the desired transfer as a citizenship right. In Indian political system, apathy of the government toward the poor and other beneficiaries of the government system is so ingrained that even accessing citizen rights—right to work, and food under the welfare system—is considered a charity by the benevolent government. Furthermore, operationalizing UBI at the current level of economic development in the country poses multiple challenges of state capacity. Many of them overlap with those of the existing social welfare programs. Lastly, if credible evidence is the yardstick for policy prescription, numerous recent studies have suggested that in asset-poor societies with deprivations on multiple counts, cash transfers only resolve the short-term constraints with no impact on long-term asset accumulation, thereby leaving the structure of poverty intact. We would, however, not like to brush aside the idea of UBI altogether as it could surely be a powerful tool of anti-poverty policy, but in the future. Currently, as India learns from the global experiments around UBI and cash transfers, a scrutiny of PM-Kisan—unconditional cash transfers to farmers—would also improve our understanding of the issue.

India's vastly heterogeneous population, high inequality, vested class interests, along with its federal structure makes it challenging to agree on common long-term goals and, how to pursue them collectively while brushing aside the divisions. As welfare programs have expanded at scale, the tensions around fiscal federalism have also risen where the central government is trying to stymie the subnational political actor's influence in program delivery which not only limits their outreach to their voters in claiming credit, but also breaches the federal spirit of the Indian constitutions. The centralization of welfare credit seeking has also worsened the position of state governments in an already asymmetric tax distribution system with much reduced fiscal power to influence developmental spending and introduce welfare programs. Central government is aggressively using its power to de-legitimize state level welfare programs—any private provisions of public services at subsidized or no cost—calling them as 'freebies' while broadcasting the developmental *scope* of similar programs run by the central government at the same time. This conflict can only be resolved in the democratic space with the center and state agreeing on a common formula for fund devolution and its periodic revision every few years which has been the norm until now. Newer frameworks must be constructed for fiscal devolution which provides subnational governments fiscal strength and autonomy which they enjoin under the federal constitution of the country.

Despite its imperfections, local welfare delivery has improved significantly with time in India. While there are areas of neglect, greater democratic competition and public accountability has collectively improved the bargaining power of citizens when it comes to public services and social welfare entitlements. Greater reach of the social welfare programs, the 'new welfare' push, especially with the expansion of technology, has provided some semblance of enhanced state capacity—notwithstanding its fragility and apathetic bureaucratic culture—which has begun to contradict the claims of India as a 'flailing' state. But improvements in the local welfare delivery system have been accompanied by a decline in the quality of apex institutions in the federal democracy through greater centralization of power which has also subdued expectations around economic potential of the country.[78]

Lastly, we are sanguine on India's fiscal prowess to continue to fund its current welfare programs and its possible expansion, but it needs to undertake fiscal modernization which would allow for a greater share of the population to be covered under the ambit of income or wealth taxation. Economic growth in the last few decades has significantly expanded the economic base and there are sufficient avenues to raise tax revenues to around 10% of the GDP, provided there is sufficient political will. It would require rationalizing spending on non-merit goods, increasing direct tax revenues through a re-structuring of tax bracket, re-introducing inheritance tax, reducing corporate tax holidays, and increasing the capacity of tax personnel to catch tax avoidance by the ultra-rich whose number is increasing rapidly. Fiscal modernization measures, however, demand significant political courage and compromises in a democracy where elections are increasingly funded by anonymous corporate money and the aspirational middle class—comprising a significant share of the voter base—falls out of the tax ambit.[79]

References

Aadil, Arshi, Alan Gelb, Anurodh Giri, Anit Mukherjee, Kyle Navis, and Mitul Thapliyal. 2019. *Digital Governance: Is Krishna a Glimpse of the Future?* Center for Global Development.

Abbink, Klaus, Gaurav Datt, Lata Gangadharan, Digvijay Negi, and Bharat Ramaswami. 2022. *Deadweight Losses or Gains from In-Kind Transfers?* Experimental Evidence from India: Monash University, Department of Economics.

[78] See Vaishnav (2022) for a discussion on the declining the quality of India's apex institutions. Lamba and Subramanian (2020) and Kapur (2020) deliberate upon the long-term potential of India's economy.

[79] https://www.bloomberg.com/graphics/2019-india-election-funds/. Accessed on January 20, 2023.

Abhishek, Anand, Vikas Dimble, and Arvind Subramaniam. 2020. "New Welfarism of Modi Govt Represents Distinctive Approach to Redistribution and Inclusion." *The Indian Express*, December 22.

Acemoglu, Daron, and James A. Robinson. 2013. "Economics versus Politics: Pitfalls of Policy Advice." *Journal of Economic Perspectives* 27 (2): 173–192.

Aiyar, Yamini. 2019. "Modi Consolidates Power: Leveraging Welfare Politics." *Journal of Democracy* 30 (4): 78–88. https://doi.org/10.1353/jod.2019.0070.

Aiyar, Yamini, and Louise Tillin. 2020. "'One Nation', BJP, and the Future of Indian Federalism." *India Review* 19 (2): 117–135. https://doi.org/10.1080/14736489.2020.1744994.

Aker, Jenny C. 2017. "Comparing Cash and Voucher Transfers in a Humanitarian Context: Evidence from the Democratic Republic of Congo." *The World Bank Economic Review* 31 (1): 44–70. https://doi.org/10.1093/wber/lhv055.

Aker, Jenny C., and Christopher Ksoll. 2019. "Call Me Educated: Evidence from a Mobile Phone Experiment in Niger☆." *Economics of Education Review* 72: 239–257.

Alderman, Harold, Ugo Gentilini, and Ruslan Yemtsov. 2017. *The 1.5 Billion People Question: Food, Vouchers, or Cash Transfers?* Washington, D.C.: World Bank Publications.

Allu, Rakesh, Sarang Deo, and Sripad Devalkar. 2019. "Alternatives to Aadhaar-Based Biometrics in the Public Distribution System." *Economic & Political Weekly* 54 (12): 30–37.

Altındağ, Onur, and Stephen D. O'Connell. 2023. "The Short-Lived Effects of Unconditional Cash Transfers to Refugees." *Journal of Development Economics* 160: 102942. https://doi.org/10.1016/j.jdeveco.2022.102942.

Anand, Abhishek, and Arvind Subramaniam. 2021. "What the Latest NFHS Data Says about the New Welfarism." *The Indian Express*, December 4.

Balboni, Clare, Oriana Bandiera, Robin Burgess, Maitreesh Ghatak, and Anton Heil. 2022. "Why Do People Stay Poor?*". *The Quarterly Journal of Economics* 137 (2): 785–844. https://doi.org/10.1093/qje/qjab045.

Banerjee, A., E. Duflo, N. Goldberg, D. Karlan, R. Osei, W. Pariente, J. Shapiro, B. Thuysbaert, and C. Udry. 2015. "A Multifaceted Program Causes Lasting Progress for the Very Poor: Evidence from Six Countries." *Science* 348 (6236): 1260799–1260799. https://doi.org/10.1126/science.1260799.

Banerjee, Abhijit. 2011. *And Esther Duflo.* Poor Economics: A Radical Rethinking of the Way to Fight Global Poverty. New York: PublicAffairs.

Banerjee, Abhijit, Esther Duflo, Clément. Imbert, Santhosh Mathew, and Rohini Pande. 2020. "E-Governance, Accountability, and Leakage in Public Programs: Experimental Evidence from a Financial Management Reform in India." *American Economic Journal: Applied Economics* 12 (4): 39–72. https://doi.org/10.1257/app.20180302.

Banerjee, Abhijit, Esther Duflo, and Garima Sharma. 2021. "Long-Term Effects of the Targeting the Ultra Poor Program." *American Economic Review: Insights* 3 (4): 471–486. https://doi.org/10.1257/aeri.20200667.

Banerjee, Abhijit, Rema Hanna, Jordan Kyle, Benjamin A. Olken, and Sudarno Sumarto. 2018. "Tangible Information and Citizen Empowerment: Identification Cards and Food Subsidy Programs in Indonesia." *Journal of Political Economy* 126 (2): 451–491.

Banerjee, Abhijit, Dean Karlan, Robert Osei, Hannah Trachtman, and Christopher Udry. 2022. "Unpacking a Multi-Faceted Program to Build Sustainable Income for the Very Poor." *Journal of Development Economics* 155: 102781. https://doi.org/10.1016/j.jdeveco.2021.102781.

Banerjee, Abhijit, Paul Niehaus, and Tavneet Suri. 2019. "Universal Basic Income in the Developing World." *Annual Review of Economics* 11: 959–983.

Banerjee, Abhijit, and Thomas Piketty. 2005. "Top Indian Incomes, 1922–2000." *The World Bank Economic Review* 19 (1): 1–20.

Banerjee, Abhijit V., Esther Duflo, and Rachel Glennerster. 2008. "Putting a Band-Aid on a Corpse: Incentives for Nurses in the Indian Public Health Care System." *Journal of the European Economic Association* 6 (2–3): 487–500. https://doi.org/10.1162/JEEA.2008.6.2-3.487.

Bardhan, Pranab. 2022. *A World of Insecurity: Democratic Disenchantment in Rich and Poor Countries*. Cambridge: Harvard University Press.

Barnwal, Prabhat. 2016. "Curbing Leakage in Public Programs: Evidence from India's Direct Benefit Transfer Policy." Working Paper. Michigan: Michigan State University

Bastagli, Francesca, Jessica Hagen-Zanker, Luke Harman, Valentina Barca, Georgina Sturge, and Tanja Schmidt. 2019. "The Impact of Cash Transfers: A Review of the Evidence from Low-and Middle-Income Countries." *Journal of Social Policy* 48 (3): 569–594.

Besley, Timothy. 2020. "State Capacity, Reciprocity, and the Social Contract." *Econometrica* 88 (4): 1307–1335. https://doi.org/10.3982/ECTA16863.

Besley, Timothy, and Ravi Kanbur. 1991. "The Principles of Targeting." In *Current issues in development economics*, 69–90. Cham: Springer.

Besley, Timothy, and Torsten Persson. 2013. "Taxation and Development." In *Handbook of public economics*, vol. 5, 51–110. Amsterdam: Elsevier.

Besley, Timothy, and Torsten Persson. 2014. "Why Do Developing Countries Tax So Little?" *Journal of Economic Perspectives* 28 (4): 99–120. https://doi.org/10.1257/jep.28.4.99.

Bhatia, Amiya, and Jacqueline Bhabha. 2017. "India's Aadhaar Scheme and the Promise of Inclusive Social Protection." *Oxford Development Studies* 45 (1): 64–79. https://doi.org/10.1080/13600818.2016.1263726.

Bhattacharya, Shrayana, and Sutirtha Sinha Roy. 2021. *Intent to Implementation: Tracking India's Social Protection Response to COVID-19*. 2107. Washington, D.C.: World Bank.

Blattman, Christopher, Nathan Fiala, and Sebastian Martinez. 2020. "The Long-Term Impacts of Grants on Poverty: Nine-Year Evidence from Uganda's Youth Opportunities Program." *American Economic Review: Insights* 2 (3): 287–304. https://doi.org/10.1257/aeri.20190224.

Brautigam, Deborah, Odd-Helge Fjeldstad, and Mick Moore. 2008. *Taxation and State-Building in Developing Countries: Capacity and Consent*. Cambridge: Cambridge University Press.

Carswell, Grace, and Geert De Neve. 2022. "Transparency, Exclusion and Mediation: How Digital and Biometric Technologies Are Transforming Social Protection in Tamil Nadu, India." *Oxford Development Studies* 50 (2): 126–141. https://doi.org/10.1080/13600818.2021.1904866.

Chancel, Lucas, Thomas Piketty, and Emmanuel Saez. 2022. *World Inequality Report 2022*. Cambridge: Harvard University Press.

Coady, David, Margaret E. Grosh, and John Hoddinott. 2004. *Targeting of Transfers in Developing Countries: Review of Lessons and Experience*. Washington, D.C.: The World Bank.

Cunha, Jesse M. 2014. "Testing Paternalism: Cash versus in-Kind Transfers." *American Economic Journal: Applied Economics* 6 (2): 195–230.

Cunha, Jesse M., Giacomo De Giorgi, and Seema Jayachandran. 2019. "The Price Effects of Cash versus In-Kind Transfers." *The Review of Economic Studies* 86 (1): 240–281.

Currie, Janet, and Firouz Gahvari. 2008. "Transfers in Cash and In-Kind: Theory Meets the Data." *Journal of Economic Literature* 46 (2): 333–383. https://doi.org/10.1257/jel.46.2.333.

Das, Upasak, Amartya Paul, and Mohit Sharma. 2021. *Can Information Dissemination Reduce Last Mile Payment Delays in the Public Works Programme? Evidence from a Field Experiment in India*. 9292569554. WIDER Working Paper.

Datt, Gaurav, Ranjan Ray, and Christopher Teh. 2022. "Progressivity and Redistributive Effects of Income Taxes: Evidence from India." *Empirical Economics* 63 (1): 141–178.

Davala, Sarath, Renana Jhabvala, and Guy Standing. 2015. *And Soumya Kapoor Mehta*. Basic Income: A Transformative Policy for India. London: Bloomsbury Publishing.

Deshpande, Rajeshwari, Louise Tillin, and K.K. Kailash. 2019. "The BJP's Welfare Schemes: Did They Make a Difference in the 2019 Elections?" *Studies in Indian Politics* 7 (2): 219–233.

Dhaliwal, Iqbal, and Rema Hanna. 2017. "The Devil Is in the Details: The Successes and Limitations of Bureaucratic Reform in India." *Journal of Development Economics* 124: 1–21. https://doi.org/10.1016/j.jdeveco.2016.08.008.

Dodge, Eric, Yusuf Neggers, Rohini Pande, and Charity Troyer Moore. 2018. *Having It at Hand: How Small Search Frictions Impact Bureaucratic Efficiency*. Working Paper, May 2018. https://www.povertyactionlab.org/sites/default.

Drèze, Jean. 2020. "Policy beyond Evidence." *World Development* 127: 104797. https://doi.org/10.1016/j.worlddev.2019.104797.

Drèze, Jean, Prankur Gupta, Reetika Khera, and Isabel Pimenta. 2019. "Casting the Net." *Economic & Political Weekly* 54 (6): 37.

Drèze, Jean, Nazar Khalid, Reetika Khera, and Anmol Somanchi. 2017. "Aadhaar and Food Security in Jharkhand: Pain without Gain?" *Economic and Political Weekly* 52 (50): 50–60.

Drèze, Jean, and Reetika Khera. 2010. "The BPL Census and a Possible Alternative." *Economic and Political Weekly* 45 (9): 54–63.

Dreze, Jean. 2013. *And Amartya Sen*. An Uncertain Glory: India and Its Contradictions. Princeton: Princeton Press.

Dvara Research, Gram Vaani, Tika Vaani, Universityof Montreal. 2021. *Delivery of Social Protection Entitlements in India Unpacking Exclusion, Grievance Redress, and the Relevance of Citizen-Assistance Mechanisms*. Dvara Research Foundation.

Evans, David K., and Anna Popova. 2017. "Cash Transfers and Temptation Goods." *Economic Development and Cultural Change* 65 (2): 189–221.

Filmer, Deon, Jed Friedman, Eeshani Kandpal, and Junko Onishi. 2021. "Cash Transfers, Food Prices, and Nutrition Impacts on Ineligible Children." *The Review of Economics and Statistics* 105 (2): 1–45. https://doi.org/10.1162/rest_a_01061.

Gadenne, Lucie, Samuel Norris, Monica Singhal, and Sandip Sukhtankar. 2021. *In-Kind Transfers as Insurance*. National Bureau of Economic Research.

Gangopadhyay, Shubhashis, Robert Lensink, and Bhupesh Yadav. 2015. "Cash or In-Kind Transfers? Evidence from a Randomised Controlled Trial in Delhi, India." *The Journal of Development Studies* 51 (6): 660–673. https://doi.org/10.1080/00220388.2014.997219.

Gelb, Alan, and Julia Clark. 2013. "Identification for Development: The Biometrics Revolution." *SSRN Electronic Journal*. https://doi.org/10.2139/ssrn.2226594.

Gelbach, Jonah, and Lant Pritchett. 2002. "Is More for the Poor Less for the Poor? The Politics of Means-Tested Targeting." *Topics in Economic Analysis & Policy* 2 (1): 1027.

Gentilini, Ugo. 2016. "Revisiting the 'Cash versus Food' Debate: New Evidence for an Old Puzzle?" *The World Bank Research Observer* 31 (1): 135–167.

Gentilini, Ugo. 2022. *Cash Transfers in Pandemic Times: Evidence, Practices, and Implications from the Largest Scale Up in History*. Washington, D.C.: World Bank.

Gentilini, Ugo, Margaret Grosh, Jamele Rigolini, and Ruslan Yemtsov. 2020. *Exploring Universal Basic Income: A Guide to Navigating Concepts, Evidence, and Practices*. Washington, D.C.: World Bank.

Ghatak, Maitreesh, Chinmaya Kumar, and Sandip Mitra. 2016. "Cash versus Kind: Understanding the Preferences of the Bicycle Programme Beneficiaries in Bihar." *Economic and Political Weekly* 51 (11): 51–60.

Ghatak, Maitreesh, and François Maniquet. 2019. "Universal Basic Income: Some Theoretical Aspects." *Annual Review of Economics* 11 (1): 895–928. https://doi.org/10.1146/annurev-economics-080218-030220.

Ghatak, Maitreesh, and Karthik Muralidharan. 2020. "An Inclusive Growth Dividend: Reframing the Role of Income Transfers in India's Anti-Poverty Strategy." In *India Policy Forum 2020*, vol. 16, 109–68. National Council of Applied Economic Research.

Government of India. 2017. *Economic Survey 2016–17*. Ministry of Finance, Department of Economic Affairs, Economic Division.

Government of India. 2021. *Report of the Comptroller and Auditor General of India on Functioning of Unique Identification Authority of India. Performance Audit*. 24/2021. New Delhi: Ministry of Electronics and Information Technology.

Grosh, Margaret, Phillippe Leite, Matthew Wai-Poi, and Emil Tesliuc, eds. 2022. *Revisiting Targeting in Social Assistance: A New Look at Old Dilemmas*. Washington D.C.: The World Bank.

Gulzar, Saad, and Benjamin J. Pasquale. 2017. "Politicians, Bureaucrats, and Development: Evidence from India." *American Political Science Review* 111 (1): 162–183. https://doi.org/10.1017/S0003055416000502.

Gupta, Aarushi, and Siraj Hussain. 2022. "A Tale of Trade-Offs: The Anatomy of the Direct Benefit Transfers System." *The Wire*. Retrieved December 14, 2022. https://thewire.in/political-economy/a-tale-of-trade-offs-the-anatomy-of-the-direct-benefit-transfers-system.

Gupta, Priyanshu, Anuj Goyal, and Rajesh Bhattacharya. 2022. "Who Moved My Welfare Scheme? Federalism and the Politics of Credit Attribution in Rural India." *Journal of South Asian Development*. https://doi.org/10.1177/09731741221113987.

Gupta, Soumya, Vidya Vemireddy, Dhiraj K. Singh, and Prabhu Pingali. 2021. Ground Truthing the Cost of Achieving the EAT Lancet Recommended Diets: Evidence from Rural India. *Global Food Security* 28: 100498. https://doi.org/10.1016/j.gfs.2021.100498.

Hanna, Rema, and Benjamin A. Olken. 2018. "Universal Basic Incomes versus Targeted Transfers: Anti-Poverty Programs in Developing Countries." *Journal of Economic Perspectives* 32 (4): 201–226. https://doi.org/10.1257/jep.32.4.201.

Haushofer, Johannes, and Jeremy Shapiro. 2016. "The Short-Term Impact of Unconditional Cash Transfers to the Poor: Experimental Evidence from Kenya*". *The Quarterly Journal of Economics* 131 (4): 1973–2042. https://doi.org/10.1093/qje/qjw025.

Hirvonen, Kalle, and John Hoddinott. 2021. "Beneficiary Views on Cash and In-Kind Payments: Evidence from Ethiopia's Productive Safety Net Programme." *The World Bank Economic Review* 35 (2): 398–413. https://doi.org/10.1093/wber/lhaa002.

Hirway, Indira. 2003. "Identification of BPL Households for Poverty Alleviation Programmes." *Economic and Political Weekly* 38 (45): 4803–4808.

Hoddinott, John, Susanna Sandström, and Joanna Upton. 2018. "The Impact of Cash and Food Transfers: Evidence from a Randomized Intervention in Niger." *American Journal of Agricultural Economics* 100 (4): 1032–1049. https://doi.org/10.1093/ajae/aay019.

Hundal, Hartej Singh, A. P. Janani, and Bidisha Chaudhuri. 2020. "A Conundrum of Efficiency and Inclusion: Aadhaar and Fair Price Shops." *Economic and Political Weekly* 55 (14): 9.

Jaffrelot, Christophe. 2022. "Populist Welfarism in India: How Modi Relates to the Poor." In *Contemporary Populists in Power*, 211–34. Cham: Springer.

Jayal, Niraja Gopal. 1994. "The Gentle Leviathan: Welfare and the Indian State." *Social Scientist* 22 (9/12): 18. https://doi.org/10.2307/3517911.

Jha, Raghbendra, ed. 2021. *Twenty K.R. Narayanan Orations: Essays by Eminent Persons on the Rapidly Transforming Indian Economy*. 1st ed. Canberra: ANU Press.

Jhabvala, Renana, and Guy Standing. 2010. "Targeting to the'Poor': Clogged Pipes and Bureaucratic Blinkers." *Economic and Political Weekly* 45 (26–7): 239–46.

Joumard, Isabelle Thomas, Alastair Morgavi, and Hermes. 2017. "Making Income and Property Taxes More Growth-Friendly and Redistributive in India." OECD Working Paper No. 1389.

Kapur, Devesh. 2020. "Why Does the Indian State Both Fail and Succeed?" *Journal of Economic Perspectives* 34 (1): 31–54. https://doi.org/10.1257/jep.34.1.31.

Khemani, Stuti. 2019. "Outsized Focus on Cash Transfers Is Missing the Point." *Brookings*. Retrieved October 29, 2022. https://www.brookings.edu/blog/future-development/2019/04/19/outsized-focus-on-cash-transfers-is-missing-the-point/.

Khemani, Stuti, James Habyarimana, and Irfan Nooruddin. 2019. "What Do Poor People Think about Direct Cash Transfers?" *Brookings*. Retrieved October 29, 2022. https://www.brookings.edu/blog/future-development/2019/04/08/what-do-poor-people-think-about-direct-cash-transfers/.

Khera, Reetika. 2011. "Revival of the Public Distribution System: Evidence and Explanations." *Economic & Political Weekly* 46 (44):36–50–36–50.

Khera, Reetika. 2014. "Cash vs. in-Kind Transfers: Indian Data Meets Theory." *Food Policy* 46: 116–128. https://doi.org/10.1016/j.foodpol.2014.03.009.

Khera, Reetika. 2017. "Impact of Aadhaar in Welfare Programmes." *Economic & Political Weekly* 52 (50): 61–70.

Khera, Reetika. 2019a. "Aadhaar Failures: A Tragedy of Errors." *Economic and Political Weekly* 54 (14): 2349–8846. https://www.epw.in/engage/article/aadhaar-failures-food-services-welfare.

Khera, Reetika. 2019b. *Dissent on Aadhaar: Big Data Meets Big Brother*. Orient BlackSwan Hyderabad.

Khera, Reetika, and Anmol Somanchi. 2020a. "A Comparable Series of Tax Revenue Foregone." IIMA Working Papers WP 2020-05-03, Indian Institute of Management Ahmedabad, Research and Publication Department.

Khera, Reetika, and Anmol Somanchi. 2020b. "COVID-19 and Aadhaar: Why the Union Government's Relief Package Is an Exclusionary Endeavour." *Economic and Political Weekly*. 55(17): 2349–8846. https://www.epw.in/engage/article/covid-19-and-aadhaar-why-union-governments-relief.

Khosla, Saksham. 2018. *India's Universal Basic Income: Bedeviled by the Details*. Carnegie Endowment for International Peace Washington.

Kishore, A., S. Saini, and M. Alvi. 2022. "Assessing Direct Benefit Transfer of Agricultural Subsidies in Bihar and Odisha." *Economic and Political Weekly* 57 (16): 36–42.

Kishore, Avinash, and Suman Chakrabarti. 2015. "Is More Inclusive More Effective? The 'New Style' Public Distribution System in India." *Food Policy* 55: 117–130. https://doi.org/10.1016/j.foodpol.2015.06.006.

Kotwal, Ashok, Milind Murugkar, and Bharat Ramaswami. 2011. "PDS Forever?" *Economic and Political Weekly* 46 (21):72–76–72–76.

Kotwal, Ashok, and Bharat Ramaswami. 2014. "Delivering Food Subsidy: The State and the Market." *The Oxford Handbook of Food, Politics, and Society* (September): 301–301.

Krishna, Anirudh. 2007. "For Reducing Poverty Faster: Target Reasons Before People." *World Development* 35 (11): 1947–1960. https://doi.org/10.1016/j.worlddev.2006.12.003.

Krishnamurthy, Prasad, Vikram Pathania, and Sharad Tandon. 2017. "Food Price Subsidies and Nutrition: Evidence from State Reforms to India's Public Distribution System." *Economic Development and Cultural Change* 66 (1): 55–90. https://doi.org/10.1086/694033.

Kumar, Rishabh. 2019. "The Evolution of Wealth-Income Ratios in India 1860–2012." *Available at SSRN 3111846.*

Kumar, Rishabh. 2020. "Top Indian Wealth Shares and Inheritances 1966–1985." *Cliometrica* 14 (3): 551–580. https://doi.org/10.1007/s11698-019-00198-7.

Kumar, Rishabh, and Ishan Anand. 2022. "The Sky and the Stratosphere: Concentrated Wealth in India during Thelost Decade'." *Available at SSRN 4042194.*

Lahoti, Rahul. 2016. "Questioning the Phenomenal Success of Aadhaar-Linked Direct Benefit Transfers for LPG." *Economic & Political Weekly* 51 (52): 24.

Lamba, Rohit, and Arvind Subramanian. 2020. "Dynamism with Incommensurate Development: The Distinctive Indian Model." *Journal of Economic Perspectives* 34 (1): 3–30.

Mani, Anandi, Sendhil Mullainathan, Eldar Shafir, and Jiaying Zhao. 2013. "Poverty Impedes Cognitive Function." *Science* 341 (6149): 976–980.

Masiero, Silvia. 2015a. "Redesigning the Indian Food Security System through E-Governance: The Case of Kerala." *World Development* 67: 126–137. https://doi.org/10.1016/j.worlddev.2014.10.014.

Masiero, Silvia. 2015b. "Will the JAM Trinity Dismantle the PDS?" *Economic and Political Weekly*. 50 (45): 21–23.

Masiero, S., & Buddha, C. 2021. "Data justice in digital social welfare: A study of the Rythu Bharosa scheme." *Proceedings of the First IFIP 9.4 Virtual Conference on the Implications of Informations and Digital technologies in Developing Countries*. 26–28.

Masiero, Silvia, and Amit Prakash. 2015. "Does Computerisation Reduce PDS Leakage? Lessons from Karnataka." *Economic and Political Weekly* 50 (50): 77–85.

McGuire, Joel, Caspar Kaiser, and Anders M. Bach-Mortensen. 2022. "A Systematic Review and Meta-Analysis of the Impact of Cash Transfers on Subjective Well-Being and Mental Health in Low- and Middle-Income Countries." *Nature Human Behaviour* 6 (3): 359–370. https://doi.org/10.1038/s41562-021-01252-z.

Mehrotra, Santosh K., Anjana Rajagopalan, and Rakesh Ranjan Kumar. 2020. *A Minimum Income Guarantee amidst Joblessness & Vulnerability: A Design for Income Transfers Post-Covid 19 and Beyond*. Working Paper.

Mittal, Neeraj, Anit Mukherjee, and Alan Gelb. 2017. "Fuel Subsidy Reform in Developing Countries: Direct Benefit Transfer of LPG Cooking Gas Subsidy in India." *Center for Global Development*. Retrieved from https://Www.Cgdev.Org/Sites/Default/Files/Fuel-Subsidy-Reformdeveloping-Countries-India.Pdf.

Mukherjee, Anit N. 2021. "Harnessing the Digital Revolution for Development: The Indian Experience." In *Theory, Policy, Practice*, 218–40. London: Routledge India.

Mullainathan, Sendhil, and Eldar Shafir. 2013. *Scarcity: Why Having Too Little Means so Much*. New York: Macmillan.

Mundle, Sudipto, and Ajaya Sahu. 2020. "Fiscal Restraint Trumps Fiscal Stimulus." *Economic and Political Weekly*, February 29.

Mundle, Sudipto, and Satadru Sikdar. 2020. "Subsidies, Merit Goods and the Fiscal Space for Reviving Growth." *Economic & Political Weekly* 55 (5).

Muralidharan, Karthik, Paul Niehaus, and Sandip Sukhtankar. 2011. "Assessing the Scope for Cash Transfers in Lieu of the TPDS in Rural and Urban Bihar." *J-PAL South Asia* 5: 25.

Muralidharan, Karthik, Paul Niehaus, and Sandip Sukhtankar. 2017. *Direct Benefits Transfer in Food*.

Muralidharan, Karthik, Paul Niehaus, and Sandip Sukhtankar. 2018. "We Need a Choice-Based Approach in the Public Distribution System." *Hindustan Times*. Retrieved November 6, 2022. https://www.hindustantimes.com/columns/we-need-a-choice-based-approach-to-the-public-distribution-system/story-RY7jEYDmXfsxOMEsZguxmJ.html.

Muralidharan, Karthik, Paul Niehaus, and Sandip Sukhtankar. 2022. "Integrating Biometric Authentication in India's Welfare Programs: Lessons from a Decade of Reforms." In *India Policy Forum 2021*, 139–66. New Delhi: National Council of Applied Economic Research.

Muralidharan, Karthik, Paul Niehaus, Sandip Sukhtankar, and Jeffrey Weaver. 2021. "Improving Last-Mile Service Delivery Using Phone-Based Monitoring." *American Economic Journal: Applied Economics* 13 (2): 52–82. https://doi.org/10.1257/app.20190783.

Muralidharan, Karthik, and Abhijeet Singh. 2020. *Improving Public Sector Management at Scale? Experimental Evidence on School Governance India*. National Bureau of Economic Research.

Narayan, Swati. 2015. "Ten Facts That Set the Record Straight on Cash Transfers." *The Wire*. Retrieved December 2, 2022. https://thewire.in/economy/the-food-or-cash-debates-fallacy-of-composition.

Narayanan, Rajendran, Sakina Dhorajiwala, and Chakradhar Buddha. 2021. "Can a Machine Learn Democracy?" *CSE WP No. 34*.

Narayanan, S. 2011. "A Case for Reframing the Cash Transfer Debate in India." *Economic and Political Weekly* 46 (21): 41–48.

Narayanan, Sudha. 2015. "Food Security in India: The Imperative and Its Challenges." *Asia & the Pacific Policy Studies* 2 (1): 197–209. https://doi.org/10.1002/app5.62.

Narayanan, Sudha. 2021. "Understanding Farmer Protests in India." *Academics Stand against Poverty* 1 (1): 133–140.

Negi, Digvijay S. 2022. "Global Food Price Surge, in-Kind Transfers and Household Welfare: Evidence from India." *World Development* 158: 106009. https://doi.org/10.1016/j.worlddev.2022.106009.

Niehaus, Paul, Antonia Atanassova, Marianne Bertrand, and Sendhil Mullainathan. 2013. "Targeting with Agents." *American Economic Journal: Economic Policy* 5 (1): 206–238.

Niti Ayog. 2020. *Accelerating Progress on Nutrition in India.*

Persson, Anna, Bo., and Rothstein. 2015. "It's My Money: Why Big Government May Be Good Government." *Comparative Politics* 47 (2): 231–249.

Piketty, Thomas. 2020. *Capital and Ideology.* Cambridge: Harvard University Press.

Piketty, Thomas, and Nancy Qian. 2009. "Income Inequality and Progressive Income Taxation in China and India, 1986–2015." *American Economic Journal: Applied Economics* 1 (2): 53–63. https://doi.org/10.1257/app.1.2.53.

Pradhan, Mamata, Devesh Roy, and Vinay Sonkar. 2015. "What Is the Effective Delivery Mechanism of Food Support in India." *Economic and Political Weekly* 54 (42): 7–8.

Prasad, M., and Deva, and Suchithra Menon C. 2020. "The Personal Data Protection Bill, 2018: India's Regulatory Journey towards a Comprehensive Data Protection Law." *International Journal of Law and Information Technology* 28 (1): 1–19. https://doi.org/10.1093/ijlit/eaaa003.

Pritchett, Lant. 2009. "Is India a Flailing State?: Detours on the Four Lane Highway to Modernization." *HKS Faculty Research Working Paper Series.*

Rahman, Andaleeb. 2016. "Universal Food Security Program and Nutritional Intake: Evidence from the Hunger Prone KBK Districts in Odisha." *Food Policy* 63: 73–86.

Ramaswami, Bharat, and Milind Murugkar. 2015. "Incremental Reforms in Food Policy: What Are the Possibilities." In *Development in India: Micro and Macro Perspectives*, edited by S. Mahendra Dev and P. G. Babu, 1–377. Springer India.

Rao, M. Govinda. 2016. "Tyranny of the Status Quo: The Challenges of Reforming the Indian Tax System." In *India Policy Forum 2015–16*, vol. 16, 12. 47–103.

Rao, M. Govinda. 2022. "Evolving Landscape of Indian Fiscal Federalism." In *Studies in Indian Public Finance*, 151–74. Oxford : Oxford University Press.

Reserve Bank of India. 2022. "State Finances: A Risk Analysis." In *RBI Bulletin*, 115–37.

Rodrik, Dani. 2007. *One Economics, Many Recipes: Globalization, Institutions, and Economic Growth.* Princeton, New Jersey: Princeton University Press.

Saez, Emmanuel. 2021. "Public Economics and Inequality: Uncovering Our Social Nature," vol. 111, 1–26.

Sandefur, Justin, Nancy Birdsall, and Mujobo Moyo. 2015. "The Political Paradox of Cash Transfers." *Center for Global Development | Ideas to Action*. Retrieved October 29, 2022. https://www.cgdev.org/blog/political-paradox-cash-transfers.

Saxena, Naresh C. 2015. "Socio Economic Caste Census: Has It Ignored Too Many Poor Households?" *Economic and Political Weekly* 14–17.

Schwab, Benjamin. 2020. "In the Form of Bread? A Randomized Comparison of Cash and Food Transfers in Yemen." *American Journal of Agricultural Economics* 102 (1): 91–113.

Scott, James C. 1998. *Seeing Like a State: How Certain Schemes to Improve the Human Condition Have Failed*. New Haven: Yale University Press.

Sekhri, Sheetal, Sisir Debnath, and Mrithyunjayan Nilayamgode. 2022. "Information Bypass: Using Low-Cost Technological Innovations to Curb." *Available at SSRN 4084289*.

Sen, Amartya. 1992. *The Political Economy of Targeting*. Annual Bank Conference on Development Economics, World Bank.

Seth, Aaditeshwar. 2022. *Technology and (Dis) Empowerment: A Call to Technologists*. Emerald Group Publishing.

Shah, Anuj K., Sendhil Mullainathan, and Eldar Shafir. 2012. "Some Consequences of Having Too Little." *Science* 338 (6107): 682–685. https://doi.org/10.1126/science.1222426.

Sheena, Chhabra, and Owen Smith. 2022. "Insuring India: PM-JAY's Targeting Problem." *Ideas For India*. Retrieved November 4, 2022. http://www.ideasforindia.in/topics/human-development/insuring-india-pm-jay-s-targeting-problem.html.

Singh, Ram. 2022. *Do the Wealthy Underreport Their Income? Analysing Relationship between Wealth and Reported Income in India*.

Sinha, Aseema. 2005. *The Regional Roots of Developmental Politics in India: A Divided Leviathan*. Bloomington: Indiana University Press.

Sinha, Dipa. 2015. "Cash for Food—A Misplaced Idea." *Economic and Political Weekly* 50 (16): 17–20.

Standing, Guy. 2014. "From Cash Transfers to Basic Income: An Unfolding Indian Agenda." *Indian Journal of Labour Economics* 57 (1): 111–137.

Subramanian, Arvind, Devesh Kapur, and Partha Mukhopadhyay. 2008. "The Case for Direct Cash Transfers to the Poor." *Economic and Political Weekly* 43 (15): 37–43.

Svedberg, Peter. 2012. "Reforming or Replacing the Public Distribution System with Cash Transfers?" *Economic and Political Weekly* 47 (7): 53–62.

Thomas, Susan, Diya Uday, and Bhargavi Zaveri. 2020. "Linking Welfare Distribution to Land Records: A Case-Study of the Rythu Bandhu Scheme (RBS) in Telangana." *Indira Gandhi Institute of Development Research, Nd.*

Totapally, Swetha, Petra Sonderegger, Priti Rao, Jasper Gosselt, and Gaurav Gupta. 2019. *State of Aadhaar Report 2019*. Dalberg.

Townsend, Robert M. 2011. *Financial Systems in Developing Economies: Growth, Inequality and Policy Evaluation in Thailand*. Oxford: Oxford University Press.

Vaishnav, Milan. 2022. "Has India's 'Flailing State' Been Turned Upside Down?" *Seminar* 749 (January).

Wilkinson, Steven I. 2021. "Technology and Clientelist Politics in India." *WIDER Working Paper Series* (2021/153).

World Bank. 2016. *World Development Report 2016: Digital Dividends*.

CHAPTER 10

Social Welfare 'Schemes' to an Economic Security 'System'

We must make our political democracy a social democracy as well. Political democracy cannot last unless there lies at the base of it social democracy.
—BR Ambedkar, at the Constituent Assembly meeting on November 25, 1949

.. so long as there are tears and suffering, so long our work will not be over. And so we have to labour and to work, and work hard, to give reality to our dreams. Those dreams are for India, but they are also for the world.
—*Tryst With Destiny*, speech delivered by Jawaharlal Nehru to the Constituent Assembly of India in New Delhi on August 15, 1947

Introduction

Contradictions of India's development trajectory are mystifying to its observers. The country's survival as a democratic nation in the postcolonial era evokes great exultation, yet the embarrassment of being home to the largest number of world's poor and malnourished warrants a scrutiny of the nature of this social democracy. While famines may be a thing of the past and hunger not as pervasive, livelihoods remain precarious keeping millions into deprivation and many others vulnerable to unforeseen economic events. Economic progress has significantly reduced infant

A. Rahman and P. Pingali, *The Future of India's Social Safety Nets*, Palgrave Studies in Agricultural Economics and Food Policy, https://doi.org/10.1007/978-3-031-50747-2_10

mortality rates; mother and child nutrition issues remain an embarrassment to the growth process. Similarly, near-universal primary education in the country has not translated into improved learning outcomes for children, and much of the labor force is unskilled and works in the informal sector with no employment-based benefits into retirement. The employment of women in the labor force remains persistently low while gender and caste norms remain archaic, thereby impeding the growth process. Rising incidence of non-communicable diseases (NCDs) and prohibitively expensive health care means households are just one illness away from losing their accumulated savings. Governance structures also exhibit a bipolar tendency. Despite a push toward digitization and citizen services, public systems and bureaucratic structure are apathetic to civic concerns and public action often thwarted by political powers. In a nutshell, India's triumph as a political democracy hasn't translated successfully into a social democracy despite equality and liberty being upheld as constitutional rights of the citizens. As a result, the imperatives of reducing economic hardship and suffering—which independent India's first democratic leader Nehru alluded to in 1947 and Ambedkar, the father of India's constitution, cautioned against its implications (see epigraph)—are as relevant now as it was 75 years ago.

Social protection programs are a central component of the citizen-state social contract wherein the government provides economic protection to the citizens against daily risks and vulnerabilities. In mature social democracies, such protections are fundamental constituents of the economic and political life which allows a level playing field between competing class interests of those who own capital and the ones which provide labor. A market-based economy where labor class is conferred a fair share vis-à-vis capital investments by the entrepreneur is considered a common ground where redistributive objectives of the state are supported by greater income growth leading to broad-based prosperity. In developing countries like India, however, the goals of social democracy are affected by the lack of financial resources, perverse political interests, and suppressed civil liberties. Economic growth and democratic deepening have however brought about a fundamental change in domestic anti-poverty policies with an increase in the importance of social welfare programs across most developing countries in the last two decades. Brazil, Mexico, India, and Indonesia have been leading this 'silent revolution' with some of the largest social welfare programs in the world. Yet, the poorest of the poor—the *focus* of these initiative—in these countries continue to be left behind contributing to greater inequality and inequality of opportunity, thereby suppressing human resilience. As a result, the social welfare architecture which has begun to take some shape in the last two decades has a long road for social democracy in the country.

In the concluding chapter of this book, we summarize our thoughts on re-imagining India's social welfare policies as a key instrument of promoting a resilient development process (*scope*). We highlight the need for a more cohesive social policy ideas around the *scope* of the social welfare, along with identifying the population at risk (*focus*), and the most effective *form* of social assistance. Our arguments are based upon a framework where structural transformation of the domestic economy—and the ensuing socio-economic, technical, and political change—necessitates a more expansive and dynamic social policy which is cognizant not only of the causes and symptoms of existing human deprivation but also the drivers of future economic insecurity. We envisage social protection strategy as akin to creating an economic security system comprising of a menu of welfare transfers (*forms*)—social assistance, social insurance, and labor regulation—which is adaptable to the nature of structural transformation and prioritizes the welfare of the vulnerable population (*focus*) with the *scope* of promoting human resilience. The systems approach to social welfare programs, which we propose here, hinges upon steady improvements in last-mile delivery, political commitment to the cause of social welfare, and complementary investments in public systems which have been the bane of India's development process. We further argue that reforms to the current social welfare programs ought to be in line with the systemic challenges of a developing country economy characterized by limited fiscal resources, underdeveloped public systems, sluggish structural transformation—decreasing farm size, informality of employment, and slow urbanization—and poor local governance.

Social Welfare Schemes to an Economic Security System

The cost of being poor has a metastasizing effect on long-term human welfare through the reduced ability to afford nutritious food, education, or health care.[1] The poor in developing countries are handicapped by market failures in key areas of human development—health, education, and infrastructure—to bootstrap their way out of deprivation. Government intervention, other hand, essential to support its citizens but developing countries lacks an effective and efficient social protection design. Fundamentally, the coverage and impact of social protection in developing countries are limited by a narrow understanding of the developmental challenge and the peculiarities of their path of structural transformation.

Advanced nations of today have a well-endowed tax-funded social protection system to safeguard the poorer citizens from a life of indignity. Developing countries with a greater need for social protection, on the other, have lower financial capability with a narrow tax base and high tax compliance. The efficacy of social protection is further eroded by poor governance structures depriving the poor of their benefits. Further, economic vulnerability in modern nation-states is principally characterized by unemployment and loss of income. During the working age, citizens contribute to the fiscal resources through taxes and avail benefits during spells of unemployment or upon retirement. In developing countries, however, an overwhelming majority is not employed

[1] Income, asset, or expenditure-based poverty estimates shy away from some of the most important factors which influence the current living conditions, such as concerns about security of livelihood, access to common property resources, and essential public infrastructure, including drinking water, health, and education. Many of these non-income factors create conditions of chronic poverty and poverty traps through food insecurity, malnutrition, mortality, and reduction in overall productivity. Food insecurity may lead to malnutrition, which causes reduced physical capacity and stunting, inhibits learning, and may have long-term nutritional, health, and productivity-related effects for present and future generations. An important finding in studies on poverty in India is that most poor households continue to be poor over time, suggesting they experience chronic conditions of poverty trap (Kapur Mehta and Shah 2003). Those suffering from chronic poverty are not necessarily poor in terms of consumption expenditure, as it is often measured, but due to very low levels of initial endowments of physical and human capital, like land, assets, education, health, and employment, which affect their risk-bearing capacities and their abilities to invest in acquiring employable skills to enhance labor productivity.

in the formal sector—devoid of any employment-based security or tax contributions—and vulnerability emerges from a variety of economic deprivations spread over the lifetime, antiquated social norms, and underdeveloped market-based institutions. The traditional state response, as a result, to such a developmental challenge in poorer countries is to provide direct social assistance—consumption or income support—through various social safety nets. The array of these independent social assistance schemes—with distinct *form*, *focus*, and *scope*—while useful, has only provided an elementary edifice of social support and the development *scope* of promoting resilience remains a work in progress.[2]

The central thesis of this book is to argue that overcoming this unrealized potential requires a re-conceptualization of social welfare as a 'system of state support' which addresses *multiple* dimensions of economic insecurity as a departure from the band-aid solutions to developmental problems.[3] We argue that the social protection policies must be restructured as a system of economic support against the various deprivations and risks across human life cycle. By safeguarding against the plausible risks—from in utero to old age—social welfare programs have the potential to arrest the decline in human capabilities, boost earning capacities, and make societies more resilient against unforeseen life events. Our arguments are rooted in the idea that the process of development is not about getting individuals over an artificially defined poverty line, but rather allowing human beings to enhance their capabilities, flourish, and make full use of their abilities to choose the means to their prosperity.[4]

[2] See Chapter 2 for more details.

[3] Organizations such as World Bank and other global development agencies now increasingly recommend building social protection systems as opposed to standalone welfare schemes to build a 'social protection floor' through a set of complementary schemes (contributory and noncontributory) harmonized in their development *scope* under a common administrative umbrella. Refer to Schüring and Loewe (2021) for more details on the various institution's definition of 'schemes to systems.' On the World Bank's ideas for social protection systems in India, see https://www.worldbank.org/en/news/feature/2019/11/21/lessons-from-social-protection-india-schemes-to-systems.

[4] Sen (1982) characterizes an individual's exchange entitlements as a combination of multiple factors such as employment status, wage earnings, the value of non-labor assets, returns on output, and the ability to buy resources. In exchange for her labor, the individual purchases food and invest in productive capital. Such entitlements could however be eroded in the wake of an exogenous shock. While the poor suffer from entitlement failure, non-poor are also likely to suffer from an erosion of this ability in the wake of unfortunate life events.

Reconfiguring the social protection question as a 'systems problem' is meaningful for multiple reasons. First, social risks and vulnerabilities for which welfare policy is designed are dynamic and multi-scalar. It has been widely accepted that independent social safety nets might temporarily reduce the extent of household vulnerability, but their longer-term benefits could be potentially eroded by macro-level economic deficiencies such as poor governance, lack of markets, and inadequate public infrastructure.[5] Moreover, resilience building social protection requires an egalitarian social order, cultural norms, and political structures where every individual especially women is empowered enough to partake in the development process. The systems approach accounts for these macro-factors which are beyond a household's micro-environment. Second, the resilience enhancing ability of isolated social safety net programs is often restrained because of the narrow developmental *scope* (say, financial protection or nutritional deprivation) of a particular safety net while economic risks and vulnerabilities emanate from multitude of factors.[6] Social protection system, as an array of interventions spread over a person's life cycle (in various *form* and *focus*), creates an incremental layer of support creating resilience against existing and potential deprivations. Third, a successful social protection system not only empowers citizens in economic terms but also increases their engagement with the state and builds trust in government leading to democratic deepening.[7] Democratic empowerment of the poor—which facilitates greater state accountability fostering a virtuous improvement in public services—in low income and poor state capacity contributes to a more deliberative political system which facilitates a more inclusive citizen-state social contract.

Social protection as a 'systems' challenge also appeals to the idea of development resilience which we present in Chapter 2 of this book. By envisaging resilience as the development *scope* of social

[5] Inadequate macroeconomic development perpetuates the existence of poverty via a multi-scalar feedback loop across the institutional, behavioral, and economic factors. See Barrett and Swallow (2006).

[6] Envisaging social protection as a system allows for a multi-faceted attack on poverty as well as its causes as opposed to the isolated welfare programs which attempt to make small improvements to human lives which "often fail to move people out of low-level dynamic equilibria unless they happen to be carefully targeted at precisely the context-specific mechanism and threshold that trap people in poverty" (Barrett et al. 2016, p. 322).

[7] Refer to Evans et al. (2019) for an overview of the debate.

welfare interventions, we broaden the *scope* of anti-poverty transfers from addressing current human deprivations to the future potential flow of people into poverty in the future as well.[8] A strong social protection system, therefore, must provide a built-in shock absorber along with acting as a facilitator of human capability through relaxing not only economic but psycho-social constraints to poverty and abet capital accumulation for long-run progress.[9]

The social protection system for developing countries which we envisage here is similar in *scope* to the graduation programs—multi-faceted interventions (*form*) which include consumption support, credit access, skills/training program, etc., to build productive capacity—but differs in its conceptualization as well as implementation. While graduation programs are designed with a *focus* on the ultra-poor and implemented through NGOs, the system of social protection is an institutional arrangement of economic security as an assurance to promote development resilience (*scope*) encompassing both the poor and the vulnerable (*focus*). In this system, independent social welfare programs (with varying *form* and *scope*) collectively form the basic edifice for the welfare transfers. Macroeconomic growth, infrastructure development, and improved governance—central to improving human development, redistribution, and economic opportunities—further act as the institutional 'enablers' of this economic security system for sustained improvements in the standard of living and broad-based prosperity. Social protection system,

[8] Scholarship on resilience approach market failures from the perspective of individual endowments but also the macro-institutional factors under which economic decisions are made by the individuals (Barrett and Constas 2014; Lade et al. 2017). Here we do not refer to a specific empirical or theoretical approach to resilience as there are many such formulations of the concept as highlighted by Barrett et al. (2021), rather we appeal to the idea that human resilience is an 'aspirational condition' where households remain unaffected by exogenous shocks and continue a sustained pursuit towards prosperity which is in sync with the economic system they are part of.

[9] For example, research has also shown that the provision of employment generates greater non-pecuniary psychosocial well-being than an unconditional cash transfer of equivalent amount (see Hussam et al. 2022). While poor in the working age group can benefit from employment through public works program, noncontributory old age pensions have been shown to reduce depressive symptoms arising out of poverty in later life years in India and other developing countries like China, Mexico, Peru, and Ethiopia among others (Banerjee et al. 2022).

therefore, becomes an integral part of broader development strategy—but not necessarily the only one—which greases the engine of growth and facilitates the structural transformation process.

Envisaging a Social Welfare System for India

A schema for India's social welfare system—comprising of several social safety nets and institutional enablers of human development—is shown in Fig. 10.1. This conceptualization highlights how public action through social welfare programs can promote human resilience in India given the country's stunted structural transformation. In Chapter 3, we highlighted the importance of various social safety nets and their *form*, *focus*, and *scope* in India. In this figure, we depict how these can work in unison as a system. Here, the 'system' works through the various individual schemes which provide social protection against the many risks and vulnerabilities over a person's life cycle.[10] While these independent schemes provide short-term support against the immediate developmental repercussions of risks, further resilience is enhanced through efficient public institutions and sustained economic growth. Household resilience is boosted when this system works in consonance—everyday risks are averted, and each form of vulnerability is deflected through a combination of state support and public systems which act as additional enablers of resilience building for transformative development outcomes. Early life nutritional assistance programs in the *form* of cash transfers for institutional delivery or child immunization can be most effective in improving welfare in the presence of adequate and quality health infrastructure. Similarly, direct welfare assistance such as cash transfers to farmers, public works program, housing subsidy, or food assistance contributes to livelihood security.

[10] Mid-term appraisal of India's 11th five-year plan (2007–2012) had a fleeting rumination around the importance of creating an effective social security system for inclusive economic growth. The report notes that "*effective social security system … is an instrument for sustainable social and economic development. It facilitates structural and technological changes, which require an adaptable and mobile labour force. With globalization and structural adjustment policies, social security assumes a renewed urgency*" (Government of India 2011, p. 218). Social security, however, was conceptualized in terms of job security, unemployment benefits, and wage protection for the informal sector workers. Our conceptualization combines the components of social security with various other forms of social assistance across the life cycle.

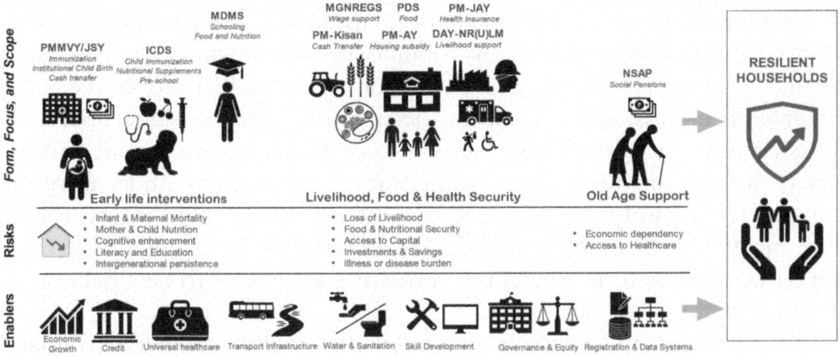

Fig. 10.1 A social welfare system for development resilience in India

An enabling infrastructure—credit markets or transport infrastructure—contributes to the potentially transformative impact of individual welfare schemes through allowing households not only to cope better against exogenous shocks thereby protecting their endowments, but also through ensuring that their productive capacity remains undiminished. The social welfare 'system' presented here not only takes a life-cycle approach—with a *focus* on early life interventions, livelihood challenges, and income support during old age—but also a multi-scalar approach to the challenges of poverty and vulnerability, wherein deprivation is understood as a symptom of poverty at birth, lack of employable skills, poor quality of infrastructure, market failures, and poor governance.[11]

Social Assistance: Central Plank of the Welfare System

Noncontributory social assistance would continue to be the focal point India's social welfare system in the immediate future for two reasons. First, with employment-based social security historically the preserve

[11] While isolated schemes might reduce the extent of household vulnerability, these interventions may not be sufficient to build the resilience required for sustained human growth. Weak governance systems, inefficiencies, or absence of the markets and poor public infrastructure typically perpetuate the existence of poverty via a multi-scalar feedback loops across the institutional, behavioral, and economic factors which explain human vulnerability. See Barrett and Swallow (2006).

of a miniscule share of the population, livelihood vulnerability intensifying with the changing employer-employee relationship, stagnant farm income, limited employment avenues for the unskilled workforce, citizens would increasingly look up to the state for social assistance. Second, persistently poor performance on some of the most important indicators of long-term development outcomes such as child undernutrition and gender inequity merits vigorous and continued state intervention. Without direct state support, the intergenerational developmental deficits and social barriers to female empowerment are unlikely to be ameliorated by economic growth alone.

In Chapters 4 and 5, we have argued that social protection to guard against the *scope* of supporting consumption and reducing income vulnerability—remunerative employment during the working age, sufficient funds for retirement, and financial protection against job loss, health shock, or disability—in a predominantly informal economy requires an array of programs. Subsidized staple food through the Public Distribution System (PDS) and public works employment through Mahatma Gandhi National Rural Employment Guarantee Scheme (MGNREGS) have proven to be of paramount importance to arrest the incidence of food insecurity and consumption support (*scope*) in rural India. Unconditional cash transfers to farmers under PM-Kisan is a new *form* of direct social assistance given stagnant farm income. While PM-Kisan is a relatively newer program, improvements in the performance of PDS and MGNREGS have only highlighted the transformative scope of direct social assistance for the country's poor and would continue to be an important source of support during uncertain times. The reliance on PDS and MGNREGS during the COVID-19 recovery for the economically stricken workers offers a shining example of the importance of these two programs and its future potential to guard against the newer risks which any economic and biophysical changes might bring.

High levels of malnutrition among young children—one of the most glaring indicators of underdevelopment—pose a conundrum to India's growth trajectory. Poverty reduction accompanied by India's growth path since economic liberalization since the 1990s has had a negligible impact on child nutrition. Clearly, higher income is not the most important determinant of nutrition. Instead, direct state intervention—nutritional support to pregnant mothers, safe childbirth, and timely—alongside greater public investments in improved sanitation and hygiene infrastructure, and social change which improves the situation of women in terms of their economic and physical well-being are key for improving child nutritional outcomes. As discussed in Chapter 6 of this book, free vaccination drives and direct nutritional support for young mothers and children (*focus*) under the Integrated Child Development Scheme (ICDS) would continue to be a major *form* of social welfare in the country to address nutritional deficits (*scope*). Similarly, the provision of hot-cooked meals at public schools under the Mid-day Meal Scheme (MDMS) is likely to remain a key *form* of social assistance for children attending public schools. These direct social assistances are further supported through complementary government schemes which include behavioral nudges such as a small cash incentive to pregnant mothers for childbirth at a safe facility under the *Pradhan Mantri Matru Vandana Yojana* (*PMMVY*) along with institutional enablers such as the Total Sanitation Campaign (TSC) and *Jal-Jeevan Mission* (JJM) which are infrastructural investments to ensure universal access to toilet and clean water access, respectively.

Progressive Universalism

A key dilemma in social policy design is whether to *focus* on the poor or have universal welfare transfers. While universalization imposes higher fiscal burden and spreads the transfers thinly to everyone rather than greater benefits to the most vulnerable, pro-poor targeting involves monetary costs associated with identifying the poor and welfare losses because of targeting errors.[12] In a low-income country like India which has limited financial resources and sources of vulnerability multifarious, a progressively universal or a quasi-universal social protection system is more suitable to strike a balance between fiscal prudence and minimizing targeting errors. Further, progressively universal programs cover poor along various dimensions of deprivation as well as those vulnerable to exogenous shocks.

While there is a strong case for universalization of welfare assistance such as school meals, nutritional assistance to pregnant women and young

[12] Human deprivation and vulnerability are differentiated along multiple axes—location, social identity, education, skill, occupation, social capital, market or information failures, etc.—and real-time identification of the poor infeasible, poverty indicators for social welfare benefits conceals wide fluctuations in a households' economic circumstances. For a discussion on inclusion versus exclusion criterions for poverty identification, see Drèze and Khera (2010).

children—child and maternal health programs such as ICDS and MDMS are universal—which have intergenerational benefits, means-tested pro-poor social transfers are more common in the case of food or income which potentially create a disincentive to reduce work effort by the beneficiaries. Besides its costs, targeting creates a fundamental—moral as well as operational—challenge of defining who ought to be classified as a poor and who isn't. Targeted social welfare programs, therefore, have not proved to be effective in the Indian case. For example, targeting errors have traditionally characterized the failures of the PDS till the 2000s and its expansion since then has led to improved performance. Similarly, the success of MGNREGS owes much to its universal eligibility. Variation in the success of social safety nets in the country—over time and across subnational regions—is a further proof of that.[13]

Preoccupation with the poverty line—an artificial boundary to classify the poor and non-poor through above poverty line (APL) and below poverty line (BPL) cards—has hampered the effectiveness of social welfare policies because of the administrative burden it imposes.[14] Despite a rich scholarship on challenges with the poverty metric, targeting errors, and the associated welfare loss, social welfare programs such as old age pensions, housing subsidy, and public health insurance continue to be focused on the poor. For the longest time, India's poverty debates remained mired in a minimum consumption requirement for a healthy diet—a historical legacy of famines and hunger incidence—despite newer sources of non-food-related insecurities, such as low wages and non-remunerative livelihoods, and costs of medical care, becoming significant as a source of economic vulnerability. The APL-BPL distinction, however, is increasingly losing relevance with more progressive population *focus* of the social welfare schemes. The National Food Security Act (NFSA) 2013 covers 'priority' households—67 percent of the households, significantly larger than the poverty figures—while the public health insurance program PM-JAY which initially focused on the BPL households is being expanded to a larger share of the population, many of whom would not classify as poor based upon the traditional asset-based metric. Some of the

[13] See Chapter 5, 9, and 10 for more details.

[14] To create a list of eligible 'poor' population, independent national scale census exercises—BPL census in 1997 and the Socio-economic and caste census (SECC) in 2011—were conducted which contained massive errors and the central government ended up discredited them as reliable sources of information.

state governments never moved to a targeted PDS while some others have already made public health insurance universal. Old age pensions, another of the targeted programs, too are being made near universal in some parts of India. Unconditional cash transfer to farmers under PM-Kisan is another *form* of social assistance which is near universal.

Progressive universalism, as an important tenet of the social protection system, allows for a combination of social assistance and insurance to the poor and the vulnerable.[15] Though some element of beneficiary selection is easily possible and deemed necessary for distributional reasons, near-universal social welfare programs create a broader coalition of potential beneficiaries. It further helps in improving welfare delivery and public accountability but also reduces targeting costs through an emphasis on easily observable indicators—taxpayers, expensive asset holders, employment, social identity, etc.—for excluding the non-beneficiaries. Addressing the various sources of vulnerability, across the life cycle with near-universal coverage—as we proclaim as the foundational basis for a social protection system—would allow social policy to beyond a narrow *focus* on the poor, and poverty reduction as the *scope* of social welfare system to a more encompassing understanding of human vulnerability and resilience building.

[15] It is important to understand that human deprivation and vulnerability are differentiated along multiple axes—location, social identity, education, skill, occupation, social capital, market or information failures, etc.—and real-time identification of the poor infeasible, poverty indicators for social welfare benefits conceals wide fluctuations in a households' economic circumstances. An accurate understanding of poverty also requires a nuanced understanding of the everyday lives of the poor which is contingent on the level of economic development (Banerjee and Duflo 2007). For example, the persistence of poverty in India has traditionally been explained through lack of land, inadequate irrigation infrastructure, frequent weather calamities, large family size, inability to accumulate productive assets, impending debt, access markets, or adverse health shocks (Adelman et al. 1985; Gaiha 1989; Krishna 2004; Naschold 2012). While these factors remain important, the composition of rural poor as well as the drivers of poverty are however changing with the spread of technology, higher education levels, urbanization, and greater wage-based labor. Newer research has begun to highlight the role of access to education and salaried employment as equally important in avoiding poverty or facilitating escape from it (Thorat et al. 2017). Apart from investing in agriculture, investing in human capital—education, acquired more skills—and physical assets, are increasingly becoming important to overcome rural poverty. In urban areas, where wages and self-employment are main sources of income, access to physical and human capital remains the most important determinant of vulnerability. See Chapter 4 for more details.

Social Assistance to Social Insurance, Rural to Urban

The *form* and *focus* of various social programs are likely to evolve with their own success—by addressing the developmental *scope* for which they were designed—and the associated changes in resilience enabling factors such as public investment in essential infrastructure, economic growth, and improved governance systems. As a result, while direct social assistance would continue to be the guardrail of social welfare policy, especially for the poorest, social insurance is likely to attain a more important role of building human resilience in the future market-based economy. The structural transformation process would also lead to a reduction in rural population, migration to urban areas, and a reduced dependence on weather vagaries but a greater risk of job and wage insecurity. With India's 'stunted' structural transformation—characterized by deindustrialization and services sector-led economy—resulting in a largely informal labor market, social protection system would exhibit greater *focus* on urban vulnerability. This transition, albeit a slower one, yet provides an opportunity to introduce newer *forms* (such as cash transfers instead of food assistance) of welfare support.

Work-related social security has been a blind spot in India's social welfare policy thereby contributing to frequent slide into poverty for the millions of citizens every year. While PDS and MGNREGS have been successful in providing consumption or income support to the poor, health shocks have been a particular important source of descent into poverty or further into poverty trap for the poor as well as non-poor. It is only in the recent times, publicly subsidized health insurance for those in the lower income strata has emerged as a potentially important form of social assistance—from the *Rashtriya Swastha Bima Yojana* (RSBY) currently known as the *Prime Minister Jan Arogya Yojana* (PM-JAY)—only in the recent times and continues to lack sufficient population and treatment coverage. In Chapter 7, we argue that PM-JAY, a publicly funded social insurance, is however, expected to become more important form of social assistance in a largely informal economy, albeit its effectiveness as a tool of financial protection remains a question. Similarly, the miniscule monthly old age pensions—again focused on those below the poverty line—as earmarked under the National Social Assistance Program (NSAP) is being revised upwards in some states. It is likely that other states would also follow suit—going by the trend in other welfare programs after 2004—making it another key component of social assistance.

Social welfare system with a transformational *scope*—development resilience—must have a broader *focus* and adaptable *form*.[16] Social welfare system, as described above, must adapt to the changing nature of poverty in cognizance of the nature of economic transformation and associated demographic, technological, and biophysical changes—urbanization, migration, informality of labor force, non-communicable diseases, aging population, climate change, globalization, etc.—which are likely to characterize future vulnerability. Social protection systems, therefore, must be adaptable to a shift from the current *focus* on rural areas with paternalistic *forms* of social welfare—toward multi-dimensional understanding of deprivation and market-based *forms* of policy intervention—engender development resilience as the overarching *scope* of the social protection. For example, greater urbanization and rising informality of employment might require a shift in *focus* from rural poverty to livelihood support programs encompassing the rural-urban binary. Similarly, rising share of old age population might necessitate more investments in old age pensions or newer initiatives such as contributory pension funds.

Necessary Institutional Enablers for Greater Economic Opportunities

While social protection programs can facilitate human resilience through guarding against deprivations across a citizen's life cycle, improvements in the quality of governance, public infrastructure, and progressive institutions have the potential to accelerate this transformative process through economic opportunities which were hitherto unavailable to them or were diminished because of their lower capabilities. Behavioral changes and infrastructural investments through promotion of safe childbirth (*Pradhan Mantri Matru Vandana Yojana*, *PMMVY*), immunization drives (under ICDS), free primary schooling and the provision of hot-cooked meals (Mid-day Meal Scheme, MDMS), access to toilets (Total

[16] In their seminal work on defining and estimating the poverty line for India, Dandekar and Rath had cautioned in favor of understanding the issue of poverty and welfare with a perspective on how economic conditions would look like in the future. Alert to the mistakes of the past, they write, "The Planning Commission's perspective for the coming decade is clearly out of line with the experience of the past decade. There is an obvious desire to close the eyes on the past failures and wishfully hope that the future will somehow be different" (Dandekar and Rath 1971, p. 47).

Sanitation Campaign, TSC), tap water (*Jal-Jeevan Mission*, JJM), rural road infrastructure (*Pradhan Mantri Gramin Sadak Yojana*, PMGSY), universal electrification and cooking gas connections, along with rural livelihood missions (*Deen Dayal Antyodaya Yojana*, DAY), and income support to the poor for housing (*Prime Minister Awas Yojana*, PMAY) are some of the key enablers of this development process which are likely to promote economic opportunities and unlock the developmental capabilities of people. These institutional enablers further act as bulwark against the newer risks which unanticipated global economic and biophysical changes are likely to bring.

In a well-oiled social protection system in India, children born to poor parents can attain far greater human capabilities. Adequate nutrition during pregnancy, institutional childbirth, timely vaccination, and good nutritional support arrest nutritional decline. Access to free primary schooling, livelihood support to parents (assured wage, food, income), and cooked meals at school imply that they neither drop out of school—because of the need to support family during bad times—nor their cognitive abilities diminish because of scarcity. Such developmental possibilities are further enhanced if the same children grow up in household with no gender discrimination, treated running water, toilet facility, and 24-hour electricity access at home. Improved quality of schooling and road connectivity add further ballast to their human potential. Robust livelihood support, social insurance against potential income loss, and the provision of retirement funds or pensions can further ensure that their future generation is neither born in poverty nor relies upon direct state assistance for sustenance. A strong social protection system is designed to be a conduit of its own declining importance in people's life with a lower share of citizens requiring that 'safety net' for survival. Higher quality of enabling mechanisms such as a physical infrastructure, economic growth, and institutional changes hastens the pace of this weaning off from social assistance. In the long run, enhancements in welfare outcomes are likely to outweigh the cost of these programs through improvements in human capital, consumption growth, and taxable income. It is therefore critical to think of these as a key component of the social protection system which act as enablers of development resilience (see Fig. 10.1).

Despite a plethora of these social welfare initiatives, India continues to be a poor country with developmental challenges of monumental proportions. While opportunities to build upon the existing social protection architecture to spur a resilient development process through furthering an 'inclusive' structural transformation of the economy are abundant, the challenges are also manifold. In Chapter 8, we delineate the glaring implementational deficits, faulty designs, and rampant corruption which characterize welfare delivery and highlight the institutional constraints—infrastructure and governance—which restrain human flourishing. Social welfare has long been relegated to secondary importance over perverse private interests and political gains. This has led to calls for bundling the multiple *forms* of welfare transfers into cash transfers which is easy to administer and cost-effective. Critics have called these proposals are premature given the country's sticky social norms, inefficient institutions, limited fiscal resources, and flailing state capacity. Any assessment of the pace of the expected socio-economic change—and the gradual evolution of the *form*, *focus*, and *scope* of social protection system—is however rife with speculation and subject to one's ideological predilection, as we argue in Chapter 9.[17] To gamble upon how long it would take for India to get there is a hazardous exercise we refrain from. What is certain, however, that improvements in the quality of life, better livelihood opportunities, higher per-capita income, development of markets, and inclusive growth process are not only likely to reduce the dependence of citizens on social safety nets—especially on paternalistic social assistance—while providing long-run overall benefits. However, without these welfare programs, economic growth is unlikely to be inclusive in a country where the first-order manifestations of poverty and deprivation emanate right before birth and persist well into adulthood and spill over to the subsequent generation.

[17] For example, if markets are ubiquitous, women carry equal agency in intra-household allocation of resources, and citizens trust government for credible welfare delivery, cash transfers are a superior *form* of social assistance to PDS for achieving food and nutritional security. Similarly, if the array of social assistance programs can succeed in *graduating* a large share of the citizens to a higher standard of living, subsidized health insurance and old age pensions (with a *focus* on those without access to employment-based health protection and the elderly population, respectively) might progressively become the key *forms* of direct social assistance, as is common in the developed world.

Resilience Through Livelihood Protection and Nutritional Enhancement

To promote development resilience, we highlight livelihood support and improved nutritional outcomes as the two overarching *scope* around which social protection system needs to be designed. Both challenges have multiple dimensions, and the future social protection system must address them considering India's slow structural transformation, persistent malnutrition among children, heightened livelihood vulnerability despite declining poverty, and the various socio-economic factors which characterize its developmental deficits.

Strengthening the Capacity of ICDS to Deliver Improved Nutrition

Persistent undernutrition among children is perhaps the biggest risk to India's growth potential. Despite state intervention in the form of supplementary nutrition to pregnant mothers and infant children, immunization, health check-up, and referral services, along with nutrition and health education to mothers, Indian children continue to be nutritionally deficient—almost 35 percent of Indian children under the age suffer from stunting (height/age)—and fare worse than children from even poorer countries. Despite the truly transformative ability of the 1.4 million *Anganwadis* (AWCs)—as ICDS centers are popularly known—through which nutritional supplementation is distributed, the program is beset with challenges of program design, staff motivation, and funding requiring reforms on multiple fronts.

AWCs need infrastructural modernization to be safe spaces for children to prosper as they are often their first centers of learning and improved health. Nearly a fourth of the AWCs lack toilet facilities while a tenth of them do not have drinking water facilities. Greater attention to the program through schemes like *Saksham Anganwadi* has been promised but needs to be sustained through financial allocation in subsequent budgets. Similarly, many of the initiatives proposed under the Prime Minister's Overarching Scheme or Holistic Nourishment (POSHAN) initiative focused on nutritional awareness, education, and behavioral change along with creating synergies across the various schemes aimed at nutritional enhancement are a welcome step in that direction. Regular social audits and community meetings are key to ensure civic participation and public accountability around the functioning of AWCs. Such administrative routines, however, require adequate funding and political commitment to the cause of mother and child nutrition which has surely gained a key place in social policy with the 2013 right to food legislation. POSHAN should be used as the platform to take the next leap in commitment to better nutrition.

With AWCs becoming the arena for fight against nutrition, *Anganwadi* workers (AWW) are increasingly at the vanguard. AWWs are responsible not only for providing immunization services and nutrition information, distributing take-home rations, act as daycare for children, cooking and serving meals to the beneficiaries, but also for providing preschool facilities and sometime home visits for consultation. The nature of services to be provided at the *Anganwadis* has increase manifold in recent years. Most recently, under the new preschool curriculum, Early Childhood Care and Education (ECCE), AWCs have been earmarked to "promote early stimulation and play-based, experiential and child-friendly provision for early childhood education and all round development" leading up to their entry into formal schooling. AWWs, as preschool teachers, are required to undertake a range of activities to develop physical, motor, social-emotional, and cognitive skills of the children. While their expanded role could be the harbinger of improved nutritional outcomes, it must be supplemented with increasing the number of staff with the necessary training. Unfortunately, work provided by AWWs is still considered as a 'community service' and their salary falls below the minimum wages leading to disgruntlement and poor motivation. Delayed payments, ad hoc recruitment for 11 months, and corruption in the hierarchy further affect their dissatisfaction. Lack of professional training—scientific understanding of issues around health and nutrition—further limits their functional capabilities to be the agents of force against nutrition. Timely and improved wages, professional training, transparent hiring, recruitment, and staff retention are some of the key organizational issues for the AWCs to improve nutritional outcomes in the country.

There must also be a focus on enhancing the nutritive component of cooked meals at the AWCs—for children and expecting mothers—with greater share of protein and micronutrients. Inclusion of eggs in the meal has been a particular bone of contention. While some states include eggs in the meal, it's a shame that social policy has not been able to overcome political hurdles to deliver the most basic and cheap form of nutrition to young children across the board. Like a hot-cooked meal for children, One Full Meal (OFM) scheme for pregnant and lactating mothers, which is being attempted in a few states, needs to be scaled up given the risks of take-home rations (THR) being shared with other family members. Given the spread of food fortification technology and cost-effectiveness, ICDS must also include micronutrient fortified meals given the high levels of micronutrient deficiencies.

Gender norms, sanitation and hygiene infrastructure, and behavioral changes associated with its use remain essential to nutritional improvements. Several noteworthy initiatives such as universal toilets and water and electricity access to every home are likely to improve nutritional outcomes. However, the success of such initiative lies in the quality of implementation and social change these schemes aim to herald. For example, toilet infrastructure without behavioral change toward sanitation practices or nutritional supplementation without associated nutritional counseling is likely to be futile. Similarly, water connection without regular services and water treatment could be rendered ineffective. Both social institutions and public systems which underpin the success of such programs are found to be sticky in India thereby slowing the process of change. It is crucial for nutrition-focused social welfare programs to focus on the social and behavioral aspects of nutrition.

Greater Focus on Learning Outcomes

Broad-based economic growth in a country is founded upon the available stock of human capital. ICDS and MDMS—with a *focus* on improving child nutrition and reducing classroom hunger—offer the initial window of opportunity for children who cannot afford better nutrition through private means. However, the scope of improved human capital must not stop only at better nutrition but also focus on improving learning outcomes among children at public school and AWCs. A resilient development process requires holistic growth where better nutrition combines with improved academic learning and skills to be employable. While free school meals under MDMS have succeeded in bringing children to school and addressing classroom hunger, their learning outcomes leave a lot to be desired. Annual Status of Education Reports (ASER) over subsequent years has highlighted poor learning outcomes among young Indian children. According to the ASER reports, less than a third of students in the third grade were able to pass tests designed for assessing reading and writing abilities for children in the second grade. Similarly, less than 30 percent of pupils in the fifth grade could solve math problems expected to be known by the second grade.

Poor learning outcomes are intensified in public schools which is characterized by poor governance—infrastructural constraints, teacher absenteeism, and low commitment remain. While right to education is a constitutional citizen right, and the quality of elementary public education system in India has improved in the last two decades, it continues to suffer from gross state neglect. Near-universal school enrollment and greater classroom attendance has not translated into improved academic performance. No wonder there is a shift in parents' preference to enroll in private schools even among the poor despite the fact that private schools do not have the provision of free school means and are often equally mediocre in quality. Yet the perceived or illusory difference in public versus private school quality by parents highlights the need to invest in public schooling which otherwise would not only lead to nutritional losses but also learning gaps.[18] Private schooling or remedial tuition classes also impinge upon the household budgets and improved quality in public schools must rectify that. The emphasis on improving the quality of public education is also important from the perspective of social justice. A large share of the students enrolled in public schools belong to the marginalized social groups who lag on most other social indicators and public schools are their only medium of education and social empowerment through education.

The remarkable transformation of public schools in Delhi offers a useful example.[19] Along with greater financial allocation to the public schools which led to a facelift of the crumbling infrastructure and adoption of technology in classroom instruction, regular teaching training, and several other organizational reforms which encouraged teacher accountability and motivation, the Delhi government schools are now competing at par with expensive private schools in terms of academic achievements. The neighboring state of Haryana has also initiated a similar drive,

[18] A study conducted by the Azim Premji University finds that perceived "quality" of teaching and learning at schooling in a low information environment is a function of parents' social and cultural aspirations. English-medium instruction remains a priority even when low-fee private schools do not deliver on the promise. See Azim Premji Foundation (2018).

[19] Refer to Aiyar et al. (2021) and Anand and Lall (2022) for greater details on the transformation of schools in Delhi.

Saksham Ghoshna, combining academic and administrative reforms to improve student learning in public schools. These reforms could motivate other states to embark upon improving the quality of public schools in the country with the *scope* of higher learning outcomes. It must, however, be ensured that school improvement programs need a spirited initiative where learning remains the central outcome of policy rather than program implementation. The failure of Madhya Pradesh *Shaala Gunvatta* (MP School Quality Assurance)—a combination of management 'best practices' which include school assessment, ratings, inspection, etc.—in improving learning outcomes should be held as a reminder that educational reforms must not end up as bureaucratic compliance checks.[20]

Adequate Supply of Public Health Facilities

It is only natural to focus on health outcomes after emphasizing the importance of superior child nutrition and learning outcomes for resilient societies as the other key component of human capital. Investment in health is central to support productive capacities of citizens and facilitate inclusive development. While health infrastructure is not a direct component of the social protection system, quality health system is paramount for the success of many social welfare programs, most notably in the context of maternal transfers for childbirth and public health insurance. The structural weakness of India's health system has been recognized for a long time which the COVID-19 only laid bare. Insufficient public health facilities—absence of trained care providers, infrastructure, medical supplies, funding, and staff motivation—have particularly diminished the effectiveness of maternal cash transfers for institutional delivery of childbirth such as the *Janani Suraksha Yojana* (JSY). A similar challenge exists with the *Pradhan Mantri Matru Vandana Yojana* (PMMVY), a conditional cash transfer to young mothers upon institutional childbirth, anti-natal care consultation, and vaccination of children. Poor administrative capacity of the health system has weakened the potential impact of PMMVY on better health-seeking behavior among pregnant women and new mothers.

[20] See Muralidharan and Singh (2020).

Maternal cash transfers can only have a limited impact in the absence of quality maternal health facilities, access to health information, and emergency obstetric care. Building and maintaining public health system fall under the purview of the National Health Mission (NHM) which aims to achieve "universal access to equitable, affordable and quality health care services that are accountable and responsive to people's needs," yet the required funding to it remains short and implementation unsatisfactory. India ranks lowest among nations in terms of public health expenditure as a share of GDP places—a little above 1 percent. Poor quality of services, rampant corruption, and lack of accountability reduce credibility of public health facilities among its targeted users. While health issues are gaining political traction, recent initiatives like *Ayushman Bharat* need to increase financial allocation to improve public health infrastructure, hire quality staff, along with better accountability mechanisms to bridge the current trust deficit patients have in the system. Put succinctly, the public health care infrastructure requires a fundamental overhaul with citizen's health and well-being at the center of it.

Regularizing 'Voluntary' Community Workers as Health Care Staff

Community health workforce—all women—play a crucial role in improving of maternal and child nutrition. While *Anganwadi* staff (AWWs) remain central to the performance of ICDS, Accredited Social Health Activist Scheme (ASHA) workers and Auxiliary Nurse Midwife (ANM) play a key role in facilitating health care access to poor women. They act as the interface between the mothers and public health centers (PHCs) especially providing the benefits of PMMVY and JSY. They are responsible for registration of mothers under the schemes, ensure and record antenatal care (ANC) check-ups, and provide advisory services toward institutional delivery, breastfeeding practices, child immunization, and reproductive health among others. However, similar to AWWs, ASHA workers and ANMs suffer from poor pay and toil hard without much recognition apart from salutary awards to sustain the local health system.

While ASHA workers were singled out by the World Health organization (WHO) with the 2022 Global Health Leaders Award for their services especially in expanding the COVID-19 vaccination coverage, these community workers do not have a regular employment contract and paid below minimum wages. It is ironic that the work situation of 1 million ASHAs, 2.6 million AWCs, and 0.2 ANMs represents the exact precarity against which social security is principally organized—casualization and informalization of labor force devoid of employment-based protections mandated by labor laws. It is unfortunate that the key frontline members among the health care workers—responsible for delivering social assistance and health advisory—lack social security themselves. For an overwhelming majority of these women, being an ASHA, ANM, or AWW is their primary employment with the 'community service' taking a disproportionate time and effort.

Community health workers must be employed on formal pay rolls with employment-based benefits instead of their current treatment as 'honorary volunteers.' The 'honorariums' which they are currently paid is significantly lower than the minimum wage rates. To improve the performance of mother and child nutrition-related social welfare programs, greater accountability measures have been adopted to monitor the scheme and staff performance—such as phone-based data entry and other administrative work—which has only led to greater time commitments on the part of AWWs, ASHAs, and ANMs. Without adequate financial rewards, such policy changes have only bred employee resentment and great dissatisfaction among the frontline health workers. The AWWs and ASHAs have regularly staged protests demanding better pay and formalization of employment along with daily allowances to food and fuel. While financial incentives in the form of fixed bonuses and performance-based monetary incentives have been added in some states, attending to these fundamental worker demands—which also includes access to other employment-based welfare entitlements such as savings and retirement fund similar to the provisions for doctors, nurses, and other medical staff—is paramount to keep their motivation high and ensure they contribute to improving nutritional outcomes in the country. Such a provision would not only improve nutritional outcomes but also increase female employment—a major developmental challenge for India—by making them a part of mainstream workforce.

Restructuring Livelihood Assistance

Access to secure and remunerative livelihood is the other essential component of human capital promotion. India's service-driven economy has not been able to create sufficient formal sector employment opportunities despite rising share of educational attainment among the youth.[21] At the same time, economic growth has reduced income poverty but farm income remains stagnant, and social institutions still hinder greater participation of women in the labor force. Response to livelihood vulnerability in the country therefore must be framed in the context of its stunted structural transformation, characterized by deindustrialization, informality in service sector employment, and stagnant farm income along with urbanization and demographic changes.

Improved Governance of Rural Social Assistance Programs
Rural livelihoods are precarious by design. Declining farm sizes, lack of employable skills for service-driven economy, and vagaries of climatic variation portend uncertain and low-income stream for the rural workers. While improved infrastructure—roads, electricity, credit access, and connectivity to markets—has provided newer economic opportunities and a reduction in poverty, livelihood vulnerability remains grave in rural areas. Assured 100 days of work to rural works under MGNREGS has been truly transformative not only in protecting income but transforming rural economy through rise in wages, creation of local infrastructure, employment opportunities to women, and improving many of the other development outcomes. However, there is a large variation across Indian states in terms of the implementation and effectiveness of MGNREGS.

A distinct advantage of MGNREGS over an unconditional cash transfer is the opportunity to use the labor to create public infrastructure such as roads, bridges, schools, *Anganwadis*, and irrigation works which enhance the quality of life, protect against environmental degradations, and diversify rural livelihood options. The transformative potential for MGNREGS can be harnessed by improving its performance in the poorer states where the program continues to be best with issues of implementation and local corruption. Despite the expansion of the program, there is a significant unmet demand for work in the poorest regions of the country.

[21] The scamper for a secure and respectful employment is conspicuous by the millions of applications which the government receives for a handful of job openings for low grade jobs every year. For example, 2.3 million people applied for a few hundred lower grade government jobs in the state of Uttar Pradesh in 2015. The applicants included many postgraduates and even PhDs which highlights not only the lack of formal employment avenues but also the poor employable skills among the educated class of workers.

Local administrative support and state capacity continue to deny work to minimum 100 days of work to citizens despite their legal entitlement to it.[22] Lack of information about the program, limited citizen voice, and rent-seeking among the local bureaucracy inhibit the creation of effective state capacity to deliver work under MGNREGS which affects household resilience in the wake of a calamity.[23] Governance reforms which increase local state capacity, bridge information asymmetry between local state actors and workers, and those which increase bureaucratic accountability such as social audits need to be pursued in a more spirited manner.

While MGNREGS is an employer of the last resort, cash transfer via PM-Kisan has emerged as the other most important livelihood support in rural areas. While the entire rural population remains the *focus* of MGNREGS, PM-Kisan was introduced as a response to stagnant farm income and hence farmers are the beneficiaries under the scheme. A relatively newer scheme, PM-Kisan offers a great opportunity to test the implementation and effectiveness of a large-scale unconditional bank-based cash transfer programs in the country—social pension being the other, albeit on a smaller scale—and is likely to become an important component of the social protection system. Its implementation, however, requires better governance systems to identify and enroll beneficiaries, make timely payments, and revise the said amount with changes in inflation.

Protecting Against Vulnerability in the Old Age Through Assured Monthly Pensions

By 2050, every fifth Indian would be over the age of 60 years, a significant increase in the total sexagenarian population from current levels. With low-wage informal employment characterizing current livelihoods, an overwhelming majority of the workers would enter into old age without recourse to any retirement pensions and miniscule savings. A large majority of them may not even have the option to retire. Henceforth, social protection system of the future ought to lean heavily toward

[22] See Narayanan et al. (2022).

[23] Afridi et al. (2022) estimate that regions with superior historical state capacity to implement MGNREGS provided more cushion against COVID-19-induced economic losses through greater work provision.

the provision of pensions for the elderly. In the absence of employment-based contributory pensions, state would be increasingly required to provide old age pensions.

Retirement age and pensions have raged an intense debate but in the more advanced countries—with formal employment—while developing countries like South Africa, Brazil, and China have initiated massive old age pension programs spending 1 percent of their GDP, close to what India spends on its most important social assistance program, PDS. Old age pensions under the current National Social Assistance Program (NSAP) provide an important, but tiny monthly sum to the most vulnerable section of the Indian population which does not affect their sustenance but influences their ability to afford health care and impinges upon the resource-constrained multi-generation households they are often a part of. The importance of old age pension is only expected to increase with greater population of sexagenarian. The current program, NSAP, needs to be upgraded with higher amount of transfer, better targeting of the program, and other administrative hurdles associated with implementation.

Future social protection policies must include the elderly as part of the system and increase the amount of noncontributory social benefits bestowed to them. The first policy challenge is however to recognize the problems of old age poverty, its implications for health, and household consumption. A 2013 Task Force on Restructuring NSAP had proposed reforms to the scheme with an expansion in coverage and pension amount as the most important ones. Yet, there was little action on that front. There are examples, however, from states like Rajasthan and Haryana which have revised the pension amount upwards. Indian government, on the other hand, has introduced contributory old age pension schemes—*PM Mazdoor Samman Nidhi* and *Atal Pension Yojana*—for the informal workers. We reckon that 'contributory' aspect of these schemes does not benefit the poorest section—lack of awareness, and certainty in income stream for regular contributions—of the population which it is aimed. An expansion in the amount and coverage of old age pensions under NSAP is path to improve resilience among the elderly population.

Addressing Urban Vulnerability

While the precarity of India's rural livelihood structure has necessitated livelihood-oriented social assistance programs such as wage-support under MGNREGS and cash transfers through PM-Kisan, there has been little concern around what ought to be a 'social minimum' in urban areas. Greater recognition to urbanization of poverty, proliferation of slums, and informality associated with urban life has only recently sparked a debate around urban livelihood vulnerability. This discourse, primarily an academic one, is crucial from the perspective of India's urbanization and social protection system for an urban labor force (Bhan 2023).

There are two school of thoughts on the potential *form* of urban social assistance. One of them proposes a cash-based social transfers envisaging this as a state support for the vulnerable income groups to protect consumption, acquire skills, and undertake entrepreneurial activities to build resilience. It assumes that cash transfers are easier to deliver in an urban setting where markets—banks and food—are easily accessible and literacy levels higher. A lump sum transfer of INR 500 (~7 USD) per month into the account of women account holders under the COVID-19 recovery package, *Pradhan Mantri Garib Kalyan*, is being a case in point. The other one has put forwarded the need for an MGNREGS-like public works program in urban India. Noted economist Jean Drèze, one of the architects of MGNREGS, has proposed a *Decentralized Urban Employment and Training* (DUET), under which tradable job stamps can be issued by the government which workers can use to work at an 'approved' institution at minimum wage rates. This would reduce unemployment among the low skilled workers and also allow for building urban infrastructure and provide basic amenities which Indian cities lack.[24] He further argues DUET can be restricted only to women to ensure self-selection by poorer section to reduce program costs while encouraging female labor force participation at the same time.

A scheme like DUET has several appealing features to create robust urban social protection system. First, skill and entrepreneurship programs historically designed to address urban poverty have been a failure and there is a need for program calibrated better to the urban realities. Schemes like the *Pradhan Mantri Awas Yojana (PMAY)* primarily *focus* on the provision of housing for the poor with negligible *scope* of addressing livelihood vulnerability. The urban livelihood program *Deen Dayal Antyodaya Yojana*-National Urban Livelihood Mission (DAY-NULM)—aimed at creating gainful self-employment and promoting skilled wage opportunities—has been unsuccessful in gaining sufficient

[24] For details of the DUET proposal, refer to Drèze (2020, 2021). For comments on the proposal, see Aiyar (2020), Bardhan (2020), Kotwal (2020), and Ray (2020).

political support and hence remains on the fringes of social policy. As a result, there is a pressing need for a social assistance program which is cognizant of current urban livelihood challenges. Second, cities are key to innovation, agglomeration economies, and attracting investment but Indian cities, especially the tier-II and tier-II cities—which are growing at a faster rate than the metropolitan towns—are characterized by grossly inadequate public infrastructure and civic amenities (especially urban commons) remain a neglected area of concern. Urban renewal schemes as implemented in the past and the current Smart Cities initiative are driven as projects with specific deliverables—increases in the number of buses, streetlights, etc.—without any adequate planning for their upkeep and its implication for the urban poor. DUET can provide the necessary impetus for improving the quality of life in urban cities by including them and their work as a key input of urban revival.[25] Third, urban poor are the most unorganized political group in the country. Residential neighborhoods are differentiated along various axes of class, occupation, and identity where associational activities are local and primarily structured around self-provisioning of services. To secure public services, the urban poor—often living in unauthorized colonies and slums—become a captive to political patronage by politicians or slumlords which limits their political power.[26] In contrast to the rural livelihood mission, where village council committees are organized political units to disseminate information on schemes and mobilize local support for implementation, urban poor are not organized along similar lines. Many of the fruit vendors, laborers, or even construction workers are itinerant workers who lack the associational ability and infrastructure to demand services from the state. DUET has the potential to foster an urban associational life around work and economic vulnerability which could facilitate deeper democratic

[25] Basole et al. (2019) describe in detail how an urban employment program could usher in urban renewal.

[26] Heller et al. (2019) argue that the pattern of urbanization and socio-economic differentiations in Indian cities—a union of rent-seeking politicians and realtor-businessmen—impede the formation of broad-based pro-poor coalitions. As a result, access to urban public services is lowest among the poorer and depressed classes in Indian cities (Bertorelli et al. 2017; Bharathi et al. 2022). Highlighting the rising economic disparity in Indian cities, Kundu and Kundu (2010) remark that "...one of the major paradoxes of urban areas is that the poor live in the cities and provide cheap labour that holds the key to the building of the city economies but enjoy no provision of safe existence or share of benefits from its development".

engagements between the urban poor and state. It must also be noted that a program like DUET is not a solution to the employment problem in the country, rather it is the first step toward ensuring the provision of decent and dignified work at a minimum wage which can provide succor in times of non-availability of better employment opportunity.

The attractiveness of DUET, however, conceals operational challenges and normative questions around how to implement such a complex program and would it suffice as a social minimum for urban poor, respectively. Identification and enrollment of workers in urban areas is a cumbersome challenge, which MGNREGS despite its presence for more than a decade continues to face. Implementing DUET entails a value chain of bureaucratic procedures, hiring of contractors, commissioning of work, liasoning with local organizations which are beset with delays, corruption, and operational inefficiencies which have traditionally plagued social welfare programs of the yore. At a normative level, it is still unclear whether DUET would be able to raise average wages for the urban workers or create the required urban infrastructure. While MGNREGS has been able to raise rural wages, its impact on creating rural infrastructure remains an area of scrutiny. Lastly, a moribund urban local governance structure in the country can potentially stifle the implementation of DUET.

Despite these challenges, DUET is an idea worth considering for its potential impact in protecting vulnerable livelihoods, promoting female labor force participation, improving urban infrastructure, and creating an urban civic consciousness which is mindful of the most marginalized citizens. It allows welfare policy to articulate a hitherto missing urban social contract. Some state governments, however, have begun to pilot similar programs.[27] Kerala's *Ayyankali Urban Employment Guarantee Scheme* was the first one which has been followed by Odisha (Urban Wage Employment Initiative, UWEI), Himachal Pradesh (*Mukhyamantri Shahri Aajeevika Guarantee Yojana*, MMSAGY), Jharkhand (*Mukhyamantri Shramik Yojana*, MSY), and Rajasthan (*Indira Gandhi Shahari Rozgar Yojana*, IGSRY). Learnings from the implementation and impact of these programs along with other ongoing pilot studies on cash transfers in urban areas would enlighten social policy on the right way to go. It

[27] Aiyar (2020) argues why the approach to DUET should be best left to state governments.

is certain, however, that a stronger *focus* on urban vulnerability would be an increasingly critical component of the future social protection system.

Social Security for Gig or Platform Economy Workers

Gig work and platform economy is omnipresent in Indian cities with Flipkart, Swiggy, Zomato, BigBasket, etc., being a household name.[28] Helmeted service providers on these platforms are seen zipping past on their motor bikes with a heavy backpacks and multiple addresses to deliver the wares. Numerous Ola and Uber cab drivers ply day and night to provide commute services. The government planning body, NITI Aayog estimates that 7.7 million workers in India were engaged in the gig economy in 2020–2021 which is expected to increase 23.5 million by 2029–2030.[29] The growth of gig work and platform economy has surely increased employment opportunities and created economic buoyancy, but the services provided by workers through these platform workers as "independent partners" hardly qualify what International Labor Organization (ILO) would classify as "decent work."[30] Regardless, we must accept—even reluctantly—gig or platform work to be the dominant source of employment in the future.

For certain, one cannot arrest the rise of e-commerce, technology, and artificial intelligence (AI) which is bound to disrupt traditional employment structures. Economic vulnerability associated with these newer employer-employee relationship, however, requires newer labor legislations and social protection frameworks which provide some form of social security benefits, retirement savings, bargaining rights, minimum wage

[28] Gig economy workers are defined as those who provide services outside the traditional employer-employee relationship which contains a written or unwritten work contract in return for money or in-kind benefit. Platform workers are identified as those who access work with organizations or individuals through an online or digital medium. While gig workers—casual or temporary workers working part-time or full-time—typically characterize Indian labor force, these terms have become popular in the wake of digitalization of the economy and the popularity of platform-based work.

[29] https://www.niti.gov.in/sites/default/files/2022-06/Policy_Brief_India%27s_Booming_Gig_and_Platform_Economy_27062022.pdf. Accessed on July 1, 2023.

[30] Research by *Fairwork*, a project based at the University of Oxford, shows that digital platform-based companies in India use the inherent information asymmetry in the system to avoid paying fair wages to the workers, and resist regulations of any kind. The service providers can rarely access their ratings and evaluate their performance to influence their future income. See Fairwork (2021).

protection, and skill development opportunities for the workers. Among the various initiatives to overhaul labor laws in the country, Social Security Code Bill 2020 for the first time has identified gig/platform workers as a distinct employment category. The bill identifies the need for every gig worker and platform worker to be part of a registry system through which social security benefits—life and disability coverage, accidental insurance, health and maternity benefits, gratuity, and creche facilities—can be conferred. However, there is no clarity on how these social security benefits would be funded and what kind of contributions would be invited from the employers and the service providers. More importantly, the code merely remains a gazette notification with no commitment on the part of government to implement it leaving millions of workers without social security. A robust social protection system requires the strong social security code to be implemented for it would protect livelihoods and reduced reliance on direct social assistance. It would also encourage greater formalization of the economy and facilitate the structural transformation process by adding to the resilience of gig or platform economy workers.

Migrants as Part of the Urban Social Protection System

Migrants are the most vulnerable of workers in urban areas who lack a fixed address, domicile, or proof of residence in the city. More than 100 million workers reside in cities as migrant laborers as part of the informal economy which characterizes urban economy and in slums or unrecognized housing colonies. Their humiliating fate—hundreds of kilometers walk back home to their villages abandoning their urban dwellings, many of them perishing on the way—in the wake of COVID-19 lockdown brought to public consciousness the precarity of migrant work, informal job contracts, poor quality of dwellings, and lack of social support leading to their status as secondary class urban citizens. A strong social protection system provides an opportunity to re-write the urban social contract with a specific focus on migrants which can improve their quality of life, reduce the barriers to migration, make cities inclusive, and spur the pace of structural transformation.[31] Strengthening social protection of migrants is also

[31] Social protection programs are tied to the original place of residence which inhibits and restricts its access by migrants. This has been found to lower migration rates in India where the pace of migration is slower than other countries of comparable per capita income.

important from the perspective of political exclusion and often violence faced by the poor inter-state migrants.

One nation one ration card (ONORC) under the PDS is the first initiative of its kind which allows for portability of welfare benefits outside of the state. Public health insurance program also incorporates migration decision of the beneficiaries using smartcards and biometric authentication. In 2021, Government of India launched a portal, eSHRAM, to create a national database of unorganized workers, which also includes migrant workers to track social assistance including portability of welfare support to the migrant workers. Given the spatial dimension of rural-urban migration, various state governments have also taken initiative to create a database of out-migrants and track their welfare benefits. However, there are serious gaps in the implementation. These initiatives rest upon awareness among the beneficiaries and service providers, logistical challenges of identification and verification in a technology reliant dynamic system, and adequate supplies with the PDS dealers. Any glitch in the system leads to a denial of benefits. Strengthening social protection for the migrants, therefore, requires greater effort in disseminating information around the portability of benefits and a string political commitment toward the political rights of migrants in the city.

Empowerment of Women Through Greater Employment Opportunities

The resilience *scope* of social protection includes greater *focus* on empowering of the most marginalized groups, especially women.[32] While maternal and child nutrition programs are particularly geared toward women, gender inequalities must be addressed through facilitating greater economic opportunities to them which also facilitate greater intra-household bargaining power. MGNREGS has been particularly empowering for women workers as they have consistently surpassed men in terms of total employment numbers since the program's inception. Female participation in the public works program has been made easier by specific provisions of a crèche facility and work within 5 kilometers of the village precinct. Despite higher domestic chores and care responsibilities in the wake of COVID-19-induced lockdown policies and the resultant reduced

[32] Refer to Gavrilovic et al. (2022) for a global review of gender-sensitive social protection system, especially in the wake of COVID-19.

economic opportunities for women, MGNREGS emerged as the principal livelihood support for women.[33] Social protection system has been inclusive of women through their contributions as community workers in key health and nutrition programs as ICDS, ASHA, and ANMS workers. Regularizing their employment contracts would add as a further boost to female labor force participation in the country and encourage more women to work outside of their home. In many states, SHGs are designed to run the PDS shops which promote female entrepreneurship.

Group-based livelihood programs have been the other key form of social protection which promote skill development and employment opportunities for women. *Deen Dayal Antyodaya Yojana* (DAY) with urban and rural suffix, National Urban and Rural Livelihood Mission (NULM and NRLM), aims to mobilize at least one member of each poor households preferably women into self-help groups (SHGs), facilitate access to financial institutions for these groups, provide skills and training to the members, and connect them to other state-run anti-poverty programs. The livelihood program primarily relies on the economies of scope associated with one group-based platform, SHGs, for multiple interventions which also includes health and nutrition information. SHG membership, by increasing a women's social capital, opens avenues for her empowerment, be it through her improved health status, access to work, or political participation. For a program which has long-term objectives through market-based means to prosperity, NRLM has been successful in improving nonfarm livelihood opportunities, greater household savings, and creating durable social capital for economic and political empowerment though its effectiveness varies across the states.[34] NRLM has also been useful example of convergence of welfare policies by encouraging participation of women in MGNREGS.[35] A singular focus on women as the transformative force behind the array of economic activities—farming, banking, entrepreneurship, etc.—in a patriarchal system however puts naively heavy burden on them which could undermine the program's long-term potential. Social protection system of the future should be gender-sensitive attuned to the differentiated needs of women and girls and build systems which address the root causes of gender inequality.

[33] See Afridi et al. (2022) and Narayan (2022).

[34] See Deshpande (2022) for a comprehensive review.

[35] See De Hoop et al. (2022).

Public Health Insurance to Promote Universal Health Coverage

As opposed to cash and in-kind social assistance, social insurance in the form of subsidized public health insurance programs has gained greater policy support. In privatized health care markets, cost of health care could be exorbitant and is identified as the principal cause of slide into poverty. In the Indian social policy, health insurance for the poor emerged as a support to the unorganized workers who lacked employment-based social security in 2008 as *Rashtriya Swasthya Bima Yojana* (RSBY) and its focus has expanded to cover a larger share of the population under *Pradhan Mantri Jan Arogya Yojana* (PM-JAY) since 2018. Publicly subsidized health insurance program has evidently emerged as an importance component of the social welfare agenda.

Demand for better health care system has emerged from a considerable decline in the quality of health care in public facilities which have not been able to meet the demand for high quality, specialized infrastructure. Private hospitals, therefore, have sprang up throughout all corners of the country, but are more expensive. While the Government of India has introduced relevant programs for health insurance, their performance leaves much to be desired. At the same time, social insurance targeted to the vulnerable—the elderly, widowed, and disabled—has been initiated; the political support for these programs remains low, as does the amount of transfers. In the future, with more market-based social protection, health insurance is expected to be the most important *form* of social insurance along with cash transfers and old age pensions as direct forms of social assistance.

There are two ways to think about the *scope* of public health insurance. Should it only be a source of financial protection? Whether it also ought to facilitate improved health outcomes? We contend it ought to be both. Currently, PM-JAY is designed as the source of financial protection against health shocks and improved health outcomes remain conditional on the health-seeking behavior of patients and the quality of care provided at the facilities. For PM-JAY to be a source of improved health outcomes, it is important first to increase enrollment in the program through greater awareness campaigns. Further, the current program with a *focus* on the poor misses a significant share of the middle-income people who are also at risk of catastrophic health shock. PM-JAY must also include a focus on the middle class even if it includes payment of a small premium. Such a move is likely to protect more households but also create a demand for private health insurance and a larger pool of insured would bring down the insurance premium.

PM-JAY only covers for hospitalization expenses while a greater share of medical expenditure in India is incurred by the households on medicines and diagnostic tests with the rise of non-communicable diseases (NCDs). Unless the program covers the cost of preventive medical care, it is expected to have little impact on either financial protection or improving long-term health outcomes. As India's health care is increasingly getting privatized further encouraged by the public health market, adequate regulatory requirements are mandatory to check overtreatment and exploitation of patients. Perverse behavior of private health care providers is common to developing countries which often diminishes the developmental *scope* of the health insurance programs.[36] India is no exception to that as the health crisis during the pandemic COVID-19 laid bare to the public eye.

In order to leverage health insurance as a means to promote universal health coverage (UHC)—a global commitment—it is important to recognize the importance of right to health in the country. Access to health, as an inalienable citizenship right, would ensure that people seeking health care are not away by service providers, which is a common practice now. We have seen how legal guarantees to education, work, and food have been instrumental in providing the basic building blocks of a social protection systems in India thereby promoting livelihood, food, and nutritional security. Health as a citizenship right would further build household resilience.

Rethinking Poverty in the Social Policy Design

The complexity of urban livelihood vulnerability and greater importance of nonfarm wage-based employment in the rural areas should act as a starting point to rethink the conceptualization of poverty in the social policy design. Poverty, vulnerability, and deprivation in an urbanizing

[36] Comparing the performance of public health insurance program across the developing countries, Das and Do (2023) find that while health insurance programs may have provided financial protection against health shocks, there is no discernable impact on improvements in overall health outcomes. The authors contend that despite a push towards better health-seeking behavior, the benefits may have been undone by the rent-seeking private healthcare providers.

world would increasingly emerge from insufficient wages and income to maintain a basic standard of living. Greater economic opportunities—in rural as well as urban areas—are expected to progressively reduce unemployment but underemployment or disguised unemployment creating a greater share of those who are vulnerable to poverty even if not identified as poor by the various metrics. Latest numbers from the Economic Survey 2022–2023 show that real wages in rural India have remained stagnant in addition to the stagnant income among farmers for more than a decade. Similarly, the oft-cited 2008 report by the National Commission for Enterprises in the Unorganized Sector (NCEUS) estimates that about 79 percent of workers in the informal sector are poor or vulnerable to future poverty because they are paid subsistence wages without any social security. According to the report, even in the formal manufacturing sector, increase in profitability has not been passed on to the workers as the wage share of the firm output. Low wages in real terms and insecure job contracts imply heightened vulnerability among those who are employed but the income is insufficient to ensure food, housing, and shelter—the three basic essential items—to their families and much less being able to invest in their own health or human capital for their children.

Working and living in poverty-like conditions is attributed to lack of gainful income opportunities, insufficient skills, poor health conditions, or lower educational levels to partake in the employment. Consider the sector that has seen the highest increase in employment share in the country—construction. Labor employment in the construction sector requires little or no education, is low productivity, and often untied with any employer-based social insurance. The long and tragic walk of the migrant workers—leaving cities for their homes accompanied by their young children, and often covering more than a 1000 kms—in the wake of COVID-19 induced lockdown remains a reminder that vulnerability to unemployment, quality of life, and social citizenship are not captured in the income dimension of poverty. It is not only lack of income, but insufficient social support—through employment or state guarantees—security which leads to fragile lives and livelihoods. It is important here to note that welfare systems emerged in the West as a response to greater insecurities around wage-based employment and urbanization of labor force. India, therefore, ought to start thinking in the same direction.

Social protection system in an urbanizing context with a greater share of wage-based employment must be based upon the evolving nature and causes of deprivation which stems not only from informality of employment, but also of temporary place of residence (often unrecognized settlements) to claim welfare (Bhan 2023). Developmental resilience as the *scope* of social protection system necessitates a broader understanding of the vulnerable population (*focus*) and the most appropriate *form* of social support. While women and children would remain the key *focus* of welfare programs, demarcation of citizens as poor and non-poor for welfare benefits needs be obliterated with the recognition than social protection is required for the poor—often unobservable and along multiple dimensions as well as those vulnerable to poverty. The APL/BPL distinction and even the priority versus non-priority households under NFSA are costly exercises and have neither improved targeting nor enhanced welfare. Different set of markers for urban and rural poverty further seems obsolete with the blurring of rural–urban distinction.[37] A robust social protection system needs to be inclusive and progressive in *focus*.

Building a Capable State with Citizen-Centric Public Systems

A transformational social protection system is built upon progressive welfare ideas, strong political commitment, efficient program design, effective implementation, and an enabling public system. Much ink has been spilled on the absence of a strong political commitment to social welfare and public services which has led to the historical failure of Indian state in improving human development outcome.[38] There have been a policy shift, however, in the last two decades with an expansion in the *focus*, *form*, and *scope* of the social welfare programs, which we have documented in this book. Greater attention to social welfare has also coincided with large-scale investments on 'hard' physical infrastructure—roads, bridges, electricity, irrigation, etc.—as well as 'soft' infrastructure—universal financial access, cheap mobile data, digital payment platforms—which have eased communication, increased the quality of life, and provided greater economic opportunities to the poor. Similarly,

[37] Despite India's urbanization rates being low as per the official classifications, rural spaces are morphing into urban at a fast pace, as typified by a change in the built-up area and livelihood structure.

[38] For canonical readings, refer to Dreze and Sen (2013) and Kohli (2012).

spirited emphasis on sanitation and hygiene practice—through universal provision of toilets and water—is expected to improve well-being of the poorest. Rising contestations around public welfare has further animated a new electoral discourse around politics of the poor and programmatic improvements in social policy.[39] In a nutshell, the citizen-state social contract is arguably more favorable to the citizens now than it has ever been in the history of independent India.[40]

Avoiding the Developmental State Impasse

While the importance of social safety nets in social policy is encouraging, we reckon rejoicing over these welfare initiatives as any giant stride toward building an inclusive social democracy would be premature. One must note that the Janus-faced transformation of Indian economy has created a veneer of success dominated by unbridled opportunities primarily restricted to a tiny minority—the upper caste, educated middle class—who have conveniently opted out of the public systems while the economically and socially marginalized groups—the vast majority—continue to rely upon the ignored, stressed, and poorly governed public systems which are as essential as social safety nets in expanding developmental possibilities.[41] In Chapter 8, we have explain how despite the improvements, delivery of social welfare and public services remains lackadaisical and its ideational foundations ambiguous with little emphasis on redistribution, empowerment, and social change.

Consider India's astounding achievements in building road and electricity network. Almost every village in the country is now on the electricity grids and is serviced by a motorable road yet evaluations of these last-mile infrastructure projects suggest that these infrastructural achievements have not translated into meaningful impact on economic

[39] See Roy (2023) for analysis of political discourse around welfare through an examination of texts from parliamentary speeches.

[40] One can argue that this is nothing but a rise in populist electoral measures than a true commitment to the cause of broad-based development through greater market-based economic opportunities. Even if one concedes to that, expansion of social welfare programs in terms of its various *forms* and the expanded *focus* is evident and its future depends on a range of factors, populism being one of them.

[41] India's paradox is nicely summed up in the following quote by Kapur (2005): "everything one can say about India is true, and so is the opposite".

impact.[42] Researchers have attributed this to lack of complementary inputs such as other investments in public goods, improvements in human capital, and economic development. The situation of health is the most glaring one. Despite economic growth, and greater investment on social welfare programs, share of public investment of health care as a proportion of GDP remains constant at around 1 percent, much lower than in many of the poorer countries. We have already discussed the importance of local public health facilities for the success of maternal and child nutrition programs whose primary beneficiaries are the poorer section of the population. A *laissez-faire* attitude to health care represents continued disregards of pro-poor public systems which must be rectified. While it is known that India's unregulated and fragmented health care system provides poor quality services overall—both in public and private sector—but the government's recent focus is on super-specialty hospitals with cutting-edge medical technology. The emphasis on high-end medical care, accessed by a tiny minority, has taken precedence over investments in public health care, primarily used by the poor. Without adequate investment in primary health care infrastructure, the burden of disease and cost of illness will continue to expose the fragility of daily lives and potentially diminish the potential effects of improved hygiene and sanitation facilities.

Similar is the state of primary education. Near-universal primary school enrollment co-exists with a 'learning crisis' which has only exacerbated by the COVID-19 pandemic.[43] Deficiencies in the quality of education in public schools has increasingly led to a preference toward 'low-fee' private schools even among the poor even if improvements in academic learning outcomes remain incommensurate.[44] The education system, therefore, has become a 'filtration' process to sort and select the more fortunate students—many of them are exemplars of global Indian professionals

[42] See Asher and Novosad (2020) and Burlig and Preonas (2016) for evaluations of the developmental effects of rural roads (***Pradhan Mantri Gram Sadak Yojana***, PMGSY) and electricity (***Rajiv Gandhi Grameen Vidyutikaran Yojana***, RGGVY) programs, respectively. Lee et al. (2020) argue that last-mile infrastructure is less likely to have a meaningful developmental impact unless complemented with other necessary infrastructural inputs and economic incentives. Adukia et al. (2020) illustrate this in the case of expansion of rural roads where the program PMGSY increased school enrollment mostly in areas which presented attractive labor market returns.

[43] See Pritchett and Viarengo (2023), Singh et al. (2022) and Muralidharan and Singh (2021).

[44] For a review of the rise of private schooling in India, refer to Kingdon (2020).

across different fields—while the median ones, disproportionate majority, are left to suffer from teacher absenteeism, outdated pedagogy, and dilapidated schooling infrastructure.[45]

The euphoria over construction of toilets and its potential impact in improving health and educational outcomes is tempered by persistence of social backwardness—archaic social norms and behavior around ritual purity, pollution, untouchability, and caste—which has not eradicated open defecation despite government sanctioned toilet construction under the *Swachha Bharat Mission* (SBM) throughout the country.[46] *Pradhan Mantri Ujjwala Yojana* (PMUY), a government initiative for cooking gas connections to the poor households to accelerate a movement away from polluting solid fuels and improve women—responsible for cooking at home—health, had little impact because people reckon cooking on solid fuel makes for a tastier meal.[47] Social norms often get prioritized over women's health. Universal financial access program, *Pradhan Mandtri Jan Dhan Yojana* (PMJDY), which created zero-balance bank account with overdraft facility to 350 million Indians has not led to improvements in access to credit and credit-deposit ratios.[48] Savings balance in the PMJDY accounts remains low and a large share of the newly opened accounts soon became dormant.

Well-meaning developmental initiatives fail because the Indian state—and its many layered bureaucracy—considers these efforts as 'projects' with clear deliverables without much concern to the socio-political processes which produce these developmental deficits. As a result, while the Indian state has been successful in delivering on milestone projects such holding free and fair elections, eradicating polio, building roads and schools, or opening bank accounts, its ineptitude is exposed when it comes to delivering on continued service delivery such as quality education or health, and changing outdated social norms (Kapur 2020). The recent techno-centric developments around public welfare delivery

[45] Das and Zajonc (2010) provide an empirical illustration of the same showing how India (the modern face of the country) shines while Bharat (the left behind) drowns on mathematics test scores.

[46] The National Family Health Survey (2019) contradicts Government of India's claim of elimination of open defecation in the country. See Coffey and Spears (2017) for more details on the sanitation preference and its behavioral correlated in India.

[47] Refer to Gupta et al. (2019) for details.

[48] See Sinha and Azad (2018).

have tried to overcome last-mile corruption, but public accountability continues to be plagued by bureaucratic compliance directed above in the hierarchy than a commitment to citizen interests.

The expansion of public goods and social welfare programs therefore must be combined with greater state capacity to deliver and maintain services with due considerations to citizen welfare and public accountability.[49] Certainly, these challenges are more obtrusive in some parts of India than in others which partly explains improved development outcomes in subnational regions where public systems are more citizen friendly. States, therefore, have much to learn from each other.

A Reasoned Articulation of the 'Social Welfare' Question

A weakened state capacity to implement social welfare programs in India primarily stems from a 'disarticulation of the state' where the 'meanings and purposes' of state intervention are obscured by the rhetoric of development and empowerment against the putative electoral appeal of distributing welfare (Naseemullah 2016). The 'rights-based' welfare agenda which emerged upon the 'politics of the poor' in the early 2000s has given way to 'new welfarism' under which the political parties are promising social transfers as a *quid pro quo* electoral bargain to the people sidelining investments in public systems (Aiyar 2019).[50] Electoral sloganeering has moved from better implementation of social welfare programs and improvements in the quality of public systems to 'free' provision of merit goods such as water, electricity, food, and even to private goods like TV sets, laptops, and cooking gas cylinders to attract voters. Political parties, even those who invoke a disdain for the 'freebie culture' (pejoratively referring to is as distribution of *revdi*, an Indian

[49] The perceived *scope* of welfare programs is conditional on changes in socio-political norms and the quality of public systems which the *new welfarism* turn is oblivious to. For example, the expansion of MGNREGS brought down civil conflict in India but only in regions with pre-existing higher state capacity (Dasgupta et al. 2017). On a similar line, MGNREGS provided greater employment protection in districts where state capacity was high (Afridi et al. 2022). Refer to Aiyar (2019), Heller (2021), and Sircar (2020) for a commentary on the centralization of social welfare and its implication for democratic politics.

[50] Using the 2019 post-election survey data, Deshpande et al. (2019) show that voters attributed the receipt of welfare benefits as an important factor in voting for the incumbent government.

sweet), are also partaking in this competitive populism—outbidding each other in making the same electoral promises—which risks a race to the bottom leading to unsustainable debts, little welfare impact, and a threat to the fledgling social protection architecture.[51] While investments in human capital through subsidizing education and health, or encouraging female labor participation through free transportation access for women and bicycle for young girls to school are 'developmental' in *scope,* new welfarism circumvents careful rationalization—via legislative debates and public deliberations—of welfare programs which often maligns the aims of a social welfare system and stigmatizes its beneficiaries.

A resilience promoting social protection system requires a clear articulation of its developmental *scope* and sustained public action to the cause of welfare, empowerment, inclusiveness, and social justice. It compels a political commitment toward ensuring a "social minimum" to the citizens which allows them to lead a decent life.[52] The social minimum must be understood as more than a pecuniary consumption floor and include protection of basic citizenship rights and political engagements. The responsibility of the state, therefore, lies not only in providing social protection but also in facilitating a political system which promotes social change apart from delivering material progress. Setting up 'collective goals' and creating political mobilization around any issue leave alone welfare, however, inhibited by the diversity of India's population, its fragmented polity, sticky social institutions, and high socio-economic inequality leading to short-termism in developmental policy and lower

[51] In the state of Madhya Pradesh, the ruling party, Bharatiya Janata Party (BJP), a strong critic of the 'freebie culture' recently announced a *Mukhya Mantri Ladli Behna Yojana,* a scheme promises a monthly transfer INR 1000 (13 USD) to every married woman in the state. Additionally, it promised biannual installments of INR 2000 (26 USD) to farmers, and subsidized pilgrimages for the elderly Hindus ahead of the elections. Such promises followed its defeat in another state, Karnataka, where the rival party promised a monthly transfer of INR 2000 (26 USD) to the female head of a family, monthly stipends for the educated unemployed, 10 kg of free rice to every member of the BPL (below poverty line) family, 200 units of free electricity to every home, and ticket-free travel for women on public buses.

[52] We have argued in the book that a striking feature of Indian social policy has been the absence of cogent redistributive strategies to reduce poverty and deprivation. Lip service to welfare has led to a classic case of "policy successions" in which several schemes and programs, without the desired impact, have been repeatedly repackaged and reintroduced by successive governments. See Chapter 2 for more details on the desired *scope* of social protection.

state capacity (Bardhan 2016). It is indeed a solemn problem which has handicapped India's growth potential. The solution to it lies in greater power to the state governments to design and implement the *focus*, *form*, and *scope* of social welfare programs.

Greater Devolution of Power and Resources to the Subnational Governments

The collective action problem is more easily solvable at subnational levels. State governments have been a laboratory of welfare reforms since the 2000s silently embarking upon initiating programs or improving its implementation which has not only influenced other states to follow suite but also the central government.[53] The historical accomplishment of the South Indian states and the recent success of welfare program implementation in poorer states such as Odisha, Chhattisgarh, or Rajasthan offer an example of successful subnational political coalitions. State governments being closer to the citizens have a better understanding of the developmental priorities of the people and therefore can use the greater autonomy to articulate a more amenable social minimum. Clearly articulated welfare goals also provide a mandate to the bureaucracy, essential to discipline administration and improve implementation. Moreover, a greater role of the subnational government in the social protection allows the *focus*, *form*, and *scope* of state support to be more attuned to their own structural transformation process and the quality of public systems. For example, with greater autonomy, economically advanced states can gradually move toward social insurance-based protection systems while the ones lagging can learn and adapt as they grow and develop. In a federal polity, however, such devolutions of power to influence welfare can result in political apprehensions, and we have begun to witness such frictions.[54]

[53] It was the popularity of Odisha's *Kaalia* and Telangana's *Rythu Bandhu* which led to the central government to take note and launch a cash transfer to farmers in the form of PM-Kisan. For example, Chhattisgarh introduced a state-level food security act before the NFSA came into effect. Rajasthan and Haryana have more expansive *focus* around health insurance and old age pension, respectively. There have many such incidents. See Deshpande et al. (2017) and Tillin et al. (2015) for subnational welfare regimes.

[54] As this book goes to press, Rajasthan government has pioneered a legislation aimed at protecting the informal workers through establishing a welfare board and a dedicated social security fund for securing the rights of gig workers in the platform economy. The

As social welfare programs have gained more importance in the lives of the poor—led principally by the initiatives of the state government—tensions in India's federal system have come to fore with regard to a competition for claiming credits and the fiscal support to finance it. Improvements in the social welfare programs emerged on the back of initiatives by the subnational governments. The rise in coalition politics since the 1990s—various state-level local parties supported the central parties to form a government in Delhi—strengthened subnational governments and the position of state Chief Ministers (CMs) as the supremacy of Prime Minister (PM) reduced.[55] A thumping majority to the *Bharatiya Janata Party* (BJP) in 2014, however, arrested this trend with a greater concentration of power at the center. Subsequent social welfare programs—new or renamed, along with greater prioritization—had a prefix PM (for "Prime Minister") added to their name to indicate the central government's munificence. At the same time, the administration of many social safety nets has been centralized—as part of the *new welfarism*—by delivering subsidies directly into the beneficiary's bank account, which has further diminished the influence of subnational government in delivering welfare.

Besides credit claiming, a more serious disagreement has emerged around the sharing of tax revenues. India's federal structure has an asymmetric center-state relationship with the central government holding disproportionately higher authority on most legal and financial matters. Recent trends suggest a decline in the financial devolution of tax revenues by the center to the state leading to political skirmishes resulting from a rising share of direct levies—cess and surcharges—in the overall tax revenues. The power to introduce such levies—to build infrastructure such as roads, health, or education—lies exclusively with the central government and the revenue proceeds fall outside the purview of the 'divisible pool' of taxes which are allocated to the state governments. As a result, there has been a reduction in the fiscal share of the subnational government which hampers their ability to spend on social welfare

state has also championed the 'right to health' through its Right to Health Bill, 2022, and guaranteed income under the Rajasthan Minimum Guaranteed Income Bill, 2023. Other states are also following suit with similar laws or electoral promises.

[55] To sustain the coalition in center, greater resources flowed to the states which initiated numerous reforms to improve program implementation (Aiyar and Tillin 2020; Tillin 2022).

programs. Goods and Services Tax (GST), introduced in 2016 to streamline sales tax collection, has further curtailed the ability of states to raise resources for their own discretionary expenses. States like Kerala which have been lauded for their social welfare-driven human development gains feel the most aggrieved as it limits their public spending on welfare.

The political contestations between greater centralization and federal independence arise fundamentally from the nature of the Indian constitution and must be resolved under the same framework. Greater attention must be paid to the issue of social welfare spending by the Finance Commission (FC), an impartial constitutional body under the President, which is set up every 5 years to suggest federal tax sharing rules. Similarly, the GST Council steps up to oversee the distribution of GST between the state and center—must be empowered and leveraged more as a deliberative space—by the state government to put up their rightful demands.[56] NITI Aayog, the government think-tank, also proclaims to be a key policy organization in fostering cooperative federalism and must push this agenda more vigorously.

Improving State Capacity for Welfare Delivery

State capacity, defined as historical investment in strengthening legal and fiscal capacity and better governance structures, is paramount to implement, monitor, and sustain a social protection system. Existence of a strong state capacity differentiates better governed states like Tamil Nadu or Kerala from states (e.g., Bihar or Uttar Pradesh) which lack citizen-centric public systems leading to inefficient last-mile welfare delivery. Limited coverage of beneficiaries, rampant corruption, absenteeism among local public workers (ICDS staff, teachers, or health workers), unannounced closure of PDS shops, delayed wage payments, or denial of work to MGNREGS workers reflect the lack of state capacity to effectively implement and monitor the delivery of welfare programs. Overcoming these and many other occurrences of gross mismanagement and negligence in social welfare delivery necessitates a stronger local state capacity which includes building egalitarian local institutions comprising of civic-minded politicians, responsive bureaucratic apparatus, and empowered citizens.

[56] See Drabu (2023) on why GST Council ought to be an importance voice of state governments to garner their jurisdictional share of federal taxes.

A citizen-centric state capacity is also about overcoming oppressive social norms and creating an egalitarian power structure as information asymmetry, poor bureaucratic accountability, insufficient grievance redressal mechanisms, and disempowered citizens have all been attributed as the reasons for an apathetic state apparatus to deliver welfare. Building state capacity to overcome last-mile delivery requires simpler bureaucratic processes, greater accountability, and empowerment of communities.

Simpler Bureaucratic Procedures, Greater Citizen Awareness
Enrollment in social welfare programs itself is a cumbersome process with lack of clarity on eligibility criteria, cumbersome paperwork, and multiple rounds to the local bureaucrat which leaves the potential beneficiary demotivated. Eligible welfare beneficiaries often lack the awareness and the agency to navigate the cumbersome and costly application process. The burdensome practice of obtaining application form, preparation of documents to prove eligibility, and get them vetted by local representatives before submitting it to the designated offices is particularly tedious for the most vulnerable—women and elderly. The ordeal is further enhanced by unclear eligibility rules and discretion of the local bureaucracy to endorse and approve the application which allows for local elite capture and clientelistic favors.

A stronger state capacity requires simplification of bureaucratic procedures to identify beneficiaries and greater information dissemination about the welfare programs. A simpler way to identify beneficiaries is to use an 'exclusion' rather than 'inclusion' criteria.[57] Instead of collecting information on multiple indicators to create a poverty score or an index, one or two simple indicators can be conveniently used to exclude the rich. Such a simplistic screening process not only puts lesser burden on the administration and reduces discretion, but also improves targeting. Linking of the unique biometric unique identification number (UID), *Aadhaar*, with the tax identification number makes it easy to exclude some section of the population. Similarly, digitization of local land records in rural areas and its linkages with the *Aadhaar* can facilitate another screening criteria.

[57] There is sufficient evidence to show that a proxy-means test in the presence of discretionary bureaucratic power is not only ineffectiveness in identifying the poor but also costly (Drèze and Khera 2010; Niehaus et al. 2013).

To increase program take-up, private and public informational campaigns can be used for awareness generation among the potential beneficiaries. While social welfare programs have an active dashboard where one can verify the details of the program implementation as part of the push toward greater transparency, beneficiaries do not use it rather they rely on peer or community networks to access information. An experimental study by Das et al. (2021) shows that personalized communications and community canvassing of the same information which is available publicly on the performance and benefits of MGNREGS enlighten the beneficiaries thereby increasing work participation. At the same time, it reduces delays in payment through increasing accountability of the local implementing authorities.[58]

Information and awareness must campaigns also be paired with opportunities for political engagement and empowerment which ease the process of citizen-state mediation. Another experimental study of social pensions targeted at poor widows and divorced women. Gupta (2017) shows the lower take-up of the program is attributable to the bureaucratic ordeals but information alone may not be sufficient enough to increase enrollment. Beneficiaries garner greater benefit through application assistance and more frequent engagement with the local politicians and important social actors.

Public Accountability Through Improved Monitoring Systems

Responsive state officials and local bureaucrats are key to strengthening local state capacity which requires greater incentive to effectively implement welfare programs and improved performance monitoring system to enhance public accountability. Performance-based pay and greater use of technology have been professed as policy tools or 'commitment devices' to improve the performance of public sector employees in India and build implementational capacity.[59]

[58] Information campaigns have proven to work elsewhere too. The demand for take-up of welfare benefits increased in Indonesia once the list of eligible beneficiaries and their entitlements was made public. Announcements through a loudspeaker and public lists created incentivized private information seeking on the welfare benefits and lowered the rent-seeking and discriminatory opportunities for the local elite (Banerjee et al. 2018).

[59] See Mansuri et al. (2023), Muralidharan and Sundararaman (2011), Singh (2015), and Duflo et al. (2012) for the developmental impact of performance-pay incentives for local service providers in India.

The proliferation of information technology (IT) and mobile services can particularly reduce the monitoring cost of social welfare programs and improve efficiency. For example, the use of mobile-based payments, linked to the biometric identification, has been instrumental in bringing down the corruption in the MGNREGA and PDS (Muralidharan et al. 2016, 2020). Governance systems can benefit from technology-enabled cost-effective, real-time information collection from multiple agents in the value chain of service delivery by allowing higher-level bureaucrats to track those at the frontline. Dodge et al. (2018) find that internet- and mobile-based monitoring of local bureaucrats reduced wage payment delays under MGNREGS by 29 percent. Phone-based monitoring of *Rythu Bandhu*, a cash transfer to farmers in the state of Telangana, led to a 7.8 percent reduction in leakages once the sub-district officials were told that there might be a cross-verification of administrative records by randomly calling up the welfare beneficiaries (Muralidharan et al. 2021). Similarly, the introduction of a daily automated Interactive Voice Response Systems (IVRS) in Bihar to monitor the performance of school meals and further corroboration by designated officials, albeit at a lower frequency, streamlined program performance in terms of improved food intake, reported self-sufficiency among students, and the overall quality of the meals (Debnath et al. 2023).

The reliance on technological innovations, however, must be envisaged as a tool to serve the interests of the citizens—downward accountability—instead of employing technology as just another means of bureaucratic control. There are polarizing views on whether technology can improve identification of intended welfare beneficiaries and improve program delivery—through disciplining local state actors typically known for corruption, discretionary biases, and little accountability—or rather the technology-enabled payment and monitoring systems impose an additional burden on the poor citizens to claim their welfare entitlements. There is research to show that technology is unlikely to deter public sector underperformance in India if there is bureaucratic or political impunity to such behavior (Dhaliwal and Hanna 2017). Such perverse incentives are common in a society which works through patronage networks, weak contract enforcements, and weak community mobilization efforts. For technology-based monitoring system to be successful in fixing the 'leaky pipes' of the social welfare delivery architecture, necessary complementary inputs—political will, citizen empowerment, and appropriate grievance redressal mechanisms, are equally vital.

Reducing Bureaucratic Overloads and Improving Deliberative Norms

The much-maligned frontline Indian bureaucracy, however, also suffers from an increasing overload of work which impedes their motivation, affects prioritization, and lowers performance. It often gets unnoticed that India has one of the lowest numbers of lower-level bureaucrats across the globe. United States and China have almost five times the number of local public employees in India (Kapur 2020). In terms of the share of local expenditure out of the total, India stands at 3 percent in comparison with 27 and 51 percent by United States and China, respectively. These numbers suggest that blaming public servant for poor services is only half the story. Proliferation of administrative units—from 466 districts in 1991 to 766 currently—and the increase in social welfare schemes and infrastructure projects have increased the managerial responsibilities of senior bureaucracy as often the same officers are entrusted with multiple departments and responsibilities. The rising time constraints lead to 'bureaucrat overload' which lowers the quality of implementation.[60] Poor implementation further lowers fiscal devolution from above thereby reducing the state capacity. Among frontline bureaucratic workers, overburdened ICDS workers are an important example where they are increasingly assigned with multiple tasks. Hiring more workers, especially those at the frontline, would certainly increase the local state capacity with improved beneficiary welfare.[61]

Recruitment of local staffs and higher bureaucrats needs to be complemented by improved culture of frontline bureaucracy. Current bureaucratic norms reflect the sticky socio-political institutions. Indian administrative structure is designed along the lines of legal compliance to the superior officers rather than accountability to the ultimate beneficiaries, the citizens (Mangla 2022). Such 'legalistic' bureaucratic norms expose a culture of strict adherence to hierarchy, procedures, and paperwork, rather than flexible problem-solving and open deliberations which foster local participation by communities and civil society.[62] These differential

[60] Refer to Dasgupta and Kapur (2020) and Somanathan and Natarajan (2022).

[61] Ganimian et al. (2021) show that hiring more ICDS workers leads to improvements in learning and nutritional outcomes for children as the AWWs can devote more time as preschool teachers and nutritional advisors.

[62] Mangla (2022) use this distinction between legalistic and deliberative norms to explain the difference in performance of schools in two comparable Himalayan states,

informal norms around the engagement of the bureaucracy with the state and citizens also contribute to subnational differences in state capacity. For better welfare delivery, a change in bureaucratic culture toward deliberative norms—which rely on iterative co-learning by the state officials working with the civil society—must be encouraged.

Facilitating Community Participation Through Decentralized Governance

The role of decentralized participatory governance institutions, therefore, is key for welfare delivery. By bringing government 'closer to the people,' decentralization of governance can potentially improve political bargaining power of the citizens and influences implementation of welfare programs thereby contributing to local state capacity.[63] Members of the village councils (or *panchayats*) are the first point of contact for a rural citizen to seek welfare programs—collect documents, find eligibility criterions, and get recognized as a beneficiary. Quotas for women and marginalized groups in these local bodies have further enabled democratic empowerment of the people.[64] Yet despite its promise, local participatory governance has not been able to command independent financial and administrative authority. In fact, the top-down approval for allocating public services and tax collection violates the basic principle of decentralization. Barring some states which have made greater progress on devolving powers to local government, local rural and urban bodies continue to be under-funded, and their influence is circumscribed by the

Uttarakhand and Himachal Pradesh. Muralidharan and Singh (2020) provide an empirical example from Madhya Pradesh where a state-of-the art educational intervention designed to improve management quality in public schools failed to improve child learning outcomes because the school authorities treated the school improvement plan as a necessary administrative task without recognizing its implication for improving the quality of education.

[63] The 73rd and 74th Amendment of the Indian parliament which give greater power to the local government. India has around 250,000 village councils (or *gram panchayats*) where representatives are elected every five years to administer the local issues and take it up with the government authorities higher up.

[64] For details on India's rural decentralization experience, refer to Bardhan (2002), Bohlken (2016), Chauchard (2017), and Rao and Sanyal (2019).

higher-order bureaucrats and politicians.[65] As a result, the empowerment of citizens to assert their rights or engage in collective action—though enhanced—remains limited despite its huge potential. It is an opportunity which India's social protection system must harness upon to empower citizens, improve participatory governance, increase bureaucratic accountability, and thereby build local state capacity. Going into the future, for any urban livelihood programs, or an idea like DUET to be implemented, the strength of participatory governance is likely to be of vital importance.

Generating Greater Fiscal Space for Financing Social Welfare

Revenue mobilization through tax collection is an essential component of building a capable state—richer countries have a broader tax base and a higher share of tax/GDP ratio—to invest in common interest public goods and redistribution among other enablers of human development.[66] India's current social protection outlay (as a share of its GDP) is considerably lower than other countries at similar levels of economic development while the opportunities for increasing revenues along with expansion in social welfare outlay remain conceivable. We suggest three broad strategies to finance India's expanding social protection system—increasing total revenues from direct taxation; ensure greater tax compliance by high net-worth individuals, and rationalization of subsidies through reduced outlay on non-merit subsidies.

In Chapter 9, we describe that an astonishingly small number of Indians (a little above 2 percent) pay income taxes. Consequently, India's tax-GDP ratio (12 percent) remains a poor comparison with other democratic nations. Total tax revenues, further, have a disproportionally high share of indirect taxation which makes it regressive in nature. A lower income tax base, limited revenues, and greater reliance on indirect taxes lead to a constricted fiscal space to finance social welfare system. It is therefore imperative that a greater share of citizens around brought under the ambit of income tax, which can be made through lowering

[65] The 'depth of decentralization' varies not only by state but also across the rural-urban spectrum. In a study comparing the perception of citizens about government responsiveness, Auerbach and Kruks-Wisner (2020) find that while half of the rural residents believe that government officials are unresponsive to their demand, in urban areas, 85 percent of the residents feel the same.

[66] See Besley and Persson (2009, 2013, 2020).

the minimum taxable income, better government efforts to increase tax compliance, and modernization of tax collection systems.

Increasing the tax base may still not yield a sufficient tax revenue if the high net-worth individuals can evade their dues. The ultra-rich Indians keep adding on to the list of global billionaires, yet they pay a miniscule amount of their wealth in taxes. While income tax evasion and misreporting of income among the rich is common, capital gains tax on wealth are rendered ineffective by loopholes in the taxation system. There are also no taxes on bequeathed assets which also contribute to concentration of wealth and perpetuation of inequality. Government must bring back the inheritance tax and identify the ultra-rich for tax collection process and introduce hefty fines for non-compliance. Digitization of land records and the use of *Aadhaar* for land transactions have certainly lowered the administrative costs of such tax collection and should be employed to coerce those at the top-end of the distribution much more vigorously than they are used to identify the poor welfare beneficiaries.

Finally, a significant share of government revenue can be mobilized through a reduction in non-merit subsidies which include the generous tax exemptions and extensive concessions provided to the large businesses at the pretext of promoting private sector incentives to spur innovation and trade. Researchers have quantified heavy financial leakages on these initiatives with little gains which calls for a rationalization of subsidies from powerful entities toward investments in social protection system.

Investing in Statistical Capacity for Policy Evaluation and Feedback

A robust social welfare architecture necessitates a strong, credible, and timely statistical system to track implementation, monitor progress, and evaluate welfare impact to complete the policy feedback loop. Statistical capacity of governments is as much a tool to govern and evaluate public programs as it is for citizens to hold public representatives accountable. In a political economy, lack of authentic data therefore can be a ploy to conceal poor governance and hinder evidence-based policymaking. When data can be used to question governance, the state—which is responsible for building credible statistical capacity—also has the power to influence or sabotage such exercise fearing a repercussion. A professional, well-trained, and independent statistical system is central to a strong social protection system not only to monitor welfare programs but also to keep track of key economic and developmental variables which determine the *form*, *focus*, and *scope* of social welfare architecture.

It is worrying to see a secular decline of India's statistical capacity. There is no official poverty figure for more than a decade, results from the most recent economic census numbers have been withheld, COVID-19-related deaths were massively underestimated because of inadequate death registration system, and the impending population census exercise supposed to be conducted every decade by the government has been put on the side burner.[67] Weakened statistical capacity has coincided with the open-data revolution led by real-time digital records of infrastructure creation and welfare delivery through government dashboards. A seminal assessment of India's statistical capacity refers to this as 'data explosion' along with 'statistical implosion' where independent data portals by various ministries publishing the latest 'real-time' numbers on their performance—punched in by local data entry operators without complete disclosures around definitions, harmonization, standardization across regions, and devoid of any scrutiny or audit—are held as substitutes for carefully designed sample surveys (Bhattacharya 2023).[68]

Lack of credible statistics has ominous consequences for the evaluation for social welfare programs and the subsequent feedback into

[67] It is a unfortunate that India, which led the rest of the world in designing sample surveys, now lacks a credible statistical system to track overall output, industrial production, poverty levels, unemployment, and other key developmental indicators on a regular basis. Revision of GDP numbers in 2014–2015 led to a controversial debate around the veracity of the overall estimates of industrial production and the statistical coverage of informal sector. Government withholding the results from 2015 to 2016 National Sample Survey Organization (NSSO) report on poverty—citing poor data quality (with no explanation) but suspecting higher poverty estimates—further made a dent on the credibility of the survey exercise and the political influence on the statistical system. Credibility of the system was further weakened by a shocking leak of the employment survey results by NSSO—which showed high unemployment numbers—by a business daily in 2018. Contrary statements by the government and the NSSO chief, and immediate resignation of the senior members of the NSSO only made the hollowing out of the country's statistical capacity and the political influence on what numbers are put out conspicuous. The decline of statistical capacity in India has been a gradual one. See Bhattacharya (2023) for a historical perspective.

[68] Imbert and Papp (2011) compare the MGNREGS administrative data as available on the program portal and compare it with the survey data to find large discrepancies in the number of workdays. They hypothesize that officials often inflate the figures on program deliverables to fulfil the legal mandates of MGNREGS.

policymaking.[69] Isolated small-scale studies by independent researchers are no substitute to national scale evaluation for evaluating social policies. For example, the absence of good quality micro-surveys has affected evaluation studies on the expansion of NFSA since 2013 and health insurance under PM-JAY, along with the introduction of many newer schemes such as cash transfers to farmers through PM-Kisan which now comprise important component of the social welfare architecture. Besides the need of micro-data for program evaluation and tracking human development outcomes, statistical prowess of the government is key for statecraft—gather information on citizen through census, draw cartographic boundaries, identify the poor and deserving, and intervene with appropriate developmental programs. For social welfare programs, such information allows for a better representation of the developmental challenges, tracks progress, and identifies the poor more efficiently.[70] Investment in statistical systems for a credible, timely, and open data—a combination of surveys, socio-economic censuses, and program implementation indicators at granular levels—which can be linked to each other for credible policy evaluations and public accountability is paramount to building a strong social protection system in India.

Gradualism in Policy Reforms

We would like to bookend our arguments by revisiting the ongoing debate on the future of India's social protection programs which veer around replacing PDS with cash, the use of technology to improve last-mile delivery, and the potential of UBI as a be-it-all welfare transfer. One observes a sense of palpable restlessness among the proponents of change in their clarion calls for greater use of digital technologies and market-based instruments of social protection to improve the lives of the poor. This impatience for policy changes surely emerges from their noble intentions, but such a missionary zeal must also consider the reality

[69] Dearth of good quality data on health and nutrition for a decade, and challenges with standardization across surveys over time, hampered the understating on these issues and hampered the development agenda for a decade. See Spears (2013).

[70] See de Souza Leão (2022) for a comparison of the data governance structures in Mexico and Brazil as utilized in implementing two of the largest conditional cash transfer programs in the world, *Progresa* and *Bolsa Família*, respectively.

of underdeveloped Indian state and sticky social norms which provide a countervailing force to modernization.

Social protection systems and their modernization—in terms of its *form, focus, and scope*—must therefore be studied in the light of India's socio-political realities. Modernization of the economic structure—markets, infrastructure, financial literacy etc.—necessitates evolution of social norms around social identity and gender, greater trust in the government, and a more empowered citizen in her interactions with the state. Social norms and political culture take time to evolve. Less than satisfactory progress in the last seven decades on this front suggests that social policy reforms require an element of gradualism while simultaneously pushing the cause of socio-political changes in a more urgent manner.

Cash Instead of Food: Future, Not the Present

Cash transfers are preferable when markets function well, citizen trust their government, and gender relations are egalitarian. There is a long way to go for India to claim success on these fronts which suggest that replacing food assistance with cash transfers would not be beneficial. In fact, the overwhelming preference of beneficiaries for cash stems from these persistent norms. The political economy challenge of how to overcome interlinked state-led procurement-distribution system further complicates any progress. But pragmatism is key to policy reforms. The feasibility of cash should however be tested in contexts where these socio-political hurdles are relatively lesser, such as the urban areas, beginning with the metropolitan cities. Similarly, it is important to investigate what happens when consumers are also provided the option of cash transfers instead when they receive food grains because households may have differential preferences regarding cash or food. A cash or food option can also familiarize citizens with the new system and build trust in delivery system, while other aspects of the welfare system evolve. State governments can take a lead in this direction and policy learnings can flow across subnational borders.

Citizen Interest: At the Heart of Technological Innovation

Indians are fascinated by digital technologies and none more than the policymakers. An aspirational class of IT technocrats has changed India's global economic positioning and multiple IT-based entrepreneurs have revolutionized the value chains, financial systems, and informational delivery in a country where internet access is ubiquitous even in the hinterland and among the cheapest in the world. This has led to an unabashed confidence in IT-based services to overcome every issue of governance and welfare delivery at the push of a button. Universal bank accounts (under the PM *Jan Dhan* scheme), unique biometric identity (*Aadhaar*), and mobile phones comprise of the digital architecture referred as the 'JAM trinity' presented as the ingenious solution to build state capacity and mitigate the last-mile challenges of identifying and delivering welfare benefits.

We have argued that such faith is often misplaced because corruption, clientelism, and last-mile implementational deficits continue to be pervasive, even if they have declined over time.[71] While technology has a key role to play in improving welfare delivery, it is neither a *sine qua non* for building state capacity, nor it necessarily prioritizes citizen interest. Moreover, there are preconditions for its effectiveness, and it must work within a particular socio-political environment, citizen grievance often remains unacknowledged, and bureaucratic indifference outlines the endemic challenges of welfare delivery. Digital technologies often serve the interests of their masters—policy elites, bureaucrats, local administrators, and politicians—than the citizens. The future of Indian social welfare ought to be the one in which citizen interests are the center. Persistence of teething issues in the digital infrastructure suggest that any sweeping change in the welfare delivery systems is likely to have an adverse impact the poor. Multiple studies, including government's own audit, have shown that there are teething problems with the JAM infrastructure; it is 'fragile,' open to manipulations, and often excludes the most marginalized. Inadequate data protection laws further pose a challenge to civil liberty and bring down trust in government systems. Having an option for those who do not want to (or face problems while doing so) link their digital identity, *Aadhaar*, along with alternative means to biometric authentication, would ease citizen access to welfare systems.

The use of technology must be prioritized for democratic empowerment of citizens, facilitate information dissemination, increasing public accountability, improve grievance redressal systems, through multiple

[71] See Chapter 9.

means such as personalized communications about welfare programs, interactive voice-response systems (IVRS) for grievance redressal, and mobile-based monitoring of delivery systems. Some of these have already been piloted by various subnational governments but require scaling up along with a strong political commitment to promptly act upon the deficiencies in delivery system.

UBI: Distal to Current Developmental Needs

The arguments against cash as a *form* of welfare assistance apply equally to the idea of Universal Basic Income (UBI) but there is more to unpack here. The altruistic idea behind providing every citizen a certain amount of cash—a *form* of social minimum, a citizenship right—is laudable but little is known about how it can be operationalized, even in the developed countries, where this idea has gained greater political traction. A fundamental challenge with UBI in India, however, is that replacement of cash transfers with all the other schemes (or even a few) pushes the welfare agenda back by a few decades by placing the developmental scope of welfare system as poverty reduction. Even when implementation is perfect and financial resources sufficient, what good is cash when undernutrition is persistent, jobs are scarce, health systems are prohibitively exploitative, and credit markets are imperfect? Current development needs of the nation are more acute and basic (food, housing, nutrition, health, and skills) for cash transfers to replace the array of social safety nets which are designed to address these fundamental aspects of underdevelopment. A revolutionary idea, which UBI is, requires an equally radical state to implement it in a context where economic risks and vulnerabilities arise often from non-income sources and the enablers of the development process still in infancy (see Fig. 10.1). Research has shown that households which lack capital endowment (human and physical) suffer from deprivations on several count. Cash transfers can ameliorate only the short-term financial constraints with questionable impact on long-term asset accumulation or building resilience against unanticipated shocks. UBI, therefore, could surely be a key component of social welfare system, but probably in the future. We must wait for more research on the effectiveness of UBI in advanced nations to have an informed debate around it.

Opportunity to Consolidate the Recent Gains in Welfare Expansion

Radical innovations to policy reforms stem from the exuberance of India's growth story—its economic modernization, bustling metropolises, construction boom, and rise of an aspiring middle class—but the other side of story—persistent undernutrition, rising informality, patriarchal norms, bureaucratic apathy, fragile technologies, lack of social mobility among the majority, etc.—suggests that pragmatism calls for a gradual and more deliberate path toward reforms. Greater use of technology, cash transfers, and eventually UBI such as citizenship rights are all desirable possibilities to make social assistance efficient but the policy must outline who are these designed to benefit. Technological innovations have not entirely disciplined bureaucracy or reduced political capture. Cash transfers in the form of social pensions and PM-Kisan to the farmers are already being implemented, but neither their implementation is perfect nor their impact transformative. But it is important to use them in unison with the *scope* of other welfare programs rather than merging all social transfers into one.

The frictions created by India's socio-political system further do not allow for sweeping reforms which is not necessarily ominous for a nation where social protection systems are still in infancy. We suggest that while future reforms are discussed and policy is learning from various pilot experiments, there is an imminent need to consolidate and build upon the existing welfare architecture through improving the performance of existing schemes and creation of credible public systems as enablers of resilience. Consolidation of current programs is likely to put India on a higher pedestal of human development gradually, create empowered citizens, and contribute toward a healthy social democracy where citizens can bargain more strongly with the state actors in designing a favorable social contract. Such propitious development process as a *scope* of the welfare system would progressively obviate the need for many social welfare schemes or enable the desired transition to more market-based *forms* of social assistance.

Conclusion

Synthesizing arguments presented earlier in the book, this chapter sketches out a schema for the future of India's social protection system. We discuss the various ways through which the fledgling social protection architecture in the country can ensure a social minimum—necessary to live a life of dignity—and facilitate a resilient development process. Guided by the historical experience of the expansion of social welfare programs in India and rest of the world, we argue for envisaging a social protection system which is inclusive, spans over an individual's life cycle, and is adaptable to the specific path of the economic structural transformation. The resilience enhancing ability of such a system necessitates a strong political coalition around progressive welfare ideas, a capable state to deliver welfare, investments in public infrastructure, empowered citizens, and sufficient fiscal capacity to fund welfare programs.

From the vantage point of history, we observe several missed opportunities where social policy occupied itself with the symptoms of poverty while skirting around the underlying structural constraints which limit human efforts at improving their situation. As India takes the pole position as the most populous nation on earth and its economic dynamism felt globally, leaving behind its poorest and the most vulnerable would lead to an unrealized potential of millions of its citizens and that of the nation-state itself. Persistence of inequality of opportunity and disenfranchised citizens can debilitate any nation. With the rise of informality, an overwhelming share of workers lacks social protection through employment. In the absence of work-based social protection, citizens increasingly look at the state for social support. Indian state, therefore, must envisage social policy reforms as citizenship rights and not merely as an employment-based benefit.

Looking into the future, a stronger social protection system is of supreme importance not only to lift people out of poverty but also to reduce vulnerability which may emerge from anticipated and unanticipated changes in the economy and environment. Drivers and manifestations of deprivation are likely to change over time, and the social policies must respond to them through a combination of direct social assistance as well as state-supported social insurance. The design of these programs—*form* and *focus*—require active deliberations in the public space, evidence generation through small-scale experiments, and greater devolution of powers to the subnational regions to implement these programs. Subnational variations are a peculiar feature of India's structural transformation which can become a source of learnings across the states in terms of building a social welfare system which is context-specific—economic, social, and political—and the central government must support the state governments within the federal framework of the Indian constitution.

We have also argued that investment in social protection system is not only crucial for the *scope* of promoting human resilience but also political roots of the nation through creating a vibrant social democracy. The citizen-state social contract is motivated by reciprocity and common goals. The democratic state provides a credible social commitment to a minimum standard of living—social protection and public services—and citizens contribute through taxes, compliance to laws, and allegiance to national sovereignty. Such a process fosters a culture of inclusive political institutions and citizen-focused civic culture—through commitment to the ideals of justice, fairness, and equity—which becomes an overarching foundational framework for greater trust in the government, equality of opportunity, and shared prosperity. The 75th anniversary of the independent Indian state might just be the opportune time to inspire such a credible social contract. One must remain hopeful even if the road is long and arduous.

References

Adelman, I., K. Subbarao, and P. Vashishtha. 1985. "Some Dynamic Aspects of Rural Poverty in India. Econom." *Economic & Political Weekly* 20 (39): A103–16.

Adukia, Anjali, Sam Asher, and Paul Novosad. 2020. "Educational Investment Responses to Economic Opportunity: Evidence from Indian Road Construction." *American Economic Journal: Applied Economics* 12 (1): 348–76. https://doi.org/10.1257/app.20180036.

Afridi, Farzana, Kanika Mahajan, and Nikita Sangwan. 2022. "Employment Guaranteed? Social Protection During a Pandemic." *Oxford Open Economics* 1: odab003. https://doi.org/10.1093/ooec/odab003.

Aiyar, Yamini. 2019. "Modi Consolidates Power: Leveraging Welfare Politics." *Journal of Democracy* 30 (4): 78–88. https://doi.org/10.1353/jod.2019.0070.

Aiyar, Yamini. 2020. "DUET: Flexible Implementation Is Key." *Ideas for India*. Retrieved July 13, 2023. http://www.ideasforindia.in/topics/poverty-inequality/duet-flexible-implementation-is-key.html.

Aiyar, Yamini, Vincy Davis, Gokulnath Govindan, and Taanya Kapoor. 2021. "Rewriting the Grammar of the Education System: Delhi's Education Reform."

Aiyar, Yamini, and Louise Tillin. 2020. "'One Nation,' BJP, and the Future of Indian Federalism." *India Review* 19 (2): 117–35. https://doi.org/10.1080/14736489.2020.1744994.

Anand, Kusha, and Marie Lall. 2022. *Delhi's Education Revolution: Teachers, Agency and Inclusion*. UCL Press.

Asher, Sam, and Paul Novosad. 2020. "Rural Roads and Local Economic Development." *American Economic Review* 110 (3): 797–823.

Auerbach, Adam Michael, and Gabrielle Kruks-Wisner. 2020. "The Geography of Citizenship Practice: How the Poor Engage the State in Rural and Urban India." *Perspectives on Politics* 18 (4): 1118–34. https://doi.org/10.1017/S1537592720000043.

Azim Premji Foundation. 2018. *School Choice in Low-Information Environments: A Study of Perceptions and Realities in Four States*. Azim Premji Foundation.

Banerjee, Abhijit, Esther Duflo, Erin Grela, Madeline McKelway, Frank Schilbach, Garima Sharma, and Girija Vaidyanathan. 2022. "Depression and Loneliness among the Elderly Poor."

Banerjee, Abhijit, Rema Hanna, Jordan Kyle, Benjamin A. Olken, and Sudarno Sumarto. 2018. "Tangible Information and Citizen Empowerment: Identification Cards and Food Subsidy Programs in Indonesia." *Journal of Political Economy* 126 (2): 451–91.

Banerjee, Abhijit V., and Esther Duflo. 2007. "The Economic Lives of the Poor." *Journal of Economic Perspectives* 21 (1): 141–67. https://doi.org/10.1257/jep.21.1.141.

Bardhan, Pranab. 2002. "Decentralization of Governance and Development." *Journal of Economic Perspectives* 16 (4): 185–205.

Bardhan, Pranab. 2016. "State and Development: The Need for a Reappraisal of the Current Literature." *Journal of Economic Literature* 54 (3): 862–92. https://doi.org/10.1257/jel.20151239.

Bardhan, Pranab. 2020. "DUET: Employment Programme in Public Works in Small Towns." *Ideas for India*. Retrieved July 15, 2023. http://www.ideasforindia.in/topics/poverty-inequality/duet-employment-programme-in-public-works-in-small-towns.html.

Barrett, Christopher B., and Mark A. Constas. 2014. "Toward a Theory of Resilience for International Development Applications." *Proceedings of the National Academy of Sciences* 111 (40): 14625–30. https://doi.org/10.1073/pnas.1320880111.

Barrett, Christopher B., Teevrat Garg, and Linden McBride. 2016. "Well-Being Dynamics and Poverty Traps." *Annual Review of Resource Economics* 8 (1): 303–27. https://doi.org/10.1146/annurev-resource-100815-095235.

Barrett, Christopher B., Kate Ghezzi-Kopel, John Hoddinott, Nima Homami, Elizabeth Tennant, Joanna Upton, and Tong Wu. 2021. "A Scoping Review of the Development Resilience Literature: Theory, Methods and Evidence." *World Development* 146: 105612. https://doi.org/10.1016/j.worlddev.2021.105612

Barrett, Christopher B., and Brent M. Swallow. 2006. "Fractal Poverty Traps." *World Development* 34 (1): 1–15. https://doi.org/10.1016/j.worlddev.2005.06.008.

Basole, Amit, Mathew Idiculla, R. Narayanan, H. Nagendra, and S. Mundoli. 2019. "Strengthening Towns through Sustainable Employment: A Job Guarantee Programme for Urban India." *State of Working India*.

Bertorelli, Ebony, Patrick Heller, Siddharth Swaminathan, and Ashutosh Varshney. 2017. "Does Citizenship Abate Class?" *Economic & Political Weekly* LII (32): 47–57.

Besley, Timothy. 2020. "State Capacity, Reciprocity, and the Social Contract." *Econometrica* 88 (4): 1307–35. https://doi.org/10.3982/ECTA16863.

Besley, Timothy, and Torsten Persson. 2009. "The Origins of State Capacity: Property Rights, Taxation, and Politics." *American Economic Review* 99 (4): 1218–44.

Besley, Timothy, and Torsten Persson. 2013. "Taxation and Development." In *Handbook of Public Economics*. Vol. 5, 51–110. Elsevier.

Bhan, Gautam. 2023. "Operationalising Social Protection: Reflections from Urban India." *Urban Studies*. https://doi.org/10.1177/00420980231186077

Bharathi, Naveen, Deepak Malghan, Sumit Mishra, and Andaleeb Rahman. 2022. "Residential Segregation and Public Services in Urban India." *Urban Studies* 59 (14): 2912–32.

Bhattacharya, Pramit. 2023. "India's Statistical System: Past, Present, Future."

Bohlken, Anjali Thomas. 2016. *Democratization from Above: The Logic of Local Democracy in the Developing World*. Cambridge: Cambridge University Press.

Burlig, Fiona, and Louis Preonas. 2016. "Out of the Darkness and into the Light? Development Effects of Rural Electrification." *Energy Institute at Haas WP* 268: 26.

Chauchard, Simon. 2017. *Why Representation Matters: The Meaning of Ethnic Quotas in Rural India*. Cambridge: Cambridge University Press.

Coffey, Diane, and Dean Spears. 2017. *Where India Goes: Abandoned Toilets, Stunted Development and the Costs of Caste*. New York: Harper Collins.

Dandekar, Vishnu Mahadeo, and Nilakantha Rath. 1971. "Poverty in India-I: Dimensions and Trends." *Economic and Political Weekly*, 25–48.

Das, Jishnu, and Quy-Toan Do. 2023. "The Prices in the Crises: What We Are Learning from 20 Years of Health Insurance in Low- and Middle-Income

Countries." *Journal of Economic Perspectives* 37 (2): 123–52. https://doi.org/10.1257/jep.37.2.123.

Das, Jishnu, and Tristan Zajonc. 2010. "India Shining and Bharat Drowning: Comparing Two Indian States to the Worldwide Distribution in Mathematics Achievement." *Journal of Development Economics* 92 (2): 175–87. https://doi.org/10.1016/j.jdeveco.2009.03.004.

Das, Upasak, Amartya Paul, and Mohit Sharma. 2021. *Can Information Dissemination Reduce Last Mile Payment Delays in the Public Works Programme? Evidence from a Field Experiment in India*. 9292569554. WIDER Working Paper.

Dasgupta, Aditya, Kishore Gawande, and Devesh Kapur. 2017. "(When) Do Antipoverty Programs Reduce Violence? India's Rural Employment Guarantee and Maoist Conflict." *International Organization* 71 (3): 605–32.

Dasgupta, Aditya, and Devesh Kapur. 2020. "The Political Economy of Bureaucratic Overload: Evidence from Rural Development Officials in India." *American Political Science Review* 114 (4): 1316–34. https://doi.org/10.1017/S0003055420000477.

De Hoop, Thomas, Garima Siwach, Chinmaya Holla, and Bidhubhusan Mahapatra. 2022. "Convergence of Social Protection Programs in India: Impact of Self-Help Groups on Access to and Employment Under the Mahatma Gandhi National Rural Employment Guarantee Scheme." Available at SSRN 4153417.

Debnath, Sisir, Mrithyunjayan Nilayamgode, and Sheetal Sekhri. 2023. "Information Bypass: Using Low-Cost Technological Innovations to Curb Leakages in Welfare Programs." *Journal of Development Economics* 164: 103137. https://doi.org/10.1016/j.jdeveco.2023.103137.

Deshpande, Ashwini. 2022. *Rural Livelihoods Programs in India: Lessons from the Past as a Guide to the Future*.

Deshpande, Rajeshwari, K. K. Kailash, and Louise Tillin. 2017. "States as Laboratories: The Politics of Social Welfare Policies in India." *India Review* 16 (1): 85–105.

Deshpande, Rajeshwari, Louise Tillin, and K. K. Kailash. 2019. "The BJP's Welfare Schemes: Did They Make a Difference in the 2019 Elections?" *Studies in Indian Politics* 7 (2): 219–33.

Dhaliwal, Iqbal, and Rema Hanna. 2017. "The Devil Is in the Details: The Successes and Limitations of Bureaucratic Reform in India." *Journal of Development Economics* 124: 1–21. https://doi.org/10.1016/j.jdeveco.2016.08.008.

Dodge, Eric, Yusuf Neggers, Rohini Pande, and Charity Troyer Moore. 2018. *Having It at Hand: How Small Search Frictions Impact Bureaucratic Efficiency*. Working Paper, May 2018. https://www.povertyactionlab.org/sites/default....

Drabu, Haseeb A. 2023. *The Goods and Services Tax Council: Dialectics and Design*. Working Paper No. 2023-10. Centre for Policy Research.

Drèze, Jean. 2020. "DUET: A Proposal for an Urban Work Programme." *Ideas For India*. Poverty & Equality, September 9. https://www.ideasforindia.in/topics/poverty-inequality/duet-a-proposal-for-an-urban-work-programme.html.

Drèze, Jean. 2021. "DUET Re-Examined." *Ideas For India*, Poverty & Equality, March 9. https://www.ideasforindia.in/topics/poverty-inequality/duet-re-examined.html.

Drèze, Jean, and Reetika Khera. 2010. "The BPL Census and a Possible Alternative." *Economic and Political Weekly*, 54–63.

Drèze, Jean, and Amartya Sen. 2013. *An Uncertain Glory: India and Its Contradictions*. Princeton: Priceton Press.

Duflo, Esther, Rema Hanna, and Stephen P. Ryan. 2012. "Incentives Work: Getting Teachers to Come to School." *American Economic Review* 102 (4): 1241–78. https://doi.org/10.1257/aer.102.4.1241.

Evans, David K., Brian Holtemeyer, and Katrina Kosec. 2019. "Cash Transfers Increase Trust in Local Government." *World Development* 114: 138–55. https://doi.org/10.1016/j.worlddev.2018.08.020.

Fairwork. 2021. *Fairwork India Ratings 2021: Labour Standards in the Platform Economy*.

Gaiha, Raghav. 1989. "Are the Chronically Poor Also the Poorest in Rural India?" *Development and Change* 20 (2): 295–322. https://doi.org/10.1111/j.1467-7660.1989.tb00349.x.

Ganimian, Alejandro J., Karthik Muralidharan, and Christopher R. Walters. 2021. "Augmenting State Capacity for Child Development: Experimental Evidence from India."

Gavrilovic, Maja, Monica Rubio, Francesca Bastagli, Roopa Hinton, Silke Staab, Ruth Graham Goulder, Charlotte Bilo, Ruby Khan, Amber Peterman, Bobo Diallo, Laura Alfers, Aroa Santiago, Zehra Rizvi, Rebecca Holmes, Juan Gonzalo Jaramillo Mejia, and Constanza Tabbush. 2022. "Gender-Responsive Social Protection Post–COVID-19." *Science* 375 (6585): 1111–13. https://doi.org/10.1126/science.abm5922.

Government of India. 2011. *Mid-Term Appraisal: Eleventh Five Year Plan 2007–2012*. Planning Commission.

Gupta, Aashish, Sangita Vyas, Payal Hathi, Nazar Khalid, Nikhil Srivastav, Dean Spears, and Diane Coffey. 2019. "Persistence of Solid Fuel Use despite Increases in LPG Ownership: New Survey Evidence from Rural North India." *Economic and Political Weekly*.

Gupta, Sarika. 2017. "Perils of the Paperwork: The Impact of Information and Application Assistance on Welfare Program Take-up in India." *Unpublished Report, Harvard University, Boston, MA*.

Heller, Patrick. 2021. "The Social Roots of the Authoritarian Turn in India." In *Routledge Handbook of Autocratization in South Asia*, 115–26. Routledge.

Heller, Patrick, Partha Mukhopadhyay, and Michael Walton. 2019. "Cabal City: Urban Regimes and Accumulation without Development." In *Business and Politics in India*, edited by C. Jaffrelot, A. Kohli, and K. Murali. Oxford: Oxford University Press.

Hussam, Reshmaan, Erin M. Kelley, Gregory Lane, and Fatima Zahra. 2022. "The Psychosocial Value of Employment: Evidence from a Refugee Camp." *American Economic Review* 112 (11): 3694–3724.

Imbert, Clement, and John Papp. 2011. "Estimating Leakages in India's Employment Guarantee." *Battle for Employment Guarantee*, 269–78. New Delhi: Oxford University Press.

Kapur, Devesh. 2005. "India's Promise." *Harvard Magazine*. Retrieved July 16, 2023. https://www.harvardmagazine.com/2005/07/indias-promise.html.

Kapur, Devesh. 2020. "Why Does the Indian State Both Fail and Succeed?" *Journal of Economic Perspectives* 34 (1): 31–54. https://doi.org/10.1257/jep.34.1.31.

Kapur Mehta, Aasha, and Amita Shah. 2003. "Chronic Poverty in India: Incidence, Causes and Policies." *World Development* 31 (3): 491–511. https://doi.org/10.1016/S0305-750X(02)00212-7

Kingdon, Geeta Gandhi. 2020. "The Private Schooling Phenomenon in India: A Review." *The Journal of Development Studies* 56 (10): 1795–1817. https://doi.org/10.1080/00220388.2020.1715943.

Kohli, Atul. 2012. *Poverty Amid Plenty in the New India*. Cambridge: Cambridge University Press.

Kotwal, Ashok. 2020. "DUET: Addressing 'Why' before 'How.'" *Ideas for India*. Retrieved July 15, 2023. http://www.ideasforindia.in/topics/poverty-inequality/duet-addressing-why-before-how.html.

Krishna, Anirudh. 2004. "Escaping Poverty and Becoming Poor: Who Gains, Who Loses, and Why?" *World Development* 32 (1): 121–36. https://doi.org/10.1016/j.worlddev.2003.08.002.

Kundu, Amitabh, and Debolina Kundu. 2010. "Globalization and Exclusionary Urban Growth in Asian Countries." Working Paper No. 2010/70, 1–23.

Lade, Steven J., L. Jamila Haider, Gustav Engström, and Maja Schlüter. 2017. "Resilience Offers Escape from Trapped Thinking on Poverty Alleviation." *Science Advances* 3 (5): e1603043. https://doi.org/10.1126/sciadv.1603043.

Lee, Kenneth, Edward Miguel, and Catherine Wolfram. 2020. "Does Household Electrification Supercharge Economic Development?" *Journal of Economic Perspectives* 34 (1): 122–44. https://doi.org/10.1257/jep.34.1.122.

Mangla, Akshay. 2022. *Making Bureaucracy Work: Norms, Education and Public Service Delivery in Rural India*. Cambridge: Cambridge University Press.

Mansuri, Ghazala, Nethra Palaniswamy, Vijayendra Rao, and Slesh A. Shrestha. 2023. "Money versus Kudos: The Impact of Incentivizing Local Politicians in India." *Journal of Public Economics* 224: 104922. https://doi.org/10.1016/j.jpubeco.2023.104922.

Muralidharan, Karthik, Paul Niehaus, and Sandip Sukhtankar. 2016. "Building State Capacity: Evidence from Biometric Smartcards in India." *American Economic Review* 106 (10): 2895–2929.

Muralidharan, Karthik, Paul Niehaus, and Sandip Sukhtankar. 2020. *Identity Verification Standards in Welfare Programs: Experimental Evidence from India*. National Bureau of Economic Research.

Muralidharan, Karthik, Paul Niehaus, Sandip Sukhtankar, and Jeffrey Weaver. 2021. "Improving Last-Mile Service Delivery Using Phone-Based Monitoring." *American Economic Journal: Applied Economics* 13 (2): 52–82. https://doi.org/10.1257/app.20190783.

Muralidharan, Karthik, and Abhijeet Singh. 2020. *Improving Public Sector Management at Scale? Experimental Evidence on School Governance India*. National Bureau of Economic Research.

Muralidharan, Karthik, and Abhijeet Singh. 2021. "India's New National Education Policy: Evidence and Challenges." *Science* 372 (6537): 36–38. https://doi.org/10.1126/science.abf6655.

Muralidharan, Karthik, and Venkatesh Sundararaman. 2011. "Teacher Performance Pay: Experimental Evidence from India." *Journal of Political Economy* 119 (1): 39–77. https://doi.org/10.1086/659655.

Narayan, Swati. 2022. "Breaking New Ground: Women's Employment in India's NREGA, the Pandemic Lifeline." *Gender & Development* 30 (1–2): 217–46. https://doi.org/10.1080/13552074.2022.2071978.

Narayanan, Sudha, Christian Oldiges, and Shree Saha. 2022. Does Workfare Work? India's Employment Guarantee during COVID-19. *Journal of International Development* 34 (1): 82–108. https://doi.org/10.1002/jid.3583.

Naschold, Felix. 2012. "'The Poor Stay Poor': Household Asset Poverty Traps in Rural Semi-Arid India." *World Development* 40 (10): 2033–43. https://doi.org/10.1016/j.worlddev.2012.05.006.

Naseemullah, Adnan. 2016. "The Contested Capacity of the Indian State." *India Review* 15 (4): 407–32. https://doi.org/10.1080/14736489.2016.1238269.

Niehaus, Paul, Antonia Atanassova, Marianne Bertrand, and Sendhil Mullainathan. 2013. "Targeting with Agents." *American Economic Journal: Economic Policy* 5 (1): 206–38. https://doi.org/10.1257/pol.5.1.206.

Pritchett, Lant, and Martina Viarengo. 2023. "The Learning Crisis of Developing Country Elites: Lessons from PISA-D." *The World Bank Economic Review* 37 (2): 177–204. https://doi.org/10.1093/wber/lhad001.

Rao, Vijayendra, and Paromita Sanyal. 2019. *Oral Democracy: Deliberation in Indian Village Assemblies*. Cambridge: Cambridge University Press.

Ray, Debraj. 2020. "DUET: Towards Employment as a Universal Right." *Ideas for India*. Retrieved July 15, 2023. http://www.ideasforindia.in/topics/poverty-inequality/duet-towards-employment-as-a-universal-right.html.

Roy, Indrajit. 2023. "How Welfare Wins: Discursive Institutionalism, the Politics of the Poor, and the Expansion of Social Welfare in India during the Early 21st Century." *Policy and Society* 42 (4): 506–25. https://doi.org/10.1093/polsoc/puad010.

Schüring, Esther, and Markus Loewe. 2021. *Handbook on Social Protection Systems*. Edward Elgar Publishing.

Sen, Amartya. 1982. *Poverty and Famines: An Essay on Entitlement and Deprivation*. Oxford, UK: Oxford University Press.

Singh, Abhijeet, Mauricio Romero, and Karthik Muralidharan. 2022. *COVID-19 Learning Loss and Recovery: Panel Data Evidence from India*. National Bureau of Economic Research.

Singh, Prakarsh. 2015. "Performance Pay and Information: Reducing Child Undernutrition in India." *Journal of Economic Behavior & Organization* 112: 141–63. https://doi.org/10.1016/j.jebo.2015.01.008.

Sinha, Dipa, and Rohit Azad. 2018. "Can Jan Dhan Yojana Achieve Financial Inclusion?" *Economic and Political Weekly* 53 (13): 165–171.

Sircar, Neelanjan. 2020. "The Politics of Vishwas: Political Mobilization in the 2019 National Election." *Contemporary South Asia* 28 (2): 178–94. https://doi.org/10.1080/09584935.2020.1765988.

Somanathan, T.V., and Gulzar Natarajan. 2022. *State Capability in India*. Oxford: Oxford University Press.

de Souza Leão, Luciana. 2022. "Optics of the State: The Politics of Making Poverty Visible in Brazil and Mexico." *American Journal of Sociology* 128 (1): 1–46. https://doi.org/10.1086/719936.

Spears, Dean. 2013. "Policy Lessons from the Implementation of India's Total Sanitation Campaign." Vol. 9, 63–104. National Council of Applied Economic Research.

Thorat, Amit, Reeve Vanneman, Sonalde Desai, and Amaresh Dubey. 2017. "Escaping and Falling into Poverty in India Today." *World Development* 93: 413–26. https://doi.org/10.1016/j.worlddev.2017.01.004.

Tillin, Louise. 2022. "Does India Have Subnational Welfare Regimes? The Role of State Governments in Shaping Social Policy." *Territory, Politics, Governance* 10 (1): 86–102. https://doi.org/10.1080/21622671.2021.1928541.

Tillin, Louise, Rajeshwari Deshpande, and K. K. Kailash. 2015. *Politics of Welfare: Comparisons across Indian States*. Oxford: Oxford University Press.

Index

A. Rahman and P. Pingali, *The Future of India's Social Safety Nets*, Palgrave Studies in Agricultural Economics and Food Policy,
https://doi.org/10.1007/978-3-031-50747-2

C

F

G

H

I

R

S

T

U

V

W

SPRINGER NATURE

GPSR Compliance

The European Union's (EU) General Product Safety Regulation (GPSR) is a set of rules that requires consumer products to be safe and our obligations to ensure this.

If you have any concerns about our products, you can contact us on ProductSafety@springernature.com

In case Publisher is established outside the EU, the EU authorized representative is:

Springer Nature Customer Service Center GmbH
Europaplatz 3
69115 Heidelberg, Germany

The manufacturer's authorised representative in the EU is Springer Nature Customer Service Centre GmbH, Europaplatz 3, 69115 Heidelberg, Germany. If you have any concerns regarding our products, please contact ProductSafety@springernature.com

Printed and bound by CPI Group (UK) Ltd, Croydon, CR0 4YY
01/10/2026
02225898-0011